Turkey's Democratization Process

Since the end of the 1980 coup d'état Turkey has been in the midst of a complex process of democratization. Applying methodological pluralism in order to provide a comprehensive analysis of this process in a Turkish context, this book brings together contributions from prominent, Turkish, English, French and Spanish scholars.

Turkey's Democratization Process utilizes the theoretical framework of J. J. Linz and A. C. Stepan in order to assess the complex process of democratization in Turkey. This framework takes into account five interacting features of Turkey's polity when making this assessment, namely: whether the underlying legal and socio-economic conditions are conducive for the development of a free and participant society; if a relatively autonomous political society exists; whether there are legal guarantees for citizens' freedoms; if there exists a state bureaucracy which can be used by a democratic government; and whether the type and pace of Turkish economic development contributes to this process.

Examining the Turkish case in light of this framework, this book seeks to combine analyses that will help assess the process of democratization in Turkey to date and will be of interest to scholars and researchers interested in Turkish politics, democratization and Middle Eastern studies more broadly.

Carmen Rodríguez is Researcher of Contemporary Turkish Studies at Election Watch OPEMAM, Autónoma University of Madrid. Her research interests include democratization, political parties and Turkey-EU relations.

Antonio Ávalos is Researcher at TEIM (Mediterranean International Studies Team), Autónoma University of Madrid. His work focuses on the political and military elite and secularism in Turkey.

Hakan Yılmaz is Professor at the Department of Political Science and International Relations, Boğaziçi University, Istanbul. His research interests include political ideologies and political culture in post-World War II Turkey; culture and identity dimensions of EU-Turkey relations; and external-internal linkages in the process of democratization.

Ana I. Planet is Professor at the Arab and Islamic Studies Department and Director of TEIM (Mediterranean International Studies Team) at Autónoma University of Madrid. Her research interests include Moroccan migration to Spain and political debates regarding Islam in Europe.

Routledge Studies in Middle Eastern Politics

Turkey's Democratization Process

Edited by
Carmen Rodríguez, Antonio Ávalos,
Hakan Yılmaz and Ana I. Planet

Routledge
Taylor & Francis Group

LONDON AND NEW YORK

First published 2014 by Routledge

2 Park Square, Milton Park, Abingdon, Oxfordshire OX14 4RN
711 Third Avenue, New York, NY 10017

Routledge is an imprint of the Taylor & Francis Group, an informa business

First issued in paperback 2018

British Library Cataloguing in Publication Data
A catalogue record for this book is available from the British Library

Library of Congress Cataloging in Publication Data
Turkey's democratization process / edited by Carmen Rodríguez, Antonio Ávalos, Hakan Yılmaz and Ana I. Planet.
    pages cm
Includes bibliographical references and index.
1. Democratization–Turkey. 2. Democracy–Turkey. 3. Turkey–Politics and government–1980- I. Rodríguez, Carmen.
JQ1809.A15.T867 2014
320.9561–dc23   2013007391

ISBN: 978-0-415-83696-8 (hbk)
ISBN: 978-1-138-37783-7 (pbk)

Typeset in Times New Roman
by Cenveo Publisher Services

Contents

Figures

Tables

Contributors

Ali Çarkoğlu is Professor of political science at Koç University, Istanbul. He received his Ph.D. at the State University of New York-Binghamton. His main research areas are voting behaviour, public opinion and party politics in Turkey. His publications appeared in *Democratization, European Journal of Political Research, Electoral Studies, Turkish Studies, New Perspectives on Turkey, South European Society and Politics, Middle Eastern Studies, Political Studies* and in edited volumes.

Ana I. Planet has a PhD in Philosophy, Arab and Islamic Studies, and holds degrees in Political Science and Arab and Islamic Studies. Professor at the Arab and Islamic Studies Department (Autónoma University of Madrid) she is currently the Director of the Mediterranean International Studies Team (TEIM). Her work deals with Moroccan migration into Spain and its impact on the origin and destination societies, the situation of Islam in Europe and the political debates regarding this.

Antonio Ávalos is Researcher at the Mediterranean International Studies (TEIM) at the Autónoma University of Madrid (UAM). He was Honorary Professor at the Department of Political Science and International Relations at UAM where he obtained his MA in Contemporary Arab and Islamic Studies. He has a degree in Law and a degree in Political Science and Administration; he also obtained a specialist Diploma in Political Science Studies (CEPC, Spanish Ministry of the Presidency). He specializes in the political and military elite in Turkey and its incorporation in the European Union regarding secularism/religion issues and in Security and International Relations. He is also concerned with cultural awareness of the military in peacekeeping and post-conflict reconstruction operations.

Aysen Çandaş Bilgen (PhD, Columbia University, 2005) is a political theorist at Boğaziçi University, Department of Political Science and International Relations, Istanbul, and a researcher at the Social Policy Forum of the same university.

Carmen Rodríguez holds a PhD from the Autónoma University of Madrid (UAM) and has conducted pre-doctoral and postdoctoral research at Boğaziçi University in Istanbul, Turkey. She is Researcher at the Mediterranean International Studies Team (TEIM/Election Watch OPEMAM) at UAM, where she teaches Contemporary Turkish Politics at the MA programme of Contemporary Arab and Islamic Studies. Her main areas of research are democratization, political parties and Turkey-EU relations.

Ceren Sözeri is a faculty member at the Communications Department of Galatasaray University. She received her Ph.D. from Marmara University. Her research areas are media economics, media policy, competition, diversity, new media and social media.

Dilek Kurban is the Stiftung Mercator-IPC Fellow at Stiftung Wissenschaft und Politik (SWP) in Berlin. She received her bachelor's degree in Political Science and International Relations from Boğaziçi University, Istanbul. She received her Master's in International Affairs (MIA) in Human Rights from Columbia University's School of International and Public Affairs, and her Juris Doctor (JD) degree from Columbia Law School. She worked at the Security Council Affairs Division of the United Nations Department of Political Affairs in New York and became Director of the Democratization Program at TESEV (Turkey). Kurban has published academic and policy-oriented research in the areas of minority rights, internal displacement, the Kurdish question, human rights law, and democratization in Turkey. She is also a columnist at Turkish national daily *Milliyet* and is a member of the European Network of Independent Experts in the non-discrimination field, supported by the European Commission.

Élise Massicard is Permanent Research Fellow at the CNRS in Paris, and Director of the Observatoire de la Vie Politique Turque at the Institut Français des Études Anatoliennes in Istanbul. Her main research areas are political sociology of Turkey, mobilization, state–society relations, identity politics and political territoriality. Among her works is *The Alevis in Turkey and Europe: Identity and managing territorial diversity* (Routledge, 2012).

Ergun Özbudun is Professor of constitutional law at İstanbul Şehir University. He has published books, articles and chapters widely in Turkish and English on constitutional law, political science, political parties and parliamentary law. He published recently *The Constitutional System of Turkey. 1876 to the Present* (Palgrave, 2011).

Fikret Adaman is Professor of economics at Boğaziçi University, Istanbul. He received his PhD. at Manchester University. His main research areas are political economy of Turkey, ecological economics and public economics. His publications have appeared in the *Cambridge Journal of*

Economics, Ecological Economics, New Left Review, New Perspectives on Turkey and in edited volumes. He is currently co-acting as an expert on social inclusion to the European Commission.

Fuat Keyman is Director of the Istanbul Policy Center, Istanbul, and Professor of International Relations at Sabancı University, Istanbul. He received his PhD. at Carleton University, Ottawa. He has published widely on citizenship and globalization. Among his books are *Hegemony through Transformation* (Macmillan-Palgrave, 2013), *Symbiotic Antagonisms: Contending discourses of nationalism in Turkey* (University of Utah Press, 2010, with Ayşe Kadioğlu) and *Remaking Turkey* (Oxford, 2008).

Hakan Yılmaz is Professor at the Department of political science and International Relations, Bogazici University, Istanbul. He received his PhD. (1996) degree at the Political Science Department of Columbia University in New York City. His main areas or research are ideologies and political culture in post-war Turkey; culture and identity dimensions of European integration and EU-Turkish Relations; and external-internal linkages in the processes of democratization. He has conducted, among others, research projects on Euroskepticism in Turkey (2004 and 2012); conservatism in Turkey (2006 and 2012); the image of Turkey (2009) and the processes of othering and discrimination in Turkey (2010).

İbrahim Saylan received his M.A. from CRIE, Siena University and his PhD. from Bilkent University. He is a lecturer at İzmir University of Economics. His main areas of interest are nationalism, citizenship, Turkish politics and the European integration process.

İlter Turan is Professor of Political Science at Istanbul Bilgi University, in which he served as President (1998–2001). He has publications in English and Turkish on comparative politics, Turkish politics and foreign policy. Lately his main research areas are politics of water, the Turkish parliament and the Turkish political parties.

Işık Gürleyen is Assistant Professor in the department of International Relations and the EU at Izmir University of Economics. Her research interests include Turkey–EU relations, foreign policy analysis, and the international dynamics of regime change. She has published *Impact of the European Union on Turkey's Democracy: Elite attitudes towards the EU and democratization* (Verlag Dr. Müller, 2008).

Marcus Graf holds a fulltime position as Associate Professor for Contemporary Art History and Theory at the Fine Art Faculty at Yeditepe University, where he has taught since 2003, and is also Resident Curator at Plato Sanat, Istanbul. After studying cultural sciences and esthetical communication in the Institute for Fine Arts, Aesthetics and Art History at the University of Hildesheim in Germany, he has worked for several institutions of art and culture as a curator, instructor, writer, project manager and artist. He received his PhD in 2010 from the Institute of Contemporary Art History, Aesthetic and Art Theory at Stuttgart Art Academy in Germany.

Mine Eder is Professor at the Department of Political Science and International Relations at Boğaziçi University in Istanbul. She received her PhD. from the University of Virginia specializing in political economy of late-industrialization. She has worked extensively on various aspects of Turkey's political economy, most recently on issues of poverty, exclusion and migration.

Pınar İlkkaracan is a researcher and activist trained both in psychotherapy and political science. She is the founding president of *Women for Women's Human Rights (WWHR)* –NEW WAYS. She initiated the *Coalition for Sexual and Bodily Rights in Muslim Societies (CSBR)*, a network of 40 leading academic and non-governmental organizations from Muslim countries around the world in 2001. Ilkkaracan has received the prestigious International Women's Human Rights Award of the Gruber Foundation in 2007.

Sabri Sayarı is Professor of political science at Bahçeşehir University in Istanbul. His research has mainly focused on political parties and party systems, political patronage and clientelism, terrorism and political violence, and foreign policy analysis. He has published in many journals and is the co-editor of *The Routledge Handbook of Modern Turkey* (Routledge, 2012).

Samim Akgönül is a historian and political scientist, professor at Strasbourg University and a researcher at the French National Centre for Scientific Research (CNRS). He is working mainly on minorities, specifically, non-Muslim minorities in Turkey, Muslim minorities in the Balkans and new Turkish minorities in Western Europe.

Senem Aydın-Düzgit is Assistant Professor in the Department of International Relations at Istanbul Bilgi University. She has published various articles in *West European Politics, Cooperation and Conflict, Alternatives, South European Society and Politics, Uluslararası İlişkiler* and *Politique Europeenne*. She is the author of *Constructions of European Identity: Debates and Discourses on Turkey and the EU* (Palgrave, 2012).

Süleyman Sözen is Associate Professor of Public Administration at the Faculty of economics and administrative sciences, Anadolu University, Eskişehir. His research interests include new public management, good governance, administrative reform and police management.

Tuba Kancı is Assistant Professor of Political Science at Yıldırım Beyazıt University, Ankara, Turkey. She received her PhD from Sabancı University and has been a Postdoctoral Fellow and Instructor at the

Department of International Relations, College of Administrative Sciences and Economics, at Koç University, Istanbul, Turkey. Her main research areas are citizenship studies, identity and gender studies, and also Political Theory and Turkish Politics. She has published among others 'The Reconfigurations in the Discourse of Nationalism and National Identity: Turkey at the turn of the twenty-first century' *Studies in Ethnicity and Nationalism*, 9 (3), 2009.

William Hale is a specialist in the politics of Turkey and the Middle East, and an Emeritus Professor in the University of London. He was a Visiting Professor, in the Faculty of Arts and Social Sciences, Sabancı University, Istanbul during 2006–8, and in the Department of Politics, University of Otago, New Zealand, in 2009. Besides a large number of papers on Turkish and Middle Eastern politics, his publications include *The Political and Economic Development of Modern Turkey* (Croom Helm, 1981), *Turkish Politics and the Military* (Routledge, 1994) and *Turkish Foreign Policy,* 1774–2000 (Frank Cass, 2000).

Yaprak Gürsoy (PhD University of Virginia) is an Assistant Professor in the Department of International Relations at Istanbul Bilgi University. Her research interests are democratization and civil–military relations. Her work has been published in several international journals, including *Democratization, Turkish Studies* and the *Journal of Political and Military Sociology.*

Preface

This book is the result of a multi-disciplinary research project carried out in the field of social sciences that aims to address the process of Turkish democratization. Academics from Turkish, English, French and Spanish universities joined forces in order to fully comprehend the global impact of the profound transformations and the interactions of different actors that have taken place in Turkey in recent years and how this is influencing the polity in its path towards democratization.

As this book was nearing publication, the May and June 2013 protests broke out in Turkey, images of which were seen around the world. The mass demonstrations and the way in which the government managed and responded to them form part of the process of Turkish democratization analysed in this book.

The seeds of this publication were planted in 2008 during the research seminar "Democracy and Democratization in Turkey" held 21–23 November in La Cristalera Residence Hall at the Autónoma University of Madrid. At that time, 14 academic experts from different fields covering Turkey's economy, culture, society and politics met under the aegis of the R&D project: "Political relations and human exchanges between Spain and the Muslim world" (1939–2004; SEJ2005–08867-C03–01/CPOL). The points raised during these seminars were developed and extended first during the R&D project "Spain in the face of political reforms and migrations in the Mediterranean and the Muslim World" (2009–11; CSO2008–06232-c03–01/cpol), then during the subsequent R&D project "The Arab-Islamic world in movement: migrations, reforms and elections and their impact on Spain" (CSO2011–29438-C05–01) and finally during a symposium held on 18 and 19 December 2009 at the Centre for Political and Constitutional Studies (CEPC) and the Círculo de Bellas Artes respectively, thanks to the public funding (Acción Complementaria) CSO2009–06186-E/SOCI. All of these projects were financed by the Spanish Ministry of Education and Science and the Ministry of Science and Innovation.

Most especially, this book has been made possible by the effort, commitment and generosity of the authors who contributed to this work with their analysis and research.

Acknowledgements

We would like to thank Bernabé López García for his help and invaluable encouragement in developing the Contemporary Turkish Studies field at the Mediterranean International Studies Team (TEIM), Autónoma University of Madrid, as well as the professors and researchers in the Faculty of Philosophy and Letters who collaborated to make this project come true. To Luciano Zaccara, with whom we have shared this field of study over many years, both as a teacher and a researcher. To Marién Durán Cenit and Inmaculada Szmolka at the University of Granada and Miguel Hernando de Larramendi at Castilla La Mancha University for their suggestions and comments. To Olivier Roy, Head of the Mediterranean Programme at the Robert Schuman Centre for Advanced Studies at the European University Institute in Florence, for his support during the research process. To the Castilla La Mancha University General Foundation for their support in finishing this project, to Pamela Lalonde, Daniel Marx and Ana Ballesteros for their language supervision and to everyone else who has contributed to making this book possible in one way or another.

Political parties

AKP (*Adalet ve Kalkınma Partisi*, Justice and Development Party)
ANAP (*Anavatan Partisi*, Motherland Party)
AP (*Adalet Partisi*, Justice Party)
BDP (*Barış ve Demokrasi Partisi*, Peace and Democracy Party)
BP (*Birlik Partisi*, Unity Party)
CHP (*Cumhuriyet Halk Partisi*, Republican People's Party),
CKMP (*Cumhuriyetçi Köylü Millet Partisi*, Republican Peasants' Nation Party)
DEHAP (*Demokratik Halk Partisi*, Democratic People's Party)
DP (*Demokrat Parti*, Democratic Party)
DSP (*Demokratik Sol Parti*, Democratic Left Party)
DTP (*Demokratik Toplum Partisi*, Democratic Society Party)
DYP (*Doğru Yol Partisi*, True Path Party)
FP (*Fazilet Partisi*, Virtue Party)
GP (*Genç Parti*, Youth Party)
HADEP (Halkın Demokrasi Partisi, People's Democracy Party)
HP (*Halkçı Parti*, Populist Party)
MÇP (*Milliyetçi Çalışma Partisi*, National Work Party)
MDP (*Milliyetçi Demokrasi Partisi*, Nationalist Democracy Party)
MHP (*Milliyetçi Hareket Partisi*, Nationalist Action Party)
MNP (*Milli Nizam Partisi*, National Order Party)
MSP (*Milli Selamet Partisi*, National Salvation Party)
Progressive Republican Party (*Terakkiperver Cumhuriyet Fırkası*)
RP (*Refah Partisi*, Welfare Party)
SHP (*Sosyaldemokrat Halk Partisi*, Social Democratic People's Party)
SODEP (*Sosyal Demokrat Partisi*, Social Democratic Party)
SP (*Saadet Partisi*, Felicity Party)
TİP (*Türkiye İşçi Partisi*, Turkish Workers Party)

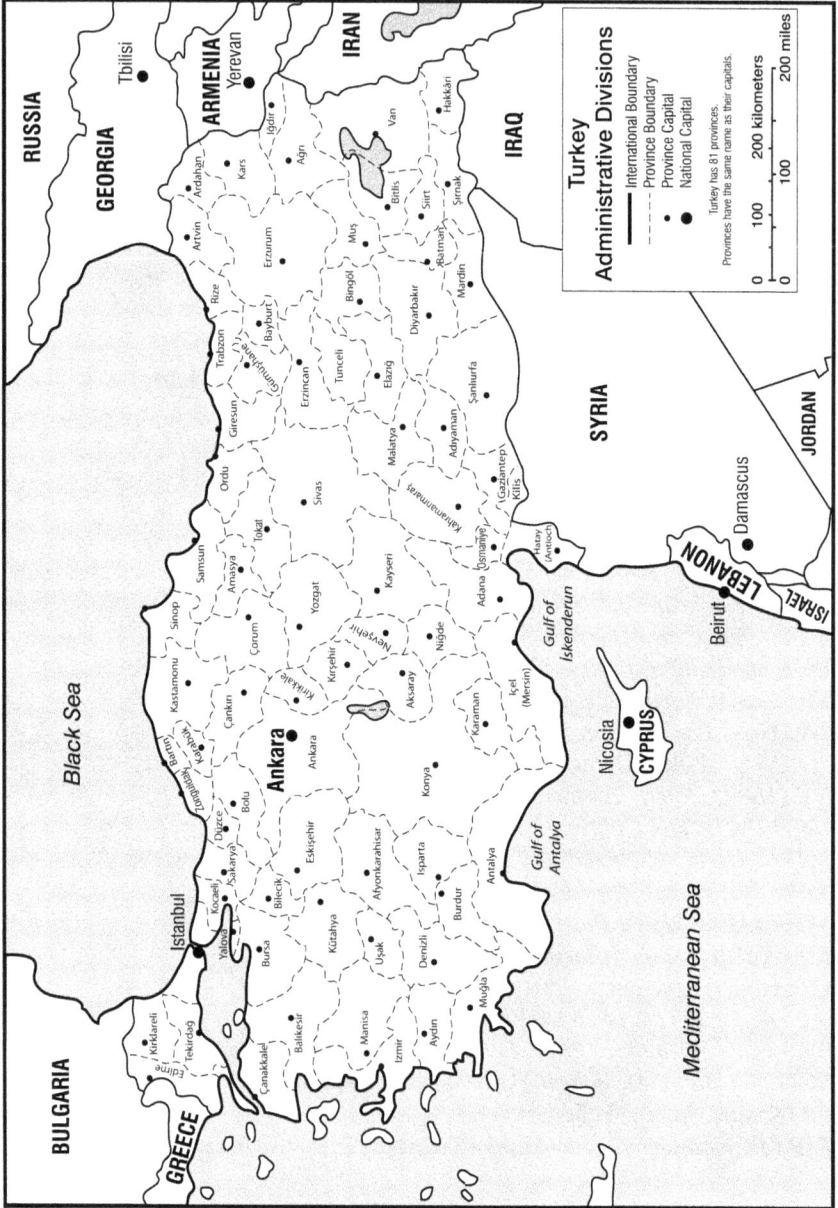

Turkey
Administrative Divisions

International Boundary
Province Boundary
Province Capital
National Capital

Turkey has 81 provinces.
Provinces have the same name as their capitals.

0   100   200 kilometers
0   100   200 miles

RUSSIA
GEORGIA
ARMENIA
Yerevan
Tbilisi
IRAN
IRAQ
SYRIA
LEBANON
Damascus
Beirut
ISRAEL
JORDAN
CYPRUS
Nicosia
BULGARIA
GREECE

Black Sea
Mediterranean Sea
Gulf of Iskenderun
Gulf of Antalya

Istanbul
Ankara

Edirne
Kırklareli
Tekirdağ
Çanakkale
Balıkesir
Manisa
İzmir
Aydın
Muğla
Denizli
Uşak
Kütahya
Bursa
Bilecik
Yalova
Kocaeli
Sakarya
Düzce
Bolu
Zonguldak
Bartın
Karabük
Kastamonu
Çankırı
Çorum
Kırıkkale
Eskişehir
Afyonkarahisar
Isparta
Burdur
Antalya
Konya
Karaman
İçel (Mersin)
Aksaray
Nevşehir
Niğde
Kırşehir
Yozgat
Kayseri
Sivas
Tokat
Amasya
Samsun
Sinop
Ordu
Giresun
Trabzon
Gümüşhane
Bayburt
Rize
Artvin
Ardahan
Kars
Iğdır
Ağrı
Erzurum
Erzincan
Tunceli
Bingöl
Muş
Van
Hakkâri
Bitlis
Siirt
Şırnak
Batman
Mardin
Diyarbakır
Elazığ
Malatya
Adıyaman
Şanlıurfa
Gaziantep
Kilis
Kahramanmaraş
Adana
Osmaniye
Hatay (Antioch)

Part I

Introduction and context

1 Democratization processes in defective democracies

The case of Turkey

Carmen Rodríguez, Antonio Ávalos, Hakan Yılmaz and Ana I. Planet

In the 12 June 2011 elections in Turkey, the AKP (*Adalet ve Kalkınma Partisi, Justice and Development Party*) claimed its third consecutive victory at the ballot box, winning a comfortable majority that once again made it possible to form a single-party government. Recep Tayyip Erdoğan, the head of the AKP, is the first political leader in the history of Turkish elections to increase the percentage of votes won by his party in three consecutive general elections. In the elections, the AKP received 49.83 per cent of the votes, giving them 326 seats. However, this overwhelming victory at the polls did not translate into the two-thirds majority needed to unilaterally adopt a Turkish constitution (which would require 367 seats) or even the 330 seats that would allow the party–after agreement in the Parliament on procedures for adoption and the president's approval–to call a referendum to endorse the change.

The main opposition parties, CHP (*Cumhuriyet Halk Partisi*, Republican People's Party), MHP (*Milliyetçi Hareket Partisi*, Nationalist Action Party) and the independent candidates backed by the BDP (*Barış ve Demokrasi Parti*, Peace and Democracy Party), were allocated 135, 53 and 36 seats respectively, corresponding to the percentage of votes they won: 25.96 per cent, 13.01 per cent and 6.63 per cent. After the elections, however, the YSK (*Yüksek Seçim Kurulu*, Supreme Electoral Board) decided to strip deputy (MP) Hatip Dicle, a candidate backed by the BDP, of his seat, since he had been sentenced to one year and eight months in prison for disseminating propaganda on behalf of the banned PKK (*Partiya Karkeren Kurdistan*, Kurdistan Workers' Party). This decision was very controversial, since it was not clear why the YSK had allowed Dicle to run in the first place. His seat was filled by Oya Eronat, an AKP candidate, thus increasing the number of deputies representing that party to 327.

The newly formed Grand National Assembly of Turkey confronted a tough challenge: to draft and approve a new constitution to replace the 1982 Turkish constitution written under the auspices of the military junta that ruled the country after the coup d'état in 1980. Although the different political groups agreed that a new constitution was needed, there was no doubt that the debates in Parliament were nonetheless going to be intense. The political parties that made up the Grand National Assembly of Turkey spoke for very different sectors of society, which made reaching an agreement more complex.

However, as other authors have noted before, a successful constitution requires the greatest possible consensus. In Turkey, then, it is crucial to reconcile different viewpoints: liberal, conservative, Turkish and Kurdish nationalist, and religious and rigidly secular sensibilities, among others. This fact is extremely important. Ozbudun and Gençkaya have already asserted that 'the Turkish experience in constitution-making can be described as a series of missed opportunities to create political institutions based on broad consensus' (2009: 3). Indeed, in a discussion of this issue in a comparative study on Italy, Spain and Turkey, McLaren asserted: 'it is consensual rule-making that would ultimately seem of utmost importance in explaining differential consolidation in Italy, Spain and Turkey' (2008: 268).

Thus, in its third term, the AKP Government faced a key moment for the Turkish political system. The objective of this book is to contribute an analysis that can help to make an assessment of the process of democratization in Turkey to date.

Theoretical framework

Gunther, Diamandouros and Puhle have singled out the different dimensions of an overall process of democratization: 'the breakdown of the previous regime,[1] democratic transition, regime consolidation, and democratic persistence', specifically noting that the transition process 'entails the creation of the basic political institutions of a new democratic system and the drafting of new rules for regulating the political behaviour of citizens, organisations and governing elites' (1995: xii). This is what O'Donnell would call the first transition, from 'the previous authoritarian regime to the installation of a democratic government' (1989: 20). During this transition process, there are expectations, as Linz says, 'that political authority will soon be derived only from the free decision of an electorate' (1990: 28). This political moment is characterised by its uncertainly, and there is no unanimity in academia in terms of establishing the end of the transition process, which includes free non-fraudulent elections and usually also involves the establishment of a new, democratic constitutional framework (Linz 1990: 28), (Huneeus 1994: 35). Linz and Stepan consider transition complete

> When sufficient agreement has been reached about political procedures to produce an elected government, when a government comes to power that is the direct result of a free and popular vote, when this government *de facto* has the authority to generate new policies, and when the executive, legislative and judicial power generated by the new democracy does not have to share power with other bodies *de iure*.
>
> (Linz and Stepan 1996a: 3)

It follows, then, that the authors caution that it is possible for a democratic transition to remain incomplete, since there may be non-elected institutions, such as the army, that unlawfully control part of the political sovereignty or there may be such a high degree of disagreement between the elites and the majority of the population about the new democratic institutions that normal evolution and consolidation are impeded by a serious threat of illegitimacy (Linz and Stepan 1996a: 4). Gunther, Diamandouros and Puhle also note in this respect that a transition 'may culminate in a new regime but that regime may not even be fully democratic' (Gunther, Diamandouros and Puhle 1995: 3).

This situation gives rise to serious disputes regarding the application of the concept of democratic consolidation to those regimes that do not possess the basic characteristics to be qualified as fully democratic. O'Donnell speaks of a second transition 'from this [democratic] government to the consolidation of democracy or, in other words, to the effective functioning of a democratic regime. I am speaking of political democracy (or polyarchy, according to Robert Dahl's useful and widely used definition)' (O'Donnell 1989: 20). Regarding democratic consolidation, Gunther, Diamandouros and Puhle argue that 'democratic consolidation, as we define it, requests full conformity with all the criteria inherent in a demanding, multifaceted procedural definition of democracy' (Gunther, Diamandouros and Puhle 1995:3). Also these authors suggested that the study of democratic consolidation is an even more complex phenomenon than that of transitions. The most recent research lines in this topic have focused on the actions of elites and on agency,[2] while 'consolidation is much more complex and it involves a much larger number of actors in a wider array of political arenas' (Gunther, Diamandouros and Puhle 1995: 3).

Linz and Stepan clearly state that it is not possible to speak of democratic consolidation unless the following three conditions are met: the existence of a state; a democratic transition that has been brought to completion (this is not the case if the freely elected government cannot impose, either *de iure* or *de facto*, its authority in certain areas because of confrontations with 'authoritarian enclaves', 'reserve domains' or military 'prerogatives'); and finally, the implementation of a democratic government that respects the constitutional framework and fundamental rights and freedoms. The authors assert that 'only democracies can become consolidated democracies' (Linz and Stepan 1996b: 14).

Schedler is one of the authors who have made an exhaustive study of the use of the term 'democratic consolidation', analysing some of the difficulties in its application. For some academics, it connotes a process, while for others it implies a point of arrival, a result, a target. This author suggests that the meaning of this concept, termed 'nebulous' by Pridham (1995: 167), depends on our empirical viewpoints and 'the type of regime we want to avoid or attain' (according to our normative horizons) (Schedler 1997: 2). For Schedler, democratic consolidation (in accordance with other authors like O'Donnell (1996) and Schneider (1995), who had already made note of this) is 'indeed an intrinsically teleological concept' (Schedler 1997: 5). The author lists five concepts of democratic consolidation: avoiding democratic breakdown, avoiding democratic erosion, institutionalising democracy, completing democracy and deepening democracy. If liberal democracies must face the challenge of preventing an 'erosion of democracy' then semi-democratic regimes[3] not only must prevent a regression to authoritarianism, but they must continue to push the evolution of the regime towards full democracy (Schedler 1998: 95). Moreover, for Schedler

> in semi-democracies which face the task of democratic completion, any talk about "the consolidation of democracy" is misleading. It suggests that a democratic regime is already in place (and only needs to be "consolidated") when in fact the issue at hand is constructing a fully democratic regime.
>
> (Schedler 1998: 99)

Merkel (2004) and Puhle (2005) use the term defective democracies to describe regimes that hold elections with a series of democratic requisites but that at the same time lack one or more of the characteristics shared by 'embedded democracies'.[4] The authors note four types of defective democracies: 1) Exclusive democracy, which contains criteria for excluding the suffrage of certain groups, usually based on questions of ethnicity, religion or gender. 2) Tutelary democracy, characterised by the existence of reserved domains outside the scope of democratically elected governments and veto players that may exercise their powers either by constitutional or extra-constitutional means, such as the military or oligarchic groups. 3) Delegative democracies, where 'the mechanisms of horizontal accountability, the checks and balances between the different powers, are out of order'. In this case, for example, a lack of judicial independence would be one of its symptoms. 4) Illiberal democracy, where the practice of the rule of law does not work well, constitutional norms are not properly implemented and human rights and fundamental liberties are not guaranteed. Some cases of defective democracies have a mixed profile that combine the characteristics defining each category.

In a regime with a defective democracy, if what Schedler calls 'completing democracy' (1998: 95) is to be produced, some alteration must occur in the existing institutions and regulations that are impeding the development of a fully democratic regime. As Valenzuela (1990) has noted, the process of democratization in this case cannot be based on the 'habituation, assimilation, or routine' of these non-democratic institutions, but some alteration must occur in the existing institutions. This alteration can be encouraged by the political class or by civil society–not just internal groups, but also external actors.

This work will study the case of a particular defective democracy, Turkey, which is undergoing a democratization process whose ideal goal would be to accomplish a full democratic regime. The term 'embedded democracies' as defined by Wolfgang Merkel (2004) and the members of the 'Defective Democracies' research project is very useful in terms of making the desired type of liberal democratic regime operational. This concept goes beyond other well-known definitions of democracy such as the one coined by Dahl as polyarchy in 1971. Still, it focuses on a specific and limited list of elements necessary to establish a democratic regime that can be taken separately, but that are also connected and mutually reinforcing.

Bearing in mind all of the positions, Linz and Stepan's theoretical framework (1996a) serves as a very useful analytical element to examine the process of democratization in Turkey at the present time, although this particular case is not one of democratic consolidation but about a prior stage. For these authors, consolidated democracies–within the essential framework of a sovereign state–have five interacting arenas in place that reinforce one another:

> first, the conditions must exist for the development of a free and lively civil society; second, there must be a relatively autonomous and valued political society; third, there must be a rule of law to ensure legal guarantees for citizens' freedoms and independent associational life; fourth, there must be a state bureaucracy that is usable by the new democratic government; fifth, there must be an institutionalised economic society.
>
> (Linz and Stepan 1996a: 7)

The analysis in this book focuses on the evolution of these five arenas in the Turkish case.

As noted on p. 5, there is some controversy regarding the use of the term democratic consolidation for regimes that are not fully democratic. However, this book starts from the premise that the arenas defined by Linz and Stepan to analyse problems of democratic transitions and consolidation are equally valid for the analysis of democratization processes in defective democracies.

In conclusion, the challenge before us is to analyse the processes of democratization that do not fully correspond to either the concept of transition or the concept of consolidation. The starting point is a regime that holds elections that meet a minimum of the democratic criteria for pluralism, inclusivity and transparent, open and contested elections, but which nonetheless have severe restrictions in other spheres, such as the existence of reserved domains, serious problems in the implementation of the separation of powers and their reciprocal control, and severe restrictions in the spheres of political and civil rights. We agree with Schedler when he asserts that if these political regimes are undergoing a democratization process, this process entails 'democratic completion' and is not about consolidating the current features of the regime (1998: 95–96).

The Turkish case

A 2012 report from Freedom House qualified Turkey as partly free, giving it a score of 3 for both political rights and civil liberties (on a scale of 1 to 7, with 1 representing the most free and 7 the least free). The Turkish state can claim prior democratic experience, a full institutional framework and a civil society capable of channelling significant proposals for change. Its history, however, has also been marked by coups d'état and severe restrictions in the sphere of political liberties and fundamental rights.

After the 1980 coup when a military junta seized power, the country underwent a transition overseen by the army that ensured that members of the military would play a decisive role and substantially cut back on individual rights and freedoms, as evidenced by the constitution approved in a 1982 referendum. This would have produced, according to the criteria of Linz and Stepan (1996a:3) mentioned pp. 4–5, an incomplete transition. The regime that emerged after the coup could be considered a 'defective' democracy (Merkel 2004 and Puhle 2005) that produced important restrictions in the sphere of rights. This defective democracy combined elements of 'tutelary democracy,' in which non-elected actors (the military establishment in Turkey's case) maintain reserved domains and act as veto players, and those of 'illiberal democracy', in which there are severe limitations in the exercise of public freedoms and fundamental rights and the effective rule of law. Although the political parties banned in 1981 were slowly rebuilt over the course of a decade, institutional weakness and/or a lack of will and conviction hindered any substantial reform of the political system. Though the democratization of the political system will continue to advance, any resulting reforms could be of limited scope and the fruit of difficult transactions between parties.

The Helsinki European Council's decision to recognise Turkey as an EU candidate country in 1999 served as a catalyst for the political parties to undertake a comprehensive process of political and economic reforms. Between 1999 and 2002, they were promoted by a difficult coalition of three parties and, after the AKP won an absolute majority in the 2002 general elections, this party determined to follow the path the previous coalition had already initiated with even greater intensity. As a result of all these changes, for the first time in Turkey, the political debate opened up significantly to issues that had been heretofore taboo (like the Kurdish question) and both the political elite and society in general seemed to come together in a synergy in favour of deep democratising changes.

Without a doubt, the Turkish regime that emerged after the 1980 coup d'état has evolved considerably since that year. Both internal democratic demands, such as those made by women's associations, which had a significant impact on the civil (2001) and penal (2005) code reforms, and the external influence of Turkey's candidacy to join the EU, have played a role. And although the Turkish constitution has been transformed in important ways, it is now commonly believed that more than a mere transformation is needed; the adoption of a new constitution that would leave authoritarian and repressive habits in the past is essential.

However, after negotiations began with the EU in 2005, the drive for democratization was slowed down, doubtless due to different factors, including most notably: messages from some EU governments ruling out the possibility of Turkey's candidacy that instead supported a different type of privileged relationship; the biased policies of the governing AKP, which, for example, while fighting to limit military power, have not been successful in establishing a legal and social framework that encourages the expansion of freedom of expression in the country (indeed, Keyman (2010: 325) believes that the AKP failed in its second term in that it did not establish the right equilibrium between its commitment to democratic consolidation and its conservative nature, thus intensifying scepticism about the objectives of its programme for democratising the regime); also during its second term in office, the AKP's erratic policies co-existed with those of an opposition that supported the status quo while wrapping itself in the discourse of national security.

The response in some sectors critical of the AKP at that time, whether political, military or judicial, was characterised by their defence of a dis-course that emphasised security (as opposed to the AKP's policies, which were seen as detrimental to the country's territorial and secular integrity) at the expense of greater democratic reforms, which would reinforce Turkish pluralism. The polarisation resulting from this process can be regarded as the inevitable consequence of a process of democratization that has opened a Pandora's box in Turkish society. Curtailed since the 1980 coup, these dif-ferent groups have been forced to openly confront their unresolved internal conflicts. Although this tension may be the natural consequence of a process in which different voices – which are not used to engaging in dialogue – must come to new agreements if they are to live together, the way in which this tension is resolved will determine the success of Turkish democratization.

Structure of the book

The analysis of the process of Turkish democratization presented in this book is designed, on the one hand, to study the recent democratic evolution not only in the Turkish political institutional arena, but also in other spheres, as defined in Linz and Stepan's classic work *Problems of Democratic Transition and Consolidation* (1996a: 7–15).[5] Using Schedler's (1998) concept, Turkey would be deep in a process that could be called 'completing democracy' and the theoretical framework advanced by Linz and Stepan makes it possible to analyse the complexity of this process in all its dimensions. This chapter is intended to provide a more detailed account of the work of these and other well known academics in the field of democratization.

If Linz and Stepan (1996a:7) consider that democratic consolidation requires much more than 'elections and markets', it is essential to begin with

10   *Rodríguez, Ávalos, Yılmaz and Planet*

a sovereign state. For this reason, the following chapter of the book is dedicated to the historical context of the formation of the Turkish nation-state. Linz and Stepan distinguish state-building from nation-building and discuss the conflicts that may arise during the evolution of these two differentiated concepts and the impact that they can have on processes of democratization: 'Whereas a state can exist on the basis of external conformity with its rules, a nation requires some internal identification' (Linz and Stepan 1996a:22). Democratic policies that emerge in the context of state-making tend to emphasise an inclusive and extensive citizenry that guarantees the equality of individual rights to citizens. On the contrary, a nation-state policy may be in serious opposition to this process of democratization if it pursues greater cultural homogeneity using repressive measures (Linz and Stepan 1996a: 25).

These questions are discussed in Chapter 2 by Ibrahim Saylan, 'The formation of citizenship in Turkey'. Following this, İlter Turan in 'Two steps forward one step back: Turkey's democratic transformation' reviews the development of both authoritarian and democratic trends in the Turkish regime since the proclamation of the Republic of Turkey, thus positioning the reader in the present day. An analysis of the international context rounds out these pieces. The outbreak of the Arab revolts has created a new situation in the region. Much speculation has been made as well about the possible influence that Turkey might have on the new regimes that are emerging, as a possible political and social model to follow. Conversely, it is essential to consider the effect that the revolts may have on Turkish internal politics, either by encouraging the democratization process with the push that may come from their spread or the so-called spirit of the times, as suggested by Linz and Stepan (1996a: 75–76), or by contributing negatively to it. This negative contribution could be due to the fact that the political instability occurring in the countries sharing borders with Turkey could intensify concerns for national security that go against democratization trends and the promotion of fundamental rights and freedoms. More time will have to pass before these recent influences can be evaluated, while other longer-term ones can be given a more unhurried and profound analysis. In Chapter 4, 'The international context of democratic reform in Turkey', William Hale takes a close look at the effect that interaction with European and transatlantic organisations and countries has had on the process of Turkish democratization.

These three chapters, then, introduce and provide context for the five relevant interconnected arenas defined by Linz and Stepan (which in this case are equally useful for the analysis of democratization processes in defective democracies). The first section includes articles relating to political society. Political parties are key actors since they carry out essential work when it comes to agreeing on the rules of the democratic game and their implementation. Chapter 5 by Sabri Sayarı, 'Party system and democratic consolidation in Turkey: problems and prospects', analyses the development of the Turkish party system. More specifically, Işık Gürleyen's Chapter 6, 'What did they promise for democracy and what did they deliver?: the AKP and the CHP 2002–11' aims to analyse the specific proposals made by the political parties to promote democratic reforms and the expansion of fundamental rights and freedoms.

The section dedicated to civil society features articles by Fuat Keyman and Tuba Kancı, Pinar İlkkaracan and Marcus Graf. Chapter 7 by Fuat Keyman and Tuba Kancı, 'Democratic consolidation and civil society in Turkey' analyses Turkish civil society's organisational capacity and the way in which civil society organisations approach democracy. Pınar İlkkaracan takes up the role of Turkish women's movements in the democratization process of Turkish society in Chapter 8, 'Democratization in Turkey from a gender perspective'. Finally, Chapter 9 by Marcus Graf, 'The Istanbul Art Scene – A Social System?', reflects on art's various functions for the palace, the state and the public and pays special attention to the interconnection between artistic and social developments in Turkey. The third major arena analysed focuses on the intersection between citizens and the idea of social justice as explained by Mine Eder in Chapter 10, 'Deepening neo-liberalisation and the changing welfare regime in Turkey: mutations of a populist, "sub-optimal" democracy'.

The fourth arena examined in the book includes an analysis of the functioning of the state apparatus. This segment includes the new public administration, the military, the judiciary and the perceptions that citizens have about corruption and the tax system in the country. Süleyman Sözen in his Chapter 11 'New public administration in Turkey' explains the substantial legal and structural changes that the Turkish public administration has undergone in the last few years in line with the democratization process in the country. Chapter 12 by Ali Çarkoğlu and Fikret Adaman: 'Determinants of tax evasion by households: evidence from Turkey' however, offers a different point of view, drawing on political culture. As a study of administrative efficiency, this piece analyses the perception that Turkish citizens have of tax evasion. Yaprak Gürsoy, in turn, in Chapter 13, 'From tutelary powers and interventions to civilian control: An overview of Turkish civil-military relations since the 1920s', provides an overview of Turkish civil-military relations primarily focusing on the post-1980 era, looking at whether or not military power is being superseded by civil power. Finally in this section, Ergun Özbudun in Chapter 14, 'The judiciary', reviews the current situation of this state power in Turkey, taking into account the developments fostered by the reforms requested by the EU.

The last arena analysed corresponds to the rule of law about which Linz and Stepan have stated:

> a rule of law embodied in a spirit of constitutionalism is an indispensable condition. A spirit of constitutionalism requires more than rule by majoritarianism. It entails a relatively strong consensus over the constitution and especially a commitment to 'self-binding' procedures of governance that require exceptional majorities to change.
>
> (Linz and Stepan 1996a: 10)

The rule of law must guarantee and promote the development of a democratic regime and the defence of fundamental rights and liberties.

In this respect, Chapter 15, by Ergun Özbudun, 'Democracy, tutelarism, and the search for a new constitution' is essential to understand the importance of the new Turkish constitutional process and the difficulties it faces. Senem Aydın in Chapter 16, 'Human rights in Turkey', provides an overview of the state of human rights in Turkey in the 1990s, followed by an account of the EU-induced reform process that accelerated in the 1999–2005 period. Ayşen Candaş Bilgen and Hakan Yılmaz in Chapter 17, 'The paradox of equality: subjective attitudes towards basic rights in Turkey' evaluate and contextualise the attitudes of Turkey's constituency with regard to basic rights from the perspective of political culture. Dilek Kurban focuses on the Kurdish issue, one of the most relevant topics influencing the democratization process in Turkey. Chapter 18 'The Kurdish question: law, politics and the limits of recognition', presents a systematic overview of the legal framework affecting the rights and freedoms of the Kurdish population in the Turkish political system and pays special attention to the current claims of the Kurdish population and whether or not the legal changes are reflecting them.

On the current situation of the minorities recognised by the Lausanne Treaty, Samim Akgönül, in Chapter 19, 'Non-Muslim minorities in the Turkish democratization process', has written about the main constraints these groups face, their demands and aspirations and the political response up to now. Elise Massicard, on the other hand, aims to analyse the question of democratization from the Alevi perspective in Chapter 20, 'Democratization in Turkey? Insights from the Alevi issue'. This piece pays special attention to the evolution not only of the legal framework affecting their rights, but also to the integration of Alevis in the political process, in particular to the Alevist movement that appeared in the late 1980s.

Ceren Sözeri in Chapter 21, 'The political economy of the media and its impact on freedom of expression in Turkey', looks at the situation of freedom of expression, a key issue concerning all democratization processes. Organisations such as Reporters Without Borders have noted a negative evolution in this area, since Turkey, which ranked 123 on the world ranking of freedom of expression in 2009, fell to 138 in 2010. Indeed, the Council of Europe's Commissioner for Human Rights Thomas Hammarberg also expressed his concern in this respect in a report published in April 2011.

Finally, the book ends with Chapter 22 'Some observations on Turkey's democratization process' in order to bring together the main ideas from the different chapters and propose some lines of analysis that can contribute to the study of the democratization processes in countries with defective democracies.

Notes

1 On the different paths to democratization, see: Stepan, A. (1986) 'Paths toward redemocratization: theoretical and comparative considerations', in G. O'Donnell,

P. Schmitter, L. Whitehead (eds) *Transitions from Authoritarian Rule, Comparative perspectives,* London: The Johns Hopkins University Press; Linz, J. J., and Stepan A. (1996) *Problems of Democratic Transition and Consolidation: Southern Europe, South America, and Post-Communist Europe,* Baltimore, MD: Johns Hopkins University Press.
2 Colomer, J. M. (1994) 'Teorías de la transición', *Revista de Estudios Políticos (Nueva Época),* 86: 243–53 and Martí i Puig, S. (2001) 'Y después de las transiciones qué? Un balance y análisis de las teorías del cambio político', *Revista de Estudios Políticos (Nueva Época)* 13: 101–24.
3 As Szmolka (2010:105–06, 117–18) notes:

The processes of political change initiated in authoritarian countries during the latest upheavals in the third wave of democratization have not always resulted in forms of democratic government. In many cases, they have produced new types of authoritarianism or near-democratic regimes that may experience significant problems in the way in which their government functions. It is difficult to classify these countries using the classic categories of political regimes established by political science, which has traditionally differentiated between democratic, authoritarian and totalitarian regimes. These new regimes have been conceptualised in different ways.

As the author explains, some scholars use terms that emphasise the democratic element: 'façade democracie', "pseudo-democracies" (Finer, 1970), "semi-democracies" (Diamond, Linz, Lipset, 1995; Mainwaring, Brinks and Pérez Liñán, 2000), among others. Other academics have stressed the adjective "authoritarian". Examples of this include the terms "competitive authoritarianism" (Levitsky and Way, 2002) and "electoral authoritarianism" (Schedler, 2002 and 2006). Finally, Szmolka mentions authors who have used the category of "hybrid political regimes". Szmolka herself differentiates between "defective democracies" and "pluralist authoritarianism" within hybrid political regimes.

For a compilation of the different definitions of hybrid regimes, see Diamond, L. (2002) 'Thinking About Hybrid Regimes', *Journal of Democracy,* 13(2): 21–35; Bogaards, M. (2009) 'How to classify hybrid regimes? Defective democracy and electoral authoritarianism', *Democratization,* 16(2): 399–423; Levitsky, S. and Way, L. (2002) 'The Rise of Competitive Authoritarianism', *Journal of Democracy,* 13 (2): 51–65.

4 Dimensions, partial regimes and criteria of embedded democracy as defined in Merkel (2004):
I. Dimension of vertical legitimacy
  A) Electoral regime
    1. Elected officials
    2. Inclusive suffrage
    3. Right to candidacy
    4. Correctly organized, free and fair elections
  B) Political rights
    5. Press freedom
    6. Freedom of association
II. Dimension of liberal constitutionalism and rule of law
  C) Civil Rights
    7. Individual liberties from violations of own rights by state/private agents
    8. Equality before the law

    D) Horizontal accountability
      9. Horizontal separation of powers
  III. Dimension of effective agenda control
    E) Effective power to rule
      10. Effective officials with effective right to rule
5 Ergun Özbudun has already applied Linz and Stepan's concept of democratic consolidation to the Turkish case in his book, Özbudun, E. (2000) *Contemporary Turkish Politics: Challenges to Democratic Consolidation*, London: Lynne Rienner.

References

Bogaards, M. (2009) 'How to classify hybrid regimes? Defective democracy and electoral authoritarianism', *Democratization*, 16(2): 399–423.

Colomer, J. M. (1994) 'Teorías de la transición', *Revista de Estudios Políticos (Nueva Época)*, 86: 243–53.

Diamond, L. (2002) 'Thinking about hybrid regimes', *Journal of Democracy*, 13(2): 21–35.

Gunther, R., Diamandouros, N. and Puhle, H. J. (eds) (1995) *The politics of democratic consolidation*, Baltimore and London: Johns Hopkins University Press.

Hammarberg, T. (2011) *Commissioner for Human Rights of the Council of Europe, Following his visit to Turkey*, from 27 to 29 April 2011, Report. Online. Available HTTP: <https://wcd.coe.int/wcd/ViewDoc.jsp?id=1814085> (accessed 7 December 2012).

Huneeus, C. M. (1994) 'La transición ha terminado', *Revista de Ciencia Política*, 16: 33–40.

Keyman, F. (2010) 'Modernization, globalization and democratization in Turkey: The AKP experience and its limits', *Constellations*, 17 (2): 313–26.

Levitsky, S. and Way, L. (2002) 'The Rise of Competitive Authoritarianism', *Journal of Democracy*, 13 (2): 51–65.

Linz, J. J. (1990) 'Transiciones a la democracia', *Reis*, 51: 7–33.

Linz, J. J. and Stepan, A. (1996a) *Problems of Democratic Transition and Consolidation: Southern Europe, South America, and Post-Communist Europe*, Baltimore, MD: The Johns Hopkins University Press.

—— (1996b) 'Toward Consolidated Democracies', *Journal of Democracy*, 7(2): 14–33.

McLaren, L. M. (2008) *Constructing Democracy in Southern Europe: A comparative analysis of Italy, Spain and Turkey*, London: Routledge.

Martí i Puig, S. (2001) 'Y después de las transiciones qué? Un balance y análisis de las teorías del cambio político', *Revista de Estudios Políticos (Nueva Época)*, 13: 101–24.

Merkel, W. (2004) 'Embedded and defective democracies', *Democratization*, 11(5): 33–58.

O'Donnell, G. (1989) 'Transiciones, continuidades y algunas paradojas', *Cuadernos Políticos*, 56: 19–36.

O'Donnell, G. (1996) 'Illusions about Consolidation', *Journal of Democracy*, 7: 34–51.

O'Donnell, G., Schmitter, P. and Whitehead, L. (1986) *Transitions from Authoritarian Rule: Comparative perspectives*, London:The Johns Hopkins University Press.

Özbudun, E. (2000) *Contemporary Turkish Politics: Challenges to Democratic Consolidation*, London: Lynne Rienner.

Özbudun,E. and Gençkaya, Ö. F. (2009) *Democratization and the Politics of Constitution-Making in Turkey*, Budapest: Central European University Press.

Pridham, G. (1995) 'The international context of democratic consolidation: Southern Europe in comparative perspective', in R. Gunther, N. Diamandouros and H.J. Puhle (eds) *The Politics of Democratic Consolidation, Southern Europe in Comparative Perspective*, Baltimore and London: The Johns Hopkins University Press.

Puhle, H. J. (2005) 'Democratic consolidation and defective democracies', Working papers online series, UAM. Online. Available HTTP: <http://portal.uam.es/portal/page/portal/ UAM_ORGANIZATIVO/Departamentos/CienciaPoliticaRelacionesInternacionales/ publicaciones%20en%20red/working_papers/archivos/47_2005.pdf> (accessed 11 March 2013).

Schedler, A. (1997) 'Concepts of Democratic Consolidation' Paper prepared for delivery at the 1997 meeting of the Latin American Studies Association (LASA), Continental Plaza Hotel, Guadalajara, Mexico, 17–19 April 1997.

—— (1998) 'What is democratic consolidation', *Journal of Democracy*, 9(2): 91–107.

Schneider, B. R. (1995) 'Democratic consolidations: some broad comparisons and sweeping arguments', *Latin American Research Review*, 30: 215–34.

Stepan, A. (1986) 'Paths toward redemocratization: Theoretical and comparative considerations', in G. O'Donnell, P. Schmitter and L. Whitehead (eds) *Transitions from Authoritarian Rule: Comparative perspectives*, London: The Johns Hopkins University Press.

Szmolka, I. V. (2010) 'Regímenes políticos híbridos. Democracias y autoritarismos con adjetivos. Su conceptualización, categorización y operacionalización dentro de la categoría de regímenes políticos', *Revista de Estudios Políticos*, 147: 103–35.

Valenzuela, J. S. (1990) 'Democratic consolidation in post-transitional settings: Notions, process and facilitating conditions', *Kellogg Institute Working Paper 150*. Online. Available HTTP: <http://kellogg.nd.edu/publications/workingpapers/WPS/ 150.pdf> (accessed 7 December 2012).

2 The formation of citizenship in Turkey

İbrahim Saylan

Introduction

Citizenship denotes a politico-legal link between state and people. In other words, it refers to membership of a political community, which provides members with a set of rights and obligations. In principle, membership to polity is universal, that is, open to everybody living within the territorial boundaries of the state. Nevertheless, the connection between people as nation and the state makes membership criteria highly contentious. Modern citizenship expresses membership to the nation-state. Although rights and duties associated with citizenship have changed in the course of history, nation-state has thus far remained the fundamental political unit defining borders and content of citizenship.

On the other hand, a number of factors have brought about questioning, or even crisis of modernist convictions, including the assumption of an indissoluble link between nation and state, which substantiated nation-state-based modern political structure. This questioning has naturally drawn attention to the institution of citizenship that has been closely bound with the state and nation in the age of nation-states.

As a part of modernity, nationalism claimed congruence of nation and state. In reality, nation was a goal to be achieved (Alter 1989). For this purpose, cultural, ethnic, religious identities were disregarded in the name of progress, prosperity, and democracy, which were defined within the context of national identity and interests. Hence, the nation-building process relegated some groups in society to minority positions in terms of religion, ethnicity, culture, and political ideology. And, unsurprisingly homogenizing attempts by the nation-states have met immediate reactions by especially autochthonous ethnic, cultural groups. Until the end of the Cold War, discontent could be hardly expressed or heard. However, for about two decades, ethnic, religious, and cultural identity claims have challenged nation-states in remarkable ways. All these demands have unavoidably related to the existing formation of citizenship, and the need to reconstruct it so to meet these diverse demands under new circumstances. Its repercussions have been more critical for the states in which the connection between nationhood and citizenship was stronger.

This chapter aims to analyze the construction of Turkish citizenship as a politico-legal institution and the discourse that links Turkish state and people in a specific way in the age of nation-states and within the context of contemporary challenges to its extant formation on various grounds. In doing this, it first gives a theoretical perspective about the relationship between nationalism and citizenship within the broader context of modernity in order to lay the ground for an analysis of the particular Turkish case. The second part focuses on the formation of citizenship in Turkey in the early republican period. In doing this, it deals with the nature and content of Turkish citizenship in relation to Turkish nationalism. Thus, while it sheds light on the tense relationship between political and cultural definitions of Turk, or state's double discourse on Turkishness, the effects of citizenship policies on various ethnic, religious minorities are examined. The third part is centered upon current debates and political struggles that relate to the reconstruction of Turkish citizenship with the effects of internal and external dynamics within the context of systemic gripes caused by increasing demands from ethnic, religious, and linguistic identities inside, and globalization processes, particularly European integration, that require the institutionalization and internalization of liberal-democratic normative\institutional framework. Thus, it is expected to denote the crucial interconnection between a democratic re-formation of Turkish citizenship and consolidation of democracy in the country.

Modernity, nationalism, citizenship

Citizenship in the modern age cannot be comprehended separately from nationalism and nation-state since they have all become entwined notwithstanding that they are conceptually differentiated. Nationalism has not only enabled establishment, and thus far reproduction, of nation-state in highly varied contexts, it has also articulated the institution of citizenship with a universalist redefinition of this new type of state since the French Revolution. Therefore, in order to have a better understanding of the notion of citizenship and related policies, one needs to scrutinize the nature, content, and mechanisms of nationalism, and then focus on the formation of nationality both at cultural and politico-legal levels within the framework of nation-state.

Nationalism

Nationalism has been one of the ideologies that put its imprint on the modern age. However, it is still a puzzling phenomenon basically since particularity, ambiguity, and resilience are features of it. Even so, one can contend that nationalism as a multifaceted phenomenon consists of mainly three aspects: sentiment, ideology, and politics. Its psychological\emotional aspect is much more related to human condition: the need for belongingness, the meaning attributed by people to their culture, language, and territory. The peculiarity of nationalism is that it exploits the emotional investment of individuals in the elements of their culture. Although there is nothing inevitable about creating national identity out of perennial cultural diversity and fluid ethno-cultural traits, nationalism reifies culture and makes a political principle out of it. This is the point where the ideological characteristic of nationalism becomes conspicuous.

Nationalist ideology basically prioritizes the nation and legitimates political authority on the basis of the will of nation. Associated with a clearly demarcated territory, nation is mobilized for self-determination. So, the idea that 'like should rule the like' (Wimmer 2002: 58) constitutes the main political objective. To put it differently, nationalism refers to a political principle ('nationality principle') which seeks to achieve congruence between cultural and political units (Gellner 1983: 1). It denotes a new mode of boundary-making according to which the legitimate unit was to be one composed of persons of the same culture. Thus, it does not only define the limits of the unit but it assumes that the unit has an institutional leadership (the state), and its main concern is that foreigners should not rule it (self-government) (Gellner 1997).

Nevertheless, despite all these naturalizing tendencies of nationalist ideology, nations are actually historical constructions. Like nation-states, nations are basically products of nationalism that emerged in the modern age through transformations in the nature of power, which led to the production and reception of nationalist politics. In this sense, nationalism is principally about politics and politics is about power (Breuilly 1993). Hence, in the struggle for power that is concentrated in the state in the modern age, there is no inevitability of the emergence of particular nations. Particular nations are the result of the defeat of alternative nationalisms (Billig 1995: 28). The establishment of the nation-state merely indicates political and/or military triumph of nationalist elites or just a specific part of them, but it does not mean that social and political integration is completed. In accordance with the ideal of congruence between political and cultural units, the process of nation-building which already started with nationalist political movement now sets about integrating and harmonizing socially, regionally, or even politically and institutionally divided sections of the people (Alter 1989: 21). Hence, nationalism as a form of identity politics by its nature politicizes cultural identity.[1] And, since homogeneity of the nation is largely fictitious, it needs to create a common culture in order to tie the inhabitants together in a national fellowship. Therefore, national identity as a construction is above all a political identity whose construction is a part of the broader process of nation-building.

The mechanisms underlying nation-building are various, and the efforts needed for this purpose vary since each case is shaped by different historical trajectories and political circumstances, and culminated in the formation of nation-states. Historically, this notion of particularity subsequently affected both the way that nation-states were established, and the conceptualization of the nation they adopted in the institutionalization of the link between the state and people through citizenship. Nation-states, as consequences of successful political movements, rose in two stages. First, they appeared as the nationalization of absolutist states of Western Europe that were relatively more homogeneous. Then, the model of nation-state was globalized through the break-up of empires that were more heterogeneous. In other words, nation-states were established in two ways: either modern state was captured by the nationalist project, or they were built on its premises by ideological and institutional copying (Wimmer 2002: 65). Actually, before nationalist ideas reached empires that led to their break-up in Habsburg, Ottoman and Russian cases, nationalism had been ramified with the emergence of the Herderian interpretation of nationalism in Germany (Greenfeld 1992).

These two historical patterns have been generally expressed on the basis of civic/ethnic dichotomy which is used to define two different conceptions of the nation, and thus citizenship regimes. This conceptualization was first used as Western and Eastern nationalisms by Kohn according to whom, while the former sees nations as associations of territorial populations governed by a single set of laws and institutions, the latter considers nations as organic wholes (Kohn 1967). Civic model is generally referred to as a standard Western model. Indeed, civicness and ethnicness have for decades been used as opposites. Recently, one can observe a relative convergence around the idea that national identity includes both civic and ethnic elements. Given that the definition of what holds the nation together varies not only from country to country, but also over time (Wimmer 2002: 56), and national identity has a culturally substantiated political character, it would be more meaningful to assert that every national identity consists of both civic and ethnic characteristics. Indeed, experiences of nation-building show that elements of both models may (and do) exist at the same time in varying degrees and differing forms. That is to say, the nation is defined not in terms of rival models but collectively signifying a cultural and a political bond (Özdoğan 2000).

Such a perspective does not totally ignore analytical usefulness of this distinction. It is apparent that the so-called civic type sees the nation as a political association based on consent and will; on the contrary, the ethnic model takes culture as its starting point, not the state.[2] Nonetheless, since the difference between ethnic and civic variants has generally been overrated, it becomes difficult to see that the civic type has also an ethnic dimension. In this sense, although only the ethnic type is labeled as exclusive, the inclusiveness of the civic type has limits. This mainly results from the fact that national 'us' vis-à-vis 'others' is constructed by particular cultural values, symbols, language, and common history.

Thus, despite the significance of the different historical trajectories followed by each case, there is always a general principle regarding nation-building that it strives to institutionalize national boundaries drawn according to the nationally defined processes of inclusion and exclusion. In Wimmer's words, national boundary-making aims at surrounding different dimensions of human life-economy, polity and society-as expression of a single entity, and in this process different forms of closure (legal, political, military, and social) are organized along the same set of nationalist principles.

(Wimmer 2002: 57)

This new type of boundary-making is so extensive and comprehensive that the nation-state model represents a unique type in history thus far in which the state, nation, and society converge, and politics becomes nation-wide politics. Furthermore, within 'the universal code of particularity' (Billig 1995), nation-states reinforce each other, making the nationalist representation of the world more and more plausible, as if this were the natural way to think and speak about society, politics, law, and so forth. Hence, the nation has gained two meanings in nationalist ideology: nation as the people living within a state, and nation as the nation-state (Billig 1995). Consequently, national 'us' is formed within a two-tiered process consisting of the construction of the nation as a cultural collective and a polity so as to complement each other and serve the same goal in the boundary-making process between 'us' and 'them'.

Nation as a cultural collectivite

The core nationalist assumption that nations are pre-existing cultural collectives contradicts with social reality, since claimed cultural homogeneity, belief in common past and future all need to be constructed and institutionalized as prevalent through a hard ideological and political struggle. Although historical evidence shows that most successful nationalisms presume some prior community of territory, language, or culture, objective elements *per se* do not lead to a distinct national identity. Nations come into existence as an amalgamation of objective and subjective elements through

cultural innovation, involving hard ideological labor, careful propaganda, and a creative imagination. (In other words), if politics is the ground upon which the category of the nation was first proposed, culture was the terrain where it was elaborated, and in this sense nationality is best conceived as a complex, uneven, and unpredictable process, forged from an interaction of cultural coalescence and specific political intervention, which cannot be reduced to static criteria of language, territory, ethnicity or culture.

(Eley and Suny 1996: 7–8)

Therefore, national identity construction is a multifaceted process resulting from a constant struggle between competing elites and aiming at obtaining the loyalty of the masses through a specific interpretation of so-called objective elements to yield a national consciousness. In this complex process of national identity construction, territory, language, and culture gain a moral meaning through manufacturing and manipulation of a particular view of the past. While ethnicity provides nationalism with an historical pedigree that it lacks (Hobsbawm 1992), nationalist construction converts the cultural traditions of everyday life into more specific claims. Historical, political, cultural, geographical, and socio-economic symbols or boundary-markers (heroes, habits, institutions, values, traditions, glories, and trau-mata) are used selectively for the present-day construction of the past (Cal-houn 1993). Thus, ethno-history is of a crucial role in the making and maintenance of the 'us' and 'them' distinction by providing the nation with a primordial aura through which the claim of historical continuity, and certain rights specific to nations, are legitimated.

The nation as polity: Nationalization of citizenship

Besides its cultural dimension, nationality is constructed at a political level, which has much more immediate and concrete consequences. This dimension is directly related to the domain of nation-states where the state and the nation are linked to each other through the institution of citizenship. With the French Revolution, citizenship, which was the symbol of freedom since the ancient Greeks, became associated with nationality (Gross 1999: 91).[3] The link established was so critical that to be a citizen of a state now meant belonging to its nation. Thus, equality derived from belonging to the same community which was culturally defined and complemented by membership to the political community.

The conflation of the state and nation in the modern (nationalist) inter-pretation of citizenship[4] was a reflection of the nationalist ideal of achiev-ing congruence between cultural and political units. In this sense, the institution of citizenship complements nationalist ideology. While the idea of nation as a cultural collective entails a great deal of cultural innovation, premises of citizenship are highly tangible. Through citizenship that enables institutional closure in legal, political, economic, and social domains (Wimmer 2002), national boundaries at an imaginary level become quite palpable. Thus, nationalism did not only imagine the nation as a horizontal comradeship (community), but also as a polity whose members are tied to each other through specific rights and duties. In this sense, we enjoy citizenship not as members of humanity, but rather as the members of particular nation-states. Therefore, modern citizenship is nationalized citizenship that includes a number of characteristics. First of all, it refers to membership of a political community. Second, this char-acteristically entails certain rights or privileges and an attendant set of duties and obligations such as social security, political representation through elections, taxation, military service, and so on.[5] Third, citizenship is usually an ascribed status given us at birth. In this sense, it is an important component of individual identity ('who I am'). (Pierson 2004).

On the grounds of these shared characteristics, one can mention at least two models of citizenship which directly relates to the conception of the nation. Therefore, historical trajectories of nationalist movements condition the conception of the nation on the civic-ethnic continuum, as a corollary, the conception of the nation shapes citizenship regimes to a great extent. Although citizenship models are conventionally analyzed in two models as civic and ethnic, the civic model also consists of two different interpretations. Therefore, we can argue that there are three models of citizenship. The first model is the French type ('republican model') that territorially defines citizenship. Rejecting ethno-cultural diversity, it is based on cultural homogeneity. Since it establishes an obligatory relationship between political authority and culture, it is culturally repressive and assimilationist. It is not exclusive but its criteria of inclusiveness may be problematic. The second type of civic model is the Anglo-Saxon type that is also based on territoriality. However, it differs from the French type, since it rests upon voluntary assimilation. It conceptualizes the nation as the unity of diversity rather than as a monolithic unity. As long as different ethnic groups are loyal to legal-political supra-identity, they are free to live their cultures (sub-identities) that are legally recognized. The ethnic model is different from the civic model in the sense that it defines the nation as a genealogical, organic entity, membership to which is not voluntary but by birth (Kurubaş 2008: 27–28).

Within this context, one can maintain that the model of citizenship in a country is connected to the prevailing characteristics of nationalism according to which both criteria for, and expectations from, membership change. In a general sense, modern citizenship has had two conflicting characteristics since its inception in the wake of the French Revolution. On the one hand, it is a reflection of a revolutionary idea, a democratizing force promoted by nationalist ideology. Despite being limited to nationally defined borders, its universalist interpretation has provided modern citizenship with a rights-based, egalitarian positive image. This implied both the democratization of the political sphere by allowing participation for each member of polity and an increasingly active role for the nation-state. Notwithstanding these positive connotations, citizenship has been actually exclusive in at least two senses. First, universalism and participation associated with citizenship have been highly ambivalent. Citizenship applies only to those who can generally be redeemed only by the particular state to which such citizenship applies. Second, citizenship has been formally or substantively exclusive. Formally, various categories of persons, such as immigrants and political refugees have been excluded from the status of citizen. On the other hand, citizens who had formally the same rights and duties have not been substantively equal to each other. Certain groups, even if they are fortunate enough to enjoy the status of citizen, on the basis of gender, ethnicity, religion, or sexual orientation have been often subject to systematic discrimination (Pierson 2004).

Equally important, citizenship policies and practices have served to complement nationalist ideologies in drawing and maintaining national boundaries. Citizenship has provided a politico-legal framework for nation-building policies oriented toward the congruence between cultural and political units. In conjunction with the prevalent conception of the nation produced and reproduced by nationalist ideology in a country, universal membership to political community has in many cases led to voluntary or forceful assimilation to the cultural unit. While the ethnic citizenship model from the very beginning closes its doors to ethnically external members, the French civic model rejects ethno-cultural diversity and demands assimilation into a politico-territorially defined French nation. Even the civic Anglo-Saxon model expects assimilation, though being voluntary in principle.

In this sense, modern citizenship that is associated with a nationality model has been exclusionary, particularistic, and/or assimilationist despite the fact that it claims to be inclusionary and universal. Citizenship, like nationalism, has also been an open-ended political practice connected to power relations. In this sense, cultural and political conceptions of nationality are contestable, subject to constant reconstruction through political struggle. Any challenges to the prevalent form of citizenship might turn into challenges to the existing form of national identity, especially in contexts where the link between ethno-cultural identity and citizenship is so strong.

The Turkish experience

Turkish nationalism

The Turkish experience constitutes a quite interesting case in order to shed light on ramifications of the close relationship between citizenship and nationalism within the broader context of modernity. Accordingly, any attempt to understand what makes up 'Turkishness', and its limits on both cultural and politico-legal grounds, requires an analysis of Turkish nationalism within the framework of Turkish modernization.

By taking modernization as almost synonymous with westernization, Turkish modernization, envisioned and led by the official ideology of Kemalism, with the foundation of the Turkish Republic in 1923, aimed at reaching the contemporary level of (Western) civilization. This meant that the making of modern Turkey was based on the creation of an independent nation-state, the promotion of industrialization, and the construction of a secular and modern national identity as an expression of 'the will to (Western) civilization' (Keyman 2005: 271). Thus, Turkish modernization emerged as a project that would be applied 'from above' by Kemalist elites to transform the Anatolian population into secular members of the emerging Turkish nation. In line with it, nationalism and secularism have constituted the core of Kemalist ideology, among its six fundamental principles symbolized by 'six arrows' (Zürcher 2004).

As one of the central tenets of Kemalism, Turkish nationalism[6] was mainly shaped by two factors which to a great extent highlight the path followed by Turkish modernization, conceptualization of national identity, citizenship practices, and particularly the Turkish official view of Muslim or non-Muslim minorities since the inception of the republican era. Modern Turkey was founded after a deep crisis during which its very existence was endangered. The gradual demise of the Ottoman Empire, and the Sevres Treaty (1920) that formally dissolved the Empire by leading to the partition of Anatolian territory by European powers, brought about a nation-state tradition that has had strong survival and threat perception. However, this perception did not turn into anti-Westernism. By contrast, while the West was the 'Other' having had designs upon the Turkish homeland, it simultaneously represented the model that should be adopted to attain contemporary civilization.[7] This ambivalent stance towards the West has been one the major factors that gives Turkish nationalism its color. On the one hand, the ultimate objective of Turkish modernization was the Kemalist will to civilize through the establishment of a nation-state. Hence, Kemalism has had a teleological character defined with the Turkish march towards the West. On the other hand, nationalism as a crucial component of Turkish modernization has consisted of anti-Western (or at least Euro-sceptic) elements,[8] which have been conspicuous but eventually overshadowed by the ultimate objective of the Kemalist project. It is not surprising that this synthesis has given rise to a self-perception and a perception of the West full of contradictions and tension. Consequently, while these perceptions embodied a particular mindset shaping the way in which Turkish nationalism and Turkish national identity were molded, they also substantiated a specific structure of power relations dominated by the Kemalist elite.[9]

The nature and ultimate objective of Turkish modernization thus imply at least two facts about Turkish nationalism. As an historical fact, the state preceded the nation in the Turkish context (Kadıoğlu 1995: 92). Therefore, national identity did not appear as an outcome of long historical processes. Instead, it was forged by the state as a prerequisite of modernization. While Turkish nationalism, on the one hand, set about reinvigorating the 'essence' through 'invention of the tradition' attuned with the 'general code of particularity' of nationalist ideology, it was first and foremost employed as an "instrument for purposes of social control and mobilization towards modernization" (Keyman and İçduygu 2005: 12). As a second fact that is interrelated to the first one, Turkish nationalism has had a state-centric character. By underlying the importance of Heper's statement that the Kemalist elite conceived the state as an active agent that shapes and reshapes the nation to the level of contemporary civilization, Keyman rightly maintains that "the Kemalist idea of the state was embedded in the question of how to activate the people toward the goal of civilization, that is, how to construct a national identity compatible with the will to civilization" (Keyman 2005: 275). Thus, state-centrism could not only be explained with the notion of survival and threat. The Kemalist attempt to forge a national identity was also attuned with the 'from-above' character of Turkish modernization.

Having an organic vision of society which was seen as essential for survival and modernization, Turkish nationalism saw the 'duties and services' to the state of different occupation groups, as the basis of the society (Kazancıgil and Özbudun 1981). More crucially, this view has underlain the official doctrine of the 'indivisible unity of the state with its territory and its nation' since the founding of the republic. According to this doctrine, there is only one people in Turkey, and it comprises the totality of the country's citizens, who enjoy the same rights and have the same obligations (Kramer 2000: 40).[10]

Nonetheless, despite official rhetoric of civic nationalism, the state-centered Turkish nationalism has had a hybrid character, combining a French-style civic nationalism based on the principle of citizenship and territoriality with ethnic nationalism of the German type. (Kadıoğlu 1993; Bora 2003). While its civilizationist dimension suggested Turkish nationality was an expression of politico-territorially defined common will, its culturalist aspect has aimed to achieve a centralist, absolutist and monist national identity.[11] This hybrid nationalist discourse underpinned formation and practices of citizenship in Turkey.

Republican understanding of citizenship

Within the framework of the aimed congruence between cultural and political units, the Turkish state's attempt to create a homogenous national identity was not very different from what happened in many other European countries.[12] Among others, Turkey was inspired especially by France in many ways. In accordance with the adopted understanding of national sovereignty in the form of supremacy of general will over particular identities and interests, the idea of 'unity-over-diversity' prevailed in the formation of nation. Nevertheless, Turkish experience developed from the above unlike the contractual French case. Strong state tradition and insufficient socio-economic development historically prevented flourishing of civil society, which implied that the invention of a Turkish nation would require much more toilsome and imaginative ideological efforts by republican elites. In the creation of a general will as an integrative force, Turkish republican elites sought to create a sense of public consciousness as the basis of common civic culture. Thus, nation-formation and citizenship formation went hand in hand in a way inspired by the assimilationist and territorial French model with quite significant particularities.

As the Turkish nation is imagined as a classless, coherent, corporate body without any privileges, Turkish citizenship was based on a non-individualized conception. Members of a Turkish nation were deemed to be organically tied to each other and were considered to be passive and obedient citizens. The masses were given civil and political rights, but the state saw citizenship primarily as an ideological device through which it attempted to transform society in line with its will to civilize (Keyman and İçduygu 2005). Primacy of state interests over individual ones reflected Gökalpian's idea that 'Turkish citizens had no right but duty'. Until the creation and consolidation of the general will, individual rights and freedoms could be dismissed. Citizens of the new-born Turkish Republic needed to be equipped with modern ideas, values and principles. When they internalized civic virtues, they would become mature enough to put into practice individual freedoms and a democratic republican regime would materialize. Hence, citizenship in Turkey has not been a liberal category safeguarding individual autonomy that is politically and culturally embodied through the language of rights. Consequently, the republican model of citizenship with the strong-state tradition, national development, and an organic vision of society established essential elements of from-above operation of Turkish modernization (Keyman and İçduygu 2005: 7).

The boundaries of Turkishness: Turkish nationality and citizenship

In search of its congruence, the Turkish nation-state faced up to the typical dilemma of nationalism: the fact of divergent ethno-cultural and political boundaries running counter to nationalist claims. Civic and ethnic models presented distinct ways to resolve this question.

In their efforts to achieve congruence between national and political units, republican ruling elites sought to transform traditional, cosmopolitan Ottoman society into a uniform, homogeneous Turkish nation. On its march to civilization, not only individuality, but also ethnic and religious diversity, at group level were marginalized or suppressed.

Turkish national identity was remarkably affected by the Ottoman millet (nation) system[13] yet with a significant epistemological change. While nationality in the Ottoman millet system was determined by a person's membership to a religious community, all Muslims of Anatolian territory were now accepted as members of the Turkish millet. Thus, while the millet gained a national character, Islam in the new secular regime turned into a nominal marker of Turkishness.[14] In line with Gökalp's conception of 'one religion and one language', all Muslims were accepted as Turks, regardless of their ethnicity and language. Ethnically non-Turkish Muslims were expected to assimilate into the Turkish nation through the Turkish language.

Nevertheless, non-Muslims were denied Turkish national identity, even if they did speak Turkish. They were seen as citizens outside the body of the Turkish nation. Ethno-religious definitions of nation excluded the non-Muslims from Turkishness and saw them fit only for Turkish citizenship. Republican ruling elites thought that the persistence of millet divisions and non-Muslim minorities were among the major causes of the fall of the Ottoman Empire. Non-Muslim minorities were considered to be unreliable and culturally "non-assimilable." They could be citizens of the Turkish state, but not be members of the Turkish nation. Non-Muslim ethno-religious groups (the Greek Orthodox, Armenian-Gregorian, and Jewish communities) were recognized as ethnic minorities with the 1923 Treaty of

Lausanne. The Treaty, that still underpins the minority regime in Turkey, granted minority status only to these non-Muslim groups by providing them with some special rights.[15] Articles 37 to 45 of the Treaty specify basic principles for the protection of minorities. These mainly include the right to use their own language, run their own schools, and maintain their social and religious institutions (Oran 2004).

Hence, although Kemalism presented itself as a radical departure from the Ottoman system, one can easily view remarkable continuities also between the national identification promoted by republican Turkey and the Ottoman millet system. The Treaty of Lausanne projected a Turkish national identity for all Muslim citizens of Turkey. The civic dimension of the emerging sense of Turkish citizenship de-emphasized the ethnic background of heterogeneous Muslim communities in Anatolia. According to the official doctrine, there were no Muslim ethnic minorities; the state therefore pursued an active policy of assimilation based on a conceptualization of Turkishness as a part of a common national, linguistic, and territorial identity. Only non-Muslim ethnic groups were recognized as minority groups who only belonged to the category of Turkish citizenship.

In this regard, citizenship expressed less than Turkishness for the Turkish state (Yeğen 2004). Moreover, although the institution of Turkish citizenship implied politico-legal neutrality, the Turkish state in practice has discriminated between 'national' and 'formal' citizens in favor of the former (Soner 2005: 290). Nevertheless, both the discourses of nationalism and citizenship have expressed this differentiation in highly ambiguous ways from the beginning of the republican period. So, 'dual practices of citizenship' were based on the state's double discourse. For instance, article 88 of the 1924 Constitution reads as follows: "the people of Turkey regardless of their religion and race would, in terms of citizenship, be called Turkish". The picture becomes more blurred when one seeks to comprehend the real meaning of the motto uttered by Atatürk, founding father of Turkish Republic: "what happiness to the one who says I am a Turk". This statement seemingly refers to civic model; but, considering the fact that Turkishness is not open to everyone, there are limitations to this ostensibly inclusive conceptualization. Yeğen (2004) convincingly argues that there has been a genetic undecidability between ethnic and political models. According to him, although Article 54 of the 1961 Constitution and Article 66 of the 1982 Constitution do not involve expression of 'in terms of citizenship', the undecidability about the notion of Turkishness did not completely disappear in these texts. In other words, dual practices of citizenship did not stem from a discord between theory and practice. An examination of the Turkish state's citizenship policies within the light of immigration and resettlement policies do not only display the state's discrimination between its citizens as full citizens and marginalized members, but also reveals its efforts for inclusionary forceful assimilation of non-Turkish Muslims elements into the Turkish nation, specifically the Kurds.

The politics of nationalism and citizenship policies

The genetic discord provided the Turkish state with a broader space for political maneuvering. Any cultural or political demands from religious and ethnic minority groups could be responded to by the establishment with the argument that the Turkish state is ethnically-blind and secular, and all Turkish citizens have the same rights and obligations. In reality, despite the equality on legal basis, Turkish citizenship policies have displayed discriminatory, unegalitarian dual and assimilative practices. Citizenship policies, as a complementary part of the politics of nationalism in the struggle for power, have been effectively used in the process of nation-building and sustaining status quo since then. While dual practices led to gradual marginalization of non-Muslims who were seen as non-assimilable, dual and assimilative practices toward non-Turkish and/or non-Sunni Muslims denied recognition, thus representation, of ethnic and cultural diversity in the public sphere.

In terms of the formation of citizenship in Turkey, the early republican years have a remarkable place. The seemingly civic conception of national identity in the 1920s was replaced by an ethnic definition of the Turkish nation with the rise of a more authoritarian, intolerant nationalism, ethnic definition of the Turkish nation in the 1930s. A number of factors, including the effects of expanding totalitarian ideologies in Europe on Turkey, and Kurdish reactions to centralization and homogenization by the modern state led to rise of Turkish nationalism. Systematic ethnicization of Turkish national identity was carried out through some significant developments at that time. The use of history in the Turkish 'invention of tradition' reached its limits. Turkish History Thesis (*Türk Tarih Tezi*) defined race, ethnicity, and long glorious history as constitutive elements of Turkishness; it claimed Turkish racial and historical continuity in Anatolia. Sun-Language Theory (*Güneş-Dil Teorisi*) put forward the thesis that all languages are descendants of a Central Asian primal language, and the only language remaining more or less the same as this primal language was Turkish. The claim of supremacy of Turkish triggered a systematic campaign for the purification of the Turkish language from Arabic and Persian words. 'Turkification' efforts were not limited to the intellectual sphere. The decade of 'High Kemalism' saw that the state put a number of specific policies into practice. The 'Citizen Speak Turkish' (*Vatandaş Türkçe Konuş!*) campaign that was started by the student union at the Darülfünun Law School in 1928, and sponsored by the Government, aimed at making Turkish the unique language spoken in public areas through the ban of speaking any language but Turkish. The Law on Last Names (*Soyadı Kanunu*, 1934, Law Nr 2741) did not oblige every Turkish citizen to take a last name but it also added that "names of foreign races and nations could not be adopted as last names" (in Çağaptay 2006: 61). Another policy at that time was the imposition of 1942 Capital Tax. The Capital Tax was levied on the wealthy Turkish citizens, with the stated aim of increasing funds for the country's defense in case of an entry into WWII. In practice, it aimed at the Turkification of the economy by giving an end to the superiority of non-Muslims, such as Jews, Greeks, and Armenians, in the economy through generally imposing higher tariffs on them. Around 2,000 non-Muslims who failed to pay huge amount demanded in a month were arrested and sent to forced labor camps (Aktar 2002).

Dual practices and an assimilationist attitude of the state were probably best represented in the policies of immigration and resettlement. Within the context of the particular synthesis of civic and ethnic elements on the basis of an ethno-religious differentiation between Muslims and non-Muslims by following Ottoman tradition, Kemalist immigration policies have seen Islam as the key factor in admitting immigrants to the country. The 1923 population exchange agreement with Greece asserted "Greek subjects, who belonged to the Muslim faith, would be exchanged with Turkish subjects of the Greek-Orthodox faith" (Çağaptay 2006: 83). In 1936, an immigration treaty with Romania allowed immigration of 'the Muslim Turkish population', having denied demands from the Greek-Orthodox Gagauz Turks for immigration to Turkey.[16]

The resettlement laws also played an important role in the Turkification of Anatolian country in conjunction with immigration policies. In 1926, the Turkish Parliament promulgated the Resettlement Law (İskan Kanunu, Nr.885) in which Turkish culture – being from Muslim faith, the Turkish language, sharing common past and values of Ottoman-Turkish Muslims {} was accepted as criteria to be admitted as immigrants (Çağaptay 2006: 84–85). Speaking Turkish is considered to be an ability that could be gained in Turkey. Within the framework of these criteria, immigrants who mainly were from the Balkans and Caucasus were settled in a planned way so that they could be Turkified. The Law Nr.885 was followed by another law for resettlement in 1934 (Nr. 2510). It primarily targeted relocation of an insurgent Kurdish population in Southeastern and Eastern Anatolia.

Consequently, the resettlement and immigration policies were designed and implemented to mold all Muslim elements into a homogeneous Turkish nation. In the interwar era, Kemalism saw both Turkishness and Turkish citizenship as privileges. In its naturalization policies, the Turkish state blended *ius soli* and *ius sanguinis*. It granted citizenship not only to ethnic Turks, but also to Ottoman Muslims who immigrated to the country. Ankara also naturalized converted East-Central European Christians and Jews, Hellenic Greeks, and both Christian and Jewish White Russians. Even if these cases seem to display that ethnicity was unimportant, the Government considered citizenship as a category exclusive to the former Muslim millet. Except for the Christians who were recognized as ethnic minorities of Turkey, Christian ex-Ottomans, particularly Armenians, were unlikely to get Turkish citizenship (Çağaptay 2006: 80–81).

Non-Muslim minorities

The Christian Communities

The Kemalists saw the Christians as a separate ethno-religious community, as citizens outside the body of the Turkish nation. Mainly composed of separate ethno-religious minority groups of Greeks and Armenians,[17] Christian minorities faced negative attitude by Turkish nationalism due to mainly recent violent conflicts with Christian minorities, ethnic cleansing of the Ottoman Muslims by the Christian powers, and collaboration of proselytizing Catholic and Protestant Churches with local people against the Sublime Porte (Çağaptay 2006: 137). With the Lausanne Treaty, Turkey recognized ethno-religious communities of Greeks and Armenians in Turkey as minorities and guaranteed to protect their rights.

In the early years of the Republic, the largest minority group in Turkey was the Greek Orthodox community. A population of 100,000 Greeks was excluded from population exchange in reciprocity with the exclusion of the Turkish community of Western Thrace. They were settled in Istanbul and the islands of Gökçeada (Imvros) and Bozcaada (Tenedos). Their number is today estimated to comprise up to a few thousand (Oran, 2004). This drastic decrease in their number can be explained through a number of significant policies and incidents. First of all, the 1942 Capital Tax that aimed at giving an end to economic superiority of non-Muslims communities in Turkish economy did not only cost the Greeks a great of deal of loss in their wealth, but also their alienation from the Turkish political community, which instigated their migration to Greece in large numbers. The Greek community of Turkey was also negatively affected by the Greco-Turkish confrontation over Cyprus. In response to persecution of Turks in Cyprus, on September 6–7 1955, a mob that was probably encouraged by the Government destroyed much of the Greek businesses, churches, schools, cemeteries, and other historical monuments. In 1971, the Government closed the Halki (Heybeliada) Department of Advanced Religious Studies which prepared appointees for office within the church (Poulton, 1997: 274). By poisoning political relations between Turkish and Greek states, the Cyprus conflict deteriorated Greeks' situation in Turkey.

The other main Christian minority in Turkey is the Armenian community. They suffered heavy losses in the mass murders during WWI. According to the census of 1960, there were 52,756 Armenian-speaking citizens in Turkey, most of whom lived in Istanbul. Today, they number around 30,000. They also suffered Capital Tax, in the riots of September 6–7, 1955. The Government's distrust of the Armenian community increased with ASALA's violent attacks on Turkish diplomats and recently with the Nagorno-Karabakh dispute between Armenia and Azerbaijan.

The Jews

Turkish nationalism was ambivalent toward the Jews in the early republican period. Jews constitute a non-Muslim minority, like Christians. However, they have had better relations with the state, so they have not been treated with the same official distrust as the Christian communities. They have never developed a separatist nationalist movement. Furthermore, they rejected calls for collaboration by Greek and Armenian Patriarchs against Turks. On the contrary, they have had a primary national identification with the Turkish majority while retaining their Jewish identity, even a sense of distant identification with Spain. In 1927, there were 81,872 Jews in Turkey; today their number is around 20,000 (Çağaptay 2006: 140).

Albeit being non-Muslim, the Turkish Government in the early years of the Republic considered Jews as an assimilable group. Citizen Speak Turkish did not only aim at assimilation of non-Turkish speaking Muslim groups but also the Jews. Nevertheless, even if they could speak the Turkish language, the legacy of the millet system put them not outside but on the margins of the Turkish nation.

Growing security concerns on Balkan borders on the eve of the impending war, increasingly ethnicized Turkish nationalism and led the Ankara Government to the Turkification of Thrace. The 1934 Thracian incidents, including the attacking and pillaging of Jewish homes and businesses, threatened many Jews in Thracian provinces causing many (around 10,000) to flee to Istanbul.[18] Turkey, in the same years, also witnessed Jewish immigration from European countries, escaping totalitarian regimes. In other words, the Thrace incidents were not inspired by anti-Semitism or racism, rather nationalism and security concerns led to the incidents. Ankara expected that Jews would assimilate into Turkishness by adopting the Turkish language, and taking over Turkish names. Then, this perspective was given up in a short period of time.

Muslim minorities

According the official doctrine, there are no minorities but Greek, Armenian, and Jewish communities that are recognized and protected as minority groups. Nevertheless, the Muslim groups that are differentiated from the Sunni-Turkish majority in terms of ethnic and sectarian divisions are analyzed as minorities since they at least sociologically constitute minority groups.[19]

The Kurds

The immediate active opposition to the Republican project that set about creating a centralized, secular and homogeneous Turkish nation-state came from religious conservatives and ethnic Kurds. Resistance to centralization and nation-building was stronger in the Kurdish provinces for several reasons. First, they were the only sizeable non-Turkish group in Turkey with an estimated population of 12–15 million (18–23 per cent of the population) (Günter 2006). Second, in Eastern and Southeastern Turkey they formed a large and adjacent Kurdish area, neighboring with majorly Kurdish populated zones of Iraq, Iran, and Syria. Finally, they had traditionally a semi-autonomous politico-economic structure with little exposure to taxation and regular conscription during Ottoman times. This structure was also facilitated by the harsh geographical features of the region that naturally isolated it from the rest of the country (Van Bruinessen 2000). Consequently, the new republic witnessed a long series of Kurdish ethno-religious rebellions between 1923 and 1938. These rebellions fed the cumulative image of the Kurdish people in the eye of the state as "socially, tribally, religiously fanatic, economically backward and most important, a threat to the national integrity of the Turkish state" (Yavuz and Günter 2001: 34). Thus, they enhanced Kemalist perspectives that Kurdish ethnicity was an impediment "to both objectives of homogenizing national territory and the Turkish nation's civilizing mission" (Moustakis and Chaudhuri 2005).[20]

After crushing the Kurdish-led Shayk Said Rebellion in 1925, the Turkish state put in place a comprehensive policy of assimilation with the goal of Turkification (Van Bruinessen 2000; Kirişci and Winrow 1997). Therefore, the existence of Kurdish ethnicity was simply denied. Besides typical means of national integration, such as nation-wide standardized (national) education and military service, the state developed specific policies aimed at forced assimilation, such as 'Citizen, speak Turkish' campaigns and the Resettlement Law of 1934. While the Kurds deemed as 'Mountain Turks' who forgot their Turkish origins, civilizing mission of the state was repeatedly confirmed. While the term "Turk" was gradually *ethnicized* in the constitutions of 1961 and 1982 (Yavuz and Günter 2001: 34), any attempt to express Kurdish identity was harshly expressed by state authorities especially after the 1980 military intervention. Until democratization reforms in the early years of the 2000s, denial and suppression of Kurdish identity had been the established state policy (Oran 2004).

Albeit gradually being ethnicized, the official definition of Turkish national identity has so far kept its hybrid character. Race never became a criterion in terms of policies of assimilation (Yavuz and Günter, 2001: 34). Ethnicized Turkish national identity both invited and forced all ethnic groups to assimilate into Turkish culture and language.[21] In this sense, official discourse has never refused to accept Kurds as Turkish citizens. But this acceptance was accompanied by the voluntary or involuntary inclusion of Kurds into the community of Turks, so the problem of Kurds in Turkey has not been exclusion (Kymlicka 1999: 134–35).[22]

Within this perspective, the Turkish state has never seen the Kurdish question as a real problem. It viewed it as "a matter of reactionary politics, tribal resistance or regional backwardness and foreign conspiracy but never as an ethno-political question" (Hirschler 2001: 148). Thus, the Turkish state saw any calls for recognition of Kurdish identity and cultural rights as separatist, terrorist acts, which should be suppressed severely. Consequently, insistence on repression not only fuelled a more militant and separatist Kurdish nationalist movement led by the PKK (Kurdish Workers' Party) but contributed to the maturing of the Kurdish national identity in the course of resistance to this policy as well.

The Alevis

Due to the nature of the link between religion and the state, Turkish citizenship has been a form of 'anomalous amalgamation' since its inception (Koçan and Öncü 2004). While a secular Turkish state chose to exclude religion from politics, it also endorsed a particular religious identity primarily as a means of fostering cultural and social solidarity among its citizens. In need of a societal glue among citizens, Turkish secular nationalism resorted to the establishment of state control over religion, and hence a bureaucratization of Turkish Islam from above. The Directorate of Religious Affairs and Directorate of Pious Foundations were founded by the state to represent a 'true' version of Sunni Islam. Hence, the state overtly adopted the Sunni Islamic identity at the expense of exclusion of non-Sunni members of the political community, such as the large Alevi population (estimated to comprise up to 20 per cent of the total population) (Poulton 1997). They were required to suppress their cultural identity and pretend to be Sunnis if they wanted to be treated as equal members of the Turkish nation in the public sphere. That is to say, the state interwove a particular form of cultural existence with political citizenship in a uniform way (Koçan and Öncü 2004: 472).

An ethno-religious definition of the Turkish nation excluded non-Muslims from the sphere of Turkishness. Although their rights, secured with the Treaty of Lausanne, were gradually limited and frequently violated, these groups could at least publicly express their cultural identities thanks to their minority status. Alevis as Muslims were both nationals and citizens but with certain specifications. Turkish-speaking Alevis were expected to accept not to express publicly their cultural identity, their exclusion from Directorate of Religious Affairs. As well as these requirements, Kurdish-speaking Alevis were also expected to suppress their ethnic identities.[23]

Despite the fact that this particular secularist transformation from above was exclusionary to them, Alevis have been the most receptive group. In spite of obvious discrepancies between theory and practice, they have seen the new republic as a key progress over their subordination to Islamic political domination during Ottoman times (Ocak 2002). Hence, they kept their loyalty to the state and chose not to question the status quo in depth until recent decades.

Current challenges: The re-forming of Turkish citizenship

To recapitulate, nationalism in Turkey has assumed a significant role in the modernization of the country. In the absence of civil society, Turkish nationalism emerged as an instrument to provide social unity and transform society rather than to connect an already existing civil society and the state as happened in Western European countries. Supported by the deep-rooted survival and threat perceptions, Turkey's state-centric nationalism sought to create a monolithic, organic society out of a culturally highly heterogeneous population. The notion of 'unity-over-diversity' has been reflected in the formation of citizenship which went hand in hand with the nation-building process. The Turkish state has made use of a double discourse that reflected a particular synthesis of French and German models by perpetuating the Ottoman millet system. This understanding declared legal equality of all citizens without any discrimination due to their ethnic, religious, and cultural identity. In practice, ethno-religiously defined Turkish national identity has aimed at getting rid of non-Muslim minorities that were seen as non-assimilable.[24] Hence it first discriminated between Muslim and non-Muslim citizens. Then, non-Turkish Muslims were invited to assimilate into Turkish culture and language. In other words, it sought for Turkification of the Kurds and other Muslim minorities. In line with this conception of national identity, citizenship policies were used as political devices for marginalization or assimilation of various elements living within the borders of the Turkish nation-state.

Nevertheless, the end of Cold War, the European integration process, internationalization of minority issues for security and humanitarian concerns, strengthening civil society, and the rise of identity politics in Turkey, among other factors, have exposed the Turkish nation-state to a still ongoing painful transformation process since the early 1990s. The 'crisis of Turkish modernity' has become obvious in many areas of its social structure. While the triumph of free market economy has gradually eroded the state's existence in economy, strengthening civil society contradicted with the 'from-above'/'state-centric' modernization. This enhanced the voices in favor of 'individual-first' rather than 'state-first ideology'. Limited but still effective political/legal globalization embodied in the increasing effectiveness of the Organization for Security and Cooperation in Europe (OSCE), European Court of Human Rights, Turkey's EU bid, and its efforts to meet Copenhagen criteria compelled the Turkish state to review its long-standing citizenship regime and policies that latently or patently contradict international democratic norms. More crucially, with the rise of identity politics, Turkey has witnessed fragmentation of the Turkish-Muslim nation that was imagined as an organic, monolithic entity. Religious, sectarian and ethno-linguistic diversity in Turkish society has become visible; Muslim ethnic groups, especially the Kurds, the Alevis, Islamist sections of an imagined Turkish nation began to demand official recognition and legal-political accommodation (Soner 2005: 302). These have been accompanied by the demands of officially recognized non-Muslim minorities that claim the state redress their up-to-now systematically violated rights.

As a part of this broader process of transformation of the Turkish state, these increased socio-political demands for re-formation of Turkish citizenship have not only interlocked with the heated debates on the nature and content of Turkish national identity; it also denotes an ongoing complicated political struggle that undermines the republican Kemalist status quo.

Ongoing questioning of the established notions of Turkish national identity and the boundaries of Turkish citizenship necessarily hinges upon the essential question of "Who are we?". There is no deffinite, fixed answer to such a question, since nationalism is a form of politics, thus national identity is a contestable identity. In other words, "who we are?", "how will define 'our' identity?" are subject to an endless political struggle. Even though nations are claimed to be homogeneous entities, they are constructed as cultural and political collectives with the use of different and ever-changing combinations of ethnic and civic elements. Besides the 'politicalness' of nationalism, its ideological aspect explains how we become, and stay, national. Nationalist ideology, always at the service of nationalist politics, is of vital importance for the construction and daily reproduction of national identity. Thus, since the forging of national identity is a product of political struggle, it is subject to constant redefinition brought about by changing power relations in national and international contexts. Extant dominant definitions of national identity can always be challenged, which may result in repression, negotiation, or violent conflict.

Current debates around a pluralistically inclusive, democratic political system above all challenge the Kemalist status quo that is based on state-centric nationalism and majoritarian democracy. A number of internal and external dynamics, particularly the AKP-led Europeanization process, since 2002, prompted a democratization process in Turkey, by displaying the vital link between citizenship, national identity, and political participation. Actually, ongoing debate is not particular to Turkey; it also refers to a globally-discussed highly contentious issue in the face of increasing transnational population movements, spreading of liberal principles through political globalization, but at the same time the rise of xenophobia and ultra-nationalism. Hence, debates on Turkish citizenship are related to the general questions about reconciliation of common citizenship identity with more particularistic group identities, democratization of the state, equal treatment to its all citizens by the state.

Within this context, modern citizenship that expresses membership to the nation-state has been criticized since it fails to accommodate increasing identity demands from black people, women, immigrants, ethnic groups and religious groups (Kadıoğlu 2005: 105). Among many arguments, two of them seem to be salient. On the one side, the post-nationalist argument maintains that parallel to the erosion of the nation, state new modalities of citizenship have become possible (Yeğen 2004: 51–53). Since national modern citizenship is considered to be an obstacle before a plural, inclusive democracy, it is proposed to cut off the link between citizenship and nationhood (Kadıoğlu 2005). The second argument hinges upon the model of constitutional citizenship. This is the one that is generally put forward as a solution against the problematic nature of the existing notions of national identity and exclusive/assimilationist citizenship understanding in Turkey. Rather than ignoring still powerful nation-states, this perspective is concentrated on enhancing civic dimensions of national identity so as to accommodate ethno-cultural and socio-cultural diversity, which is a sine qua non for a democratic political system. This model does not see minorities and diversities as a threat to national integrity and security, thus it decouples security concerns and discriminatory/authoritarian notions and practices. Moreover, it is aware of the fact that prioritization of identity in itself has its own disadvantages given that identity politics is essentially not for everybody but only for the members of a specific group (Hobsbawm 1996: 44). Hence, claiming that citizenship has five dimensions: civil, political, social, cultural, and economic rights, it stresses egalitarianism as well as satisfaction of identity claims (Kaya 2008).

Hence, constitutional citizenship can be viewed as a sound response to the demands for re-formation of Turkish citizenship as to be reshaped toward a system of substantive equality. Naturally, there is a crucial interconnection between a democratic re-formation of Turkish citizenship and the consolidation of democracy in the country, and a realization of such a model of citizenship is a matter of political struggle that revolves around the debates about a new constitution. Hinging on a series of such fundamental issues as national identity, sub-national and religious identities, gender issues, and secularism, debates regarding citizenship are thus related to deep-seated socio-political and cultural problems of the country.

Nevertheless, there are remarkable difficulties before the democratization of the political system and citizenship regime with a more civic type of Turkish nationalism. While traditional forces express their reaction in the form of 'ulusalcilik' or ultra-nationalism, Islamist, liberals, Kurds, and Alevis agree on the need for a new constitution that would bring along a more democratic, identity-friendly, inclusive understanding of citizenship. Yet, given that most Kurdish nationalists claim a kind of cultural and/or territorial autonomy, and most Alevis have been traditionally close to secular nationalism of Kemalism, it would be too optimistic to foresee a fruitful consensus among these groups at least in the near future. Thus, the lack of consensus regarding recognition and accommodation of identity demands seems to be the major factor that hinders elite convergence for a new democratic constitution, and a new model of citizenship. Despite these difficulties, however, the need for articulation of identity claims to citizenship has been increasingly expressed. Today, adoption and implementation of the constitutional citizenship model is no longer a far-reaching ideal in Turkey that has been undergoing a comprehensive reshaping of state-society relations towards a democratic, liberal and pluralist structure.

Notes

1 One should stress the fact that nationalism defies strict generalizations. Nationalism in the countries of immigration such as the USA, Australia, and New Zealand conceived the nation primarily as a territorially-based voluntary association. Nevertheless, it does not mean that these nations do not identify themselves through particular cultural values, symbols, language and common history.

2 Brubaker (1992: 13) maintains that the French and the Germans arrived at their nation-states from opposite ends. While the French have defined themselves territorially in terms of a country created by a state and then productive of a nation, the Germans have defined themselves ethnocentrically in terms of a community of descent, of language, which is the productive of a state.

3 Turner (1990: 208) states that the transfer of sovereignty from the body of the king to the body politics of citizens is a major turning point in Western democracies. Two parallel movements experienced at that time denote that 'a state is transformed into a nation at the same time subjects are transformed into citizens.

4 Even if some nationalists reject it, these two dimensions are so interwoven that the modern concept of the nation is inextricably linked to the concept of the state. Therefore, nationality connotes membership of a nation only because it can connote membership of a state (Gilbert 2000: 61).
This conflation is so obvious in international law that does not recognize any distinction between nationality and citizenship (Bendix 1977).

5 Marshall (1965) identifies 3 species of citizenship rights: civil, political, and social. Within the light of British experience, he observes cumulative expansion of citizenship rights as to it include civil rights (eighteenth century), political rights (nineteenth century), ans social rights (twentieth century).

6 By rightly maintaining that it is neither a fixed nor a homogenous discourse, Bora distinguishes five variants of Turkish nationalism, namely official (Atatürk), Kemalist left-wing, liberal, ultranationalist, and Islamist (Bora, 2003). In this study, Turkish nationalism refers to official nationalism, or Ataturkist nationalism, focusing on the mission to establish and perpetuate the nation-state.

7 In contrast to the anti-colonial sentiment that fuelled the majority of third world national movements, Turkish nationalism did not exhibit an anti-Western nativism. Instead, it aimed to locate a Turkish presence in an already accomplished model. (Keyder 2005: 12).

8 Anti-Europeanism has been most conspicuous among Turkish ultra-nationalists, for more information see: Canefe and Bora (2003).

9 The term 'establishment' denotes all those actors within the executive and the administration, the judiciary, the military, the security services and intelligence community, political parties, the media and academia, which ascribe to the Kemalist republican values. The establishment is so heterogeneous that it consists of actors clinging to different political ideologies ranging from liberalism to ultranationalism. In this sense, as Bozarslan maintains, Kemalism constitutes a metaideology in Turkey (Bozarslan 1999: 20).

10 The emphasis made on monolithic cultural unity is clearly seen in Afet İnan's *Medeni Bilgiler ve Atatürk'ün El Yazıları* (Civics and Atatürk's Manuscripts), which was actually penned by Atatürk himself. See *Medeni Bilgiler ve Atatürk'ün El Yazıları* (Civics and Atatürk's Manuscripts) 2nd ed. Ankara: TTK, 1988.

11 Ziya Gökalp is the well-known ideologue of this two-track conceptualization of Turkish national identity. According to him, while civilization (medeniyet) is universal, culture (hars) is national (Gökalp 1970).

12 Nation-building process typically consists of a range of means such as a single official language, a secular public school system, an ethno-culturally based national history, the establishment of official institutions of history and language,

38   *İbrahim Saylan*

creation of national holidays, erecting public monuments, a compulsory military service (Hobsbawm 1990). Like European cases, Turkish ruling republican elite made use of these means in a particular context to create a common sense of nationhood.

13 Nationality in the Ottoman system was determined by a person's membership to a religious community.

14 While nationalism was incorporated into the constitution as a principle of Turkish state, Turkish state ceased to have Islam as state religion. Unity of the state and nation thus replaced unity of the state and religion (Köker in Ünsal, 1998).

15 According to the 1924 Constitution, everybody living in national territories was deemed as Turk. Therefore, politico-territorial (civic) conception of nation was adopted. However, non-Muslims, albeit being Turks according to the constitution, they have not been ethno-culturally seen as Turks.

16 Living in ex-Ottoman territories, however, did not guarantee access for all Muslims. Çağaptay (2006) states that Ankara has tended to prefer the non-Turkish Muslims from the Balkans to those from Caucasus for various reasons.

17 Since the official understanding in Turkey has recognized only Armenians, Greeks, and Jews as minority groups, other Christian communities (Eastern Christians), namely, Assyrians, Chaldeans, and Jacobites could not enjoy official recognition and protection of their rights. According to Oran, this is an obvious violation of the Treaty of Lausanne that actually refers to all non-Muslims, not specifically the three largest groups (Oran 2004).

18 There is no consensus on government's role in Jewish exodus from Thrace. Bali sees it as a result of well-planned government policy for Turkification of the region. Likewise, Aktar asserts that it was a part of Ankara's long-term strategy and it was executed by CHP cadres and local government. In contrary to these views, Toprak does not see Ankara as the major responsible. For more information see: Aktar, A. (December 1996) 'Cumhuriyet'in İlk Yıllarında Uygulanan Türkleştirme Politikaları' (Turkification Policies during the Early Years of the Republic), *Tarih ve Toplum*, 156: 4–18; Bali, R. (1999) *Cumhuriyet Yıllarında Türkiye Yahudileri (1923–45)* (Turkish Jews under the Turkish Republic), İstanbul: İletişim; Toprak, Z. (October 1996) '1934 Trakya Olaylarında Hükümet'in ve CHF'nin Sorumluluğu' (The Responsibility of the Government and the CHF in the 1934 Thracian Incidents), *Toplumsal Tarih*, 34: 19–33.

19 Turkey consists of various Muslim groups that are differentiated from Turkish-Sunni majority according to the internationally accepted objective criteria (Oran 2004). Due to mainly Ottoman legacy and varied and complex combinations of ethnicity and Islamic sects, these groups object to be defined as minorities. While main sectarian division is between Sunnism and Alevism, Turkish society is composed of various Muslim ethnic groups as well as non-Muslim ethnic groups of Greeks, Armenians, Jews, and Assyrians/Syriacs. Main Muslim ethnic groups are Kurds, Arabs, Lazs, Circassians, Chechens, Georgians, Albanians, Macedonians, Bosniaks, the Roma people. (Andrews 1989). This study focuses on Alevis and Kurds as major representatives of sectarian and ethnic divisions in Turkey.

20 Actually, the report, based on observation and investigation in the southeastern and eastern regions and prepared by İsmet İnönü (then prime minister of Turkish Republic) reflects this type of image of the Kurds and the impending 'Kurdish threat' against ongoing republican project. For instance, İsmet İnönü states in his report that "if Erzincan becomes a center for the Kurds, I fear that Kurdistan would be established" (İsmet Pasha's Kurdish Report in Saygi Öztürk 2007: 51). This statement typically reflects survival and modernization concerns together. Another influential work in terms of official ideology belongs to Kazım Karabekir Pasha (one of the heroes of National Independence War). In his 'Kurdish Problem', he underlines the main role of foreign conspiracy in Kurdish insurgencies (1995). For detailed information on major reports on Kurdish question see

Belma Akçura. *Devletin Kürt Filmi 1925 – 2007 Kürt Raporları* (the State's Kurdish Movie 1925–2007 Reports On Kurdish Issue), Ankara: Ayraç, 2008.
21 Paul Dumont states that rejecting criterion of race, Kemalists hoped coalescence of different ethnic groups into a single Turkish nation through policies of Turkification based on culture and language (Dumont, 1984).
22 It is not to argue that ultra-nationalist version of Turkish nationalism has been totally rejected by official nationalism. There have been always osmoses and syntheses, which makes impossible to elicit a pure form of nationalism (Bora 2003). But even this articulation did not severe the invitation to the Kurds.
23 Dersim, today the Province of Tunceli in Eastern Turkey, witnessed a rebellion by Kurdish-speaking Alevis, or Alevi Kurds in Dersim against Turkish state in 1937. It was harshly repressed by state authorities.
24 This view has been recently reexpressed by the Minister of Defence, Vecdi Gönül as follows: "Bugün eğer Ege'de Rumlar, Türkiye'nin pek çok yerinde de Ermeniler yaşamaya devam etseydi, acaba Türkiye aynı milli devlet olabilir miydi? (If Greeks had continued to live in the Aegean, and Armenians in various part of the country, could Turkey have become the country it is?) Online. Available HTTP: <http://www.cnnturk.com/2008/turkiye/11/10/vecdi.gonul.nufus.mubadelesine.dikkat.cekti/499977.0/index.html> (accessed 11 January 2013).

References

Akçura, B. (2008) *Devletin Kürt Filmi 1925 – 2007 Kürt Raporları* (the State's Kurdish Movie 1925–2007 Reports On Kurdish Issue), Ankara: Ayraç.
Aktar, A. (December 1996) 'Cumhuriyet'in İlk Yıllarında Uygulanan Türkleştirme Politikaları' (Turkification Policies during the Early Years of the Republic), *Tarih ve Toplum*, 156: 4–18.
—— (2002) *Varlık Vergisi ve 'Türkleştirme' Politikası*, 6th edn, İstanbul: İletişim.
Alter, P. (1989) *Nationalism*, London & New York: Edward Arnold.
Andrews, P. A. (1989) *Ethnic Groups in the Republic of Turkey*, Wiesbaden: Dr Ludwig Reichert Verlag.
Ayata, A. (1998) 'Türkiye'de Kimlik Politikalarının Doğuşu' in A. Ünsal (ed.), *75 Yılda Tebaa'dan Yurttaş'a Doğru*, İstanbul: Tarih Vakfı.
Bali, R. (1999) *Cumhuriyet Yıllarında Türkiye Yahudileri (1923–45)* (Turkish Jews under the Turkish Republic), İstanbul: İletişim; Toprak, Z. (October 1996) '1934 Trakya Olaylarında Hükümet'in ve CHF'nin Sorumluluğu' (The Responsibility of the Government and the CHF in the 1934 Thracian Incidents), *Toplumsal Tarih*, 34: 19–33.
Bendix, R. (1977) *Nation-building and Citizenship*, Berkeley: University of California Press.
Billig, M. (1995) *Banal Nationalism*, London: Thousand Oaks & New Delhi: Sage Publications.
Breuilly, J. (1993) *Nationalism and the State*, 2nd edn, Manchester: Manchester University Press.
Bora, T. (Spring/Summer 2003) 'Nationalist Discourses in Turkey', *The South Atlantic Quarterly*, 102 (2/3): 433–51.
Bozarslan, H. (1999) 'Why Armed Struggle? Understanding the Violence in Kurdistan of Turkey' in G. Gürbey and F. Ibrahim (eds), *The Kurdish Conflict in Turkey*, New York: St. Martin's Press.
Brubaker, R. (1992) *Citizenship and Nationhood in France and Germany*, Cambridge, MA: Harvard University Press.

Calhoun, C. (1993) 'Nationalism and Ethnicity', *Annual Review of Sociology*, 19 (1): 211–39.

Canefe, N. and Bora, T. (2003) 'The Intellectual Roots of Anti-European Sentiments in Turkish Politics: the Case of Radical Turkish Nationalism', *Turkish Studies*, 4(1): 127–48.

Çağaptay, S. (2006) *Islam, Secularism, and Nationalism in Modern Turkey*, London & New York: Routledge.

Dumont, P. (1984) 'The Origins of Kemalist Ideology' in J. Landau (ed.), *Atatürk and the Modernization of Turkey*, Boulder: Westview Press.

Eley, G. and Suny, R. G. (1996) 'Introduction: From the Moment of Social History to the Work of Cultural Representation' in G. Eley and R. G. Suny (eds), *Becoming National*, Oxford & New York: Oxford University Press.

Gellner, E. (1983) *Nations and Nationalism*, Oxford: Blackwell.

—— (1997) *Nationalism*, New York: New York University Press.

Gilbert, P. (2000) *Peoples, Cultures and Nations in Political Philosophy*, Washington: Georgetown University Press.

Gökalp, Z. (1970) *Türkçülüğün Esasları* (The Principles of Turkism), İstanbul: Milli Eğitim.

Greenfeld, L. (1992) *Nationalism: Five Roads to Modernity*, Cambridge and London: Oxford University Press.

Gross, F. (1999) *Citizenship and Ethnicity*, Westport & London: Greenwood Press.

Günter, M. M. (2006) 'The Kurdish Problem in International Politics' in J. Joseph (ed.), *Turkey and the European Union*, Palgrave Macmillan: Basingstoke.

Hirschler, K. (July 2001) 'Defining the Nation: Kurdish Historiography in Turkey in the 1990s', *Middle Eastern Studies*, 37 (3): 145–66.

Hobsbawm, E. J. (1990) *Nations and Nationalism since 1780 – Programme, Myth, Reality*, Cambridge: Cambridge University Press.

—— (February 1992) 'Ethnicity and Nationalism in Europe Today', *Anthropology Today*, 8 (1): 3–8.

—— (May / June 1996), 'Identity Politics and the Left', *NLR*, 217: 38–47.

Kadıoğlu, A. (1995) 'Milletini Arayan Devlet: Türk Milliyetçiliğinin Açmazları', *Türkiye Günlüğü*, 33: 91–100.

—— (2005) 'Can We Envision Turkish Citizenship as non-Membership?' in E. F. Keyman and A. İçduygu (eds), *Citizenship in a Global World – European Questions and Turkish Experiences*, London & New York: Routledge.

Karabekir, K. (1995) *Kürt Meselesi* (Kurdish Question), 2nd edn, İstanbul: Emre Yayınları.

Kaya, A. (2008) 'Avrupa Birliği Bütünleşme Sürecinde Yurttaşlık, Çokkültürcülük ve Azınlık Tartışmaları: Birarada Yaşamanın Siyaseti' in A. Kaya and T. Tarhanlı (eds), *Türkiye'de Çoğunluk ve Azınlık Politikaları*, 3rd edn, İstanbul: TESEV Yayınları.

Kazancıgil, A. And Özbudun, E. (1981) *Atatürk: Founder of a Modern State*, London: C. Hurst

Keyder, Ç. (2005) 'A History and Geography of Turkish Nationalism' in F. Birtek and T. Dragonas (eds), *Citizenship and the Nation-State in Greece and Turkey*, New York: Routledge.

Keyman, E. F. (2005) 'Articulating Citizenship and Identity – The "Kurdish Question" In Turkey' in E. F. Keyman and A. İçduygu (eds), *Citizenship in a Global World – European Questions and Turkish Experiences*, London & New York: Routledge.

Keyman, E. F. and İçduygu, A. (2005) 'Introduction – Citizenship, Identity, and the Question of Democracy in Turkey' in Ed. E. F. Keyman and A. İçduygu (eds), *Citizenship in a Global World – European Questions and Turkish Experiences*, London & New York: Routledge.

Kirişci, K. (1998) 'Majority\Minority Discourse – The Case of the Kurds in Turkey' in D. C. Gladney (ed.), *Making Majorities – Constituting the Nation in Japan, Korea, China, Malaysia, Fiji, Turkey, and the United States*, Stanford: Stanford University Press.

—— (July 2000) 'Disaggregating Turkish Citizenship and Immigration Practices', *Middle Eastern Studies*, 36 (3): 1–22.

Kirişci, K. and G. M. Winrow (1997) *The Kurdish Question and Turkey: An Example of Trans-state Ethnic Conflict*, Portland, Oregon: Frank Cass.

Koçan, G. and Öncü, A. (December 2004) 'Citizen Alevi in Turkey: beyond Confirmation and Denial', *Journal of Historical Sociology*, 17 (4): 464–89.

Kohn, H. (1967) *Prelude to Nation-States: The French and German Experience, 1789–1815*, New Jersey: Van Nostrand Company.

Kramer, H. (2000) *A Changing Turkey – The Challenge to Europe and the United States*, Washington D.C.: Brookings Institution Press.

Kurubaş, E. (April 2008) 'Etnik Sorunlar: Ulus-Devlet ve Etnik Gruplar Arasındaki Varoluşsal İlişki', *Doğu Batı*, 44: 11–41.

Kymlicka, W. (1999) 'Misunderstanding Nationalism' in R. Beiner (ed.), *Theorizing Nationalism*, New York: SUNY Press.

Marshall, T. H. (1965) *Class, Citizenship, and Social Development*, New York: Anchor Books.

Medeni Bilgiler ve Atatürk'ün El Yazıları (Civics and Atatürk's Manuscripts) 2nd ed. Ankara: TTK, 1988.

Moustakis, F. and Chaudhuri, R. (2005) 'Turkish-Kurdish Relations and the European Union: An Unprecendented Shift in Kemalist Paradigm', *Mediterranean Quarterly* 16 (4): 77–89.

Ocak, A. Y. (2002) *Türk Süfiliğine Bakışlar* (Perspectives on Turkish Sufism), İstanbul: İletişim Yayınları.

Oran, Baskın (2004). *Türkiye'de Azınlıklar* (Minorities in Turkey), İstanbul: İletişim Yayınları.

Özdoğan, G. G. (2000) 'Civic Versus Ethnic Nation: Transcending the Dual Model?' in G. G. Özdogan and G. Tokay (eds), *Redefining the Nation State and Citizen*, İstanbul: Eren.

Öztürk, S. (2005) *İsmet Paşa'nın Kürt Raporu* (İsmet Pasha's Kurdish Report), İstanbul: Doğan Kitap.

Pierson, C. (2004) *The Modern State*, 2nd edn, London and New York: Routledge.

Poulton, H. (1997) *Top Hat, Grey Wolf and Crescent – Turkish Nationalism of the Turkish Republic*, London: Hurst & Company.

Soner, B.A. (2005) 'Citizenship and the Minority Question in Turkey' in E. F. Keyman and A. İçduygu (eds), *Citizenship in a Global World – European Questions and Turkish Experiences*, London & New York: Routledge.

Soyarık-Şentürk, N. (2005) 'Legal and Constitutional Foundations of Turkish Citizenship – Changes and Continuties' in E. F. Keyman and A. İçduygu (eds), *Citizenship in a Global World – European Questions and Turkish Experiences*, London & New York: Routledge.

Taşpınar, Ö. (2005) *Kurdish Nationalism and Political Islam in Turkey*, New York and London: Routledge.

Ünsal, A. (1998) 'Yurttaşlık Zor Zanaat' in A. Ünsal (ed.), *75 Yılda Tebaa'dan Yurttaş'a Doğru*, İstanbul: Tarih Vakfı.

Van Bruinessen, M. (2000) *Kurdish Ethno-Nationalism versus Nation-Building States*, İstanbul: The Isis Press.

Wimmer, A. (2002) *Nationalist Exclusion and Ethnic Conflict – Shadows of Modernity*, Cambridge: Cambridge University Press

Yavuz, H. M. and Günter, M. M. (January 2001) 'The Kurdish Nation', *Current History*, 100: 33–39.

Yeğen, M. (2004) 'Citizenship and Ethnicity in Turkey', *Middle Eastern Studies*, 40(6): 51–66.

Zürcher, E. J. (2004) *Turkey: A Modern History*, London: I.B. Tauris.

3   Two steps forward one step back: Turkey's democratic transformation[1]

İlter Turan

Turkey began to be counted among democracies long before democracy was elevated to the level of being the only respectable form of government in the world after the demise of the Warsaw Pact and the fall of the Soviet Empire. Ruled by a single party since its founding in 1923 and a track record of two failed experiments in initiating opposition parties, Turkey might not have come to mind as the most outstanding candidate to make a transition to political democracy after the Second World War. Yet, by all accounts, it managed to achieve a peaceful transition to political competition during the 1946–50 period. At a time when many of the underdeveloped countries, as well as those becoming independent as a result of decolonization, were becoming targets of a rivalry between the 'Free World' and the 'Communist World', the Turkish success was quickly seized upon by the advocates of political democracy as a model demonstrating that moving to democracy in a developing country was possible. The case of Turkey was studied and analyzed to uncover the secrets of democratic transition.[2] Within a decade, it became evident that the smooth transition did not necessarily lead to smooth operation. Turkey went through a long period of democratic breakdowns, military governments, and returns to civilian rule between 1960–83. Since 1983, the country has been spared military interventions and has been going through a process such that democracy appears to be on its way to becoming the only game in town.

This chapter will analyze the processes through which Turkey has evolved into a reasonably democratic system. Two intertwined processes may be discerned in Turkey's democratization. First, the several stages of democratization, breakdown, and restoration have all begun with a major political problem that needed to be addressed and solved. The particular solutions devised, however, while taking care of the initial problem, led to the emergence of another major problem that could not be solved within the existing political framework. We will be looking at the stages of evolution of Turkish democracy with this problem-solution-new problem in mind.[3] Second, solutions have been devised within the broader framework of paradigms. It will be argued that Turkey has shifted from a security maximization to a prosperity maximization paradigm, and that along with such a paradigm shift, democratic consolidation may have become more likely.

The background to democratic transition

Turkish politics from 1946 to today contains periods marked first by the expansion and then by the contraction of the role of the citizens in the political decision-making processes of society. These movements, resembling the movements of a pendulum, are the product of competition between men of state and those of politics as regards maintaining the upper hand in ruling society. Turkish modernization, having its origins in Ottoman modernization, was a process initiated by the state to avert military defeat in the hands of Western powers. As piecemeal attempts to modernize proved insufficient to turn the tide of defeat, measures grew more comprehensive. The salient aspect of the modernization attempts from the perspective of our analysis is that change was state driven, implemented by a growing corps of military-bureaucratic elites through an expanding system of public institutions. A split between radical and conservative modernizers was lost by the latter with the founding of the republic symbolizing the victory of the former.

The single party period from 1923 to 1946–50 was a long period of cultural transformation. The Caliphate was abolished, religious orders were banned and their convents closed, a universal civil law replaced religion-based rules, education was placed under the direction of the Ministry of National Education and given a secular nationalist content, the traditional schools of Islamic education the *medreses* were closed down, the Latin alphabet replaced the Arabic alphabet, the traditional headgear called the *fez* was banned in favor of the western hat. Other changes were also introduced.[4] In this process, the citizens were conceptualized as a passive body who should comply with the centrally made and directed policies.

The fundamental concern of the founders of the republic was the consolidation of the regime and their own power. By abolishing the imperial system, they had eliminated the basis on which traditional political authority was built. Now, a new legal-rational basis needed to be constructed. The policies of cultural transformation they pursued were designed mainly to eliminate the sources of support for the *ancien régime*, and to open the way for further modernization of society. While they were successful in this endeavor, they were not able to overcome a fundamental political difficulty which was, to some extent, their own doing. The masses that had been treated as passive recipients of modernization were far removed from the ruling elite. They were not persuaded that the series of modernization measures that were effected necessarily benefited them (Turan 1969). They were incapable of relating their responses, needs, demands, and expectations to the Government without the intermediation of the local notables. The notables, being at the receiving end of a Government-Party patronage network, provided the link between the ruling CHP (*Cumhuriyet Halk Partisi*, Republican People's Party) and the Government. They often functioned, however, as spokesmen for the Party and the Government. In this way, they were able to strengthen their position vis-à-vis the ordinary citizens.[5] In the final analysis, the intended cultural transformation failed to transform the population homogeneously. It remained confined mainly to the elite as had been the case during the Ottoman Empire. A dramatic example is the immediate and without exception restoration of the Arabic call to prayer to replace the Turkish version once a choice became available. The Turkish version had been favored by the modernizing elite, but the use of the Arabic version was allowed in response to massive popular demand once the Government changed hands through elections.[6] Herein then lay the problem that could not be solved within the existing framework: the masses were not integrated into national political life.

Transition to competitive politics (1946–50)

What prompted the single-party Government to make a transition to competitive politics? Three broad and different answers have been given to this question (Özbudun 2000). Some observers have emphasized the socio-economic effects of the Second World War. One line of socio-economic analysis has pointed out that the war helped create a stratum, mainly located in provincial centers that accumulated wealth by trading in export commodities that were in high demand during the War.[7] This stratum, socially, economically, and politically insecure, wanted to secure a place for itself in the political arena but failed since local party organization of the CHP was already staffed by traditional local notable families who had cooperated with the Nationalists during the War of Independence. Its economic insecurity was heightened by the arbitrary exercise of governmental power in the economic domain. Specifically, in the middle of the war in 1942, ostensibly to meet its needs for revenue to finance a fully mobilized military, but probably to also promote the Turkification of commerce and trade (Barutçu 1977), the Government had introduced a wealth tax whose incidence particularly on non-Muslim citizens had proven devastating. Then, in 1945, came a land reform which, if fully implemented, would have given away land from large holdings, the major source of power of the local notables, to landless peasants. The implications of these actions were not lost on the new wealthy whose sense of insecurity was heightened. Hence, this new socio-economic strata evolved into a rival elite and making a common cause with the economically more liberal wing of the CHP, to lobby for the introduction of political competition (Turan 1988: 68–72).[8] Their troops were the disaffected voters, especially peasants, who had suffered most under the extractive and authoritarian policies of the single party.

In examining Turkey's democratic transition, one group of scholars have focused on the attitudes and preferences of the political elite as well as the nature of the political system. They remind us that the CHP did not possess an ideology that mandated the perpetuation of a single-party system. Rather, the overall goal of westernization, operationally meaning becoming like a Western European state, included the democratization of the system as a long-term aspiration. During the single-party years, an electoral system had been well set in place; therefore an infrastructure for conducting competitive elections already existed. Those who emerged as leaders of the opposition movement, having all been members of the CHP, had full republican credentials and were not suspected of harboring covert goals to weaken the secular republic. Therefore, when an internal challenge came, a democratic opening did not present an option that was fully out of line with the cognitive maps of the leaders or their ideologies. Without such a background, the regime might well have grown more authoritarian (Özbudun 2000: 13–24).

Finally, some analysts have pointed out that the international context pressured Turkey into making a democratic transition (Yılmaz 1997). During the War, the Soviets made known their intention not to renew the Turco-Russian Friendship and Non-Aggression Treaty of 1925. They had been frustrated by Turkey's policies that were oriented toward keeping the country out of war and therefore not sufficiently cooperative toward the Allies. Being on the winning side, they thought that they could force a reconsideration of the status of the Turkish Straits so as to have a role in their operation as well as bring about a revision on Turkey's border with Georgia. Under the circumstances, Turkey felt compelled to become a part of the emergent Western Bloc. Allowing a transition to political competition was no more than a tactical move to render Turkey an acceptable candidate in the eyes of the Americans for being included in the western defense system.

These three frameworks need not be treated as rivals but as complementary explanations. Demands for political change were supported by a newly emerging provincial economic elite which also constituted the cadres of the rival DP (*Demokrat Parti*, Democratic Party) The ideological dispositions of the ruling elite did not preclude a positive response to demands for political change. The economic and/or political liberals within the governing single party might not have been able to bring about a democratic opening if international conditions did not favor Turkey's making a transition to democracy.

In 1945, the Government allowed the opening of new parties. During the next five years changes were made in a number of laws to render elections free and fair as government changed hands between the proponents and opponents of the democratic opening. On May 14, 1950, the DP scored a landslide victory against the CHP. Turkey had entered a new phase in its political history. It was now a democracy.

Cycles of Turkish democracy: 1950–80

The overarching concern of the modernizing state elites during the 1945–83 period can best be described as security maximization. While the concern with regime consolidation and sustenance that had characterized the single-party period had not fully disappeared from the agenda of the state elites after the advent of democracy, an external concern with Soviet expansionism created a new basis for adopting security as the guiding concept in the politics of the country. The outcome may best be described as cyclical democracy. As the name indicates, during 1950–80 there were cycles during which the system first moved toward the expansion of the power and the activities of elected governments and then a period of turmoil and a military intervention. Each cycle (1950–60, 1961–71 and 1973–80) began with an **election of transition** (1950, 1961, 1973), an election that marked the transition to competitive politics. The next **elections** were one **of consolidation** where one party achieved a prevalent position or strengthened an already existing prevalence (DP in1954, AP (*Adalet Partisi*, Justice Party) in 1965 and CHP in 1977). Then the performance of the Government began to falter, the relations between the Government and opposition parties grew intense and an **election of polarization** was held (1957, 1969). After these elections, came a military intervention. In fact, after the elections of 1977, public order was so weakened and political stability so undermined, that the military intervention came before an election of polarization even took place.

The first experiment with democracy (1950–60)

During the 1946–50 interim, the Government changed hands between proponents and opponents of democratization no fewer than four times as the factions within the governing single party tried to direct developments to conform to their own preferences. Significant changes were eventually introduced in the electoral laws, law of associations, Duties and Powers of the Police Force Law among others, making a reasonably fair election possible. The CHP experienced an astounding defeat at the hands of the opposition Democrats in the elections of May 14, 1950.[9] The peaceful transfer of power was met with relief and initially a mood of optimism prevailed.

The DP Government led by Adnan Menderes liberalized the import regime to meet the demand for manufactured goods in a market that had been starved of them since the beginning of the World War, pursued policies favorable to the farmers, including the introduction of price supports for major agricultural commodities, and invested in building plants that produced basic commodities that were short in supply such as sugar and cement. A comprehensive highway construction program was started with American economic assistance. A string of years with favorable climate conditions produced bumper crops that brought in high revenues since the demand for foods and raw materials remained high owing to a Europe that was still trying to recover from the devastation of the World War and the ongoing Korean War. The improved economic conditions paid off and the DP returned to power in 1954 with even a higher percentage of the vote than in 1950.

The economic achievements of the DP had proven possible by deficit financing at home and borrowing abroad. As production fell on account of unfavorable climate and the commodity prices on account of falling demand after 1955, the Government began to experience difficulties in sustaining economic growth and keeping inflation under control. This unfavorable turn in the economic conditions was reflected in the elections of 1957, moved a year ahead so that the Government could get a new lease on life before losses in electoral support cost it its parliamentary majority. By 1958, the country was experiencing a major foreign currency shortage, much needed goods could not be imported and prices were going up. The Government was forced to devalue the Turkish Lira by nearly 300 percent and to introduce austerity measures. It did not manage to stabilize the economy (Zürcher 1993: 234–41). Its electoral support appeared to continue to erode.

On the political front, from the very beginning, tensions had emerged between the bureaucracy and elected politicians. The deputies, as elected politicians, felt they were given an unlimited mandate by the voters to command the bureaucracy as they wished. The top level of the bureaucracy made their peace with the Government and accommodated itself to electoral politics. But starting from just below them, the bureaucrats, conditioned to thinking that their utmost priority was to serve the interests of the state, were not appreciative of political masters who looked at them with disdain, suspected them of being CHP loyalists, expected them to dish out public goods and resources as patronage to supporters while draining the public treasury of funds and mismanaging the economy. The unhappiness of the bureaucrats was exacerbated by their declining income in the face of high rates of inflation which were not compensated by the meager raises they were given.

Particularly after the elections of 1957, the DP began to feel less secure about its ability to sustain itself in power and turned increasingly to authoritarian measures such as harassing the opposition in and out of parliament including suspending its leader from attending sessions for a week for obstructing the sessions; banning visits of the opposition leader to provincial centers to hold rallies; removing from their positions and sometimes demoting judges who rendered verdicts not to the liking of the government and forcing bureaucrats to join the Homeland Front, an instrument designed to force voters, especially the bureaucrats, to declare publicly their support to the government party. But most importantly, in 1960, the government forced a law in through parliament, empowering the DP to form a parliamentary committee comprised exclusively of DP members and equipped with judicial powers to investigate, and if necessary punish, the so-called 'subversive' activities of the opposition. These actions constituted the background to student protests against the Government in May which, in turn, constituted the pretext for a military committee of lower ranking officers calling itself the National Unity Committee (NUC) to assume power and imprison the leaders and the deputies of the DP (Weiker 1963: 8–13). Apparently, the NUC was born in 1954 (Seyhan 1966: 42) but began to grow strong after the elections of 1957.

Restructuring the political system (1960–61)

The first Turkish experiment with democracy had ended in failure. Political competition had shown voters that competitively elected governments were responsive to their needs, mobilizing them to become more active participants in politics. In this way, the passive citizens of the single-party era were integrated into national political life. It had also become evident, however, that the determination of governments through elections was only one aspect of political democracy that would not by itself check tendencies to authoritarian recidivism. In an ironical way, the NUC identified constructing a more stable democratic system as one of its main goals. This approach derived from the diagnosis that political problems that had prompted their intervention had derived from DP's corruption of democracy and the legal loopholes in the system that had made such an outcome possible.

The DP was closed by a court decision at the end of September.[10] By this time, the military leadership had already put the DP deputies in prison. Later, it set up an extraordinary court to try them for violating the constitution and a variety of laws. These trials culminated in fifteen death sentences including the president, the prime minister, the ministers of finance, interior and foreign affairs (Seyhan 1966: 25–47). The sentence of the President, Celal Bayar, was commuted for reasons of age but others were carried out, leaving a scar on the memories of many who recalled the DP rule with favor. Furthermore, a body of experienced politicians was eliminated from Turkish politics. But, the long-term effects of the military intervention became manifest in the constitution prepared by law professors, approved by the NUC and then ratified in a public referendum. The new constitution contained a significant number of changes which distinguished it from the one it replaced (Özbudun 2000: 53–57; Weiker 1963: 64–81).

One major change was the introduction of proportional representation in the electoral system. The plurality system used during the 1950–60 period was singularly insensitive to shifts in voter preferences owing to the multi-member districts, varying in size, in which the winner took all the seats. The change would serve to reduce distortions the electoral system introduced in translating votes to seats in the parliament. Furthermore, the responsibility of running of elections was taken away from the Ministry of Interior bureaucracy and given to a High Council of Elections comprised of members of the judiciary.

A second change related to the establishment of a constitutional court with powers to review acts of parliament. This American innovation had been incorporated into some European systems, particularly after the Second World War. The military leadership judged that this mechanism would constitute a check against laws that conflicted with the constitution but accepted by a parliamentary majority such as the setting up of a special investigation committee described above. Access to the court was rather generous. Parties, universities, labor unions among others could turn to the court to challenge the constitutionality of legislative acts.

A third area of change pertained to the setting up of a set of autonomous institutions that would be reasonably free of the intervention of elected politicians. These included the universities which were rendered autonomous and pretty much self-governing, a state broadcasting company that was to be neutral, a state planning organization that would free public investments from the haphazardness which a patronage system had generated, and an independent body named the High Council of Judges to deal with the appointing, the promotion and relocation of judges. The new institutions also included a MGK which brought the security agencies and concerned ministries together under the leadership of the prime minister to coordinate activities pertaining to national security and advise the government on these.

Fourth, a new legislative institution called the Senate of the Republic was created to have a two tier system of law making, so as to render law making a more deliberative process. The new chamber also incorporated all members of the NUC as lifetime senators, providing a way for them to exit to normal political activity and constitute a parliamentary group that would protect the values the NUC harbored and project them into the working of elected governments.

Finally, the constitution contained an elaborate list of the rights and obligations of citizens. While citing obligations of citizens in a constitution is usually not deemed necessary, it is important to recognize that for the first time Turkish citizens got constitutionally guaranteed civil liberties. Many observers feel that in its initial form, the constitution of 1961 was the most liberal constitution Turkey has ever had. By using constitutional engineering, the military leaders had hoped that they could build a democratic system in which elected politicians would run the country but checked by a set of rules and autonomous institutions to prevent them from turning authoritarian and from undermining the prevalence of the state in some critical domains like the judiciary and education (Kalaycıoğlu 2005: 93–95).

The second try at democracy (1961–80)

The 1961–73 period

The 1961 military intervention had tried to improve upon the achievement of the first democratic period (i.e. the integration of the masses to national politics) by devising a system that would also stand against the authoritarian proclivities of elected governments. After the ratification of the constitution in 1961, the CHP and newly organized parties contested the elections. The CHP led the polls but by a small margin and Turkey got introduced to coalition governments. Twice the more radical elements in the military who felt that the modernizing tradition of the republic was not sufficiently strengthened before returning to civilian rule attempted to stage coups. Prime Minister İnönü, the head of the CHP, respected by the military as a hero of the war of national independence, proved key in averting imminent military takeover. As the probability of military intervention receded, the AP, claiming to be the inheritor of the DP tradition and votes, began to enhance its popular standing. Its appeal owed also to its young leader, Süleyman Demirel who had assumed the presidency of the party in late 1964. Without losing time, he led his party into undoing the existing coalition led by the CHP and became the vice premier in a new coalition led by a neutral figure. Shortly afterwards, in the elections of 1965, despite an electoral system that was highly protective of small parties, the AP managed to get a majority of seats in the parliament. One-party government was restored by a party that claimed the heritage of the DP which the NUC had banned in 1961. The AP won also the 1969 elections, though by a smaller margin.

The liberal atmosphere generated by the 1961 Constitution had produced an environment in which many ideas and ideologies began to make their way into different segments of Turkish society. Not surprisingly, one of the first places where severe clashes of ideas began to occur with increasing frequency was the universities. Students soon organized into rival ideological camps, their quarrels quickly being transformed into fighting between groups associated with different student and youth organizations. Non-student youth groups and occasionally labor unions also began to join them. As public order eroded, the Government complained that the too liberal constitution tied its hands in addressing public disorder. Yet, there was little consensus among parties in the parliament as regards how the constitution should be changed and the Government did not have the needed votes by itself to effect the change.

The political impasse provided the conditions under which the top leadership of the military gave an ultimatum to the Demirel Government in March 1971 to resign and make room for a government of national unity whose explicit duty would be to address public disorder and violence and to amend the liberal features of the constitution which presumably stood in the way of effective action. This indirect intervention of the military, in addition to the distaste of the military leadership for being called in to perform law enforcement duties in the face of mounting violence, may have derived from the fear of the commanders that if they failed to react to the prevailing conditions, the junior officers might seize the initiative as they had done in 1960.

The resignation of the Demirel Government constituted the beginning of a period of uneasy relations between the military and elected politicians for the next two and a half years during which no fewer than five governments held office. Constitutional changes aiming to narrow down civil liberties and enhancing the powers of government were affected. As the elections of 1973 began to approach, the military leadership recognized their indirect intervention was not sustainable, particularly after their demands for amending the constitution had been met. They judged that placing a trusted general in the presidency that was soon to become vacant might constitute the most effective way of exercising oversight of the Government. Accordingly, the chief of staff General Faruk Gürler resigned his post to become a candidate. Despite the possibility that his failure to get elected might lead to a more direct military intervention, the parliament fell one vote short of electing him. A more neutral retired admiral Fahri Korutürk, untainted by political ambitions, was then elected president and the country moved on to early elections.[11]

The 1973–80 period

The outcome of the elections was a surprise. The CHP under its new leader Bülent Ecevit and its new ideology of 'Left of Center' came out first. The religiously Oriented MSP (*Milli Selamet Partisi*, National Salvation Party) whose predecessor MNP (Milli Nizam Partisi, National Order Party) had been closed by the Constitutional Court for having used religion for political ends, also achieved parliamentary representation. Furthermore, barring the coalition of the two major parties, i.e. the AP and the CHP, no coalition government could form without the participation of the MSP. The initial coalition was formed between the CHP and the MSP who had not held office during the troublesome period that had led to the indirect military intervention. Half a year after its forming, Turkey staged an intervention on Cyprus in July 1974 to stop the unification of the island with Greece as a result of a coup against President Makarios. The success of the military operation enhanced the popularity of Mr Ecevit who wanted to translate it into a more substantial electoral victory than in 1973. His partners did not agree to a new election and the coalition collapsed. A new coalition of all parties save the CHP, calling itself the Nationalist Front, was soon established.

Turkish political history from 1974–80 was characterized by highly polarized politics and intensifying public disorders which the successive governments failed to bring under control. The Nationalist Front governments were comprised of partners that had very little in common with each other except a desire to be in government so as to dispense public goods and resources to their supporters as patronage blended with strong anti-left rhetoric. Attempts to formulate policy only served to reveal their differences. Therefore, they chose three-dimensional strategy to prolong their rule. The first element of this strategy was to polarize the political field into left-right camps in which they represented the right. Polarization served to cement their cohesion by precluding any other coalition formulae and kept the voters within the camp and prevented them from moving to the opposite pole. The second element was to render the parliament ineffective. A parliament that met regularly and carried out its routine activity would only reveal how seriously divided the partners were on questions of policy. And finally, the council of ministers met infrequently for the same reasons as the parliament. The cabinet functioned as a confederation of ministries, each with its own domain, rather than a team of ministers developing and implementing a common government policy.

A brief interlude to the Nationalist Front governments came in 1978 when the CHP leader Mr Ecevit lured 11 deputies from the AP into defecting by giving them cabinet posts in a Government he would establish. The new Government proved ineffective, however, and felt obliged to resign when it did not gain a single seat in a by-election in 1979, making room for a return of the Nationalist Front.

From 1974 until 1980, polarized politics permeated all aspects of Turkish political life. Deep political cleavages took hold not only among students and labor unions, but also among the faculties of universities, high school and primary school teachers, semi-public agencies such as the bar associations, the bureaucracy itself, including even the police force and the publicly paid preachers. Urban life in particular came to be characterized by increasing political violence such that daily death toll had begun to exceed ten by 1980. The Government and the opposition accused each other of fanning violence. There was no indication that all major political actors could come together to address the emergency the country was facing. The military leadership kept issuing warnings but these became additional ammunition to the contestants each of whom said that the military meant not them but the other. The polarized politics also locked the country in a struggle regarding the election of a new president by the parliament. After incessant rounds, there were no results. The military, within its existing chain of command, assumed political power on September 12, 1980 (Zürcher 1993: 266–82).

The political economy of change

What was happening on the political front was not entirely unrelated to what was happening on the economic front. The military administration of 1960–61 had formalized an earlier economic aspiration of the republic to be self-sufficient into a policy of import substitution. This choice derived from the security maximization paradigm which assumed that import substitution would render Turkey less dependent on the outside world. What in fact occurred was a change in the nature of goods Turkey imported, not a reduction of import dependency. The importing of finished goods was now replaced by imports of investment goods, semi-finished goods, raw materials and more energy. As the economy expanded during the 1960s, so did the need for hard currency to finance imports. There was no corresponding increase in the export earnings of the country which was comprised of agricultural products and raw materials. The industrial goods produced in the protected market hardly proved suitable for export. These conditions constituted the background conditions of an economic cycle. At the beginning of the cycle, external borrowing was available, new industries were established and the economy expanded. Current account deficits were financed by external borrowing which became progressively more difficult as the country's creditworthiness declined. Finally, a point was reached where it became nearly impossible to borrow. A stabilization program in compliance with IMF expectations including the devaluation of the Turkish lira, a consequent standby agreement and austerity measures followed so as to restore the creditworthiness of the economy. Once that was achieved, the process started again with economic expansion, increasing external borrowing, an eventual inability to finance the external needs of the economy, economic crisis and the adoption of an austerity program.

Three developments came together to render the continuation of the above strategy of economic development unsustainable. First, there was a built-in tendency in the model to require ever greater infusion of hard currency for it to function which the economy did not generate. With each cycle the industry would expand; crises would naturally lead to its temporary contraction, but then the next wave of expansion would come, necessitating an even more substantial external cash supply. Second, the coming of the oil crisis in 1973 constituted a shock, necessitating the allocation of almost all of Turkey's external earnings to the importing of energy. Third, the state expenditures kept growing without a corresponding increase in public revenue. The patronage system that prevailed in Turkish politics pressured governments to engage in intensifying acts of generosity toward the voters, especially after Turkey began to be ruled by coalition governments. The budget deficits were covered by public borrowing at ever spiraling interest rates which propelled inflation while starving the country of the much needed private investment funds.

The expansionary industrialization policies coupled with the exodus from rural areas to the cities had brought about a shift in the centers of power in Turkish society. The prevailing AP and the smaller parties of the right had rural and small town orientations and were somewhat out of tune with the needs and concerns of the new urbanites. This may be one of the significant reasons behind the turning of the tide in favor of the CHP during the 1973 and 1977 elections, as voters mistook the new left of center ideology as turn for social democracy rather than a restatement of the modernizing philosophy of the early republic. When the expected policies were not forthcoming, they began to move back to the traditional parties of the right.

With electoral volatility high, fragmented party system, ineffective governments, political chaos also stood in the way of taking measures to cure the economic problems the country was facing. As Turkey scrambled around for funds to send the salaries of its diplomats, the prime minister confessed: 'Turkey is in need of seventy cents'. The severity of the crisis that appeared to pose an existential threat to the country must have persuaded Prime Minister Demirel to adopt a drastic reform proposal designed by Turgut Özal, one time head of the state planning organization who had later pursued a career in business before returning to government service. A set of changes in the rules and regulations protecting the value of the Turkish Lira prepared in utmost secrecy was presented on January 24, 1980 as a *fait accompli* to the Council of Ministers. Many of the restrictions on hard currencies were suspended. People could send or take money out of the country, exporters could keep their earnings abroad and bring them back at a time they deemed appropriate, private banks could buy and sell foreign currency.

Revolutionary as they may seem, these changes were not perceived as having a fundamental effect on the political transformation of Turkish society, yet they marked the beginning of a paradigmatic shift not only in economics but also in Turkish politics as we shall see later.[12]

Wearing the straightjacket: Military rule 1980–83 and the institutionalization of the political role of the military

The makers of the 1960 military intervention, building what they considered to be a model liberal democratic framework through devising a new constitution, felt that they had opened the way to the growth of liberal democracy, an outcome which the political leaders of Turkey's first experiment with democracy had failed to achieve. No one anticipated at the time that the new atmosphere would encourage a 'debilitating pluralism'[13] in party and associational life, excessive fragmentation of political parties and the breakdown of trust among all political actors, gradually leading Turkish politics to both over-politicization and intense polarization. This transformation was accompanied by violence that successive governments failed to contain. It is far from being certain that such a state of affairs was the direct outcome of the liberal constitution. Nevertheless, the military leadership that ended Turkey's second experiment with democracy identified the constitutional order, the political parties and civil society organizations as some of the major culprits for the state of affairs in which the country found itself.

The military adopted a two-step strategy to restore order in public and especially political life. The first step comprised bringing the violence that had seized the country to an end. The already existing martial law began to be applied with growing strictness, many who were suspected of having taken part in violent public manifestations as well as those suspected of having committed acts of terrorism were pursued, caught, taken into custody, questioned, and were handed heavy sentences by military courts where high standards of justice hardly prevailed. Within a year, violence had virtually disappeared.[14] As a second step, the military leadership introduced comprehensive measures to restructure not only political institutions but also other 'troublemakers' such as the universities to prepare a future which would be characterized by political stability. These deserve closer examination.

Just like the NUC in 1960, the National Security Committee[15] engaged major constitutional engineering. The military rulers of 1960 had addressed the problem of strengthening the democratic features of the constitution so as to insure that a parliamentary majority would not be used to build an authoritarian government. The overall goal of the 1980 military administration, on the other hand, became eliminating for good the polarization that had characterized Turkish politics during the 1970s. The particular formulae they devised toward that end, however, was highly questionable.

First, the military leadership turned to using unrestrained coercion to pacify those who were thought to be associated with organizations that contributed to political polarization and the accompanying violence. Those who were taken into custody were often subjected to inhumane treatment, becoming objects of torture in prisons many of which were run by the military. Such maltreatment continued and intensified for those who were given prison sentences by special National Security Courts charged with dealing with broadly defined 'terrorism'-related crimes.

Second, the commanders judged that the root problem was too much politics which in turn was a product of too many and too broad liberties. Concluding that society had to be depoliticized, they determined that the surest way to achieve it was the narrowing down of liberties. Therefore, the new constitution put limits on individual liberties, particularly as regards engaging in political activity by any organization other than political parties. Associations, labor unions, universities, activists, workers, university students and faculty were all placed under severe restrictions so as to prevent them from any activity that could be construed as being political.

Third, after initially asking political parties to put their house in order, the military leadership judged that this was impossible and decided to set up an entirely new party system. In 1981, all political parties were dissolved. When their leaders insisted on carrying on with politics, they were placed under custody in military camps near the Dardanelles on different occasions. Believing that a proper democracy needed only two parties, one on the center right and the other on the center left, the National Security Committee devised laws which it thought would contribute to the evolution of a moderate two-party system. To that end, a political parties law with strict organizational requirements was enacted to insure that all parties would have national rather than exclusively regional bases of support. The electoral law, redesigned, also introduced a national electoral threshold of 10 percent with an additional provision for local thresholds to prevent fragmentation of the vote and therefore parliamentary parties. But most importantly, the generals empowered themselves to approve of the members of the national organs of political parties as well as their list of candidates for the elections that would be held in November 1983. With such powers, they could determine whether a party would actually be considered as formally born, whether it could participate in the upcoming elections and who could get on party tickets. Taken together, these measures were intended to prevent the participation of other parties in the elections. In this way, the Committee made sure that its favored parties would be in power for an entire legislative term (Turan 1988).

Fourth, the military leadership expanded the scope of intervention of the state and reduced the scope of intervention of elected politicians in public life. To that end, the powers of the MGK (*Millî Güvenlik Kurulu*)[16] that brings the high command with the prime minister and several others together to discuss broadly defined matters of national security were enhanced. The universities were placed under the guidance and oversight of the Council on Higher Education to which the MGK also appointed a member; access to the Constitutional Court was narrowed while the system of National Security courts that included military judges and Military Courts was strengthened (Özbudun 1988: 25–28).

The military leadership appears to have envisioned a society in which the scope of politics would be narrow and a modestly competitive style of politics among parties representing 'moderate' political tendencies would prevail. The military itself, on the other hand, would exercise oversight of the political process through several instruments. To begin with, the MGK would function as a veto group to reject policy choices elected governments favored but the military leadership found objectionable. In this way, the commanders found opportunities to pressure the government to adopt policies and pursue courses of action which the governments themselves did not favor.[17] Next, through a set of representatives in state agencies like the universities, the state broadcasting system and the national security courts, the MGK would scrutinize the activities of some key organizations to insure that their activities remained within the bounds of their visions. The military leadership also appointed retired officers to a number of public positions to reinforce their ability to exercise oversight of the governmental-political process. Finally, military courts, empowered to try cases that would ordinarily be dealt with in civilian courts in other democracies, constituted an additional means, pointing to the expanded role of the military in the political process.

The political role of the military was considerably enhanced by acts of terrorism carried out by the PKK (*Partiya Karkerên Kurdistan*, Kurdistan Worker's Party). Civilian governments incapable of developing non-military responses turned over total responsibility to the military leadership to exterminate the movement. Rather than offering leadership in devising policies in which the military might be given a role, governments abdicated any role, extending instead comprehensive powers for the military to operate in domains that are seen to belong to the elected politicians in democratic societies. Elected governments did not often hesitate to accede to military demands for limiting individual liberties and tolerate frequent cases of unrestrained coercion by law enforcement agencies in the name of fighting terrorism.

In part intentionally and in part inadvertently, the military placed itself in a superior position to those of elected politicians. The fragmented nature of politics from 1991 until 2002 and the apprehension that the military might intervene once more if challenged too much by politicians, allowed the military leadership to possess and display autonomy not characteristic of societies where electoral politics prevail. Such autonomy was further enhanced by a system of recruitment-promotions-appointments-dismissal from service which was not subject to judicial review and with which politically weak governments chose generally not to interfere.

Return to civilian politics and rebuilding of party life (1983–95)

The elections of 1983 marked yet another transition to competitive politics. The military leadership was clearly committed to building a two-party system under their tutelage. How and why they decided to allow a third party not appearing to have their backing to take part in the elections remains a mystery to this day, but the ANAP (*Anavatan Partisi*, Motherland

Party) established by the architect of economic reform Turgut Özal was allowed to take part in the 1983 elections along with the 'officially approved' MDP (*Milliyetçi Demokrasi Partisi*, Nationalist Democracy Party) of General Turgut Sunalp and the HP (*Halkçı Parti*, Populist Party) of Necdet Calp, a former high-ranking bureaucrat. The ANAP based its campaign on integrating or synthesizing the pre-1980 rival political tendencies into a new political formula. It attacked the interventionist state and argued for its downsizing. Such themes appealed to the masses who had become tired of the bickering among the pre-1980 parties and the heavy hand of government in everyday life that had only become worse during military administrations. The charismatic dynamism of Mr Özal contrasted sharply with the insipid and didactic styles of Mr Sunalp and Mr Calp. The elections confirmed what had appeared to be a foregone conclusion. The ANAP won an overwhelming victory with 45 percent of the vote and 53 percent of the seats in the parliament (Ergüder 1988: 127–32; Ahmad 2006: 189–92).

The aspiration of the military leadership to build the ideal two-party system, however, proved unworkable. In the local elections of 1984 in which other parties that had been barred from the national elections of 1983 were allowed to participate, the two parties which the military had favored hardly received electoral support, producing a unique situation: two opposition parties in the parliament with almost no electoral basis in society and two opposition parties with voter support but no parliamentary representation. This anomaly invited attempts for mergers. The HP and the Social Democrats were united in 1985 in the SODEP (*Sosyaldemokrat Halkçı Parti*, Social Democratic Populist Party). Many of the deputies belonging to the MDP, on the other hand, left their party to join either the ANAP or the pre-1980 AP reborn under the name of DYP (*Dogru Yol Partisi*, True Path Party).

The primary policy goal of the Özal Governments was to complete a liberal economic reform agenda. To that end, legal and institutional structures that had been developed during the period of import substitution and autarchy were dismantled, many state economic enterprises were privatized and foreign investment was encouraged. A new class of industrialists and exporters emerged whose interests dictated the consolidation of a liberal market economy. Under the circumstances, questions of political liberalization were given lower priority. Nevertheless, Mr Özal could not resist pressures to restore the political rights of the former political leaders that were suspended by the military for 10 years. Rather than working to meet the two-thirds majority a direct constitutional amendment required, he chose to achieve a lower qualified majority that would submit the final decision to a public referendum. The proposition that brought back such figures as Süleyman Demirel, Bülent Ecevit, and Deniz Baykal back to politics barely passed. Mr Demirel quickly assumed the leadership of the DYP. Mr Ecevit replaced his spouse as the leader of the DSP (*Demokratik Sol Partisi*, Democratic Left Party). The Ecevits had decided to distance themselves from the CHP that Mr Ecevit had headed prior to 1980. Mr Baykal, a former minister of public finance and energy and natural resources, joined the SODEP. Rather impatiently, he tried to become the party chief but failed on three occasions. Then in 1992, when the reestablishment of pre-1980 parties became possible, he led the effort to reconstitute the party and became its president at a reopening convention in 1992. In 1995, the SODEP and the CHP merged with an interim president who was replaced by Deniz Baykal six months later (Ergüder 1988: 133–40; Ahmad 2006: 189–95).

The ANAP, victorious in the 1983 elections of transition, achieved a parliamentary majority again in 1987 though with a much slimmer margin. Mr Özal was undeterred, however, in the pursuit of his liberal economic policies. His familiarity with the workings of the Turkish state and the bureaucracy and the private sector, enabled him to identify potential sources of resistance and overcome them with relative ease. The expiration of the term of General Evren as president posed a dilemma for Mr Özal. His tenure as prime minister was uncertain since there were elections two years later. The presidency, on the other hand, was not an active policy position. It seems that he chose to offer his candidacy for president with the expectation that he might be able, informally, to run the parliamentary system as a presidential system.

The election of Mr Özal to the presidency was not an easy process. Ever since the 1960 military intervention, the position had been occupied by retired generals who kept their distance from daily politics and perceived their job to be guarding the fundamental values of the republic. Mr Özal did not inspire confidence among the ranks of the opposition as someone who could fit the description of a figure above politics. He managed to be elected only in the third round at which point the qualified majority requirement reverted to a simple majority. In retrospect, his election appears to have constituted a watershed event. On later occasions, leaders of majority parties no longer hesitated to offer their candidacy, with similar accompanying political tensions and lack of consensus between Government and opposition.

Mr Özal, as predicted, tried to behave as if he were the president in a presidential system. He handpicked a successor in the person of Yıldırım Akbulut, but Mr Akbulut lost his position to Mr Mesut Yılmaz at the next party convention. The declining fortunes of the party were reflected in the elections of 1991. It seemed that the country had gone to full round and come back to where it had started from in 1980 before the military intervention. Surely, the widespread violence that had been characteristic of pre-1980 was lacking but the dispersal of the vote and the fragmentation of the party system had come back. No fewer than five parties had placed deputies in the parliament with the DYP leading, and government by coalition had become a necessity.[18]

The realignment (1995–2002)

By 1995, the political party system that the military leadership had tried to construct had totally broken down; the parties they had tried to create had disappeared, parties that were revived forms of the pre-1980 parties had come back, the party system had become fragmented and the need for coalition governments returned. The restrictive political environment, however, comprised of constitutional provisions and laws that narrowed down political space and reduced opportunities for political participation remained somewhat intact. Furthermore, what the military leadership and the secularist elite had perceived as a problematical tendency, a major religiously oriented party, had not only reappeared but seemed to be getting stronger.

The rise and fall of the National Salvation Party and its successors and the emergence of the AKP

Religiously oriented parties had become a part of the Turkish political scene after 1970. The first such party, the MNP, was closed down in 1972 by the Constitutional Court having used religion for political ends. The MSP soon took its place and became a major actor after the elections of both 1973 and 1977. During the 1973–77 interim the distribution of the seats in parliament was such that, excepting a coalition between the two major parties, a government could not be formed without the support of the MSP. During 1977–80, the MSP was again included in all right wing coalitions that were in power most of the time. It was closed down with all others in 1981, but reconstituted itself as the RP (*Refah Partisi*, Welfare Party) in 1983. It began with a modest showing in the 1987 elections of 8.7 percent but rose to 16.9 percent in 1991, and to 21.4 percent in 1995. The strengthening of a religious party, its skills in mobilizing large number of voters to become involved in the political process, and its inclusion in governments, culminating in the premiership of its leader Mr Erbakan in 1996, caused grave concern among the highly secular military establishment. Mr Erbakan's references to Turkey joining an Islamic world which it would lead in founding increased suspicions as regards where he would lead the country. After a stormy meeting of the MGK in 1997, he was forced to resign in what has often been referred to as a 'post-modern coup'. In 1998, the party suffered the fate of some of its predecessors and was closed down by the Constitutional Court.

The party soon reappeared as the FP (*Fazilet Partisi*, Virtue Party) under the leadership of Mr Recai Kutan since Mr Erbakan had been barred from politics for five years. In the 1999 elections, the rising fortunes of the party appeared to have been reversed, falling down to 15.4 percent from 21.4 in 1995. Then in 2001 came another blow when the Constitutional Court closed down the party once again for exploiting religion for political ends. The routine of proceeding to establish a new party to replace the defunct organization did not fully operate, however, on this occasion. In 2001, while those loyal to Mr Erbakan founded the SP (*Saadet Partisi*, Felicity Party), a larger group of mainly younger people chose to reject the conservative leadership and proceeded to establish the AKP (*Adalet ve Kalkınma Partisi*, Justice and Development Party) under the leadership of Recep Tayyip Erdoğan, a young and charismatic personality who had been elected mayor of metropolitan Istanbul in 1994, only to be convicted later for inciting religious hatred by citing a poem with religious symbolism in a public speech. By pursuing a moderate line, keeping an open door to all who wanted to join the party and focusing on bread and butter issues, the AKP soon developed into a major political force and led the elections of 2002 with 34.3 percent of the vote. With the national electoral threshold of 10 percent that kept small parties out of the parliament, such a percentage gave the AKP a comfortable majority to achieve power by itself. Electoral studies have shown that the AKP succeeded in building a coalition of voters that resembled that which was built by Turgut Özal in 1983 (Özbudun 2006: 546).[19]

The AKP repeated its 2002 electoral success but more impressively in 2007 by getting 46.6 percent of the vote. The elections moved several months ahead because of the failure of the Grand National Assembly to elect a vice premier and foreign minister, Abdullah Gül the president of the republic appeared to have enhanced voter support for the Government party. Mr Gül was elected president after the elections and a short time later a constitutional amendment was ratified that moved the election of the president from the parliament to the voters.

The consolidation of political parties under the ANAP in 1983 following the 1980–83 military intervention had given way by 1991 to a party system that resembled in many ways the pre-1980 configuration. The ensuing period of coalitions during 1991–2002 caused deep voter dissatisfaction with the old parties. In the meantime, the AKP, having drawn lessons from the experience of religiously oriented parties from National Salvation to Felicity Party, managed to present a pragmatic, socially conscious but conservative image. Combined with the charisma of the party's leader, Recep Tayyip Erdoğan, the party succeeded in bringing back one-party government to Turkish politics.

Death of the center-right and the enigma of the center-left

The 2002 and 2007 elections showed that despite attempts to resuscitate them, the center-right Motherland and True Path Parties had lost the potential to become once again important actors in national politics. Similarly, the Felicity Party continues to give the appearance of a fringe party of the religious right. The CHP with its strict secularism and the MHP (*Milliyetçi Hareket Partisi*, Nationalist Action Party) with a philosophy occasionally bordering on jingoism represent the opposition. It seems a gradual realignment of voters and parties is on its way. The first part of this alignment, the transformation of the center right into a pragmatic political party that incorporates religious conservatism into its orientation has already taken place. The overall process of realignment, however, is continuing.

The process of post-1983 alignment was found lacking in one fundamental aspect. The ANAP of Mr Özal in 1983 and the AKP of Mr Erdoğan in 2002 were both born against a set of parties whose politics were to a large extent shaped within the framework of a security maximization paradigm.

Both reflected a preference for prosperity considerations. The reconstituted pre-1980 parties, on the other hand, have maintained their security focus. Their failure to transform themselves has constituted an Achilles heel of Turkish democracy. It is imperative in this context to examine the case of the CHP, the major opposition, claiming to represent the social democratic choice in Turkish politics.

The CHP, as the founding political organization of the republic, had taken upon itself the defense of the values of the republic and the principles of Atatürk's revolution after the transition to competitive politics. This approach representing a continuation of the defense of centrally directed cultural modernization policies paid little attention to questions of economic prosperity. The loss of three elections in a row in 1950, 1954, and 1957 did not result in a reconsideration of party ideology. The military intervention of 1960 against the DP and the failure of its adherents to organize into an effective political organization under the watchful eyes of the military made it the plurality party in 1961 only to suffer defeat once again in 1965 and in 1969.

It was the then secretary general of the party Mr Ecevit who recognized that, if it wanted to improve its electoral standing, the party had to appeal to specific socio-economic constituencies by addressing their concerns rather than pursuing an exclusively ideological line. It is thus that the party was introduced to the timidly named 'left of center' ideology. As discussed earlier, the new line of thinking produced immediate results. The electoral fortunes of the party improved so much that it became the plurality party in both the 1973 and 1977 elections. In retrospect, neither its electoral success nor the military intervention of 1980 appears to have constituted sufficient stimulus, however, for the party to reconsider seriously, or alter fundamentally, its ideology and its basic approach to politics.

When the CHP came back to life first as the SHP (Sosyaldemokrat Halk Partisi, Social Democratic People's Party), its leadership expressed some interest in bringing the thinking of the party in line with the social democratic trends that prevailed in Europe. Once the CHP was reconstituted, however, the new leaders reassumed the role of the defending what they thought comprised the fundamental values of the republic. Two dominating values were a rather strict interpretation of laicism and strong nationalism sometimes bordering on xenophobia. To the extent that the voters were not attracted by the party's ideology, the party chose to rely on the institutions of the state such as the military and the courts (especially the Constitutional Court) as resources in its conduct of politics.

It is interesting that the CHP displayed insensitivity to major changes that were occurring both in Turkish society and the world. After 1980, the Turkish economy had grown in leaps and bounds and Turkey had evolved into an industrial economy led by the private sector. More than three-quarters of the population had moved to centers that were classified as urban. The party took little notice of these changes and did not engage in an effort to review its ideology and programs, and adjust them to the widely altered domestic political environment.

The party was equally insensitive to changes in the international environment. The restructuring of social democratic political movements in various parts of Western Europe after the end of the bipolar world, the adjustments to the prevalence of liberal economics after the disappearance of the socialist alternative, failed to stimulate similar debate and changes in the party.[20]

The CHP has displayed little electoral success since its reconstitution. It has failed to pass the electoral threshold in 1999 and has registered modest achievements in the elections of 2002 and 2007 (19.4 and 20.9 percent respectively). The party gets its widest support from the educated, modern urban middle classes rather than the working class. In its daily pronouncements, the prevailing themes are strict secularism and nationalism rather than those of social justice, redistribution and the defense of the less well-off. The recent change of leadership has generated hope that the party's line of thinking may come under review. It is too early to tell whether those hopes will be fulfilled.

Asymmetric competition: Paradigm shift in Turkish politics

Any observer of contemporary Turkish politics may be puzzled by the fact that the agenda of Government and opposition often diverge as does their basic approach to societal problems. The Government party usually displays a pragmatic, problem solving approach in politics in contrast to the opposition that is frequently characterized by focusing on ideological issues or conceptualizing of all political problems in terms of ideology. This leads to what may be called asymmetric competition to the extent that Government and opposition base their programs, policy preferences, and even their rhetoric on different mindsets that I have described earlier as two rival paradigms of security and prosperity maximization. Security maximization focuses on internal and external dangers a country encounters and therefore places priority on the development, maintenance and expansion of the instruments of the state in order that security can be achieved. In this scheme, society is seen to be held together by a strong central administration and state regulation. The attitude toward civil society is characterized by distrust and pluralistic political competition is viewed with suspicion. The scope of politics is limited. Prosperity maximization paradigm, on the other hand, gives primary emphasis to the economic well-being of society. By its nature, it is society-centered and the state is seen as an instrument that serves to enhance the prosperity of society and individuals. The bureaucracy is public service oriented rather than assuming a commanding posture toward the citizenry. Under this scheme, society is thought to be best held together by the economic division of labor in society, mutual interdependence and the complementarity of economic interests. The room for political action is broad and civil society is seen as an indispensable part of the political process.

Turkish society has been making a long-term transition from a security-maximization to a prosperity-maximization paradigm. The decision regarding the shift to export-led growth initiated the shift and the end of the Cold War reduced the appeal of security maximization as motivation and justification of public policy. Increasing number of voters have found a bread-and-butter-issues oriented pragmatic political approach more appealing than ideological approaches. The social and economic environments in which Turkish politics occur have been changing. As is the case in all transitions, first the proponents of change are in the minority, but gradually despite occasional setbacks, they assume the upper hand. Some of those who have resisted change eventually admit to the necessity of change and make adjustments; others either disappear or become inconsequential.

The Turkish transition to a prosperity driven politics gained momentum with the rise of the ANAP after the economic reforms of 1980. After setback in the form of coalition governments in which recreations of pre-1980 political parties was a major force in between 1991–2002, prosperity driven paradigm became prevalent once again. Whether and how opposition parties will adjust to the altered circumstances remain to be seen. A failure to complete the transition is likely to prolong asymmetric politics and promote political fragmentation if the support for the government party dwindles. A more broadly based internalization of prosperity maximization than now, on the other hand, is likely to reduce the salience of ideological issues in the political agenda and to encourage further deepening of democracy.

The prevalence of a prosperity maximization paradigm whose emergence have been stimulated by socio-economic change, may facilitate the emergence of a political context characterized by pragmatism, negotiation and comprise, and also expand the public space that is allocated to politics, thereby creating suitable conditions for further consolidation of Turkey's democracy. In this context, the increasing understanding that the so called Kurdish question is not so much a uni-dimensional problem of law and order as security maximization would dictate, but one of recognizing the ethnic pluralism in society as well as achieving socio-economic betterment, constitutes an example that the prosperity maximization is slowly becoming the prevalent paradigm. It is important to remember, however, that change of paradigm is yet to be completed and some political turmoil is still to be expected on the way.

Notes

1 I would like to thank my colleague Boğaç Erozan of İstanbul Bilgi University for his helpful remarks on the first draft of this chapter.
2 Turkey was one of the two countries studied in the celebrated volume of the Princeton series on political development. Ward, R.T. and Rustow, D. (1964) *The Political Modernization of Japan and Turkey*, Princeton: Princeton University Press.
3 This framework was initially developed in Turan, İ. (1988) 'Stages of Development in the Turkish Republic' in *Perspectives on Democracy in Turkey*, Ankara: Turkish Political Science Association, pp. 59–112.
4 For a more elaborate treatment of these changes see Turan, İ. (1984) 'Atatürk's Reforms as a State and Nation Building Process', *Southeastern Europe*, 1: 169–89.

5 For an empirical study of the relationships between government-party-local notables, see Güneş-Ayata, A. (1992) *CHP: Örgüt ve İdeoloji*, Ankara: Gündoğan, esp. pp. 63–74 and 127–29.
6 This clarification and example come from the comments of my colleague Boğaç Erozan.
7 A very vivid description of the rival elite groups and their role in the emergence of competitive politics may be found in Leder, A. (1976) *Catalysts of Change: Marxist versus Muslim in a Turkish Community*, Austin: University of Texas at Austin, *Middle East Monographs 1*, esp. pp. 6–11.
8 See also Karpat, K. H. (1996) *Türk Demokrasi Tarihi*, İstanbul: Afa, pp. 98–122.
9 For changes paving the way to free and fair elections, see Eroğul, C. (1970) *Demokrat Parti: Tarihi Ve İdeolojisi*, Ankara: Ankara Üniversitesi, Siyasal Bilgiler Fakültesi, pp. 51–52.
10 Interestingly, a DP member had taken his party to court in March 1960 for having failed to hold a party convention for five years, a violation of the Law of Associations. The court rendered a decision to close down the party. It is doubtful that such a decision would have been rendered if the DP were still in power. I owe this clarification to Boğaç Erozan.
11 A more comprehensive account may be found in Kalaycıoğlu (2005), pp. 101–8.
12 This account has relied heavily on Krueger, A. O. and Turan, İ (1993) 'The Politics and Economics of Turkish Policy Reforms in the 1980s' in Bates, R. H. and Anne O. Krueger, A. O. (eds), *Political and Economic Interactions in Economic Policy* Reform, Oxford: Blackwell, pp. 333–86.
13 The expression comes from Bianchi, R. (1984) *Interest Groups and Political Development in Turkey*, Princeton: Princeton University Press, p. 346.
14 There has been some speculation that the military tolerated and in some instances even instigated the violence to justify its intervening in politics. While such a contingency cannot be ruled out, currently available evidence is not sufficient to substantiate such a suspicion.
15 To avoid confusion, National Security Committee is used to refer to the military command that took over government in 1980 while MGK refers to the constitutional organ that brings the military leadership with some key ministers and security bureaucrats to discuss security related policy questions.
16 Note that here reference is to the constitutional organ and not the ruling junta.
17 A case in point is forcing in 1998 Mr. Erbakan, head of the religiously oriented Welfare Party and prime minister at the time, to raise the length of primary school education from five to eight years, thereby closing down the middle school sections of the preacher training schools.
18 For a more detailed account cf. Turan, İ. (1994) 'Leadership Change in Turkey', *Mediterranean Politics* 1, London: Pinter Publishers, pp. 232–45.
19 The current and the preceding paragraph about the history of religiously oriented parties have benefited extensively from Özbudun (2006), esp. pp. 544–47.
20 A more comprehensive discussion of the recent life of the CHP may be found in Turan, İ (2006) 'Old Soldiers Never Die: The Republican People's Party of Turkey', *Southern European Politics*, September-December, 559–78.

References

Ahmad, F. (2006) *Kimlik Peşinde*, İstanbul: İstanbul Bilgi Üniversitesi Yayınları.
Barutçu, F. A. (1977) *Siyasi Anılar, 1939–1954*, İstanbul: Milliyet Yayınları.
Bianchi, R. (1984) *Interest Groups and Political Development in Turkey*, Princeton: Princeton University Press.

Ergüder, Ü. (1988) 'Post-1980 Parties and Politics in Turkey' in Özbudun, E. (ed), *Perspectives on Democracy in Turkey*, Ankara: Sevinç Matbaası.

Eroğul, C. (1970) *Demokrat Parti: Tarihi Ve İdeolojisi*, Ankara: Ankara Üniversitesi, Siyasal Bilgiler Fakültesi.

Güneş-Ayata, A. (1992) *CHP: Örgüt ve İdeoloji*, Ankara: Gündoğan.

Kalaycıoğlu, E. (2005) *Turkish Dynamics: Bridge Over Troubled Lands*, New York: Palgrave-Macmillan.

Karpat, K. H. (1996) *Türk Demokrasi Tarihi*, İstanbul: Afa.

Krueger, A. O. and Turan, İ (1993) 'The Politics and Economics of Turkish Policy Reforms in the 1980s' in Bates, R. H. and Anne O. Krueger, A. O. (eds), *Political and Economic Interactions in Economic Policy* Reform, Oxford: Blackwell.

Leder, A. (1976) *Catalysts of Change: Marxist versus Muslim in a Turkish Community*, Austin: University of Texas at Austin, *Middle East Monographs 1*.

Özbudun, E. (1988) 'Development of Democratic Government in Turkey: Crises, Interruptions and Reequilibrations' in Özbudun, E. (ed), *Perspectives on Democracy in Turkey*, Ankara: Sevinç Matbaası, pp. 543–557.

—— (2000) *Contemporary Turkish Politics: Challenges to Democratic Consolidation*, Boulder: Lynne Rienner.

—— (2006) 'From Political Islam to Conservative Democracy: The Case of the Justice and Development Party in Turkey', *Southern European Society and Politics*, September-December.

Seyhan, D. (1966) *Gölgedeki Adam*, İstanbul: Uycan Matbaası, 1966, p. 42.

Turan, İ (1969) *Cumhuriyet Tarihimiz*, İstanbul: Çağlayan.

—— (1984) 'Atatürk's Reforms as a State and Nation Building Process', *Southeastern Europe*, 2: 169–189.

—— (1988) 'Political Parties and the Party System in Post-1983 Turkey' in Metin Heper, M. and Evin, A. (eds), *State, Democracy and the Military: Turkey in the 1980s*, Berlin: deGruyter.

—— (1988) 'Stages of Development in the Turkish Republic' in *Perspectives on Democracy in Turkey*, Ankara: Turkish Political Science Association.

—— (1994) 'Leadership Change in Turkey', *Mediterranean Politics* 1, London: Pinter Publishers.

—— (2006) 'Old Soldiers Never Die: The Republican People's Party of Turkey', *Southern European Politics*, September-December: 559–578.

Ward, R.T. and Rustow, D. (1964) *The Political Modernization of Japan and Turkey*, Princeton: Princeton University Press.

Weiker, W. F. (1963) *The Turkish Revolution, 1960–1961*, Washington, D.C.: The Brookings Institution.

Yilmaz H. (1997) 'Democratization from Above in Response to International Context in Turkey, 1945–50', *New Perspectives on Turkey*, Fall: 1–37.

Zürcher, E. J. (1993) *Turkey: A Modern History*, London: I. B. Tauris.

4 The international context of democratic reform in Turkey

William Hale

How important is the international context in determining a transition to democracy in societies without a democratic political tradition? Classical social contract theory assumes that political structures emerge from bargains from within society: hence, as Phillippe E. Schmitter notices, it assumes that 'democratization is a domestic affair *par excellence*', so that the academic literature on democratisation has 'largely reflected this nativist tendency'. However, as he goes on to argue, the establishment of democratic government in the formerly communist countries of eastern Europe during the 1990s would hardly have been imaginable without the collapse of the USSR's previous regional hegemony (Schmitter 1996: 27). Geoffrey Pridham extends this proposal to cases in southern Europe (Greece, Spain and Portugal), arguing that the 'simultaneous process of democratic transition' in these countries drew on a 'common geopolitical environment', aided by the role of the then European Community as an integrative organisation. He cautions that although 'the salience of the international context of democratic transition may be ... easily recognised, analysing its real impact or influence on this process is no easy task, either theoretically or empirically' (Pridham 1991: 1–2) The problem is illustrated by the fact that, while the collapse of communism produced a transition to what has become consolidated democracy in most of Eastern Europe, it has failed to do so in most of the former USSR. The implication is that, either domestic conditions and historical traditions were quite different in the two sets of cases, and critically influential, or that the international context was quite different – for instance, that the goal of European Union membership was not held out to the former Soviet republics outside the Baltic, so they had little external incentive to democratise. Clearly, a full explanation requires careful examination of both the internal and external factors, weighing the relative importance of each.

To put the argument very crudely, we might be able to establish the relative importance of external and internal factors by comparing cases where the external environment was (a) neutral (or maybe even anti-democratic) with (b) those in which there was a positive international pressure for democratisation. If there were important moves towards liberalisation in instances of (a) but no such moves in instances of (b) then we could decide that the international context had no influence on democratisation; *per contra,* if cases of democratisation corresponded fairly closely to an international context which favoured it, we could conclude that there appeared to be a positive relationship between democratisation and the international environment. Even then, caution would need to be exercised. There may be doubts, for instance, as to whether the international environment was positive or otherwise, and coincidence does not prove causation. What constitutes democratisation may also be regarded as highly problematic. For present purposes, it would be useful to assume that it includes such things as the establishment of the rule of law, and equality before the law, as essential preliminaries to the evolution of democratically elected government, and of individual and collective civil rights.

The Turkish experience, from the Tanzimat to the Cold War

With all these reservations born in mind, the Turkish case is nonetheless an instructive one, since the process of political reform in Turkey goes back almost two centuries, with the international context a critical (albeit not always positive) factor for most of this period. During the first half of the nineteenth century, faced with the existential threat posed by European imperialism, a succession of Ottoman Sultans and statesmen began a process of reform known as the 'Tanzimat' or 'reorganisation'. The prime purpose of this project was to strengthen the state, primarily by modernising its army and administrative bureaucracy, rather than strengthening the rights of the citizens against it. Nevertheless, by changing the patterns of thought, especially among a new elite educated on western lines, the reforms came to have effects more far-reaching than those originally intended, culminating in the proclamation of the first Ottoman constitution in 1876.

For most of this period, the external environment was ambiguous. Western, especially British, statesmen may have seen the reform programme as a result of their own initiatives, but Ottoman internal policies were almost certainly more autonomous than they supposed (Bailey 1942: 228). Of the foreign powers most closely involved in what was called 'the eastern question', Russia was an irresponsible autocracy, hardly likely to back the cause of political reform in the Ottoman Empire or anywhere else. Against this, the British government generally favoured the Tanzimat, as a means of strengthening the empire against Russia. However, like most of the European powers, when the British spoke of reform, what they normally meant was the improvement of the position of the Christian communities. If the rights of all citizens, regardless of their religion, were improved as a result, then this was a by-product of the original aim. This point was illustrated in 1839 when the young Sultan Abdul Mejid issued the first of the 'Tanzimat charters', known as the 'Noble Rescript of the Rose Chamber' (*Hatt-i Şerif* of Gülhane). Designed to win the support of the western powers against the Sultan's nominal vassal and governor of Egypt, Mehmet Ali Pasha, who had come close to taking over the empire, the rescript proclaimed the principles of security of life and property of the subject, fair and public trial of those accused of crimes, and the equality of all before the law, regardless of religion. The same principles were repeated in an 'Imperial Rescript' (*Hatt-i Humayun*) issued in 1856 as part of the preliminaries for the Treaty of Paris which ended the Crimean war.[1] This was very far from democracy, but the principles of the rule of law and the legal equality of all citizens were essential foundation stones.

The background to the proclamation of the constitution of 1876 was more complex. In 1874 a revolt broke out in Bosnia-Herzegovina, which spread to Bulgaria in the following year. This threatened to produce a military intervention by Russia, supposedly to protect its fellow Orthodox Christians in the Balkans. The Western European governments badgered the Ottoman rulers to put their house in order, in the hope of staving off a Russian takeover of south-east Europe. Within the empire, liberal intellectuals, led by the writer Namık Kemal and known as the Young Ottomans, argued that representative democracy was quite compatible with Islamic principles, and would help to save the empire. With the senior Ottoman statesman Midhat Pasha supporting the cause, a section of the army deposed the autocratic Sultan Abdul Aziz in May 1876. In the following September, after the brief reign of Abdul Aziz's nephew Murad, who proved to be mentally unstable, his brother Abdul Hamid was brought to the throne, on the promise that he would proclaim a constitution. On 23 December 1876, as representatives of the powers were meeting in Istanbul to discuss peace terms between the Ottoman government and the Balkan rebels, with possible territorial concessions by the empire, their deliberations were interrupted by the booming of guns announcing the proclamation of the Ottoman constitution. The constitution could thus be seen as a defensive reaction to European ambitions, rather than a positive result of benign European diplomatic influence.[2]

Despite the brave hopes of its supporters, the constitutional experiment of 1876 turned out to be stillborn. The threatened war with Russia broke out in April 1877, producing defeat for the Ottoman armies. In February 1878 Abdul Hamid used this as an excuse to dissolve the parliament indefinitely. His grip on power lasted until July 1908 when a revolt by army officers in the Balkans, known in Europe as the Young Turks, forced him to re-proclaim the constitution. After an abortive counter-revolution by army units loyal to the Sultan, Abdul Hamid was deposed in April 1909. This renewed attempt at constitutional government was ended in 1913 when the Young Turk triumvirate headed by Enver Pasha seized power, only to drag the Empire into its fatal involvement on the German side in the First World War. In all this, there were no signs that the European powers were acting to promote democratic government – rather the reverse. In the Balkans, Austria seized the opportunity of turmoil in the empire to annex Bosnia-Herzegovina in October 1908. On their side, the Young Turks were deeply suspicious of all the European powers, including Britain. The British reciprocated, as their ambassador in Istanbul, Sir Gerard Lowther, intrigued constantly against the

Young Turk government, convinced that the revolution was part of a sinister global conspiracy by Jews and Freemasons to undermine the established order (Ünal 1996: 31–36; Kedourie 1971:89–104). In short, it appears that the constitutional movement was re-launched in spite of, rather than because of, the external environment, and was internally, not externally driven.

In the aftermath of the First World War, the attempt by the former entente powers to divide up Turkey's remaining territory among themselves was defeated by the national resistance movement, led by Kemal Atatürk, who then established the Turkish republic on the ruins of the old Empire. Following the peace treaty of Lausanne, signed in July 1923, the new regime sought to establish cooperative relations with all the main European powers, including the nascent Soviet Union. However, the events of 1918–23 had left them with almost no influence over Turkey's domestic politics, and no apparent desire to intervene. With America's return to isolationism in the 1920s, there was virtually no international pressure for the adoption of democratic values. 'Realist' power politics were the basis of the international system. In November 1924 the Progressive Republican Party (*Terakkiperver Cumhuriyet Fırkası*) was formed in parliament in opposition to the ruling People's Party (later Republican People's Party, or CHP) but in June 1925 it was suppressed by the government, following a Kurdish rebellion which had broken out the previous February. In August 1930, on Atatürk's initiative, a second opposition party was formed in the shape of the Free Republican Party, but this was also suppressed in the following November, since it attracted the support of Islamist groups who were basically opposed to the secular republic. Admittedly, the lack of an opposition party drew some European and American criticism in 1930, but on neither occasion did any of the European governments attempt to influence the outcome, either for or against democracy.[3]

A fundamental change in the Turkish political system occurred in 1945–46, when İsmet İnönü, Atatürk's successor as president, allowed the formation of another opposition party. Led by Adnan Menderes, the DP (*Demokrat Parti*, Democrat Party) won a landslide victory in the general elections of 1950, marking the start of a new era in which the locus of power was decided by a free vote of the people. By this time the external environment had changed radically. Until the end of the 1930s, Turkey had been able to remain neutral between the main European states, but the start of the Cold War, and a clear territorial threat from the Soviet Union, now forced it to seek an alliance with the Western powers. This it eventually achieved with its admission into NATO in 1952. This inevitably prompts the conclusion that the internal and external transformations were causally connected – that İnönü opted for multi-party democracy so as to make Turkey acceptable as a Western ally.

While the connection may have been there, however, it is very hard to prove. Although President İnönü appears to have been deeply impressed by the defeat of fascism in 1945, with the conclusion that Turkey must catch up with the democratising wave of world politics,[4] there is no evidence that the

Western powers specifically made Turkey's admission into the Western alliance conditional on its adopting democratic politics internally.[5] İnönü had strong domestic motives for the change of direction, since wartime privations and mismanagement had built up strong public resentment against the CHP (*Cumhuriyet Halk Partisi*, Republican People's Party) government, and the president correctly concluded that it would be better to provide a controlled saftey valve rather than risk an explosion of the whole republican system. On the other hand, it is very hard to believe that the external environment had nothing to do with İnönü's decision. As the American scholar Dankwart A.Rustow relates

> [D]uring a lengthy private interview in Ankara in 1954 İnönü at first angrily denied any suggestion that foreign policy considerations had influenced his decision: 'All that slander spread about me, as if I had been swimming with the stream!' Then he visibly relaxed, and with a shrewd smile added 'And suppose I had been swimming with the stream, that, too is a virtue'.
>
> (Rustow 1988: 245)

Although the available evidence is not conclusive, it suggests that the decision to opt for a multi-party system was due to powerful domestic pressures, plus İnönü's conclusion that Turkey should be 'swimming with the stream', rather than a clear agenda directly dictated by the Western powers.

After its election victory in 1950, the DP continued to rule Turkey until 27 May 1960, when it was overthrown by a military coup nominally led by General Cemal Gürsel. Although this was a clear case of the removal by force of a democratically elected government, and in a NATO country, none of Turkey's western allies made any protest. Almost certainly, the need not to alienate an essential Cold War ally was the main motivation for this reticence. Within NATO, the US played a clearly dominant role, and normally put strategic considerations at the top of its agenda. Once the western governments were assured by Gürsel's first broadcast that Turkey would remain faithful to its alliances (Weiker 1963: 20–21) they had no difficulty in recognising the new government. Paradoxically, the military regime also oversaw the preparation and enactment of a new constitution which extended civil liberties, introduced a new range of social and economic rights, and established a Constitutional Court to provide judicial review of government decrees and acts of parliament. This document is widely judged to have been Turkey's most democratic constitution, but there is no evidence that it resulted from external pressure. At this stage, it appears that Turkey's external alliances had very few, if any, effects on its internal politics.

Turkey's return to democratic government lasted until March 1971, when another military intervention forced the resignation of the government of Süleyman Demirel, the successor to Menderes as the leader of the centre-right of Turkish politics. On this occasion, the generals did not openly take over the government, but instead set up a series of puppet administrations which normally followed offstage directions by the military. There is some evidence that this caution may have derived from the fear that if an outright military regime were installed this would create difficulties in relations with Turkey's allies, but this is not conclusive.[6] By this stage, international human rights organisations were active in publicising the numerous cases of torture, arbitrary arrests and dismissals which occurred under the military-directed regime, but these protests seem to have had little or no effect on the reactions of western governments.[7] Once again, Cold War *Realpolitik* overruled moral misgivings. Turkey returned to elected civilian government, following, general elections held in October 1973, but this was the result of disagreements within the military on how to proceed, plus the fact that the regime had simply run out of an agenda, not external pressure.

Turkey's third post-war military coup occurred on 12 September 1980, following several years of brutal terrorism from the ideological fringes, economic crisis, and political incapacity by successive governments. On this occasion, US military officials had for some time been privately prompting the Turkish armed forces to act, in order to stave off national collapse. Once the coup had been launched by the Chief of the General Staff, General Kenan Evren, the Carter administration in Washington was relieved, although it regretted the necessity for the coup and privately urged Evren to make it clear that there would be a return to elected government in due course (Birand 1987: 124–27, 185–86; Spain 1984: 12–14, 19, 21–24).[8] The military regime lasted until November 1983, when it handed over to an elected government headed by Turgut Özal, founder and leader of the newly formed ANAP (*Anavatan Partisi*, Motherland Party).

In 1983 the military rulers argued that the return to civilian rule was purely their own decision: as ex-Admiral Bülend Ulusu, the Prime Minister under the military, claimed, 'the Turkish nation has adopted parliamentary democracy as its political system without any external influence'.[9] On the other hand, the external reaction to the coup was far less uncritical than it had been on the two previous occasions, as international human rights pressure groups like Amnesty International had become far more active and vociferous in reporting cases of torture and arbitrary arrest. Government spokesmen were forced back onto the defensive, suggesting that they took the criticisms seriously. As a result, Turkey was obliged to withdraw from the Parliamentary Assembly of the Council of Europe: within the Council, there was serious consideration of expelling Turkey from the organisation, although the eventual decision was to avoid this, so as to keep up a dialogue with the regime. In the European Community, pressure from the European Parliament to suspend the Association Agreement which Turkey had signed with the then EEC in 1963, did not prevail. However, in November 1981 parliamentary pressure forced the Commission to suspend a 600 million ECU aid programme which had been announced earlier, until democracy was restored: (in the event, the suspension remained indefinite, due to objections from Greece). In Washington, the Reagan administration was not openly critical of the military government, although it kept up some behind-the-scenes pressure urging the eventual restoration of democracy (Dağı 1996: 127–36). As İhsan Dağı concludes, it is impossible to say definitely that European pressure forced the regime to restore elected government, but it is virtually certain that they were heavily influenced by it, in spite of their denials (Dağı 1996: 136). It thus seems that, by the 1980s, Cold War strategic priorities were less influential than they had been previously, with Turkey's European allies more prepared to act independently of the United States. This was to prove a crucial factor in subsequent years.

After the Cold War: the European Union and Turkish democracy

In spite of the return to elected civilian government in 1983, during the 1990s Turkey remained a highly illiberal democracy, with draconian constitutional and legal restrictions on freedoms of speech, communication, and association. In the south-east, a dirty war erupted in response to terrorist attacks by the PKK (*Partiya Karkerên Kurdistan*, Kurdistan Worker's Party), with flagrant human rights abuses on both sides, the displacement of as many as 3 million internal refugees, the widespread torture of suspects, and hundreds of extra-judicial killings. On the other hand, the European Union was beginning to play a bigger role in Turkey's foreign policy. Its first application for admission to the then European Community, which was submitted by Turgut Özal's government in 1987, was unsuccessful, but in 1992 the Association Council, which handled Turkey's relations with what was now the EU, agreed to re-start the process of constructing a customs union between the two sides, in accordance with the Association Agreement signed in 1963. This was eventually achieved in 1995, coming into effect at the beginning of the following year. Although its main purpose was economic, political factors were of primary importance, since it would require ratification by the European Parliament, which was highly critical of Turkey's human rights record (Müftüler-Baç 1997: 90–91; Kramer 1996: 60, 67). In an attempt to meet some of these criticisms, the Turkish parliament discussed a series of constitutional amendments, of which 15 were adopted in July 1995. These included a repeal of the bans on political activities by trades unions and trade associations, permission for public employees to join labour unions and alteration of the rules for the closure of political parties by court order.[10] However, they left most of the serious constitutional restrictions on civil rights intact, and did little to assuage criticisms in the European Parliament and elsewhere. Hence, it was only under intense pressure from the member state governments that the EP eventually ratified the customs union agreement in December 1995 (Müftüler-Baç 1997: 94; Kramer 1996: 68–69).

In Ankara, the customs union was only accepted as a stepping stone on the path to EU membership, but for the next four years the Turkey-EU relationship remained stalled. During 1996–97 the pro-Islamist RP (*Refah*

Partisi, Welfare Party), the lead partner in a chaotic coalition government, was opposed in principle to the idea of EU accession, and in December 1997 the European Council, meeting in Luxembourg, pointedly left Turkey off the list of potential new members. This position was not reversed until December 1999 when, after years of dithering, the European Council finally decided that Turkey could become a candidate for full membership of the EU on the same basis as other applicant countries. Before accession negotiations could start, Turkey would need to meet the democratic norms which the Council had drawn up at its meeting in Copenhagen in June 1993.

While originally designed to govern the accession process of the former communist countries of Eastern Europe, the 'Copenhagen criteria' applied equally to the Turkish case, by stipulating that 'membership requires that the candidate country has achieved stability of institutions guaranteeing democracy, the rule of law, human rights and respect for a protection of minorities'.[11]

In line with the Helsinki decisions, the EU Commission issued an Accession Partnership Document in November 2000, detailing the political reforms it expected Turkey to make over the short and medium term. The Turkish government responded in March 2001 when the cabinet approved a 'National Programme' for the implementation of the EU *acquis*. This set off a far more concerted and directed programme of liberalising reforms than any which had succeeded it, providing a striking example of the powerful impact of an external stimulus. The process began with a raft of constitutional amendments passed in 2001 under the coalition government led by Bülent Ecevit, and extending into nine 'harmonisation packages' of legal and constitutional reforms under the AKP (*Adalet ve Kalkınma Partisi*, Justice and Development Party) government which was elected in November 2002: ('harmonisation' referred specifically to the need to bring Turkish laws and practices into 'harmony' with those of the EU). Since these changes have been described in detail elsewhere (Hale 2003; Hale and Özbudun 2010: ch. 5; Özbudun and Gençkaya 2009: ch. 3–5),[12] they will only be summarised here. They included, most notably, the revision of the constitution so as to enhance freedoms of speech and association and the passage of a new Law of Associations, the enactment of new Criminal and Civil Codes, the complete abolition of the death penalty, legal changes to facilitate the prosecution of public officials responsible for torture and maltreatment of prisoners, and the passage of legislation allowing broadcasting in languages other than Turkish, as a first step towards the recognition of Kurdish cultural rights. In the institutional field, there were important moves designed to restrict the political role of the military, primarily by reducing the National Security Council, which brings together the military commanders and government ministers, to a purely advisory role, plus some moves to extend civilian control over military expenditures.

So far as Turkey's foreign relations were concerned, this programme succeeded in its main purpose, since accession negotiations between the EU and Turkey were formally launched in October 2005. After this, however, there was a notable slow-down in the reform process, leading the experienced German observer Heinz Kramer to conclude gloomily that whole mechanism of 'conditionality compliance' which is considered central to the accession process had broken down (Kramer 2009: 1). In the 2007 election campaign, the AKP had committed itself to introducing a new constitution, to replace the highly restrictive document issued by the military regime in 1982. It asked a group of academic experts, headed by Professor Ergun Özbudun, to prepare a new text, but then quickly shelved the prepared draft.[13] This is not to suggest that the process of reform came to a complete stop. Thus, in 2006, parliament passed a bill providing for the establishment of an Ombudsman's office, which had long been urged by the EU: in the event, this was vetoed by the Constitutional Court in 2008, but the blame for this could not be laid at the government's door. In 2008, a new Law on Foundations substantially improved freedoms of association, as well as the property rights of charitable and religious foundations of the non-Muslim minorities in Turkey.[14] The government also attempted to meet widespread complaints, both domestically and abroad, by revising Article 301 of the new Penal Code which had been used to prosecute dozens of writers and intellectuals for alleged 'insults' to 'Turkish identity' and state institutions.[15] Nonetheless, as the European Commission complained, this reform did not go far enough. Other serious shortcomings which the EU pointed out included the failure to improve the cultural and other rights of the Kurdish minority, the continuation of compulsory school classes in religious culture and ethics (ignoring the complaints of the Alevi community) and restrictions on the Greek Orthodox Ecumenical Patriarchate.[16]

This sharp slowdown in the reform programme could partly be explained by domestic political developments. Up to 2005, the CHP, as the main opposition group in the Turkish parliament, had generally supported the reforms, giving the government the two-thirds majority which is required to change the constitution without calling a referendum. After this, the party switched to a strongly nationalist and generally anti-liberal line, in which it was joined by the MHP (*Milliyetçi Hareket Partisi*, Nationalist Action Party) which entered parliament in the 2007 general elections. The AKP government was also preoccupied by a crisis over the presidency in the spring of 2007, the general elections of that year, and the attempt by the Chief Public Prosecutor of the Court of Cassation to have the ruling party closed down by the Constitutional Court in 2008 (Hale and Özbudun 2010: 62–65, 74–75). Changes in the external environment had a highly negative effect. In Germany, the Christian Democrat party (CDU-CSU), which opposes Turkish membership of the EU in principle, came to power in September 2005. In practice, Chancellor Angela Merkel could not go back on the commitment of her Social Democrat (SPD) predecessor, Gerhard Schröder, to start accession negotiations with Turkey: moreover she was obliged to cooperate with the SPD, as her coalition partners. This situation remained unchanged when she formed her second coalition government, this time with the Free Democrat Party (FDP) in 2009. Nevertheless, in public statements she repeated support for her party's policy, which favoured an ill-defined 'privileged partnership' for Turkey as an alternative to full membership – in effect, a polite way of saying 'no' to the Turks. In France, the ruling UMP party (*Union pour un mouvement populaire*) also supported 'privileged partnership', although in practice Jacques Chirac, the President up to May 2007, joined the other EU leaders in accepting full membership for Turkey as the eventual aim. However, after this the new President, Nicolas Sarkozy, was an outspoken supporter of 'privileged partnership'. Austria could also be expected to oppose full membership for Turkey, although experience suggested that it could be persuaded to back down under pressure from other member states.

To make matters worse, although Turkey and the Turkish Cypriots reversed previous Turkish policy by supporting the Annan Plan for a settlement of the Cyprus dispute in 2004, this was not reciprocated by the Greek Cypriot side, which joined the EU in May 2004 without any representation of the Turkish Cypriots. Cyprus thus became yet another stumbling block in the path to EU membership. Thanks to a complex dispute over Turkey's refusal to open its airports and harbours to Greek Cypriot aircraft and shipping, negotiations on eight Chapters of the *acquis communautaire* were blocked as from December 2006. In 2007 the French government unilaterally blocked discussion of another five Chapters (Hale and Özbudun 2010: 121–28). All these developments raised serious doubts in Turkish minds as to whether the EU would stand by its commitments to Turkey, resulting in a serious loss of public support for the EU project.[17]

Events between the 1990s and 2009 thus support the argument that there was a strong and positive relationship between the external environment – in particular, relations between Turkey and the EU – and the pace of democratisation in Turkey. Prior to 1999, with the EU still reluctant to accept Turkey as a candidate for membership, the external incentive was slight, and the reforms correspondingly limited and hesitant. Once the EU had given Ankara a clear commitment to the effect that full membership was a long-term possibility, then both the Ecevit and AKP governments responded with an impressive succession of constitutional and legal reforms. After 2005, however, the EU began to send out mixed and confusing signals, with the Commission and most member-state governments still supporting the aim of Turkish accession, but France and Austria opposed, and Germany ambiguous, at best. As a reaction, the reform programme flagged, with many wondering whether it had petered out entirely.[18]

Fortunately, this assumption turned out to be too pessimistic. As Hugh Pope reported in January 2010, in spite of the disappointments in the EU relationship, the AKP government 'slowly re-started its EU engines in 2009' by issuing its own 'National Programme' for the adoption of the *acquis,* and appointing Eğeman Bağış as its chief negotiator with Brussels, separating this job from that of the foreign minister.[19] During 2009–10 the government revived the internal political reform process, first by attempting to address the Kurdish problem, and then by re-launching a package of crucial reforms to the 1982 constitution. Although the reforms could be expected to have important and positive effects on Turkey's relationship with the EU, this was not used by the government as the main reason for launching them (for instance, the term 'harmonisation package' was quietly dropped) and that the new effort did not correspond to any clear or more positive signals from the EU itself. The conclusion is that the reform programme had now been partly uncoupled from the Turkey-EU relationship, having acquired an internal dynamic, based on domestic rather than external pressures and demands.

In the case of the so called 'Kurdish initiative' (in Turkish, *açılım*, or 'opening') some of the incentive came from the United States rather than the EU, since the Obama administration was beginning the drawn-out process of extricating itself from Iraq, and wished to avoid the risk of conflict between Turkey and the Iraqi Kurds after it had done so. Equally, the Turkish government took pains to re-build its bridges with the Iraqi Kurdish leadership, and was largely successful in this. Nonetheless, a large part of the incentive was purely domestic, since the continuing Kurdish problem, and the alienation of much of the Kurdish public from the Turkish state, was still the major defect of Turkish democracy. The government made it clear that it was not prepared to concede to Kurdish demands for the establishment of a federal state, with autonomy for the south-east, or to end the provision that Turkish is the sole state language. While the details still had to be worked out, it was nonetheless expected that the 'initiative' would probably include the reduction of the much-criticised 'village guards' units (that is, pro-government militia in Kurdish villages) and wider use of the Kurdish language.[20]

Previously, the armed insurgents of PKK and its supporters had insisted that they would not lay down their weapons unless they were granted a full and general amnesty. The government could not go this far, but in breaking another taboo by striking up direct and more cooperative relations with the autonomous Kurdistan Regional Government in Iraq, as well as the Iraqi government, there was a chance that it would be able to bring the PKK militants in Northern Iraq 'down from the mountains'. As a first step, 34 PKK members and their relatives (including four children) presented themselves at the Turkish-Iraqi border crossing post of Habur on 19 October 2009. After questioning by the Turkish judicial authorities, they travelled on to Diyarbakır, the main city in the Kurdish-inhabited south-east. Here they received a rapturous reception clearly orchestrated by the DTP (*Demokratik Toplum Partisi*, Democratic Society Party), Turkey's main pro-Kurdish overground organisation, which has unofficial links with the PKK. This reaction backfired severely, however, since the government quickly realised that the PKK was turning the 'initiative' into a propaganda coup for itself. As Prime Minister Tayyip Erdoğan told a group of journalists travelling with him to Pakistan on 24 October, 'Let's take a break ... We will continue the process after reviewing the situation'.[21] This turned out to be the start of an indefinite postponement of the 'Kurdish initiative'. On 3 December the DTP announced that it no longer supported it.[22] Worse was to come on 11 December, when the Constitutional Court concluded a closure case against the DTP which had originally been launched in November 2007. As expected, the Court ordered the dissolution of the party on the grounds of 'its links with a terrorist organisation and being the focal point of activities contrary to the indivisible integrity of the state'. Although he was identified as leader of the more moderate faction of the DTP, Ahmet Türk, along with another of the party's MPs, Aysel Tuğluk, were deprived of their seats in parliament.[23] The party then re-founded itself as the BDP (*Barış ve Demokrasi Partisi*, Peace and Democracy Party).

Apparently aware of the fact that if its plans for reform were presented as being addressed purely to the Kurds then they might fail to win the support of the ethnic Turks who constitute around 80 per cent of the population, the government tried to re-launch the programme as a more broadly-based 'national unity and brotherhood project' or (more commonly) the 'democratic initiative'. This resulted in a raft of proposed constitutional amendments which was presented to parliament at the end of March 2010. It included, most notably: changes to Articles 10 and 41 to allow for 'positive discrimination' in favour of women and children, and to protect children from abuse: to Articles 53, to allow civil servants and retired workers to enter into collective labour contracts (although not to go on strike): to Article 74, to allow the establishment of an Ombudsman's office: to Article 145, to allow civilian courts to try military officers for 'crimes against the security of the state, constitutional order and its functioning', and to Article 148, to allow individuals to apply to the Constitutional Court for legal redress 'on the grounds that one of the fundamental rights and freedoms within the scope of the European Convention on Human Rights which are guaranteed by the Constitution has been violated by public authorities'.[24] The most controversial of the amendments included: to Article 69, to restrict the conditions under which political parties could be closed down by the Constitutional Court: to Articles 146, 147 and 149, affecting the structure and membership of the Court, and the methods of appointments to it: and to Article 159, affecting the composition and appointment of the Supreme Council of Judges and Public Prosecutors (known by its Turkish initials as HSYK) which carries out the crucial function of appointing judges and public prosecutors. Finally, the draft included the withdrawal of Provisional Article 15 of the 1982 constitution, which had given members of the former military junta of 1980–83 immunity from prosecution for any of their actions while they had been in power.[25]

Parliament opened its full debate on the amendments on 19 April 2010. Since the opposition parties refused to support the package, there was virtually no chance that it would receive the two-thirds majority which is needed to enact a constitutional amendment on the floor of the House. However, amendments passed by a three-fifths majority (that is, 330 votes) can be enacted if they are later approved in a national referendum. Since the

ruling AKP had 336 seats, it could resort to this method as the only practical way of pushing the package through. The first ballot on each of the
individual articles was completed on 29 April.[26] This process was repeated
in a second round of voting, but with a crucial casualty on 4 May when the
proposed amendment to Article 69, affecting the closure of political parties,
received only 327 votes. Nonetheless, the Government pressed ahead with
the rest of the package, which was finally passed on 7 May.[27]

Following the parliamentary debate, a referendum was scheduled for 12
September 2010 (ironically, the thirtieth anniversary of the coup d'état of 12
September 1980). In the run-up to the referendum the CHP and MHP, as the
two main opposition parties, fiercely urged a 'no' vote, while the BDP pressed
its Kurdish supporters to boycott the polling stations. In the event, Prime
Minister Erdoğan and his colleagues presented a far more convincing case, so
that the 'yes' votes carried the day, by a majority of 58 to 42 per cent. AKP
spokesmen acknowledged that many of those who had voted 'yes' – as they
claimed, around 13 per cent of the total – would have voted for other parties
if this had been a general election. Nonetheless, the results suggested that, as
is usual in referendums, most voters had followed party loyalties, rather than
being swayed by the merits or demerits of the constitutional package itself.
With a few notable exceptions, the 'no' votes were in the majority in those
areas where the opposition parties had won in previous elections, in the western and coastal districts, with the 'yes' votes dominating in the AKP's traditional strongholds in Istanbul, the Black Sea region, and central and eastern
Anatolia. For the government, the worrying aspect of the results was that the
BDP's boycott campaign appeared to have been successful in several, albeit
far from all, of the south-eastern provinces, with turnout rates well below
those of the rest of the country.[28] This underlined the need for the government
to revive the 'Kurdish opening' as part of the overall democratic initiative.

More broadly, it was recognised that, by itself, the reform package did not
go far enough, since most of the restrictive 1982 constitution remained
intact. This was acknowledged by Prime Minister Erdoğan who, immediately
after the referendum results became known, announced that the government
would begin work on preparing a completely new constitution. This would be
presented to parliament after the next general elections, which could be
expected in July 2011.[29] Needless to say, the referendum results were warmly
welcomed by the European Commission.[30] However, it was notable that, in
its referendum campaign the AKP had urged that the reform package should
be adopted on its own merits, and not because democratisation was part of
the EU's agenda. Evidently, its main motivation was Turkey's internal
dynamics (more crudely, its own interests) rather than external pressures.

Summing up: Democratic reform and the international environment

This brief historical survey enables us to suggest some answers to the questions raised in the first section about the role of external forces in pushing

forward democratic reforms in Turkey and the late Ottoman Empire. For the Ottoman period the record is a mixed one. During the Tanzimat period, between the 1830s and 1860s, the western powers, notably Britain, pushed for reforms of the Ottoman administrative and judicial system. Nevertheless, there was also an important internal momentum for this process, since the Ottoman statesmen clearly realised the need for reform, and initiated most of it themselves. Moreover, the prime original purpose of the Tanzimat was to strengthen the state against its internal and external enemies, rather than the rights of the citizen. The European powers were mainly concerned with the treatment of the Christian minorities, rather than the population as a whole. When Ottoman reformers like Midhat Pasha pressed for the introduction of the first constitution in 1876 they were partly motivated by the fear that if they failed to do so then the European powers would partition the empire's Balkan territories among themselves. In this sense, the constitution was used as a defence mechanism *against* European diplomatic tactics, rather than harmonisation with them. As it was, the constitutional order rapidly collapsed, and the European powers did nothing to save it. Nor did they do anything to encourage the attempted re-launch of the constitution after 1908 – in fact Britain, the power which ought to have projected itself as the champion of democracy, actively tried to undermine the Young Turk government. If foreign diplomacy had a role in democratic reforms in the Ottoman state – such as they were – it was more often negative than positive, especially during the final years of the empire.

This story continued after the foundation of the republic in 1923. Once the Treaty of Lausanne was signed, bringing a formal end to the First World War between the former Ottoman Empire and the entente powers, Atatürk sought to re-build Turkey's bridges with the main European states, and had largely succeeded in doing so by the 1930s. On the other hand, the European governments had virtually no influence over the course of domestic politics in Turkey, or any desire to exercise it. The experiment of establishing an opposition party which Atatürk launched in 1930 may have been partly inspired by the need to emulate the western democracies, but the initiative had come from within Turkey, not outside, and the western powers did not react when it was ended.

Moving forward to the post-war period, it is likely that foreign policy considerations were important in İnönü's decision to open up the political system, but domestic incentives were equally significant, and there is no clear evidence that the western powers specifically made democratisation a *sine qua non* for Turkey's admission to the NATO alliance. As the western reaction to the 1960 *coup* demonstrated, the other members of NATO, especially the United States, were preoccupied with the need to ensure the loyalty of a crucial cold war ally. If this were assured, then Turkey's internal politics were its own affair. By 1971–73 human rights pressure groups and their supporters had become more active in advertising human rights abuses by the semi-military regime, but this appears to have had little or no effect on the policies of Western governments. The 1980 coup was not resisted by the other NATO governments, but by this stage criticisms by non-governmental organisations of Turkey's internal regime were more widespread and influential. This effect was heightened by the fact that the European NATO members, notably through such bodies as the European Parliament, now played a more significant role in overall Western policy towards Turkey, and were less inhibited than the US government by Cold War priorities. Comparing the experiences of 1980–83 with those of 1960–61, it is also clear that the striking development of human rights NGOs like Amnesty International also had important effects on western policies, opening up a 'second track' in the relationship.

It was only after the EU governments had accepted Turkey as a candidate for full membership, and had presented the Turkish government with a clear road map of conditionality, that they began to have a definite, concerted and generally impressive effect in speeding up the democratisation process in Turkey. This had important results. Without the EU incentive, it is unlikely that the Turkish reform programme would have been nearly as fast or determined as it actually was. Domestically, liberal opinion would have supported democratisation anyway, but the need to 'harmonise' with the EU almost certainly helped to persuade the more reluctant to speed up the process of reform This effect was significantly weakened between 2005 and 2009, as serious doubts about the whole accession project began to cloud the horizon on both sides. After this, however, an important shift occurred, as the AKP government decided to re-launch the democratisation process in its own way, and without any clear change in the external environment which could have prompted this. By this stage, 'harmonisation' had virtually dropped out of the vocabulary of democratisation in Turkey, suggesting that external incentives were now less influential than domestic ones.

Experiences since 1999 had other two other important implications. The first was that if the external factor was to have its full effect, there must be a clear commitment to a goal valued by both sides. To put it bluntly, the effectiveness of the EU's road map depended on the fact that the EU could offer Turkey full membership of the Union as an incentive: without this, it had no more than vague and weak moral force. In contrast with the Turkish experience, the failure of the EU's Mediterranean Partnership Programme to achieve democratic progress in those Mediterranean countries which were not candidates demonstrated that the mere offer of 'partnership' was far too feeble an incentive (Grigoriadis 2009: 173–74). Once the European leaders – or at least some of them – began to speak of 'privileged partnership' for Turkey, then the external incentive for democratisation was similarly and significantly weakened. The second was that if domestic factors became the primary motive for reform, then the shape of the programme, and the commitment to achieve it, would naturally be shaped by domestic conditions. As an example, the AKP government launched the 'Kurdish opening' on its own initiative, or at American rather than European prompting, but effectively shelved it once the PKK and its supporters first tried to exploit it, and then abandoned cooperation. Similarly, the emphasis in the 'democratisation package' of 2010 on reform of the judiciary resulted from the AKP's reasonable resentment of its own treatment by the Constitutional Court, not EU priorities. The idea that democratisation, like globalisation, was purely 'driven by the West and imposed on the rest' was clearly inapplicable in the Turkish case. Meanwhile, the main hope was that if democratic transformation could be achieved through conflict and compromise between internal forces, rather than external prompting, then it would be all the more robust and effective.

Notes

1 An English translation of the *Hatt-i Şerif* of 1839 is printed in Landen, R. G. (1970) *The Emergence of the Modern Middle East: Selected Readings*, New York, NY: Van Nostrand, pp. 38–42: for a summary and analysis of the Tanzimat reforms, see Lewis, B. (1961) *The Emergence of Modern Turkey*, London: Oxford University Press, pp.104–25.
2 On the Young Ottomans, see Mardin, Ş. (1962) *The Genesis of Young Ottoman Thought*, Princeton NJ: Princeton University Press, (repr. (2000) Syracuse NY: Syracuse University Press). On the constitutional movement, see Devereux, R (1963)*The First Ottoman Constitutional Period*, Baltimore MD: Johns Hopkins Press. The English text of the constitution is printed in Kili, S. (1971) *Turkish Constitutional Developments and Assembly Debates of the Constitutions of 1924 and 1961*, Istanbul, Robert College Research Center, pp.150–62, with a critical explanation on pp.14–17.
3 On the first point, see Weiker, W. F.(1973) *Political Tutelage and Democracy in Turkey: the Free Party and its Aftermath*, Leiden: E.J. Brill, p.58; on the Progressive Republican Party, see Zürcher, E. J. (1991) *Political Opposition in the Early Turkish Republic: the Progressive Republican Party, 1924–1925*, Leiden, E.J. Brill.
4 As he later put it, 'I used to see other countries around us holding free elections and had become very ashamed of ourselves': quoted, Robinson, R. D. (1965) *The First Turkish Republic: a Case Study in National Development*, Cambridge MA, Harvard University Press, p.142: see also Heper, M. (1998) *İsmet İnönü, the Making of a Turkish Statesman*, Leiden, E.J. Brill, pp. 184–93.
5 For instance, the exhaustive study of the contemporary diplomatic record by Athanassopoulou, E. (1999) *Turkey-Anglo-American Security Interests, 1945–1952*, London and Portland OR: Frank Cass reveals no clear demand by Britain or the US to this effect, although she refers to the possibility (p. 73).
6 In his memoirs, General Muhsin Batur, the Airforce Commander who played a major role in issuing the '12 March memorandum' which overthrew the Demirel government, relates that he had earlier turned down a plan for a full military takeover which had been prepared in Army Headquarters, on the grounds that it would be rejected by Turkey's western allies: Batur, M. (1985) *Anılar ve Görüşler*, Istanbul, Milliyet, pp. 224–25. Batur's version of events is strongly disputed by Gürkan, C. (1986) *12 Mart'a Beş Kala*, Istanbul: Tekin, pp. 216–18, 230–49; Batur's reply is on pp. 422–33.
7 See Cousins, J. (1973) *Turkey: Torture and Political Persecution*, London Pluto Press, esp. pp. 6, 22–23, 39–41, 58–77, 94–97.
8 Spain was US Ambassador in Ankara at the time of the 12 September coup.
9 Quoted, *Newspot* (weekly bulletin issued by the Directorate of Press and Information, Ankara), 21 October 1983.

10 Other amendments included the reduction of the voting age to 18 years, and an increase in the membership of the Grand National Assembly, Turkey's unicameral parliament, to 550. For the details, see Özbudun, E. and Gençkaya, Ö. F. (2009) *Democratization and the Politics of Constitution-Making in Turkey*, Budapest and New York NY: Central European University Press, pp. 39–40.

11 Presidency Conclusions, Copenhagen European Council, 21–22 June 1993 (from www.europarl.europa.eu/enlargement/ec/pdf/cop_en.pdf).

12 For a critical account of the reforms affecting the military, see Michaud-Emin, L. (2007) 'The Restructuring of the Military High Command in the Seventh Harmonization Package and its Ramifications for Civil-Military Relations in Turkey', *Turkish Studies*, Vol.8, No.1, pp. 27–28, 30–32.

13 See Hale, W. and Özbudun, E. (2010) *Islamism, Democracy and Liberalism in Turkey: the Case of the AKP*, London and New York NY: Routledge, pp. 65–67. For the text of the draft, with relevant explanations by the committee, see the website of the organisation 'Yeni Anayasa İçin' (www.yenianayasicin.org). For a comparison with other proposed constitutional drafts, such as that of the Union of Turkish Bar Associations, see Yazıcı, S. (2009) *Yeni bir Anayasa Hazırlığı, Seçkinlikten Toplum Sözleşmesine*, Istanbul: Istanbul Bilgi Üniversitesi Yayınları.

14 See *Turkey 2008 Progress Report* (Brussels, Commission of the European Communities, 5 November 2008, SEC [2008] 2699) pp. 17, 23: *Turkey 2009 Progress Report* (Brussels, Commission of the European Communities, 14 October 2009, SEC [2009] 1334) pp. 9, 15.

15 *Turkey 2008 Progress Report*, p. 15. Those in the dock had included the Nobel prize-winning novelist Orhan Pamuk, and the Turkish-Armenian journalist Hrant Dink, who was later murdered by Turkish nationalist fanatics.

16 See the frequent references in the *Turkey Progress Reports* for 2005, 2006, 2007, 2008 and 2009.

17 According to data collated by Ali Çarkoğlu and Ersin Kalaycıoğlu, the percentage of Turkish respondents who said they would vote in favour of Turkish membership of the EU if a referendum were held dropped from a high point of 74 percent in January-February 2003 to 50 percent in July 2007: Çarkoğlu, A. and Kalaycıoğlu, E. (2009) *The Rising Tide of Conservatism in Turkey*, New York NY, Palgrave Macmillan, p. 122.

18 E.g. Kramer, H. (2009) op. cit., p. 3

19 Pope, H. (2010) 'EU and Turkey Edge Back from the Brink', (2 January 2010): report for the International Crisis Group (www.crisisgroup.org).

20 *Radikal*, (Istanbul, daily) 16 September 2009: *Today's Zaman*, (Istanbul, daily) 18, 24 September 2009.

21 *Hürriyet Daily News*, (Istanbul, daily) 25 October 2009.

22 *Radikal*, 1 November 2009: *Today's Zaman*, 4 December 2009.

23 *Hürriyet*, (Istanbul, daily) 11 December 2009.

24 For the full text of the proposals, as originally laid before parliament, see Prime Ministry, Secretariat General for European Affairs, *Constitutional Amendments Proposal (5 April 2010)* (from www.abgs.gov.tr/files/BasinMusavirlik/const_amendments.pdf).

25 In practice, the last change would be purely symbolic, since a statute of limitations would come in to effect on 12 September 2010.

26 For the exact voting figures, see *Radikal*, 30 April 2010.

27 *Hürriyet*, 4 May 2010: *Today's Zaman*, 8 May 2010.

28 For the details, see *Radikal*, 13 September 2010.

29 Ibid.

30 BBC News website (www.bbc.co.uk/news) 13 September 2010.

84   *William Hale*

References

Athanassopoulou, E. (1999) *Turkey-Anglo-American Security Interests, 1945–1952*, London and Portland OR: Frank Cass.
Bailey, F. E. (1942) *British Policy and the Turkish Reform Movement: a Study in Anglo-Turkish Relations, 1826–1853*, Cambridge MA: Harvard University Press.
Batur, M. (1985) *Anılar ve Görüşler*, Istanbul, Milliyet.
Birand,M. A. (1987) *The General's Coup in Turkey; an Inside Story of 12 September 1980*, London, Brassey's Defence Publishers (tr. Dikerdem, M. A.) (Adapted translation of Birand,M. A. (1984) *12 Eylül, Saat 04.00*, Istanbul: Karacan).
Çarkoğlu, A. and Kalaycıoğlu, E. (2009) *The Rising Tide of Conservatism in Turkey*, New York NY, Palgrave Macmillan.
Commission of the European Communities. (2005) *Turkey 2005 Progress Report*, Brussels, Commission of the European Communities, 9 November 2005, SEC [2005] 1426.
Commission of the European Communities. (2006) *Turkey 2006 Progress Report*, Brussels, Commission of the European Communities, 8 November 2006, SEC [2006] 1390.
Commission of the European Communities. (2007) *Turkey 2007 Progress Report* , Brussels, Commission of the European Communities, 6 November 2007, SEC [2007] 1436.
Commission of the European Communities. (2008) *Turkey 2008 Progress Report*, Brussels, Commission of the European Communities, 5 November 2008, SEC [2008] 2699.
Commission of the European Communities. (2009) *Turkey 2009 Progress Repot* , Brussels, Commission of the European Communities, 14 October 2009, SEC [2009] 1334.
Cousins, J. (1973) *Turkey: Torture and Political Persecution*, London Pluto Press.
Dağı, İ. (1996) 'Democratic Transition in Turkey, 1980–83: the Impact of European Diplomacy', *Middle Eastern Studies,* Vol.32, No.2: 127–36 (reprinted in Kedourie, E. (ed.), *Turkey: Identity, Democracy, Politics*, London and Portland OR: Frank Cass).
Devereux, R (1963)*The First Ottoman Constitutional Period*, Baltimore MD: Johns Hopkins Press.
Grigoriadis, I. N. (2009) *Trials of Europeanization: Turkish Political Culture and the European Union*, New York, Palgrave Macmillan.
Gürkan, C. (1986) *12 Mart'a Beş Kala*, Istanbul: Tekin.
Hale, W. (2003) 'Human Rights, the European Union and the Turkish Accession Process', *Turkish Studies,* Vol.4, No.1, (Spring): 111–23. (Reprinted in Çarkoğlu, A. and Rubin, B. (eds) (2003) *Turkey and the European Union: Domestic Politics, Economic Integration and International Dynamics*, London and Portland OR: Frank Cass).
Hale, W. and Özbudun, E. (2010) *Islamism, Democracy and Liberalism in Turkey: the Case of the AKP,*London and New York NY: Routledge.
Heper, M. (1998) *İsmet İnönü, the Making of a Turkish Statesman*, Leiden, E.J.Brill.
Kedourie, E. (1971) 'Young Turks, Freemasons and Jews', *Middle Eastern Studies,* Vol.7, No.1: 89–104.
Kili, S. (1971) *Turkish Constitutional Developments and Assembly Debates of the Constitutions of 1924 and 1961*, Istanbul, Robert College Research Center.

Kramer, H. (1996) 'The EU-Turkey Customs Union: Economic Integration Amidst Political Turmoil', *Mediterranean Politics,* Vol.1, No.1.

—— (2009) 'Turkey's Accession Process to the EU: the Agenda behind the Agenda', Berlin, Stiftung Wissenschaft und Politik, SWP Comments 25, October.

Landen, R. G. (1970) *The Emergence of the Modern Middle East: Selected Readings,* New York, NY: Van Nostrand.

Lewis, B. (1961) *The Emergence of Modern Turkey,* London: Oxford University Press.

Mardin, Ş. (1962) *The Genesis of Young Ottoman Thought,* Princeton NJ: Princeton University Press, (repr. (2000) Syracuse NY: Syracuse University Press).

Michaud-Emin, L. (2007) 'The Restructuring of the Military High Command in the Seventh Harmonization Package and its Ramifications for Civil-Military Relations in Turkey', *Turkish Studies,* Vol.8, No.1: 25–42.

Müftüler-Baç, M. (1997) *Turkey's Relations with a Changing Europe,* Manchester and New York, NY: Manchester University Press.

Özbudun, E. and Gençkaya, Ö. F. (2009) *Democratization and the Politics of Constitution-Making in Turkey,* Budapest and New York NY: Central European University Press.

Pope, H. (2010) 'EU and Turkey Edge Back from the Brink', (2 January 2010): report for the International Crisis Group (www.crisisgroup.org).

Pridham, G. (1991) 'International Influences and Democratic Transition: Problems of Theory and Practice in Linkage Politics', in Pridham, G. (ed), *Encouraging Democracy: the International Context of Regime Transition in Southern Europe,* Leicester and London: Leicester University Press.

Robinson, R. D. (1965) *The First Turkish Republic: a Case Study in National Development,* Cambridge MA, Harvard University Press.

Rustow, D. A. (1988) 'Transitions to Democracy: Turkey's Experience in Historical and Comparative Perspective', in Heper, M. and Evin, A. (eds), *State, Democracy and the Military: Turkey in the 1980s,* Berlin and New York NY: Walter de Gruyter.

Schmitter, P. C. (1996) 'The Influence of the International Context upon the Choice of National Institutions and Policies in Neo-Democracies', in Whitehead, L. (ed), *The International Dimensions of Democratization: Europe and the Americas,* Oxford: Oxford University Press.

Spain, J.W. (1984) *American Diplomacy in Turkey,* New York: Praeger.

Ünal, H. (1996) 'Young Turk Assessments of International Politics, 1906–9', *Middle Eastern Studies,* Vol.32, No.2: 31–36, reprinted in Kedourie, S. (ed.), *Turkey: Identity, Democracy, Politics,* London and Portland OR: Frank Cass.

Weiker, W. F. (1963) *The Turkish Revolution, 1960–1961,* Washington DC: Brookings Institution.

Weiker, W. F.(1973) *Political Tutelage and Democracy in Turkey: the Free Party and its Aftermath,* Leiden: E.J.Brill.

Yazıcı, S. (2009) *Yeni bir Anayasa Hazırlığı, Seçkinlikten Toplum Sözleşmesine,* Istanbul: Istanbul Bilgi Üniversitesi Yayınları.

Zürcher, E. J. (1991) *Political Opposition in the Early Turkish Republic: the Progressive Republican Party, 1924–1925,* Leiden, E.J. Brill.

Part II
Political society

5 Party system and democratic consolidation in Turkey

Problems and prospects

Sabri Sayarı

Political parties have existed in Turkey since the last decades of the Ottoman Empire during the late nineteenth and early twentieth centuries. However, a party system with universal suffrage, free and honest elections, and multiplicity of political parties emerged only in the late 1940s following the transition from an authoritarian single-party regime to democracy. Thus, Turkey represents the case of a country of relatively early party formations but one of late democratization in its historical development. It is also worth noting that in the post-World War II era, Turkey was one of the first countries in the 'developing world' to experience a regime change from authoritarian rule to democratic politics. Yet, despite this early start, the consolidation of Turkish democracy has encountered serious problems, as evidenced most notably in the three regime breakdowns through military interventions in 1960, 1971, and 1980. In comparison with the transitions to democracy in Southern Europe during the late 1970s and early 1980s, for example, where consolidation took place within a relatively short time following the end of authoritarian rule, the consolidation process in Turkey has taken a very long time and it has not yet reached its final phase. Turkey's protracted unconsolidated democracy has had a major impact on the development of the country's party systems as well as on the survival or demise of individual parties during more than six decades of electoral politics.

The origins and development of a party system

Turkish democracy was born within a two-party system. Following President İsmet İnönü's decision, at the end of 1945, to liberalize the country's authoritarian regime, scores of parties emerged on the political scene. However, the majority of them failed to survive and become serious contenders in party competition. Instead, the emerging party system was dominated by two major players: CHP (*Cumhuriyet Halk Partisi*, Republican People's Party), the 'single party' of the authoritarian regime from 1923 until 1946, and DP (*Demokrat Parti*, Democratic Party), which was formed following a factional split from the CHP in 1946. In Turkey's first free and honest elections in 1950, the DP ended nearly three decades of

CHP rule by scoring a major victory. The strong trend toward a two-party system remained in force in the 1950, 1954, and 1957 elections when the two major parties collectively received more than 90 per cent of the votes and won nearly 98 per cent of the seats in the TBMM (*Türkiye Büyük Millet Meclisi*, Turkish Grand National Assembly), or the country's parliament in Ankara. Several factors contributed to the emergence of a two-party system during the democratization process (Sayarı 2002: 11–12). Historically, beginning with the initial phase of party formations in the Ottoman Empire, rival elites competing for power, had organized their activities around two major parties. The legacy of political dualism in Turkish politics became apparent following the transition to democracy. The existence of bifactional divisions in many rural communities based on competition for power and status among the leading notable families also played a role in the trend toward bipartism after 1946. Last, but not least, the electoral system that was used between 1946 and 1960, contributed to the strength of the two-party vote: The simple plurality electoral system with multimember electoral districts clearly favoured the largest parties, especially the party that finished first, and it greatly limited the chances of the minor parties to gain representation in the parliament.

The initial phase of Turkish democracy ended in 1960 as a result of the country's first experience with a military coup in its modern history. The 1960 military coup had important consequences for party politics. After the return to democracy in 1961, one of the two largest parties, the DP, was no longer on the political scene since it was outlawed by the military regime. The DP's unnatural death led to an intense competition between several newly-formed parties which sought to capture its popular support and party activists. Eventually AP (*Adalet Partisi*, Justice Party) succeeded in establishing itself as the main successor to the DP. The military coup also led to a change in the electoral system from plurality to proportional representation. In addition, it ushered in a new constitution which expanded the ideological space of party competition. As a result of these developments, the post-1961 party system was more fragmented and displayed a wider ideological spectrum than the party system of the 1946–60 period. Unlike the previous decade when majority party governments were in power, Turkey had its first experience with coalition politics in the early 1960s. The party system also became more structured along the left-right ideological spectrum: the CHP officially identified itself as a centre-left party while the AP adopted a more discernible ideological position on the centre-right. At the same time, newly-formed minor parties on the radical-left and far-right expanded the ideological space in party competition. In the 1965 elections, the extreme left and the far-right gained access to parliamentary representation through the newly-formed Marxist TİP (*Türkiye İşçi Partisi*, Turkish Workers Party) and the ultra-nationalist MHP (*Milliyetçi Hareket Partisi*, Nationalist Action Party), respectively. The organizational drive to win votes at the extremes was followed by attempts to legitimize religious-sectarian interests through the establishment of new minor parties. For example, while the BP (*Birlik Partisi*, Unity Party) sought to defend the interest of the Alevis, MSP (*Milli Selamet Partisi*, National Salvation Party) was formed to promote a greater role for Sunni Islam in Turkish society and politics (Sayarı 1978: 39–57).

In 1971, Turkey had its second military intervention when the officers ousted the AP from power and replaced it with a civilian government that was largely staffed by technocratic ministerial elites. As in the case of the 1960 coup, there was transition back to democracy after a relatively short military interregnum in politics. When electoral politics resumed in 1973, the party system displayed a basic continuity with the pre-1971 era: the AP and the CHP remained the two major parties on the centre-right and centre-left, respectively, and they alternated in power through coalition partnerships with minor parties, such as the pro-Islamist MSP and the ultra-nationalist MHP. The major distinguishing characteristic of electoral and party politics during the 1970s was the growing left-right ideological polarization. The CHP, under Bülent Ecevit's leadership, increasingly moved to a more discernibly leftist position and adopted a strong "anti-fascist" rhetoric against its rivals on the right, especially the MHP. The centre-right AP, led by Süleyman Demirel, became a bitter opponent of leftist ideologies and moved further to the right on the party spectrum by assuming the leadership of the so-called 'National Front' coalition governments from 1974 to 1977. During the latter part of the decade, Turkey experienced one of its worst crises in the history of the Republic: political violence and terrorism spread from the major cities to the provincial towns in Anatolia, the country was hit by a severe economic and financial crisis, and political instability became endemic through short-lived and ineffective coalition or minority governments (Sayarı 1978: 39–57).

Amidst the deepening political and economic crisis, Turkey had its third military intervention within two decades. The 1980 coup, which led to a three-year long military rule, administered a strong shock to party politics. The military regime banned all existing parties and excluded their leading elites from politics up to ten years in an effort to create a new party system from scratch. The officers also drafted a new constitution which weakened Turkey's parliamentary system by granting extensive powers to the president, provided a greater role for the military in the policy-making process, and instituted a 10 per cent national electoral threshold that was intended to hinder fragmentation in the party system and produce majority party governments. The party system which emerged following the gradual return to democracy after 1983 initially bore little resemblance to the party system of the pre-coup era: none of the former parties were on the political scene, fragmentation and ideological polarization appeared to have disappeared, and the newly-formed ANAP (*Anavatan Partisi*, Motherland Party) led by Turgut Özal assumed a dominant role in national and local politics (Turan 1988: 63–80). However, as the grip of the military on the transition process gradually loosened during the latter part of the decade, the pre-1980 parties re-emerged under their former leaders but mostly under new names. On the political right, the DYP (*Doğru*

Yol Partisi, True Path Party) replaced the AP, the MSP re-emerged as the RP (*Refah Partisi*, Welfare Party), and the MHP resurfaced first as the MÇP (*Milliyetçi Çalışma Partisi*, National Work Party) before returning to its previous name, *Milliyetçi Hareket Partisi* (Nationalist Action Party). On the political left, two new parties, SODEP (*Sosyal Demokrat Halkçı Parti*, Social Democratic Populist Party) and DSP (*Demokratik Sol Partisi*, Democratic Left Party) competed for the political loyalties and organizational personnel of the outlawed CHP (in 1992, the CHP re-emerged under its original name and SODEP merged with it three years later).

The 1980 coup had several major consequences for the party system. Most importantly, the bans imposed by the military undermined the strength of two-party dominance in the party system which had been a distinguishing feature of party competition since the transition to democracy in the late 1940s. In the absence of the CHP and the AP, the party system entered into a new phase in which a dominant party, Özal's ANAP, controlled power between 1983 and 1991. Until 1980, the centre-left and the centre-right were represented by the CHP and the AP, respectively. A decade later, the centre-right was divided between ANAP and DYP, while CHP and DSP competed for the centre-left votes. Once they got established, these divisions proved to be resistant to change despite the similarities in the ideological outlooks and policy orientations of the parties within the centre-right and the centre-left blocs (Sayarı 2002: 18–19).

ANAP's dominance in party competition came to an end in 1991 when it finished second in the parliamentary elections after the DYP, its chief rival for the centre-right votes. In addition to ending nearly a decade-long ANAP rule, the outcome of the 1991 elections marked the rise of several new trends that were to shape party politics in Turkey for the next 10 years. Most importantly, fragmentation and ideological polarization, which had contributed to the collapse of Turkish democracy in 1980, returned to the party system in full force. In sharp contrast to the period from 1983 to 1991 when ANAP had enjoyed large parliamentary majorities, no single party managed to win a majority of the seats, five to six relevant parties succeeded in clearing the 10 per cent electoral threshold, and political power was exercised through coalition or minority governments. The increase in fragmentation was accompanied by the steady weakening of the electoral support for the centrist parties throughout the 1990s. The four centre-right and centre-left parties (ANAP, DYP, CHP, and DSP) collectively received 82.7 per cent of the votes in 1991. In the 1999 elections, their electoral support declined to 56.1 per cent. The erosion of support for the centre-right was an important indicator of the shifting balance of forces in Turkish politics because most of the governments since the 1950s had been formed by the centre-right parties.[1]

The decline of the centre-right's popular support was accompanied by the increase in the votes of the RP. Under its veteran leader Necmettin Erbakan, the RP finished first in the 1995 elections after winning 21.4 per cent of the votes. A year later, Erbakan became prime minister in the coalition

Table 5.1 Percentage of votes and number of seats won by parties, 1991–2001

Party	1991		1995		1999		2002		2007		2011	
	% of Votes	Seats	% of Votes	Seats	% of Votes	Seats	% of Votes	Seats	% of Votes	Seats	% of Votes	Seats
AKP	–	–	–	–	–	–	34,43	365	46,47	341	49,95	326
CHP	–	–	10,71	49	–	–	19,41	177	20,84	112	25,94	135
MHP	–	–	–	–	17,98	129	–	–	14,26	71	12,98	53
SHP	20,75	88	–	–	–	–	–	–	–	–	–	–
DSP	10,75	7	14,64	76	22,19	136	–	–	–	–	–	–
ANAP	24,01	115	19,65	132	13,22	86	–	–	–	–	–	–
DYP	27,03	178	19,18	135	12,01	85	–	–	–	–	–	–
RP	16,88	62	21,38	158	–	–	–	–	–	–	–	–
FP	–	–	–	–	15,41	111	–	–	–	–	–	–
SP	–	–	–	–	–	–	2,49	–	2,34	–	1,25	–
Others	0,58	–	14,44	–	19,19	–	43,67	–	16,09	–	9,88	–
Indep.	0,13	–	0,48	–	0,87	3	0,96	8	5,19	26	6,58	36
All	100	450	100	550	100	550	100	550	100	550	100	550

Party Names and Acronyms

AKP (*Adalet ve Kalkınma Partisi*-Justice and Development Party), CHP (*Cumhuriyet Halk Partisi*-Republican People's Party), MHP (*Milliyetçi Hareket Partisi*-Nationalist Action Party), SHP (*Sosyal Demokrat Halkçı Parti*-Social Democratic Populist Party), DSP (*Demokratik Sol Parti*-Democratic Left Party), ANAP (*Anavatan Partisi*- Motherland Party), DYP (*Doğru Yol Partisi*-True Path Party), RP (*Refah Partisi*-Welfare Party), FP (*Fazilet Partisi*-Virtue Party), SP (*Saadet Partisi* -Felicity Party).

government which the RP formed with the DYP. The rising electoral popularity of the RP, a party which advocated a greater role for Islamic norms, values, and lifestyles, highlighted a major new development in Turkish politics and the party system. The political ascendancy of the RP was a major cause of increased polarization in the party system between the defenders of the Republic's secularist foundations and those whose worldview and lifestyles reflected their strong religious beliefs and piety. Two decades earlier, the polarization in the Turkish party system was based on the growing ideological distance between the left and the right in party competition. In the 1990s, polarization in the party system stemmed largely from the conflict between the secularist and pro-religious parties. The RP's growing electoral strength produced a strong backlash from the country's secularist political and social forces, led by the CHP, the military, and the judiciary. Following a crisis-ridden year during 1996–97, the RP-DYP coalition was ousted from power amidst increasing pressures from the secularist forces that were largely mobilized by the armed forces against the government. The RP was subsequently banned by the Constitutional Court in 1998 for violating the secularist principles of Turkey's constitutional order. Erbakan quickly formed a new party called FP (*Fazilet Partisi*, Virtue Party) that was similarly banned by the Constitutional Court in 2001. His followers then split into two groups: The Erbakan loyalists established the SP (*Saadet Partisi*, Felicity Party), while Tayyip Erdoğan, the former Mayor of Istanbul, founded the AKP (*Adalet ve Kalkınma Partisi*, Justice and Development Party) (Sayarı 2007: 204–5).

The AKP and the emergence of new party dynamics

The 2002 election was another turning point in the Turkish party system.[2] The outcome of the elections propelled the AKP to power with a large parliamentary majority, dealt a severe blow to several parties which had played a prominent role in the making and breaking of coalition governments during the preceding decade, and led to single-party majority rule. The electoral victory of the AKP, a party with an Islamist pedigree, was one of the most important developments in Turkey since the transition to democracy in the late 1940s.[3] As noted earlier, the popular appeal of the parties which emphasized Islamist norms, values, and practices had increased significantly in the post-1991 era. This trend was clearly highlighted by the fact that Erbakan's RP became the largest party in the 1995 elections. Despite the efforts of the secularist forces, led by the military and the judiciary, the RP and its successors remained a principal player in party politics. In the 2002 parliamentary elections, the AKP, which sought to differentiate itself from the parties which were formed by Erbakan previously, adopted a more 'moderate' stand on issues such as Turkey's membership of the European Union and its relations with the West, finished first with 34.2 per cent of the votes and a comfortable parliamentary majority (363 out of 550 seats). Although political parties with a religious orientation had shared political power in the coalition governments during 1973–77 and 1996–97, the AKP's victory marked the first time a party which had its roots in the Islamist movement formed a majority party government. The AKP repeated its success in 2007 by winning 46.5 per cent of the votes and 62 per cent of the seats. In addition to being in the government, the AKP also controlled the office of the presidency following the election of Abdullah Gül, one of its founders and leading members, as president of Turkey in 2008. Moreover, Turkey's governing party extended its power to local and municipal politics after it finished first in the 2004 and 2009 local elections as well.

The party system that has come into existence since the 2002 elections displays a number of important characteristics.[4] First, the most distinguishing feature of party competition has been the dominant role of the AKP in electoral politics. Since there has been no alternation in government in the 2002, 2007, and 2011 elections, other parties have been excluded from sharing power for nearly a decade. Consequently, the Turkish party system in the post-2002 era has acquired the characteristics of what Sartori has defined as a 'predominant party system' in which 'the same party manages to win, over time, an absolute majority of seats (not necessarily votes) in parliament' (Sartori 1976: 195). Alternation in power through a shift in voter alignments remains a possibility in predominant party systems. However, this does not happen so long as the governing party continues to maintain its parliamentary majority in election after election. In the Turkish case, the AKP's success owes to a variety of factors. They include its ideological appeal and organizational strength, the popularity of its charismatic leader Tayyip Erdoğan, the failure of the opposition parties to offer a credible alternative, and its easy access to resources for patronage distribution in return for electoral support as a result of its control of governmental power (Gümüşçü 2013).

Second, in the predominant party system that has come into existence during the past 10 years, the parliamentary political opposition has been marginalized. Turkey's main opposition party, the centre-left CHP, has been unable to expand its electoral strength significantly in the three elections held since 2002. The shift in the ideological preferences of the Turkish voters from left to right has adversely affected the chances of the CHP to pose a serious challenge to the dominance of the AKP in electoral politics. Moreover, the CHP has made matters worse for itself by failing to maintain party unity due to incessant infighting and factionalism under its former leader Deniz Baykal. The replacement of Baykal and his coterie of party activists prior to the 2011 elections by Kemal Kılıçdaroğlu and a new team of leadership cadres initially raised expectations about the CHP's chances of coming to power. Although the CHP's seats in the parliament increased from 112 in 2007 to 135 in the 2011 elections, its strength in the legislature still compared poorly with that of the AKP which won 326 seats out of 550. The CHP's failure to formulate new strategies and policies to broaden its popular appeal continues to undermine its chances to present itself as a credible alternative to the AKP (Sayarı 2007).

Third, the emergence of a predominant party system has been accompanied by a significant decline in fragmentation of the votes and seats. During the 1990s, the party system was highly fragmented since Turkish voters chose to divide their support among a multiplicity of parties on the left and the right of the ideological divide in electoral politics. As a result, despite the use of the 10 per cent national threshold, five to six relevant parties gained representation in the parliament and participated in the successive coalition governments that came to power. Although fragmentation of voter preferences was still evident in 2002, it declined noticeably in the next two elections. In 2002, only two parties, the AKP and the CHP, entered the parliament. In 2007 and 2011, they were joined by the MHP and a bloc of independents who subsequently joined the pro-Kurdish parties. However, the parliamentary strengths of both the MHP and the pro-Kurdish parties remained considerably less than those of the AKP and the CHP.

Fourth, the 2002 elections marked the collapse of the 'old order' in the party system since several parties that had played prominent roles in the coalition politics during the period from 1991 to 2002, have largely disappeared from the political scene. The two centre-right parties, ANAP and DYP, have failed to pass the 10 per cent electoral threshold since 2002. Their merger in a newly-established *Demokrat Parti* (DP-Democratic Party) has, so far, had little impact on national politics. Similarly, the centre-left DSP, which had been the senior partner of a coalition government from 1999 to 2002, has lost much of its electoral and organizational strength.

Fifth, the electoral geography of the predominantly Kurdish populated provinces in southeastern Turkey has undergone a major change as a result of the popular support enjoyed by the pro-Kurdish parties. The electoral strengths of the major parties, such as the centre-left CHP, that used to be competitive in this region until the 1990s, have virtually disappeared during the last decade. In addition to the pro-Kurdish parties, only the AKP has managed to command the political loyalties of a significant number of voters in the predominantly Kurdish electoral districts.

Although the post-2002 party system differs considerably from that which existed between 1991 and 2002, it displays a basic continuity with respect to the high degree of polarization in interparty relations. As had been the case during the 1990s, the polarization in the party system is largely based on the conflict between the major parties over the issue of religion. Although the AKP strongly objects to being identified as an 'Islamist' party and prefers, instead, to refer to itself as 'conservative democratic', its secularist critics remain adamant in their conviction that the AKP's ultimate goal is to transform Turkey's secular political institutions, educational system, and lifestyles by promoting Sunni Islam's norms, values, and practices. Consequently, in the parliamentary and electoral arenas, the heated debates between the governing AKP and the main opposition CHP have centred less on economic policy or foreign affairs than on the issue of Islam's role in society and politics.[5]

Political parties and regime changes

Political parties have played an important role in the regime changes which Turkey has experienced over the years. During the transition from authoritarian single-party rule to democracy in the late 1940s, the emerging party system and electoral politics proved to be the main catalysts for opening up the political space, providing citizens with the means to exercise their newly-acquired political rights and freedoms, and for the legitimization of the democratic regime. The roles performed by the parties and the party system continued to be important during the transitions back to democracy after each regime breakdown in 1960, 1971, and 1980. The party system survived the draconian measures adopted by the military regimes against parties, such as the closing of the DP following the 1960 coup or the bans imposed on all existing parties in the aftermath of the 1980 military takeover. After every military intervention, the revival of party activities proved to be the key to the resumption of electoral politics and the re-democratization process. Although the party system was affected by the shocks that were administered by the armed forces, it did not always conform to the political engineering projects of the military officers. This was best exemplified by developments in party politics following the 1980 coup when the military regime sought to create a new party system. However, two of the three new parties which were 'licensed' by the ruling junta to compete in the elections failed to command popular support and quickly withered away. More important, the major parties which were banned in 1981 re-emerged on the political scene with their veteran leaders, after a relatively brief hiatus.

It is also worth noting, however, the strategies pursued by the political parties have also contributed to regime breakdowns through military interventions. During the first decade of Turkish democracy from 1950 to 1960, the intensity of the conflicts between the two major parties, the DP and the CHP, had serious adverse effects on the stability and legitimacy of democratic politics (Sunar and Sayarı 1986). The governing DP, led by Prime Minister Adnan Menderes, increasingly adopted authoritarian measures against the CHP under its veteran leader İsmet İnönü. The DP Government's efforts to silence its critics reached a point whereby the very survival of the main opposition party was threatened. The CHP, for its part, provoked the DP into a politics of confrontation, endeavoured to undermine the legitimacy of the government, and hinted at the possibility of a military coup during the escalation of the political crisis in early 1960. Had the two major parties, and especially the governing DP, adopted different strategies in party politics, Turkey might have avoided the 1960 coup which seriously weakened the prospects for an early consolidation of democracy since it set a precedent for further military interventions in politics.

Two decades later, there was a repetition of a somewhat similar scenario when the two major parties, the centre-right AP and the centre-left CHP, failed to reach an accommodation to defend the democratic regime against the extremist parties and terrorist groups. The high level of polarization in the party system, based on a left-right ideological conflict, led the two major parties to pursue policies and tactics that further exacerbated the mounting political and economic crisis which Turkey faced in the late 1970s (Sunar and Sayarı 1986). In particular, the democratic regime experienced growing strains when the AP and the CHP chose not to unite against the radical leftist and far-right terrorist organizations which strove to create political instability and provoke an authoritarian response by the military.[6] Amidst growing fatalities from political violence and terrorism, the military stepped in and ousted the AP from the government in September 1980.

Parties and democratic consolidation

The problems and weaknesses of the political party system in Turkey have hindered progress toward the consolidation of democracy. The weakness of the party system is best revealed in its relatively weak institutionalization. As Mainwaring and Scully suggest, 'the institutionalization of a party system is important to the process of democratic consolidation ... It is difficult to sustain modern mass democracy without an institutionalized party system' (Mainwaring and Scully 1995: 1). According to Mainwaring and Scully, an institutionalized party system should meet four conditions. First, there should be stability and regularity in party competition. High levels of electoral volatility, accompanied by wide swings in the preferences of voters, are the main characteristics of relatively weak party system institutionalization. Second, there should be strong linkages between major parties and citizens. In institutionalized party systems, major parties have strong roots in society. Third, the legitimacy of parties and electoral processes should be accepted by all major actors in politics. Four, parties should have strong and autonomous organizational structures which do not simply serve the personalistic exercise of power by leaders who dominate the party organization (Mainwaring and Scully 1995: 4–6).

Judged by these criteria, the Turkish party system is notably less institutionalized than its counterparts in West European democracies. To begin with, one of the major features of party competition in Turkey has been the absence of regularity and stability in mass electoral behaviour. As a result, some established parties have suffered major drops in their votes from one election to the next. One of the most dramatic examples of this phenomenon was the spectacular drop in the votes of the centre-left DSP, the senior partner of the coalition government between 1999 and 2002, from 22.3 per cent in 1999 to 1.2 per cent in 2002. Other major Turkish parties have also experienced wide swings in their popular support. Consequently, electoral volatility rates in Turkey have been much higher than those observed in the more institutionalized Western European party systems. For example, during the period from 1954 to 1995, the average volatility rate in Turkey (21.2 per cent) was nearly three times higher than the average rate in Western Europe

(8.7 per cent) (Sayarı 2002: 22). In the 2002 elections, electoral volatility reached an astonishing 50.2 per cent which was the highest in Turkish political history, and one of the highest in contemporary democracies.

The instability of mass electoral behaviour in Turkey also reflects the relative weakness of the party organizations and their failure to establish strong and durable roots in society.[7] During the early phase of electoral politics in the 1950s, the two major parties, DP and the CHP, extended their organizations from the large cities to the local political arenas in the provincial small-towns and villages throughout the country. As a result, party organizations had relatively strong roots in society. However, the 1960 coup significantly altered this picture: the newly-enacted Political Parties Law of 1965 prohibited parties from forming local units below the sub-province (*ilçe*) level which meant that they could no longer have organizations in nearly 40,000 villages. The prohibition of village party organizations reflected the view, shared by the military and some civilian politicians, that party activities at the grass-roots level during the 1950s had exacerbated the social and political conflicts among the villagers, thus undermining national unity and solidarity.

The banning of all existing parties by the military regime in 1981 had an even more devastating impact on party organizations: It undermined continuity in organizational life, weakened the ties between parties and voters, and led to a decline in party identification. The 1982 constitution, which was drafted under the aegis of the military regime, similarly contributed to the weakening of party organizations. As a reaction to what the officers viewed as the 'excessive politicization' of Turkish political life during the late 1970s, the new constitution prohibited parties from forming youth and women's branches, and it barred students, university faculty, and civil servants from party membership. These measures, together with the restrictions on the political activities of organized interest groups, such as the labour unions, further limited the capability of parties to develop strong organizational roots in society. However, the parties that have been the products of Turkey's Islamist movement have been the exceptions to this trend. The RP, and more recently the AKP, have managed to establish strong grass-roots units that are organized in the neighbourhoods of large urban metropolises as well as in the provincial cities and small towns. The neighbourhood local units of the RP and the AKP have played a particularly important role in the distribution of political patronage and the mobilization of voters in the elections.

As Mainwaring and Scully suggest, in institutionalized party systems, the legitimacy of parties and electoral politics is accepted by the major political actors. Consequently, 'political elites base their behaviour on the expectation that elections will be the primary route to governing' (Mainwaring and Scully 1995: 5). However, this cardinal rule of the game in democracies has often been breached in contemporary Turkish politics. The military has ousted popularly elected governments from power through its interventions in politics. These have resulted in the replacement of elected politicians with unelected military and civilian officials as key policy-makers. Therefore, elections have not necessarily been 'the primary route to governing' in the Turkish politics and party system. Moreover, following the transition back to democracy after military interregnums in politics, the officers have been able to act independently of the popularly elected officials in the absence of strict civilian control over the military by retaining their 'exit guarantees'.[8] Although the officers have repeatedly stressed their commitment to democracy, they have generally refrained from according full legitimacy to the electoral process and parties. More importantly, military interventions in politics have been primarily responsible for the weakness of the Turkish party system and its relatively low level of institutionalization. The 1960, 1971, and 1980 military coups have disrupted the natural evolution of party politics, they have weakened the organizational capabilities of parties, and they have prevented the strengthening of the links between parties and voters. Moreover, the military's political engineering efforts in the aftermath of the coups have led to disarray in the party system which, in turn, has contributed to its weakness.

One of the prominent characteristics of Turkish political parties concerns the dominant role of the party leaders who can easily subordinate party organizations to their own interests and ambitions. This contrasts sharply with the established practices in the institutionalized party systems where party organizations 'acquire an independent status and value of their own' and where they play an important role in the political recruitment of the parliamentary elites (Mainwaring and Scully 1995: 5). In the Turkish case, the autonomy of party organizations vis-à-vis the leaders is severely restricted due to the virtual absence of internal party democracy. Party activists who express views that are different from those of the inner party leadership are usually expelled or they are forced to resign. The dominant role of the leader stems from several sources: the annual party congresses where leaders are elected are usually controlled by the faction led by the incumbent leader, party executives have the legal means to close local party units (usually those which dissent from the decisions made by the leadership), and access to party patronage requires absolute loyalty to the leader. More importantly, party leaders personally control recruitment to the parliament. Due to the centralization of the candidate nominating process, party leaders usually manage to exclude large number of incumbent deputies from the party lists in the elections or demote them to the lower, electorally hopeless places on these lists (Sayarı and Alimov 2008: 347). Personalistic leadership has been the case with almost all Turkish political parties, irrespective of their ideological orientation. Leaders such as Özal, Ecevit, Erbakan, Demirel, Çiller, Yılmaz, Baykal, and Erdoğan have exercised almost unlimited power and authority over their parties. Some, such as Ecevit, Çiller, Baykal, and Yılmaz, have held on to the top leadership positions in their parties for an excessively long time even after losing successive elections. The subordination of the party organization to the personal interests and ambitions of the leader has been a problem for the strengthening of party organizations and for the institutionalization of the party system.

In addition to its weak institutionalization, the Turkish party system also has had several additional problems which have adversely affected the consolidation of democracy. To begin with, the question of 'inclusiveness' in party competition has yet to be fully addressed and resolved. Including or excluding some parties from competition has significant implications for representation and for the quality of democracy. As Linz and Stepan note,

> for a democracy, it is a critical choice whether to make an inclusionary decision to allow all political forces to participate in the political process, or to make an exclusionary decision to enact rules against parties that might, in view of one or another important sector of the regime or society, be perceived as threatening to them or democracy.
>
> (Linz and Stepan 1996: 97)

Turkey has generally chosen to exclude those parties which the state elites have viewed as threatening to the two fundamental principles of the Republic, namely, secularism and a unitary state. The strategy of exclusion has been implemented through two principal means: by the Constitutional Court's decisions to outlaw parties and by the 10 per cent threshold in the electoral system.

Since its establishment in 1962, Turkey's Constitutional Court has closed 24 political parties. 15 of these closures took place during the 1990s when there was a sharp rise in the political activism of the pro-Islamist and pro-Kurdish parties (Sayarı 2008: 412). The behaviour of the pro-Kurdish and pro-Islamist parties raised doubts in the minds of many secularist Turks about their commitment to the country's unitary and secular constitutional order. Although the court has not referred to them as 'anti-system parties', it has clearly viewed these parties as being basically disloyal to the existing constitutional system. In the case of the pro-Kurdish parties, this perception has become even stronger when they have increasingly become legal façades for the Kurdish-based terrorist organization, the PKK (*Partiya Karkerên Kurdistan*, Kurdistan Worker's Party). In 2009, the Constitutional Court closed the pro-Kurdish DTP (*Demokrasi ve Toplum Partisi*, Democratic Society Party) 'due to its connections with the terror organization and because it became a focal point for terrorism against the indivisible integrity of the state'.[9] The Court also banned the DTP's chairman, Ahmet Türk, and 36 members from politics for five years. Subsequently, BDP (*Barış ve Demokrasi Partisi*, Peace and Democracy Party) became the main representative of the pro-Kurdish political forces in the party system.

The Turkish constitutional and legal system is not unique with respect to the proscriptions against extremist or anti-system parties. Several established democracies, such as Germany, Austria, and Ireland, as well as transitional democracies such as Chile, Estonia, and Romania have constitutional provisions that exclude extremist parties from participation in politics. In the 1950s, Germany (then West Germany) banned the Nazi and the Communist parties, and more recently the Spanish Government banned the radical Basque nationalist Herri Batasuna Party because of its ties to the terrorist group, ETA. However, banning political parties is rarely practiced in contemporary democracies. What makes the Turkish case unusual is the frequency with which parties have been banned from politics. Moreover, unlike its counterparts in some other countries such as Germany where the parliament plays an important role in the selection of the judges who serve on the Constitutional Court, in Turkey, members of the Court were, until 2010, chosen by the President of the Republic without any input from the elected representatives of the people.[10]

The electoral system represents the other main instrument for excluding some parties from the political arena.[11] As noted earlier, the Turkish electoral law changed from plurality to PR system in 1961. Since 1961, the PR system has been used with a number of changes in the methods used for calculating the translation of votes into seats. The 1982 constitution retained the PR system based on the d'Hondt formula but it introduced a 10 per cent national electoral threshold which meant that a party had to get at least 10 per cent of the national votes in order to gain seats in the in the parliament. The change in the electoral laws was partly designed to prevent the fragmentation of the party system which had been a source of governmental instability during the pre-coup era. However, it also reflected the ruling military's belief that minor extremist parties should be excluded from the parliament. Electoral thresholds, ranging between 1 to 5 per cent, are used in many democratic countries. In comparison, Turkey's 10 per cent threshold is unusually high: it is arguably one of the highest in the world. By winning more than 10 per cent of the votes since the mid-1990s, the parties with Islamist pedigrees have managed to evade one of the intended goals of the change in the electoral system. However, the excessively high threshold has prevented some of the other parties from gaining access to the parliament. In the 2002 elections, for example, a lower threshold, such as 5 per cent, would have enabled five other parties—DYP, MHP, GP, ANAP, and DEHAP (*Demokratik Halk Partisi*, People's Democracy Party)—to enter the parliament along with the AKP and the CHP. As a result of the high threshold, nearly 45 per cent of the votes cast by the voters were 'wasted'.

The high threshold used in the elections has been criticized extensively in Turkey and by various international organizations, such as the European Union, for undermining fair representation of different social and political forces (Hale 2008: 237). Although many smaller parties have been adversely affected by the electoral system that is currently in use, the criticism of the high threshold has been particularly strong on the grounds that it excludes the pro-Kurdish parties from participating in politics. Since the early 1990s, the electoral support or the pro-Kurdish parties have averaged around 6 per cent of the national vote. As a result, they were unable to enter the parliament until the 2007 elections. The Turkish parliaments have traditionally included sizeable number of deputies with Kurdish ethnic background who belonged to various centre-right and centre-left parties. But a party which explicitly sought to represent Kurdish interests was unable to gain representation. In the 2007 elections, the candidates for pro-Kurdish DTP ran as independents and managed to win 23 seats since there is no 10 per cent threshold for the independents. Once in the parliament, they abandoned their independent status and formed the DTP's parliamentary group. The precedent set by the DTP was followed by the BDP in the 2012 elections whereby it won 20 seats in the parliament. Nevertheless, the 10 per cent threshold remains a major problem for the fair representation of diverse social and political interests. Despite the strong criticisms directed against it, however, it has remained unchanged for nearly three decades. The main reason is that it benefits the largest parties and punishes the smaller ones. Consequently, the major parties have been reluctant to lower the electoral threshold.

The under representation of women in the parliament is another significant shortcoming of electoral and party politics in Turkey. Turkish women obtained the right to vote in the national elections in 1935. However, this was not accompanied by an increase of women deputies in the parliament: during the late 1930s and early 1940s, women representatives accounted for about 4.0 per cent of all the parliamentarians (Sayarı and Alimov 2008: 351–53). In the parliament that was formed after the first free and honest elections in 1950, women deputies constituted only 0.6 per cent of the legislature. The representation of women in the parliament has remained limited. In the 2002 elections, there was a slight increase when women deputies accounted for 4.4 per cent of the members serving in the TBMM. The increase in the number of women parliamentarians was largely due to two factors. First, the AKP and the CHP decided to nominate more women candidates and to place them on the more winnable places on the party lists than before. As a result, the percentage of female deputies increased from 3.6 to 8.8 and from 6.2 to 9.2 in the parliamentary groups of the AKP and the CHP, respectively. Second, the pro-Kurdish DTP used a 40 per cent affirmative action quota in choosing its candidates. Consequently, women constituted 40 per cent of the DTP's parliamentary representatives (or 9 out of 23) which was the largest among all the parties which managed to win seats in the legislature (Sayarı and Alimov 2008: 351–53). In the 2011 elections, the number of women parliamentarians increased to 14.1 per cent (or 78 out of 550 seats). The AKP had the largest women deputies (45), followed by the CHP (19), BDP (11) and MHP (3).

The fact that women have been vastly underrepresented in the parliament has also led to their underrepresentation among Turkey's cabinet ministers. No woman held a ministerial post during the first 50 years of the Republic. The first time a woman held a cabinet seat was in 1971 when the elected civilian government was ousted from office by the military and replaced by a cabinet composed of technocrats. The increase in the number of women parliamentarians during the past 10 years has also resulted in a modest rise in the percentage of women ministerial elites from 3.3 during the 1980–2002 period to 6.5 in the years between 2002 and 2009. In Prime Minister Erdoğan's Government that remained in office from 2007 to 2011, only 2 ministries (Ministry of Education and the State Ministry responsible for Women and Family) were headed by a woman. However, Erdoğan's new government that he formed after the 2011 election included only one woman minister (Ministry for Family and Social Policy).[12] Despite the recent increase of women parliamentarians in Turkey, the fact that they account for less than 15 per cent of the deputies serving in the legislature and less than 5 per cent of the cabinet members compares very poorly with the recent trends in Western European democracies where the number of women parliamentarians and ministerial elites has increased significantly during the past 20 years (Norris 2004: 179–208).

Conclusions

Instability and weak institutionalization were the two major characteristics of the Turkish party system from its emergence in the late 1940s until the first decade of the twenty-first century. The outcome of the 2002 parliamentary elections underscored the continuity of these characteristics: the party (AKP) that won nearly two-thirds of the parliamentary seats was founded only one year before the elections, the votes of the party (DSP) that had finished first in the 1999 elections plummeted drastically, and an upstart in electoral politics, GP (*Genç Parti*, Youth Party), that was established only a few months before the elections, made a respectable showing by capturing 7.2 per cent of the national vote. Equally telling was the fact that, with one exception, none of the major contenders for power in 2002 was founded before 1983 although several had organizational links with the parties that had been established earlier. Only one of the major parties (CHP) in 2002 was also present at the time when a party system came into in the immediate aftermath of the Second World War. Other prominent indicators of instability and weak institutionalization of the party system over more than six decades of electoral politics included high rates of electoral volatility, which were well above those in West European democracies, the disappearance of what were once considered major parties from the political scene and their replacement by new ones, the large number of party switching by the deputies serving in the parliament, and the frequent changes and rotation in party names and labels.

However, the outcome of the 2007 and 2011 elections suggest that there has been a noticeable change toward increasing stabilization of the electorate and party competition in Turkey. This was best exemplified by the decline in the rate of volatility among the voters and the level of fragmentation in the party system. While the electoral volatility dropped sharply from the record-high 50.2 per cent in 2002 down to 17.3 per cent in 2007, the number of relevant parties in the parliament was halved in comparison to the 1990s (Kalaycıoğlu 2008: 300).[13] Moreover, the outcome of the 2007 and 2011 elections have shown that party competition has gained greater regularity and stability. Unlike in previous years, there have been no wild swings in the votes received by parties from one election to the next. Similarly, the high frequency of party switching among the deputies that increased the number of parties in the parliament between the elections during the period from 1991 to 2002 has largely subsided in the past decade. If the trend toward greater regularity and stability in electoral politics continues, it will make an important contribution to the institutionalization of the party system. This, in turn, is likely to facilitate progress toward democratic consolidation in Turkey.

As discussed in this chapter, arguably the most important reason for the weakness of the Turkish party system has been military interventions in politics since the first coup in 1960. In addition to disrupting the natural evolution of party politics, the fact that the military officers retained the power to veto the decisions made by the elected representatives of the people seriously undermined the consolidation of democracy in Turkey. During the past decade, and especially since 2008, there has been a major change in civil-military relations. Empowered by its broad popular support and determined to prevent the occurrence of new military interventions, the AKP has initiated a number of measures that have ended the tutelary control of the Turkish military in politics. The critical turning point was the imprisonment of nearly 350 retired and active-duty soldiers, including several four-star generals, due to their alleged involvement in coup-plotting against the government. In the past, serious confrontations between the civilian and military leaders usually resulted in the overthrow of the elected civilian governments by the officers. In this respect, the 'Ergenekon Case' represents the beginning of a new phase in civil-military relations in Turkey since for the first time in memory a civilian government managed to take punitive action against the country's military establishment. The restructuring of the civil-military relations and the subordination of the officers to elected politicians in the decision-making process is likely to strengthen the legitimacy of party competition and prevent the recurrence of military interventions in politics which, in the past, had debilitating effects on the party system and hindered progress toward the consolidation of democracy.

The stabilization of the party system and the restructuring of civil-military relations represent important new developments concerning the institutionalization of democratic processes and institutions in Turkey. However, recent years have also witnessed the growing tendency of the governing AKP to silence its critics in the media, to subordinate the judiciary, and to identify democracy with a crude understanding of majority rule that ignores the importance of protecting minority rights and the need for checks and balances in the exercise of political power. The AKP's insensitivity to some of the central features of modern democracy represents a troubling development regarding the prospects for Turkish democracy. The strengthening of the party system and the withdrawal of the military from active involvement in the policy-making process have moved Turkey closer to a point when democracy, to use the classic formulation of Linz and Stepan, becomes 'the only game in town' (Linz and Stepan 1996). However, if the AKP continues to equate democracy only with elections and ignores some of the fundamental requisites of democratic governance, the quality of the game in town in Turkey is likely to leave much to be desired.

Notes

1 For developments in the party system during the 1990s, see Özbudun, E. (2000) *Contemporary Turkish Politics: Challenges to Democratic Consolidation,* Boulder, Lynne Renner, pp. 73–103; Çarkoğlu, A. (1998) 'The Turkish Party System in Transition: Party Performance and Agenda Transformation', *Political Studies,* vol. 46, pp. 544–71; and Akgün, B. (2001) 'Aspects of Party System Development in Turkey', *Turkish Studies,* vol. 2, pp. 71–92.

2 For analyses of the 2002 elections, see Çarkoğlu, A. and Kalaycıoğlu, E. (2007) *Turkish Democracy Today. Elections, Protest and Stability in an Islamic Society,* London: I. B. Tauris, pp. 22–42; and Öniş, Z. and Keyman, F. (2002) 'A New Path Emerges', *Journal of Democracy,* vol. 14, pp. 95–117.

3 On the AKP, see Özbudun, E. (2006) 'From Political Islam to Conservative Democracy: The Case of the Justice and Development Party in Turkey', *South European Society and Politics,* vol. 11, pp. 543–87, and Tepe, S. (2005) 'Turkey's AKP: A Model for a "Muslim-Democratic" Party?', *Journal of Democracy,* vol. 16, pp. 69–82.

4 For an analysis of the post-2002 party system, see Sayarı, S. (2007).

5 For a discussion of the ongoing controversy over the issue of religion, see Heper, M. (2009) 'Does Secularism Face a Serious Threat in Turkey?', *Comparative Studies of South Asia, Africa, and the Middle East,* vol. 29, pp. 15–22.

6 On the impact of political violence on regime breakdown in 1980, see Sayarı, S. (2010) 'Political Violence and Terrorism in Turkey, 1976–80: A Retrospective Analysis', *Terrorism and Political Violence,* vol. 22, pp. 198–215.

7 On the organizational characteristics of political parties in Turkey, see Sayarı, S. (1976) 'Aspects of Party Organization in Turkey', *The Middle East Journal,* vol. 30, pp. 187–200, and Özbudun, E. (2000), pp. 80–87.

8 On the "exit guarantees" retained by the Turkish military, see Özbudun, E. (2000), pp. 105–23.

9 *Guardian,* 12 December, 2009.

10 Ibid. In 2010, a nationwide referendum approved several changes in the constitution including the article on the selection of judges for the Constitutional Court. The parliament now has the power, to choose two of the seventeen judges who serve on the Constitutional Court.

11 For an analysis of the electoral system, including the consequences of the 10 per cent threshold, see Hale, W. (2008) 'The Electoral System and the 2007 Elections: Effects and Debates', *Turkish Studies,* vol. 9, pp. 233–46.

12 S. Sayarı and H.D. Bilgin, 'Paths to Power: The Making of Cabinet Ministers in Turkey,' *Parliamentary Affairs,* vol. 64, (2011), pp. 751–52. The one notable exception to the underrepresentation of women among the ministerial elites and party leadership was Tansu Çiller who served as Turkey's first woman prime minister from 1993 until 1995. She also served as the leader of DYP between 1993 and 2002, and as foreign minister during 1996–97.

13 Kalaycıoğlu, E. (2008) 'Attitudinal Orientation to Party Organization in Turkey in the 2000s,' *Turkish Studies,* vol. 9, p. 300.

References

Akgün, B. (2001) 'Aspects of Party System Development in Turkey', *Turkish Studies*, vol. 2: 71–92.

Çarkoğlu, A. (1998) 'The Turkish Party System in Transition: Party Performance and Agenda Transformation', *Political Studies*, vol. 46: 544–71.

Çarkoğlu, A. and Kalaycıoğlu, E. (2007) *Turkish Democracy Today. Elections, Protest and Stability in an Islamic Society*, London: I. B. Tauris.

Gümüşçü, Ş. (2013). 'The Emerging Predominant Party System in Turkey' *Government and Opposition*, vol. 48.

Hale, W. (2008) 'The Electoral System and the 2007 Elections: Effects and Debates', *Turkish Studies*, vol. 9: 233–246.

Heper, M. (2009) 'Does Secularism Face a Serious Threat in Turkey?', *Comparative Studies of South Asia, Africa, and the Middle East*, vol. 29, no. 3: 15–22.

Kalaycıoğlu, E. (2008)"Attitudinal Orientation to Party Organization in Turkey in the 2000s," *Turkish Studies*, vol. 9: 297–316.

Linz, J. J. and Stepan, A. (1996a) 'Toward Consolidated Democracies', *Journal of Democracy*, vol. 2: 14–33.

—— (1996b) *Problems of Democratic Transition and Consolidation*, Baltimore: The Johns Hopkins University Press.

Mainwaring, S. and Scully, T. R. (1995) 'Introduction' in Mainwaring, S. and Scully, T. R. (eds.), *Party Systems in Latin America*, Stanford: Stanford University Press.

Norris, P. (2004) *Electoral Engineering: Voting Rules and Political Behaviour*, Cambridge: Cambridge University Press.

Öniş, Z. and Keyman, F. (2002) 'A New Path Emerges', *Journal of Democracy*, vol. 14: 95–117.

Özbudun, E. (2000) *Contemporary Turkish Politics: Challenges to Democratic Consolidation*, Boulder, Lynne Renner.

—— (2006) 'From Political Islam to Conservative Democracy: The Case of the Justice and Development Party in Turkey', *South European Society and Politics*, vol. 11: 543–87.

Sartori, G. (1976) *Parties and Party Systems: A Framework for Analysis*, Cambridge: Cambridge University Press.

Sayarı, S. (1976) 'Aspects of Party Organization in Turkey', *The Middle East Journal*, vol. 30: 187–200.

—— (1978) 'The Turkish Party System in Transition', *Government and Opposition*, vol. 13: 39–57.

—— (2002) 'The Changing Party System' in Sayarı, S. and Esmer, Y. (eds), *Politics, Parties and Elections in Turkey*, Boulder: Lynne Rienner.

—— (2007) 'Towards A New Turkish Party System?' *Turkish Studies*, vol. 8: 197–210.

—— (2008) 'Non-Electoral Sources of Party System Change' in *Prof. Dr. Ergun Özbudun'a Armağan: Essays in Honor of Ergun Özbudun*, Ankara: Yetkin Yayınları.

—— (2010) 'Political Violence and Terrorism in Turkey, 1976–80: A Retrospective Analysis', *Terrorism and Political Violence*, vol. 22: 198–215.

Sayarı, S. and Hasanov, A. (2008) 'The 2007 Elections and Parliamentary Elites in Turkey: The Emergence of a New Political Class?', *Turkish Studies*, vol. 9, issue 2: 345–361.

Sayarı, S. and Bilgin, H. D. (2010) 'Paths to Power: The Making of Cabinet Ministers in Turkey', paper presented at the annual conference of the Midwest Political Science Association, Chicago, April.

Sunar, İ and Sayarı, S. (1986) 'Democracy in Turkey: Problems and Prospects' in O'Donnell,G., Schmitter, P. and Whitehead, L. (eds), *Transitions from Authoritarian Rule: Southern Europe*, Baltimore: The Johns Hopkins University Press.

Tepe, S. (2005) 'Turkey's AKP: A Model for a "Muslim-Democratic" Party?', *Journal of Democracy*, vol. 16 pp. 69–82.

Turan, İ. (1988) 'Political Parties and the Party System in Post-1983 Turkey' in Heper, M. and Evin, A. (eds.), *State, Democracy, and Military: Turkey in the 1980s*, Berlin: Walter de Gruyter.

6 What did they promise for democracy and what did they deliver?

The AKP and the CHP 2002–11

Işık Gürleyen

Introduction

There is a general, possibly global, cynicism about the incongruence between the pre-election promises and post-election behavior of political parties. This chapter explores the validity of this belief in the Turkish case by analyzing the words and deeds of two political parties, namely the AKP (*Adalet ve Kalkınma Partisi*, Justice and Development Party) and the CHP (*Cumhuriyet Halk Partisi*, Republican People's Party). More specifically, it analyzes the level of congruence between the two parties' democratization-related election pledges and their subsequent legislative actions in the period between 2002 and 2011.

Although political parties in Turkey enjoy an active role in the political system as they hold legislative power, the level of public distrust of them is quite high, particularly during times of political instability, for many reasons. The most important is the politicians' perceived failures to keep their pre-election promises. This observation has applied to all political parties in the Turkish parliament, particularly during the 1990s, although it can be argued that public distrust has been diminishing since 2002. The ruling party, the AKP has increased its votes to win three consecutive elections since 2002 with an increasing share of votes cast. This suggests that public trust in this party has not fallen, if it has not actually increased. The following question is whether or not the increased public trust can be related to pledge fulfillment.

This chapter addresses the question by analyzing whether or not the AKP and the main opposition party, the CHP, keep their pre-election promises in relation to one particular field, democratization. Election manifestos and legislative activities of the political parties are two sources in analyzing the degree of their fulfillment of election pledges. On the one hand, to identify the pre-election promises, election manifestos are analyzed as the public declaration of the intentions, opinions, objectives, and motives of the political parties. On the other hand, to understand what the elected parties have actually delivered, draft laws made by the party are analyzed. Proposal, rather than actual enactment of a law, is the criterion employed. In other words, enactment is not a condition to be considered as legislative activity.

The chapter is composed of three parts. It starts with a brief literature review establishing the theoretical grounds of this study. The second part presents the empirical data that is the words and deeds of the AKP and the CHP. In this section, the democratization-related pledges of the parties are identified, and then the corresponding legislative actions of the parties are explored. This section compares the two parties regarding fulfillment of election pledges between 14 November 2002 and 12 June 2011. The chapter concludes with an overall evaluation of the role of political parties regarding the liberalization and consolidation problems of Turkish democracy.

Literature review

The literature on pledge fulfillment generally focuses on the party manifestos, the official written statements published by a political party in which they announce their aims and policies. As Walgrave and Nuytemans argue, 'party manifestos matter because they affect the political agenda and steer policy attention towards certain issues' (Walgrave and Nuytemans 2009: 191). They are also important for clarifying party policies. As, Budge and Bara note, 'the party position for elections [is] most clearly and authoritatively stated in the only document parties ever [issue] the manifesto, platform or election program' (Budge and Bara 2001: 6). Finally, manifestos are significant also in terms of specifying how political parties differentiate themselves from each other in the competition for government.

In short, manifestos present a list of policy preferences to the electorate, which allows political scientists to trace whether they are fulfilled or not. Accordingly, there is mounting literature on party manifestos that grew particularly in the 1990s following the completion of the project of the Manifesto Research Group (MRG). MRG rightly concludes that the manifesto research literature should focus on relating party programmatic pledges to actual legislative and administrative policy-making (Budge and Bara 2001: 72). The literature on pledge fulfillment converges on a number of hypotheses, whether in single cases or comparatively. The hypotheses tested in the literature generally focus on the following independent variables: incumbent versus opposition parties, single party versus coalition governments, pledges preserving status-quo versus pledges requiring policy change, level of pledge saliency, and regional versus nation-wide parties (Libbrecht et. al 2009: 62–63; Thomson 2001: 173–77; Royed and Borelli 1999: 116–17; Walgrave and Nutemans 2009: 191).

Although several studies have found a significant positive relationship between the party manifestos and subsequent policy change implementations, variation in pledge fulfillment across parties and over time has been under-researched (Royed and Borelli 1999: 116–17). In the literature, there are two basic approaches to analyzing pledge fulfillment: phrase identification and saliency approaches. As Thomson puts it, '[i]n many such studies, the specific policy commitments, election pledges, made by parties in their election programs are identified. The extent to which these pledges are congruent with subsequent government policy is then evaluated' (Thomson 2001: 171–72). This direct approach, identifying specific pledges in party manifestos and determining whether or not they have been carried out, is the dominant method in the literature (Royed and Borelli 1999). Another method is the saliency approach, which examines the congruence between the emphasis parties place on different policy themes and subsequent government spending patterns on related policy areas (Thomson 2001: 172). Budge and colleagues exploit the saliency approach to reveal the level of emphasis on categorized policy areas based on a left-right scale (Budge et al. 2001: 8, 22).

Regardless of the methodology, the focus of the pledge fulfillment literature is on advanced democracies and their ideological positioning of the political parties (Conti 2008; Brunner and Debus 2008; Libbrecht et al. 2009; Thomson 2001). Regarding democracy specifically, Allen and Mirwaldt analyzed three consolidated democracies and identified the following references to democracy in party manifestos: democracy as a form of government, the institutional characteristics of the domestic democratic system and workplace or industrial democracy (Allen and Mirwaldt 2010). They added to these references the role of people in formal governmental decision-making (Allen and Mirwaldt 2010: 875). Although the literature focuses on national parties, there are also studies that analyze the inter-party differences in regional campaigning, such as Libbrecht et. al (2009). Existing research on the fulfillment of election pledges also suggests a distinction between single-party and coalition governments, although the latter has not been studied as much (Thomson 2001: 171–72). Overall, the literature on pledge fulfillment focuses on consolidated democracies, national parties and single-party governments.

As with other multi-party democracies, political parties in Turkey publish electoral manifestos (i.e. election platforms) which specify their policy preferences and sketch projected legislative proposals. There are numerous studies analyzing the election manifestos of political parties in Turkey. However, there are few systematic analyses linking Turkish political parties' election manifesto pledges to fulfillment evidence. Among them, Budge and Klingemann argue that Turkey represents a particular case because of the military's repeated political interventions, over alleged threats from Islamic traditionalists and Kurdish secessionists (Budge and Klingemann 2001). Thus, Turkey in the 1990s, is considered as a semi-democracy, in which parties supporting civil liberties and related reforms in the state structure are less tolerated in the system (Budge and Klingemann 2001: 35). Recurrent military interventions and the related problems with Turkey's democracy may also account for the lack of academic attention to the fulfillment of election pledges.

This chapter aims to contribute to the literature both on pledge fulfillment and Turkish politics by analyzing the linkage between two distinct sets of data, pledges and legislative actions. Therefore, the rest of the chapter first presents the political parties' pledges on democratization by using phrase identification methods and analyzes the AKP's and CHP's manifestos for elections held on November 3, 2002 and June 12, 2011. After identifying their pre-election pledges, the parties' legislative actions are explored in terms of draft laws and parliamentary bills related to democratization. In this way, the relationship between party manifestos and subsequent legislative behavior can be comprehensively investigated.

Empirical evidence

This section identifies the election pledges made by the two main Turkish parties in their election manifestos for the 2002 and 2007 national parliamentary elections, and the legislative actions taken to fulfill these promises. The period between 2002 and 2011 was chosen because comprehensive democratization reforms were implemented in this period. These two parties were selected because they both passed Turkey's ten percent electoral threshold, allowing them to be represented in the parliament. Following its initial success in the 2002 elections, the AKP has remained in office, with an absolute majority, winning two subsequent elections with an increased vote, most recently in 2011. Since 2002, the CHP has been the main opposition party in parliament, holding the most number of seats after the AKP. Like the coalition Government that preceded it, the first AKP Government largely focused on long-awaited democratization reforms. However, the pace of democratization legislation slowed somewhat after 2005.

Democratization-related pledges in election manifestos: 2002 and 2007

Democratization-related election pledges of the two parties are assessed according to whether they explicitly propose testable constitutional and/or legal changes (Thomson 2001). Distinguishing democracy pledges from others is relatively complicated. In this study, the same references to democracy that Allen and Mirwaldt list are considered as democratization-related: references to democracy as a form of government, institutional characteristics of domestic democratic systems, industrial democracy and citizen participation in formal governmental decision-making (Allen and Mirwaldt 2010: 875).

The democracy pledges of the parties consist of changes not only to the legal system but also changes in the implementation of already-existing regulations. However, for analytical purposes this chapter only considers pledges requiring legislative action. The reason for focusing only on the legislative process is that implementation involves administrative actors, beyond the limits of this study. Accordingly, this section explores the election manifestos of the AKP and the CHP in 2002 and 2007 to identify those election pledges relating to democratization requiring legal and/or constitutional change. A thematic typology categorizing these pledges is developed on the basis of the party's respective positions on various democratization issues.

Such phrase identification is useful in addressing several issues. First, this data allows a comparison between two political parties regarding the range of their concerns about Turkish democracy. It will also help determine which party made the largest or smallest number of pledges on various democratization items. Second, it will reveal the specific reform issues that these parties focus on more. The most emphasized phrases help to demonstrate the democratization issues that have a high profile in the parties' manifestos. Lastly, it helps to address the issue of whether or not Turkish political parties have been consistent in their democracy-related promises over time.

The AKP

Shortly after the party's establishment, the AKP's leaders declared that they supported democratization and Turkey's EU membership bid. Senior party members stated that being a victim of undemocratic practices in the past is the main motive behind the AKP's supportive position (Gürleyen 2008). Because it has been in power since November 2002, the AKP has played a crucial role in the recent democratization process. Being the incumbent party, the AKP has brought the entirety of the so-called 'democratization packages' to the Parliament. The question addressed in this section, however, is what kind of democratization promises were made by the AKP prior to the elections.

In 2002, aside from general references to democracy, the AKP leadership promised various legislative changes to strengthen Turkish democracy. First, it emphasized the need for a new constitution as the 1982 Constitution has been criticized for being the source of many anti-democratic practices in Turkey. Accordingly, the party advocated a new constitution guaranteeing fundamental rights and freedoms based on universal standards. This aim was also repeated in the 2007 manifesto, but with more details about the content of the new constitution:

Our party favors the new constitution having the nature of a social contract regulating the relationship between state-society-individual on the basis of right, freedom and responsibility. The new constitution should be short, concise and clear; the relationship between legislative, executive and judicial powers should be determined on the basis of a parliamentary system and in an open, clear and comprehensible manner; the status and powers of the president should be re-defined in this context; the transition from representative democracy to participatory democracy should be achieved. The new constitution should be prepared on the basis of a wide social consensus.

(AKP Election Manifesto 2007: 7–8)

Alongside such large-scale constitutional reforms, the AKP also suggested constitutional and legal regulations pertaining to a wide array of problems in Turkey's democratic system. Among these, the AKP's leadership placed special emphasis on fundamental rights and freedoms in both 2002 and 2007. In 2002, under the title of 'Fundamental Rights and Freedoms', the leadership promised to undertake the necessary measures to end torture, maltreatment under arrest, extrajudicial killings, and other human rights violations, while promising to make all the necessary constitutional and legal changes to raise fundamental rights and freedoms to international standards specified in international agreements, particularly in the EU's Copenhagen Criteria. Another pledge was 'to remake the legal rules that restrict the right to live and property rights, freedoms of thought, expression, conscience, entrepreneurship, association in accordance with universal law and freedom perception' (AKP Election Manifesto 2002: 6).

Similarly to the 2002 manifesto, in 2007, the AKP stated that it believed in the full implementation of fundamental rights and freedoms which are guaranteed under international conventions, presenting itself as a party which believes that 'political power and bureaucratic structures cannot hinder the use of fundamental rights and freedoms in democratic regimes' (AKP Election Manifesto 2007: 10). The AKP declared its intention to guarantee the actual implementation of promised constitutional and legal guarantees of fundamental rights and freedoms, and to make them an essential element of Turkish political culture. Even though the actual implementation of legislation lies outside the scope of this chapter, such statements are useful for clarifying vague pledges in this respect. For instance, the AKP declared its determination to continue its 'zero tolerance' policy for human rights violations, such as torture, disappearance or death in detention, and extrajudicial killings (AKP Election Manifesto 2007: 10).

> The AKP will fully realize the right to life and property rights, freedom of thought, expression, conscience, enterprise and association, which have been re-regulated with universal legal [principles] and understanding of freedom. Shortcomings regarding freedoms and rights lie at the root of controversial practices regarding religion, sect, gender and ethnic discrimination issues. Such shortcomings shall be removed by establishing a state mentality 'based on human rights', which will raise our democracy to a universal level.
>
> (AKP Election Manifesto 2007: 10)

Furthermore, the AKP promised to continue the extension of freedoms that were not legislated for in their first term of office. For instance, it promised to enact a new Law on Public Meetings and Demonstrations, in line with international standards (specifically, the European Convention on Human Rights) in the following legislative period (AKP Election Manifesto 2007: 11).

Closely related to, or sometimes overlapping with fundamental rights and freedoms are reforms that aim to strengthen civil society. The AKP perceives the public monitoring and strengthening of civil society as essential because it views itself as having a 'good governance' outlook. Accordingly, both manifestos contain a specific section reserved for strengthening civil society. This apparent embrace of participatory values is noticeable in both the 2002 and 2007 manifestos, although with increased emphasis in the latter. Civil society was praised in the context of public participation in government, while pluralism and participation were articulated as major characteristics of a truly democratic system.

In both manifestos, the AKP promised to abolish the legal and administrative obstacles that prevent active citizen participation in government. To increase citizen participation and accountability, it proposed 'the Law on Right to Information' and legal regulations for ombudsman. The party also promised to establish the necessary mechanisms to allow communication between societal organizations, such as trade unions, business associations and voluntary organizations, and public offices to solve their respective sectorial problems. Furthermore, the party envisaged 'a transition from representative to participatory democracy' by introducing legal mechanisms to increase the active participation of civil society in public administration (AKP Election Manifesto 2002: 7, 14). Both manifestos included the media under the title of civil society. However, the 2002 manifesto merely mentioned the party's view of media-government relations while not promising any legal changes in this respect, and the 2007 manifesto offered only the vague statement that 'the AKP would take necessary steps for a pluralist, competitive and transparent media' (AKP Election Manifesto 2002: 7; 2007: 13).

While civil society was discussed in the 2002 manifesto in terms of improving communication between society and government, the 2007 manifesto emphasized it in the context of freedom of association. Another change was that, in contrast to the 2007 manifesto, the 2002 manifesto only mentioned civil society-related issues vaguely in broad pledges, while specific legislative changes were not listed (AKP Election Manifesto 2002: 6–7; 2007: 11–12).

The 2002 manifesto declared that establishing rule of law was one of the AKP's priorities. The document noted that 'by changing the legal system, which prohibits fundamental rights and freedoms, the Turkish state would become a true rule of law and, therefore Turkey would have a respectable status in the international community' (AKP Election Manifesto 2002: 7–8). The manifesto further stated that a new constitution clearly defining the powers of the executive, legislative and judiciary branches should be the first step towards legal reforms. The AKP also suggested restructuring the judicial system to simplify court procedures and to reduce the burden on courts. To achieve this aim, the party suggested enacting 'the Administrative Procedure Act' to clarify authority and obligations in administrative affairs

(AKP Election Manifesto 2002: 8–10). Regarding anti-corruption measures, the AKP promised to fight corruption and bribery (AKP Election Manifesto 2002: 21). Similarly to the 2002 election manifesto, the 2007 manifesto emphasized the rule of law principle listing the related laws that the AKP government had enacted in the previous period. Although such pledges had not in fact been clearly specified in 2002, some were noted in 2007 retrospectively, such as the new criminal code and the establishment of regional courts of appeal. In another marked difference from the 2002 manifesto, the AKP placed a greater importance on corruption in 2007 (AKP Election Manifesto 2007: 117–18).

The AKP was particularly vocal in championing reform of the judicial system, stating in its 2002 manifesto that one of its priorities was to accomplish a full-scale reform of Turkey's legal system. The main aim put forward was to bring the judicial system in line with the rule of law principle. A secondary aim of reform was stated as simplification through revision of all constitutional and legal provisions that were incompatible with judicial independence and the legal guarantee of judges and implementation of measures ensuring the impartiality of judges and preventing the politicization of the law. For example, the 2002 manifesto promised to repeal all legal clauses that are incompatible with judicial independence, while a new regulation would be enacted concerning re-election of the members of the Constitutional Court. In the proposed regulation, Parliament would have the authority to appoint members to the Constitutional Court with a view to establishing a better balance between legislative, executive and judicial powers (AKP Election Manifesto 2002: 8–9). The 2002 manifesto also promised to bring the implementation of judicial legislation in line with modern norms, in which the rights of detainees and convicts would be clearly defined, and if amnesty were to be declared, it would be limited only to those crimes committed against the state. Also promised were the abolishment of the State Security Courts and the transfer of their functions and powers to criminal courts specializing in organized crime and terrorism (AKP Election Manifesto 2002: 9–10). Finally, the AKP promised legal regulations envisaging alternative [to judicial system] solutions for legal disputes in order to ensure fast, simple, and effective resolution of disputes at minimum cost, thereby reducing of the workload of judicial organs (AKP Election Manifesto 2007: 15). However, what would exactly constitute such alternative dispute settlement systems was not specified.

Restructuring the government is another priority listed in the 2002 manifesto, with the party proposing to enact a Statute for Council of Ministers. Related to this issue, the AKP also championed decentralization noting that it was necessary to reinforce the authority of local administrations in line with the European Charter of Autonomy of Local Governments. It promised 'all the necessary legal regulations' to achieve this aim (AKP Election Manifesto 2002: 15–16). Another recurring manifesto theme was enhancing balance of power between the President and the Parliament through a promised Code of Political Ethics and Asset Declaration (AKP Election Manifesto 2007: 18).

A final issue for democratization was gender equality. The AKP promised to introduce regulations necessary for the implementation of the principles of the Convention on the Elimination of All Forms of Discrimination against Women (AKP Election Manifesto 2002: 49). However, the party seemed to give this issue less priority than others, and its emphasis reduced even more in 2007.

While approximately one-quarter of the 2002 manifesto was devoted to democratization issues, by 2007, this had fallen to one-eighth, although some of the themes that emerged in the 2002 manifesto were still present in 2007. The 2002 manifesto expressed a belief in democratic practices in a section entitled 'the AKP is democratic', in which the AKP was proclaimed to be an opponent of party closures as long as parties act within constitutional and legal boundaries. Likewise, the AKP affirmed that it opposed any intervention in democracy from forces outside the system, hinting at the political authority of Turkish Armed Forces (AKP Election Manifesto 2002: 3). Both election manifestos emphasized the democratic nature of the party, although the degree of emphasis considerably diminished in 2007.

The CHP

With its long-standing history, the CHP has played a significant role in Turkish politics and has continued to be an important actor since 2002 as the main opposition party in the parliament. Perceiving itself as the leading social democratic party in Turkey the CHP has taken a positive stance on democratization, particularly in the last decade. This section discusses the democratization-related pledges of the CHP during the 2002 and 2007 election campaigns.

The CHP emphasized its commitment to democracy and secularism in both election manifestos. In 2002 manifesto, the CHP declared that its aim was to 'create a peaceful, cooperative and an egalitarian society; to implement a liberal and pluralist democracy based on human rights … ' (CHP Election Manifesto 2002: 47). To achieve this, the CHP promised 'to lead in the preparation of a new, modern, pluralistic and liberal Constitution' and 'to dismantle all persisting anti-democratic institutions and practices of the 1980 military regime, including its legal outlook that still persists' (CHP Election Manifesto 2002: 48).

The CHP leadership promised to match all international standards such as the European Convention on Human Rights and the EU's Copenhagen Criteria, in Turkey's legal system, administrative and internal security practices. The CHP also promised to remove all legal and administrative barriers obstructing freedoms, particularly the freedom of expression and the freedom of association. Regarding freedoms of the press and communication, the CHP promised to propose legal and institutional regulations to prevent media monopolies (CHP Election Manifesto 2002: 25–26). Similarly, in 2007, its pledges included the elimination of legal and administrative obstacles to fundamental rights and freedoms. However, few of its proposals overtly mentioned legal changes. Instead, the pledges were general promises aiming to eliminate remnants of the 1980 Military Regime, such as a 'total purge of the distorted conception of law, anti-democratic institutions and practices' (CHP Election Manifesto 2007: 17). There was also a specific section on cultural pluralism in 2002, which was not repeated in 2007. In it, the CHP promised to eradicate politically motivated or arbitrary bans and censorship and lift any type of administrative pre-audits, potentially including some legal changes along with implementation. However, the CHP also stated that it would adhere to judicial verdicts on this issue (CHP Election Manifesto 2002: 24). Thus, this pledge can be assessed as regarding implementation rather than legislative action.

Another priority for the CHP was labor rights. The CHP leadership promised to annul all anti-democratic clauses of the Trade Union Act and regulations regarding collective bargaining, strikes, and lockouts on the basis of EU standards, including collective bargaining and strike rights for public employees (CHP Election Manifesto 2002: 22; 2007: 42). In its 2007 manifesto, the CHP also promised to lift all the reservations of the AKP Government on the Revised European Social Charter; to realize the legal regulations regarding severance pay with consensus; and to re-organize the Economic and Social Council (consisting of business, labor representatives and public authorities) to reduce the influence of the state (CHP Election Manifesto 2007: 42–43).

The CHP pledges also include a number of reforms regarding the rule of law. However, most of these again took the form of general promises, such as 'removing the impediments against rule of law', rather than specified reforms (CHP Election Manifesto 2002: 47). One specific pledge that was made in 2002 concerned three reforms of the judiciary: the reorganization of High Council of Judges and Prosecutors, the establishment of ombudsman, and the speeding up judicial process (CHP Election Manifesto 2002: 25–26). In 2007, the pledge to reform the judiciary was made more specific: terminating the memberships of the Minister of Justice and the Undersecretary on the High Council of Judges and Prosecutors. Another specific pledge was to annul the regulations that made judges and prosecutors administratively subservient to the Ministry of Justice. Third, the CHP leadership criticized the Law of the Regional Court of Appeals as damaging the unitary nature of the state, promising to amend this law establishing specialized courts (CHP Election Manifesto 2007: 18).

The 2002 election manifesto promised to democratize the state, describing the principles supporting this goal as the 'modern, participatory, pluralistic, democratic rule of law' (CHP Election Manifesto 2002: 6). In order to achieve this goal, the CHP leadership intended to restructure the state by reducing the number of ministries and unnecessary bureaucracy, and introducing measures that would make the state more publically accountable. Finally, the party's Local Government Reform pledge called for a number of legislative changes promoting transparency and public participation in local governing (CHP Election Manifesto 2002: 6).

Like the AKP, the CHP made major pledges concerning reform of public administration. However, one important difference was the CHP's insistence that such reform had to be achieved on the basis of Kemalist principles and 'with an understanding of the unitary and secular social state that follows the rule of law' (CHP Election Manifesto 2007: 58). That is, the CHP clearly opposed federalism, viewing the AKP Government's policies relating to local administrations as a threat to the unitary characteristics of the Turkish state. Thus, the CHP pledge was limited to the financial autonomy of the local administrations (CHP Election Manifesto 2007: 58).

The CHP's 2002 election manifesto placed great importance on the issue of corruption. The promise to amend Articles 84 and 100 of the constitution aimed at ending the use of parliamentary immunity as a shield against prosecution for non-political crimes. Accordingly, the CHP leadership promised to restrict parliamentary immunity to issues of freedom of thought and expression. In this way, ex-ministers could be held accountable if they had committed a crime during their office. The CHP claimed to be the only party running for office that made such a promise regarding the lifting of parliamentary immunity (CHP Election Manifesto 2002: 4). In 2007, the CHP repeated its promise to lift the legal immunity of parliamentarians for non-political illegal activities and restrict it to issues of freedom of thought and expression only (CHP Election Manifesto 2007: 20).

In its 2002 manifesto the CHP promised to enact immediately a 'Clean Politics Law' to prevent parliamentarians becoming involved in any profit-producing relations with public offices. This law would also establish the TBMM (*Türkiye Büyük Millet Meclisi*, Turkish Grand National Assembly) Ethics Committee to review parliamentarians' non-political actions and relationships. The law also would restrict and audit the election campaign expenditures of political parties and parliamentary candidates in line with western democratic norms. Lastly, the law would ensure the transfer of the asset portfolios of commercial enterprises belonging to prime minister and other ministers to a trustee for the duration of their office (CHP Election Manifesto 2002: 4). In 2007, the party repeated its promise to enact a Political Ethics Code requiring the declaration of the business connections of all parliamentarians, auditing of election expenditures in line with Western norms and public declaration of the assets of MPs (CHP Election Manifesto 2007: 20).

In addition, the CHP promised to restructure the Court of Accounts in order to ensure effective auditing of public expenditure, and proposed to ban media owners from tendering for public procurement contracts to ensure that the media performed its actual function without a conflict of interest. The CHP criticized the earlier Public Procurement Law as not being transparent and possessing discriminatory elements, and promised to amend it in line with EU norms (CHP Election Manifesto 2007: 20). The CHP also promised to ensure the absolute independence of the judiciary in order to punish political support for corruption. Both 2002 and 2007 manifestos contained many other related pledges on corruption, but, they mainly related to implementation rather than legislative changes.

Gender equality was another priority area for the CHP leadership both in the 2002 and 2007 manifestos. In 2002, the party stated that gender equality was an undeniable human right and an indispensable prerequisite of democracy. Accordingly, the CHP's leadership promised to introduce a constitutional amendment making gender equality a state obligation. Another promise was the promulgation of a new law, the 'Equality Framework Act' (CHP Election Manifesto 2002: 25–26). This pledge was extended in 2007 with a promise to include gender equality considerations in all party policies. 2007 manifesto also promised to redesign the Turkish legal system in line with the principles of 'the Convention on the Elimination of All Forms of Discrimination against Women' and to make constitutional amendments ensuring the state's obligation to provide an 'opportunity priority' for women (CHP Election Manifesto 2007: 55). Finally, the CHP promised to enact a law allowing Turkish citizens living abroad to vote (CHP Election Manifesto 2007: 69).

Although the CHP emphasized democratization in both its manifestos, the 2002 manifesto contained more pledges on this issue. It can be argued that there was a change of emphasis in 2007 due to the perceived threat from some of the reforms made by the AKP Government to the unitary nature of the state. The emphasis on corruption in 2002, for example, was replaced by an emphasis on terror, security, and peace in 2007.

Both the AKP and the CHP have been consistent over time regarding their pledges. However, following a change in the leadership of the CHP in 2010, there has been a shift towards the rule of law category. Under the previous leader, Deniz Baykal, the CHP opposed the draft laws proposed by the governing AKP on decentralization, arguing that they would lead to the disintegration of the country. Baykal's CHP argued that decentralization would aid terrorism, while some laws would damage secularism if implemented. A leading political scientist labeled such opposition as 'defensive nationalism' (Öniş 2009). In contrast, under Kemal Kılıçdaroğlu's leadership, the CHP's focus has shifted to corruption-related issues although its emphasis on secularism has also continued.

Both parties favor writing a new constitution criticizing the exiting constitution as the source of many undemocratic practices in Turkey, particularly regarding its constraints on civil rights. However, parties differ remarkably in the nature of their manifesto statements. Those of the CHP are more general and relate to problems stemming from the inappropriate implementation of laws, while the AKP's pledges are usually specific and related to legal changes. A second difference between the two parties concerns the type of democratization issue they emphasized. Civil liberties and restructuring the state are the most cited specific pledges of the AKP, while rule of law and corruption issues were manifesto priorities for the CHP. Although both parties mentioned reform of state organization, reform of the judiciary is a particularly high-profile topic inthe AKP manifestos. In contrast to this emphasis on fundamental rights and freedoms, the CHP stressed corruption-related legal changes in both manifestos, although, the degree of importance placed on corruption declined considerably in the 2007 manifesto.

Both parties' democracy related pledges can be classified under seven headings: civil liberties and human rights, political liberties, civil – military relations, citizen and civil society participation, state organization restructuring, rule of law, and gender rights. Although some of the reform items can be placed in two, or even more headings, such categorization is analytically useful for comparing the pledges of the two parties. The next section assesses the fulfillment of the election pledges on the basis of the political parties' parliamentary legislative activities subsequent to their pledges. Such an analysis addresses five related questions. First, are the legislative proposals of these political parties consistent with their election manifestos? To put it differently, to what extent do the parties attempt to fulfill their pre-election promises? The second question regards the content of pledges: Which issues are translated into legislative bills – high-profile or rarely mentioned ones? The third question concerns the timing of pledge fulfill-ment: Are the legislative actions to fulfill pledges only taken just before elections? Fourth, is there any variation in the fulfillment of pledges between different ruling periods? Finally, is an incumbent party more likely to fulfill its election pledges than an opposition party? If yes, what accounts for it?

Legislative action for pledge fulfillment: Draft laws and law propositions of MPs

In the literature, pledge fulfillment is usually defined as enacting the pledge-related law. However, defining fulfillment of pledges as enactment ignores an intervening variable, which would distort such an evaluation to the advantage of the party holding the majority of seats in the parliament. That is, a party that is a minority in the parliament may also have proposed legislation, but lost in the parliamentary vote. Taking this into account, fulfillment is defined in this study as starting legislative action on a related pledge during a specific legislative period. Thus, fulfillment includes the introduction of draft bills and proposals of law rather than actual enactment of legislation. By considering the initiation of legislative action, rather than its enactment, it is assumed that the bias against minority parties can be avoided. In the same way, non-fulfillment is defined as the situation where the party does not even begin the process of introducing a draft bill or law proposal related to its pledges in its election manifesto. Even in cases where other parties in the parliament draft a law on the same issue, the pledge is considered unfulfilled.

Table 6.1 summarizes fulfilled and unfulfilled pledges relating to democratization. Legislative data for this study was gathered from the online database of the parliament (TBMM). This database contains detailed descriptions of all legislative activity,[1] including signatory MPs of and the justification for the draft law and the date of submission to the parliament. Each of the above explained pledges are matched with draft laws during 22nd and 23rd legislative periods, respectively referring to November 14, 2002–July 22, 2007 and July 22, 2007–April 7, 2011.

The table indicates that the AKP drafted laws for most of its electoral pledges. In general, the AKP submitted a constitutional amendment proposal in 2010. The proposal included most of the AKP's democratization-related pledges.[2] In particular, during both of the legislative periods, the AKP Government initiated legislation improving civil liberties and human rights. For example, one fulfilled pledge is related to the right to property. To this end a draft law was prepared in 2003 envisaging changes 'improving the investment environment, promotion of foreign investment, strengthening the financial structures of local governments and individuals aimed to solve their grievances regarding the use of property rights'.[3] There were also draft bills on broadcasting and education rights in languages other than Turkish in 2003; extension of freedom of expression in 2003, 2009, and 2010; protecting human rights in 2003 and 2005; and extension of the right to assembly in 2003 and 2010. Regarding freedom of conscience, AKP MPs drafted various laws in 2008 lifting restrictions on Muslim religious practices such as wearing headscarves in higher education institutions. Such initiatives caused controversy over Turkey's secularism principle. However, they were defended by the AKP as strengthening freedom of conscience. The AKP also fulfilled its electoral pledge concerning freedom of conscience through draft laws in 2003 and 2006 extending the rights of non-Muslim foundations, such as to build places of worship.

Closely related to civil liberties are pledges that aim to strengthen citizen participation in government and civil society. As they view referendum as an instrument for direct citizen participation in decision-making process, the AKP drafted laws for a referendum on constitutional amendments in 2007 and 2010. The AKP drafted laws also for the establishment of city councils in 2005. However it should be noted that, the AKP has promised city councils also in its 2007 manifesto, even though these had been already established two years earlier.

The issue of political liberties was another focus of the AKP's draft laws in 2010 particularly clarifying the Constitutional Court's auditing of party expenditures, which had been a frequent ground for party closures, and restricting other grounds for party closures. Regarding civil-military relations, the AKP drafted a number of laws in 2003 and 2004 on modifications

Table 6.1 Fulfillment of election pledges on democratization

Summary of pledges (party, year of manifesto)		Pledge fulfillment	
		AKP	CHP
Civil Liberties and Human rights	Fundamental rights and freedoms (AKP 2002, 2007; CHP 2002, 2007)	F	F
	Freedom of expression (AKP 2002; CHP 2002)	F	F
	Freedom of conscience (AKP 2002; CHP 2002)	F	F
	Right to property (AKP 2002)	F	O
	Right to assembly – Law on Public Meetings and Demonstrations (AKP 2007; CHP 2002)	F	F
	Prevention of torture and maltreatment (AKP 2002; CHP 2002)	F	F
	Liberalization of Trade Union Act (CHP 2007)	O	F
	Right to strike and collective bargaining for public employees (CHP 2007)	O	F
Political Liberties	Party closures (AKP 2002)	F	O
	Voting rights of Turks abroad (CHP 2007)	O	NF
Civil-Military Relations	Restricting Turkish Armed Forces' political powers (AKP 2002)	F	O
	Abolishing State Security Courts (AKP 2002)	F	O
Strengthening citizen participation and civil society	Increased citizen participation in local government (CHP 2002)	O	F
	Extending the scope of direct democracy by more frequent use of referendums (AKP 2002)	F	O
	Setting up city councils (AKP 2007)	F	O
Restructuring state organization	Decentralizing the polity, empowering local authorities (AKP 2002)	F	O
	Financial autonomy of local authorities (CHP 2007)	O	NF
	Administrative Procedure Act (AKP 2002)	F	O
	Statute for Council of Ministers (AKP 2002)	F	O
	Reducing the number of ministries (CHP 2002)	O	NF
	Reform of Judiciary – repeal of clauses incompatible with impartiality (AKP 2002, 2007; CHP 2002)	F	NF
	Reform of Judiciary – Establishing alternative mechanisms for legal disputes (AKP 2007)	F	O
	Reform of Judiciary – New Regulation for Election of Members of Constitutional Court (AKP 2002)	F	O
	Reform of Judiciary – Re-organization of High Council of Judges and Prosecutors, HSYK (CHP 2002) Terminating membership of the Minister and Undersecretary in the HSYK (CHP 2007)	O	NF
	Reform of Judiciary – Autonomy of judges and prosecutors from Ministry of Justice (CHP 2007)	O	NF
	Reform of Judiciary – Establishing new courts with special authority (AKP 2002)	F	O
	Reform of Judiciary – Modify the Law of Regional Court of Appeals as they pose a threat to unitary characteristics of state (CHP 2007)	O	NF

Table 6.1 (continued)

Summary of pledges (party, year of manifesto)		Pledge fulfillment	
		AKP	CHP
Rule of Law	Abolishing parliamentary immunity for non-political activities (CHP 2002, 2007)	O	F
	Political Ethics Code (AKP 2007; CHP 2007)	NF	F
	Establishment of Parliamentary Ethics Commission (CHP 2007)	O	F
	Anti-corruption regulations (AKP 2002, 2007; CHP 2002)	F	F
	Public Procurement Law (CHP 2007)	O	NF
	Measures against media-politics-business relations (CHP 2007)	O	NF
	Restructuring of Court of Accounts (CHP 2007)	O	F
	Law on Right to Information (AKP 2002)	F	O
	Ombudsman (AKP 2002; CHP 2002)	F	NF
Gender Equality	Enacting Gender Equality Framework Act (AKP 2002; CHP 2002, 2007)	NF	NF
	Constitutional amendments regarding opportunity priority for women (CHP 2007)	O	F

Key: NF (Not fulfilled), indicates the party did not propose any draft law or bill on the related issue in the 22nd and/or 23rd legislative periods. F (Fulfilled), indicates the party submitted a draft law on the related issue in the 22nd and/or 23rd legislative periods, whether or not the draft was passed into law. O (No Pledge), indicates the party did not make a relevant pledge.

to the structure of the National Security Council and military courts, and the abolishment of state security courts.

One of the main concerns of the AKP leadership has been re-organization of state functions, among which reform of judiciary is priority. Regarding the non-judicial state functions, the AKP drafted the Administrative Procedure Act in 2003 and 2010, laws concerning empowerment of local administration in 2005 and 2006 and reorganization of ministries in 2006 and 2011. The AKP's electoral pledges to reform the judiciary were all fulfilled: AKP MPs drafted laws on the establishment of Regional Court of Appeals in 2003, 2004 and 2005, regarding reform of the Constitutional Court in 2010, and on the establishment of alternative mechanisms for legal disputes to reduce the burden on the judiciary, in 2011. Regarding the repeal of clauses incompatible with impartiality, the AKP drafted a law making the Court of Accounts and the HSYK (*Hâkimler ve Savcılar Yüksek Kurulu*, High Council of Judges and Prosecutors) as autonomous bodies, respectively in 2005 and in 2010. However, it should be noted that the new law was heavily criticized by the opposition for allowing the Government to choose four members of the HSYK, which damages the HSYK's independence from the executive.

As regards rule of law, the AKP drafted laws on three of its pledges: the right to information in 2003, anti-corruption regulations in 2003 and 2004 and the establishment of an ombudsman repeatedly in 2005, 2006, 2010 and 2011, although it did not draft any law on the Political Ethics Code. Last but not least, the AKP failed to fulfill its pledge regarding gender rights that is to pass the Gender Equality Framework Act. Thus, overall, the AKP fulfilled all of its electoral pledges but two; ethics and gender.

In comparison to the governing party the main opposition party the CHP performed less well in fulfilling its electoral pledges. One of the areas in which the CHP did perform well concerns civil liberties and human rights violations. The party drafted laws on extending freedom of conscience in 2005; on recognition of churches, *cemevis*, synagogues, etc. as places of worship in the same way as mosques in 2005, 2008 and 2010; on prevention of torture in 2006 and 2008; on limiting the authority of police in 2008; on restricting bans on travel abroad in 2008; on improving conditions for fair trials in 2009; on compensation for damages caused by the 1980 military regime in 2010; on limiting detention periods in 2011; on limiting the powers of the High Criminal Courts Having Special Authority in 2011; and on extension of freedom of expression in 2011.

Regarding labor rights, the CHP drafted laws on extension of labor rights, such as simplifying red tape in 2004; the right to strike for public employees in 2007 and 2010; and collective bargaining rights for public employees in 2010. Furthermore, the party drafted a law extending political rights in 2004 by lifting restrictions on political participation of TOBB (*Türkiye Odalar ve Borsalar Birliği*, The Union of Chambers and Commodity Exchanges of Turkey) and another one in 2010, allowing re-establishment of associations that were closed down by the military regime. On the issue of civil society, the CHP fulfilled its single pledge of extending citizen participation in local government by drafting two laws in 2004 and 2008. The CHP also drafted legislation in 2010 aiming to compensate for damage caused by the 1980 military regime. Thus, it generally fulfilled its promises regarding the extension of civil liberties, labor rights and civil society.

The CHP performed quite well in fulfilling its promises on gender equality and anti-corruption. In 2009, the CHP drafted a law to oblige municipalities to establish women's shelters; to establish commissions to study this aim in 2010; to require half of all party organs and commissions to be made up of women in 2010; to extend protection from domestic violence to those in non-marital relationships in 2011; to reform the marital property regime in 2011; and to increase penalties for those found guilty of domestic violence in 2011.

Regarding corruption, the CHP drafted laws on the enactment of the Political Ethics Code and the establishment of a Political Ethics Commission in the parliament in 2002 and 2007; the efficient use of right to information in 2003; specifying December 9 as a day for raising awareness against corruption in 2003; defining match-fixing in football games as bribery in 2006; requiring asset declaration by political party leaders in 2006; developing a strategy to fight corruption in 2009. Of the area in which the CHP fulfilled the least of its pledges was restructuring state organization. Finally, a few of the pledges were categorized as unfulfilled because the relevant laws were enacted having been drafted by other parties. For instance the DSP (*Demokratik Sol Partisi*, Democratic Left Party) drafted the law giving the right to vote for Turks abroad in 2008, so in Table 6.1 it is recorded as unfulfilled for the CHP.

The analysis shows that on the whole, both parties fulfilled a majority of their democratization-related pledges. However, it is also clear that the governing party performed much better than the main opposition party in this. While the AKP fulfilled all but two of the pledges considered here, the CHP fulfilled only slightly more than half of its pledges regarding democratization. Before drawing of general conclusions on the relative poor performance of the main opposition party, research limitations should be taken into account.

One of the limitations in the research that may hinder the findings is that it gives credit to the party which submitted a particular draft law earlier than the other one, which can be the case for reform items promised by both parties in their manifestos. Clearly, if one party has already drafted legislation, there is no need for the second party to do so. Thus its pledge is categorized as unfulfilled. For instance this might be the case for the AKP, regarding the political ethics code, or for the CHP regarding impartiality of the judiciary. Nevertheless, this limitation does not hinder the findings because such cases were very few in this study; only three pledges are promised by both parties and fulfilled only by one of them.

A second shortcoming is that the above analysis does not shed light on cases in which contradictory draft laws were submitted. In some cases, MPs from the same party may initiate legislation which contradicts other bills, particularly regarding freedom of expression. In both legislative periods studied here, bills aiming to extend freedom of expression were undermined by other bills; some of which were even enacted. For instance, the AKP Government fulfilled its pledge on freedom of speech. However, the governing party also drafted or enacted laws restricting freedom of expression such as the Article 301 of the Turkish Penal Code, which penalizes 'insulting Turkishness'. The governing party amended this clause in 2008 following heavy international criticism, particularly from the EU.

A final methodological concern relates to the fact that pessimism might lead to non-fulfillment, which can be labeled as reverse anticipation.[4] That is, opposition MPs, having only a minority of parliamentary seats, might foresee failure of their draft bill and therefore prefer inaction. That is to say, simply by holding the majority of seats the ruling party, the AKP in this case, can block any legislative initiative by opposition parties. The expectation of such failure could discourage opposition parties from drafting laws on certain issues. Unfortunately, there is not any mechanism to verify a possible reverse anticipation in case of the CHP.

Despite these methodological weaknesses the above analysis allows us to conclude that both parties by and large fulfilled their democratization-related pledges in the 22nd and 23rd legislative periods. Those issues which received more attention in the respective manifestos–i.e. higher profile issues–were most likely to be translated into legislative bills. For the AKP, pledges related to high profile issues, such as state reorganization, were all fulfilled while rarely mentioned promises on corruption and gender equality were not fulfilled. Similarly, while the civil liberties and corruption pledges of the CHP were fulfilled, relatively less emphasized promises regarding the judiciary were not. As for the timing of pledge fulfillment legislative actions to fulfill pledges were dispersed throughout the legislative periods rather than concentrated nearer to elections.

Concluding remarks

This chapter analyzed the relationship between the electoral pledges and the legislative activities of Turkey's current governing party and the main opposition party regarding democratization. Such an analysis contributes to the pledge-fulfillment literature, which is significantly under-researched in Turkish political science. For the sake of simplicity, the analysis was limited to democratization pledges in two consecutive legislative periods, 2002–7 and 2007–11. It was not straightforward process to establish linkages between two distinct sets of data, party positions and legislative behavior on democratization, because few of the draft laws made direct reference to respective election pledges. However, all draft laws included a document called 'legal grounds' justifying the draft law. Since the purpose of each draft law was clearly stated within these documents, it was possible to infer the manifesto pledge to which the draft law referred.

Both political parties referred to democracy in various ways in their 2002 and 2007 manifestos. Such references are grouped together under seven general themes: civil liberties and human rights, political rights, civil-military relations, civil society, restructuring state organizations, rule of law, and gender equality. Overall, the two parties were consistent, in terms of their democratization pledges in their party manifestos, over time. The AKP's manifestos contained more promises than the CHP's. In contrast to pledges regarding the quality of democracy that parties tend to make in advanced democracies (Allen and Mirwaldt 2010) the pledges of these two Turkish political parties focused more on the institutional characteristics of democracy.

As demonstrated by this analysis, there is in general a high degree of congruence between the political parties' election pledges and their subsequent legislative bills. Both the AKP and the CHP, by and large, fulfilled their pre-election promises. In addition to the above pledges, there were also some democratization-related draft laws which were not promised in the election manifestos. One noteworthy example concerned reducing the election threshold. Although the manifestos included no related pledge on reducing the ten percent threshold, it was one of the concerns of CHP MPs. Another example was the AKP's draft law in 2010 on aligning labor rights and trade union law with EU standards.

Although, the governing party and the main opposition party collaborated to enact many of the democratization-related bills, there were fierce debates over some of the reform items. One of the most controversial issues was decentralization. Opposition parties viewed some of the reforms regarding fundamental rights and freedoms as either damaging the secular characteristics of the state or conceding to separatists. The governing party's 'democratic opening' towards Kurdish citizens of Turkey was a remarkable example in this regard. Under Deniz Baykal, the CHP had opposed this reform package arguing it would lead to the territorial disintegration of the country. However, such disagreements were reduced with the change in the CHP's leadership in 2010 in that under Kemal Kılıçdaroğlu, the CHP appear to have shifted its political focus. Consequently, some of the previous differences with the governing party have been overcome. This may result in lessening of polarization in parliamentary debates on democratization-related reforms.

The findings of this analysis challenge the common perception that Turkish political parties do not fulfill their pledges. Nevertheless, it should be stressed that this is a study of the parliamentary practice of politics rather than the implementation of democratic reforms. Fulfillment in this study refers merely to taking legislative action not to the actual implementation of democratization reforms. Therefore, it would be overstretching to argue that the fulfillment of pledges discussed here means a more democratic Turkey. Such conclusions cannot be drawn from the present study and will have to be revealed by future research. However, it can be confidently argued that these two parties are bound by their election manifestos and translate their pre-election promises into legislative action.

Notes

1 Regarding legislative procedure in Turkey, Article 7 of the Constitution states that 'Legislative power is vested in the TGNA on behalf of the Turkish Nation. This power cannot be delegated.' Article 88 clarifies the proposing and debating of laws: 'The Council of Ministers and deputies are empowered to introduce laws. The procedure and principles relating to the debating of draft bills and proposals of law in the TGNA shall be regulated by the Rules of Procedure.' Online. Available HTTP: <*http://www.tbmm.gov.tr/english/about_tgna.htm#*> (accessed 30 June 2013).
2 for details of this proposal see Yazıcı, S. (2010) 'Turkey's Constitutional Amendments: Between the status quo and Limited Democratic Reforms', *Insight Turkey* 12 (2), pp. 1–10.
3 http://www.tbmm.gov.tr/develop/owa/tasari_teklif_gd.sorgu_yonlendirme
4 I owe this argument to Philippe Schmitter, who kindly read an earlier version of this study and provided many valuable insights.

References

AKP Election Manifesto (2002). Online. Available HTTP: <http://www.akparti. org.tr> (accessed 30 June 2013).

—— (2007) Online. Available HTTP: <www.akparti.org.tr> (accessed 30 June 2013).

Allen, N. and Mirwaldt, K. (2010) 'Democracy-Speak: Party Manifestos and Democratic Values in Britain, France and Germany', *West European Politics*, 33 (4): 870–93.

Brunner, M and Debus, M. (2008) 'Between Programmatic Interests and Party Politics: The German Bundesrat in the Legislative Process', *German Politics* 17 (3): 232–51.

Budge, I. et al. (2001) *Mapping Policy Preferences: Estimates for Parties, Electors and Governments 1945–1998*, Oxford, New York: Oxford University Press.

Budge, I. and Bara, J. (2001) 'Manifesto-based research: A Critical review', in Budge, I. et al. *Mapping Policy Preferences: Estimates for Parties, Electors and Governments 1945–1998*, Oxford, New York: Oxford University Press.

Budge, I. and Klingemann, H. (2001) 'Finally! Comparative over-time mapping of party policy movement', in Budge, I. et al. *Mapping Policy Preferences: Estimates for Parties, Electors and Governments 1945–1998*, Oxford, New York: Oxford University Press.

CHP Election Manifesto (2002). Online. Available HTTP: <www.chp.org.tr> (accessed 30 June 2013).

—— (2007) Online. Available HTTP: <www.chp.org.tr> (accessed 30 June 2013).

Conti, N. (2008) 'The Italian Parties and Their Programmatic Platforms: How Alternative?' *Modern Italy* 13 (4): 451–64.

Gurleyen, I. (2008) *Impact of the European Union on Turkey's Democracy:Elite Attitudes towards the EU and Democratization*, Berlin: VDM.

Keyman, E. F. and İçduygu, A. (2003) 'Globalization, Civil Society and Citizenship in Turkey: Actors, Boundaries and Discourses', *Citizenship Studies* 7, no. 2: 219–234.

Libbrecht, L. et al. (2009) 'Issue Salience in regional party manifestos in Spain', *European Journal of Political Research* 48: 58–79.

Onis, Z. (2009) 'Conservative globalists versus defensive nationalists: political parties and paradoxes of Europeanization in Turkey.' *Journal of Southern Europe and the Balkans Online* 9 (3): 247–61.

Royed, T. J. and Borelli, S. A (1999) 'Parties and Economic Policy in the USA: Pledges and Performance, 1976–92', *Party Politics* 5 (1): 115–27.

Thomson, R. (2001) 'The programme to policy linkage: The fulfillment of election pledges on socio-economic policy in Netherlands, 1986–98', *European Journal of Political Research* 40: 171–97.

——(2011) 'Citizens' Evaluations of the Fulfillment of Election Pledges: Evidence from Ireland', *Journal of Politics* 73 (1): 187–201.

Turkish Grand National Assembly. (2010) *The Functions and Powers of the Turkish Grand National Assembly*. Online. Available HTTP: <www.tbmm.gov.tr> (accessed 2 February 2010).

Walgrave, S. and Nuytemans, M (2009) 'Friction and Party Manifesto Change in 25 Countries, 1945–98', *American Journal of Political Science* 53(1): 190–206.

Yazıcı, S. (2010) 'Turkey's Constitutional Amendments: Between the status quo and Limited Democratic Reforms', *Insight Turkey* 12 (2): 1–10.

Part III
Civil society

7 Democratic consolidation and civil society in Turkey

E. Fuat Keyman and Tuba Kancı

Turkey, in the last decades, has been undergoing significant changes and transformations lived and felt in each and every sphere of life. As a country carrying on accession negotiations with the European Union, Turkey has embraced a proactive foreign policy ranging from contributing to peace and stability in the Middle East to becoming a new 'energy hub', being one of the architects of 'the inter-civilization dialogue initiative', envisioning a world based on dialogue, tolerance and living together. Its regional power role in world politics has become more important with its active, multidimensional foreign policy as well as its identity as a modern secular nation-state with parliamentary democratic governance, secular constitutional polity and a primarily Muslim population (Keyman 2009). However, besides this active, multi-dimensional, pro-peace foreign policy and the global attraction that it has brought, internal politics in Turkey have recently become subject to political impasses and societal polarization; the interactions between the state elite and the elected governments have increasingly been patterned by conflict. From assassinations to post-modern military coups, from party closures to the rising power of reactionary nationalism, Turkey has been confronted by serious problems leading to domestic instability. Hence, the transformation process has been marked by a paradox: global attraction and visibility *versus* domestic instability and polarization.

The solution to this paradox lies in fact in the consolidation of democracy in Turkey. The global dynamics and active multi-dimensional foreign policy alone cannot pave the way to the settlement of political and social polarization that has been generating severe obstacles to living together as a plural and multi-cultural society. The growing complexity of Turkish modernity and politics indeed necessitates governance based on democratic consolidation, realized through a discourse and regime of citizenship founded upon the equal rights and freedoms of diverse identities. In this chapter, we will seek an answer to the question of democratization, the solution to which requires the consolidation of democracy not only as a political regime, but also as a process by which state, society and individual relations are regulated. In doing so, we will discuss democracy and its consolidation in Turkey by focusing specifically on civil society.

Articulating democracy and civil society

The site of civil society has attracted significant attention in the recent decades both from academic and public circles. The transitions to democracy, which had taken place during the 1980s and early 1990s, from authoritarian rules and military regimes to democracy in Latin America and Eastern Europe, have contributed to this revival. Yet it is globalization that has constituted an effective foundation for the increasing importance of civil society for coping effectively with the serious problems and dangers confronting humanity. Civil society has been treated as a major actor in democratic transition and sustainable economic development; and the site of civil society served as an important space for analyzing social change. Turkey does not constitute an exception at this point; on the contrary, the recent transformation process of Turkey has involved the emergence and widening of civil society. In what follows, we will first briefly discuss democratic consolidation and its links with civil society. We will then proceed with the Turkish case, and discuss the making of state-centric modernity in Turkey in the 1920s. The analysis will focus on the continuities and changes in Turkey's experience with modernity by specifically focusing on civil society. The effects of the globalization processes of the 1980s, as well as the Europeanization processes of the 2000s will be specifically taken into consideration with respect to their impact on civil society in Turkey and on the consolidation of democracy in the country.

Turkey's historical experience with democracy displays an ambivalent course of development. The modern political and institutional structures necessary for 'political modernity', which can be defined along the emergence of the nation-state, modern state bureaucracy, secularism and citizenship, were created successfully. The making of Turkey involved contradictions and tensions, and when coupled with the global and local developments, it has been subject to a number of political, economic and cultural crises, leading to significant transformations. The transition to parliamentary democracy in 1945–50 has been one of these important transformations; the history of Turkey from 1950s to the present times came to be defined as a process of democratization.

The end of World War II marked the beginnings of the transition from one-party rule to democracy in Turkey. Alongside the international context, the domestic factors such as mass discontent in the country, and factions in the ruling coalition exacerbated the calls for political change. As Ergun Özbudun states, this was a peaceful democratic transition realized through a movement of reform in the single-party political system in the late 1940s (2000: 13–14). However, democracy was experienced mainly as a procedural system, and it has not been deepened (Sunar 2004; Özbudun 2000; Ahmad 2003; Keyman and Öniş 2007). This failure in consolidating democracy has manifested itself in the regime breakdowns of the multi-party parliamentary system, which were experienced in 1960, 1971, and 1980; and from the

1980s onwards, in the emergence of identity-based conflicts, the question of Islamic resurgence and the Kurdish question. Although there have been some governmental initiatives for democratization in the last decade, most of these attempts remained abortive. Nevertheless, despite frequent regime breakdowns, and significant democratic deficits which show themselves primarily through the issues related to representation and identity, the history of Turkey from the 1950s to the present has been a process of democratization which first involved the practice of procedural democracy with parliamentary system of rule, then a move towards consolidation and deepening of democracy through the development of the language and practice of rights and freedoms.

Scholars of democracy and democratization generally have defined democracy through four main approaches: procedural, constitutional, substantive, and process-oriented (Tilly 2007). The procedural approach focuses on governmental practices, and specifically on the existence of regular, free, and fair elections. Such an understanding of democracy indeed fits the definition of democracy outlined by the Austrian economist Joseph Schumpeter in the 1940s. The existence of competitive elections, 'on the thin side, in a minimal sense', can account for the mere existence of 'electoral democracy' (Diamond 2008). However this thin conception of democracy can hardly led towards democratic consolidation; as Larry Diamond has pointed out, democracy

> [...] is not just a system in which elites acquire power to rule through a competitive struggle for the people's vote, as Schumpeter defined it. It is also a political system in which government must be held accountable to the people, and in which mechanisms must exist for making it responsive to their passions, preferences and interests.
>
> (Diamond 1999: 219)

Advocates of the constitutional approach in defining democracy and democratization pay specific attention to the laws that design a regime. Although constitutions and laws are not among the necessary preconditions of democracy, they are among the requisites of democracy, and have utmost importance in making democracy thrive and in consolidating it. What should be noted at this point are the enactment of announced principles and laws. In fact, significant discrepancies exist between laws and daily practices in most countries even today.

Substantive approaches identify 'the conditions of life and politics a given regime promotes' (Tilly 2007: 7). As Charles Tilly notes, this societal conception of democracy focuses specifically on 'human welfare, individual freedom, security, equity, social equality, public deliberation, and peaceful conflict resolution' (Tilly 2007: 7). It foresees a specific type of society in which the language of 'rights, freedoms, and responsibilities' constitutes a dominant normative and legal norm concerning not only the question of 'the regulation (or the governance) of societal affairs' but also the question of 'the creation of unity in a diverse and multicultural social setting' (Keyman and Öniş 2007).

Process-oriented approach signifies a minimum set of processes as the defining criteria of democracy. Robert Dahl defines these minimum set of processes under five categories as effective participation, voting equality, enlightened understanding, control of the agenda, and full inclusion of adults (Dahl 1998: 37–38). However these criteria refer mainly to democracy in local contexts and/or in small-scale formations. Dahl's explanation focuses on institutions as he discusses the minimum requirements of a large-scale democracy (Dahl 2005). According to this argument, a large-scale democracy requires elected officials, free, fair, and frequent elections, freedom of expression, access to alternative sources of information, associational autonomy, and inclusive citizenship. In a unit as large as a country, these six political institutions are necessary for 'a full transition to modern representative democracy'. According to Dahl, '[a]s a country moves from a nondemocratic to a democratic government, the early democratic *arrangements* gradually become *practices*, which in due time turn into settled *institutions*' (Dahl 2005: 187). As Dahl's definition of institution consists of settled practices, we can argue that he approaches democracy as a working process. Thus these institutions are also the ones that need to be 'strengthened, deepened and consolidated' to realize the criteria he has set in his five categories as the democratic minimum (Dahl 2005: 193, 197).

A full transition to democracy, and its strengthening and consolidation as well as its continual deepening, in fact, necessitate, besides a procedural and constitutional operation of democracy, a simultaneous existence and operation of both substantive and process-oriented understandings of democracy. Considering transition to, and consolidation of, democracy in Turkey, Özbudun, in his widely referred work, moves beyond a procedural approach to democracy as he adopts Juan J. Linz and Alfred Stepan's comprehensive framework which defines democratic consolidation in behavioral, attitudinal, and constitutional terms:

> Behaviorally, a democratic regime in a territory is consolidated when no significant national, social, economic, political, or institutional actors spend significant resources attempting to achieve their objectives by creating a non-democratic regime or turning to violence or foreign intervention to secede from the state.
>
> Attitudinally, a democratic regime is consolidated when a strong majority of public opinion holds the belief that democratic procedures and institutions are the most appropriate way to govern collective life in a society such as theirs and when the support for anti-system alternatives is quite small or more or less isolated from the pro-democratic forces.
>
> Constitutionally, a democratic regime is consolidated when governmental and non governmental forces alike, throughout the territory of

the state, become subjected to, and habituated to, the resolution of conflict within the specific laws, procedures, and institutions sanctioned by the new democratic process.

(Linz and Stepan 1996, p. 6, quoted in Özbudun 2000: 4).

Linz and Stepan further argue that, in addition to a well-functioning state, 'five other interconnected and mutually reinforcing conditions must also exist or be crafted' for consolidation of a democracy:

First, the conditions must exist for the development of a free and lively civil society. Second, there must be a relatively autonomous and valued political society. Third, there must be a rule of law to ensure legal guarantees for citizens' freedoms and independent associational life. Fourth, there must be a state bureaucracy that is usable by the new democratic government. Fifth, there must be an institutionalized economic society.

(Linz and Stepan 1996, p. 7, quoted in Özbudun 2000: 5).

The behavioral patterns and reinforcing conditions indicate that democratic consolidation involves a simultaneous existence and operation of procedural, constitutional and substantive understandings of democracy, and they also coincide with the political institutions that Dahl notes as necessary for a 'full' democracy. Within the context of Turkey, and considering Turkey's experience with democracy, democratic consolidation has less to do with the procedural operation of democracy. Dahl's process-oriented approach, and his institutional requirements (elected officials, free, fair and frequent elections, freedom of expression, access to alternative sources of information, associational autonomy, and inclusive citizenship) set themselves as the minimum necessary criteria for democratic consolidation, whereas its deepening requires further progress in substantive terms.

Dahl's process-oriented approach also implicitly points to civil society as a necessary actor in democratic transition and consolidation. Although he does not treat civil society as the major actor in democratization, civil society, especially since the transitions to democracy in Latin America and Central and Eastern Europe (1980s and early 1990s), has an utmost importance. In the last decades, we have seen the increasing number of civil society organizations, whose scale of operations range from local to global levels, whose functions involve social, political, economic, and environmental issues. Civil society has been viewed as an effective actor for eradicating poverty, promoting democracy and good governance, resolving social conflict, securing human rights and freedoms, and protecting the environment (CIVICUS 1999). However, recently, its real 'effectiveness' in contributing to the creation of a better world, and its 'easy articulation' into different and even antagonistic political and economic ideological discourses of modernity, democracy, and development have started to be questioned.

In his influential essay on the theoretical and philosophical construction of the idea of civil society and its historical development, Charles Taylor suggests that there are three 'modes' in which civil society has been defined in Western modernity. In broadest terms, 'civil society exists where there are free associations, not under the tutelage of state power' (Taylor 1990: 98). This definition, however, exemplifies a narrow and minimalist approach to civil society. It views civil society as an 'associational life' operating on the basis of civil rights and freedoms, and thus, does not assign it a political and ethical role, such as the creation of a democratic and just society. This first mode can be observed in the emergence of European modernity. Here, civil society is defined in relation to the modern society as a market society, perceived as a domain of rights and freedoms of the new urban class vis-à-vis the state, and giving meaning to the emerging individualist and secular culture. What is important here is that civil society is located against the state, related to market and individualism, defined on the basis of individual rights and freedom, but not connected or associated to democracy.

In the second mode, however, civil society is perceived politically and ethically as being an integral part of good society. In this mode, civil society is considered to exist where 'society as a whole can structure itself and coordinate its actions through such associations which are free of state tutelage' with a view towards good society (Ibid.). This politically and ethically loaded definition implies that social life in any given country can organize itself independently of any state interference, coordinate its activities through voluntary organizations and transfer its demands to the political sphere again via these organizations. This mode can be traced in the democratization movements that have taken place in Central and Eastern Europe and Latin America throughout the 1980s. Civil society gave meaning to the transition to democracy from military rule or authoritarian political regimes. Within the framework that draws a strict separation between state and society, and locates civil society against the state and its power, civil society symbolizes the existence of an ethically and politically free and good society, and functions as the sufficient condition for democratization and democratic governance aiming at limiting state power in order to secure and expand the domain of individual liberties and freedoms. In this mode, civil society also constitutes a sufficient basis for comparing and classifying political regimes; whereas a strong and influential civil society with a limited state defines democracy, the strong state creates either totalitarian or authoritarian political regimes, depending on its approach to civil society (Konrad 1989, Cohen and Arato 1992).

However, the politically and ethically loaded definition of civil society, while correctly locating it in relation to the process of democratization, underestimates and ignores the fact that civil society also constitutes an associational life with a variety of social, political, and economic functions (Edwards 2004). To put it differently, if in the first mode of defining civil society only with reference to the associational life is too minimalist, the second mode, in which civil society is directly associated with democracy is too maximalist and ethically-loaded. In the second mode of defining, civil society and minimal state together have been linked to democracy, however, it should be noted that a limited state in, and by, itself does not necessarily lead to the latter, and can be related only to neoliberal ideologies. It may mean the dismantling of the welfare state other than democratization. These problems have led to the emergence of the third mode of thinking about civil society as 'an alternative or supplement to the second sense', and referring to 'the ensemble of associations that can significantly determine or inflect the course of state policy' (Taylor 1990: 98).

In this chapter, we follow the third line of approach to civil society which provides a suitable conceptual framework for exploring the ways in which civil society and democratic consolidation articulate with one another. Employing some aspects of minimalist and maximalist approaches to civil society, the third approach nonetheless attempts to link civil society as an associational life with the larger context of good and democratic governance of society. In doing so, this third approach (i) regards civil society as an effective tool in solving social problems; (ii) emphasizes that civil society may cooperate with the state and political actors in the solution of these problems; (iii) stands against the use of civil society by the state and political actors as a factor to legitimize their position and holds that civil society should be a leading actor in efforts to give effectiveness, efficiency and transparency to the state; (iv) suggests that civil society plays an important role in ensuring that society is organized on the basis of 'active citizenship' from micro-local issues to macro-national level; (v) adds that civil society is also important in grounding the relations between different identities, social actors and sections of society on democratic principles; and (vi) concludes that in our present world civil society is a key in ensuring the democratic and fair sharing of rights and responsibilities by the state, society and individuals as well as by the different identities (Edwards 2004; Ehrenberg 1999). This mode of thinking of civil society derives from the recent debates on democracy, modernity, and globalization, locates it outside the political society as well as the economic society, and perceives it as a third space where civil associational life is organized and public deliberation in search of a better society is initiated (Ehrenberg 1999; Kaldor 2003; Keyman and İçduygu 2005).

In what follows, we will provide a brief reading of Turkish modernity from the perspective of democracy and civil society. This will enable us to demonstrate the historical unfolding of civil society from being simply an associational life under state tutelage to being a third space formed by an ensemble of associations with the potential to make a contribution to the good and democratic governance of society. Such a reading will also show how, in recent years, civil society and democracy have been increasingly articulated with one another.

State-centric modernity, democracy, and civil society in Turkey: 1923–80

Although displaying certain continuities with its Ottoman past, the emergence of Turkey constitutes a break with the past, insofar as it was made in the image of the Kemalist elite as a modern republican nation-state. In the nineteenth century, the aim of preserving the Ottoman state led to partial and/or wholesale adoption of Western European goods, institutions, and ideas. The Western European-inspired changes defined the boundaries of the 'modern', even though the attempts at institutional and social change were the foci of controversies, contradictory aspirations, and reactions. As Mardin argues, nineteenth century reformers 'succeeded in producing a well-trained, knowledgeable bureaucratic elite guided by the interests of the state' (2006: 308). These Western-educated elite were followed by succeeding generations that were much more radical and impatient with respect to reform measures (Mardin 2006: 309). At the same time, they were much more influenced by the diffusion of nationalist ideologies throughout Europe, and thus, by the end of the nineteenth century, the aim of modernization in the Empire increasingly became the realization of a nation-state in the image of the West for the purposes of 'saving the state'.

The Kemalist elite followed the lines of Ottoman experience with social engineering, and as Keyder points out, focused on the ideal of 'saving the state' (1989: 160). They undertook a rapid modernization effort carried out through reforms from above with the intention of 'attaining the level of Western civilization'. Republican Turkey was both the outcome of the modernization efforts and a response to wars and the dismemberment of the Empire that took place in the nineteenth and early twentieth centuries. The process of 'making' of the Republican Turkey included establishing the political, economic, and ideological prerequisites of Western modernity, such as the creation of an independent nation-state, the fostering of industrialization, and the construction of a secular and modern national identity. Western modernity was regarded as 'the way' of making modern Turkey and its existence as a modern nation-state in its fullest form.

Four epistemic and normative parameters, the strong-state tradition, national developmentalism, the organic vision of society, and the republican model of citizenship, together established the basis of the state-centric mode of operation of Turkish modernity. This state-centric mode not only defined the early republican period, but became consolidated and marked the future of state-society interactions.

(i) In the making of modern Turkey, the state has acted as the privileged and sovereign subject operating independently from society and assuming the capacity of transforming it. In this process, the state has constituted the primary context of politics, defined its boundaries, and it has played the dominant role in the reproduction of societal affairs. National interest was formulated by the state elite in such a way that it was identified as state interest. Thus, the 'strong-state tradition' meant a state-centric way of governing society from above by assuming a unity between state and nation, as well as between national interest and state interest (Keyman 2008).

(ii) National developmentalism was the ideology for rapid modernization and industrialization, as well as the basic vehicle for the top-down transformation of society into a modern, industrial, civilized totality. It involved, as the 'proper prescription for development', a 'planned, import-substituting industrialization' (Keyder 1997: 40). The state acted as the developmental state, creating a state-directed economy and taking substantial decisions for the regulation of economic activities for industrialization. National developmentalism ensured and secured the role of the state as a dominant economic actor. In this context, the state in its national developmentalist intervention into society assumed full autonomy with providing neither transparency nor accountability.

(iii) As the strong-state and national developmentalism together established the institutional foundation of the state-centric Turkish modernity, modernity and its rapid implementation into social relations also required, in the minds of the Kemalist elite, an 'organic vision of society' that defines society not with reference to such categories as class or individual but on the basis of the 'duties and services' of different occupation groups to the state. Thus, in their attempt to modernize Turkey, the Kemalist elite did not approach to society in terms of individual rights and freedoms, nor did they see society as containing individualism, pluralism, participation and claims to difference. Instead, society had to be organic; societal affairs were to be organized in a homogenous and monolithic way to serve for the national interest – the making of Turkey as a 'civilized' and modern nation.

(iv) The making of modern Turkey involved the transformation of the masses into citizens; yet citizenship referred to a morally-loaded category, rather than a liberal category framed by the language of rights, and aimed at creating a secular and rational national identity compatible with the project of modernity as civilization. The 'republican model of citizenship', while giving the masses political rights, concomitantly demanded that they had to accord normative primacy to national interest over individual freedoms, duties over rights, and state sovereignty over individual autonomy. It served, first, as a link between the state and society; second, as an articulatory principle connecting people with different religious, ethnic, and cultural origins; and third as an effective ideological device by which the state had attempted to disseminate its will to civilization throughout society.

The making of modern Turkey in fact still continues today, and within time it has been a continuous, multi-dimensional, and complex process as it involved a number of significant ruptures (Keyman 2008). The first rupture was the transition to parliamentary democracy in 1945–50. Despite frequent regime breakdowns and significant democracy deficits, the history of modern Turkey has been, and today remains as, a process of modernization which entails a significant reference to the question of democratization. Turkey's exposure to globalization in the 1980s led to a new rupture, and globalization came to constitute the world-historical context of the transformation process of Turkey. It has brought into existence the squeeze of 'the national' between the global forces and local dynamics. Thus, throughout the 1980s, and especially since the 1990s, the process of modernization involved not only the question of democratization, but also a reference to globalization. In the year 2000, Turkey has faced another rupture. In the Helsinki Summit of December, 1999, the country has been granted candidate status for full membership of the EU by the European Council. Since then, Turkey has been undergoing a process of European transformation, covering almost all the areas of the governing structure and the state-society/individual interactions.

If we approach the period from 1923 to 1950 from the angle of civil society, in the first instance it can be argued that the site of civil society was even non-existent. In this period, there has been no civil society development leading to the increasing participation of societal groups into politics (Kalaycıoğlu 2002). Nor was there a civil society as independent of the state and prepared to demand the protection of civil rights and freedoms (Yarasimos 2000). However, to suggest that civil society in the way it operates in modernity, did not appear in Turkish modernity, is not to imply that in the period of the emergence and the consolidation of modernity no associational life had emerged in Turkey. On the contrary, both the strong-state tradition and national developmentalism assumed an active society to support the process of modernization and contribute to the process of Turkey's attempt to reach rapidly the level of contemporary civilization. This associational life involved (a) public professional organizations, (b) foundations, (c) cooperatives, and (d) associations (İçduygu and Keyman 2005). These organizations were the constitutive units of the organic vision of society, acted in accordance with the principle of 'a division of labor among services and duties' to modernity, and aimed at activating the top-down transformation of what is regarded as a backward-traditional society into a progressive-modern social formation. Moreover, they also served as an institutional space within which the unity between the state and republican model of citizenship was reproduced. In fact, the associational life went hand in hand with the duty-based understanding of citizenship which operated by giving moral primacy to the services to state and nation over rights and freedoms.

The state-centric model of associational life in Turkish modernity, whose defining features and characteristics were embedded in the organic vision of society and the duty-based understanding of citizenship can be said to have prevailed its dominance after the transition to democracy in Turkey up until the 1980s. The transition to the parliamentary multi-party system did not alter the existing associational life. Even though the transition to democracy symbolized a set of developments in which the political life began to be organized on the basis of the right-left axis and the economic life involved a certain level of liberalization, the cultural and social life did not have civil society organizations independent of the state (Özbudun 2000). It was only with the radical economic and cultural changes in Turkish modernity during the 1980s that Turkey witnessed the emergence of the idea of civil society as a vital area for democratization and different civil society organizations as actors of a new associational life based on civil rights and freedoms.

Globalization and the transformation of Turkish modernity: 1980–2000

In the aftermath of the 1980 military coup and the restoration of democracy, internal developments such as the economic liberalization of 1980s and 1990s, and the global developments such as the end of the Cold War, the emergence of 'New World Order', and the rise of the European integration paved the way for the transformation of modernity in Turkey. Throughout the 1980s and especially during the 1990s, Turkish modernity and its state-centric governing of society from above faced a serious legitimacy and representation crisis (Keyder 1997: 47). A number of important changes and transformations gave rise to this crisis. First, parallel to the changes in the world economy during the 1980s, framed to a large extent by the emergence and consolidation of the neoliberal discourse of free market rationality, the ideology of national developmentalism became untenable. The move from import-substitution industrialization to export-promotion industrialization in the 1980s, and the exposure of the Turkish economy to economic globalization significantly reduced the power and legitimacy of national developmentalism. It was no longer possible to use this ideology as an effective device of the strong-state to dictate the rules of the economic sphere in its regulation of economy. On the contrary, since the 1980s, the Turkish economy has been increasingly framed by the free market-based economic rationality. The regulation of state-economy relations came to be dictated by neoliberal discourse of individualism, free-market and the minimal state. This transformation also gave rise to societal calls for individual rights and freedoms, it underlined the importance of the democratization of state-society relations, and set the stage for the positive and transformative impacts of the European integration process for creating an efficient and effective state (Özbudun and Keyman 2002: 303–5).

Second, in this period, the organic vision of society also collapsed, and a concomitant emergence of the politics of identity/difference was observed. In this context, both the resurgence of Islam and the 'Kurdish question' initiated in their own ways a strong challenge to the organic vision of society, and thus contributed to the process of the fragmentation of political culture in Turkey. The resurgence of Islam as a strong political, economic, and cultural actor criticized the secular foundation of the strong-state tradition. The Kurdish question, articulated both as a language of ethnic difference and a form of ethnic violence, challenged the organic vision of society and its basic assumption of the unity of the state and nation.

Third, since the 1980s there has been a steady increase mainly in the quantitative development of civil society organizations along with the societal calls for the needed democratization of the state-society relations in Turkey (Gönel 1998, Turkish Economic and Social History Foundation 2000 and 2003). Despite the depoliticizing measures of the post-1980 era, civil society started to flourish by the mid-1980s with the women's movement being one of its forerunners. This began as an effort at intervening at the level of everyday beliefs and practices, and a way to establish a link between the everyday life and politics. As Sirman argues, these 'non-hierarchical and independent forms of associations, consciousness-raising groups, issue-oriented *ad hoc* committees' of the Turkish scene were 'clearly reminiscent of the Western experience', whereas the '*ad hoc* organizations were instrumental at a time when state repression discouraged all forms of extra-parliamentary political activity' (1989: 19). Besides contributing to the rise of such elements of civil society as woman rights activists, ecologists, and Islamists, economic liberalization also resulted in the emergence of 'a multiplicity of economic actors and economic pressure groups' that accepted the rules and norms of economic globalization and demanded minimum state intervention. (Keyman and İçduygu 2005: 7). In this period, civil society organizations have been extremely important in introducing to Turkish society the language of rights and freedoms, the discourse of individualism, and the idea of participatory democracy. Moreover, they have challenged the dominance of the state-centric model of associational life which was embedded in the organic vision of society. Contrary to this vision, civil society organizations have attempted to activate societal life as independent of the state, present critiques of the strong-state tradition and its top-down governing of society, and transform the republican duty-based design of citizenship to an active one. The latter was to involve a democratic emphasis placed upon the philosophical principles of rights and freedoms which included both individual and group-based claims to autonomy, pluralism and democracy (Göle 1994).

It can be suggested in this context that it was only during the 1980s and 1990s that the idea of civil society in Turkey gained definitional and institutional resemblances with the ways in which civil society function in modernity, and constituted itself both as an associational life independent of the state and as the vital area for democratization. However, during this period, the quantitative development of civil society was not transformed into qualitative importance due partially to the organizational and financial capacity problems of civil society organizations. Yet, the main reason was the organization of the Turkish political landscape, especially during the 1990s, on the basis of clash between the strong-state tradition and the politics of identity/difference (Kramer 2000). Especially during the 1990s, what marked the nature of the state-society relations in Turkey were the mutual efforts of the strong-state tradition and the politics of identity/difference 'to cannibalize each other' (Appadurai 1996) to define the future of Turkey. The politics of identity/difference was initiated either in the form of the Kurdish question, whose activities have ranged from the demands for the recognition of cultural rights and freedoms to the ethnic assertiveness involving terrorist activities, or as the process of Islamic resurgence whose political activities were perceived by the state-elite as a major danger for the secular foundation of the Turkish Republic. Thus, in the 1990s, as identity questions rather than civil society were becoming the central focus of Turkish politics, the protection of the secular identity and the territorial integrity of the state had become the main and primary motive of the state in its governing of Turkish society. As a result, identity replaced civil society, security replaced democracy, and the will to protect the republic replaced the protection and enlargement of the rights and freedoms. The more the state aimed for ensuring the secular and territorial integrity of the republican regime by privileging security over democracy, and the more the state-society relations were framed by the politics of identity/difference, the less civil society and civil society organizations were supported and promoted as vital and important for democracy and stability. Civil society was in fact 'abused' by the state elite, political actors and the politics of identity/difference (Keyman and İçduygu 2003, Özbudun and Keyman 2002).

Civil society, democratization and Europeanization: 2000 to the present

In the last decade, Turkey have been subject to a number of important historical processes which led the state elites and political actors to conceive security, democracy, and economic sustainability as intertwined, and also to perceive civil society and civil society organizations not instrumentally but, on the contrary, as effective actors for democratization. These historical developments include the AKP (*Adalet ve Kalkınma Partisi*, Justice and Development Party) majority government since 2002 (despite significant problems of trust and ambiguity); the deepening of Turkey-EU relations since 2000 (taking the form of full accession negotiations); the institutional restructuring of Turkish economy since the economic crisis of February 2001; the increasing global visibility of the pivotal state role of Turkey since the September 11, 2001 terrorist attacks on the USA; and the growing foreign policy activism of Turkey since 2005. As a result of these processes, the strong state has been subject to a radical restructuring, placing the questions of democracy, economic stability and social cohesion at the center of Turkish modernity.

In this transformation process, throughout the decade, the site of civil society has widened considerably. The range of issues civil society organizations focus upon has multiplied along with the quantitative increase in the number of associations. Although these historical processes, which originated from international and domestic developments, did not necessarily have direct impacts on the development of civil society, they affected it to the extent that they resulted in underlining the significance of democracy for a politically and economically stable state. They also provided a suitable context for the increasing importance–in the minds of state elites, political and economic actors–of civil society in making Turkey a democratic and economically stable country.

This quantitative development of civil society in Turkey can be observed from the records of the Ministry of Interior Affairs. In year 2000, the total number of voluntary associations was around 60,931; this number rose to 71,832 by 2003. In the second half of the decade, by 2006, the number of voluntary associations summed up to 73,378; a year later, it rose to 77,849, and the increasing trend continued until the current times. The total number of associations by the early 2010 amounted to 84,521 (Ministry of Interior Affairs 2010). However a quick glance at the nature of these associations shows that this quantitative development is not necessarily matched in the qualitative side. Most of these voluntary associations are embedded in religious networks and/or in territorial solidarities; they are mainly associations for realizing religious services, i.e. mosque building societies, or solidarity associations for village and small town development (Ministry of Interior Affairs 2010; Kalaycıoğlu 2007). This dichotomy between the quantitative and qualitative capacities of civil society in Turkey is also evident in the findings of the Civil Society Index Project (CSI), which was conducted between 2003–5 and which undertook a thorough and comprehensive research of the site of civil society (Bikmen and Meydanoğlu 2006).

Despite the recent widening of the site of civil society, the CSI report shows that civil society in Turkey is still in a nascent stage of development. Especially the involvement of citizens in civil society, when measured along membership levels to organizations, continues to be rather low. This number, for the first half of the decade, according to the CSI report is around 5 per cent. The records of the Ministry of Interior Affairs indicate a different number; according to the Ministry's statistics, the card holding members of the voluntary associations by the end of 2005 amounts to 7,035,375 people, which is 9.6 per cent of the population (Kalaycıoğlu 2007). However, the 2006 survey of 'socio-political orientations in Turkey' points to a lesser percentage than the official statistics. Kalaycıoğlu argues that this discrepancy is due to underreporting in surveys as well as multiple counting of the members of associations by the official authorities. What should be underlined here is the fact that more than 90 per cent of the population declines to have an affiliation with a voluntary association (Kalaycıoğlu 2007). The primary reasons of low levels of membership are identified in the CSI report, depending on the focus groups of the research, as the ongoing negative socio-economic conditions and the restrictions on freedom of association. Nevertheless, the percentage of citizen involvement in civil society seems to increase when participation is taken not on membership basis but on voluntary grounds. In this case, the women's organizations, which in fact have the lowest membership percentage, attract the greatest number of volunteers along with the human rights organizations (Bikmen and Meydanoğlu 2006).

Despite the positive aura brought by the new Law of Associations of 2004 (İçduygu 2007), civil society in Turkey continues to suffer from various obstacles. Besides extremely low levels of citizen involvement, the civil society organizations are faced with acute structural problems that range from lack of professional staff, financial resources and organizational management skills to inefficient management of resources. The current legislation indeed presents opportunities for dialogue and financial cooperation between the civil society organizations, local governments, and central government. The municipalities can include civil society organizations in the city councils, civil society organizations can undertake joint projects with municipalities and governorships, or they can provide expertise to specific commissions set up by the Government (which includes preparing reports, draft policies or laws). Although these recent changes in the legislation are quite positive developments, especially when compared with legal status in the beginning of the decade, the channels of communication between the state and civil society are not yet well-established and institutionalized. Although examples such as the Prime Ministry initiating a joint commission in 2003 with the participation of civil society organizations to examine and monitor human rights issues exist, when the state seeks dialogue, it generally gets into communication with trade unions, chambers and private sector business organizations (Bikmen and Meydanoğlu 2006: 72). Furthermore, the site of civil society continues to be subjected to government interference and control, rather than regulation. In fact, a gap exists between the laws and their actual practice. Laws and regulations set forth a 'vague language' which work to increase the discretionary powers of the state agencies and authorities (Bikmen and Meydanoğlu 2006: 71). Government interference and control seems to be the case especially with respect to human rights organizations.

These discrepancies, coupled with the structural problems of civil society, negatively affect the civil society's contribution to the policymaking processes in Turkey. As the results of the CSI project point, the levels of civil society activity in holding the state accountable and promoting state transparency are rather low, and the impact of civil society organizations on public and social policy remains considerably limited. Even though the civil society organizations are quite active in areas related to human rights, women and children rights, the gains acquired remain moderate. But it can, nevertheless, be argued that there is a positive trend in their impact on policymaking with respect to the rights related areas (Bikmen and Meydanoğlu 2006: 18). The human rights organizations' efforts to expand civic liberties, as well as the women's organizations' struggle for the realization of reforms based on gender issues and human rights can be counted among the most notable endeavours of the civil society in Turkey with respect to societal policy making. Here we must specifically mention the civil code amendments in 2001, the 2004 changes in the penal code which define acts of sexual violence as acts committed against the integrity of individuals and 'not as acts committed against the general morality and family order', and the increase in the terms of punishment for crimes committed in the name of 'honour' (Arat 2001, Altınay and Arat 2009).

The Human Rights Association (İHD, *İnsan Hakları Derneği*), Human Rights Foundation of Turkey (TİHV, *Türkiye İnsan Hakları Vakfı*), Association for Human Rights and Solidarity with the Oppressed (Mazlum-Der, *İnsan Hakları ve Mazlumlar İçin Dayanışma Derneği*), Helsinki Citizen's Assembly (HYD, *Helsinki Yurttaslar Dernegi*), Human Rights Platform (İHOP, *İnsan Hakları Ortak Platformu*), Amnesty International Turkey (UAÖ, *Uluslararası Af Örgütü Türkiye*), Human Rights Agenda Association (İHGD, *İnsan Hakları Gündemi Derneği*), and the Human Rights Institute of Turkey (TİHAK, *Türkiye İnsan Hakları Kurumu*) can be counted among the most influential human rights organizations in Turkey. These human rights organizations have implemented various programs aimed at increasing and improving the use of international human rights mechanisms. İHD, for instance, traditionally focuses on extending civil liberties such as the right to freedom of expression and peaceful association, and on the situation in prisons, torture, disappearances, and political killings. The main forms of İHD activities have recently been monitoring and reporting, lobbying and participating in legislative drafting, providing legal assistance (i.e. to victims of state violence, to internally displaced persons, asylum seekers and refugees), as well as organizing various forms of pickets (International Helsinki Federation for Human Rights, 2007). Mazlum-Der's works focus on similar areas with the İHD; the organization is known to be moderate Islamist. TİHV provides treatment and rehabilitation services for torture victims. All of these organizations publish periodical human rights reports. Most of the applications from citizens of Turkey to the European Court on Human Rights (ECtHR) have been filed by İHD and Mazlum-Der lawyers; the two organizations work closely with the Kurdish citizens in the southeast region of Turkey (Isyar, Keyman and Rumelili 2009). Both Mazlum-Der and TİHV, as well as HYD, were members of the joint committee on human rights (Human Rights Advisory Council) founded by the Government in 2003.

The accession negotiations with the EU, and the need to fulfill the conditionalities for membership such as the necessity to harmonize with the *acquis communautaire* (i) acted as a positive impetus for the state to undertake the legal changes such as the Law of Associations, as well as the civic liberties and gender-based reforms, (ii) helped the civil society organizations to develop their skills and coping mechanisms through the funds it provided, as well as through the joint projects, and networking. It should be noted here that the funding opportunities were regarded as limited by the civil society organizations, and the cumbersome procedures, bureaucracy and lack of transparency were noted as the problems in using these funds (Bikmen and Meydanoğlu 2006: 18). Access to the EU funds was sometimes regarded as problematic by nationalists and/or conservative circles with EU being perceived as a Trojan horse. Thus some civil society organizations chose not to be involved with the EU funding in order to avoid being attacked by these circles (Özkan 2006). Nevertheless both the human rights associations and women's organizations worked through different strategies to become a part of European networks in order to put the reforms related to civil liberties and rights and gender issues to the agenda of the EU institutions. They acted not as passive participants but as active demanders of European standards and norms on human rights and gender issues, and they tried to enter the EU reporting processes in order to make their demands of civil liberties and gender-based reforms more pressing for the government. The 2009 Progress Report, especially in the case of the women's civil society organizations, marks their success in this sense (EurActiv 2009).

Conclusion

As seen in the above discussion of civil society in Turkey, the state-centric Turkish modernity and its organic vision of society acted as the main obstacles to the emergence of civil society, and they continued to hamper its growth as independent of the state and its tutelage well into the 1980s. Moreover, as our historical and thematic account of civil society has indicated, the development of civil society during the 1980s and 1990s occurred under the shadow of the politics of identity/difference. The state, aiming to ensure the secular and territorial integrity by privileging security over democracy, led the state-society relations to be framed increasingly by the politics of identity/difference, and which, in turn, resulted in the abuse of civil society by the state elite, political actors and the politics of identity/ difference. Yet in the recent years, the site of civil society has started to be regarded as a third space formed of associations which can affect the course of state policy. It is promoted as a way of transforming what has been the main obstacle to its development, namely the state-centric Turkish modernity and its organic vision of society; and it is also glorified as a way of contributing to the solution of identity/recognition problems and difference claims within a democratic platform, and, thus, expected to act as the major actor of democratic consolidation.

Despite such high expectations, as discussed in our analysis, the site of civil society in Turkey is still subject to a handful of problems, and the impact of civil society organizations in affecting the course of state policies remains quite limited. Paradoxically, this very moment in which there are high expectations from civil society in terms of its positive role in the democratic transformation process of Turkish modernity, is also the time when the need to initiate a constructive and critical discussion of civil society arises. Such a discussion is timely and necessary for arriving at a civil society which exists outside of state tutelage, which structures and coordinates its actions through the ensemble of its associations, and influences the course of state policy in accordance with the needs of the society as a whole. As Edwards (2004) suggests, revival of civil society necessitates the development of an 'integrative model', which requires that civil society associations not only focus on their own organizational and financial capacity problems, but instead operate by linking their own particular functions with the general aim of contributing to the process of democratization in both national and global domains. Qualitative effectiveness of civil society with transformative power depends on the realization of the double-functions of civil society–civil society as an associational life and civil society as an integral part of a (global, national and local) democratic society–and their simultaneous and reciprocal operation. Today, for the development of an effective civil society in Turkey, we should bear in mind that it is this simultaneous presence of associational life and democratic society from which civil society obtains its transformative power.

Since the year 2000, there has emerged a growing and active civil society in Turkey, which has the capacity of contributing to the good and democratic governance of the country. However, it seems that this capacity of civil society has indeed been limited. For the moment, the civil society in Turkey is far from being truly vibrant, and is not wholly capable of making its necessary contribution to democratic consolidation by yielding social capital, producing alternative solutions to societal problems, generating civic values, and linking itself to society at large. No doubt, civil society has the potential to realize these aims, and play a significant role in the needed democratic consolidation and transformation of Turkey. In fact, as the recent research on civil society in Turkey reveals, even if limited, civil society organizations have begun to play this role effectively. Yet how civil society will contribute to the democratic consolidation in Turkey at large still remains to be seen. It is actually demanding that the state creates mechanisms to facilitate the structural development of the civil society organizations (i.e. fiscal benefits and incentives), improvement of laws and their implementation, active citizenship and citizen involvement in public policy making.

Consolidation of democracy and strengthening and deepening of civil society are indeed mutual and reciprocal processes. The more democracy becomes the only game in town, the more civil society consolidates its presence and importance in the process of democratization, and *vice versa*. A strong and vibrant civil society feeds into democratic consolidation, but it requires from the civil society actors and organizations a commitment to democracy as a process, which requires, as a minimum, the actualization of the five categories/processes set forth by Dahl, as well as the embracement of the integrative model. An autonomous and valued political society with effective and representative political parties, legal guarantees for citizens' freedoms and their active participation in political and public life, a stable and institutionalized economy able to establish at least minimum welfare for the public are key to democratic consolidation as the existence of a vibrant civil society–which invigorates active participation to associational life and produces informed and creative policies to solve societal problems effectively, with a view to contribute to the good and democratic governance of Turkey.

References

Ahmad, F. (2003) *Turkey: The Quest for Identity*, Oxford: One World.

Altınay, A. G. and Arat, Y. (2009) *Violence Against Women in Turkey.* Istanbul: Punto.

Anheier, H.K. (2004) *Civil Society: Measurement, Evaluation, Policy*, London: Earthscan.

Appadurai, A. (1996) *Modernity at Large: Cultural Dimension of Globalization*, MN: University of Minnesota Press.

Arat, Y. (2001) "Women's Rights as Human Rights: The Turkish Case" *Human Rights Review* 3(1): 27–34.

Bikmen, F. and Meydanoğlu, Z. (eds) (2006) *Civil Society in Turkey: An Era of Transition – CIVICUS Civil Society Index Report for Turkey*, Istanbul: TUSEV Publications.

Bilgi Üniversitesi, Sivil Toplum Kuruluşları Eğitim ve Araştırma Birimi (2005) *Avrupa Birliği Müzakere Sürecinde Sivil Toplum Kuruluşları* [NGO's in the European Union Negotiation Process], İstanbul: Bilgi University Publications.

CIVICUS (World Alliance for Citizen Participation) (1999) *Civil Society at the Millennium*, West Hartford: Kumarian Press.

Cohen, J. L. and Arato, A. (1992) *Civil Society and Political Theory*, London: The MIT Press.

Dahl, R.A. (2005) "What Political Institutions Does Large-Scale Democracy Require?" *Political Science Quarterly* 120: 187–97.

—— (1998) *On Democracy.* New Haven: Yale University Press.

Diamond, L. (2008) *The Spirit of Democracy*, New York: Times Books/Henry Holt and Company.

—— (1999) *Developing Democracy: Toward Consolidation*, Baltimore: Johns Hopkins University Press.

Edwards, M. (2004) *Civil Society*, Oxford: Blackwell.

Ehrenberg, J. (1999) *Civil Society: The Critical History of an Idea*, New York: NYU Press.

EurActiv. (2009) "AB raporu'nda Türkiye kadın haklarında hala sorunlu ülke". November 11, 2009. Online. Available HTTP: <http://www.euractiv.com.tr/ab-ve-turkiye/analyze/dr-selma-acuner-ab-raporunda-trkiye-kadn-haklarnda-hala-sorunlu-lke-007752> (accessed 30 June 2013).

Heper, M. (1985) *The State Tradition in Turkey*, North Humberside: The Eothen Press.

Göle, N. (1994) 'Toward an Autonomization of Politics and Civil Society in Turkey', in Heper, M. and A. Evin, A. (eds), *Politics in the Third Turkish Republic*, Boulder, Westview.

152 *Keyman and Kancı*

Gönel, A. (1998) *Önde Gelen STK'lar,* İstanbul: Türkiye Tarih Vakfı Yayınları [Turkish History Foundation Publications].

İçduygu, A. (2007) "The Anatomy of Civil Society in Turkey", in Keyman, E. F. (ed.), *Remaking Turkey: Globalization, Alternative Modernities, and Democracy,* Lanham, MD: Lexington Books.

International Helsinki Federation for Human Rights. (2007) "Human Rights Defenders in Turkey." 1 August 2007. Online. Available HTTP: <http://www.unhcr.org/refworld/pdfid/46963ae5d.pdf> (accessed 30 June 2013).

Isyar, B., Keyman, F., Rumelili, B. (2009) *Kurdish Acts of European Citizenship.* FP7–SSH–2007–1–217504, ENACT: Enacting European Citizenship, Deliverable: WP6. Online. Available HTTP: <http://www.enacting-citizenship.eu/index.php/sections/deliverables_item/288/> (accessed 30 June 2013).

Kalaycıoğlu, E. (2007) "State, Civil Society and Political Participation in Turkey", paper presented at the 48th Annual Convention of International Studies Association, Chicago, Illinois, February 27 – March 3, 2007. Online. Available HTTP: <http://www.isanet.org> (accessed 30 June 2013).

—— (2002) "State and Civil Society in Turkey: Democracy, Development and Protest", in Sajoo, A. B. (ed.), *Civil Society in the Muslim World,* London: I. B. Tauris Publishers.

Kaldor, M. (2003) *Global Civil Society,* Oxford: Blackwell.

Keane, J. (2003) *Global Civil Society,* Oxford: Blackwell.

Keyder, Ç. (1997). "Whither the Project of Modernity?" in Bozdogan, S. and Kasaba, R. (eds), *Rethinking Modernity and National Identity in Turkey,* London: University of Washington Press.

—— (1989) *Türkiye'de Devlet ve Sınıflar* [State and Class in Turkey], İstanbul: İletişim.

Keyman, E. F. (2009) "Globalization, Modernity and Democracy", *New Perspectives on Turkey* 40: 7–27.

—— (2008) *The Good Governance of Turkey.* İstanbul: Bilgi University Publications.

Keyman, E. F. and İçduygu, A. (2005) *Citizenship in a Global World: European Questions and Turkish Experiences,* London: Routledge.

—— (2003) "Globalization, Civil Society and Citizenship in Turkey: Actors, Boundaries and Discourses", *Citizenship Studies* 7, no. 2

Keyman, E. F. and Öniş, Z. (2007) *Turkish Politics in a Changing World.* İstanbul: Bilgi University Publications.

Konrad, G. (1989) *Antipolitics,* New York: Harcourt Brace Javanovic.

Kramer, H. (2000) *A Changing Turkey,* Washington: Brookings Institution Press.

Linz, J. J. and Stepan, A. (1996) *Problems of Democratic Transition and Consolidation.* Baltimore, London: The Johns Hopkins University Press.

Mardin, Ş. (2006) "Center-Periphery as a Concept for the Study of Social Transformation", in Mardin, Ş., *Religion, Society and Modernity in Turkey,* Syracuse, NY: Syracuse University Press.

Ministry of Interior Affairs, Republic of Turkey. (2010) *Derneklere İlişkin İstatistikler.* Online. Available HTTP: <http://www.dernekler.gov.tr/index.php?option=com_content&view=category& layout = blog& id = 52& Itemid = 12& lang = tr> (accessed 30 June 2013).

Özbudun, E. (2000) *Contemporary Turkish Politics: Challenges to Democratic Consolidation,* London: Lynne Rienner.

Özbudun, E. and Keyman, E. F. (2002) "Cultural Globalization in Turkey", in Berger, P. L. and Huntington, S. P. (eds), *Many Globalizations*, Oxford: Oxford University Press.

Özkan, F. (2006) "Muhafazakar Kesimde Kadınlar Artık Hareketli". *Yeni Safak Daily*, May 9.

Rosenblum, N. L. and Post, R. C. (2002) *Civil Society and Government*, New Jersey: Princeton University Press.

Sirman, N. (1989) "Feminism in Turkey: A Short History", *New Perspectives on Turkey* 3, no.1: 1–34.

Sunar, I. (2004) *State, Society and Democracy*, İstanbul: Bahçeşehir University Publications.

Taylor, C. (1990) "Modes of Civil Society", *Public Culture* 3, no.1: 95–118.

Tilly, C. (2007) *Democracy*, Cambridge, New York: Cambridge University Press.

Türkiye Tarih Vakfı Yayınları [Turkish History Foundation Publications] (2003) *AB Uyum Süreci ve STK'lar*, İstanbul.

Türkiye Tarih Vakfı Yayınları [Turkish History Foundation Publications] (2000) *Avrupa Birliği, Devlet ve STK'lar*, İstanbul.

TÜSEV. (2006) *Türkiye'de Sivil Toplum: Bir Değişim Süreci* [Civil Society in Turkey: A Process of Change]. Uluslararası Sivil Toplum Endeksi Projesi Ülke Raporu. Türkiye Üçüncü Sektör Vakfı.

Yarasimos, S. (2000) *Civil Society in the Grip of Nationalism*, İstanbul: İletişim.

8 Democratization in Turkey from a gender perspective

Pınar İlkkaracan

Introduction

At a meeting with 60 representatives from women's organizations on July 18, 2010, Turkish Prime Minister Tayyip Erdoğan said: 'I do not believe in equality between women and men. Sorry! I believe only in equal opportunity for women and men. How can they be equal? Women and men are different, they complement each other.'[1] Erdoğan's statement had a shocking and a freezing effect on women's organizations——as captured by *Cumhuriyet*'s headline 'Words Like Ice' (Kaplan 2010). Despite the criticisms and protests that followed, Erdoğan repeated his statement at a campaign rally in July 2010, and at a party meeting in October 2010 (Oral 2010; Tuksal 2010).[2]

The women's movement in Turkey is considered by many researchers as one of the leading forces in Turkish civil society (Tekeli 1990; Arat 1994; Yeşilyurt-Gündüz 2004; Bikmen and Meydanoğlu 2006). Yet, interestingly, Erdoğan's statements have not yet triggered the level of criticism that would be expected from a women's movement that successfully realized nationwide campaigns and wide-ranging legal reforms over the past decade despite a the strong opposition of various governments. As someone who has been involved in the struggle for gender equality and democratization in Turkey for almost two decades, both as an activist and a researcher, I contend that the slow and less-than-expected reaction to Erdoğan's statements reflect a tiredness, a slowing of reaction and—perhaps—a temporary loss of vitality in the women's movement as a result of the AKP (*Adalet ve Kalkınma Partisi*, Justice and Development Party) Government's insistent conservatism and resistance to implement policies to realize 'actual' gender equality since 2002, despite the extensive legal reforms towards gender equality achieved by the women's movement.

The feminist movement in Turkey has been involved in tireless efforts to establish gender equality in Turkish laws through extensive national campaigns in the last decade. Its hard-won successes include the enactment of the law on protection orders[3] in 1998, the reform of the Turkish Civil Code in 2001, the reform of the Turkish Penal Code from a gender perspective in 2004, and the reform of the Turkish Constitution from a gender perspective in 2010. These campaigns were exemplary in terms of civil society participation in the democratization of law-making processes in Turkey. Yet, despite the strength of the feminist movement and its widely recognized accomplishments, the response of the Turkish state until now has remained far from meeting the demands of the women's movement for gender equality.

Another social movement that has become increasingly vocal in the struggle for gender equality in Turkey is the LGBT movement, which has focused its demands on freedom from discrimination in the legal sphere, police violence against transgender people, and hate crimes. The wide-ranging discrimination that LGBT people face in Turkey—compared to their counterparts in other Western countries—constitutes a significant barrier in formulating their demands for liberties and rights in positive terms rather than negative ones. For instance, issues related to citizenship rights of LGBT people, such as the right to marriage or marriage benefits and the right to adopt or foster children—which top the agenda of Western LGBT movements—have not yet been asserted by the LGBT movement in Turkey. Since 2005, many existing LGBT groups in various cities across Turkey that wanted to make use of the new 'democratic' Law of Associations to establish a legal entity—contrary to their expectations—received threats to be shut down by public authorities on the grounds that they were harmful to 'general morality' and 'protection of the family.'

It seems that the AKP administration's acclaimed ideology of 'conservative democracy'[4] is in fact far removed from conservatism in many aspects—for instance in terms of economic and political institutions or national values, other than family, Islam and morality. Indeed, a conservative attitude towards gender relations seems to be the only pillar of the AKP's conservatism. Moreover, the key role in the creation of this morality is accorded to women, that is, on the morality of women themselves (Çıtak and Tür 2008). While the AKP and its leader Erdoğan are highly praised for their role in Turkey's democratization process by many researchers and commentators at home and abroad, the AKP Government, despite much lip service, undeniably did not perceive the realization of gender equality as an integral component of this process. The AKP administration played a significant role in the Turkish democratization process, mainly by decreasing the role of the Turkish military in Turkish politics, an achievement that has been widely supported by the women's and LGBT movements. However, as this chapter seeks to demonstrate, democratization in terms of gender is excluded from the AKP Government's understanding and definition of democracy despite the EU membership process and its requirements on gender equality.

Despite the growing interest in democracy and the processes of transition to democracy through the third wave of democratization, there is yet little empirical research that has addressed the relationship between democracy and gender equality. The existing research provides conflicting evidence.

Most studies assume a causal relationship, where a higher level of democratization would lead to more gender equality. However, case studies and comparative research provide controversial findings on the issue. For instance, Paxton, who hypothesized that democracies will have more women in parliaments because democracies reduce artificial and arbitrary barriers to power and are therefore more likely to promote the interests of those not in power, found democracy to be either insignificant or in some instances negatively related to women's representation in national legislatures (Paxton 1997). McDonagh finds that democracy is most beneficial to women only when it is combined with the constitutionalized provision of social welfare (McDonagh 2002). Waylen, comparing processes of transition in Latin America and Eastern Europe, also points to the importance of women's strong mobilization as a factor that contributes significantly to democratic transition, especially in the initial phases, as in the case of Latin America (Waylen 1994). However, as the transition proceeds, women might face difficulties in achieving institutional representation, 'especially if' political parties do not place gender issues on the political and electoral agenda and adopt policies expected to appeal to women voters.

The findings of this case study examining the relationship of democratization and gender equality in Turkey strongly supports some of the evidence provided by previous research, in particular that democratization does lead to more gender equality–in fact, the opposite might be the case; and that while a strong women's movement contributes significantly to the democratic transition, as the transition proceeds, women might face severe difficulties in achieving gender equality in institutional representation if political parties do not place gender issues on the political and electoral agenda.

Examining the engagement of women and LGBT activists in the Turkish democratization process, both in terms of their successes and the obstacles they face, I argue that the experience of women's and LGBT movements sheds light on the particular problems regarding the institutionalization of democracy in Turkey.

My analysis is based on NGO reports and press statements, governmental reports on gender equality, statistical indicators, newspaper and media articles, e-mail communications in various gender activist list-servers, and interviews with women and LGBT activists.

The contribution of the feminist movement to Turkey's democratization

The feminist movement in Turkey was the first new social movement to emerge after the military intervention in 1980. According to Tekeli, the feminist movement has played a major role in the democratization process in Turkey as it was not only the first, but also a leading social opposition movement for the democratization process in the aftermath of the 1980 military coup (Tekeli 1990).

A significant achievement of the new feminist movement in Turkey was its criticism of the patriarchal and authoritarian nature of the Kemalist regime. Feminists claimed that women's rights, granted by Kemalists, were rather intended to destroy links to the Ottoman Empire and strike at the foundations of the religious hegemony rather than to promote the actual liberalization of women in everyday life (Tekeli 1982). Thus, women were instrumentalized in line with the Republican ideology–as the 'protectors' of secularism and the 'new Republic'—just as they have been instrumentalized by the conservatives, for whom women serve as 'protectors' of family values and the social *status quo*. Although women were granted many rights on paper, the mechanisms to facilitate the use of these rights were not realized.

Throughout the decades after the new feminist movement emerged in the 1980s, the power and dynamism of the women's movement contributed significantly to the development and extension of a civil society in Turkey. The movement's successes, particularly concerning the legal reforms realizing gender equality in the legal sphere and the EU-accession process have been praised by many researchers (Arat 1994; Yeşilyurt-Gündüz 2004). A major study on the status and progress of civil society in Turkey in the 2000s highlights that women's organizations deserve particular attention for their achievements regarding the progress and impact of civil society:

> Civil society initiatives on a broad array of issues from freedom of expression to criminalization of torture, women's rights or the right to sexual orientation are taking the rights-based agenda to a new level ... Most notable efforts include human rights CSOs [Civil Society Organizations] efforts on expanding civic liberties, and women's CSOs that succeeded in their plight for gender-based reforms to the Turkish Penal Code.
>
> (Bikmen and Meydanoğlu 2006: 14)

Until the late 1990s, the national legislation in Turkey contained various discriminatory provisions and an overarching patriarchal perspective, be it in civil, penal, or labor laws, despite the constitutional gender equality principle,[5] and numerous international documents of which Turkey is signatory.[6] This situation has undergone a rapid change in the last decade, beginning with the adoption of the Law on Protection Orders aiming to prevent domestic violence in 1998, followed by the reform of the Civil Code in 2001, and most recently the Turkish Penal Code Reform in 2004. None of these reforms were easy, ready-made accomplishments for the women's movement in Turkey. Often faced with a combination of resistant conservative forces from parliament and government officials, women's coalitions had to overcome the challenge not only of finding effective and diverse advocacy strategies, but also of making their demands heard and publicizing their agenda in a rather volatile political atmosphere.

The new feminist movement of the 1980s brought the issue of women's human rights in the private sphere to public attention for the first time in Turkish history. The first widespread campaign of the new feminist movement targeted domestic violence.[7] This was followed a year later by another widespread and energetic feminist campaign against sexual harassment and sexual violence; it began in November 1989 with a press conference held on a ferryboat in the Bosporus, the waters separating the two halves of Istanbul, which straddles Asia and Europe. The highlight of the press conference was selling pins sporting purple ribbons, to be used by women to prick harassers. The campaign brought about an important achievement in the legal arena. Article 438 of the Turkish Penal Code, which reduced the sentence given to rapists by one-third if the victim were a sex-worker, was repealed by the Grand National Assembly in 1990. Another legal gain of the first feminist campaigns in the 1990s was the Constitutional Court's annulment of Article 159 of the Turkish Civil Code, which decreed that married women needed to have their husband's implicit or explicit consent to be able to work.

After this point, despite the success of the first campaigns and the foundation of numerous feminist NGOs in the 1990s, no other significant legal change regarding gender equality was realized in Turkey, except for a special law concerning protection orders that aimed to protect victims of domestic violence, which passed in 1998 as a result of another feminist campaign.

Throughout the 1990s, feminist advocacy and lobbying for legal reform in Turkey concentrated mainly on the reform of the civil code, which declared husbands as the head of the family and contained several provisions violating both the constitutional guarantee for gender equality, and international conventions to which Turkey was signatory, such as the Convention on the Elimination of All Forms of Discrimination against Women (CEDAW).[8] Although civil code reform and amendments for gender equality became an issue on the public agenda and several drafts were prepared by various governments after 1984, none of these attempts were concluded until the fully-fledged civil code reform in 2001, which resulted from a broad and intensive campaign by the women's movement.

The reform of the Turkish civil code: The impact of the EU or domestic actors?

After a decade of activism by women's organizations for the reform of the civil code, the coalition Government of the DSP (*Demokratik Sol Partisi*, Democratic Left Party), the ANAP (*Anavatan Partisi*, Motherland Party) and the MHP (*Milliyetçi Hareket Partisi*, Nationalist Action Party) finally prepared a draft civil code integrating women's demands for full gender equality in 2000. Women's groups perceived the civil code reform providing full gender equality as fail-safe. This perception was based on several facts: for one, their years of advocacy for full equality in the civil code seemed finally to be recognized by the Government, which had integrated their demands into the draft. Moreover, the Government enjoyed absolute majority in parliament, thus even if all of the opposition, including the religious-right RP (*Refah Partisi*, Welfare Party), voted against the new civil code, the votes of the MPs in the coalition parties would be sufficient for the acceptance of the Government's draft by parliament. Finally, just a few months before the draft law was expected to be discussed in parliament, Turkey was officially named as a candidate for EU accession in December 1999, a development that was expected to intimidate opponents of gender equality in Turkey.

Despite the supporting evidence, it soon became clear that the optimism of the women's movement was unfounded. As soon as the draft law was submitted to parliament for discussion in April 2000, an alliance of male MPs belonging to the coalition parties took the lead in opposing the clauses aimed at gender equality proposed by their own government. The opposition was led by the MHP, though strongly supported not only by the members of the Islamist opposition, the RP, but also numerous male MPs from coalition parties. They argued that the provisions aiming at equality between men and women would create anarchy and chaos in the family and thus threaten the foundations of the Turkish nation.

After its initial shock, the women's movement was quick to respond. Within a very short time, more than 120 women's NGOs from all around the country joined together to initiate a major campaign, the widest coalition ever formed for a common cause since the emergence of the new feminist movement in the 1980s. The campaign was effective in gaining the support of the media and the public, creating an atmosphere where resistance to equality between men and women was viewed with scorn. In consequence, the opposition had to step back, and the campaign played a key role in the ultimate realization of the civil code reform (WWHR-NEW WAYS 2005). The new Turkish Civil Code, approved by parliament in November 2001, abolished men's supremacy in marriage and established full equality between men and women in the family. It also raised the minimum age for marriage to 17 for both women and men (previously 17 for men and 15 for women); set the equal division of property acquired during marriage as a default property regime, assigning an economic value to women's hitherto invisible labour in the household; allowed single parents to adopt children; and gave equal inheritance rights to children born outside and within marriage. Another gain of the campaign was the amendment of article 41 of the Constitution in October 2001, redefining the family as an entity that is 'based on equality between spouses'.

The reform of the Turkish penal code from a gender perspective

Inspired and motivated by the successful outcome of the campaign to reform the civil code—despite the strong opposition—Women for Women's

Human Rights (WWHR, in Turkish *Kadının İnsan Hakları*), an organization that was one of the coordinators of the civil code campaign, initiated the Women's Coalition for the Reform of the Turkish Penal Code in early 2002, which included representatives of fifteen NGOs and bar associations, as well as academics from the various regions of Turkey.

The coalition was also encouraged by the national program prepared for the government in agreement with the EU on reforms that Turkey pledged to carry out by late 2004 to fulfil EU membership criteria. This program included the reform of the Turkish Penal Code, among others. However, the European Commission was concerned mainly with the abolition of the death penalty, pre-trial detention provisions, and expansion of the scope of freedom of expression in the penal code, and not with issues related to gender equality. Yet, WWHR–NEW WAYS and the Women's Coalition perceived the planned reform of the penal code as a window of opportunity to push for gender equality in the code, especially in terms of women's right to bodily and sexual autonomy.

The 1926 Turkish Penal Code, adapted from the Italian Penal Code of the time, constituted the most striking evidence of the divergence between the rhetoric and practice of the Turkish republic on gender equality. Despite the narrative that the Kemalist regime granted women equal rights, the code included several articles that aimed to protect men's honour and the so-called moral values; sanctioned practices such as honour crimes, and the abduction and rape of women; and constructed women's bodies as the property of their families, husbands and society. Many articles reflected the construction of sexuality, in particular women's sexuality, as a potential threat to public order and morality, and in need of regulation by laws. For instance, all sexual crimes were regulated under the section entitled 'crimes against society', subsection *Adab-ı Umumiye ve Nizam-ı Aileye Karşı Cürümler* (crimes against traditions of morality and family order) instead of under the section 'crimes against individuals'. The regulation of crimes such as rape, abduction or sexual abuse against women as crimes against society, and not as crimes against individuals, was a manifestation of the code's foundational premise that considered women's bodies and sexuality as the property of men, the family or society.

The terminology and phrasing in several articles on the old penal code regarding sexuality referred to traditional notions, all adapted into Turkish from Arabic, commonly associated with religious—i.e. Islamic—morality. The notion of *ırz*, defined by the Ottoman-Turkish dictionary as 'honour' or 'purity,' was the key concept in definition of sexual crimes. For instance, the term used for rape in the code was 'penetrating one's honour', instead of the common word used for rape in Turkish, meaning also violation or attack. If a man who had raped or abducted a woman subsequently married his victim, the code granted a suspension of the sentence (Art. 434), the underlying logic being that while a raped woman suffered a loss of honour, this could be restored and hence the offence undone if the rapist ultimately married her. In cases where a woman or girl under 15 was abducted or raped by a group of men, if one of the perpetrators accepted to marry her, charges against all of them would be dropped (Art. 434). These provisions not only sanctioned the crimes of rape and abduction, but also encouraged men to abduct or rape women who refused them, thus virtually forcing women to marry their rapists in order to preserve their honour. The code assigned less value to unmarried women than to married women. The minimum sentence required for abducting a married woman was seven years of imprisonment, but if the abducted woman was unmarried, the sentence could be anything from three to ten years (Art. 429).

Notions of *haya* (shame) and *ar* (things to be ashamed of, especially in relation to sexuality) were the main criteria for specification of criminal sexual behaviour. An article in the old penal code referring to a general, undefined notion of 'shameless behaviour' provided for up to one year's imprisonment for 'anyone who acts or engages in a sexual relationship without *haya*' (Art. 419). In practice, this article was often used to justify human rights violations by police against LGBT people, although homosexuality was not criminalized by law.

Moreover, while the Code included a very broad definition of sexual behaviours considered criminal, it failed to penalize crimes of marital rape, sexual harassment at the workplace, virginity tests, discrimination based on sexual orientation or sexual crimes by security forces.

In the seventy-eight years following its first introduction in 1926, until its full-fledged reform in 2004, several articles in the old Turkish Penal Code were amended; but except for two, none of these amendments concerned women's rights or women's right to bodily autonomy. The Women's Coalition undertook a thorough review of the penal code and its underlying philosophy, identifying all the articles that violated women's right to sexual and bodily integrity and autonomy. It also prepared a detailed publication with word-by-word formulated articles, new sections and new provisions, with justifications to be integrated in the new law to be sent to all MPs.

As the Coalition continued its work, the November 2002 elections in Turkey ended with a stunning victory for the newly formed AKP. As soon as the new parliament was formed, the Women's Coalition sent its publication—including the thorough review of the old penal code, new word-by-word formulated demands and justifications based on international human rights law and conventions—to all deputies of the AKP and the opposition Republican People's Party, asking for an appointment with Justice Minister Cemil Çiçek to present its work and demands. Repeated requests for an appointment through letters and faxes to the Minister of Justice and other members of government remained unanswered and ignored until two prominent female columnists, Zeynep Oral in *Cumhuriyet* and Ferai Tınç in *Hürriyet*, wrote an open letter to the Justice Minister, criticizing him for not responding to women's organizations' demand for a meeting. Finally, five months later, the head of the Justice Commission,

Köksal Toptan, and several key MPs agreed to meet with coalition representatives on April 28, 2003.

Meanwhile, the Women's Coalition learned that the AKP government had drafted a new penal code. Obtaining a copy of the draft law prepared by AKP proved to be an impossible task. Several formal requests to the Ministry of Justice and to parliament asking for a copy on behalf of the Working Group were left unanswered. The Parliamentary Justice Commission and the government seemed to handle the new draft law as a private initiative to be concealed from the public and from women's NGOs. As it slowly became clear that the coalition would be unable obtain a copy of the new draft law by official means, it resorted to alternatives. A copy of the draft law was finally obtained through the covert action of a liberal journalist friend who had access to certain key people in the AKP administration.

An analysis of the AKP's draft law exposed that none of the group's demands were integrated in the draft; instead, all articles pertaining to women were again copied verbatim from the old penal code. Faced with these dramatic setbacks and intense opposition from the AKP government, the Women's Coalition decided to transform its efforts into a massive public and media campaign; to set up a wider national Platform by the addition of other NGOs that supported its demands; and to raise awareness on the issue throughout the country by organizing conferences and meetings in various cities.

The resulting three-year campaign (between 2002 and 2004) and the accompanying controversial discourses on gender equality, sexuality, and law drew great public and media attention, especially after the Platform's first press conference in May 2003, with several front-page headlines and daily coverage by a majority of newspapers and TV and radio outlets (İlkkaracan, 2010). It triggered numerous public debates and generated the widest discussion on issues related to sexuality in Turkey since the foundation of the Turkish Republic in 1923, and broke several taboos on issues such as the constructions of morality, honour, virginity, sexual orientation and adultery. It was also successful in garnering the support of the majority of the public and the media despite the resistance of the AKP government. Finally, the new penal code was accepted in the TBMM (*Türkiye Büyük Millet Meclisi*, Turkish Grand National Assembly) on the 26th of September, 2004.

The Women's Platform for the Reform of the Turkish Penal Code from a Gender Perspective succeeded in realizing a revolutionary change in the philosophy of the code, from one that regarded women's bodies and sexuality as belonging to their families, husbands, fathers or society, to one that accepts their right to bodily sexual autonomy. As such, it constitutes a leading example of a triumphant advocacy campaign led by civil society–in this case by the Turkish women's and LGBT organizations–that resulted in groundbreaking reforms at the national level despite strong governmental opposition. The campaign was also a pioneering example of an effective democratic opposition initiative that involved a long process of awareness-raising and efforts to gain public and media support in Turkey, and it has been exemplary of a long-term, sustained democratic political bargaining between two politically opposed social actors: feminists and a conservative government.

Yet, just as parliament accepted the new penal code that integrated women's demands, Prime Minister Erdoğan expressed sharp anger towards the campaigners, signalling the first signs of the government's resistance to the reform. At a meeting organized by his party's women's branch, he accused the Women's Platform that had realized the reform of being 'a marginal group that does not have any right to represent the Turkish women', referring to the rally organized by the Platform on the 14th of September, 2004 in front of the Turkish Parliament with the slogan 'our bodies and sexuality belong to ourselves'. He said: 'There were even those who marched to Ankara, carrying placards that do not suit the Turkish woman. I cannot applaud behaviour that does not suit our moral values (*ahlak*) and traditions [...] A marginal group cannot represent the Turkish woman', implying that by demanding ownership of their bodies and sexuality, the campaigners had proved that they were immoral and not worthy of representing 'the Turkish woman'.[9]

Turkey's growing gap between legal and actual gender equality

Despite all the extensive and highly praised legal reforms realized in the past decade ensuring gender equality in the legal sphere, Turkey not only notoriously lags behind in various international indexes related to gender equality, but has also been steadily falling in the rankings since 2006. According to 2009 figures, Turkey ranks 101st out of 109 countries in the gender empowerment measure (GEM) of the United Nations Development Program (UNDP) and 129th out of 134 countries in the Global Gender Gap Report of the World Economic Forum (UNDP 2009; Hausmann, Tyson and Zahidi 2009). According to the 2009 Gender Equity Index (GEI) of Social Watch, Turkey is among the countries that have been in severe regression since 2004 in terms of gender equity (Social Watch 2009).

Turkey has been steadily falling in the rankings, especially since 2006. For instance, in the gender empowerment measure (GEM) ranking of the UNDP, Turkey ranked 64th in 2000, 72nd in 2006 and 101st in 2009. In the Global Gender Gap Index of the WEF, Turkey held the 105th place in 2006, was 123rd in 2008 and 129th in 2009, while more than two-thirds of 115 countries included in the report have posted gains in overall index scores (Hausmann, Tyson and Zahidi, 2009). The deterioration in these indexes shows that despite the wide-ranging legal reforms in the past decade, there has been a steady decline in these measures to the disadvantage of women, accelerating especially since 2006. Thus, a close look at various gender equality measures common to these indexes–women's participation in political and decision-making mechanisms, women's participation in the labour force and the gender gap in education–requires special attention. Below, I provide a review of recent statistics, as well as–the lack of–present government policies on these issues to reflect on factors that lead to the wide gap between gender equality in the legal sphere and actual gender equality.

Women's participation in political and decision-making mechanisms

Turkey ranks very low in terms of women's participation in political and decision-making mechanisms compared to many other countries. The percentage of women in parliament in Turkey rose from 4.2 per cent in 2001 to 9.1 per cent in 2010. Yet, Turkey ranks 92nd in 190 countries with regard to the rate of women's representation in parliaments, after 2011 elections, the rate of women in the TBMM is 14.3 per cent (most of them members of AKP) remaining below the average of all regions but Pacific countries, and being close to the average of the Middle East and Arabic countries, which is 14.9 per cent (as it is shown in the web of Inter-Parliamentary Union, 2012).[10] Women's participation in local governments in Turkey is even worse. Only 2 of 81 greater municipalities have a female mayor after 2009 elections. The total number of women mayors is 27 out of total number of 2,948 mayors, according to a 2012 report by the Department for Women's Status (KSGM, *Kadının Statüsü Genel Müdürlüğü*).[11]

Apart from factors such as the lower educational and economic status of women compared to men, and the extreme burden of care on women, there are numerous structural obstacles to women's political participation in Turkey. A major reason is that the area of social responsibility for women has been defined as the family and women's major role as wife, mother and caregiver. A public perception survey conducted in Turkey among members of political parties and parliaments before the 2007 general elections shows that the roles given to women politicians replicate those they held at home and in their communities.[12] Thus, gender stereotypes play a significant role in deterring women from participating in the political sphere. The AKP government's conservative policies and various statements by government officials serve to further exacerbate such gender stereotypes. A major dispute between Prime Minister Erdoğan and the women's movement has been his call to women in 2008 that every Turkish woman should bear at least three children, to stop the Turkish population from decreasing. Although he has been extensively criticized for it, Erdoğan has repeated this call many times in recent years (Can 2008; Yener and Kaya 2010).[13]

Political parties do not consider women's representation in the political sphere as an issue of democracy, and lack the political will to increase women's participation in political processes. Women's branches of political parties, which aim to increase women's participation in political life, are not perceived as effective organs of decision-making processes in the party, but rather as insignificant secondary units. They do not even have the authority to suggest female candidates as representatives to the Grand National Assembly or as a member of party executive boards. In order to change this situation, new legislation on political parties is essential. While the number of women candidates remains low, in cases where women do become candidates, they face various obstacles. They are usually selected as candidates on the lists where they have no chance to be elected.

Under these conditions, the major solution to increasing women's participation in political and decision-making mechanisms lies in applying supportive policies like gender quotas (TÜSIAD, 2001). Other necessary measures include the reform of the Law on Political Parties to allow for more democratic decision-making mechanisms in political parties and lowering the 10 per cent threshold in elections. Yet, improvement on these matters does not seem to be forthcoming in the near future. Various demands by the women's movement for political quotas for women have been vehemently rejected both by various women's ministers and by Prime Minister Erdoğan since 2002. The AKP government is also resistant to a reform of the Law on Political Parties or lowering the election threshold of 10 per cent, although these are demands made not only by women's organizations, but many national and international institutions as well, the EU included.

Women's participation in the labour force

Women's employment rate in Turkey is the lowest among the OECD (Organization of Economic Cooperation and Development) countries. Female employment is declining in absolute terms, and the number of women that stay out of labour force is increasing rapidly. From 1995 to 2006, total female employment dropped by 166,000 (Toksöz 2007). The percentage of women in the labour force has been steadily falling in the past two decades, from 36.1 per cent in 1989 to 30 per cent in 1999, and to 24.5 per cent in 2008 (Turkstat 2009). A joint report by Turkey's State Planning Organization and the World Bank refers to this situation as the 'puzzle of low female labour participation in Turkey' despite the increasing level of women's education, women getting married at a later age, the declining fertility rate and the changing attitudes towards working women (State Planning Organization and World Bank 2009: 1). The report states that many women in Turkey would like to work, but face many difficulties that prevent them from doing so. Women without university education, especially in urban areas, generally have access to jobs that offer low wages, require long and hard working hours, and do not provide social security.

The low rate of women's employment in Turkey is widely recognized as a significant and urgent problem that requires an urgent solution by major civil society organizations or international bodies, including the EU, the International Labour Organization and the United Nations Committee on the Elimination of Discrimination against Women (TÜSİAD 2000;

TÜSİAD and KAGİDER 2008; CEDAW 2005; Toksöz 2007; Commission of the European Communities, 2008). Yet, despite various calls and demands both from domestic and international actors, the AKP government has failed to develop and implement policies regarding the recruitment, promotion, and on-the-job training for women in work life, or to oversee and eliminate the gender gap in wages (TÜSİAD and KAGİDER 2008). Buğra and Yakut-Cakar note that the AKP Government seems to be faced with a trade-off between continuing adherence to patriarchal values, and the objective of increasing women's labour force participation (Buğra and Yakut-Cakar, 2010).

In this context, it should also be mentioned that the already low level of women's access to social security has been further curtailed during the AKP era. Between 2006 and 2008, the AKP administration's neoliberal restructuring of Turkey's social security system through the adoption of a new law on social security and health insurance drew intense criticism from civil society groups, mainly the Labor Platform and the Initiative to Improve Women's Labor and Employment, and academics. The new Law on Social Security and General Health Insurance[14] is criticized as privatizing social security; curtailing the rights of the working population and worsening the situation of the most disadvantaged (Buğra 2007; Coşar and Yeğenoğlu 2009). Women, already among the most disadvantaged, were further excluded from the new social security system. Revisions made under the guise of establishing formal equality based on EU directives, included the elimination of articles that had offered positive discrimination to women, though they were not replaced by new incentives to improve women's situation in the labour force. Thus, the law in fact contributes to existing gender inequalities in society (KEİG 2008, Kılıç 2008; Savran 2008). Despite widespread criticism and protests – mostly ignored by the Government – the law was passed in April 2008.

An example of recent AKP policies that constitute a further barrier to women's participation in the labour force instead of eliminating them, is the Government's major policy change since 2007 regarding the care of the disabled and the elderly, prioritizing and promoting family-based care through cash transfers to unemployed family members–which should be read as women–instead of care provided at public or private institutions. Cash transfers for care have become popular in many developing countries in the last decade, as the policy is also supported by the World Bank. They are framed as a measure for poverty alleviation, rather than as a tool for facilitating care. An inevitable problem with such an approach is that it is gender and class biased. That is, as payments are very low, women who have little or low earning power or are unemployed are most likely to take them up.

While some might argue that cash transfers can be a form of poverty alleviation for poor women, such measures will contribute to their being further excluded from the labour force and public life, and also strengthen existing gender inequalities, as they make care a duty for poor women, reducing their chances for employment even more and reinforcing traditional gender roles. Cash-for-care policies have particular disadvantages when considered from a gender equality perspective, including absolving the state of its responsibilities for care, and shifting the burden of care to women through very low payments that do not allow for social security or employment rights and thus reinforce traditional gender roles that depict women as natural caregivers (Daly 2001: Molyneux 2007; Razavi 2007; Kabeer 2008).

In addition to the disadvantages of cash-for-care policies for women cited above, an analysis of the AKP model for care shows that it has an additional characteristic that differentiates it significantly from models in other countries, working even more to the disadvantage of women; namely, the cash assistance for care requires the beneficiaries – mostly women – to be unemployed. By making it conditional that the caregiver should be unemployed, the AKP policy significantly clashes with the government's declared aim of increasing the extremely low rate of women's participation in the labour force in Turkey.

Gender discrimination in education

Closing the gender gap in education still constitutes a major challenge for Turkey. In theory, primary school attendance is compulsory for eight years and free of charge. Across the country, however, there were gender gaps of 8 per cent in primary education and 17 per cent in secondary education according to 2003 figures (Otoran et al. 2003). The gender gap in primary education has since closed by 15 per cent due to various efforts by the government, but a great deal of work remains to be done if the Millennium Development Goals (MDGs) of universal primary education and gender equality are to be achieved, according to a UNICEF report (UNICEF, 2010). A comparison of the gender parity index (GPI) for all three education levels shows that the gender gap in education becomes much more pronounced in higher education.

Gender stereotypes constitute a significant obstacle to closing the gender gap in education. Education, particularly in lower income bracket and rural areas, is seen as irrelevant or in conflict with the accepted roles of girls and women in society. The enrolment of boys is preferred to girls, particularly in cases where a choice between the two has to be made. Early marriages, which are still very common despite the legal minimum age of 17, constitute another factor that negatively affects girls' access to education.

According to a UNICEF review of gender and education in Turkey, gender discrimination is frequently observed in education processes as well. Research indicates that teachers tend to overlook issues as to whether or not their schools are male-dominated, or question the gender biased content in textbooks. Thus, it is possible to conclude that schools in Turkey actually contribute significantly to the reproduction of traditional gender roles. Textbooks still contain elements that attribute an active role to men and a passive role to women. The teaching of stereo-typical gender roles also occurs within the scope of literacy courses for adults. Course materials often perpetuate and reinforce the traditional roles that prevail amongst learners (Otaran et al. 2003). Yet, despite the requirements put forward by various international documents and con-ventions Turkey is signatory to, such as the Beijing Plan of Action or CEDAW, and various advocacy efforts by the women's movement, no effective gender cleansing of the curriculum, textbooks or teacher-training materials has taken place until 2010.

To summarize, a review of statistical measures on women's participation in political and decision-making mechanisms, women's participation in the labor force and the gender gap in education, which are common to various gender equality or gender gap indexes, show that while such measures reflect significant discrimination against women and girls in these areas, policies to realize actual gender equality and eliminate such discriminations in Turkey are either non-existent or unsatisfactory, and in some cases, even contra-dictory or detrimental for gender equality.

Certainly, there are many other issues to be considered regarding Tur-key's failure to implement measures to realize de-facto gender equality; for instance, its notorious inadequacy in developing and enforcing procedures to prevent domestic violence against women, although the legal framework is progressive and in line with many EU countries. Despite the enactment of the Law on the Protection of the Family enabling protection orders for victims of domestic violence in 1998 as a result of feminist campaign between 1995 and 1998–earlier even than some other European countries such as Germany, Turkey has failed to enact effective policies for the enforcement of this law. In a landmark decision of the European Court of Human Rights (ECHR), *Opuz vs. Turkey*, Turkey was found guilty not only of not providing mechanisms to protect women from domestic vio-lence, but also of 'discriminatory judicial passivity' that creates 'a climate conducive to domestic violence' and the state's 'insensitivity in preventing gender discrimination against women'.[15]

Another interesting example is a court case which Nimet Çubukçu, former Minister for women, filed against women's activists for faxing pro-tests on gender inequality to parliamentarians. Çubukçu sued four repre-sentatives of three leading women's organizations[16] at an Ankara court in 2004, claiming that they had committed the offence of insult for criticizing her for opposition to their demand of an article to the Turkish constitution that 'the state is responsible for taking all necessary measures to realize de-facto equality between women and men'. Interestingly, shortly after the court case, which was widely criticized by the women's movement, the media and the public at the time, she was appointed as the State Minister responsible for Women's Affairs by the Prime Minister Erdoğan in June 2005. After her appointment as the Women's Minister, Çubukçu refused to withdraw her complaint against the women activists despite criticisms identifying her as 'the only women's minister of the world who has a court case with women's organizations' (Armutçu 2006). The women activists were finally acquitted by the Ankara 10th Court of First Instance in April 2006, as the prosecutor in the case concluded there was no intent for insult on part of the defendants who were using their right to criticism, which he referred to as 'democratic expression', and demanded their acquittal on the charges. The judge agreed with the prosecutor's argument. Upon that, Çubukçu's lawyer informed the court that the Minister would no longer pursue the case (Durukan, 2006).

The incidents portrayed above exemplify the present severe controversies between the women's movement and the AKP government on the under-standing, definition and scope of gender equality, as well as policies required to achieve its realization.

The struggle of LGBT people for recognition and democratization

The lack of recognition of LGBT people and their rights, despite an LGBT movement that has been increasingly successful in voicing its demands in the public sphere, illustrates Turkey's failure to integrate demands by minority groups for equality in the democratization process. The demands of the LGBT movement are still regarded as marginal issues. The leaders of the LGBT movement in Turkey name the misrecognition of LGBT people as 'the last denial of the Turkish Republic' (Erol 2008).

In fact, since 2005, all LGBT groups in Turkey that aspired to utilize a new Law of Associations, which was supposed to support the transition to democracy—contrary to their expectations—were sued to be shut down by public authorities on the grounds that they threaten 'general morality.' Many LGBT groups, including KAOS GL and the Pink Life Association in Ankara; The Rainbow Association in Bursa; Lambda in Istanbul; and Black Pink Triangle in Izmir, which applied to officially register as a non-governmental organization, faced official law suits for their closure. In almost all cases, public authorities cite Article 56 the Turkish Civil Code and Article 33 of the Constitution, which stipulate that freedom of association can be restricted on ground of general morality, among others and to protect the family, respectively. In some cases, they also refer to articles of EHRC on 'general morality' and 'morals' as possible grounds of restriction of freedom of association in the case of LGBT organizations. In all of the cases, the LGBT groups succeeded in winning the cases, yet, in some cases, this proved to be a quite hard and exhausting process. For instance, Lambda Istanbul had to go through a very tough three-year court case to be finally registered as a non-governmental organization.

It is worthwhile noting that the term used for morality (*genel ahlak*) in Turkish laws differs from the terms used in Western or international law (public morality or morals). The correct translation of 'public morality' into Turkish would be *kamu ahlakı*. However, *genel ahlak* can be translated into

English as 'general morality', a term roughly meaning morality as accepted by the majority of a society. 'General morality', in contrast to 'public morality', blurs the distinction between the private and the public, leaving it open to various interpretations based on one's subjective prejudices or values.

An exhaustive analysis of the legal context regarding LGBT rights and human rights violations against LGBT people is beyond the scope of this paper, therefore my aim below is rather to briefly sketch the legal situation of LGBT people in Turkey, in particular on issues related to the lack of anti-discrimination provisions and the often arbitrary application of various laws and statutes used to discriminate against LGBT people and groups. While there are no laws that criminalize homosexuality in Turkey, Turkey does not recognize same-sex marriages, civil unions or domestic partnership benefits for gay and lesbian couples.[17] A 1982 decision of the Supreme Court ruled that lesbian mothers cannot have the custody of their children. This decision has set a precedent for further decisions regarding custody rights of lesbian women.

Since the Campaign for the Reform of the Turkish Penal Code between 2002 and 2004, the LGBT movement in Turkey has been advocating for various anti-discrimination provisions in the Turkish Constitution and other laws. As of 2010, there are no laws or provisions that aim at preventing discrimination or violence against LGBT people in Turkey. Although the European Commission Directive 2000/78/EC explicitly demands Turkey to enact an anti-discrimination legislation on the ground of sexual orientation in the Labour Law within the framework of Turkey's accession process, such a legislation has not yet been realized.[18] As the new Labour law was enacted in 2003, provisions for prohibition of anti-discrimination on grounds of race, religion and disability were added to the Article 5 of the law, however, anti-discrimination on grounds of sexual orientation and age, also required by the directive, were left out.[19] The lack of anti-discrimination provisions on the basis of sexual orientation has been criticized by various progress reports of the European Commission on Turkey since 2002, including the 2008 Progress Report (Commission of the European Communities 2008).

Various laws and statutes are used to discriminate against gay, lesbian, transgender and transvestite people. Article 225 of the Turkish Criminal Code on 'public exhibitionism' is often misused by security forces as grounds for harassment, abuse, violence, detention or criminal charges against transvestites or transsexuals who are dressed as females (Altıparmak and Öz 2007, Human Rights Watch 2008). Legislative changes in recent years have given the police additional authority to arrest people based on perception or prejudice. The 'Misdemeanor Law' (*Kabahatler Kanunu*) which was passed by the AKP government and entered into force in March 2005 states that it 'aims to protect public order, general morality, general health, the environment, and the economic order'.[20] The law has given the police additional powers to misuse their authority to arrest or fine transgender or transvestite people based on prejudice, for example with fines starting from 58 YTL, recently raised to 140 YTL. Furthermore, the Law on the Powers and Duties of the Police (*Polis Vazife ve Selahiyet Yasası*) was amended in June 2007, for the first time formally giving the police discretionary powers to stop and ask for identification in order to 'prevent a crime or a misdemeanor (*kabahat*)'. As a recent Human Rights Watch report states, these discretionary powers substantially increase the scope of policing without judicial scrutiny in Turkey, by leaving how 'general morality', 'public order' or 'misdemeanor' can be interpreted to the authoritative power of the police, thus providing them with the authority to limit (or violate) human rights (Human Rights Watch 2008). The provisions in legislation that include 'general morality' and are often used to violate the human rights of LGBT people and groups require special attention. Reference to 'general morality' in various laws, for example in the Turkish Civil Code, or laws regulating the duties of the police as mentioned above, lead to serious human rights violations of LGBT people and groups, as well as arbitrary restrictions of their rights (Altıparmak and Öz 2007).

The AKP Government's policy towards LGBT people has ranged from non-recognition to absolute discrimination, in a rather increasingly hostile fashion. On the eve of International Women's Day in 2010, Turkey's women's minister, Selma Aliye Kavaf, triggered a huge public debate and garnered wide criticism by declaring that she believes homosexuality is a biological disorder, which should be treated, in an interview she gave to the daily *Hürriyet*. In the same interview, she accused women's organizations of exaggerating domestic violence in what they perceive as violence (Bildirici 2010). Other criticisms against the minister included her seeming tolerance for violence. She stated, 'I only watch "Kurtlar Vadisi" (The Valley of Wolves)', a popular television series about the mafia and 'deep state' affairs, in which scenes of murder and torture are common. Her comments came only shortly after she had been broadly criticized for stating her discomfort with kissing and love scenes in Turkish soap operas, which in her belief were inappropriate for Turkish family values.[21] Kavaf was protested widely by the country's LGBT movement and women's groups through press statements and demonstrations, demanding her resignation and trial for insult, and incitement to enmity and hate crimes against LGBT people (Jones 2010). The LGBT association KAOS GL in Ankara filed a criminal complaint against the minister at the Office of the Ankara Public Prosecutor for inciting the public to hatred and hostility against homosexuals according to Articles 216 and 218 of the Turkish Criminal Code.

A positive development, on the other hand, is the increasing support for the LGBT groups and organizations by other social movements, including an ever-growing collaboration between the LGBT and women's movement and the support of two major worker's unions, the Confederation of Progressive Trade Unions (DİSK, *Türkiye Devrimci İşçi Sendikaları Konfederasyonu*) and Public Employees Trade Union (KESK, *Kamu Emekçileri Sendikaları Konfederasyonu*) for LGBT demands.

Conclusion

A strong and dynamic women's movement since the 1980s has significantly contributed to the democratization process in Turkey through its intense criticism of the patriarchal and authoritarian nature of the Kemalist regime, extension of civil society and realization of wide ranging legal reforms for equality between women and men, including the enactment of the law on protection orders in 1998, the reform of the Turkish Civil Code in 2001, the reform of the Turkish Penal Code from a gender perspective in 2004, and the reform of the Turkish Constitution from a gender perspective in 2010. Yet, despite the strength of the feminist movement and its widely recognized accomplishments, the response of the Turkish state until now has remained far from meeting the demands of the women's movement for actual gender equality. The AKP Government's conservative ideology has played a significantly negative role in resisting the implementation of recently realized legal reforms or adapting holistic policies to increase de-facto equality between and men. It seems that the AKP administration's acclaimed ideology of 'conservative democracy' is in fact far removed from conservatism in many other aspects–for instance in terms of economic and political institutions or national values–but is rather based on a conservative attitude towards gender relations.

A clear evidence of the AKP's government's resistance to developing policies to improve gender equality in line with the reformed laws is the fact that Turkey has been steadily falling in rankings of various international indexes related to gender equality since 2006. An analysis of statistical measures – women's participation in political and decision-making mechanisms, women's participation in the labour force and the gender gap in education, common to various international gender equality or gender gap indexes of UNDP, World Bank or Social Watch show that while women are faced with multiple discriminations in these areas, policies to realize actual gender equality or to eliminate such discriminations in Turkey are either non-existent or unsatisfactory, and in some cases, even contradictory or detrimental for gender equality.

The LGBT movement has also become increasingly vocal in the last decade, focusing on demands for freedom from discrimination in the legal sphere and freedom from police violence and hate crimes. Yet, they are faced with even increasing social discrimination during the AKP era, as exemplified by the Women's Minister Kavaf's remark that homosexuality is a disease that should be treated on the eve of the International Women's Day in 2010. Since 2005, all LGBT groups in Turkey that aspired make use of a new and supposedly more democratic Law of Associations to officially register as non-governmental organizations, faced legal suites for their closure by public authorities on the grounds that they threaten 'general morality.' All groups have won the legal suites until now, succeeding in registering as NGO's, yet it seems that the political struggle for the recognition of LGBT people and their rights will increasingly become a topic of public and political debates in the near future.

Obviously, gender equality constitutes the weakest point of the Turkish democratization process in the present political context. Examining obstacles to, and problems of, the democratization process in Turkey through the lens of the experiences of the women's and LGBT movements that contributed significantly to the Turkish democratization process, this chapter sheds light on problems of institutionalization of democracy in Turkey.

Notes

1 The author was present at the meeting.
2 'Yaratılışımız Farklı Bayan' (We are Created Differently Misses), *Bugün*, October 17, 2010; 'Kadının Çilesini Anamdan Biliyorum' (I Know Women's Suffering From My Mother), *Hürriyet*, November 6, 2010.
3 'The Law for the Protection of the Family', Law no. 4320.
4 In 2003, a year after it came to power, the AKP constructed a new ideology under the motto of 'conservative democracy', declared as the party's ideological manifesto through the publication of a book titled *Conservative Democracy* by one of Prime Minister Erdoğan's chief consultants, Yalçın Akdoğan. See Akdoğan (2003).
5 Article 10 of the Turkish Constitution.
6 For example, the Convention on the Elimination of All Forms of Discrimination against Women (CEDAW) or The Universal Declaration of Human Rights.
7 In February 1987, a judicial ruling cited the Turkish proverb 'one should not leave a woman's back without a stick or her womb without a baby', and rejected a woman's application for divorce on grounds of domestic violence. This triggered a feminist campaign against domestic violence.
8 Turkey ratified CEDAW in 1985, with several reservations but with a promise to remove them shortly; yet this was not realized until 2002.
9 'Türk Kadınını, Marjinal Bir Kesim Temsil Edemez' (A Marginal Group cannot Represent the Turkish Woman), *Zaman*, September 25, 2004.
10 http://www.ipu.org/wmn-e/classif.htm
11 http://www.kadininstatusu.gov.tr/upload/mce/trde_kadin_2012_ekim.pdf
12 'Turkey Needs Affirmative Gender Policies', *New Horizons*, 52, April 2010.
13 'Erdoğan Yine 3 Çocuk İstedi', *Yeni Şafak*, October 26, 2010.
14 *Sosyal Sigortalar ve Genel Sağlık Sigortası Yasası*, Law no. 5510, which became effective on the 1st of October, 2008.
15 ECHR, *Opuz c. Turquie*, No: 33401/02, 9th of June, 2009. Online. Available HTTP: <http://www.echr.coe.int/NR/rdonlyres/3483DE4C-3CCC-4DCB-ACC4-A24CBABFB9E5/0/Rapport_annuel_2009_versProv.pdf> (accessed 30 June 2013).
16 The four women activists were from Women for Women's Human Rights (WWHR)–NEW WAYS, the Women's Solidarity Foundation, and the Amargi Women's Cooperative.
17 In comparison, a total of 24 European countries have legalized same sex marriages, civil unions or other forms of recognition for same-sex couples as of 2009.
18 Council Directive 2000/78/EC of 27 November 2000, Establishing a General Framework for Equal Treatment in Employment and Occupation, *Official Journal of the European Communities*, L 303/16, December 2, 2000.
19 The EC Directive states that the principle of equal treatment in the area of employment covers disability, religion or belief, sexual orientation and age.

174   *Pınar İlkkaracan*

20 *Kabahatler Kanunu*, Law No. 5326, Article 1, enacted March 13, 2005.
21 'Homosexuality is a Disease Says Turkish Minister', *Hurriyet Daily News*, March 7, 2010.

References

Altıparmak, Özlem and Öz, Yasemin (2007). "Türk Hukuk Mevzuatında LGBTT Bireylere Yönelik Ayrımcılık Yaratan Düzenlemeler" [Regulations that Discriminate against LGBTT Individuals in Turkish Statutes], unpublished report.
Akdoğan, Yalçın (2003). *Muhafazakar Demokrasi* [Conservative Democracy], Ankara: AK Parti Yayınları, 2003.
Alvarez, Sonia E. (1990). *Engendering Democracy in Brazil: Women's movements in transition politics.* Princeton: Princeton University Press.
Arat, Y. (1994). 'Toward a Democratic Society: The Women's Movement in Turkey in the 1980s', *Women's Studies International Forum*, 17 (2/3): 241–48.
Armutçu, E. (2006). 'Kadın Örgütleriyle Değil, Bazı Kadınlarla Sorunum Var' [I Have a Problem Not with Women's Organizations, Only with Some Women], *Hürriyet*, February 12, 2006.
Bikmen, F. and Meydanoğlu, Z. (2006) *Civil Society in Turkey: An Era of Transition*, Civicus Civil Society Index Country Report for Turkey, Istanbul: TÜSEV Yayınları.
Bildirici, F. (2010). 'Eşcinsellik Hastalık, Tedavi Edilmeli' [Homosexuality is an Illness, Must Be Treated], *Hürriyet*, March 7, 2010.
Buğra, A. (2007). 'AKP Döneminde Sosyal Politika ve Vatandaşlık' [Social Policy and Citizenship in the AKP Era] *Toplum ve Bilim*, 108: 143–66.
Buğra, A. and Yakut-Çakar, B (2010) 'Structural Change, the Social Policy Environment and Female Employment in Turkey', Development and Change, 41 (3), pp. 517–38.
Can, E. (2008). 'Attali'den Erdoğan'a 3 Çocuk Uyarısı' [Attali Cautions Erdoğan against 3 Children] *Referans*, May 15, 2008.
CEDAW (Committee on the Elimination of Discrimination against Women) (2005) 'Concluding Comments: Turkey', CEDAW/C/TUR/CC/4–5, New York: United Nations CEDAW.
Commission of the European Communities (2008) 'Turkey Progress Report 2008', SEC (2008) 2699 final, Brussels, November 5, 2008.
Coşar, S. and Yeğenoğlu, M. (2009) 'The Neoliberal Restructuring of Turkey's Social Security System', *Monthly Review*, April. Online. Available HTTP: <http://www.monthlyreview.org/090420-cosar-yegenoglu.php> (Accessed May 30, 2009).
Çıtak, Z. and Tür, Ö. (2008) 'Women between Tradition and Change: The Justice and Development Party experience in Turkey', *Middle Eastern Studies* 44 (3): 455–69.
Daly, M. (2001) *Care Work: The Quest for Security.* Geneva: International Labor Organization.
DİSK (2009) 'Özgürlükçü-Eşitlikçi, Demokratik ve Sosyal Bir Anayasa İçin Temel İlkeler Raporu' [Report on the Fundamental Principles for a Libertarian-Egalitarian, Democratic and Social Constitution], Disk Yayınları, no: 57. Istanbul: Türkiye Devrimci İşçi Sendikaları Konfedarasyonu (DİSK).
Durukan, A. (2006). 'Women Activists Acquitted in Insult Case', *Bianet*, April 19. Online. Available HTTP: <http://bianet.org/english/women/77916-women-activists-acquitted-in-insult-case> (Accessed 17 June 2010).

Erol, A. (2008). 'Cumhuriyetin Son İnkarı: Eşcinsel Realitesi' [The Last Denial of the Republic: the Homosexual Reality], *Birgün*, November 17.

Friedman, E. J. and Hochstetler, K. (2002) 'Assessing the Third Transition in Latin American Democratization: Representational regimes and civil society in Argentina and Brazil', *Comparative Politics*, 35 (1): 21–42.

Hausmann, R., Tyson, L. D. and Zahidi, S. (2009) *The Global Gender Gap Report.* Geneva: World Economic Forum.

Human Rights Watch (2008) 'We Need a Law for Liberation: Gender, Sexuality, and Human Rights in a Changing Turkey', New York, Human Rights Watch.

İlkkaracan, P. (2010) 'Re/forming Laws to Secure Women's Rights in Turkey: The campaign on the penal code', in Gaventa, J. and McGee, R. (eds), *Citizen Action and National Policy Reform.* London: Zed Books, pp. 195–216.

Jaquette, J. S. (1994) *The Women's Movement in Latin America: Participation and democracy.* Boulder: Westview Press.

Jones, D. (2010) 'Turkish Activists Want Minister Tried for Derogatory Comments on Gays', *Deutsche Welle*, March 16.

Kabeer, N. (2008) *Mainstreaming Gender in Social Protection for the Informal Economy.* London: Commonwealth Secretariat.

Kaplan, E. (2010). 'Buz Gibi Sözler' [Words Like Ice], *Cumhuriyet*, July 19, 2010.

KEİG – Kadın Emeği ve İstihdamı Girişimi (2008) *Sosyal* Sigortalar ve Genel Sağlık Sigortası Yasa Tasarısı Kadınlara Nasıl Bir "Sosyal Güvenlik" Vaat Ediyor? [What Does the Law on Social Security and General Health Insurance Promise Women in Terms of "Social Security?] Istanbul: KEİG.

Kılıç, A. (2008) 'Toplumsal Cinsiyet Gözüyle Sosyal Politika Reformu' [The Social Policy Reform from a Gender Perspective] *Toplum ve Hekim*, 23 (5): 396–400.

McDonagh, E. L. (2002) 'Political Citizenship and Democratization: The gender paradox', American Political Science Review, 96 (3), pp. 535–52

Molyneux, M. (2007) 'Change and Continuity in Social Protection in Latin America: Mothers at the Service of the of the State?', UNRISD *Gender and Development Programme* paper no: 1, Geneva: United Nations Research Institute for Social Development (UNRISD).

Oral, Z. (2010) 'Kadın Hareketi mi? Hadi Canım … ' [Women's Movement? Come On …], *Cumhuriyet*, July 25, 2010.

Otoran, N., Sayın, A., Güven, F., Gürkaynak, İ. and Atakul, S. (2003). *A Gender Review in Education.* Ankara: UNICEF.

Paxton, P. (1997) 'Women in National Legislatures: A Cross-national Analysis', *Social Science Research*, 26 (4): 442–64.

Razavi, S. (2007) 'The Political and Social Economy of Care in a development Context: Conceptual Issues, Research Questions and Policy Options', UNRISD Gender and Development Programme, paper no: 3, Geneva: United Nations Research Institute for Social Development (UNRISD).

Savran, G. A. (2008) 'SSGSS, Görünmeyen Emek ve Feminist Politika' [SSGHI, Invisible Labor and Feminist Politics], *Amargi* 8: 16–19.

Social Watch (2009) *Social Watch Gender Equity Index 2009*, Montevideo: Social Watch.

State Planning Organization and World Bank (2009) 'Social and Economic Benefits of More and Better Job Opportunities for Women in Turkey'. Online. Available HTTP: <http://siteresources.worldbank.org/ECAEXT/Resources/Turkey_FemaleReport_3_pager_final_final.pdf> (Accessed 31 March 2010).

Tekeli, Ş. (1982) *Kadınlar ve Siyasal Toplumsal Hayat* [Women and Socio-political Life] Istanbul: Birikim Yayınları.

—— (1990) '1980'ler Türkiye'sinde Kadınlar' [Women in Turkey in the 1980s] In Tekeli, Ş. (ed.), *Kadın Bakış Açısından 1980'ler Türkiye'sinde Kadın* [Women in Turkey in the 1980s from a Gender Perspective] Istanbul: İletişim Yayınları.

Toksöz, G. (2007) *Women's Employment Situation in Turkey*, Ankara: International Labour Office.

Tuksal, H. Ş. (2010) 'Kadın Erkek Eşit Değil mi?' [Are Women and Men not Equal?], *Star*, October 21.

Turkstat (2009) *Statistical Indicators 1923–2008*, Ankara: Turkish Statistical Institute.

TÜSİAD, Türk Sanayicileri ve İşadamları Derneği (2000) *Kadın–Erkek Eşitliğine doğru Yürüyüş* [The March towards the Equality of Women and Men] Istanbul: TÜSİAD.

—— (2001) *Towards Gender Equality: Education, Working Life and Politics*. Istanbul: TÜSİAD.

TÜSİAD and KAGİDER – Türkiye Kadın Girişimciler Derneği (2008) *Türkiye'de Toplumsal Cinsiyet Eşitsizliği: Sorunlar, Öncelikler ve Çözüm Önerileri* [Gender Inequality in Turkey: Problems, Priorities, and Proposed Solutions], Istanbul: TÜSİAD and KAGİDER.

UNDP (United Nations Development Program) (2009) *Human Development Report 2009*, New York: UNDP.

UNICEF (2010) 'UNICEF in Turkey: Country profile'. Online. Available HTTP: <http://www.unicef.org/turkey/ut/ut2_2010.html#nt14> (Accessed 7 April 2010).

Waylen, G. (1994) 'Women and Democratization: Conceptualizing gender relations in transition politics', *World Politics*, 46 (3): 327–54.

Women for Women's Human Rights-NEW WAYS (2005) *Turkish Civil and Penal Code Reforms from a Gender Perspective: The success of two nationwide campaigns*, Istanbul: WWHR-NEW WAYS.

Yener, T. and Kaya, S. (2010) 'Erdoğan: En az 3 tane çocuk istiyoruz' [Erdoğan: We Want at Least 3 Children], *Hürriyet*, July 19, 2010.

Yeşilyurt-Gündüz, Z. (2004) 'The Women's Movement in Turkey: From Tanzimat towards European Union membership' *Perceptions*, 9, Autumn 2004: 115–34.

9 The Istanbul art scene – a social system?

Marcus Graf

Introduction

Visual art has always been an action of a minority for another, mostly educated minority. Nevertheless, the state of an art scene shows the state of democratization and modernization. It can function as an important parameter for illustrating the situation of a civic society. If the scene is not socially engaged and integrated it can only play a minor role in the democratization and modernization process. It is obvious that except for film, art has never been popular, and has never been a media for the masses. Though, since the 1990s, contemporary artists, curators, theorists and art managers increasingly deal with the question of how to integrate art into social life. Current biennials, museum shows and large scale exhibitions, often present artists who deal with political and social issues and imagine alternative models for a liveable civic society.[1] Nevertheless, the audience they reach is limited and the general social impact is of minor importance compared to other actors of our visual culture like film or pop stars.

This chapter discusses the socio-political dimension and role of visual art in the history of Turkey from the first westernization of the Ottoman Empire in the middle of the nineteenth century through the various phases of Turkey's modernization in the twentieth century until its current status quo, that is to say, under the impact of internationalization and globalization. While reflecting shortly on art's various functions for the *saray*, the state and the public, this chapter also concentrates on the interconnection between artistic and social developments in Turkey by reviewing the history of public exhibitions. As the exhibition space is the meeting point of the artist and the public it is per se a communication platform, in which artistic and social processes intermingle and is regarded as a Social Space by Nina Möntmann (Möntmann 2002: 109) in the Operating System Art by Thomas Wulffen (Möntmann 2002: 12), where it becomes, following Hans Dieter Huber a Social Construction (Huber 2007: 10), which deals with art as a Social Medium as Niklas Luhmann states (Rebentisch 2003).

The text concentrates on the situation of visual art in Istanbul by making a short and exemplary analysis of certain parameters in its art scene such as art education, the art market or exhibition institutions. Here, it must be underlined that the art community in Istanbul is better financed and more strongly developed than in other cities of Turkey and therefore cannot easily be compared with the situation in Anatolia.

After analyzing some aspects of governmental art and cultural policies, the focus will move to the Istanbul Biennial, as an example of an important civil art initiative dating from the late 1980s. Finally, insight will be given into the current state of the art system, its audience, artistic education, governmental support for the arts, as well as the danger of its unbalanced sponsorship system and cultural *festivalization.*

A few thoughts on the politics and social integration of art in western countries

During the progress of European modernism, art gained freedom by demanding an independent system. The slogan 'art for art's sake' liberated the artists from the former patrons in the religious and royal contexts. During the evolution of modernism in the eighteenth century, the artist changed from a court-artist to an exhibition-artist. He/she now was supposed to be a free person whose work belonged to the people (Bätschmann 1997: 6). First in central European countries, art then claimed to be a social system, as it developed its own education (academy), its own language and review system (art criticism), its own science and research field (art history), its own space (museum, gallery, exhibition space) and its own market creating its own value system (art market) (Schmidt 1987: 10). This system is today both interwoven with other social systems as well as to a certain degree autarchic. That is why art and culture became a differentiated industry and a very important factor of the socio-economy in the so-called developed and post-industrial countries, where often spectacle, excitement and entertainment help the public swallow the difficult and sometimes bitter pill called contemporary art.[2] In this context, art institutions and biennials, for example, have to struggle with the paradox of being a forum for reviewing society, a platform for showing the latest trends in art as well as being an instrument that is promoting the (cultural) life of the city and entertaining its audience on a high level (Graf 2008).

A few thoughts on the social dimension of the ottoman and Turkish art scene since the nineteenth century

The history of modern art in Turkey can be divided into *Westernization* (Ottoman, mid-nineteenth century), *First Modernization* (early Turkish Republic, 1923–1950), *Second Modernization* (1950–1980s), and *Third Modernization* (1987–today). The text will now point out some important historical events that played major roles in the development of the art scene and its interconnection with society.

During the period of Westernization in the nineteenth century, art styles and cultural behaviors from central Europe played an influential role in the cultural politics and the artistic life at the Ottomans court. After 1839, the reforms caused by the *Tanzimat-i Hayriye* (Administrative Reforms) aimed to change the visual appearance of the Ottoman Empire in order to integrate into a close relationship with European partners France, Germany, and Italy (Steinbach 2003:18). During this period, the Empire not only tried to bring western technologies and industries into the country, but also foreign artists and art styles. After the first exhibition held in 1845 by the Austrian artist Oreker at the Saray of Sultan Abdülmecit, who himself was a talented painter, gradually, a group of Ottoman and foreign painters started to work, teach and exhibit in Istanbul. In this context, since the nineteenth century, various educational institutions like the school of engineering (*Mühendishane-i / Berr-i Hümayun*, 1795), the military academy (*Mekteb-i Harbiye-i Şahane*, 1834) the medical school (*Mekteb-i Tibbiye*, 1835) as well as the educational institution for orphans (*Darüşşafaka*, 1873) began to give painting lessons. Initially, the classes were characterized by a mainly formal and technical focus on the use of geometrical projection, perspective or map drawing, but later, these schools started also to teach free painting (Tanyeli 2003: 84). Some successful soldier-painters such as Osman Hamdi Bey or Şeker Ahmet Paşa were sent for a couple of years to France to study in the studio of orientalist painters like Jean-Léon Gérome. The most important event in the 19th century was the opening of the art academy *Sanayi-i Nefesi Mektebi* in 1882, which was responsible for the education of western orientated painters. According to Mustafa Cezar, the academy was to teach painting in a country whose only traditional figurative art was miniature paintings that where concealed from public view in the libraries of sultans and statesman. The academy was also to play an important role in preparing the ground for the modernization of society in Turkey through these artists and their work (Cezar 2004: 9). Compared to Europe, a time-difference of more than 300 years exists since the first European academy, the Academy of the Arts of Drawing (*Accademia delle Arti del Disegno*), promoted by the first art historian Vasari and protected by Cosimo dei Medici, opened in 1563 in Florence. From the beginning, the Ottoman art academy was solely focusing on and teaching western painting styles like Orientalism and Neo-Classicism. Until the present, this tradition of western orientated education is predominant at Turkish art academies, which are today integral parts of universities.

Besides the state-built and organized art academy, some civil art initiatives were important for artistic development as well as for the social integration of art. In 1873 to show works of Ottoman and foreign painters, the first public art exhibition in the history of Ottoman art was organized by Şeker Ahmet Ali Paşa in Beyoğlu. Besides this, in 1874, the painter Pierre Desire Guillemet, for example, opened a private art academy in Beyoğlu, Istanbul. At the beginning of the twentieth century, the Second *Meşrutiyet*

(Constitution) marked a fundamental break in social history, because it loosened censorship and widened the scope for freedom of speech and expression in public. This positively influenced the development of art. As a result, the Ottoman Painter's Union (1909) was formed, which printed the Ottoman Painter's Union Newspaper and from 1916 onwards organized the Galatasaray Exhibitions (Gören 2003: 83).

We see that during the period of Westernization, the art and cultural scene in the Ottoman Empire was deeply influenced by foreign artists and art practices. As a tool for cultural as well as socio-politics, it was directly instrumental in the first attempts at modernization of the country and for the Westernization process.

Since the 1923 ending of the sultanate and the declaration of the Turkish Republic through Mustafa Kemal, during the actual first phases of Modernization, art and culture played an even more direct fundamental role in reforming the country and creating a new nation. Links to the Ottoman Westernization continued as the new government also mainly imported western art styles like Post-Impressionism and Realism as well as oriented itself on predominant cultural behaviors of the West. At the same time, it forbade traditional cultural behaviors such as Islamic dress as well as the Islamic judicial system and Arabic writing. During this early period of the Turkish Republic, art helped to shape and modernize the country according to the canons of Kemalism. On January 1, 1923, Mustafa Kemal declared in public that a nation without painting, sculpture and scientific research would not be able to claim a place in the modern world (Sanlier 2003: 105). According to Ahmet Kamil Gören, an attempt to create a new nation, and in this process to include all relevant institutions was taking place (Gören 2003: 82). Besides opening art museums in Ankara (1930) and Istanbul (1937) with collections of modern Turkish artists, the state organized exhibitions like the *İnkkılap Sergileri* (Exhibitions of the Revolution) (1933 – 1936), *Yurt Gezileri ve Sergileri* (National Tours and Exhibitions (1938 – 1943) or *Devlet Resim ve Heykel Sergileri* (State Painting and Sculpture Exhibitions) (since 1939). Especially the Yurt Gezileri ve Sergileri illustrated the cultural policy of the state to use art for reformation. Since they were given the opportunity to witness first-hand the physical and human geography of Anatolia, Erol Turan stresses that these excursions into Anatolia made it possible for Turkish artists, who were then overwhelmingly concentrated in Istanbul, to break out of the confines of the clichéd picturesque of the city and its environs. That an artist and his art should go to the people to gain strength from the dynamics of national energies were notions generally supported by the Republican intellectuals. It was also believed that all the arts should make efforts to promote the ideologies of the 'new way of life' and 'new culture' that were envisaged from the beginning of the Republic (Erol 1998: 8). The official state declaration of its cultural policy supports Turan's thesis. On the fifth of September 1923, the government announced that the organization of national culture was to be given primary emphasis and national education should be based on national culture. A cultural administration was founded that began to research various fields, to install national museums, to collect national works, and to support the development of national creativity and art (Katoğlu 2003: 180). The stressing of the word 'national' in connection to the establishment of art institutions shows that the state understood the power of art in forming a visual culture to support the process of *Türkleştirme* (Turkification or becoming Turkish in a Turkish nation) and the construction of the country according to the ideology of Kemalism (Kortun and Kosova 2004: 88).

During the second phase of modernization, the Turkish art scene started to develop a more differentiated system. As the 1950s showed the end of the one-party system, and the beginning of a multi-party system, the Turkish art scene began to create original artistic strategies parallel to developments in the West and formed civil art institutions and festivals.[3] Since it constructed a constitution that supported the production of art publications and art exhibitions outside the official national galleries where young artists had started to exhibit, the first of the military coups that took place on May 27, 1960, made a strong impact on the Turkish art scene (Özsezgin 1989: 407). Furthermore, due to the rising level of political conflicts that often resulted in violent eruptions between right and left wing factions, artists became more socially and politically engaged. At the former art academy now known as Mimar Sinan University, Altan Gürman became a leading figure for introducing contemporary art practices to a conservative academic environment (Erdemci 2007:47).

On March 12, 1971, the second military coup that aimed to stop the escalation of violent political conflicts, forced the Prime Minister Süleyman Demirel to resign. A new and stricter constitution was formulated resulting in the imprisonment of numerous artists and intellectuals. Nevertheless, the new changes to the constitution could not prevent the ongoing conflicts and over 5.000 people in politically motivated homicides lost their life by the end of the 1970s. In spite of the difficult social, economic, and political situation, due to the innovative work of gallery founders like Yahsi Baraz (Gallery Barz) or Rabia Capan (Maçka Art Gallery), from as early as 1975 notable development of the art gallery sector took place (Tanzug 2003: 362). Also due to the work of Sarkis and Füsun Onur, more contemporary art practices such as installation art were introduced to the Turkish art scene. Turkish artists born after 1945 helped the public become interested in contemporary art allowing a foundation for a slowly evolving art market to develop. In addition, a general increasing positive attitude towards art was noted (Turani 1989: 311). Nevertheless, in Turkey a professional system for the collection of art did not yet exist (Gören 2003: 93).

Seen as a trauma by many Turkish artists and intellectuals, the third military coup took place on the 12th of September 1980 and lasted for two years (Kortun and Kosova 2004: 91). Subsequently, in the following years, political or critical discussion was forbidden or restricted and the highly politicized youth of the 1970s was forced to become an a-politic generation during the 1980s. Censorship was strict and all artistic or intellectual expression was evaluated according to the canon of the military that was seen as the protector of Kemalism. This resulted in a nationalistic, closed art scene, in which the remaining local artists produced elitist, non-political and conceptual art works (Kortun and Kosova 2004: 18).

The 1980s were a diffuse and complex period for Turkey. After the restrictive period of military dictatorship, dating from the mid 1980's onwards and beginning with the political era of Turgut Özal, the country developed a neo-liberal economic system and opened its borders to foreign companies. At the same time conflict between the PKK (*Partiya Karkerên Kurdistan*, Kurdistan Worker's Party) and the military led the country especially in the southeast towards civil war. Simultaneously, neo-conservatism and Islamism was on the rise. Nevertheless, this 'opening' of the economic system influenced developments in the Turkish art scene (Kortun and Kosova 2004: 18).

Important exhibitions during this period were the *Sanat Bayramı* (Art Festival) at Mimar Sinan University as well as the *Günümüz Sanatçıları* (Artists of today) competition exhibition. In both shows, a younger generation of artists doing experimental work found a forum for their work. Although at the opening it did not receive much attention or appreciation, the most important art event was the 1987 1st International Istanbul Biennial that is still organized by the Istanbul Foundation for Culture and Art (İKSV, *İstanbul Kültür Sanat Vakfı*).

The International Istanbul Biennial and its socio-political impact on the civic society

As one example of a cultural institution, which plays a major role in the Turkish art scene as well as in its civic society, I would like to review the Istanbul Biennial regarding its sociopolitical impact. It is a fundamental part of the Turkish art scene, in which since 1987, every two years, at different locations within the old and modern part of Istanbul, the inhabitants and thousands of foreign visitors have had the chance to experience the latest forms and concepts of contemporary art as well as plural facets of the city. Since its first organization, it introduced first western and now international contemporary art to the local scene, promoted Turkish art to the global network and presented Istanbul as a modern, open minded and democratic city, which is merged with the evolution of European art and culture.

The International Istanbul Biennial was born in a time of rapid social and political transition. Historically situated at the end of the Cold War and before the biennial boom of the 1990s, it opened its doors to a public currently experiencing an explosive mixture of right and left extremism, economic liberalism and religious fundamentalism. In this social context, the

Figure 9.1 Istanbul Biennial, Former Feriköy Greek School, 2009. Photo by
Marcus Graf

International Istanbul Biennial strived to promote the further evolution and
improvement of Turkish society through contemporary local and international art. It aimed at developing an exchange between the Turkish and the
international art world in order to enhance the national art scene and art
market as well as the city of Istanbul itself. The need for an inter-cultural
and inter-artistic exchange to lead Istanbul out of its isolation from the
international art world spurred its organization (Eczacıbaşı 1987: 10).

Looking at points of conceptual and formal references and comparing it
to other large-scale exhibitions, in a politico-cultural sense, the International
Istanbul Biennial showed more parallels to the 1st documenta in Kassel
than to the 1st Venice Biennial, the mother of all biennials originally developed by the city Government of Venice to honor the King and his marriage.
Inspired by the success of the world exhibitions of the nineteenth century in
London and Paris, the Venice Biennial aimed at being a platform for cultural and artistic exchange as well as an art competition. Designed to be a
huge and glamorous art festival, it became an exhibition of national culture
and propaganda as well as a place for international comparison. The Documenta on the contrary was organized as a counter-exhibition to the fascist
exhibitions '*Entartete Kunst*' (Degenerated Art) and '*Grosse Deutsche Kun-
stausstellung*' (Great German Art Exhibition) held in 1937 in Munich. Since
the end of fascism, Germany aimed to reunite with Europe and again play
an important role in the evolution of international modernism, for Werner

Haftmann, the documenta served the welfare of Germany. Through this international artistic exchange, Germany not only faced its recent past, but also became familiar with the contemporary tendencies of other European countries. In other words, the documenta aimed to make the nation familiar with its modern past as well as the developments of the neo-modern present in Europe.

In particular, the motivation for the International Istanbul Biennial shared similarities with documenta's function in post-war Germany of the 1950s. Likewise, the founder and president of the board of directors of IKSV, Nejat F. Eczacıbaşı, stressed the biennial's aim to be an international and intercultural exchange in the first exhibition catalogue. Sezer Tansuğ, a prominent art critic of the time, idealistically concluded that the Turkish artist would perhaps for the first time, be able to reach the status he deserves in the world (Tansuğ 1987: 25).

Seeing itself as a follower of the ideological path of Mustafa Kemal Atatürk, the International Istanbul Biennial wanted to be a politico-cultural instrument for the promotion of the national art scene as well as to propel the (western) modernization process of society. Also having internal artistic goals, it aimed to introduce international contemporary art to the Turkish people and the local art scene in order to change its conservative, sometimes hostile attitude towards today's artistic strategies. The International Istanbul Biennial wanted to create interest in contemporary art, acceptance of its strange, often difficult and yet unknown character as well as build a platform to analyze and discuss today's art. Through the exhibition, Turkish artists should be able to gain easier access to the international network of artists, curators, critics, museum directors, gallery owners, and collectors. In this way, it aimed to bring the local art world in touch with the international art scene, to internationalize its characteristics into the Turkish context, and attract foreign collectors thus strengthening the local art market. For this reason, during the first and second biennials, galleries from Istanbul and Ankara participated in the exhibitions. Since the 1990s, cultural spectacle and artistic entertainment has been used as an urban marketing strategy for city promotion, the biennial played an important role in presenting Istanbul as a modern metropolis. Nevertheless, neo-orientalistic tendencies could be seen in this exhibition series that underlined Istanbul's function as a bridge between the Orient and Occident by using this cliché as the conceptual core. With the exception of the third biennial, during its first years, in general, the International Istanbul Biennial aimed to create a modern and western orientated image while at the same time, attaining international attention by using neo-oriental clichés to construct a post-oriental identity.

My investigation over the last year shows that some concrete problems endangered the realization of these goals. After 26 years, there is still no substantial governmental financial support. This makes the biennial extensively dependent on corporate or private sponsoring. A system dependent on the good will of sponsors hinders the formulation of criticism and brings the

Figure 9.2 Istanbul Biennial, Antrepo Nr. 3. Photo by Marcus Graf

degree of self-censorship into question. Furthermore, limited collaboration with the city's various municipalities prevents a deeper and more effective involvement of the biennial into everyday city life. In addition, the organizational team of the biennial needs to be enlarged, its working conditions facilitated, permanent exhibition spaces must be found, and the financial situation improved in order to ensure a professional and sustainable situation. Since a main part of the biennial workforce consists of freelance, low-paid assistants and employees, the motivation of its workers and the execution of the exhibition is adversely affected. Nevertheless, the successful work and individual efforts of a few individuals, especially those in the biennial office and on the production team who share a deep belief in the importance of the biennial guarantees the success of the International Istanbul Biennial.

The comparatively low number of visitors to the biennial proves that it is not as yet integrated into public awareness and consciousness and is still an alien event in Istanbul. Of course, the fact that the number of visitors has increased from around 10,000 at the first biennial to 110,000 including around 10,000 foreigners at the 12th biennial proves the event to be a success on its own terms. This significant increase in numbers also shows a general tendency towards popularization and social integration of the biennial. Nevertheless, when we take into account the increased amount of public relation efforts including a huge number of posters, television spots, and free entrance for students, the number of visitors at the International Istanbul Biennial compared with other western biennials shows it is not yet fully accepted by the public. Since there is still an underdeveloped art market with only a few professional working galleries, Istanbul appears uninteresting as a place to either buy or sell artwork. Conservative, sometimes hostile older generations of non-biennial or anti-biennial artists, some of whom teach at the various art academies in Istanbul, prevent the possibility of a closer interconnection between the academies and the biennial. The lack of governmental or private funding for residency programs or intercultural exchange programs prevents an international interconnection of artists, curators and researchers.[4] Furthermore, the struggle and cost of acquiring a passport and a visa often prevents the free flow of Turkish artists traveling abroad.

The Istanbul Biennial as catalyst

Since Istanbul attracts artists and visitors, beginning with the first organization in 1987, the lure of the city itself outbalanced the many financial, organizational, and conceptual difficulties of the International Istanbul Biennial. This attraction was one of the main reasons that this young biennial became one of the most popular among artists and visitors. After going through an initial phase of strong local hostility, my investigation of relevant articles written in the national and international press proved that the International Istanbul Biennial could create a firm and important place in the local art scene. Since the 1990s, the international press in particular has been favorable towards the International Istanbul Biennial and has seen a positive impact on the Turkish art scene. In recent years, the International Istanbul Biennial has been evaluated as one of the strongest and most important biennials in the world and even described as being in the same league with Venice.

The biennial also plays an important socio-political role in the representation of Turkey. Especially during the 1980s and 1990s, a period of increasing religious fundamentalism and political extremism, the biennial was seen by the foreign press as an important symbol of the western orientated elite's claim that Turkey is a modern, democratic and liberal society.

After a phase of polemic during the first three biennials in the mid-1990s, the biennial has sparked a lively discussion between modern and postmodern artists, or biennial-artists and non-biennial artists, who have become more professional. Art historical and art theoretical research has been enhanced in recent years by the numerous panel discussions, publications and research projects about the biennial and its context.

Every two years, the International Istanbul Biennial functions as a catalyst for the whole art scene. The more than 40 exhibitions and symposiums normally organized during the biennial prove this assertion. As Ahu Antmen pointed out during the 2003 International Association of Art Critics (AICA) conference, 'Art Criticism and Curatorial Practices, East of the EU', the impact on the younger generation of artists and art students is significant. She describes the biennial as an 'art magazine' for students in which alternative

Figure 9.3 Istanbul Biennial, Antrepo Nr.3 (above), Antrepo Nr. 5 (middle and bottom). Photo by Marcus Graf

concepts and forms of contemporary art are legitimized and later used by students as direct links to or inspiration for their own production of 'biennial art' (Antmen 2004: 251).

Until the exhibitions 'Centre of Gravity' (2005) and 'Venice–İstanbul' (2006) curated by Rosa Martinez for the Istanbul Modern Museum, the International Istanbul Biennial was the only opportunity for the Turkish art scene to see large-scale exhibitions showing contemporary foreign art. Since 2001, a number of exhibition spaces, commercial galleries and museums have been opened and today a lively exhibition scene exists in Istanbul. Local as well as an increasing number of foreigners can now find venues to show their works. Regardless of this situation, since most of the museums and exhibition spaces present either classic-modern or national-local artists, the International Istanbul Biennial is still the most important institution exhibiting contemporary, international art in Turkey.

In addition, the biennial gave numerous young people the chance to step into the contemporary art world. The fact that thousands of young Turks worked as assistants for the biennial and came into direct contact with contemporary art and artists underlines the socio-cultural meaning of the biennial for the past 26 years. Already in 1999, during the 6th biennial, both former biennial directors, Fulya Erdemci and Melih Fereli, realized that 'the Biennial […] opened many doors for our artists [Erdemci] [and] caused an enormous acceleration of artistic development in our country [Fereli]' (Erdemci 1995).

The current situation of the art scene in Istanbul

According to Christoph Tannert, the Turkish art scene has found it easier to overcome the general crisis of the period directly following the Cold War than other countries of the Balkans or former USSR. It has even turned this difficult time of reorientation into a chance for strengthening itself (Tannert 2004: 14). The 1990s showed the emergence of a new generation of young artists, who worked in a more conceptual, ironical and critical fashion. Artists like Hale Tenger or Halil Altındere were no longer afraid to create socially and political engaged works. At the same time, the younger generation had a stronger international orientation than the previous ones (Kortun and Kosovo 2004: 9). Also, at the end of the 1990s the artist Selda Asal (*Apartman* Projects) as well as the curator Vasıf Kortun (Istanbul Contemporary Art Projects) opened the first alternative off-space galleries. In these spaces artists and art lovers could experience a platform for a non-exclusive and non-elitist discussion of art. Functioning as catalysts for the communication and social integration of contemporary art, these types of non-profit and non-governmental spaces have been very common since the 1970s in the western art scene. Even though today more than 15 art initiatives and off-spaces exist in Istanbul, since they cannot rely on official support and funds, the general engagement of the public, officials or possible sponsors is low, their future is uncertain, and their social impact limited.[5] Nevertheless, providing a platform for artistic experiment and freedom, they are meaningful for the local art scene. For many young curators and artists, these off-spaces provide the only opportunity for presenting their work. Also, for foreign artists, and EU supported art projects from abroad, spaces like 5533, Pist or Galata Perform function as bridges to the local art community.

Since the beginning of the millennium, hosting the largest number of art institutions and exhibitions, Istanbul became the capital of contemporary art in the country. Still, artists today are struggling with various hegemonies under a conservative government. The academies are traditional, the general art market is underdeveloped, and as they assume the former role of the art patrons, sponsors attempt to use art as a form of public relations (Graf 2009). In Istanbul, we see the local art scene being used as an attraction, as a symbol and also as a kind of entrance-ticket to the club of global cities. The International Istanbul Biennial is in this context the strongest symbol for promoting Istanbul as an established modern and western city that is developing into a global metropolis (Yardımcı 2005). Shaped by inner and outer migration and emigration, western metropolises shelter huge numbers of minorities and foreigners who live together in these cultural cosmopolite areas. In contrast, in Istanbul, we see a huge impact from inner migration and a very low impact from foreign immigration. Compared with Berlin, New York, and London, Istanbul still has a low number of foreigners who live and work in the city. At present, only a few foreign owners run galleries

Figure 9.4 Istanbul Biennial, Antrepo Nr.3, 2012. Photo by Marcus Graf

and just a few international collections exist. As yet, Istanbul does not have an international art museum. Not yet having become a part of a global network of communication, trade 'and' culture, with artists free to travel as global citizens, the art scene is still shaped by national art and cultural production (Cameron 2003). Global citizenship open to western artists who have access to supporting funds, social security systems and passports requiring no visa for travel abroad, remains closed to young Turkish artists who lack these parameters. The expensive involved in getting a passport and the difficulties encountered when attempting to obtain a visa makes these simple tasks impossible.

Since 2005 the artwork exhibited in the Istanbul biennials showed that today's art is deeply engaged in political, social and urban discussions. Contemporary art can function as a communication medium for reviewing the given socio-political status quo and constructing proposals for a 'better' way of living. In 2007, the title of the 10th Istanbul Biennial 'Not only possible but necessary: Optimism in the age of global war', and the title of the 11th Istanbul Biennial 'What keeps Mankind Alive?' clearly showed the socio-political scope of the exhibitions, which were looking for answers to the today's various crisis. Functioning as a fundamental part of the platform on which a civic and civil society stands, it supplies information needed for surviving in times of global crises (Yuko Hasegawa) and also serves as an important tool for the ongoing modernization and democratization processes in Turkey (Hasegawa 2001). To achieve this, a balanced relationship among the three important players of the art scene is required. The government should provide the laws that guarantee contemporary cultural policies, corporate sponsors and partners should provide financial and infrastructural support for the art scene and art initiatives should increase the public participation in art. Since governmental support is missing and off-spaces, art initiatives and art associations are low in number and weak in power, a very unbalanced situation exists in Istanbul. Most exhibition spaces and museums either belong to companies or are financed by them. The Istanbul biennial, e.g. generally receives around 5 per cent (mostly in-kind) support from the municipalities, 25 per cent from foreign ministries and cultural institutions and 70 per cent from local and international sponsors.

Conclusion

This text pointed out that visual arts in Turkey has always had a strong connection to cultural political interests with the aim of strengthening the position of the country and presenting it as a modern nation among the others of the Western sphere. A comparative analysis between fifteenth century onwards European and North American art and exhibition history and that of the nineteenth century onwards late Ottoman and Turkish Republic proves that due to the lack of interested Turkish politicians, the failure to integrate art into society, the weakness of the art market and the poor infrastructure of the art system, the Turkish art and exhibition scene has not as yet developed a sustainable relationship with society and cannot be evaluated as a fully developed social system. Nevertheless, since 2001, rapid progress with an increase in professionalism and differentiation in the Turkish art and exhibition scene can be recognized. The Turkish art market that depends on private and corporate sponsorship resembles the North American rather than the European art and cultural model.

The analysis of the Istanbul Biennial has shown that its impact on the local art scene is fundamental and caused a change in the production and reception of contemporary art. Therefore, it is an important motor within the Turkish art scene that propels the evolution of art and culture. At the same time, it is an important socio-political tool for the integration of contemporary art in society.

In order to create an effective and critic civic society within Istanbul, the number of off-spaces and art initiatives has to be increased, funds have to be provided and in order to create an audience for integrating art in society, art education in schools has to be strengthened.

Notes

1 See e.g. the 10th and 11th Istanbul Biennial as well as the 10th and 11th documenta.

2 Fort the Turkish context see: Yardımcı, S. (2005), *Kentsel Değişim ve Festivalizm, Küreselleşen Istanbul'da Bienal*, Istanbul: Iletişim Yayınları.
3 In contrast to the time before the 1950/ 60's, in which the Turkish art scene was mainly concerned with a delayed import of western styles, some Turkish art experts consider the period after the 1950's as the beginning of a real modernity inside the Turkish art scene, because the artists would work increasingly deal with original themes and concepts.
4 Exceptions are the residence program at the art centre *Garanti Platform* and the bilateral 'Transfer' program between NRW, Germany and Turkey.
5 See e.g.: Aylık, A. Apartman Projesi, Artık, Atıl Kunst, BAS, Caravansaray, Daralan, Hafriyat, Galata Perform, Kop-Art, Masa, Nomad, Pist, Oda Projesi, Videoist, 5533.

References

Antmen, A. (2004) 'Discussion Session 2' in Madra, Beral (ed.), Istanbul: Art Criticism and Curatorial Practices, East of the EU, AICA TR.
Bätschmann, O. (1997) *Der Ausstellungskünstler*, Köln: DuMont, Köln.
Cameron, Dan (2003) *Poetic Justice*, in: Istanbul Foundation for Culture and Arts (Ed.), *The 8th International Istanbul Biennial* (Exhibition Catalogue), Istanbul Foundation for Culture and Arts, Istanbul.
Cezar, M. (2004) *From the Academy of Fine Arts to Mimar Sinan University*, in Mimar Sinan University (Ed.): *Sanayi-i Nefise Muallimleri Resim ve Heykel Sergisi*, Promat, Istanbul.
Eczacıbaşı, N. F. (1987) 'Why Contemporary Istanbul Exhibitions? ... ' in Istanbul Foundation for Culture and Arts (Ed.), *1. International Contemporary Art Exhibitions*, Istanbul: Istanbul Foundation for Culture and Arts.
Erdemci, F. (1995) 'Ali'ce Now/ Here' in Istanbul Foundation for Culture and Arts (ed.), *The 4th Istanbul Biennial* (exhibition Catalogue), Istanbul: Istanbul Foundation for Culture and Arts.
—— (2007) *Büyü Bozmak, Yeniden-Yön Vermek*, in: *Modern ve Ötesi*, Istanbul: Istanbul Bilgi University.
Erol, T. (1998) *Yurt Gezileri ve Yurt Resimleri*, Istanbul: Milli Reasürans T.A.S.
Gören, A. K. (2003) 'Cumhuriyet'in İlk Yıllarında Sanata Yaklaşım ve Sonuçları', *Sanatdünyamız*, No. 89, Spring.
Graf, M. (2008) *From the Periphery to the Centre* in European Culture Association (Ed.), *After All, Herşeyden Sonra*, Istanbul: Mimar Sinan Güzel Sanatlar University.
—— (2009) "Sanat ve Kültür Politikaları", in Outlet (ed.), Istanbul: Dersimiz Güncel Sanat, Outlet.
Hasegawa, Y. (2001) *7th International Istanbul Biennial*, in Istanbul Foundation for Culture and Arts (ed.), *The 7th International Istanbul Biennial* (Exhibition Catalogue), Istanbul: Istanbul Foundation for Culture and Arts.
Huber, H. D. (2007) *Kunst als soziale Konstruktion*, München: Wilhelm Fink.
Katoğlu, M. (2003) 'Cumhuriyet'in İlk Yıllarında Sanat ve Kültür Hayatının Oluşumunda Kamu Yönetiminin Rolü', *Sanatdünyamız*, No. 89, Spring.
Kortun, V. and Kosova, E. (2004) *Abseits aber Tor*, Jahresring 51, Köln: Walter König.
Kosovo, E. (2004) *Abseits aber Tor*, Jahresring 51, Köln: Walter König.
Möntmann, N.(2002) *Kunst als sozialer Raum*, Köln: Walter König.
Özsezgin, K. (1989) *Türkische Malerei heute*, in *Geschichte der türkischen Malerei*, Genf: Palasar.

Rebentisch,J. (2003) *Ästhetik der Installation*, Frankfurt am Main: Edition Suhrkamp.

Sanlier, Z. (2003) 'Sanat ve Toplum Açısından On Yıllık Bir Dönem', *Sanatdünyamız*, No. 89, Spring.

Schmidt, S. J. (1987) *Kunst: Pluralismen, Revolten*, Bern: Beneteli.

Steinbach, U. (2003) *Geschichte der Türkei*, München: C. H. Beck (3rd edition).

Tannert, C. (2004) 'berlin.istanbul.vice.versa' in *berlin.istanbul.vice.versa*, Calbe: GCC.

Tansuğ, S. (1987) *Contemporary Exhibitions in Historical Monuments*, in: Istanbul Foundation for Culture and Arts (ed.), *1. International Contemporary Art Exhibitions*, Istanbul: Istanbul Foundation for Culture and Arts.

—— (2003) *Çağdaş Türk Sanatı*, Istanbul: Remzi Kitabevi, (6th Edition).

Tanyeli, U. (2003) 'Cumhuriyet'in İlk Yıllarında Sanat Yaklaşım ve Sonuçları', *Sanatdünyamız*, No. 89, Spring.

Turani, A. (1989) *Die Türkische Malerei nach dem Zweiten Weltkrieg*, in *Geschichte der türkischen Malerei*, Genf: Palasar.

Yardımcı, S. (2005), *Kentsel Değişim ve Festivalizm, Küreselleşen Istanbul'da Bienal*, Istanbul: Iletişim Yayınları.

Part IV
Economic arena

10 Deepening neoliberalization and a changing welfare regime in Turkey

Mutations of a populist, "sub-optimal" democracy[1]

Mine Eder

T.H. Marshall's notion of 'social citizenship' where political, economic and social rights are seen as constantly reinforcing each other, can serve as an effective 'ideal type' to assess the social policy environment and the transformation of the welfare regime in Turkey. Placing social rights at the heart of citizenship, Marshall argued that social elements refer to:

> the whole range, from the right to a modicum of economic welfare and security, to the right to share to the full in the social heritage and to live the life of a civilised being according to the standards prevailing in the society.
>
> (Marshall 1950:149)

Though the language of 'a civilised being', and 'standards prevailing in society' might appear rather vague, and our understanding of citizenship has evolved considerably since then, this chapter is based on a similar assumption: that citizenship as a concept includes a notion of social justice. Marshall's proposition that regardless of the apparent tension between capitalism and the unequal social classes it creates, political and civic citizenship are intertwined with a notion of equality, raise further questions regarding the scope and extent of social policy and welfare regimes: What are the 'proper' boundaries between public and private in terms of social services and welfare provisions? What kind of an institutional welfare mix is necessary for full-fledged citizenship? Or more broadly, what kind and degree of social justice is necessary for a consolidated democracy where citizens can enjoy social, economic and political rights?

Existing welfare regimes around the world offer different institutional welfare mix which often oscillate between two poles. One is based on Marshall's vision of social rights, and provision of universal and equal entitlements and the other one is Bismarkian, based on selective, minimalist, family-based, conservative, and often charity-based welfare services.[2] In the Turkish context, Buğra, Keyder and Candaş articulate this very well as they refer to the constant tension between the universalist, egalitarian and rights-based approach to social policy, and what they call the 'conservative liberal tendencies', a combination of Islamic notions of charity and family-based conservative values, the roots of which go back to the Ottoman Empire (Buğra and Keyder 2006; Buğra and Candaş 2011).

This chapter explores the modalities through which this Marshallian 'social' element in the concept of citizenship has systematically been 'hollowed' in Turkey. Indeed, as Buğra indicates, Turkey's immature welfare state, as in most of the developing countries, never even came close to this ideal type (Buğra 2007). With more than half of its workforce employed in the informal sector (a staggering 87 per cent of those employed in the agricultural sector) almost 40 per cent of its overall population not having any access to any healthcare, Turkish Governments have long struggled with the challenges of addressing the social security needs of its rapidly growing population since the 1950s and rising expectations from the state. (All numbers are from TUIK, *Türkiye İstatistik Kurumu*, the Turkish Statistical Institute, unless otherwise indicated). Nevertheless, the fact that abject poverty (defined as below one dollar a day according to UNDP) has been relatively small even during the worst of economic times (a little above 2 per cent) suggests that, despite its limitations, some the informal welfare mechanisms, have worked effectively to cushion some of the more drastic effects of rapid social and economic transformation that the country underwent.

Indeed, Turkey's welfare governance has increasingly moved towards the latter type, towards a more liberal, residual, mean-tested, 'workfare' state particularly since the 1980s (Jessop 1993). Liberalization of Turkey's economy since the 1980s has intensified significantly in the aftermath of the 2000/2001 financial crises. This 'deepening' liberalization has hollowed the concept of citizenship even further, transforming the individuals to 'loyal' subjects, vulnerable to the whimsical powers of charity providers and often-murky mechanisms of social assistance schemes. What is new in the neo-liberal era is not the inegalitarianism, informality and the duality that has long characterized Turkey's welfare regime but almost an eradication of social rights as 'rights' and the clear faith in the 'market rationality' in welfare provision.

The unprecedented expansion of social assistance mechanisms to address poverty (without ever acknowledging or addressing the structural causes of poverty to begin with) combined with the proliferation of charity groups, community-based philanthropic activities, have significant implications for the quality of democracy and democratic engagement as well. In a society that already operates through informal networks and does not trust the state in its ability to provide basic social services equally for all, such arrangements, this chapter suggests, are likely to undermine the trust and legitimacy in the state institutions.

Second, in an environment where inequalities have become ever more entrenched, hybrid and evermore interdependent, the ability of the citizens to demand redistributive policies and use their democratic rights diminish as well (Candaş et al. 2010). In fact, there is growing evidence that for democracy to work and generate political pressures for redistribution, you need a minimal level of social risk protection (Brooks 2010).[3] In the absence of such a risk protection, existing democracies can actually entrench the existing inequalities even further. After all, at the micro-level, there will be a trade-off between economic survival and political engagement. It is not clear whether that threshold has been reached in Turkey. What is certain, however, is that growing inequality, its sticky and hybrid nature coupled with the persistent problem of poverty poses a serious threat to both stability and democracy in the country, and existing democratic institutions does not seem adequate in addressing the needs of the genuinely insecure and vulnerable segments of society. As Brooks summarizes:

> the gravest risk to democracy may arise not from the destabilizing cycles of mass mobilization but from malaise and demobilization, along with declining confidence in the democratic regime itself. Even if a reversion to authoritarianism is not in the offing, this research suggests that the declining *quality* of democracy may pose an even greater threat to the longer-term processes of social and economic development in the vast portions of the world where citizens are confronted daily by the threats of violence, poverty and exclusion.
>
> (Brooks 2010)[4]

Given its persistent inequalities, a typical hollowing out of the democratic citizenship might indeed be at work in Turkey. Finally, as will be shown below, the shift towards a marketized welfare regime in Turkey also leaves enormous room for patronage politics, clientelism and populism.

The first part explores the way through which the deadly combination of highly informal economy with deepening structural problems and minimalist welfare state – whose main functions have either been privatized and/or subcontracted to private charities or families – raises significant questions on the quality of democracy. The second section describes the main contours of the populist/corporatist welfare regime that Turkey had prior to the transition to a liberalising economy in 1980. Here, the populist strategies based on agricultural subsidies as well as strategies of deliberate negligence on informal housing in the cities coupled with a heavy reliance on the family unit have played a created a highly dualistic, unequal welfare regime. The third part analyses the social and economic consequences of liberalization experience in the country since the 1980s, with particular emphasis on the changes since the 2000/2001 financial crisis and aims to provide preliminary data as how Turkey has started moving towards a more privatized, individualized and charity-based welfare governance.

The fourth and final section of this chapter reviews some of the changes in the welfare governance in Turkey which can be broadly summarized as the increasing retreat of the state from direct welfare provision which culminated in the 2008 social security reform, and most importantly increasing subcontracting of most of the welfare services by the state to the family, to non-state actors, philanthropic organizations, private volunteers and community-based charity groups as well as well-known micro-credit schemes such as Grameen Bank model (Adaman and Bulut 2007). This section ends with the implications of this type of welfare governance for the quality of democracy. Apart from the State Statistics TUIK numbers, the data that is presented in this chapter is based on a national survey on urban informality conducted in March 2004 (with Ali Çarkoğlu).[5]Some of this data has later been updated by a World Bank survey in December 2009 (Adaman, Çarkoğlu and Eder 2009).

An underdeveloped welfare regime and challenges in Turkey's political economy

The limitations of Turkey's social policy framework are all but evident from the very start. Simply put, the formal social policy in Turkey has long been based on the provision of free primary, secondary and tertiary education, coupled with public healthcare and pension system which were all linked to the employment status. Retirement Chest, founded in 1949 has provided health care and pension for civil servants, Social Insurance Institution, founded in 1946 covered the workers whereas Bağkur, founded in 1971 covered the self-employed.

Nearly half of the working population are still not covered by any these insurance schemes, hence working informally. High dependency ratios also indicate strikingly low employment rate in the country. Between 1980 and 2004, the working age population grew by 23 million but only 6 million jobs were created. The result is a 44 per cent employment ratio, which has climbed up to only 48.1 per cent in 2011, among the lowest in the world. The declining female labour participation is partly responsible for low employment rates. Female employment rate has been declining since the 1960s and has hovered around 25 per cent, (26.6 per cent as of 2011) almost half of it European counterparts (World Bank 2006:4–7 and 2010).

It is not surprising then that low employment ratio, coupled with high degree of informality in the labour markets has really widened the gap between those employed formally, whose insurance premiums are being paid by the employer (until the 2007 social security reform, the Turkish state did not contribute at all to the insurance schemes) and those who have no coverage, are either employed in the informal sector and does not have access to basic health care (as of 2006, 19.8 per cent of population did not have any health insurance). The numbers are particularly striking in the rural sector where the on average, the lack of any social insurance has systematically been around 85 per cent of the agricultural labour force. In the case of women who are counted as 'employed in family farms as unpaid family workers', nearly 100 per cent do not have any insurance.[6] Given the fact that until very recently, rural employment still counted for 40 per cent of total employment, the contrast becomes even greater.

This stark contrast between the fully insured and employed worker versus the rest also becomes clear when the distribution of employment according to status at work is analysed. Self-employed and unpaid family workers constitute 25per cent and 20 per cent of total employment respectively. Unpaid family workers are predominantly agricultural women picking up cotton and working in the fields and is the largest category among the informal workers. (That is why when the overall agricultural employment began to decline, as will be elaborated below, the women unemployment began to decline as well, as these women began to appear as unemployed in the urban setting.)

Self-employed is also a category where informal work is abundant. It is important to note, however, that informality does not only manifest itself in the informal labour markets or among the self-employed. Informality is also evident in most business practices, daily life and most importantly in perceptions. Many businesses admit that they would not have survived in the business if they were to pay their taxes in full. On the consumer end, 87 per cent of all the daily shopping is done in cash; people mostly shop in neighbourhood bazaars where almost all transactions are done in cash and where *veresiye* (an oral promise of payment) is common. More than half of the population does not have a bank account or a savings account, which is as much a sign of economic vulnerability as it is of informality (Çarkoğlu and Eder 2006), and not picking up receipts in return for VAT deduction is prevalent.

Thus it is not surprising that despite ongoing controversies on measuring and assessing poverty, there is a general consensus that the risk of poverty, particularly in the aftermath of the financial crisis, has been on the rise in the country. More than 1 million jobs were lost and many small businesses went bankrupt. The 2008 OECD report, for instance, has underscored that Turkey has the highest rate of increase in child poverty (5 points increase since 1995 reaching 25 per cent) and urgently called for a targeted poverty alleviation programme (OECD, 2008). According to 2003 Eurostat data, the percentage of children in Turkey under the age of 16 at poverty risk was 34 per cent which is twice the EU-25 average.

In our 2004 urban household survey, for instance, when asked their last six month's average family income including all of the wages, pensions and rental income of all the family members, 51.6 per cent all the households indicated that their income is below 600 dollars/month. While a good one-third of the household reported income levels between 600–1200 dollars, only 13.3 per cent reported income higher than 1200 dollars. Based on these declared incomes, those who have a per capita household income of approximately 2.5 dollars a day or less (approximately 100 YTL) can be considered economically vulnerable. Though most economic vulnerability indexes are based on consumption and the cost of basic and non-basic goods, we used income numbers but have used a much lower threshold since the individuals are very likely to understate their income. Based on the threshold of 100 YTL and less declared income, we found that 24 per cent

Table 10.1 Different measurements of poverty in Turkey

Methods	Rate of poor individuals (%)							
	2002	2003	2004	2005	2006	2007	2008	2009
Food poverty	1..35	1..29	1..29	0..87	0..74	0..48	0..54	0..48
Complete poverty (food+nonfood)	26..96	28..12	25..60	20..50	17..81	17..79	17..11	18..08
Below 1 $ per capita per day (1)	0..20	0..01	0..02	0..01	0..00	0	0	0
Below 2..15 $ per capita per day (1)	3..04	2..39	2..49	1..55	1..41	0..52	0..47	0..22
Below 4..3 $ per capita per day (1)	30..30	23..75	20..89	16..36	13..33	8..41	6..83	4..35
Relative poverty based on expenditure (2)	14..74	15..51	14..18	16..16	14..50	14..70	15..06	15..12

Source: TUIK: 2009 Poverty Statistics

(1) Purchasing power parity (PPP) has been used. 1 Dollar PPP is converted as 0.917 TL for 2009 50% of the median value equivalent of individual consumption expenditures has been used.

of households had a per capita household income of 100 YTL, which is comparable to TUIK numbers of 2009 (See Table 10.1.)

When asked whether this income can meet the needs of their respective households, only 13.8 per cent among the household responded positively, underscoring both the insufficiency of earnings in providing for the basic needs of the families but also the resilience of the families in making ends meet no matter how difficult the economic conditions might be. Most striking finding, however, was the reported length of time they could manage, if their income was cut off for some reason. 69.8 per cent the household report that they could survive 30 days or less if their source of income was depleted suddenly. This intense economic vulnerability, (absence of security money or savings) can be one of the important factors that can explain why people prefer, or better yet, do not have another option but to work in the informal sector.

Ownership patterns reflect a very similar picture in terms of degree of economic vulnerability and poverty. 76.2 per cent in our survey did not have a car in the household, and approximately 40 per cent of the urban households do not own their houses. These findings are also in line with

> risk-of-poverty rates, which is defined as 60% of median of the net income of all households. In 2003, 26% of the Turkish population is found below this line. More striking is the high rate observed among the working population, which amounts to 23%, implying that approximately one out five individuals (among those who are employed) is a 'working poor'. This number is threefold the EU-25 average
>
> (Adaman and Keyder 2006: 16).

In cases of health-care issues, the importance of family also becomes very visible. When asked in our household survey, how will the healthcare costs be paid is a family member is ill, 47.6 per cent indicates that it will be paid through one of the insured members in the family. 8.3 per cent suggests that they will borrow from relatives, 7 per cent from friends but 30.4 per cent said that they will have to pay out of their own pockets (which actually means that no one is insured in the family). In face-to-face interviews with urban informal female workers, we also found out that in the case of young women married to uninsured men, it is common for the women either to fake-divorce or fake-marry so as to benefit from a family member's insurance. Though this clearly brings an extra burden on the health-care system it also underscores the importance of family ties in cases where the welfare state has failed to provide sufficient health care.

It is also important to note that most household members consider it normal to rely on friends and relatives in cases of poverty. One asked which one of the following you would consider acceptable for the head of a poor household when state aid is unavailable, nearly 72 per cent suggest that to get by with family and relative help is acceptable, 64 per cent expressed that getting by neighbour's help is also acceptable but only 17.3 per cent find begging acceptable.

Finally, as yet another indication of family ties, when asked to identify the different sources of incomes in the household over the last six months, 10 per cent identified help from the family, and another 10 per cent suggested that they received goods and foods from their original province as supplemental income which underscores that the ties with the rural sectors continues to be important.

Apart from the intense economic vulnerability described above, Turkey has also become extremely unequal on all very different dimensions. In a recent report on entrenched inequalities in Turkey, Candaş and others have argued that the persistent 'bundling' of inequalities in the country constitute a major challenge (Candaş et al. 2010). It is not surprising to find, for instance, that food and non-food poverty rate[7] is about 9.5 per cent in urban areas while it is about 34.5 per cent in rural areas, that women are much poorer and lower paid than men, that poor and working children are much more likely to drop out of school, that 46 per cent of citizens whose mother tongue is Kurdish are not primary school graduates, while that ratio is only 9 per cent among native Turkish speakers. Regionally, Southeast and Central/East Asia fare considerably lower than the country average on a whole range of social statistics, such as students per teacher, patients per doctors, patients for hospital beds, infant or mortality rates and years of schooling (Candaş et al 2010). National surveys, and World Values Surveys also suggest that Turkey is a highly intolerant country complicating this picture of the economic vulnerability with visible patterns of 'other'ings and exclusions (Çarkoğlu and Kalaycioğlu 2009 and Esmer 2010). This bundling of inequalities and rising intolerance raise significant questions over quality of democracy and prospects of full-fledged citizenship for all.

In the midst of this degree of economic vulnerability and entrenched inequalities, it is not surprising that the expectations from the state would rise as well. In terms of the perceptions, our survey data revealed that there are solid expectations from the state. 50 per cent of the households indicate, for instance, that taking care of the poor is primarily the state's responsibility followed by all the citizens (support for solidarity 23.8 per cent) and by wealthy citizens (support for charity, 21.3 per cent). When asked about the extent to which the state can meet the health, infrastructure and education needs of the population, on a scale of one to ten where one indicates, does not meet at all and 10 refers to meets the expectations fully, on average has been 4.4. Among those who believe that state's performance has been below 5, nearly 30 per cent indicate that the primary reason as to why the state cannot meet the expectations is that it is wasteful and cannot use its resources effectively. Another 16 per cent suggest that the state uses the public funds not for the general public but for small groups. A very strong sense of inequality and corruption also appears to breed this scepticism of the state. Approximately 70 per cent of the public agrees or agrees strongly with the following statements: 'The public officials protect their individual interests', 'no matter how much tax we pay, unless the state is reformed, our taxes will be wasted', 'when it comes to paying taxes, the businessmen do not do their share in comparison to workers and civil servants'. Nearly 63 per cent of the household thinks that the biggest tax evaders in the country are either holdings or big companies. A 2010 survey also revealed that well above half of the population in Turkey see the tax system as unfair, find the fact that high income groups having access to better education and healthcare as unfair. More than 90 per cent of the population sees inequality as a major problem in the country (Çarkoğlu and Kalaycıoglu, 2009).[8]

Needless to say, such high levels of state scepticism and mistrust are highly problematic, and are likely to undermine the long-term legitimacy of the institutions and public trust. It appears that the vicious cycle of scepticism and mistrust on the one hand and very high level of informality and perception of injustice keep feeding on each other. As noted, coupled with this scepticism is also a growing evidence of immense economic vulnerability and growing dependence of either on social assistance or charity handouts. This level of economic vulnerability and distrust in the fair distribution of state's resources raise significant doubts on the prospects of 'vigilant citizenship' demanding accountability and transparency. As Margaret Levi has argued:

> To achieve legitimacy requires the rule of law and the provision of infrastructure, justice, education and other services that make populations better off than they would be without government. But law and services are insufficient without government commitments to procedural

fairness and relative transparency. This, in turn, involves public servants with pay and other incentives to withstand corruption and to serve constituents, all constituents. And that in turn rests on the symbiotic relationship with an alert citizenry willing to make demands and hold their public servants accountable. They will do so only if they believe— and for a good reason—that they are getting something in return for their compliance and active citizenship.

(Levi 2005: 25)

Instead of this virtuous cycle of procedural fairness and relative transparency leading to vigilant citizenship, Turkish case reflects a vicious combination of informality, and perceptions of state inefficiency and inequality in terms of provision of public services. It is clear that establishing a rights-based universal social policy framework with an egalitarian framework might be the starting point for breaking the vicious cycle and help reduce the scepticism and inegalitarian perception of public services. But trapped in informality and economic vulnerability with growing dependence on state assistance schemes, the prospects for making universal social rights and claims for fully-fledged social citizenship are likely to decrease as well.

Populist/corporatist welfare solutions until the 1980s

Given such a high level of informality, it is not surprising to see that welfare provision and social policy framework in Turkey have also been based on informal strategies, implicit social pacts, compromises, as well as family ties, and informal personal networks The existing literature on poverty in Turkey all suggest that three main factors, namely, agricultural subsidies along with tax exemptions for the rural sector, the possibilities of informal housing in the urban areas where the public land could easily been invaded by migrant settlers and most importantly family and social networks, which have long been the foundation of the countries' welfare regime, have largely been responsible for the relative absence of violent dispossession, extreme poverty, rapid commodification and/or social unrest.

Rant distribution through agricultural subsidies and deliberate negligence and acceptance of migrant squatters on the public land not only constituted a welfare cushion but also fundamental pillars of Turkey's populism. This political compromise was populist in a sense that it included a 'direct appeal to the people', a mechanism for material support for the targeted popular sector (regardless of the economic program) and an anti-elitist rhetoric. Despite the changing political coalitions, and very different economic programs, these three features of populism have remained constant. (Eder 2006).

Indeed, Turkey's rural populism was based on a combination of persistently high product subsidies which were well above the world prices and the habitual registration of the non-performing farmers' credits as 'duty losses' of the Ziraat Bankası, (a national bank predominantly designed to provide credits and receive deposits from the farmers) These were characteristics largely held accountable for the huge fiscal deficits in the country since the 1960s. Non-existing or extremely low levels of taxation from agriculture and the production still based on small land ownership are the other two unique characteristics of Turkey. About 60 per cent of the rural families own fewer than 5 hectares of land and another 20 per cent between 5 and 10 hectares (Kasnakoğlu 1994; Eder 2003). Mostly because of the availability of land and to policies and concerns dating back to the Ottoman era (large land-owners were always perceived as threats to the central government), small landownership has persisted until now with the only exception of the Kurd-ish southeast regions and a few valleys in Söke and Çukurova. The persis-tence of a large rural population thanks to small landownership also meant that agricultural policies and subsidies became prime areas of political and populist contestation. So much so, that the politicians since the 1950s have consistently found themselves in a populist competition in outbidding each other in terms of agricultural base prices (prices at which the government guarantees to buy from the farmers) (Eder 2004).

Nevertheless and despite its high costs and the ample opportunities such a political compromise, based on the successive governments foregoing their tax revenues and spending huge sums for product subsidies, have created for political patronage, these policies have managed to cushion the rural popu-lation from extreme forms of poverty by providing them with some sort of unemployment insurance. Yet, this type of rural populism had serious poli-tical consequences. As Güven argues, similarly to Sandbrook and colleagues, these compromises constitute a 'deformed substitute for social democratic options' (Güven 2009; Sandbrook et al. 2007: 28–29). As predominantly centre-right parties used rural incorporation through subsidy and support regimes as a fundamental part of their political strategy, combining urban and rural discontent to formulate social democratic alternatives became very difficult. Peasants could easily be appeased and their democratic participa-tion was firmly entrenched on the nature of the populist compromise. The economic and social consequences of this compromise were not any better. Turkey's economy is still considered as semi-industrial with more than 26 per cent of the working population still employed in agriculture while the sector only accounts for 9 per cent of the GDP in 2009. The rural popula-tion in the country, by all comparative accounts remained relatively poor, undereducated and unskilled. In short, it might have prevented extreme forms of poverty, but agricultural policies in Turkey and informal welfarism were hardly any substitute for full-fledged institutionalized social policy framework and have come at a high economic and political cost.

If agricultural policies aimed at keeping the peasants at the countryside, overlooking or what one can call deliberately neglecting informal housing in the urban areas has been the predominant strategy to ease the pressures of migration and integration to the cities. As in most of the irregular settlements in the developing world, *gecekondu*s (literally means landed-overnight in Turkish) was an outcome of the inability of the governments to provide low income housing address the problem of rapid urban migration, which despite all the agricultural strategies cited above, began to skyrocket in the 1960s. As Buğra (1998: 307) reports, 'In the first half of the 1960s, 59% of the population in Ankara, 45% in Istanbul and 33% in Izmir lived in irregular settlements'. The peculiar aspect of *gecekondu*s in Turkey, however, was the fact that they were mostly built on available public land in the cities (75–80 per cent (Buğra 1998: 309)). The land was simply invaded and appropriated mostly by the new migrants into the city.

This deliberate negligence of informal housing was again a result of a political compromise. The governments could manage a possible urban social unrest through informal housing and ease its burden of having to deal with the immediate implications of migrations to the cities, while the new migrants found a way, however immoral and unfair it might be, to ease their transition to the cities and experience what came to be classically dubbed as 'poverty-in turns' where the old migrants move to better and improved houses and integrate into the city leaving room for the new migrant poor (Pınarcıoğlu and Işık 2001). Once again, however, such a political compromise, created an enormous opportunity of political patronage mechanisms and clientelism.

A total of seven amnesty laws were passed since the 1950s, in effecting regularizing, legitimizing and legalizing the *gecekondu*s and allowed them to receive equal municipal services (Tekeli 1993). The distribution of land titles in return for votes became of typical political strategy. What is more, *gecekondu*s themselves eventually became commercialized themselves (Öncü 1988; Buğra 1998). Through improving the physical conditions of the buildings, (however ugly they remain), at times even turning themselves into semi-cities as Erder as aptly demonstrated in the case of Ümraniye, these buildings created additional income, rent opportunities and eventually additional income through sales to the newcomers, most of whom would often be their *hemşeris* (provincial brothers) (Erder 1996). In short, to some extent, the combination of agricultural subsidies which de facto worked as unemployment insurance in the countryside, the availability of urban public land for incoming migrants and strong family ties compensated for the absence of a full-fledged welfare regime. The result was a highly costly, but intensely populist welfare system

From liberalization to 'deepened' neoliberalism in the aftermath of the 2000/2001 financial crisis

These informal pillars of the welfare regime began to come under strain in the 1980s as the country started to undergo its most visible structural economic and social transformation which combined a move from domestic market oriented import substitution policies to export orientation with wide range of deregulation, privatization and liberalization initiatives (Pamuk 2008; Öniş 2004). Many argued, however, that Turkey's liberalization experience has been 'unorthodox' as it failed to carry out extensive privatizations, push for public sector reforms and genuinely integrate the economy into global commodity chains-?foreign direct investment and financial liberalization (Öniş 1991). However, as typical in most of its Latin American counterparts, as neoliberal policies such as limits of fiscal spending, wage freezes, opening the economy to global competition became politically unsustainable, most of the policies of the previous era returned with vengeance in the 1990s, with all of its side effects such as unsustainable debt burden, skyrocketing public sector borrowing ratios, and of course, high inflation. The proliferation of global financial instruments in the early 1990s, coupled with the global financial boom, and interest in the newly emerging markets, allowed the successive governments to borrow much more easily than they normally would also contributed to the brewing and rather inevitable fiscal crisis. The first major hick-up in the economy came in 1994, unfortunately followed by more deregulation and borrowing bringing the country on the brink of a virtual collapse with its worst financial crisis in 2000/2001.[9] Hence despite its initial neoliberal push in the 1980s, Turkey's neoliberal restructuring really began to be put in place since the 2000/2001 financial crisis with much more visible and significant social and economic consequences.

Unable to cope with and resolve its skyrocketing domestic and international debt, the fragile coalition government led by Bülent Ecevit requested an IMF loan and signed a stand-by agreement. This 1999–2002 IMF stand-by agreement was the seventeenth of its kind in the history of the republic and envisioned severe belt-tightening measures, fiscal discipline, and an ill-fated pegged currency system that fixed the value of the Turkish lira vis-à-vis the dollar. The inability of the government to implement bitter pill of structural reform, the false consumption boom that emerged with the pegged currency system, and the crisis in the Turkish banking system that failed to adjust to the low-interest environment ushered in the worst economic crisis in the republic's history.

With a 9 per cent decline in GDP and more than one million jobs lost, it was no surprise that the political parties of the coalition were literally wiped out of the political scene in the 2002 elections. The AKP (*Adalet ve Kalkınma Partisi*, Justice and Development Party) government came to power with the promise of economic stability. Fully implementing the IMF program, the AKP indeed brought down inflation to single digits, lowered the interest rates, and managed to achieve an average annual GDP growth of 6 per cent during the 2002–7 period, before the global crisis hit the Turkish economy in 2008 only to be followed by a new round of economic growth.

The most remarkable change occurred in external economic ties as Foreign Direct Investment (FDI), which on average had hovered at $1 billion annually in the 1990s. Annual FDI reached $10 billion in 2005, $20 billion in 2006, $22 billion in 2007, and another $18 billion in 2008.[10] Most of this FDI, however, came in through the sales of State Economic Enterprises (SEEs) or through the sales of banks whose asset values more than halved after the 2000–2001 financial crisis. Another big increase was in Turkey's international trade. Although Turkey's trade deficit continued to grow, both imports and exports increased exponentially: exports jumped from an annual $34 billion in 2001 to $114 billion in 2010, and imports from $38 billion to $186 billion in the same years. The post-financial crisis in Turkey ushered in a much deeper and extensive liberalization of the economy.

Given its fiscal burden, it is no surprise that the agricultural policies became the main target of reform in the aftermath of the 2000/2001 financial crisis. The fact that the implementation of agricultural reform implementation program (ARIP) designed by the World Bank (ARIP) became a structural benchmark for IMF lending in the aftermath of the crisis also accelerated this process. In fact, World Bank became the single most important player in the reform process both in terms of policy advice and the financial support. The program aimed at replacing the product subsidies with direct Income Subsidy (DIS) program, eliminated most of the state-owned cooperatives, established independent regulatory boards on cash crops, extensively liberalised agricultural trade bringing in major international agro-businesses into the country. The Agricultural Bank was also privatised which meant the elimination of privileged credit conditions for the farmers. DIS program, which ended in 2008, has not really achieved its targeted goals and was far from addressing some of the perennial problems such as the absence of innovation, and rural training in the country. (Eder 2003; Akder 2007).

Nevertheless, the result has been the precipitous decline in agricultural employment. The ratio of agricultural workers in total employment declines from 40 per cent in 1998 to 29.5 per cent in 2005 and 25.2 per cent in 2010 (www.treasury.gov.tr). An estimated 3 million agricultural jobs have been lost since the financial crisis of 2001 (in the same site). Furthermore, since the corresponding job growth in the urban sectors was insufficient (in effect, Turkey went through the experience of jobless growth along with many of the countries around the world), the pressures of unemployment remained constant and high. All these developments, in effect, meant that informal welfare mechanisms through agricultural policies would no longer be available which is also visible in the persistently high degree of poverty in agriculture in comparison to the other sectors. Ratio of poor individuals among the employed members (15 years old and above) in agriculture were 33 per cent in 2009, but 9.6 per cent among those employed in the industry and 7.2% of those employed in services. Clearly, deepening commodification of Turkey's agriculture has intensified the uncertainty and vulnerability in the countryside (Keyder and Yenal 2010).

Meanwhile, the prospects of using informal housing as a welfare measure had long started dimming as urban landscape started becoming rapidly saturated and commodified as well (Keyder 2005a and 2005b). Two major trends accelerated this process and transformed the urban land into an area of social and political contestation. One was the increasing devolution of power to the municipalities. In 1984, the Motherland Party who enjoyed the parliamentary majority passed a Construction law enabling the municipalities to prepare and approve urban construction and land development. Needless to suggest that this change has opened a flurry of rent seeking activities and allowed the municipalities to subcontract giant urban development and construction projects, residential complexes to the private sector. As the urban real estate became a highly valuable commodity and became fully privatized, the so called regularization of irregular settlements had turned into expanding the city limits and building middle and upper middle class suburban houses with often dire environmental consequences (Buğra, 1998:312). Globalization and influx of foreign capital into the cities, which once again increased the prospects for rent seeking for the municipalities, also fastened this process of appropriation of land.[11]

Two more developments further expanded the privatization of land in the city and extended the opportunities for political patronage even further. One was the changes in the Public Procurement Law. The law was passed in 2002 and aimed at making public procurements more transparent. However, a total of sixteen changes were made to the law since 2002 one of which included a change to take the municipality biddings out of the scope of the law in effect eliminating all the pressure on them for transparent tendering. It is since then the municipalities have begun to enter into giant infrastructure projects together with foreign partners (Ercan and Oğuz 2006). The second was the rising power and visibility of Mass Housing Authority (TOKİ, *Toplu Konut İdaresi Başkanlığı*), which has taken over the properties and assets of Emlak Bank, a national bank that was supposed to provide credits for affordable mass housing projects and largely proved inefficient. Though the institutional origins of TOKİ go back to 1984, it was the AKP, in power since 2002, which has equipped TOKİ with extraordinary powers. The authority is tied to the office of Prime Ministry and its financing comes from extra-budgetal Mass Housing Fund, which means it cannot be supervised regularly by the parliament. And virtually all urban state lands are now rendered available to TOKİ free of charge, for planning and executing housing projects, in cooperation with the Privatization Administration. Though some of TOKİ's activities is meant to provide cheap houses for the poor, a long needed demand in most cities, the lack of transparency particularly in bidding for TOKİ projects, the continued rampaging of the public land for private purposes has significantly accelerated the commodification of urban land eliminating prospects for informal housing as an exit from poverty. In fact, some of the initial research indicates that far from its presumed social integration impact, that was observed through informal housing, TOKİ's projects have become turned into new zones of exclusion. (Yılmaz 2009; Candan and Kolluoğlu 2008). Whether it is the private developers building new office spaces or shopping malls, or the municipalities undertaking giant infrastructure projects, or sprawling mass housing projects, or giant *gecekondu* transformation projects dubbed as 'urban renewal', pathways of social integration and upward social mobility through informal housing have clearly been closed for good (Kuyucu and Ünsal 2010).

Reforming the social security system: Privatization, social assistance and charities[12]

Without the informal/populist welfare mechanisms, the growing severity of the poverty problem described above, coupled with the insufficiency of the existing social security system that still relies on 'workfare' and family, one would have thought that time had come for new type of welfare governance based on social rights and equal access. However, the changes in welfare governance since the financial crisis of 2000/2001 and the social security reform package that passed the parliament in April 2008 suggests that entirely contrary trends are underway. In fact, profound changes in the social security system in Turkey, has been instrumental in deepening neo-liberalization of the country's political economy.

One reason as to why the social security reform agenda did, once again, emerge in this context was fiscal constraints and debt sustainability. The deficit in the social security system has risen as high as 6 per cent of the GDP as of 2006, which became the primary motive behind the reform. Once again, the World Bank was one of the major architects of the reform. The final version of the reform package had all the blueprints of the World Bank proposals.

Two aspects of the reform package became extremely controversial. One was over the increase in retirement age and the increase in the minimum number of days for which premiums are to be paid before retirement. Not surprisingly, the package received intense criticism from labour unions and the general public. Increased premiums and caps on existing pension payments, recalculation of some of the pension payments were particularly unpopular. The ones who were never covered by a social security system to begin with, were also left empty-handed and the provision of a universal healthcare insurance for the poor was postponed.

In fact this minimal universal healthcare for the poor, which was expected to replace the current Green Card program in two years, was still not in operation as of 2011.[13] Introduced in 1992, and albeit very mixed in its record and quality of services, "The Green Card program" is one of the very few means?-tested social assistance programs and perhaps the most far-reaching one in the country, giving access to hospitals and doctors (though not medicine) to more than 12 million card holders. As in most social assistance schemes, however, there were serious problems and concerns in the implementation of the program based on arbitrariness of card distribution and subjective evaluations of who constitutes the 'real poor'. In some of the fieldwork that has been done on this issue, for instance, a "deserving poor" is defined as divorced, orphaned, elderly and handicapped. A young man of working age is asked to 'find work' and 'persuaded' to find a micro credit and is hardly ever granted a 'Green Card' (Buğra and Keyder, 2008:21). The emphasis on 'work' has not really disappeared. How new universal healthcare scheme will be implemented on the ground and how such problems will be addressed still remain to be seen.

Second controversy was over access to health care. Under the reform package, all the three social insurance funds, SSK (*Sosyal Sigortalar Kurumu*, Social Insurances Administration), Bağkur and Emekli Sandığı and their corresponding hospitals were institutionally united under the management of SGK, (*Sosyal Güvenlik Kurumu*, Social Security Administration) linked to the Ministry of Labour and Social Security. The idea was to increase administrative efficiency and coordinate between highly scattered funds. This did, however, raised questions about creating a giant bureaucracy. When one considers the fact that social security deficits were not only due the early retirement age, which has indeed part of the populist politics in the country, or to the pending demographic concerns over an aging population, but also thanks to the use and abuse of these funds for political purposes, the degree to which such an institution can remain autonomous from political pressures remain to the seen.

Nevertheless, the unification of the social insurance organizations and their hospitals was a positive development as it allowed everyone to have equal access to the hospitals, which have hitherto been exclusive to the respective social insurance beneficiaries. Similar egalitarianism was also observed in the offer of a minimal universal healthcare for everyone who can confirm that they earn below the minimum wage.

Final aspect of the social security reform with regards to the healthcare was the fact that that package, in effect, pushed for the spread of supplementary private insurance schemes and brought an array of arrangements with private hospitals to open them up to the general public. Many opposed such cooperation, most vocal opposition among them was the Turkish Union of Medical Doctors, and interpreted such private-public cooperation as the creeping privatization of health care. The private hospitals, clinics have been a booming business and that international insurance companies such as AIG and Allianz had flooded the market. The number of private hospitals has skyrocketed from 270 in 2002 to, 365 in 2007 and 450 in 2009.[14] One of the primary reasons for this unexpected rise was that 'the transformation of health program' had turned public hospitals into autonomous business institutions competing with both university hospitals and private hospitals and SSI had become the largest customer buying and financing *both* public and private hospitals. The result was the explosion of public health care expenditures, which increased 200 per cent between 2002 and 2007.[15]

Meanwhile, one of the striking feature of Turkey's welfare regime, in a stark contrast to it counterparts in Latin America and Southern Europe, has been minimal role public social assistance programs have played in overall welfare provision. Main reason was the continued reliance of the family. Even the 1976 Legislation on Social Disability and Old Age Pension Funds, for instance, defined eligibility only when there was 'no close relative' to take care of them. (Buğra and Keyder 2006: 222). Partly because of the informal welfarism described above and the reliance on family networks,

> social expenditure categories such as survivors' benefits, incapacity, family support, active labour market policies, unemployment benefits and housing is very low or almost non-existent in Turkey in comparative terms, even in relation to Mexico and Korea. It constitutes 1.3% of the GDP while the OECD average is 7.9% and comparable figures for Mexico and Korea are 3.1 and 1.6% respectively.
>
> (Buğra and Adar 2008: 96)

There has been an explosion, however, of social assistance expenditures since 2002. While the total public social transfers amounted to 2.5 million TL in 2002, this increased to 8.5 million TL in 2008 bringing the ratio of total social transfers to GDP from 0.007 to 0.009 per cent (Sarısoy and Koç 2010: 338). Currently, General Directorate of Social Services and Child Protection is in charge of all the central social assistance schemes in the country. The founding of the directorate itself in 1986 was, Buğra and Keyder rightly argue 'an implicit admission that the family-based solidarity may no longer be sufficient' (Buğra and Keyder 2006: 222). Institutionally, however, it was first the 'Fund for Encouragement of Social Cooperation and Solidarity' which later became the General Directorate of Social Assistance and Solidarity (SYDGM, *Sosyal Yardımlar Genel Müdürlüğü*). While the fund had been previously administered by a secretariat under the Prime Ministry, in 2004, the government founded an independent Directorate General, and passed an associated law governing the directorate. What was most remarkable about this institutional transformation was the degree of autonomy the directorate gained as it began drawing a significant part of its resources from the extra-budget funds. With the exception of transfers to the Ministry of National Education and Ministry of Health for social transfers, SYDGM and its Fund Board were beyond public scrutiny and were only accountable to the Office of Prime Ministry (Yilmaz and Cakar 2008).

According to Law 25665, passed in 2004, and Law 25913 in 2005, the Fund Board and SYDGM are expected to fund and supervise a total of 973 Social Aid and Solidarity Foundations (SYDV, *Sosyal Yardımlaşma ve Dayanışma Vakıfları*) located at the city and provincial level that work in quasi autonomy from each other as well as the Directorate General. These

SYDVs could also work very closely with local private partners and develop joint projects for targeted groups. While a small part of the fund is allocated for specific purposes, education material for children, coal, project supports, the majority is handed over as regular periodic transfers and were left for the discretion of SYDVs. In 2008, the money transferred to SYDV's paid for food for 2.1 million families, fuel for 2.3 million families, education materials for an estimated 2 million students, and helped 28,000 families for rebuilding their shelters.[16] Among the most popular programs run by SYDGM is the conditional cash transfer to poor families to send their children to school. Yagci reports that an estimated 2 million children saw their families receive cash, bringing the total number of people – albeit with overlaps – to approximately 10 million (Yagci 2009: 83). Though the effectiveness and targeting in most of these programs have not been studied systematically and lack of transparent procedures makes data collection and tracking extremely difficult, these numbers clearly reflect the populist reach and scope of these social assistance schemes.

Yet another example of the unaccountable welfare institutional arrangements was the increasing visibility of the municipalities in social assistance schemes. In 2005, with the laws concerning provincial administration and greater municipalities, local municipalities assumed greater responsibilities in social assistance. More importantly, they were allowed to use private sector and/or wealthy organizations for various services and funding. Municipalities have indeed become very visible by way of organizing soup kitchens for the poor, building giant food tents for *iftar* meals during the month of Ramadan, and, most importantly, in-kind assistance to the poor. Very little of the funding for these services, however, actually come directly from the municipalities but from those who contribute to the municipalities' charity funds.

Clearly, such arrangements have created enormous welfare governance problems. First, since the funding is dependent on charity, such programs have been inconsistent and unreliable. Furthermore, given the fact that 30 per cent of the public procurements were bid by the municipalities in 2007, it would naïve to think that charity would not become a substitute for bribery, leaving ample room for corruption and political arbitration. A typical arrangement then would be generous donations to the municipality charity fund in return for a lucrative infrastructure and a real-estate bid.

The general agreement on how the social assistance is distributed and monitored in Turkey has been that they have been very scattered, that they occur through uncoordinated channels and perhaps more importantly for our purposes, is based on quite arbitrary definitions of who constitutes the 'real poor'. Hacımahmutoğlu (2009) documents, for instance, that there are significant variations in the definitions of the needy even among the different programs implemented by the same SYDVs. There is also very little coordination among the local SYDVs and the municipalities. There is no systematic mechanism of means testing and targeting is usually arbitrary. Even more problematic is that there is growing evidence to support that such social assistance schemes, particularly in the distribution of in-kind assistance such as in coal and food, leaves enormous room for political patronage. The downside of such programs, however, is that they creates 'subjects' who have to constantly prove that they are poor to state authorities so as o be eligible for aid, who are utterly dependent on the state assistance rather than 'citizen' who demand these social services as basic rights.

Meanwhile, the AKP government along with the municipalities, have, in principle, supported such private initiatives and welcomed the private sector involvement as a way to address poverty issues. Projects such as Project Rainbow, in which the Ministry of Education and the General Directorate for the disabled jointly appealed to philanthropic groups, for instance, aimed to finance the integration of the disabled into the labour markets. 100per cent tax rebates on the donations of generous individuals on education and schools is yet another example (Buğra and Adar, 2008). There was also an enthusiastic support for applying the Grameen Bank model which is based on providing micro-credits to poor women and encouraging entrepreneurship, to poor women in Diyarbakir, a major city in the Kurdish southeast. This was yet another sign that the Government was still convinced that poverty can be eradicated through private entrepreneurship and work.

Equally problematic is the meteoric rise in the number of charity associations, philanthropic groups, NGOs, and predominantly Islamist community movements such as the Gülen movement, which aim to fill the social vacuum, left by the absence of a full-fledged welfare state. Fetullah Gülen community has by far become one of the richest Islamist communities. According to Rose Ebough and Koç,[17] it is estimated that some 500 big firms in wide range of sectors from finance to textiles, more than 2000 schools, and seven universities in ninety countries, TV channels, newspapers, magazines and 100 foundations are all affiliated with the Gülen movement commanding more than 20 billion dollars' worth of an international empire.[18] Another famous NGO, known for its Islamic tendencies, *Deniz Feneri*, for instance, boasts of having collected millions of dollars in charity and provided aid to thousands of poor children and the needy (www.deniz-feneri.org).[19] In 2004, the organization has been given the authority by the Council of Ministers, to collect donations from the public without prior permission. This recognition of an association as an 'association of public interest' which can only be done by the Council of Minister, decision also allows significant tax deduction and privileges. Yet another large scale Islamist charity organization, *Kimse Yok mu* received the same status in 2006 (Göçmen, 2010). These explicitly religiously motivated charity NGOs have become not only more visible but much more organized over the last decade. The umbrella organization for NGOs, Turkish Foundation for Voluntary Organizations lists more than one hundred NGOs, which use religious references and are religiously motivated (Buğra and Candaş, 2010). As was the case with municipalities and SYDVs, however, problems on definition of the poor, dubious means-testing and arbitrary implementations constitute are common problems with the NGOs and charity associations.

Neoliberal populism?: Implications of the new welfare regime for the quality of democracy

The 'new welfare mix' that has emerged in Turkey in the aftermath of the 2000/2001 financial crisis has important repercussions for quality of democracy as well. As noted earlier, AKP governments have implemented a neoliberal economic program engaging in intensive privatization, including privatization of some social services and health care. In fact, most of the social security and agricultural reform programmes have been blueprinted from the World Bank. Nevertheless, social assistance and health care expenditures have also 'increased' during this period, which suggest that the party has combined neoliberalism with new kind of populism. Though this 'neoliberal populism' does not have the fiscally very expensive redistributive characteristics, as was the case in agricultural subsidies or can open social integration channels through urban populism, as was the case in informal housing policies, it still preserves the main features of populism. First, the explosion of social assistance programs and anti-poverty alleviation strategies allowed the party to appeal directly to the 'masses' and the poor. These programs, though arbitrary, discretionary and highly problematic as discussed above, were extremely popular and managed to entrench AKP's image as the party of the poor. Though there was no significant improvement in quality of health care, the merging of all the public hospitals and allowing the individuals to have access private hospitals through public funding also made these reforms popular.

It is important to note, however, combining neoliberal economic programs, which frequently creates poverty, adjustment and transition problems, with anti-poverty programs is quite typical and constitutes one of the core strategies of international financial institutions. In fact, even the institutional design of SYDVs has been adopted from the World Bank's 'social risk mitigation' project designed to address the social fall-out after the 2000/2001 financial crisis (World Bank 2005). What is unique in the case of AKP is not necessarily the effective ways through which this deepened neoliberalism has been 'packaged' through wide-scale social assistance programs. Rather, AKP has managed to couple these strategies with an intense anti-elitist rhetoric, anti-institutional, and anti-elitist rhetoric, which is yet another important feature of populism. The discussion of how this anti-elitism and anti-establishment rhetoric has merged and was intertwined with Islamist ethos is beyond the scope of this chapter. Suffice to suggest, however, that there is a growing literature on how urban migration and poverty and Islamist politics has managed to create a rather harmonious marriage between deepening neoliberalism and Islamist communitarianism (Tuğal 2009).

Two aspects of new welfare institutional mix with an Islamist dent, however, are problematic. First, the combination of privatization of social services and the increasing role of the NGOs in social assistance and poverty alleviation can also be seen as the retreat of the state, where the state appears to be subcontracting some of its welfare provision functions to the third sector. Such organizational retreat, however, does not mean that the political power of the state is anyway reduced. On the contrary, by enabling 'certain' NGOs to get involved and collect private money and donations for various causes, the state also appears to extend its political power 'through' the NGOs. The extent to which this move toward further philanthropy is in line with the Islamist, conservative ideals of the government is beyond the scope of this chapter. What is clear, however, is that through the legal changes that allowed some NGOs to assume more responsibility in social assistance, the government has increased its political reach and, in a way, has also genuinely compensated for its lack of institutional capacity to provide sufficient social assistance for the poor and the needy. Hence instead of a universal, right-based social policy framework, a fragmented, institutionally dispersed yet highly politicized welfare provision mechanism emerges, leaving plenty of room for political patronage and clientelism.

Second, this fragmented institutional design tends to be non-transparent which raises questions of accountability. (Why and how, for instance, are certain causes are prioritized for charity? How exactly are they administered?) Perhaps more importantly, however, is the familiar problem of conditionalities being attached to getting access to these services? As typical in any community organization, community affiliation and loyalty are expected in return for access. The subcontracting of some of the welfare provisions to charity groups and NGOs is simply incompatible with the right-based of approach where access to services has to be provided to 'everyone' irrespective of their identity, ethnicity, race, gender or any other affiliation. There is also growing evidence that such communities can create new patterns and layers of social exclusion (Toprak 2008). Such litmus tests in return basic social assistance or social services are simply incompatible with the notion of Marshall's social citizenship. This inegalitarian and particularistic distribution of social benefits breeds, in return, perceptions of government ineffectiveness. If government cannot provide public services, becoming a member of a community becomes much more attractive. But Rawls (2003:3) reminds us 'a democratic society cannot be a community, when a community is posited as a body of persons united in affirming the same doctrine'.

Thus, the persistent problem of poverty and economic vulnerability along with with the sticky nature of inequality in Turkey combined with this new welfare mix is in fact changing the very basis of the state–citizen relationship. As citizens become needy subjects waiting for hand-outs from the state or the voluntary donors, as they become willing and ready to accept any litmus tests or community loyalty in order to survive, universalistic welfare provision through all-encompassing state institutions start to evaporate as well. The prospects for the emergence of vigilant citizenship demanding social justice and accountable institutions diminish rapidly. What is worse, as Turkey moves from classic populism to 'neoliberal populism' with an Islamist ethos, the prospects for addressing the structural causes of poverty and economic vulnerability as well as the questioning of neoliberal policies, disappears. As the poor become ever more entangled with everyday survival, demanding political and civic let alone social rights becomes secondary. As the country diverges further and further away from the Marshallian ideal type, a transition towards a consolidated democracy based on rule of law, equality and fully-fledged citizenship becomes all the more unlikely.

Notes

1 The author would like to thank Ellen Lust and Yale University, Council for Middle East Studies for their encouragement and getting me involved in welfare state issues. I also would like to thank Ali Çarkoğlu and Fikret Adaman for allowing me to use the data collected from our research on informality in Turkey. Final thanks go to the editors of this volume for their input and patience.
2 See, for instance, Esping-Anderson (1990) in which he discusses three types of welfare capitalism.
3 The author uses 1960–2007 global data and Latinobarometro 2007 data to test her arguments.
4 Online. Available HTTP: <http://www.yale.edu/leitner/resources/PMF-papers/Brooks_Democracy%20Risk%20Protection%20Inequality.pdf> (accessed 11 February 2011).
5 This project was funded Ford Foundation's Middle East Resarch Competition. There were actuallly 4 samples, 1232 household, 630 shopkeepers, 300 bazaaris and another 300 street vendors.
6 As these women migrate to the cities, they will be recorded as unemployed which explains the further decline in female labor participation as rural employment numbers decrease particularly since 2000.
7 This is based on 'the Cost of Basic Needs' method which values an explicit bundle of foods typically consumed by the poor at local prices first. To this, a specific allowance for nonfood goods, consistent with spending by the poor, is added.
8 Carkoglu, A. and Kalaycioglu, E. (2009) *Turkiye'de Toplumsal Esitsizlik*, Istanbul: Sabanci Universitesi – IPM, 2010: 19.
9 It is no wonder that the economists have called the 1990s 'the lost decade.'
10 Central Bank of Turkey.
11 Keyder (2005a: 128) describes the physical transformation of Istanbul as 'globalization: gated communities, five-star hotels, city packaged as consumption artifact for tourists, new office towers, expulsion of small business from central districts, beginnings of gentrification in old neighborhoods and world images on billboards and shop windows.'
12 For further elaboration of some of the arguments in this section, see Eder (2010).
13 The new program, which is expected to be implemented in 2012, would require more than half of the existing Green card holders to pay health care insurance premiums.
14 http://www.saglik.gov.tr/TR/dosya/1–72059/h/siy2009.pdf
15 http://www.ekutuphane.teb.org.tr/pdf/eczaciodasiyayinlari/izmir/8.pdf
16 See http://www.sydgm.gov.tr/tr/html/236/Aile+Yardimlari
17 Cited in Helen Rose Ebough and Doğan Koç 'Funding Gülen-Inspired Good Works: Demonstrating and Generating Commitment to the Movement' 27

October 2007H. Yavuz, *Islamic Political Identity in Turkey* (London: Oxford University Press, 2003) http://www.fethullahgulen.org/conference-papers/contribu tions-of-the-gulen-movement/2519-funding-gulen-inspired-good-works-demonstrat ing-and-generating-commitment-to-the-movement.html.

18 Filiz Baskan, The Political Economy of Islamic Finance in Turkey: The Role of Fethullah Glen and Asya Finans, in: C. M. Henry & R. Wilson (Eds) *The Politics of Islamic Finance* (Edinburgh: Edinburgh University Press).

19 The German affiliation of Deniz Feneri has been charged and found guilty for corruption and embazzlement by the German courts. Similar charges have been brought in Turkey in 2011.

References

Adaman, F. and T. Bulut (2007) *500 Milyonluk Umut Hikayeleri: Mikrokredi Maceraları (Hope stories of 500 million: Microcredit Adventures)* Istanbul: İletişim.

Adaman, F. and C. Keyder (2006) *Poverty and Social Exclusion in the slum areas of Large Cities in Turkey*. A research report prepared for the European Commission, Employment, Social Affairs and Equal Opportunities.

Adaman, F., A. Çarkoğlu and Eder, M. (2008) *National survey on informality* (World Bank Project.

Akder, H. (2007) 'Policy formation in the process of implementing agricultural reform in Turkey', *International Journal of Agricultural Resources, Governance and Ecology* 6. no.4/5: 514–32.

Brooks, S. (2010) 'Insecure Democracy: Risk Protection and the Politics of Inequality in Developing Countries' Working paper http://www.yale.edu/leitner/resources/ PMF-papers/Brooks_Democracy%20Risk%20Protection%20Inequality.pdf [last accessed 2nd November, 2011].

Buğra, A. (1998) 'Immoral economy of housing in Turkey', *International Journal of Urban and Regional Research* 22.2.

—— (2003) 'The place of the Economy in Turkey', *The South Atlantic Quarterly* 102. 2/3: 453–70.

Buğra, A. and A. Candaş (2011) 'Change and Continuity under an Eclectic Social Security Regime: The Case of Turkey', *Middle Eastern Studies*, 47(3): 515–28.

Buğra A., and C. Keyder (2003) *New Poverty and Changing Welfare Regime in Turkey*, UNDP.

Buğra, A. and C. Keyder (2008) 'Kent Nufusunun en yoksul kesiminin istihdam yapısı ve geçinme yöntemleri', [The employment structure and the survival strategies of the urban poor"] (Unpublished TUBITAK report).

Buğra, A. and S. Adar (2008) 'Social policy change in countries without mature welfare state: The case of Turkey', *New Perspectives on Turkey* 38: 83–106.

Buğra, A., (2007) 'Poverty and Citizenship: An overview of the social policy environment in Turkey', *International Journal of Middle East Studies* 39.1: 33–52.

Candan, A. B. and B. Kolluoğlu (2008) 'Emerging Spaces of neoliberalism: A gated Town and a Public Project in Istanbul', *New Perspectives on Turkey* 39, pp. 5–47.

Candaş, A, et al. (2010) *Türkiye'de eşitsizlikler: Kalıcı eşitsizliklere genel bir bakış*, (A general look at entrenched inequalities in Turkey), Istanbul: Bogaziçi Üniversitesi, Sosyal Politika Forumu.

Çarkoğlu A., and E. Kalaycıoglu (2009), *Turkiye'de Toplumsal Esitsizlik*, Istanbul: Sabanci Universitesi - IPM, 2010.

Çarkoğlu, A. and E. Kalaycıoğlu (2009) *Rising Tide of Conservatism in Turkey* Palgrave, Macmillan.

Çarkoğlu, A. and M. Eder (2006) 'Urban Informality and Economic Vulnerability, The Case of Turkey', unpublished article.

Eder, M. (2003) 'Political Economy of Agricultural Liberalization in Turkey' in İnsel, A. (ed.) *La Turquie et le development*, Paris: L'harmattan, pp. 211–44.

—— (2004) 'Populism as a Barrier to Integration with the EU: Rethinking The Copenhagen Criteria' in Uğur, M. and Canefe, N. (eds). *Turkey's Europe: An Internal Perspective On EU-Turkey Relations*, London: Routledge, pp. 49–74.

—— (2010) 'Retreating state: Political economy of welfare regime change in Turkey', *Middle East Law and Governance* 2. 2: 152–85.

Eder, M., Parla, A. and Danış, D. (2008) 'Forms of organization among new migrants in Turkey: A comparative analysis of Bulgarian Turks, Iraqi Turks and Moldavians in Turkey' (TUBITAK Project, 106K162).

Ercan, F. and Ş. Oğuz (2006) 'Rescaling as a class relationship and process: The case of public procurement law in Turkey' *Political Geography* Vol. 25:6, August 2006: 641–56.

Erder, S. (1996) *Istanbul'a bir kent kondu: Ümraniye (A city landed in Istanbul)* Istanbul: İletişim.

Erder, S. and Incioglu, N. (2008) *Türkiye'de Yerel Politikanın Yükselişi: Istanbul Büyükşehir Belediyesi Örneği* (The rise of Local politics in Turkey: The Case of Istanbul Metropolitan Municipality) Istanbul: Istanbul Bilgi Üniversitesi Yayınları.

Esmer, Y. (2010) 'Diversity and Tolerance: Rhetoric versus reality' in Jensens, M. et al. (eds) *Sustainability of Cultural Diversity: Nations, Cities and Organizations* Edward-Elgar Publishing, pp. 131–59.

Esping, A. G.(1990) *Three Worlds of Welfare Capitalism* Princeton University Press.

Göçmen, I. (2010) 'Politics of Religiously Motivated Welfare Provision', Doctoral Thesis, University of Köln.

Güven, A. B. (2009) 'Reforming Sticky Institutions: Persistence and Change in Turkish agriculture', *Studies in Comparative International development* 44: 162–87.

Hacımahmutoğlu, H. (2009) *Türkiye'deki Sosyal Yardım Sisteminin Değerlendirmesi* [An evaluation of the social assistance system in Turkey] Ankara: State Planning Organization http://www.aciktoplumvakfi.org.tr/pdf/turkiyede_esitsizlikler.pdf [last accessed 22nd October, 2011].

Jessop, B. (1993) 'Towards a Schumpeterian Workfare State? Preliminary Remarks on Post-Fordist Political Economy', *Studies in Political Economy* 40, pp. 7–40.

Kamu İhale Kurumu [Public Procurement Administration]. (2007) *Activity Report 2007*. Ankara: Public Procurement Office.

Karapınar, B. (2007) 'Rural transformation in Turkey 1980–2004: case studies from three regions' *International Journal of Agricultural Resources, Governance and Ecology* 6.No.4/5:483–513.

Kasnakoğlu, H. (1994) 'The impact of agricultural adjustment programs on agricultural development and performance in Turkey' Ankara: FAO June.

Kasnakoğlu, H. and E. Çakmak, E. (1999) *Tarım Politikalarında yeni denge arayışları ve Türkiye*. Istanbul, TUSIAD Publications.

Keyder, C. (ed.) (1999). *Istanbul: between the global and the local*. Lanham, Md.: Rowman & Littlefield.

—— (2005a) Globalization and Social Exclusion in Istanbul, *International Journal of Urban and Regional Research*, 29(1): 124–34.

—— (2005b) 'Transformations in Urban Structure and the Environment in Istanbul' In F. Adaman and M. Arsel (eds) *Environmentalism in Turkey: Between Democracy and Development?* Aldershot: Ashgate, pp. 201–15.

Keyder, C. and Yenal, Z. (2010) 'Agrarian change under globalization: Markets and insecurity in Turkish agriculture', *Journal of Agrarian Change* 11.1: 60–86.

Kuyucu, T. and Ünsal, Ö. (2010) 'Urban transformation as state-led property transfer: Analysis of two cases of urban renewal in Istanbul', *Urban Studies* 47.7: 1479–99.

Leitman, J. and Baharoğlu, D. (1998) 'Informal Rules: Using Institutional Economics to Understand Service Provision in Turkey's Spontaneous Settlements', *The Journal of Development Studies* 34:5: 98–122.

Levi, M. (2005) 'Achieving good government and Maybe Legitimacy'. Online. Available HTTP: <http://siteresources.worldbank.org/INTRANETSOCIALDE-VELOPMENT/Resources/ACHIEVINGGOODGOVERNMENT.pdf> (accessed 30 June 2013).

OECD (2000) *Agricultural Policies in OECD Countries: Monitoring and evaluation 2000* Paris: OECD Publications.

—— (2008) Online. Available HTTP: <www.oecd.org/els/social/family/database and http://www.oecd.org/dataoecd/52/43/41929552.pdf> (accessed 30 June 2013).

Öncü, A. (1988) 'The politics of the urban land market in Turkey:1950–80', *International Journal of Urban and Regional Research* 12: 38–64.

Öniş, Z. (1991) 'The Political Economy of Turkey in the 1980s: The Anatomy of Unorthodox Liberalism' in Heper, M. (ed.) *Strong State and Economic Interest Groups. The Post-1980 Turkish Experience,* New York and London: Walter de Gruyter.

—— (2004) 'Turgut Özal and his economic legacies: Turkish Neoliberalism in Critical Perspective' *Middle Eastern Studies* 40.4: 263–90.

Pamuk, S. (2008) 'Economic Change in Twentieth Century Turkey: Is the glass more than half full?' in Kasaba, R. (ed.) *Cambridge History of Modern Turkey* (vol. 4), Cambridge-New York NY: Cambridge University Press, pp. 266–300.

Pınarcıoğlu, M. and O. Işık (2001) *Nöbetleşe Yoksulluk: Gecekondulaşma ve Kent Yoksulları, Sultanbeyli örneği. (Rotating poverty: Slums and Urban Poverty)* Istanbul: Iletisim.

Rawls, J.(2003) *Justice as fairness* [Kelly, E. (ed.)] Cambridge: Harvard University Press.

Sandbook, R., Edelmen, M., Heller, P., and Teichman, J. (2007) *Social democracy in the periphery: origins, challenges and prospects* Cambridge University Press.

Sarısoy, İ., and Koç, S. (2010) 'Türkiye'de Kamu Sosyal Transfer Harcamalarının Yoksullug?u Azaltmadaki Etkilerinin Ekonometrik Analizi', *Maliye Dergisi* 158. Ocak-Haziran, pp. 326–48.

Tas, H. and Lightfoot, D. (2005) 'Gecekondu Settlements in Turkey: Rural-Urban Migration in the developing European Periphery' Journal of Geography Nov/Dec. 104(6): 263–71.

Tekeli, I. (1993) 'Gecekondu maddesi', *Istanbul Ansiklopedisi*, Istanbul, Tarih Vakfi.

Toprak, B. (2008) *Din ve Muhafazarlık eskeninde ötekileştirme (Othering on the nexus of religion and conservatism)*, Bogazici University Fund and Open Society Institute.

Tuğal, C. (2009). *Passive Revolution: Absorbing the Islamic Challenge to Capitalism*, Stanford, Stanford University Press.

World Bank (2005) *Joint Poverty Assessment Report*, Washington DC.

—— (2006) *Labor Market Study: Summary Turkey* World Bank Document April 14th, 2006. Online. Available HTTP: <http://siteresources.worldbank.org/INTTURKEY/Resources/361616–1144320150009/Ozet-Overview.pdf> (accessed 30 June 2013).

Yagci, A. (2009) 'Packaging neoliberalism: Neopopulism and the case of Justice and Development Party' MA Thesis, Department of Political Science and International relations, Bogazici University, Istanbul.

Yazıcı, B. (2008) 'Social work and social exclusion in Turkey: An overview', *New Perspectives on Turkey* 38: 107–34.

Yılmaz, B. (2008) 'Türkiye'de sınıf-altı: Nöbetleşe yoksulluktan müebbet yoksulluğa', [From rotating to permanent poverty], *Toplum ve Bilim* 113: 127–46.

Yılmaz, V. and Çakar, B. Y. (2008) 'Türkiye'de Merkezi Devlet Üzerinden Yürütülen Sosyal Yardımlar Üzerine Bilgi Notu', Istanbul: Social Policy Forum, Boğaziçi University.

Yoltar, Ç., (2009) 'When the Poor Need Health Care: Ethnography of State and Citizenship in Turkey' *Middle Eastern Studies* 45.5: 769–82.

Part V
State apparatus

11 New public administration in Turkey

Süleyman Sözen

Introduction

In the first decade of the new millennium, Turkey experienced an intensive change process in political, social and economic areas with the influence of external and internal dynamics. Democratization reforms have been one important aspect of the change process. There is a strong link between democratization and public administration reform. In other words, one essential component of the democratization process involves public administration reform. Therefore, in line with the democratization process Turkish public administration has also undergone substantial legal and structural changes.

The main purpose of this chapter is to consider the public administration dimension of democratization reforms in Turkey. The study focuses on the impact of democratization on public administration as well as the implications of administrative reforms for the consolidation of democracy. The chapter is organized in the following way. In the first part, the democracy and public administration relationship will be broadly discussed with particular reference to the Turkish politico-administrative culture. After this, current administrative reforms will be briefly outlined. Finally, the implications of the current public administration reforms on the Turkish democratization process will be considered.

Democracy and public administration in Turkey

Public administration plays a crucial role within the state. The state relies upon public administration to perform its functions. Governments carry out their policies with their administrative machinery. Meier and O'Toole consider bureaucracies, as an abstract institutional form, which can serve any master, indifferent to whether that master is authoritarian or democratic (Meier and O'Toole 2006: 2). Then, the important question for the purposes of this study is: what is the role and place of public administration in a democratic regime?

With regard to the relationship between democracy and public administration two crucial points need to be addressed. First of all, effective and well developed public administration is an essential prerequisite for the functioning of democracy. More precisely, there is no modern democracy that does not also have an effective bureaucracy. Joseph A. Schumpeter argued that modern democracies are best served when elected politicians are supported by professional bureaucrats. Therefore, it is argued that the presence of an effective and well-functioning administration is considered as a necessary condition for democratic consolidation. According to Linz and Stepan, one of the five conditions for a democracy to be consolidated is to have a state bureaucracy that is usable by democratic governments (Linz and Stepan 1996: 7–11).

Indeed, in a political system competent bureaucracy plays a central role in developing a high level of internal regulation, distribution, or extraction (Heady 1984: 410). Public administration acts as an apparatus to implement public policies and enforce the laws.

One essential function of public administration is to deliver services to the public. Without an effective public administration the state cannot deliver sufficient public services. In addition to the function of delivering public services, another crucial role that public administration plays in a democratic state is that public institutions function as the principal interface between state and society. Citizens almost daily come into contact with public officials but they rarely contact their democratically elected representatives. These encounters with public officials play a major role in defining how the public considers government and the legitimacy of the state (Peters 2010: 216). In this sense, democracy and public administration are bound together. Modern democracies need an effective and well-functioning bureaucracy. In other words, the presence of a competent administration is vital for a democracy to function well. To be effective and competent, it is generally accepted that public administration should have the characteristics of Weberian legal-rational bureaucracy. Similarly, Linz and Stepan suggest that public administration should operate according to legal-rational bureaucratic norms (Linz and Stepan 1996).

The second point in relation to democracy and public administration relationships is that in a democratic state public administration should be subservient to the political authorities. Democratic values stress sovereignty of the people and, in turn, the subservience of bureaucrats to the elected politicians who are the representatives of the public. This is called democratic accountability of public administration. In a democratic state public administration is viewed as an instrument for the effective and efficient execution of the policies of democratically elected governments.

To sum up, the relevant literature on the democracy and public administration relationship indicates that democratic political systems require, on the one hand, an effective public administration and, on the other hand, the political control of public administration by democratically elected bodies.

Through taking the two points addressed above into consideration, it might be argued that two fundamental characteristic features of Turkish political culture, which evolved in the history of the Ottoman-Turkish polity, have great implications for the relationship between democracy and public administration in Turkey. These characteristics are strong state tradition and political patronage/party politics (Özbudun 1981; Heper, 1990; Güneş-Ayata 1994).

Strong state tradition and its implications for public administration

The Turkish Republic inherited from the Ottoman Empire a strong, centralized, and highly bureaucratic state (Mango 1977; Heper 1987, 1992; Özbudun 1996; 2000). For Inalcık, the Ottoman state tradition can be defined as recognition of the state's absolute right to legislate on public matters (Inalcık 1980). Heper and Keyman point out that

> Turkey has had a strong state tradition in the sense that, from the time of the Ottoman Empire to the present, there has always been a particular category of elite, who acted in the name of the state by assuming virtually complete autonomy from other groups in the polity, including the political elite.
>
> (Heper and Keyman 1998)

Following the proclamation of the Republic, the CHP (*Cumhuriyet Halk Partisi*, Republican People's Party) leadership, and the military and civilian bureaucrats representing the state vigorously pursued state-centred policies in order to establish a modern Turkish nation-state based on secular and Western precepts. They also placed great emphasis on issues of national unity and territorial integrity (Heper 1990; Sakallıoğlu 1997).

In this respect, politico-cultural issues have always taken precedence over social and economic issues. For the state elites, the foremost concern has always been for the preservation of the state ideology, unity and integrity. Thus, the emphasis has been placed on the obligations of citizens towards the state-such as paying taxes and being subject to military conscription-rather than on the rights of individuals as citizens. As a result, the state apparatus relating to national security policies has been over-institutionalized and over-developed, while that relating to the provision of public services has remained weak and underdeveloped. In this respect, it can be argued that the state in Turkey might be perceived as having a weak capacity for providing sufficient public services to its citizens. After all, the term 'strong state' in the Turkish context does not mean that the state has the capacity to successfully penetrate society and extract resources from it (Heper 1992: 189).

The predominance of a strong state tradition has had important consequences with regard to the state and society relations. Some of them can be expressed as follows: the weakness of civil societal and individualist elements vis-à-vis the state, the creation of a highly centralized administrative structure, the establishment of autonomous state institutions, such as the military, the Constitutional Court, the National Security Council and the civil service and their dominance over civil society.

With respect to public administration, another consequence of having a strong state tradition has been the development of an administrative culture which is not responsive to the needs of the citizens. A culture of secrecy has constituted a crucial aspect of Turkish administrative culture. Furthermore, public officials generally see themselves as a state official representing the state rather than servants of the public. As one reflection of such a notion of the state, extensive immunities have been granted to public officials. Indeed, public officials have considerable legal safeguards in relation to performing their duties.

Within this polity, the military and civil bureaucracy acquired a pre-dominant position in the structure of state power. They have traditionally seen themselves as guardians of the state and protectors of general interest and acted as an independent political actor rather than an instrument. In particular, the single party era (1923–46) was viewed as the golden years of the bureaucracy. Besides, the ruling Party (CHP) itself was dominated by the military and civilian bureaucrats (Şaylan 1974: 76–77). The intertwined relationships between the CHP and the bureaucracy reached its peak in 1935 when Minister of Interior also officially became the general secretary of the Party and provincial governors became at the same time, the Party's provincial chairmen. With this move, the CHP and the bureaucracy became identical. Thus, in the eye of people, the Party was considered as not the people's party but the party of bureaucracy. Although the practice of making governors the Party's provincial leader was put on an end in 1939 the intertwined relations continued by 1950 (Eryılmaz 2002: 137–39).

Nevertheless, with the introduction of the multi-party system in 1946, the DP (*Demokrat Parti*, Democratic Party) came to power in 1950 and the new political elite began to replace the state elite as the major public policy-makers (Heper and Keyman 1998). Since then, Turkish politics have witnessed a struggle between the intellectual-bureaucratic elite aspiring to represent the state and the political elites as representatives of the people. The confrontation between the state elites and the political elites has not manifested the characteristics of a positive-sum game, but has rather become a zero-sum game (Heper 1990: 608). In due course, the bureaucratic elite, in particular the military, has made concerted efforts including military coups, to continue their dominance over the policy-making function. On the other side, political elites also sought to pursue policies that led to the politiciza-tion of public administration.

As mentioned above, in a consolidated democracy the essential function of public administration is not to make public policies but to execute gov-ernment policies in an efficient, effective and impartial way. In this respect, the Turkish bureaucracy, particularly the military plays a political role within the Turkish polity. However, it should also be addressed that with the current measures taken by the AKP (*Adalet ve Kalkınma Partisi*, Justice and

Development Party) government the predominant position of the military in the public policy-making structure has begun to debilitate.

Political patronage and its implications for public administration

Political patronage and clientelism has been a prominent feature of the Turkish political culture. Özbudun argues that 'Turkey provides a fertile ground for the formation and maintenance of a wide variety of clientelistic relationships' (Özbudun 1981: 252). Indeed, patronage affiliations have always been important in Turkish social structure and culture. With the transition from an authoritarian one-party rule to a competitive multi-party system in 1945 a new clientelistic pattern, which has been called 'party-directed' patronage has come into existence (Sayarı 1977). As a result of polarized socio-political structure and party politics, political parties in power have pursued pragmatist and populist policies based on short-term political interest rather than modernizing the administrative system. It can be argued that the patrimonial and clientelist nature of the political culture, coupled with the absence or weakness of any civil society, produced a relationship between the state (the ruler) and society (the ruled) resembling that of father with son. In folklore, 'Devlet Baba' meant 'Papa State' (Sunar 1974).

The prevalence of political patronage and clientelistic relations within Turkish politics has important implications for administrative system. Overall, such a relationship has hampered the development of a legal-rational bureaucracy. Instead, the emphasis has been placed upon personal rule rather than impersonality, loyalty rather than merit, informal networks rather than formalized structures, and partisanship rather than impartiality.

Indeed, one consequence of political party patronage practices has been the politicization of public administration. With political considerations, the governments of the day implemented the policy of favouritism by appointing their supporters in administrative positions instead of meritocratic recruitment and promotion. In turn, politicization and partisanship emerged as a great problem in the Turkish public administration. When we look at the previous reform studies we see that most of them including the first reform study of the Neumark Report in 1949, the MEHTAP (*Merkezî Hükümet Teşkilâtı Araştırma Projesi*, Central Government Organization Research Project) Report, and the Five Year Development Plans proposed the need for the establishment of the principle of merit in public personnel regime. The absence of the principle of merit can be attributed to the patrimonial nature of public administration (Sözen 2005).

With respect to the politics and administration relationship, another related issue is political interference into the day-to-day management of administration. This is also a crucial problem in Turkish public administration. Such practices have had adverse effect on public administration and created favourable condition for incompetence, corruption and partisanship in administration.

As mentioned above, an efficient, professional and politically neutral administration is critical for a democratic state to perform its functions, but party patronage practices and clientelistic relations in Turkey impede the development of a merit based and professionalized bureaucracy.

Overall, it can be argued that strong state tradition and political patronage undermine the legitimacy and effectiveness of state bureaucracy. They constitute an important impediment to the development of modern legal-rational bureaucracy.

The impact of the democratization process on public administration: A brief overview of current reforms

Democratization and public administration reform are closely linked. Democratic reforms and administrative reforms go hand in hand. Hence, along with democratic reforms Turkish public administration has recently experienced immense changes. Undoubtedly, one of the most important reasons behind these reforms is the EU membership process starting with the candidate status being granted to Turkey at the Summit of the Council of Europe held in Helsinki in December 1999. Following the Summit, a new era began in the Turkey-EU relations and Turkey undertook comprehensive reforms in many areas including public administration in order to fulfil the membership criteria and ensure harmony with EU norms. Moreover, the relations stemming from the loan agreements signed by Turkey with international organizations such as IMF and the World Bank are another external factor pushing for public administration reforms.

On the domestic sphere, the strong political commitment and leadership demonstrated with regard to restructuring of public administration by the governments set up by the AKP, which secured a landslide majority of the seats in the TBMM (*Türkiye Büyük Millet Meclisi*, Turkish Grand National Assembly) at the general elections of 3 November 2002 and 22 July 2007, played an important role in pursuing administrative reforms. Administrative reform has been one of the key priorities of the AKP governments. In addition, growing demands and expectations for effective and higher quality provision of public services raised by the various segments of the society and mainly by the business world and the NGOs were also influential in making administrative reforms happen.

When we look at the content of current public administration reforms, we can clearly see that the emphasis is on transparency, accountability, decentralization and participation, which are the main tenets of good governance.

Reforms to strengthen transparency and accountability of public administration

In line with the democratization process, several new legal regulations have been introduced in order to enhance the transparency and accountability of Turkish public administration. The Right to Information Act, the Law on

Public Financial Management and Control and the Law on the Establishment of the Ethics Committee of Civil Servants are some of these arrangements.

With regard to transparency and accountability one important legal regulation has been the introduction of the Law on the Right to Information (*Bilgi Edinme Hakkı Kanunu*, BEHK) into the Turkish legal system. The Law was adopted on 9 October 2003 (Law No. 4982) and came into force on 24 April 2004. Furthermore, the Regulation, adopted on 27 April 2004 laid down the principles and procedures for the implementation of the law.

It is widely suggested that one of the indispensable elements of modern democracies is to have the right to information. The right to information is a prerequisite for ensuring the voice and participation necessary for a democratic governance. The Law on the Right to Information entitles the individual to access to information held by public authorities, while putting the administration under obligation to give information. The aim of the Law, according to the Article of 1, is to establish 'the principles and procedures regarding the right of individuals to receive information in accordance with the principles of equality, objectivity and openness, which are the requisites of a democratic and transparent government' (art. 1). All public organizations are identified as responsible parties in the exercise of this right (art. 2). The Law provides citizens and legal persons with a right of access to recorded information held by public authorities. Within the framework of reciprocity, foreign citizens residing in Turkey and foreign legal entities operating in Turkey also have a right to information related to themselves or their field of activity (art. 4). The Law also makes public organizations responsible for taking necessary administrative and technical measures to ensure effective exercise of the right to information. In this regard, public organizations are obliged to publish their basic decisions and legal regulations falling under their duty domains, and annual activity reports, through using information and communication technologies.

In addition, the Law stipulates a time limit for the administration to provide the requested information or documents, setting it at 15 days and at maximum 30 days in exceptional cases (art. 11). The Law also established the Right to Information Review Board (BEDK, *Bilgi Edinme Degerlendirme Kurulu*) for the supervision of whether the public agencies properly fulfil their obligations regarding the right to information and for the review of any objections raised to this effect (art. 14).

Apart from the Law on the Right to Information, the Law on Public Financial Management and Control (*Kamu Mali Yönetimi ve Kontrol Kanunu*, KMYKK) (Law No. 5018) also have included noteworthy measures in ensuring transparency in the financial management system. In order to ensure control in acquisition and use of any public resource the Law required public authorities to inform the public in a timely manner. The Law also envisaged that public authorities shall prepare strategic plans through participatory methods; measure their performance against pre-determined indicators and monitor and evaluate the process (art. 9). Another novelty provided for in KMYKK with regard to accountability is the new obligation for public administrations to prepare and publicly announce annual activity reports that demonstrate the outcomes of their activities (KMYKK, art. 41).

Besides, the establishment of the Ethics Committee for Civil Servants in 2004 with the Law (No. 5176) on the Establishment of the Ethics Committee for Civil Servants and Amendment of Some Laws has been another notable development for public administration. In 2005, the related Regulation set forth the ethical codes of conduct for public officials and laid down the principles and procedures to regulate applications to the Ethical Board. The overall aim is to increase public trust in public administration, to inform citizens as to what they are entitled to expect from public officials. The concerning Regulation identified the principles in the discharge of duties as justice, integrity, transparency and impartiality.

In addition to these legal arrangements, we can also address some reform attempts which have not yet become a law due to various reasons. Among them, the Draft Law on the Fundamental Principles and Restructuring of Public Administration, the Draft Law on General Administrative Procedures and the Draft Law on Public Inspection (Ombudsman) Authority are noteworthy to mention. They also include substantial arrangements to make public administration more transparent, accountable and participative. For example, in the Draft Law (No: 5227) on the Fundamental Principles and Restructuring of Public Administration, it stated that the establishment of a participatory, transparent, accountable public administration based on human rights and freedoms is aimed for (art. 1). In fact the concerning draft law was adopted by the General Assembly of the TBMM on 15 July 2004 but the draft law was sent back to the Parliament for re-discussion by the President of the Republic who claimed some of the articles were in violation of the Constitution. Later on, the Parliament never got to re-discuss it, so, the draft law failed to become a statutory law.

In a democratic system, accountability mechanisms are multi-dimensional and the ombudsman institution is one of them. In Turkey the establishment of an Ombudsman institution was discussed for many years but the first concrete step was taken through the Draft Law (No. 5227) on the Fundamental Principles and Restructuring of Public Administration. The Law foresaw the establishment of public ombudsman in every province for local authorities to assist in resolving the conflicts arising from the acts and operations of local authorities (art. 42). However, as stated above, this Law failed to come into force as it was sent back to the TBMM by the 10th President of the Turkish Republic and hence a local Ombudsman institution could not be established (Sözen and Algan 2009).

Following this failed attempt, the government initiated a new legal arrangement and in 2006 the Public Inspection (Ombudsman) Institution (*Kamu Denetçiliği Kurumu*, KDK) was established under the Law (No. 5548) on Public Inspection Institution. Nevertheless, the Constitutional Court first stayed the execution of the Law and later annulled it on 25 December 2008 (Resolution No. E. 2006/140, K. 2008/185). But the story goes on. With the 2010 Amendments to the Constitution, the Article 74 of the Constitution, titled 'Right of Petition' changed as 'Right of Petition, Right to Information and Appeal to the Ombudsman'. As such, the constitutional reform provided the basis for establishment of an Ombudsman institution. Finally, Ombudsman institution acting as a link between public administration and citizens was established with the introduction of the Law (No. 6328) on the Ombudsman Institution adopted on 16 June 2012.

The main responsibility given to the Institution is upon a complaint to review and investigate the actions of the both central and local administration and to advise the administration accordingly. The Ombudsman Institution examines complaints and makes suggestions concerning the functioning of the administration with respect to the rule of law and human rights. The Law regulates the Ombudsman Institution (KDK) as a public legal entity attached to the Presidency of the TBMM with a special budget and its central office in Ankara, the capital city. In addition, the Institution is asked to prepare a report at the end of each calendar year on its activities carried out and recommendations offered.

Another important reform attempt is the Draft Law on General Administrative Procedure (GİUKT, *Genel İdari Usul Kanun Tasarısı*) which includes crucial principles aiming at enhancing the transparency and accountability characteristics of administration. Predetermination of procedural rules that need to be adhered to during administrative acts and ensuring that these rules are known by citizens is an important requirement for a transparent administration. In Turkey, despite a long history of efforts to establish the principles and procedures regarding the acts of the administration, law on administrative procedure has not yet been issued. However, it can be said that preparations are at the final stage following the work on which has been continuing since 1990s. The Draft Law on General Administrative Procedure was submitted to the Prime Ministry by the Ministry of Justice in November 2003. The last version of the Draft Law was sent to the Prime Ministry in September 2008. The 2008 version of the Draft Law contains significant provisions oriented to ensure transparency of the administration. In the 2008 Program of the Government, under the section 'Increasing Quality and Effectiveness in Public Services', it was stated that the work on the Draft Law on General Administrative Procedures will be concluded by the end of the year. There is no doubt that when the Draft Law becomes as a statutory law, there will be substantial implications for public administration. The Law will reinforce transparency in public administration and foster the transition from secrecy to transparency in the relations between the administration and the individual. However, the Draft Law has not become a statutory law as of 2012.

Reforms to ensure participation of and cooperation with civil society

Citizen participation is one of the core values of democracy. Democratization in a sense means an increase in citizen participation in public affairs. The presence of a strong and effective civil society is vital for monitoring public administration and overseeing its activities. One essential component of democratic public administration is to have legal and institutional mechanisms for ensuring the participation and cooperation of non-governmental organizations. However, due to its unitary state structure, strong state tradition and highly centralized organization, it is difficult to say that Turkish public administration system has the mechanisms to ensure effective participation of the civil society. Moreover, it is also difficult to say that there is a strong civil society tradition that can fulfil the function of overseeing administrative machinery.

Nevertheless, this situation has started to change in recent years. Current administrative reforms in Turkey have included some mechanisms for ensuring civil society participation and cooperation. Two arrangements in particular deserve to be paid attention. One is the creation of City Councils in 2005 by the Law (No. 5393) on Municipalities (art. 76). The related Regulation was published by the Ministry of Interior to regulate the working principles and procedures of City Councils. In the Regulation, City Councils are defined as democratic structure and governance mechanism where the local branches of central government, local government and civil society organizations meet with an understanding of partnership and within the framework of a community (townsmanship). In short, City Councils are seen as a platform to enhance public participation in local government, and strengthening local governance structure. However, the EU Progress Report points to the little progress on establishing operational city councils (European Commission 2009).

The second step taken to improve cooperation between public sector, private sector and NGOs is the establishment of Regional Development Agencies (*Kalkınma Ajansları*) in 2006. The Law (No. 5449) on Establishment, Coordination and Duties of Development Agencies identified their founding purpose as to develop cooperation between public, private and civil society organizations, to ensure appropriate and effective usage of resources and mobilize the local potential and thereby accelerate regional development and ensure its sustainability in harmony with the principles and policies foreseen in national development plans and programs and close the developmental gap within and between regions. These Agencies have legal status and are subject to private law provisions in all their acts and transactions that are not regulated in the Law (art. 3). The Agency is represented by the Chairman of the Board of Directors. The Board of Directors, which is the decision-making body of the Agency, is comprised of the provincial governor, the mayor of the greater city, chairman of the provincial general assembly, chairman of the chamber of industry, chairman of the chamber of commerce and three representatives selected by the board from private sector and/or non-governmental organizations. The board of directors is chaired by the governor (art. 10) (Sözen and Algan 2009)

Reforms to improve human rights

Progress in democracy is closely linked to progress in protecting human rights. Improvements in the protection of human rights contribute to the consolidation of democracy. In the field of human rights there have been important developments in the recent period. Reforms undertaken for protection and improvement of human rights occupy a noticeable place in the overall public administration reforms. In this respect, restrictions on human rights and freedoms have been eliminated to a considerable extent and significant progress has been made towards achieving the universal standards in human rights through extensive constitutional and law amendments in many areas that are directly associated with human rights and particularly through the Constitutional amendments of 2001 and 2004 (İnsan Hakları Başkanlığı 2008).

In addition to legal reforms, some structural arrangements have been also made in the area of human rights. The TBMM Human Rights Review Committee, the National Committee for the Decade for Human Rights Education, the Prime Ministry Human Rights Presidency and the provincial and district Human Rights Boards can be listed among these new structural arrangements. Furthermore, human rights units have also been established within the related public departments. For example, the Bureau for Review of Allegations of Human Rights Violations was established in 2004 under the Inspection Board of the Ministry of Interior. The latest development in the field of human rights has been the establishment of the Human Rights Institution of Turkey with the Law on the Human Rights Institution of Turkey (No. 6332), adopted on 21 June 2012. The Human Rights Institution of Turkey replaced the existing the Prime Ministry Human Rights Presidency. The Institution, linked to the Prime Ministry, has a public legal personality, administrative and financial autonomy as well as a special budget. The Institution is authorized to carry out activities for protection and development of human rights as well as for prevention of violations; to fight against torture and ill-treatment; and to review the complaints and applications.

Reforms to strengthen decentralization

An essential ingredient of democratization is decentralization. Decentralization policies can remove barriers to participation; enhance the responsiveness and accountability of government. Following criticisms that the centralized bureaucratic structure is far from being responsive to the needs of the citizens, strengthening local governments has been a key priority within the AKP Government's reform agenda. In this context, the former laws regulating local governments were totally changed and the duties, responsibilities and powers of local governments were expanded with the Law (No. 5302) on Provincial Special Administration, and the Law (No. 5393) on Municipalities, Law (No. 5216) on Greater City Municipalities and the Law (No. 5355) on Local Government Unions. The new laws narrowed the administrative tutelage control of the central government on local governments and also included provisions providing participatory mechanisms for local community.

Implications of administrative reforms for democratic consolidation

As briefly outlined above, in recent years substantial legal and structural reforms have been introduced into the Turkish public administration. These reforms have brought about considerable changes in the role and functions of public administration. In other words, the content and spirit of the reforms reflect a new understanding of administration that is quite different from the traditional form of administration.

It can be argued that current administrative reforms might have important implications for Turkish democracy to be consolidated. Above all, with new legal and structural arrangements, the Turkish administrative system has been moving from a "state-centred" administration to a more 'people-centred' administration. Traditionally, the control function of administration has taken primacy over service delivery function but current reforms have put emphasis on service delivery function of administration. Thus, the primary role of administrative apparatus has been changing from being the one serving to the state to serving to the people. Citizens in a democratic polity expect public administration to be responsive to their requests and demands. In this respect, in addition to the reforms mentioned above, another important step towards making public administration more responsive was taken in July 2009. The Council of Ministers issued a regulation establishing the principles and procedures for the administration to deliver better public services to citizens. They focused on enhancing e-services and information, establishing standards for public services. 170 regulations have been simplified and 421 administrative documents were eliminated (European Commission 2009).

Without doubt, transparent, accountable and responsive administration is an essential component of a democratic state. This is mainly because having such an administration, in turn, builds public trust in government and enhances the legitimacy of the regime. Current reforms include some provisions and mechanisms to make public administration more accountable, transparent and participative. Besides, there are ongoing attempts in improving civilian oversight of internal security forces-the police and the gendarmerie.

Table 11.1 Transparency International Corruption Perceptions Index

Years	Turkey's Score	Turkey's Rank	Number of Countries
2000	3.8	50	90
2001	3.6	54	91
2002	3.2	64	102
2003	3.1	77	133
2004	3.2	77	146
2005	3.5	65	159
2006	3.8	60	163
2007	4.1	64	179
2008	4.6	58	180
2009	4.4	61	180
2010	4.4	56	178

The Corruption Perceptions Index (CPI) ranks countries according to perception of corruption in the public sector. The CPI score ranges from 10 (highly clean) to 0 (highly corrupt).

Source: Transparency International

What has changed on the ground?

After all these reforms have been introduced, so far what has changed on the ground? This is a critical question to which attention needs to be paid. Unfortunately, there is no adequate research in Turkish public administration literature on the outcomes of recent administrative reforms. Thus, we can only make some general points. When we look at the practice of the Right to Information Law since its introduction in 2004 we can say that the right to information was welcomed enthusiastically by the Turkish public. This is clearly demonstrated by the annual reports prepared and made public by the Right to Information Review Board (BEDK). When the Law came into force on April 2004 the total number of applications in that year was 395,557. In the coming years the interest has been grown and the total number of applications has been increased to 626,789 in 2005, 864,616 in 2006, 939,920 in 2007, 1,099,133 in 2008 and 1,091,589 in 2009. Furthermore, more than 80 per cent of applications have resulted in access granted to information and documents requested by applicants. Besides, with this Law, it has now become possible to access many information and documents that were previously inaccessible or confidential. For example, now public employees have access to their employment records, personnel files and inspector review reports. Then, it would not be wrong to say that the Right to Information Law, to some extent, has increased openness of public administration.

Furthermore, given Turkey's recent Transparency International (TI) Corruption Perceptions Index (CPI) scores and ranks it can be said that good governance reforms have had some relatively positive impact on corruption. As shown in Table 11.1, there are some improvements in the score and rank of Turkey. Nevertheless the score is still below 5 out of 10.

In relation to financial transparency it is difficult to assert that there have been significant improvements even though the Public Financial Management and Control Law was passed in 2003 and has been in principle fully in force since 2006. In a recent OECD Report on Turkey it is stated that

> As of May 2010, the full degree of transparency in fiscal accounts does not yet match its initial objectives. Major progress was achieved at the central government level. The Ministry of Finance started to publish many components of general government accounts. However, a consolidated set of general government accounts are not yet published.
>
> (OECD, 2010 p. 84)

In general, it can be said that good governance reforms have brought some improvements but they are far from being at a satisfactory level. Thus, in the wake of these rapid changes, the effective implementation and enforcement of laws has become a critical issue in Turkey. In this regard, increasing importance of civil society organizations within Turkish social and political life is one encouraging sign to put recently introduced legal and structural arrangements into practice.

Obstacles to effective implementation: New rules and old habits?

There is no doubt that making legal reforms is a significant development on its own but without effective implementation of them it is unlikely to achieve the desired changes aimed with these reforms. In Turkey it can be argued that the discrepancy between legality and reality on the ground in some instances might be considerable. In this respect, it can be argued that there are some difficulties and obstacles to put new legal arrangements into practice. First of all, the prevalent state-centred administrative culture might pose great difficulties in implementing reforms because of incompatibility between traditional administrative structure and recent reforms which reflect good governance approach. Human Rights Boards can be a good example to illustrate this point. The provincial and district Human Rights Boards were first established in 2000 with a Regulation titled the Establishment, Duties and Working Principles of Provincial and District Human Rights Boards. A significant portion of the board members were consisted of public officials including police and gendarmerie commanders. With a new regulation issued in 2003 the composition of Human Rights Boards earned largely a civil character with representatives of bar associations, local governments, professional organizations, universities, political parties and other civil society organizations.

Human Rights Boards as a platform for bringing together the representatives of civil society and public administration could potentially play very important role in promoting human rights at local level. In this regard, the regulation in question gave provincial/district governors the primary responsibility in the work of the Boards. Indeed, they chair the Boards, determine the meeting agenda, and select representatives from applying civil society organizations. Furthermore, secretarial services shall be carried out by secretariats in provinces and districts; consultation and application desks shall be set up within the secretariats of provincial and district governorates and running costs shall be borne by the governorate. In this situation, it is clear that provincial/district governors play a key role in the effective functioning of Human Rights Boards. In other words, effective functioning of the Boards depends largely on the perceptions and attitudes of provincial/district governors toward human rights reform. A governor might think that creating participation mechanisms for civil society organizations in local government weakens state authority and endangers the unitary structure of the state. He might also be thinking that human rights related legal arrangements have been forcefully dictated by the EU. Even, he would personally think that inclusion of civil society organizations in administration process strips his powers and leaves him weak. If so, governors would not perform their responsibilities in a vigorous way. Instead, they will most likely adopt the tactic of 'act as if doing' to avoid to be blamed. In fact, a civil society organization representative member of a Human Rights Board who worked with different governors experienced the differences in the Board's work. He pointed out that the interest, leadership and commitment shown by the previous governor with regard to the works of the Board made quite a difference, which is reflected directly on the board's works (Sözen and Algan 2009). Today, there are 973 Human Rights Boards, 81 in provinces and 892 in districts. In 2010, only 2,446 people claiming human rights violations applied to these Boards (İnsan Hakları Başkanlığı 2011). Hence, the number of applications demonstrates very clearly that Human Right Boards are not functioning effectively.

Second, in relation to the design and scope of recently established mechanisms and structures there are some weaknesses which are adversely affecting their effectiveness. It can be argued that new mechanisms are not equipped with sufficient authority, autonomy and resources so as to undertake their functions in an efficient and effective way. For example, both the Ethics Committee for Civil Servants and the Board of Review of Access to Information do not have the status of a distinct public entity. They had neither their own budget and nor permanently assigned staff. Both of them are affiliated with the Prime Minister's Office and the secretariat is provided by the Office. In its evaluation report, the Council of Europe's Group of States against Corruption (GRECO) recommended that an appropriate budget and sufficient staff should be provided to them and independence of the Board of Review of Access to Information and the Ethics Committee for Civil Servants should be strengthened (GRECO, 2006). Similar points have also been made in the EU Reports. For example, in the EU 2007 Progress Report, it was stated that

The Ethical board of civil servants established in 2004 is still dependent on the Prime Ministry, with no separate budget or personnel of its own. It thus incurs limitations as to the proper fulfilment of its tasks of monitoring the respect of ethic principles and investigating complaints.

(European Commission, 2007: 60)

It might be argued that Turkish Governments are very reluctant to create autonomous agencies in public administration. Political parties in government desire to have a firm control on public bureaucracy. Thus, the challenge is not simply to establish a structure on paper but to give it the authority, autonomy, and resources with which to do its job.

Conclusion

In line with the democratization process the Turkish public administration has recently undergone significant reform. Now, public administration in Turkey is in a constant flux even though the failure of administrative reforms has a long tradition. The internal as well as external dynamics involved in the change process. More precisely, the main driving forces for change have been Turkey's aspiration for the EU full membership and the AKP Governments' strong political commitment to reform. Without doubt, the prospect of EU membership has been an effective instrument in the initiation of public administration reform. Domestically, the AKP Governments' anti-statist, pro-democracy and pro-EU political stance has been also an influential factor. Indeed, the AKP Governments have vigorously pursued the reform policies aimed at curbing the entrenched power of bureaucratic oligarchy within the politico-administrative system. In this regard, the goal and policies of AKP Governments have been in congruence with the EU's accession criteria. Hence, recent administrative reforms have provided citizens substantial legal rights and established new mechanisms to make public administration more transparent, accountable and participatory. Nevertheless, the AKP Governments have not been so enthusiastic in taking necessary measures aiming at making public administration more professionalized, autonomous and meritocratic. This is a crucial missing part in the recent public administration reform policies.

In general, recent legal and structural reforms have a potential to alter not only the role of public administration but also the nature of relationship between state and society. It can be said that when implemented effectively current administrative reforms can be a facilitating factor for the consolidation of Turkish democracy. However, effective implementation of administrative reforms is a challenging task and that is as important as making these arrangements. Within the existing administrative culture, the attitudes and behaviours of public officials towards these reforms might be obstructing one. Thus, successful implementation of current reforms relies heavily on the adaptation of public officials to their new roles. This requires changes in existing administrative culture. Moreover, the persistence of patrimonial patterns in the Turkish state and party patronage constitute another impediment to the introduction of administrative reforms aiming at the formation of legal-rational administration. To consolidate Turkish democracy political neutrality of bureaucracy is a crucial necessity.

To what extent do recent administrative reforms indicate the signs of the emergence of a 'new' public administration? As Turkey's unique geographic position where the East meets the West demonstrates, the Turkish public administration system includes modern as well as deep-rooted traditional elements. In other words, the 'old' public administration has largely coexisted with the 'new' public administration elements. Recent reforms, however, suggest that the direction of change is towards modernization and democratization of the politico-administrative system.

References

Eryılmaz, B. (2002) *Bürokrasi ve Siyaset*, İstanbul: Alfa yayınları.

European Commission (2007) *Turkey 2007 Progress Report*, Brussels: Commission of the European Communities. Online. Available HTTP: <http://ec.europa.eu/enlargement/pdf/key_documents/2007/nov/turkey_progress_reports_en.pdf> (accessed 11 January 2010).

—— (2009) *Turkey 2009 Progress Report*, Brussels: Commission of the European Communities. Online. Available HTTP: <http://ec.europa.eu/enlargement/pdf/key_documents/2009/tr_rapport_2009_en.pdf> (accessed 21 July 2010).

—— (2010) *Turkey 2010 Progress Report*, Brussels: Commission of the European Communities. Online. Available HTTP: <http://ec.europa.eu/enlargement/pdf/key_documents/2010/package/tr_rapport_2010_en.pdf> (accessed 3 February 2011).

Ezra, S. (2003) *Dismantling Democratic States*, Princeton: Princeton University Press.

GRECO (2006) *Joint First and Second Evaluation Report*. Online. Available HTTP: <http://www.coe.int/t/dghl/monitoring/greco/evaluations/round2/GrecoEval1-2 (2005)3_Turkey_EN.pdf> (accessed 3 February 2011).

Günes-Ayata, A. (1994) 'Roots and trends of clientelism in Turkey', in L. Roniger and A. Günes-Ayata (eds) *Democracy, Clientelism, and Civil Society*, Colorado: Lynne Reinner.

Hamilton, M. R. (2007) 'Democracy and public service' in Box, R. C. (ed.) *Democracy and Public administration*, New York: M.E. Sharpe, Inc.

Heady, F. (1984) *Public Administration: A Comparative Perspective*, New. York: Marcel Dekker.

Heper, M. (1987) 'State, democracy, and bureaucracy in Turkey', in M. Heper (ed.), *The State and Public Bureaucracies: A Comparative Perspective*, New York: Greenwood Press.

—— (1990) 'The state and debureaucratization: the case of Turkey', *International Social Science Journal*, 42 (4): 605–15.

—— (1992) 'The strong state as a problem of democracy: Turkey and Germany compared', *Comparative Political Studies*, 25 (2): 169–94.

Heper, M. and Keyman, F. (1998) 'Double-faced state: political patronage and the consolidation of democracy in Turkey," *Middle Eastern Studies*, 34(4): 259–77.

İnalcik, H. (1980) 'Turkey between europe and middle east', *Foreign Policy,* 7(7).

İnsan Hakları Başkanlığı (2008) 2007 *Türkiye İnsan Hakları Raporu, Ankara: Başbakanlık İnsan Hakları Başkanlığı.* Online. Available: http://www.humanrights.gov.tr/raporlar.htm (accessed 21 September 2009)

—— (2011) 2010 *Türkiye İnsan Hakları Raporu, Ankara: Başbakanlık İnsan Hakları Başkanlığı.* Online. Available: http://www.ihb.gov.tr/DuyuruGoster.Aspx?AdvID= 86&AdvBaslik, (accessed 24 February 2011).

Linz, J. J. and Stepan, A. (1996) *Problems of Democratic Transition and Consolidation,* Baltimore: The John Hopkins University Press.

Mango, A. (1977) 'The state of Turkey', *Middle Eastern Studies,* 13: 261–73.

Meier, K. J., and O'Toole, L. J. (2006) *Bureaucracy in a Democratic State: A Governance Perspective,* Baltimore: The Johns Hopkins University Press.

OECD (2010) *Economic Surveys: Turkey,* Paris: OECD. Online. Available HTTP: <http://www.oecd-ilibrary.org/economics/oecd-economic-surveys-turkey-2010_eco_-surveys-tur-2010-en> (accessed 20 January 2011).

Özbudun, E. (1981) 'Turkey: The politics of clientelism' in S. N. Eisenstadt and R. Lemarchand (eds), *Political Clientelism, Patronage and Development,* London: Sage.

—— (1996) 'Turkey: How far from consolidation?', *Journal of Democracy,* 7 (3): 123–38.

—— (2000) *Contemporary Turkish Politics: Challenges to Democratic Consolidation,* Colorado: Lynne Rienner Publishers.

Peters, B. G (2010) 'Bureaucracy and democracy', *Public Organization Review,* 10: 209–22.

Sakallıoğlu, U. C. (1997) 'The anatomy of the Turkish military's political autonomy' *Comparative Politics,* 29 (2): 151–66.

Sayari, S. (1977) 'Political patronage in Turkey' in Gellner, E. and Waterbury, J. (eds), *Patrons and Clients in Mediterranean Societies,* London: Dockworth's.

Şaylan, G. (1974) *Türkiye'de Kapitalism Bürokrasi ve Siyasal İdeoloji,* Ankara: TODAİE.

Schumpeter, Joseph A. (1949) *Capitalism, Socialism and Democracy,* 3rd ed. New York: Harper.

Sözen, S. (2005) 'Administrative reforms in Turkey: Imperatives, efforts, and constraints', *Ankara Üniversitesi S.B.F Dergisi,* 60(3).

Sözen, S. and Algan, B. (2009) *Good Governance,* Ankara: The Ministry of Interior.

Sözen, S. and Shaw, I. (2003) 'Turkey and the European Union: modernizing a traditional state?' *Social Policy & Administration,* 37(2): 108–20.

SPO (2010) *2010 Annual Programme,* Ankara: Undersecretariat of State Planning Organization. Online. Available HTTP: <http://ekutup.dpt.gov.tr/program/2010/2010_program_i.pdf> (accessed 22 October 2010).

Sunar, İ. (1974), *State and Society in the Politics of Turkey's Development,* Ankara: AÜSBF.

12 Determinants of tax evasion by households

Evidence from Turkey

Fikret Adaman and Ali Çarkoğlu

Introduction and setting out the problem

Tax evasion, defined as intentional and fraudulent activities by economic agents to escape paying taxes, has been of great importance to Turkey, bringing about considerable economic and societal costs. It is now clear that both business and households in the country are indeed looking for ways to evade taxes of all sorts, thereby contributing to the shrinking of revenues collected through the tax system. More specifically, collected tax revenues in Turkey barely reach one-quarter of the national GDP (it was 23.7 per cent in 2007), while figures for OECD and EU countries fluctuate at close to two-fifths of their GDPs (the EU15 and OECD figures for 2007 were 38.8 per cent and 35.8 per cent, respectively) (Zenginobuz *et al.* 2010). This difference comes about not because the state lacks the desire to collect taxes at levels comparable to the EU average, but because it is largely unable to do so. Zenginobuz and Tokgöz offer a striking example of the extent of tax evasion, arguing that in 2008 in Turkey, VAT evasion was at 41 per cent (calculated as the difference between the potential income tax people should normally pay – based on consumption figures revealed in a country-wide comprehensive household survey – and the actual amount of collected taxes) (Zenginobuz and Tokgöz 2010). Furthermore, since income tax evasion seems to be relatively easier than consumption tax evasion in a value-added tax environment, the composition of tax revenues in Turkey hinges on another anomaly: Roughly speaking, only one-third of tax revenue is generated through direct taxes, while the remainder comes from indirect taxation – a picture that is almost completely reversed in most developed countries (Zenginobuz *et al.* 2010).

Informality, defined as a set of economic activities that take place outside the framework of bureaucratic establishments (see, e.g., Hart 2008), complements tax evasion in many ways. Although the difficulty of formulating a causal link between tax evasion and informality needs to be acknowledged, it can nonetheless be argued that these two dimensions are closely correlated in the Turkish case.

Informality manifests via a vast array of mechanisms that have been invented and are in effective use in many sectors of the Turkish economy. Apart from the non-registration of workers with the social security system, it may be claimed that the most important forms of informality are the underreporting of revenues and wages. Note also that the main fiscal effect of informal employment translates to losses of personal income tax (as firms underreport or completely conceal wages, and the self-employed, their income). Currently, according to the Turkish Statistical Institute (TURK-STAT) household survey conducted with people who work, 44 per cent of the working force is informally employed (Ercan 2010; TURKSTAT 2010; World Bank 2010). This figure alone could be taken as a headline measure of informality in the country. Despite the very presence of methodological problems in estimating the magnitude of informality by virtue of the subject, the existing literature on Turkey reveals that compared to national GDP, informality is at about 35 per cent (Schneider 2007).

In addition to fiscal losses from tax evasion, informality brings additional social costs. First, in a social protection system largely indexed to employment in the formal sector, a considerable portion of the informally employed are vulnerable to social exclusion due to various reasons (Adaman and Ardıç 2008). Informal workers are also excluded from the welfare system and cannot benefit from union protection in relations with their employers. Exclusion from both the welfare system, and unionized employment and wage negotiations, means informal-sector employees are at major risk when exposed to exploitative motives and erratic changes in market conditions. Second, loss of respect for public institutions and increased feelings of injustice will inevitably lower social morale in general and encourage more people to evade taxes. Third, massive informality leads to productivity losses in the economy (for a general assessment, see Oviedo *et al.* 2009; for a study conducted on Turkey, see World Bank 2010). A further complication may also arise, exacerbated by dynamics that accompany a reckless social consciousness, where informality and tax evasion are not considered reprehensible acts. Consequently, a lop-sided conception of citizenship may slowly take shape, and foundations of a sustainable tax system leading to a capable state – which undertakes social and economic responsibilities for its citizens – may disappear.

Within this broader picture, the objective of this chapter is to try and understand why households in Turkey, qua ordinary citizens, opt to evade taxes. In their role as producers and/or consumers, households may decide to evade taxes due to a myriad of reasons. They have, at their disposal, a rich palette of options to choose from to this end, including underreporting (or completely hiding) their income; employing informal labour; underreporting rent contracts; or evading VAT simply by relying on cash transactions without a receipt. It goes without saying that any reform initiative aiming to tackle the problem of tax evasion in Turkey should question the motives that underlie public attitudes toward tax evasion. The present study aims to answer this exact question.

More specifically, the aim here is to evaluate the dynamics that lead to tax evasion in Turkey. Using data from a survey conducted in 2008 with a sample of households in Turkey, the relevance of two reasons are assessed in explaining people's attitudes toward tax evasion. The first is the extent to which people's trust in the Turkish Government impacts their attitudes toward tax evasion. People's perceptions of how well their taxes are used in the provision of public goods and services ultimately explain their tax evasion behaviour. Inefficiencies in the public sector – as perceived by households – is therefore likely to create low 'tax morale' in people, as a result of which they refrain from paying taxes (see, e.g., Torgler 2007; World Bank 2010). Coined as the 'we-pay-for-what-we-get' attitude, the link between low levels of trust in the Government and tax evasion is depicted in the literature that uses cross-country analyses (that convincingly show the correlation between low institutional quality – as proxied by corruption, weak rule of law, and lack of accountability and transparency – and the extent of tax evasion – as proxied by the proportion of informality in the country) (see, e.g., Buehn and Schneider 2007). Alternatively, micro-level survey data is used in this study across an urban sample from Turkey, to test whether the link between trust in the Government and tax evasion is also valid for a given country. Provided that people's level of trust will vary, a negative relationship between level of trust and tax evasion is expected.

The second reason why people may choose to evade taxes is linked to their perceptions regarding the extent to which their fellow citizens contribute to collected taxes. If people believe that the bulk of taxes will not be collected, will they be ready to pay their taxes promptly or evade payment? Conversely, what if people believe that the overwhelming majority will pay their taxes appropriately; what would their reaction be then? This is obviously largely a collective action issue, with the related matter of the free-riding problem at the heart of it. Theoretical findings and empirical evidence are vague on this subject; while a higher number of taxpayers (that is to say, a low free-riding problem) may conceivably provide an incentive to free-ride (thinking that a large amount of funds will be collected anyway), it may also induce people to act as responsible citizens, and in a way reciprocate the positive attitudes of others by making their contribution more likely. However, presumably no one would like their contribution to be used by opportunistic people, implying that if one thinks only a small fraction will pay their taxes, one may choose to evade them as well (Sugden 1984; Wiser 2007). The present paper also aims to look at this dimension of collective action through the results of the survey conducted.

The remaining part of this chapter is structured as follows: The next section briefly presents the survey that was conducted in 2008, outlining the sampling procedure and establishing its statistical significance in representing the whole country. The conducted econometric study follows; the main model and the way in which parameters have been characterized are introduced at the beginning of the section. The final section evaluates the findings and offers some concluding remarks.

Research design, sampling and survey administration

The fieldwork consisted of face-to-face interviews that were administered by a professional research company between 14 October and 26 November 2008, with 1,004 persons from the urban areas of the following cities in Turkey: Istanbul, Izmir, Ankara, Kocaeli, Bursa, Denizli, Mersin, Konya, Gaziantep, Malatya, Trabzon and Adiyaman (representing 47 per cent of the total population).[1] The targeted number of interviews was first distributed across the statistical regions (Nomenclature of Territorial Units for Statistics – NUTS Level 1) of TURKSTAT according to urban population share. Based on urban population figures, a representative province was then selected from each region using probability proportionate to size (PPS).[2] Once interviews across cities had been determined, PPS was used once again to select two districts per province. Block data were obtained from TURK-STAT for each district, and household addresses were randomly chosen from each block. The unit of analysis was the household, thus respondents aged 18 and above from each household were determined by random sampling. If the selected person was unavailable at the time of the visit, an appointment was made and the household was visited for a second time. If the selected person was still unavailable, a new replacement address was again randomly chosen from the block of addresses obtained from TURK-STAT. Prior to finalizing the questionnaire, a set of pre-tests was conducted. Interviews lasted approximately 30 minutes on average and rejection rate was 25 per cent.

The main descriptive demographic statistics were as follows: Of the respondents, 47.3 per cent were female and 52.7 per cent male; regarding educational background, 6.6 per cent had no formal schooling and thus hold no diploma, 42.7 per cent had a primary school diploma, 13.1 per cent a middle-school diploma, 24.7 per cent a high-school diploma, and the remaining 13.4 per cent a university degree or higher. These results conform to census data compiled by TURKSTAT, for the rejection rate is almost always higher for women than for men in Turkey (thus explaining the slight bias towards men in our distribution).

Econometric analysis

The model

We propose to estimate the following multinomial logit model:

$$\Pr(Y_i = j) = F(\alpha P_i + \beta T_i + \sum \lambda_i \, SD_i),$$

where Y_i denotes tax evasion by the respondent, and is equal to either 'I tend not to pay tax," or "I neither pay nor refuse to pay tax (inconclusive answer)', or 'I tend to pay tax'; F(.) is the standard normal distribution; and i denotes individuals.[3] Following the literature, the error term is assumed to be independent across individuals. The explanatory variables are grouped into three categories: P denotes participation index, indicating the extent to which respondents think their fellow citizens pay taxes; T corresponds to respondents' trust index for central government officers; and finally SD corresponds to individual characteristics that include age, gender, education, household size, wealth, and respondents' level of satisfaction with the economic conditions of their family. These parameters are elaborated next.

The parameters

At this point it should be noted that the dependent variable represents a categorical tendency of the respondents to report the extent to which they paid their taxes. The subjectivity of these assessments should be underlined. The wording here takes the subjective judgment of the amount other people should be paying in taxes as a reference point. If there had been any tax inspectors among the respondents, they might have had a clear idea as to the amount of taxes their colleagues should be paying. However, this judgment is likely to be quite a challenge for non-expert laypersons especially in Turkey, where, as underlined above, pervasive informality undermines the whole tax system and individuals' taxes are typically deducted from their salaries or wages, and people do not fill out income tax forms to pay their taxes. The wording again does not differentiate between direct income tax and indirect taxes like the VAT. Thus the wording of the question attempts to simplify the real world complexity concerning taxation in the Turkish context, and an overall subjective assessment is targeted concerning the extent to which respondents feel they are paying their taxes. The midpoint (5 and 6 on the 1-to-10 scale) category represents here an inconclusive judgment by the respondent. Respondents who scored either 5 or 6 on the original 1-to-10 scale seemed to reach no conclusive judgment about their tendency to pay taxes. Those who scored between 7 and 10 (or alternatively between 1 and 4) on the original scale appear to be reporting that they tend to pay (not pay) their taxes. In short, respondents were asked to roughly judge whether or not they felt they actually were or were not paying taxes.

This may sound like an easy question, but an overall judgment may in fact be quite difficult to reach for a conscientious respondent. The results are reported in Figure 12.1, which indicates that 8 per cent tend to feel that they are not paying their taxes, while 5 per cent are inconclusive about their stance on taxes and the rest apparently feel they tend to pay their taxes. There might of course be an upward manipulation in the answers; respondents may have felt pressure to appear as responsible citizens and inflated their answers. However, since the aim here is to explain variances in the answers (and not the absolute values), and since there is no *a priori* expectation that some subgroups (say women or relatively more educated groups)

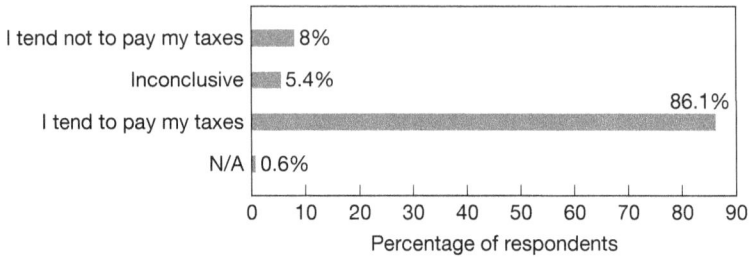

Figure 12.1 Of the taxes you know you should be paying, how much do you actually pay?

might inflate their responses more than others, this possible manipulation was considered negligible.

The aim here was to explain the variations in the rate of people's self-reported tax payments by the two dimensions that were outlined above. The first dimension is the extent to which respondents believed tax revenues would be spent efficiently and effectively. Perceived level of trust in officers attached to the central government was used as a proxy (since it is the government that levies the bulk of the taxes), and a scale of 1-to-10 was employed, where 1 represented no trust and 10, complete trust. Figure 12.2 shows the respondents by groups and the average points for each entry. A factor analysis was applied, and two factors obtained. One consisted of government officers, judges, police officers, finance/tax officers, politicians, and members of the armed forces; this factor was named trust in agents of the central government. Finally, factor loadings of that group were taken as the proxy for respondents' level of trust in the central government.

Findings related to the above summary measures of trust are telling in that confidence toward politicians is very low. As illustrated in Figure 12.2, politicians received an average score of 2.6 on a scale of 1-to-10. Furthermore, leaving aside members of the armed forces who have historically been somewhat idolized, none of the items in the central government category managed to obtain an average score of 7 or above. In passing let us note that low levels of trust in members of the central Government and its related organs have been observed in previous studies; therefore, the current set of results simply confirms them (see Adaman et al. 2009, and references cited therein). Obviously, a low level of trust in the central Government may arise if the Government is not considered competent enough to provide high quality public services, and/or if it is perceived as corrupt. A detailed inquiry on the underpinnings of low trust levels is beyond the scope of this paper; knowing the overall level of trust for the central government is sufficient for our purposes.

The second dimension is the extent to which individuals perceive their fellow citizens will contribute to the collective action case by paying their

Members of the Armed Forces — 8.3
Judges — 6.5
Police officers — 6.2
Neighborhood craftsmen — 5.8
Government officers — 5.4
Municipal officers — 5.3
Finance/Tax officers — 5.0
Street vendors — 3.2
Politicians — 2.6

1 2 3 4 5 6 7 8 9 10
No   Full
confidence   confidence

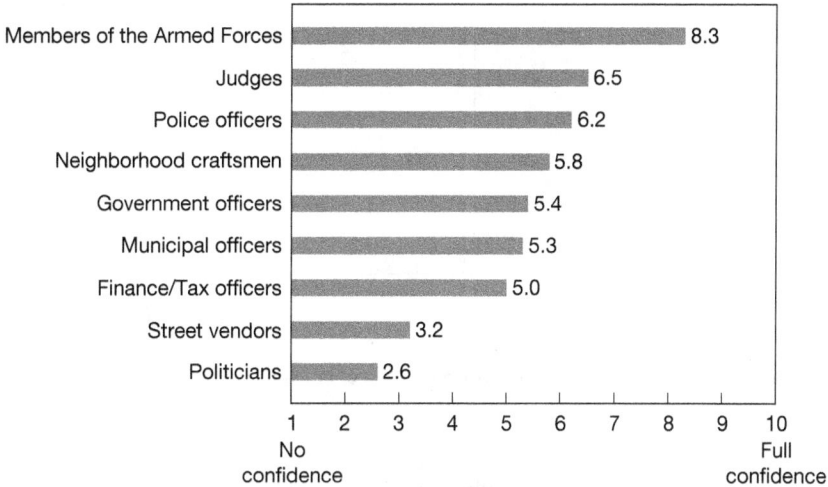

Figure 12.2 On a scale of 1 to 10, how much confidence do you have in the following people and institutions? (Mean values)

taxes. Responses are again on a 1-to-10 scale, where 1 denotes that respondents think their fellow citizens pay no taxes at all, and 10 indicates views that they pay their taxes in full. As seen in Figure 12.3, only 23.2 per cent reported that they felt other people paid their taxes promptly or near-promptly (by marking scores of 7 and above – 5 and 6 were the inconclusive

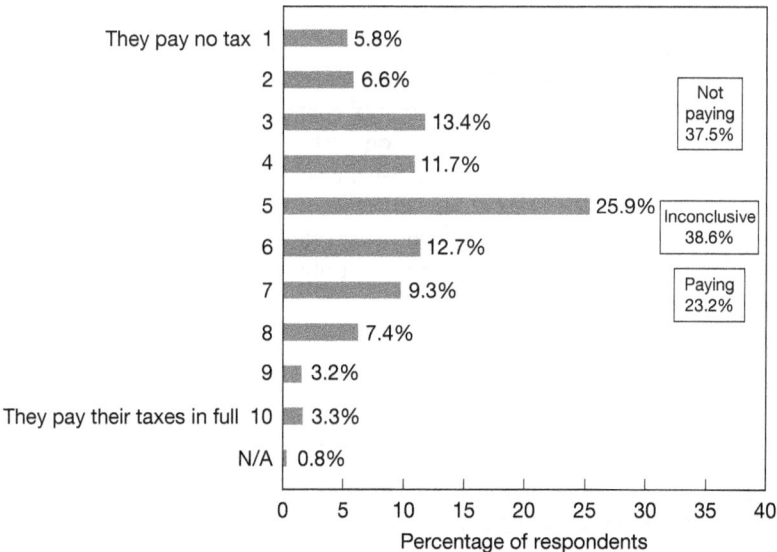

They pay no tax 1 — 5.8%
2 — 6.6%
3 — 13.4%
4 — 11.7%
5 — 25.9%
6 — 12.7%
7 — 9.3%
8 — 7.4%
9 — 3.2%
They pay their taxes in full 10 — 3.3%
N/A — 0.8%

Not paying 37.5%
Inconclusive 38.6%
Paying 23.2%

0   5   10   15   20   25   30   35   40
Percentage of respondents

Figure 12.3 To what extent do you think people pay their taxes?

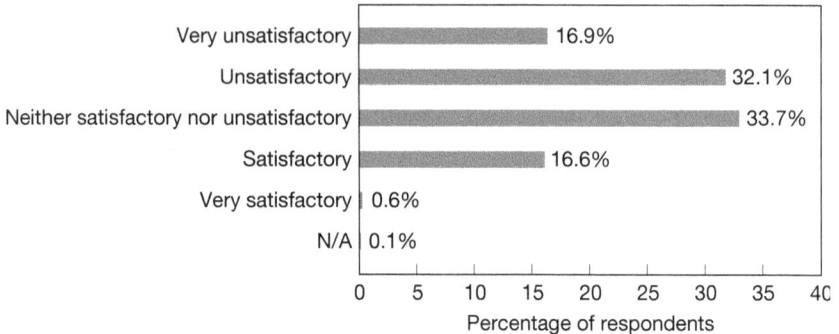

Figure 12.4 Level of satisfaction with economic conditions of the family.

midpoints). This is a rather striking finding; people apparently feel that an important portion of their fellow citizens evade taxes fully or partially.

To control the net effects of the above introduced parameters, as set out in the model, it was necessary to filter the possible effects of a set of 'controlling parameters'. In addition to standard parameters such as age, gender, household size, and education, it was decided to consider two other dimensions. The first was wealth of households. To this end, the possession of household items consisting of dish washers, DVD players, microwaves, plasma TVs, computers, internet access, air conditioners and summer homes were coded for each household, and a total wealth score was computed for each household based on the total number owned items. Respondents that had all the wealth items on the list were given a score of 100, and those who had only half of the items were given a score of 50. Hence, the wealth score indicates the percentage of items owned by the respondents.

The second parameter, somewhat complementary to the wealth dimension, was respondents' level of satisfaction with the economic conditions of their family. As depicted in Figure 12.4, more than half the respondents indicated dissatisfaction with the economic conditions of their family. Although this indicator (a subjective measure) can be seen as correlated with the wealth indicator (an objective measure), both capture different aspects of wellbeing in the given sample.

The econometric analysis and the results

The results of the multinomial logit regression conducted will be presented here, with the aim of determining which parameters have explanatory power and which do not in explaining respondents' tax evasion attitudes. The results are offered in Table 12.1. As discussed above, our point of interest is to ascertain the possible effects of the perceptions of the magnitude of free-riding in the community and the level of trust in the government. To filter

Table 12.1 Econometric results

How much tax do I pay?	I tend not to pay my taxes			I tend to pay my taxes		
	B	Sig.	Exp(B)	B	Sig.	Exp(B)
Intercept	2.31	0.19		-0.95	0.49	
Participation	-0.45	**0.00**	0.64	0.00	0.96	1.00
Trust	-0.12	0.52	0.89	0.51	**0.00**	1.67
Age	0.00	0.80	1.00	0.02	**0.09**	1.02
Gender (1=female)	0.05	0.90	1.05	-0.26	0.41	0.77
Family size	0.20	0.11	1.23	0.21	**0.05**	1.23
Wealth	0.02	0.12	0.98	0.00	0.52	1.00
Education (ref. group = University degree or higher)						
Illiterate	-0.85	0.43	0.43	-2.17	**0.01**	0.11
Literate with no diploma	-1.77	0.16	0.17	-2.04	**0.03**	0.13
Primary school graduate	-0.95	0.22	0.39	-0.90	0.16	0.41
Middle school graduate	0.10	0.91	1.10	-0.36	0.63	0.70
High school graduate	-1.14	0.12	0.32	-1.21	**0.04**	0.30
Satisfaction from the surrounding economic conditions (ref. group = Very satisfactory)						
Very unsatisfactory	0.39	0.77	1.48	2.80	**0.01**	16.43
Unsatisfactory	0.21	0.88	1.23	3.40	**0.00**	29.84
Neither/nor	0.57	0.67	1.77	3.57	**0.00**	35.65
Satisfactory	0.54	0.69	1.72	2.74	**0.01**	15.46
Cox and Snell			0.14			
Nagelkerke			0.22			
McFadden			0.15			

any possible effects of socio-demographic characteristics, a set of parameters was included in the regression to control for them.

The first observed result is that if free-riding is believed to be widespread (viz., a shift toward 1 on the 1-to-10 'participation' scale), people would tend to avoid paying their taxes – an observation in line with the literature. Quite interestingly, however, the reverse does not hold: the fact that free-riding is believed to be less widespread, that is if it is believed that people do pay their taxes (viz., a shift toward 10 on the 1-to-10 'participation' scale), does not make people shift toward a tendency to duly pay their taxes. This implies that tax evasion has a self-fulfilling nature in the sense that bad perceptions exacerbate the tax evasion problem, but correcting perceptions would not induce people to pay their taxes promptly.

Second, it was seen that increased confidence in bureaucrats attached to the central Government was likely to make people report a tendency to pay taxes. It is again interesting to note that the reverse does not hold in this case either – viz., a decreased level of trust in the central government does not make individuals more likely to report they do not pay their taxes. Therefore, as will be further elaborated in the next session, the only policy that would be effective in combating tax evasion at the individual level is one that alters people's perceptions on both free-riding and trust in government officers. Partial improvement would only bring about partial success.

Finally, with regards the effects of the control variables used in this analysis, those found to be significant were also in the expected direction: Although gender and wealth were found not to be significant, other parameters were. Older respondents tended to report that they paid their taxes; this was also true of families with a large number of family members. Education levels of university degree or higher also made it more likely that taxes would be paid. Lastly, respondents who were rather dissatisfied with the economic conditions of their family were more likely to report that they paid taxes. In summary, while there appears no difference between men and women and no impact of relative household wealth in terms self-reported likelihood of tax payment, older people, people with higher education, and people who are relatively less satisfied with their family's economic conditions are more likely to report that they paid their taxes.

Evaluation and concluding remarks

The above discussion makes it clear that tax evasion at the household level in urban Turkey, as the main manifestation of informality, is deeply rooted in two perceptions ordinary people have. The first is a common view that 'a large number of ordinary citizens are evading taxes'. This perspective clearly creates a disincentive for anyone to pay his/her taxes, and is an indication of a coordination failure among people. The second, on the other hand, is based on the expectation that public services will be provided efficiently only if there is a trust in the central government. If people trust in governments, then they will tend to pay their taxes properly. But if a significant number of people do not trust their government, tax collection will not be properly secured – and likely other forms of informality as well – tax evasion will simply be legitimatized and normalized in the country, creating a vicious cycle that has so far proven difficult to break. A typical household that supposes a significant number of other households are informal will not pay their taxes properly. In a similar vein, people who believe that the government is simply either incompetent or too corrupt, and would thus waste the monies collected, would *ceteris paribus* not pay their taxes properly. Given this attitude of households, the state machinery will at the end of the day be unable to meet the expectations throughout the country because of this inability to collect taxes. As a result, lacking or low-quality public services will in turn further create low tax morale.

The questions of 'how does one break this vicious cycle, change this perception, improve the quality of state services, provide more formal jobs or create incentives to shift towards a more formal economy?' remain as challenging as ever. Our survey made it clear that to make people responsible citizens and induce them to pay taxes, securing their commitment is as vital as making long-term investments to build trust in ordinary citizens.

On a pessimistic note, it could be said that the short-run vision of democratically elected governments may not favour such long-term policies of building trust in people for the merit and efficiency of their government apparatus. Improving the responsiveness and efficiency of the policy machinery, and especially rendering the bureaucracy more efficient and trustworthy, requires long-term investments, the returns of which may only be observed beyond any government's tenure. Thus, a natural disincentive seems to exist that does not favour such policy reforms.

Yet on an optimistic note, several mechanisms may already be underway that naturally create a favourable atmosphere for reform. First among these is the global investment environment that creates ready funds for countries like Turkey to use for long-term development and growth. Such funds naturally seek a business environment that is free from corruption and ask for formalization of the economy for a predictable and fair competition environment. Turkey, being part of this environment, is already feeling the need, and already has a heavy dose of incentives to ameliorate its corrupt and informal economy in order to attract readily available investment funds for its long-term development. Second is the economic environment that the EU membership seeks to create in newly acceded countries, which formalizes and reforms the corrupt policy machinery in member states. As Turkey moves along the treacherous negotiation chapters, concerning especially economic issues, a reform of the tax system that would bring about formalization and anti-corruption measures could create the long-term momentum it requires.

Notes

1 The survey was prepared for the World Bank Ankara Office by a team consisting of ourselves and Prof. Mine Eder (of Boğaziçi University) for a project on informality in Turkey. We are thankful to the World Bank as well as to Prof. Eder for their consent in letting us use the data. Frekans Research Company, Istanbul, conducted the survey.

2 In a companion survey, administered again by the same team, the business community was interviewed and 12 cities were selected to represent the contributions of businesses to the country. The household survey used the same set of cities.

3 Our dependent variable was obtained from a question about the extent to which individuals actually pay their taxes. The answers were obtained on a 1-to-10 scale, where 1 represents "I don't pay any taxes" and 10 represents 'I pay all my taxes'. All our analyses were first ran with an ordered logit model as the scale used was an ordinal one. Yet, in none of our estimates was the assumption of parallel regression maintained. We thus regrouped the scale values into three categories. Values between 1 and 4 were coded in the 'doesn't pay tax' category; 5 and 6 were coded as 'neither pays nor refuses to pay tax', and values between 7 and 10 were coded in the 'pays tax' category. Following Long's (1997, pp: 145–49) suggestion, we then estimated our models with the multinomial logit model using the middle category of neither paying nor refusing to pay as our reference category. Our consequent finding of a positive (negative) coefficient in comparing the 'doesn't pay taxes' category with our reference category indicates a tendency to switch from (to) the inconclusive reference category towards (from) tax evasion. Alternatively, in the second comparison of the reference category with the 'pays taxes' category, a positive (negative) coefficient indicates a tendency to move from (to) the inconclusive reference category to (from) the pays taxes category.

References

Adaman, F. and Ardıç, P. (2008) 'Social exclusion in the slum areas of largecities in Turkey', *New Perspectives on Turkey*, 38: 29–60.

Adaman, F., Çarkoğlu, A., and Şenatalar, B. (2009) *Türkiye'de Kamu Reformu (Public Sector Reform in Turkey)*, Ankara: TEPAV.

Buehn, A. and Schneider, F. (2007) 'Shadow economies and corruption all over the world: Revised estimates for 120 countries', *Economics: The Open-Access, Open-Assessment*, E-Journal, Vol. 1, 2007–9 (Version 2). Online. Available HTTP: <http://www.economics-ejournal.org/economics/journalarticles/2007–9> (accessed 30 June 2013).

Ercan, H. (2010) 'Crisis and self-employment in Turkey', report prepared for European Employment Observatory.

Hart, K. (2008) 'Informal economy' in S.N. Durlauf and L.E. Blume (eds.) *The New Palgrave Dictionary of Economics*, Second Edition, Palgrave Macmillan.

Long, J.S. (1997) *Regression Models for Categorical and Limited Dependent Variables*, Thousand Oaks, CA.: Sage Publications.

Oviedo, A.M, Thomas, M.R., and Karakurun-Özdemir, K. (2009) *Economic Informality: Causes, Costs, and Policies-A Literature Survey*, World Bank Working Paper no 167, Washington D.C.

Schneider, F. (2007) 'Shadow economies and corruption all over the world: new estimates for 145 countries', *Economics: The Open-Access, Open-Assessment E-Journal.*

Sugden, R. (1984) 'Reciprocity: The supply of public goods through voluntary contribution', *The Economic Journal*, 94 (376): 772–87.

Torgler, B. (2007) *Tax Compliance and Tax Morale: A theoretical and empirical analysis*, Cheltenham, UK: Edward Elgar.

TURKSTAT (2010) *Labor Force Survey 2009*, Ankara: TUIK.

Wiser, R.H. (2007) 'Using contingent valuation to explore willingness to pay for renewable energy: A comparison of collective and voluntary payment vehicles', *Ecological Economics*, 62 (3–4): 419–32.

World Bank (2010) *Turkey: Country Economic Memorandum: Informality: Causes, Consequences, Policies*, Ankara.

Zenginobuz, Ü., Adaman, F., Gökşen, F., Savcı, Ç., and Tokgöz, E. (2010) *Türkiye'de Vergiler, Temsiliyet ve Demokrasi (Taxation, Representation, and Democracy in Turkey)*, Istanbul: Boğaziçi University Publications.

Zenginobuz, Ü. and Tokgöz, E. (2010) 'Trends in tax revenues and rates in OECD countries: A comparative assessment of the Turkish tax system', mimeo, Istanbul: March 2010.

13 From tutelary powers and interventions to civilian control

An overview of Turkish civil-military relations since the 1920s

Yaprak Gürsoy

Any account of democracy and democratization in Turkey must also focus, among other factors, on civil-military relations and the role of the Turkish Armed Forces (TAF) in politics. The influence of the military could be analyzed from two perspectives. While the interventions and powers of the armed forces could be seen as *obstacles* to democratization, they can also be perceived as important *indicators* of lack of full democracy in the country. The TAF have had political autonomy since 1923 and intervened in politics through two different mechanisms; first, by staging overt coups (1960, 1980) and, second, by pressuring the elected governments to resign through implicit or explicit threats of coups (1971, 1997). For much of the republican period, the military also exercised tutelary functions without intervening in democracy. Such military influence in politics and coups has prevented the establishment of a stable democracy in the country. As Linz and Stepan argue, transition to democracy is not complete if the 'elected government ... [does not have the] *de facto* ... authority to generate new policies, and when the executive, legislature and judicial power generated by the new democracy share power with other bodies *de jure*' (Linz and Stepan 1996: 3). The involvement of the TAF in politics as a veto player and as a possible power that could overthrow the government has been a significant impediment of full democratization in Turkey since the Government and other elected bodies have had important limitations in generating certain policies, especially on security, and have shared power with the military.

However, at the same time, the circumstances that led to military intrusions have also been important indicators of an unconsolidated democracy. In other words, not just the fact that the military has intervened in politics, but also the reasons that led to these interventions are significant for understanding why Turkish democracy has not been consolidated. According to Linz and Stepan's definition of democratic consolidation, all significant actors in a polity must behaviorally, attitudinally, and constitutionally support democracy so that it becomes the 'only game in town.' In such a definition, there are three important criteria. First, behaviorally, 'no significant group attempt[s] to overthrow the democratic regime and secede from the state.' Second, attitudinally, 'the overwhelming majority of the people believe that any further political change must emerge from within the parameters of democratic formulas.' Finally, constitutionally, 'all the actors in the polity become habituated to the fact that political conflict will be resolved according to the established norms and that violations of these norms are likely to be both ineffective and costly' (Linz and Stepan 1996: 5).

Given this definition, Turkey has not consolidated its democracy. Significant groups in society and also within the military has made attempts to overthrow the regime, at least temporarily. Supporters of leftist ideologies, political Islamists or Kurdish activists have been suspected of attempting to overthrow the secular, republican, and democratic regime. It has been believed that these radical groups could violate democratic institutions and norms. Their support for democracy has been seen as instrumental rather than being a goal in itself. Such arguments, then, have justified military interventions and support for TAF's role in politics. It is not a coincidence that military interventions followed intense polarization of politics into rival camps, such as left versus right, secular versus religious, separatist versus nationalist. Such conflicts have demonstrated that democracy was unconsolidated in Turkey because civilian groups in society have not regarded democracy as the only game in town. But at the same time, polarization also has made the very act that undermined democracy, military intervention, a credible option, ironically in order to protect the regime.

This chapter will analyze civil-military relations from the perspective that military interventions have been both obstacles and indicators of an unconsolidated democracy in Turkey. The first section will provide an historical overview of the development of the military in the Ottoman Empire, its increasing autonomy during the republican period and the military interventions of 1960, 1971, 1980, and 1997. This section will provide both a background to current Turkish civil-military relations and also a partial explanation of why Turkish democracy has failed to consolidate after the transition to multi-party politics in 1946. The second part of the chapter will focus more on recent developments and especially the reforms in civil-military relations and the trial of retired and active-duty military officers suspected of being involved with coup conspiracies in the early 2000s. This section will try to assess whether or not civilian control over the military is increasing and what these current events mean for democratic consolidation.

The era of direct interventions: Civil-military relations up until the 1980s

Turkey made a transition to multi-party politics in 1946 and to democracy in 1950. However, the regime has not been consolidated partly because of the role of the military in politics. The autonomy of the TAF, their involvement in democracy, and their ideological stance can be traced back to the Ottoman Empire and the early republican period. The military interventions between 1960 and 1997 left significant legacies in shaping the powers of the military, with important implications for democratic consolidation. This section will analyze this historical legacy in order to shed better light on subsequent developments.

The birth of a new civilian and military bureaucracy in the Ottoman Empire and the founding of the Turkish Republic

Understanding Turkish politics necessarily entails analyzing the rise of a new group of political and military elites during the later stages of the Ottoman Empire. These elites, characterized by their secular stance, came into existence during the reform period of the nineteenth century. In 1908, they captured the Ottoman Government despite the opposition of the old elite, whose ideological power over the predominantly rural population stemmed partly from its religious authority. After the First World War, the new rulers simultaneously fought against the Ottoman state elite and the Allied forces who had distributed the territories of the Empire among themselves. At the end of the war of independence, the new elites had succeeded in attaining international recognition, eliminating the majority of the Ottoman ruling elite, and dominating the country.

At the beginning of the nineteenth century, the weakness of the Ottoman army in comparison to its European counterparts led the Sultanate to reform the military organization. In 1826, the Janissary corps was abolished and, in its place, a new military with modern weapons imported from Europe was established. Prussians were invited to train this military and a new War College was established (Zürcher 1993: 63–71). Through the creation of an intensive European-style education system, the newly trained military students were introduced to Western thinking, and along with it, they became acquainted with liberal ideas of parliamentary constitutionalism. From the mid-nineteenth century onwards, the staff colleges and especially the medical school of the army became the centers of secret political organizations determined to modernize the Empire (Rustow 1959: 515; Hale 1994: 13–34).

In the 1820s, the Ottoman state began to reform its bureaucracy as well. In 1835, Sultan Mahmut II created a hierarchical bureaucracy with the minister of the interior at the top, and introduced a new division of labor among the offices. In addition, the Sultan established new advisory councils, increasing the political powers of the bureaucrats. Meanwhile, similar to the changes in military schooling, fundamental modifications were made in the educational system of the civilian bureaucrats. In 1833, the Interpretation Office, which taught French to the civil servants, was established. In the 1850s and 1860s, new secular schools (modeled on the French *lycées*) were opened to train the bureaucrats (Zürcher 1993: 89–97).

These efforts created a new class of civilian and military elites. Between 1826 and 1871, the Empire saw the creation of a pool of military officers, administrators, tax collectors, and school teachers trained in Western ideologies and dedicated to modernizing the Empire in order to prevent its gradual collapse. However, just when these elites were ready to influence politics, the Ottoman state under Sultan Abdülhamit II started to curtail their powers and put an end to the reform program. In response, a group of exiled civilian officers calling themselves the Young Turks established the Committee of Union and Progress (CUP, *İttihat ve Terakki Cemiyeti*) in Paris. The Committee increased its strength substantially when, in 1907, military officers from the Third Army in Thessaloniki and the Second Army in Edirne joined forces with them. In 1908, the civilian and military arms of the CUP staged a coup against Sultan Abdülhamit and made him agree to re-open the Ottoman parliament (Zürcher 1993: 130–36). The first year of the CUP rule was turbulent. Internal divisions within the Committee and the challenge of the old conservative rulers culminated in an attempted countercoup. However, in 1909, with the help of the Macedonian army, the CUP consolidated its power in the parliament and managed to rule the Empire until the end of the First World War (Rustow 1959: 516; Hale 1994: 35–58).

After the defeat of the Ottoman Empire in the war, the top leadership of the CUP fled the country while the victorious Allied powers prepared to carve up the Empire. However, the organizational base of the CUP in the provinces remained solid and the Ottoman army was reorganized in inner Anatolia (Rustow 1959: 519). Thus, a group of civilian and military bureaucrats was available when Mustafa Kemal Atatürk, a commander of the Ottoman army in the First World War and an ex-CUP member, started to organize the national resistance movements under one association (Tunçay 1999: 19–29). The new association, which was formed against the Allied forces, managed to obtain representation in the 1920 Istanbul parliament. Thus, when the Allied forces seized the capital, the parliament (after new elections) was forced to move to Ankara on the 23rd of April 1920.

From that day onwards, a new battle started between the Ankara and Istanbul governments. Given their bureaucratic backgrounds, the Ankara elites organized under the CHP (*Cumhuriyet Halk Partisi*, Republican People's Party) were well entrenched in the country, both administratively and militarily, to carry out a 'revolution from above'. In 1922, the Ottoman Sultanate was abolished and in 1923 the Turkish Republic was declared. In 1924, the caliphate (the religious title of the Sultan) was annulled and religious schools were banned. In the subsequent years, the political power base of the religious leaders (*ulema*) was gradually eliminated with such reforms as the adaptation of the new Latin alphabet, confiscation of religious endowments (*vakifs*), and elimination of religious courts (Trimberger 2003: 49–51).

During the transition from the Ottoman Empire to the Turkish Republic, the military and the civilian leaders were fused into one group. Mustafa Kemal Atatürk held the title of commander-in-chief of the Turkish army along with his civilian positions. In addition, in 1920, the post of chief of the General Staff became a regular cabinet position. Accordingly, Chief of the General Staff İsmet İnönü acted as a minister and General Fevzi Çakmak (who became İnönü's successor as the chief of the general staff) served as prime minister between 1921 and 1922. During this period, the position of minister of national defense was always held by 'an active duty officer concerned primarily with political matters rather than command' (Harris 1965: 55 ff3). Among the 17 commanders of the Ottoman army who fought during the First World War, only two continued to pay allegiance to the Sultan in Istanbul. Seven commanders joined the Ankara government and five were exiled or deceased (Rustow 1959: 533). This demonstrates that the generation of military officers who were trained during the Ottoman reform period and the Young Turk era became part of the ruling coalition between 1920 and 1923.

After the declaration of the Republic in 1923, the union of military and civilian elites in one group continued. Atatürk, İnönü, Kazim Özalp (the minister of national defense and the president of the assembly) and two other deputies retired from the military only in 1927 (Harris 1965: 59). Indeed, in the 1923 and 1927 parliaments, 20 percent and 19 percent of the deputies, respectively, had military backgrounds (Frey 1965: 181). The fusion of the army with the political elite is also evident from the fact that, during this period, at least three governors and two ambassadors were active-duty army officers (Tunçay 1999: 120–23).

A single-party authoritarian regime was established in the 1920s and 1930s as a response to the preferences of the mostly rural population. The peasants who formed the majority of the electorate did not overwhelmingly support the secular elite who won the National Independence War (Ahmad 1993: 75–76). Trials of multi-party politics in 1924–25 and 1930 proved that if democracy with free and fair elections were allowed, the electorate would not vote for the CHP and the dominant elites (Weiker 1973; Zürcher 1991). Additionally, democracy was likely to bring about resistance and sporadic revolts–especially in eastern Turkey among the Kurdish population–against the reforms of the seculars and nationalists. These factors caused the CHP, with the support of the TAF, to establish a single-party regime.

During the single-party years of 1923–46, the military acted as the guardian of the nascent regime against rebellions (Harris 1965: 55–56; Özdağ 1991: 87–95; Hale 1994: 78–81). As Mustafa Kemal stated in November 1925, 'when activity occurs, it is evident that the army of the Republic is busy with bringing to reason and cleansing the reactionary incident.' Mustafa Kemal believed that 'the power and strength of the army, navy and air force … is the main instrument which safeguards and secures beloved Turkey's work towards the road to prosperity and development' (quoted in Özdağ 1991: 76 ff128). Accordingly, in 1925 the military was given judicial powers to approve and execute death sentences passed by the martial law courts. Aside from the guardian role, it is clear that Atatürk wanted the military on his side when he carried out crucial reforms. For instance, nine days before the declaration of the republic, the salaries of the military officers were increased. Similarly, before the abolition of the caliphate, Atatürk went to Izmir to meet with army generals and, only after their approval, did he take the issue to the assembly. During the single-party era, even such seemingly unrelated matters as construction of factories, railroads and bridges were sometimes approved by the military (Harris 1965: 57, 60; Özdağ 1991: 44–47, 95 ff 200).

In return for supporting and guarding the reforms, the Turkish military was given autonomy. In March 1924, the chief of the General Staff became responsible only to the president, and thus, was removed from the supervision of the parliament. The chief of the General Staff was responsible for almost all military matters (such as education, maneuvers, and inspection) while the only role of the ministry of defense 'was to serve principally as a channel for the communication of the military's views to the government' (Harris 1965: 58). Even the authority to prepare the defense budget (which made up around 30 percent of the state expenses between 1926 and 1938) was given to the office of the chief of the General Staff and not to the ministry of defense (Özdağ 1991: 105–8).

The legacies of this period continued into the subsequent years. The modernization of the Ottoman military gave this institution the capability to establish the republic based on the principles of secularism, nationalism and Westernization. These principles later became the basic tenets of the Kemalist ideology – an ideology which the TAF has continued to support and protect. Indeed, the guardian role of the military was set during the early republican period and, in the years to come, the TAF intervened in order to preserve the principles that the founding fathers had established. Moreover, the practice of giving high political autonomy to the military was first founded during this period as well. In the subsequent years, the TAF came to demand political autonomy and to interfere in politics when its privileges were perceived to be under threat.

Transition to multi-party politics and the military interventions of 1960, 1971, and 1980

The single-party regime came to an end in 1946, when a group of politicians split from the CHP and established the DP (*Demokrat Parti*, Democratic Party), with the support of economic elites (Karpat 1959; Timur 2003). The DP won the elections in 1950, and received the authorization to form the government in democratic elections again in 1954 and 1957. The rule of the DP, however, came to an end in 1960 with a military intervention. In fact, this coup was the first of several other military interventions that followed.

Even though the reasons for the 1960, 1971, and 1980 interventions were quite different, they all shared three characteristics. First, all of the coups were preceded by polarization in society and politics. In 1960, the rivalry was between two political parties; but in the 1971 and 1980 coups, the conflict was more ideological, between leftists and rightists. These conflicts were also reflected in opposing factions in the military and, except for the 1980 coup, the military was split into rival groups as well. These types of polarizations in politics were both important reasons for the coups and also significant indicators that democracy was not consolidated in Turkey.

A second common element in all three coups was that, as a legacy of the early republican period, they were all carried out in the name of guarding the regime, secularism, unity of the nation with its territory, and Kemalism. In addition, protecting and enhancing military autonomy and privileges were important considerations in the coups. Consequently, each military coup further increased the political powers of the TAF. This was made possible by the third common element in each coup, namely the transition paths to democracy that followed each intervention. Given the guardian (as opposed to the ruler) role of the military in Turkey, the TAF returned to their barracks after a short period of time. However, the decision to withdraw came from the military itself, which as Linz and Stepan argue, 'possesses the greatest ability to impose "reserve domains" on the newly elected government, and this by definition precludes democratic consolidation' (Linz and Stepan 1996: 67). Since the military led the transitions, it also increased its autonomy and powers in democracy after each coup. As a result, the obstacles to full democratization were amplified after the interventions.

The 1960 military intervention was caused by the grievances of the middle and lower ranking officers in the military and the CHP. The DP came to power after the authoritarian regime in 1950 with promises of democratic freedom and with assurances that the interests of the CHP members would not be attacked. However, as time went on, the party both defied its pledges and started to flirt with Islamic ideas in order to increase its votes. But perhaps the most pronounced disappointment with the DP was its repressive practices, which were meant to stop the advance of the parliamentary opposition. These measures of the DP threatened the well-being and security of politicians (especially the CHP) and caused them to support the military intervention of 1960 in order to oust the Democrats from power (Eroğul 2003).

The DP had also disappointed the military officers. There were serious imbalances within the military remaining from the CHP era that the DP did not attempt to change. There were insufficient numbers of lower ranking officers, but the middle ranks and higher ranks were swollen, which challenged the promotion of the juniors. Throughout the DP rule, the military officers were also affected by decreases in their real incomes and their declining social prestige. A law of 1949, prior to DP rule, subordinated the chief of the General Staff to the minister of defense. The behavior of the ministers and Prime Minister Menderes were at times dismissive of the officers, which was perceived as insulting (Özdağ 1997: 23–32; 52–54).

On 27 May 1960, a military clique led by junior officers took over the Turkish government and deposed the Democratic Party. Turkey returned to parliamentary democracy with the 1961 national elections. After a period of unstable coalition governments, the AP (*Adalet Partisi*, Justice Party, heir of the DP) came to power alone. However, the AP's success failed to bring regime stability. First, the government parties of the 1960s and 1970s were in almost constant conflict with the bureaucracy especially with institutions such as the State Planning Organization, Ministry of Finance, and the Constitutional Court which had been given considerable autonomy and power by the 1961 constitution. Governments did not accept the challenge these non-elected institutions posed to their authority to determine and implement state policies. In the 1970s, a common practice to deal with the bureaucracy was to place political party sympathizers in bureaucratic positions. Even such institutions as the police and education services fell into partisan conflict (Tachau and Heper 1983: 24).

Second, during this period the AP broke up into splinter groups (Ahmad 1992: 236–44). New rightist parties, such as the ultra-nationalist MHP (*Milliyetçi Hareket Partisi*, Nationalist Action Party), the Islamist MSP (*Milli Selamet Partisi*, National Salvation Party), and the DP, caused the AP to loose considerable power after 1973. As a result, the 1970s witnessed unstable coalition governments and a growing rivalry between the major leftist party of the decade (the CHP) and the rightist parties. When combined with the conflict identified above (bureaucracy versus government), this led to the paralysis of the state and the government and unintentionally allowed extreme movements to grow in an unrestrained manner.

In the late 1960s, an extreme movement that involved a group of lower ranking officers became a major concern. Influenced by leftist intellectuals, a military clique came into existence. The officers in the clique believed that the economic reforms of the constitution could not be carried out in a parliamentary system and that a coup was necessary in order to initiate the change toward socialism. The military commanders were aware of the activities of the clique and informed the AP government of the coming threat. However, the government was too weak to avert a leftist insurgency either by force or by socioeconomic reforms. As a result, in 1971 the military commanders intervened by means of a memorandum in order to prevent the execution of the leftist conspiracy, and forced the government to resign (Akyaz 2002: 235–330). After the 1971 memorandum, the two major parties of the time, the AP and the CHP, did not overtly support the intervention. However, they collaborated with it by giving a vote of confidence to the caretaker government the military established, by providing ministers to it, and by helping to enact constitutional amendments. Democratic elections were held in 1973, with the hopes that politics would become more stable.

However, contrary to expectations, the seven years after the military's withdrawal from active politics in 1973 (that led up to the 1980 intervention) were characterized by extremism and radicalism in the streets. In these years, leftist activities spread to the lower classes. At the same time, rightist movements came into existence, fuelled by radical political parties. The leftist versus rightist clashes in the streets terrorized the common people as well as the politicians, intellectuals, and economic elites. The spread of what was considered in the past radical ideologies, such as religious fundamentalism and Kurdish separatism, intensified the terror and perceptions of threat that the military and the majority of the population experienced. In 1978, more than 800 people died and thousands of people were wounded. The number of victims increased in the following years, reaching more than 20 deaths per day during the weeks just before the 12 September 1980 coup (Tachau and Heper 1983: 25).

The political behaviors and attitudes of the mainstream political parties, especially the AP and CHP, were seen as one of the primary causes of increasing terrorism. Because neither party held the majority in the parliament, their cooperation was essential to deal with violence. However, rather than cooperating with each other, both parties formed coalition governments with the radical parties, namely the Islamist MSP and the ultra-nationalist MHP. One major result of this type of cooperation was the paralysis of the parliament and the state. The national assembly could not select a president for several months despite multiple voting sessions, which completely disabled legislative work for six months prior to the coup. Similarly, with increased powers as government coalition partners, radical political parties infiltrated bureaucratic organizations and placed their own sympathizers in administrative positions (Heper 1985: 114–23). Dealing with terrorism became problematic because state institutions and even the police forces were not impartial anymore. Even when governments called in the military to help with violence, the CHP and AP could not agree on how much power the military commanders should have or enact the necessary laws that would increase the powers of the martial law commanders.

Another issue the major political parties could not agree on was economic policy. During the last two years of democracy, the economic situation worsened as a result of the exhaustion of Import Substitution Industrialization (ISI). ISI strategy in Turkey was combined with strong anti-export bias thanks to an overvalued exchange rate, government financing of inefficient state economic enterprises, and expansionary policies funded by short-term external borrowing. Increases in the world oil prices at the beginning of the 1970s led to inflation, unemployment, and shortage of many goods, such as fuel, coal, and even basic food supplies (Roy 1989: 3–11). GNP growth rates declined from 10.7 percent in 1971 to 1.1 in 1980. Growth in the industrial sector decreased from an average of 9.3 percent in the first half of the 1970s to 1.9 percent in the second half. While the inflation rate was 6.7 percent in 1970, it increased to 107.2 percent in 1980. Unemployment, on the other hand, reached 14.8 percent (Roy 1989: 8, 33).

In this highly violent and unstable context where there was no personal or economic safety, the military staged a coup. This intervention was the most repressive one that the country had ever witnessed. The military closed down all political parties, suppressed most of the civil society organizations, and restructured the legal framework of the country, including the constitution. In 1983, restrictive elections were held, in which old politicians and political parties were prevented from participating. Turgut Özal and his ANAP (*Anavatan Partisi*, Motherland Party) won these elections and Turkish politics entered a new phase.

Military interventions in Turkish politics in the post-1980 era

After the 1980 coup, the TAF did not stage another overt coup. However, this did not mean that Turkey was moving towards a more consolidated democracy. First, the autonomy of the military continued, and in fact increased, after the 1980 coup. As a result, civilian control of the military, a significant condition of democracy, was not achieved. Second, the political powers that the military was able to carve up for itself during the transition to democracy in 1983 made it possible for the TAF to intervene in politics without the need to stage an overt coup.

The political system and the constitution that was created in Turkey after the 1980 coup retained important spheres of political autonomy for the military. Some of these privileges had been first established by the previous coups. For instance, since the 1960 intervention, the military was responsible to the prime minister instead of the minister of defense; civilians had limited oversight over the military budget; and decisions pertaining to defense policy, arms procurement and production, military promotions and discharges were made by the General Staff (*Türkiye Cumhuriyeti Genelkurmay Başkanlığı*) and the YAŞ (*Yüksek Askerî Şûra*, High Military Council) (Cizre Sakallıoğlu 1997).

After the 1980 coup, the areas in which the military had tutelary powers were extended. The military continued to have the legal right and duty to protect Turkey against internal and external threats. While this tutelary function of the military was stated in its Internal Service Act, the increased powers of the MGK (*Millî Güvenlik Kurulu*, National Security Council) in the constitution made security *de facto* a reserve domain of the military. The MGK, which was first established by the 1960 coup, functioned as a forum that facilitated communication between the chief of the general staff, commanders of the armed forces and cabinet ministers. The MGK was also an institution that made it possible for the military to communicate its policy choices to the government. With the 1982 constitution, the cabinet was legally required to give precedence to the Council's decisions. The number of armed forces representatives was greater than that of civilians in the MGK meetings, which translated into the dominance of the military in security issues. The secretary general of the Council was a full general of the armed forces and the personnel of the MGK general secretariat consisted mostly of active or retired members of the military. These officers kept watch over civilian bodies through the MGK (Gürsoy 2009: 47–75).

The powers of the MGK were so significant that in 1997, the military pressured the coalition government of the RP (*Refah Partisi*, Welfare Party) and DYP (*Doğru Yol Partisi*, True Path Party) to resign, by using its role in the Council as the principal mechanism. The RP was an openly Islamist party, and its chairman, Necmettin Erbakan, had led the Islamist MSP in the 1970s that was closed down by the military intervention of 1980. In 1996, the RP entered a coalition government with the right-wing DYP and Erbakan became the prime minister. While in office, Erbakan took measures that intimidated the military and secular elites. For instance, the prime minister and the party in government made gestures to the Islamist groups by official visits to Iran and Libya, planning to end the ban on headscarves in public institutions, inviting leaders of the religious brotherhoods to dinner in the residence of the prime minister, and allowing (or organizing) religious demonstrations, such as the one in Sincan in January and in Istanbul in May 1997.

The military perceived the rise of the RP and the increasing visibility of Islam as a danger to the secularism principle of the republic. On 28 February 1997, during the MGK meeting, commanders handed an 18-point recommendation list to Prime Minister Erbakan and asked the Government to put an end to Islamic activities and to repress religious groups. The list of recommendations resembled an ultimatum since it implicitly threatened to use force unless the coalition government refused to carry out the military's proposals. After the military handed in its recommendations, it started to organize a series of briefings for selected members of the civil society. Members of the business community, judiciary, media, universities, and labor unions participated in the briefings. Faced with growing military and civilian opposition, on 18 June 1997, Erbakan resigned from his post and a new government, consisting of the secular parties in the parliament, was established (Heper and Güney 2000: 642–47; Bayramoğlu 2007). The constitutional court then closed down the Welfare Party and banned Erbakan from politics.

The events of 1997 were significant in demonstrating that polarization continued in Turkey after the 1980 coup. Whereas in the 1960s and 1970s the primary conflict was between the left and right, in the 1990s the focus shifted to the ascendancy of Islam. Secular elites, including the military, judiciary and political parties such as the CHP and their supporters, started to perceive the visibility of Islam in politics as a threat to the regime. This polarization, regardless of the involvement of the military, is an important indicator that democracy was not consolidated in Turkey. As in past interventions, political conflict again led to the intervention of the military. The TAF pressured the RP to resign by using its tutelary powers in the MGK, which continued to be an important obstacle to democratization in Turkey.

New dynamics in civil-military relations in the 2000s

In the late 1990s, two important developments changed civil-military relations and prospects for democratic consolidation in Turkey. The first significant event was the decision of the European Union to declare Turkey an official candidate for membership at the Helsinki Summit of 1999. After this date, the coalition government of the DSP (*Demokratik Sol Partisi*, Democratic Left Party), MHP and ANAP started a reform process and amended the constitution and laws in order to adopt the *acquis communitaire* and the Copenhagen criteria. Some of these reforms were in the realm of Turkish civil-military relations.

The second important development in Turkish politics has been the continuation of the conflict between seculars and Islamists after the closure of the RP in 1998. The party, in fact, split into two groups and the moderate faction established the AKP (*Adalet ve Kalkınma Partisi*, Justice and Development Party) in 2001. The AKP won the 2002, 2007 and 2011 elections and became the governing party. In its first term in office, the AKP continued the reform process on civil-military relations, tying it to the EU accession. The party's pro-EU stance was in part strategic: the Islamist background of the AKP leaders was a cause for concern among secular groups in society and the state, including the armed forces. What appeared as liberal and democratic policies within the framework of the EU insulated the Government from accusations that it was undermining secularism by reducing the powers of the guardians of secularism (Özel 2003: 93). Since EU membership has been seen as an important part of the Westernization goal of the secular establishment, AKP's pro-Europe stance seemed to safeguard the party from doubts about its intentions. Thus, polarization in politics has continued in the past decade, reminiscent of the earlier historical trends in Turkey, but this time it has also been combined with a debate on democratization. Whereas the pro-Islamist government justified its politics with democracy, the secular factions believed that the AKP was undermining secularism and the regime itself.

Past military interventions in Turkey have been preceded by polarization in politics. The TAF staged coups and pressured governments to resign in the name of guarding the regime and its basic pillars. At the same time, before the interventions, the TAF perceived threats to its political autonomy and, after the putsches, took measures to increase its powers. If the past could be seen as an example of what is going to happen in the future, it was natural to expect a coup in Turkey after the AKP won the elections and carried out reforms in civil-military relations. In fact, events that unraveled in the second half of the decade demonstrated the possibility of such coups in 2003–4. The exposure and failure of alleged coups, however, brought the tutelary powers of the military to an end. Civilian control over the armed forces increased to historically unprecedented levels, making it possible to talk about democratic civil-military relations in Turkey.

Reforms in civil-military relations

The constitutional and legal reforms in civil-military relations have covered a wide range of areas since the early 2000s. The tutelary powers of the armed forces over elected politicians have been severely restricted by several amendments to the 1982 Constitution, Law of the MGK, and other laws and regulations. The following list provides a chronological summary of the most significant legal reforms that have been carried out:

- In October 2001, Article 118 of the constitution was changed so that the number of civilians participating in the MGK meetings was increased relative to the military members (Türkiye Büyük Millet Meclisi 2001);
- An EU reform package brought into force in August 2003 added a new article to the Law on the Court of Auditors, paving the way for inspections of TAF properties albeit 'in consistency with the principles of confidentiality' (Türkiye Büyük Millet Meclisi 2003a);
- In the same reform package, a new clause was added to the Law of Foundation and Adjudication Procedures of Military Courts, stating that if crimes defined in the military penal code were committed by people who are not soldiers, they would not be tried in military courts (Türkiye Büyük Millet Meclisi 2003a). This addition to the Law restricted the jurisdiction of the military courts;
- The same package also changed Articles 4, 5, 9 and 15 of the Law of the MGK and abolished Articles 9, 14 and 19 of the same law. These amendments introduced the following (Türkiye Büyük Millet Meclisi 2003a):
  - The Council would only provide its recommendations to the government, without obliging the prime minister and the council of ministers to follow its policy suggestions;
  - The frequency of the MGK meetings was reduced;
  - The task of MGK personnel to follow up and oversee the implementation of MGK decisions by civilian bodies was eradicated;
  - The appointment procedures of the secretary general of the MGK were changed and the requirement that the secretary general must be a full general or admiral of the military was deleted;
  - The duty of the secretariat was reduced to carrying out the secretarial functions of the MGK;
  - The obligation of all public and private legal entities to share information with the MGK whenever the Council requested was eliminated;
- In December 2003, the words referring to the confidentiality of personnel appointments and the by-laws of the MGK were deleted in Articles 16, 17 and 21 of the Law (Türkiye Büyük Millet Meclisi 2003b);
- Another EU reform package, which was brought into force in May 2004, changed Article 131 of the constitution and removed the seat

appointed by the general staff to the YÖK (*Yükseköğretim Kurulu*, Higher Education Council);

- In the same constitutional package, Article 143 regarding the State Security Courts was annulled, abolishing the courts altogether. The courts included a military judge, however this seat of the armed forces had already been revoked in 1999;
- Article 160 of the constitution restricting the Court of Auditor's authority to oversee the state properties of the TAF was deleted (Türkiye Büyük Millet Meclisi 2004b);
- In March 2004 and July 2005, the relevant laws were amended, removing the seats representing the MGK secretariat and the General Staff in the Cinema, Video and Musical Works Supervisory Board and the Radio and Television Supreme Board (Türkiye Büyük Millet Meclisi 2004a and 2005);
- In July 2006, a significant number of the articles in the Law of Foundation and Adjudication Procedures of Military Courts was amended to the effect that military courts would not be able to try civilians in peacetime, unless they committed crimes together with armed forces personnel (Türkiye Büyük Millet Meclisi 2006);
- In February 2010, the AKP government and the General Staff together abolished the 1997 Protocol (*Hürriyet* 2010) that had given the armed forces the privilege of taking action against social events and collecting intelligence without consulting civilians (*Zaman* 2010);
- The 2010 Constitutional Reform Package, which was approved in parliament in May and by a referendum in September, changed Article 145 of the constitution. The new Article reinforced the changes made in the Law on Military Courts and stipulated that crimes committed by military personnel 'against state security, constitutional order and the functioning of that order' would be tried in general courts, and military courts would only hear cases related to the discipline of the armed forces (Türkiye Büyük Millet Meclisi 2010);
- The same Constitutional Package also added to Article 125 of the constitution a clause making it possible for military personnel who had been dismissed from the armed forces to seek judicial remedies;
- In December 2010, a new Law on the Court of Auditors was enacted, removing restrictions on the Court to oversee and inspect TAF properties, procurements, assets, equipment and budget.

Besides these legal reforms, important changes also took place in practice. The YAŞ meetings, which decide on personnel appointments and promotions, began to be chaired by the prime minister in 2011. In the past, the chief of staff and the prime minister together headed the meetings. The new seating arrangement indicates that the civilians are in charge of assignments in the armed forces. Accordingly, since August 2010 the government had played a more active role in personnel decisions, even causing the chief of staff to resign over a possible disagreement with civilians before the August

2011 meeting. Another significant change in practice has been on the procedures that were followed in the preparation of the MGSB (*Milli Güvenlik Siyaseti Belgesi*, National Security Policy Document). In the past, the military bureaucracy of the MGK had been responsible for this document and identifying internal and external threats. In 2010, for the first time, the civilians took charge of authoring the MGSB, hindering another of the tutelary powers of the armed forces.

While the significance of reforms in civil-military relations cannot be underestimated, it cannot be claimed that civilian control over the military is fully complete. As of January 2013, for instance, the military is responsible to the prime minister, not the ministry of defense; the Internal Service Act of the military, which states that it is the duty of the TAF to intervene against internal threats, remains unchanged; the parliament does not debate the military budget in detail (even though they have the legal right to do so); and the High Military Administrative Court (*Askeri Yüksek İdare Mahkemesi*) still has jurisdiction over the decisions of civilian institutions when these decisions involve military personnel. Despite these shortcomings, however, in important respects Turkish civil-military relations have come close to a consolidated democracy and the era of military interventions in politics has come to an end for the foreseeable future.

Reactions of the general staff to the reforms

Despite the fact that the powers of the military have been reduced by the reform process, the overall stance of the General Staff has been neutral to the changes. Why did the General Staff refrain from responding to the reforms? Why did the military hierarchy decline to intervene in politics and prevent a decrease in its powers by what it perceived as an Islamist political party? There are three primary reasons why the General Staff has not reacted. First, there was initial belief among the military hierarchy that the reform process could be controlled and in important respects it would still be possible to maintain prerogatives (Ünlü-Bilgiç 2009). The changes were accomplished piecemeal, allowing the General Staff to adjust and use other mechanisms to replace the powers it has lost. For instance, after the NSC reforms in 2004, the General Staff began to raise its concerns over internal and external threats not in the MGK but in the YAŞ, which until 2010 was still controlled by the military bureaucracy (Özcan 2006: 40–41). Similarly, the General Staff held regular press briefings informing the media of the security concerns of the TAF. Until July 2012 only accredited newspapers were allowed to participate in these meetings, thus making it possible for the general staff to control information disseminated from the hierarchy of the TAF. Media networks reported these briefings, as well as other comments of the generals, extensively, leading to the continued influence of the TAF on political matters.

The second reason why the General Staff has not reacted to its decrease in power is because until 2006, the reform process was tied to European Union

(EU) membership. The General Staff has been historically supportive of integration with the West and Turkey's EU endeavor (see, for instance, the declaration of Chief of the General Staff Yaşar Büyükanıt in *Milliyet* 2002: 17). EU membership has been supported as long as Turkish national unity, security interests, and secularism are protected. Even though the officers' understanding of democracy 'is much more closer to the maintenance of order than democracy per se,' the military 'accepts the legitimacy and supremacy of democratic ideals and civilian rule … due to the strong Kemalist legacy that it inherited' (Güney and Karatekelioglu 2005: 443). As a result, from an ideological perspective, the democratic principles of the EU match the military's vision for Turkey.

Moreover, as explained above, the Turkish military has played the role of modernizer since the 19th century. Indeed, the military was the first institution in the Ottoman Empire to modernize. After its own transformation was complete, the armed forces established the Republic and led the entire country in the path of modernization (Heper and Güney 2000: 636–37). The officer corps internalized this leadership role, but the EU accession process created a challenge requiring the military to abandon its 'other' role, namely that of guardian. While this dilemma put the officer corps in a difficult position, the hope that Turkey could eventually become an EU member has provided a prospect in which both goals of the military could be realized at the same time. The eventual membership of Turkey in the EU would be the final confirmation that Turkey has attained the modern civilization of Western nations and that political Islam and separatism are no longer threats (Aydınlı, Özcan and Akyaz 2006). In sum, the General Staff has chosen the option of staying in the barracks because once Turkey became part of the EU, the tutelary powers of the military would not be necessary. Combined with the difficulty of being against the EU reforms, which would openly contradict the Kemalist ideology of the TAF, the General Staff has accepted the reforms that directly attacked its tutelary powers.

Not all officers, however, agreed with the stance of the general staff. The constitutional changes that weakened the role of the MGK in accordance with the *acquis communitaire* were seen as a mistake by some of the generals. A visible split occurred between those members of the armed forces who publicly criticized the amendments and Chief of the General Staff Hilmi Özkök, who took a more liberal and pro-EU stance (Aydınlı 2009: 591–94; Heper 2005: 37–43).[1] In later years, those officers who made declarations against the reform process were implicated in coup plots. Two separate trials were initiated against hundreds of military officers and civilians. These trials are the third reason why the TAF did not react to the reform process. In 2006, the EU declared that negotiations with Turkey would be frozen in 8 accession chapters (out of 35) and none of the chapters would be closed until Turkey accepted signing the Customs Union agreement with the new members of the EU. After this decision of the EU, the political reform process in Turkey moved separately from EU conditionality, and the Government ceased referring to EU membership as one of the primary reasons for the amendments. The effects of this were felt when adjustments in civil-military relations slowed in pace until 2010. The court cases that started in 2008, however, gradually strengthened the hands of the civilians and led to a new phase of reforms.

The first trial, known as *Ergenekon*, has involved more than 300 civilians and retired and active military officers who have been accused of forming a terrorist organization with the purpose of staging a coup that would displace the AKP Government. From 2008 until 2013, more than 20 different indictments were prepared against the suspects. In April 2012, a separate court case, accusing seven generals including former Chief of the General Staff İlker Başbuğ with setting up internet websites against the government, was combined with the *Ergenekon* trial. At the time of this writing, the *Ergenekon* trial has not been concluded and the fates of the suspects are still unknown. However, there is no doubt that *Ergenekon* has ushered in a new era in civil-military relations, since it is the first of its kind where high-ranking military officers are being tried for coup plots.

After the start of the *Ergenekon* case, in July 2010 a second trial was started that implicated more than 350 officers in an incomplete attempt to overthrow the Turkish government by planning a conspiracy known as *Balyoz*. On 21 September 2012, the court decided that 325 suspects were guilty and condemned them to prison. The former first army commander and former commanders of the air force and navy were sentenced to 20 years in prison, while other officers received sentences ranging from 6 to 18 years (*Hürriyet* 2012b). Despite the verdict of the court, the controversies over the *Balyoz* trial have not come to an end. There are claims that some of the documents implicating suspects were forged and that due process was not followed in the examination and sharing of evidence with the court (Ergin 2012). The defendants are expected to start an appeals procedure, which could take several years to finally settle the issue.

A final set of legal actions were taken against the perpetrators of the past military interventions. With the 2010 amendment package to the 1982 constitution, it had become possible to try the officers who had staged the 1980 coup. In January 2012, the indictment prepared against the 1980 coup makers was accepted by the Ankara 12th High Penal Court. The chief of the General Staff during the 1980 coup (and later the president of the Republic) Kenan Evren and former Commander of the Air Force Tahsin Şahinkaya are being tried with the charge of attempting to overthrow the constitution and parliament by force (*Hürriyet* 2012a). A similar procedure was initiated against those who were responsible for the 28 February 1997 military intervention. Even though an indictment has not been prepared and the trial has not started at the time of writing, there is an ongoing investigation, which has led to the arrest of more than 60 retired military officers. The chief of the General Staff in 1997, İsmail Hakkı Karadayı, was also taken into custody but he was released after an interrogation (*Posta* 2012; *Hürriyet* 2013). It is not entirely clear if there will be a separate trial for the 1997 intervention and how the court case for the 1980 coup will come to an end. However, it is certain that there is an ongoing process of reckoning with the past. In this respect, it is also significant that a Committee for the Investigation of Military Coups and Memorandums was established by the parliament in May 2012. After listening to more than 150 people about the 1960, 1971, 1980 and 1997 military interventions, the Committee prepared a report with a set of reform suggestions in November of the same year (*HaberTürk* 2012).

The *Ergenekon* and *Balyoz* trials and investigations of past coups led to the detainment, prosecution and sentencing of military officers, generals, retired commanders, and former chiefs of General Staff on an unprecedented scale. These developments clearly signify a change in the balance of power between the military and civilians. Increasing numbers of people in Turkey have started to openly question the involvement of the military in politics. The judiciary's willingness to go after those who have been implicated, intellectuals' readiness to analyze the events, and the media's determination to expose the coup plans have been other indicators of this change in the balance of power. The TAF lost their previous status in public and politics, making it almost impossible for them effectively to resist new reforms and reductions in their tutelary powers. Indeed, some of the reforms after 2008 were directly related to the trials. For instance, the changing seat arrangement in the 2011 YAŞ meetings was the result of a dispute between the government and the generals over the promotion of suspects in the coup trials, which led to the resignation of the chief of General Staff and commanders of the army, navy and air force. The resignations created a power vacuum in the MGK that was filled by the civilians, who found the opportunity to expand their own influence. Other reforms, however, were indirectly related to the trials and point to more implicit and long-term changes, such as the annihilation of threats of future military interventions, which in the past had caused civilians to be cautious in their relations with the TAF.

Concluding remarks: The future of civil-military relations and democracy in Turkey

This chapter has argued that military involvement in Turkish politics could be perceived from two perspectives. First, the role of the military in Turkey and its powers are important obstacles to democratization. Turkey experienced two overt coup d'états and two military interventions that led elected governments to resign. Since the founding years of the Republic, the military had played important political roles as a modernizer and guardian of the nation and the state. Its tutelary powers restricted the decisions of civilians, especially in areas where the TAF perceived threats to the secular Kemalist principles. The reforms that have been carried out in civil-military relations initially due to EU conditionality, then with the coup trials, are significant democratic developments precisely because they have the

potential to increase civilian control of the TAF and fulfill one of the conditions of democracy that Turkey had failed in for decades.

However, this chapter also argued that all of the past interventions of the
TAF in politics were due to polarization in Turkish politics, and thus, military involvements are not only the causes of a failed democracy but also
indicators of it. Prior to the 1960 coup, the polarization was primarily due to
the conflict between two political parties. In the following decades, confrontation between leftist and rightist groups within the military, in parliament, among political parties, and in the streets led to an intervention by
memorandum in March 1971 and the most repressive coup in Turkish history
in September 1980. In the 1990s, conflict between secularists and Islamists led
to the continued involvement of the military in politics. In the past decade,
despite increasing civilian control of the military, conflict between secularists
and the AKP Government have continued. This polarization in society shows
that despite the fact that one reason for the failure of democracy in Turkey
(military tutelage) is being gradually eliminated; another important problem
that caused previous military interventions in the first place is still ongoing.
As long as this polarization in politics and society continues, past events lead
to the pessimistic conclusion that Turkish democracy will fail to consolidate
regardless of changing civil-military relations.

Notes

1 Özkök provided his testimony in the Ergenekon trials (*Milliyet* 2012) and also
made declarations to the dailies *Milliyet* and *Radikal* about the conspiracies. In
these statements he neither confirmed nor denied the existence of coup attempts,
but pointed to the divisions among the generals (Bila 2008; Yetkin 2008; Bila
2009). His account of the events confirms that there was a split between Özkök
and some of the generals who have been accused of military conspiracies.

References

Ahmad, F. (1992) *Demokrasi Sürecinde Türkiye (1945–1980)*, trans. Ahmet Fethi,
Istanbul: Hil Yayın.
—— (1993) *The Making of Modern Turkey*, London and New York: Routledge.
Akyaz, D. (2002) *Askeri Müdahalelerin Orduya Etkisi: Hiyerarşi Dışı Örgütlenmeden
Emir Komuta Zincirine*, Istanbul: İletişim Yayınları.
Aydınlı, E. (2009) 'A Paradigmatic Shift for the Turkish Generals and an End to the
Coup Era in Turkey', *Middle East Journal*, 63: 581–96.
Aydınlı, Özcan, N. A. and Akyaz, D. (2006) 'The Turkish Military's March Toward
Europe', *Foreign Affairs*, 85: 77–90.
Bayramoğlu, A. (2007) *28 Şubat: Bir Müdahalenin Güncesi*, Istanbul: İletişim Yayınları.
Bila, F. (2008) 'Özkök: Ne Vardır, Ne Yoktur Derim', *Milliyet*, 9 July: 16.
—— (2009) 'Özkök: Bırakalım Soruşturmayı Yargı Yapsın', *Milliyet*, 17 January.
Online. Avaliable HTTP: <http://www.milliyet.com.tr/default.aspx?aType=YazarDe
tay&ArticleID=1048193> (accessed 09 January 2013).
Cizre-Sakallıoğlu, Ü. (1997) 'The Anatomy of the Turkish Military's Hierarchy',
Comparative Politics, 29: 151–66.

Ergin, S. (2012) 'Balyoz Davası Asıl Şimdi Başlıyor', *Hürriyet*, 22 September: 26.

Eroğul, C. (2003) *Demokrat Parti: Tarihi ve İdeolojisi*, Ankara: İmge Kitapevi.

Frey, F. W. (1965) *The Turkish Political Elite*, Cambridge, Massachusetts: The M.I.T. Press.

Güney, A. and Karatekelioglu, P. (2005) 'Turkey's EU Candidacy and Civil-Military Relations: Challenges and Prospects', *Armed Forces and Society*, 31: 439–62.

Gürsoy, Y. (2009) 'Civilian Support and Military Unity in the Outcome of Turkish and Greek Interventions', *Journal of Political and Military Sociology*, 27: 47–75.

HaberTürk (2012) 'Darbe Raporu Tamam', 28 November. Online. Available HTTP: <http://www.haberturk.com/gundem/haber/798461-darbe-raporu-tamam> (accessed 09 January 2013).

Hale, W. (1994) *Turkish Politics and the Military*, London: Routledge.

Harris, G. S. (1965) 'The Role of the Military in Turkish Politics (Part I)', *Middle East Journal*, 19: 54–66.

Heper, M. (1985) *The State Tradition in Turkey*, Beverley: The Eothen Press.

—— (2005) 'The European Union, the Turkish Military and Democracy', *South European Society and Politics*, 10: 33–44.

Heper, M. and Güney, A. (2000) 'The Military and the Consolidation of Democracy: The Recent Turkish Experience', *Armed Forces and Society*, 26: 635–57.

Hürriyet (2010) 'EMASYA Protokolü Kaldırıldı', 4 February. Online. Available HTTP: <http://www.hurriyet.com.tr/gundem/13684829.asp> (accessed 09 January 2013).

Hürriyet (2012a) '12 Eylül İddianamesinin Tam Metni,'', 10 January. Online. Available HTTP: <http://www.hurriyet.com.tr/gundem/19651524.asp> (accessed 09 January 2013).

Hürriyet (2012b) 'Cezada da Balyoz … Tahliye Yok', 22 September: 26.

Hürriyet (2013) 'İmzası Yok Diye Serbest Kaldı', 04 January. Online. Available HTTP: <http://www.hurriyet.com.tr/gundem/22288901.asp> (accessed 09 January 2013).

Karpat, K. (1959) *Turkey's Politics: The Transition to a Multi-party System*, Princeton: Princeton University Press.

Linz, J. J. and Stepan, A. (1996) *Problems of Democratic Transition and Consolidation: Southern Europe, South America, and Post-Communist Europe*, Baltimore and London: The John Hopkins University Press.

Milliyet (2002) 'PKK terör listesine karşı isim değiştirdi', 26 March: 17.

Milliyet (2012) 'Ben de Tedirgindim', 3 Ağustos: 15.

Özcan, G. (2006) 'Milli Güvenlik Kurulu', in *Almanak Türkiye 2005: Güvenlik Sektörü ve Demokratik Gözetim*, in Ü. Cizre (ed.), Istanbul: TESEV Yayınları.

Özdağ, Ü. (1997) *Menderes Döneminde Ordu – Siyaset İlişkileri ve 27 Mayıs İhtilali*, Istanbul: Boyut Yayıncılık.

Özdağ, Ü. (1991) *Ordu-Siyaset İlişkisi (Atatürk ve İnönü Dönemleri)*, Ankara: Gündoğan Yayınları.

Özel, S. (2003) 'Turkey at the Polls: After the Tsunami', *Journal of Democracy*, 14: 80–94.

Posta (2012) '28 Şubat Soruşturması Nasıl Başladı?', 2 October. Online. Available HTTP: <http://www.posta.com.tr/siyaset/HaberDetay/28-Subat-sorusturmasi-nasil-basladi-.htm?ArticleID=142420> (accessed 09 January 2013).

Roy, J. (1989) 'The Turkish Economy: Assessment of a Recovery under a Structural Adjustment Program', *EDI Working Papers*, Washington, D.C.: The Economic Development Institute of the World Bank.

Rustow, D. A. (1959) 'The Army and the Founding of the Turkish Republic', *World Politics* 11: 513–52.

Tachau, F. and Heper, M. (1983) 'The State, Politics, and the Military in Turkey', *Comparative Politics*, 16: 17–33.

Timur, T. (2003) *Türkiye'de Çok Partili Hayata Geçiş*, Ankara: İmge Kitapevi.

Trimberger, E. K. (2003) *Tepeden İnmeci Devrimler*, trans. Fatih Uslu, Istanbul: Gelenek Yayınları.

Tunçay, M. (1999) *Türkiye Cumhuriyeti'nde Tek-Parti Yönetiminin Kurulması (1923–1931)* Istanbul: Tarih Vakfı Yurt Yayınları.

Türkiye Büyük Millet Meclisi (2001) 'Türkiye Cumhuriyeti Anayasasının Bazı Maddelerinin Değiştirilmesi Hakkında Kanun, Kanun No. 4709', Online. Available HTTP: <http://www.tbmm.gov.tr/kanunlar/k4709.html> (accessed 10 December 2012).

Türkiye Büyük Millet Meclisi (2003a) 'Çeşitli Kanunlarda Değişiklik Yapılmasına İlişkin Kanun, Kanun No. 4963', Online. Available HTTP: <http://www.tbmm.gov.tr/kanunlar/k4963.html> (accessed 10 December 2012).

Türkiye Büyük Millet Meclisi (2003b) 'Milli Güvenlik Kurulu ve Milli Güvenlik Kurulu Genel Sekreterliği Kanununun Bazı Hükümlerinin Yürürlükten Kaldırılmasına Dair Kanun, Kanun No. 5017', Online. Available HTTP: <http://www.tbmm.gov.tr/kanunlar/k5017.html> (accessed 10 December 2012).

Türkiye Büyük Millet Meclisi (2004a) 'Çeşitli Kanunlarda Değişiklik Yapılmasına İlişkin Kanun, Kanun No. 5101', Online. Available HTTP: <http://www.tbmm.gov.tr/kanunlar/k5101.html> (accessed 10 December 2012).

Türkiye Büyük Millet Meclisi (2004b) 'Türkiye Cumhuriyeti Anayasasının Bazı Maddelerinin, Kanun No. 5170', Online. Available HTTP: <http:// http://www.tbmm.gov.tr/kanunlar/k5170.html> (accessed 10 December 2012).

Türkiye Büyük Millet Meclisi (2005) 'Radyo ve Televizyon Kuruluş ve Yayınları Hakkında Kanunda Değişiklik Yapılmasına Dair Kanun, Kanun No. 5373', Online. Available HTTP: <http://www.tbmm.gov.tr/kanunlar/k5373.html> (accessed 10 December 2012).

Türkiye Büyük Millet Meclisi (2006) 'Askeri Mahkemeler Kuruluş ve Yargılama Usulü Kanununda Değişiklik Yapılmasına Dair Kanun, Kanun No. 5530', Online. Available HTTP: <http://www.tbmm.gov.tr/kanunlar/k5530.html> (accessed 10 December 2012).

Türkiye Büyük Millet Meclisi (2010) 'Türkiye Cumhuriyeti Anayasasının Bazı Maddelerinde Değişiklik Yapılması Hakkında Kanun, Kanun No. 5982', Online. Available HTTP: <http://www.tbmm.gov.tr/kanunlar/k5982.html> (accessed 10 December 2012).

Ünlü Bilgiç, T. (2009) 'The Military and the Europeanization Reforms in Turkey', *Middle Eastern Studies*, 45: 803–24.

Weiker, W. (1973) *Political Tutelage and Democracy in Turkey: The Free Party and Its Aftermath*, Leiden: E.J. Brill.

Yetkin, M. (2008) 'Özkök'ten "Savunma": Beni 28 Şubat'takiler Gibi Davranmamakla Suçladılar', Radikal, 25 December. Online. Avaliable HTTP: <http://www.radikal.com.tr/Radikal.aspx?aType=RadikalYazar&ArticleID=914193& CategoryID = 98> (accessed 09 January 2013).

Zaman (2010) 'İşte Darbecilerin Güvendiği EMASYA Protokolü', 25 January. Online. Available HTTP: <http://www.zaman.com.tr/newsDetail_getNewsById.action?haberno=944296> (accessed 09 January 2013).

Zürcher, E. J. (1991) *Political Opposition in the Early Turkish Republic: The Progressive Republican Party, 1924–1925*, New York: E.J. Brill.

Zürcher, E. J. (1993) *Modernleşen Türkiye'nin Tarihi*, Istanbul: İletişim Yayınları.

14 The judiciary[1]

Ergun Özbudun

Introduction

The roots of the independence of the judiciary go back to the Constitution of 1876. Article 81 stated that judges cannot be dismissed. Other articles in the section entitled 'The Courts' also adopted such guarantees as the public nature of the court proceedings (Art. 82), the right to use all legitimate means in self-defence (Art. 83), the prohibition of denial of justice (Art. 84), the principle of the legal judge (Art. 85), the prohibition of all outside interference in court proceedings (Art. 86), and the prohibition of establishing extraordinary courts or commissions with judicial powers (Art. 89).

The Constitution of 1924 regulated the judicial branch under the title of 'judicial power.' The Constitution stipulated that

> judges are independent and free from any kind of intervention in the proceedings and judgements of all cases, and subject only to the provisions of law. Decisions of the courts shall in no way be changed or postponed or their execution be prevented by the Turkish Grand National Assembly and the Council of Ministers.
>
> (Art.54, 1924 Constitution)

According to Article 55, 'judges cannot be dismissed except for the cases and procedures defined by law'. And, under Article 56, the qualifications, rights and duties, salaries, and the method of their appointment and dismissal are to be regulated by a special law.

It thus appears that the Constitution of 1924, while recognizing the independence of the judiciary in principle, left many vital areas, notably the tenure guarantees for judges, to the regulation of ordinary laws. Since such laws did not provide sufficient tenure guarantees and the executive authorities often dismissed or retired judges whom they found politically undesirable, the independence of the judiciary was a major political issue before the Constitution of 1961. Therefore, much stronger constitutional guarantees were provided by the 1961 Constitution. The 1982 Constitution broadly maintained such guarantees with some modifications.

The constitutional court

Turkey was one of the first European countries to adopt a system of the judicial review of the constitutionality of laws. The Turkish Constitutional Court (*Anayasa Mahkemesi*) was established by the Constitution of 1961, and was conceived as an effective check over the often arbitrary power of parliamentary majorities. Since then, the Constitutional Court has played a major role in Turkish politics and often pursued an activist approach that put it in collision with the elected branches of government, as will be spelled out below.

The Constitution of 1982 maintained the essential features of the constitutional review system with some modifications. Both Constitutions opted for a centralized review system by giving this task to a special court rather than to general courts. Only, under the 1961 system, general courts were also empowered, in exceptional cases, to render a decision on the constitutionality of a particular law applicable in a pending trial. Thus, if a plea of unconstitutionality was raised by one of the parties during the trial, the trial court had to refer it to the Constitutional Court; but if the Constitutional Court did not render its decision in six months, the trial court was empowered to decide on the plea according to its own judgement (Art. 151). No such power was granted, however, to general courts by the 1982 Constitution; thus, the review system was fully centralized.

Structure

Another difference between the 1961 and 1982 Constitutions concerns the mode of selection of the judges. Thus, the 1961 Constitution had provided for a mixed body, partly chosen by the other high courts, and partly by elected branches of government (the two chambers of parliament and the President of the Republic). All members had to carry the necessary legal and professional qualifications stipulated by the Constitution. The Constitution of 1982 changed this system radically by completely eliminating the role of the parliament in the selection of judges and giving the President of the Republic a dominant role in the process, as referred to in Chapter 15 p. 297.

The composition of the Court and the method of selecting its members were changed considerably by the constitutional amendment of 2010, as described in Chapter 15 pp. 297–98. The amendment to Article 147 also changed the term of office for the Constitutional Court judges. While under the original text of the Article they served until the mandatory retirement age of 65, now their term of office is limited to twelve years with no possibility for re-election. This is in line with the practice in most Western democracies, and will make it possible that changes in the public opinion will be reflected on the composition of the Court. The amendment maintains full security of tenure for the judges. Thus, their office may be terminated only upon conviction of an offense entailing dismissal from the judicial profession or for reasons of health. In the latter case, the Constitutional Court itself decides on the termination of office (Art. 147).

The 2010 amendments concerning the Constitutional Court are, in general, in line with the proposals put forward by the Court itself in 2004, including a modest role for parliament in the selection of judges, a two-chamber structure, and the introduction of constitutional complaint.

Powers

In addition to its main function of reviewing the constitutionality of laws, the Constitutional Court is also granted certain other important powers. One is to try cases on the prohibition of political parties, as was alluded to in Chapter 15 p. 296. The Constitutional Court also exercises financial control over the legality of the acquisitions, incomes, and expenditures of political parties (Art. 69). Another such function is that of the High Court, namely trying certain high office-holders for crimes connected with their official duties. These officials are the President of the Republic (only in case of high treason), the Prime Minister and ministers; presidents, judges, and chief prosecutors of the Constitutional Court, Court of Cassation, Council of State, Military Court of Cassation, High Military Administrative Court; the deputy Chief Public Prosecutor; presidents and members of the HSYK (*Hâkimler ve Savcılar Yüksek Kurulu*, High Council of Judges and Public Prosecutors), and of the Court of Accounts. The 2010 amendment to Article 148 broadened the competence of the High Court to include the Speaker of the TBMM (*Türkiye Büyük Millet Meclisi*, Turkish Grand National Assembly), the Chief-of-the-General Staff, and the commanders of the Army, Navy, Air Force, and the Gendermary for crimes connected to their office. The amended paragraph also provided an appeal procedure against the decisions of the High Court, to be examined by the same body.

In addition, the Constitutional Court is empowered to decide on appeals against parliamentary resolutions on the lifting of parliamentary inviolability or the forfeiture of the parliamentary membership (Art. 85), and selects one of its members to preside over the Court of Conflicts (Art. 158).

The main function of the Constitutional Court is, of course, to review the constitutionality of laws. The Court is also competent to review the constitutionality of the law-amending ordinances, and the Standing Orders of the TBMM. Its competence over constitutional amendments is limited to specific procedural defects, as discussed in Chapter 15 p. 305. Similarly, the Constitutional Court has in general no competence over parliamentary resolutions, with the exception of those involving the removal of parliamentary inviolability or the forfeiture of parliamentary membership, and the Standing Orders of the TBMM. The Court, however, has extended its competence over parliamentary resolutions in cases where it deems that a parliamentary resolution is a *de facto* change in the Standing Orders or creates a new rule in the nature of the Standing Orders.

Excluded from the competence of the Court are the reform laws of the Atatürk period considered as essential elements of the Turkish modernization project and enumerated in Article 174 of the Constitution, including laws on the unity of education, the wearing of hat, the closing of the *derviş* convents, civil marriage, the adoption of international numerals and of Latin alphabet, the abolition of certain traditional titles, and the banning of certain garments. Even though such laws can amended by the legislature, their unconstitutionality cannot be claimed before the Constitutional Court. Thus, in a sense, they are put somewhere between constitutional norms and ordinary legislation. Another such immunity from judicial review was provided for the laws and decree-laws passed during the MGK (*Millî Güvenlik Kurulu*, National Security Council) regime (1980–83) as an important exit guarantee; it was repealed by the constitutional amendment of 2001.

The law-amending ordinances (decree laws) passed during the periods of emergency rule, martial law, and war are also excluded from the review of the Constitutional Court (Art. 148). Given the fact that most serious human rights violations are likely to occur during these periods, such an exclusion severely conflicts with the principle of the rule of law. Once they are approved by parliament, however, such ordinances become ordinary laws and subject to the constitutionality review. Finally, under Article 90 of the Constitution, the unconstitutionality of international agreements that are duly put into effect cannot be claimed before the Constitutional Court.

The Court's jurisdiction encompasses both substantive and procedural review. Procedural review is limited to ascertaining whether in the final vote on the bill the requisite majority was obtained. Other procedural defects committed during the legislative process are not subject to constitutional review (Art. 148). This limitation introduced by the 1982 Constitution may be considered as a reaction to the Court's tendency to annul laws on the grounds of minor procedural irregularities under the 1961 Constitution.

The modes of constitutional review

Access to the Constitutional Court can be secured in two ways: principal proceedings, namely, those instituted by a government organ; and incidental proceedings, arising out of a pending trial. Principal proceedings (abstract norm control) can be initiated by the President of the Republic, parliamentary groups of the government party and the main opposition party, or at least one-fifth of the full membership of the TBMM (Art. 150). Suits of unconstitutionality must be initiated within sixty days following the publication of the law in question in the *Resmî Gazete* (Art. 151). However, appeals on procedural grounds may be initiated only within ten days following publication and only by the President of the Republic or one-fifth of the full membership of the TBMM (Art. 148).

In contrast to principal proceedings incidental proceedings (concrete norm control), can be initiated by any individual and are not subject to any time limitation. In other words, an individual may, during proceedings in a regular court, secure judicial review of legislation which is applicable to the case and allegedly infringes upon his rights. Access to the Court by way of incidental proceedings is dependent on two conditions. First, a plea of unconstitutionality must be put forward in the course of a pending trial. Second, the regular court trying the case must determine whether access to the Constitutional Court is justified (that is, whether the plea seems serious). In the event that it does so, the court adjourns the proceedings and refers the matter to the Constitutional Court, which must decide the matter within five months. The trial court may also decide to refer the matter to the Constitutional Court on its own initiative, if it thinks that the applicable law in the case is unconstitutional. If no decision is reached by the Constitutional Court within this period, the trial court has to render its judgement on the basis of the existing law. If the Constitutional Court reaches a decision before the judgement of the trial court becomes final (that is, upheld by the relevant high court in case of an appeal), the trial court must comply with this decision. This is one of the points where the present Constitution departed from its predecessor, which permitted the trial court to decide upon the question of constitutionality by an *inter partes* ruling if the Constitutional Court did not reach a decision within six months. Another such departure is that, in the event the Constitutional Court dismisses the case on substantive (not procedural) grounds, no plea of unconstitutionality for the same law can be put forward until a ten-year period elapses (Art. 152). Although the framers of the Constitution defended this innovation as contributing to 'legal stability', it is, in fact, a serious limitation upon defendants' rights.

The original text of the 1982 Constitution did not recognize the right to put forward a constitutional complaint for individuals. The 2010 amendment to Article 148 introduces this right. Thus, it is stipulated that

> Everybody has the right to appeal to the Constitutional Court claiming that one of his/her fundamental rights and liberties guaranteed by the Constitution and covered by the European Convention of Human Rights is violated by a public authority. For such an appeal, it is required that all regular ways of judicial appeal must be exhausted. In individual applications, no examination shall be made in areas that have to be evaluated in regular judicial appeals.
>
> (Art. 148, 1982 Constitution, as amended in 2010)

The details of constitutional complaint have been regulated by Law no. 6216, dated 30 March 2011 on the 'Organization and Trial Procedures of the Constitutional Court' (Arts. 45–51).

The introduction of constitutional complaint had long been advocated by a majority of legal scholars and human rights activists, even though the two high courts remained cool to the idea for fear that this would elevate the

Constitutional Court to the position of a super appellate court over the decisions of the two high courts. Clearly, however, the Constitutional Court's examination will not be extended to the facts of the case, but will be limited to an examination of the question of unconstitutionality.

The introduction of constitutional complaint also required certain changes in the structure and working methods of the Constitutional Court, as it would considerably increase the workload of the Court. Thus, the amended Article 149 stipulated that the Court shall work in two chambers and a plenary. Chambers convene with the presence of four members under the chairmanship of the Vice-President of the Court, and the plenary convenes with the presence of at least twelve members under the chairmanship of the President, or the Vice-President authorized by him. Constitutional complaints are examined by chambers and sub-commissions may be established to examine their admissibility. Chambers and the plenary make their decisions with their absolute majority. However, decisions to annul a constitutional amendment, or to close a political party, or to deprive it from state subsidies require a two-thirds majority of the participating judges. The 2010 amendment also abolished substitute judges, and stipulated in its provisional article 18 that the current substitute members shall become regular members, and that all current members shall continue to serve until the mandatory retirement age of 65; in other words, the 12-year term of office shall not apply to the present members.

The effects of constitutional court decisions

The decisions of the Constitutional Court are final. In case of an annulment ruling, the law becomes ineffective as of the date of the publication of the annulment ruling in the Official Gazette. However, if the Court deems it necessary, it can determine the effective date of the annulment decision as a date not later than one year from the date of its publication. This provision aims at giving the legislature the opportunity to adopt a new law in cases where a legal vacuum is deemed dangerous for public order.

The decisions of the Constitutional Court have *erga omnes* and *ex nunc* effect. In other words, they are binding for everybody and not retroactive (Art. 153). The Court's competence to render *inter partes* decisions (binding only for the specific case and for the parties of the conflict) under the 1961 Constitution is abolished by the 1982 Constitution. Non-retroactivity (*ex nunc* effect) means that transactions made under the annulled law remain valid. However, in case of the annulment of a criminal law provision, persons convicted under that law benefit from the annulment judgement. Article 153 of the Constitution also states that when the Constitutional Court annuls a law, it cannot act as the legislature and lead to a 'new practice'. This rather vague provision has to be interpreted in the sense that the Court is not allowed to interfere with the legitimate margin of appreciation of the legislature.

It is a matter of debate whether the Court, when upholding a law, can issue a binding interpretation of it 'in conformity with the Constitution', a technique used by certain European constitutional courts, for example the German Constitutional Court. Again, the Constitution contains no provision permitting such an option. On the contrary, the above quoted rule in Article 153 to the effect that the Court cannot act as the legislature and establish a new practice, may be cited as evidence against such an interpretation. In fact, 'interpretation is conformity with the Constitution' puts the Court in the position of a 'positive legislator' rather than its normal role of a 'negative legislator'. There are cases, however, where the Turkish Court used this technique. A perfect example of this is a 1991 ruling of the Court in which it did not annul a law abolishing the headscarf ban at universities, but interpreted it in such a way, referring to a previous ruling, that the ban persisted.[2]

Finally, it is also a matter of debate whether the Constitutional Court is competent to issue stay orders, namely to suspend the application of the challenged law pending the trial. The Constitution is silent on the matter and until 1993, the Court refused to issue stay orders. It changed its view, however, in 1993,[3] and since then it has exercised this power liberally. Thus, between 1993 and 2005, the Court accepted such requests in 52 out of 92 cases. The Court has argued in these cases that the power to issue stay orders is 'inherent in the judicial process' to prevent irreparable damages and consequences, and that the Court is competent to fill in a 'constitutional vacuum' in the absence of a clear provision prohibiting it. It may be argued, however, that in the absence of a clear constitutional or legal authorization, the Court has no such power. According to the wording of the Constitution, the Court has only two options in cases of the review of constitutionality, namely, either annulling the law, or rejecting the request for annulment.

The judicial activism of the constitutional court

The Turkish Constitutional Court, one of the earliest and most powerful in Europe, was established by the Constitution of 1961, made by a Constituent Assembly strongly dominated by the state elites, as an effective check against popularly elected parliamentary majorities, always seen suspect and untrustworthy by the dominant state elites. In its history of half a century, the Turkish Court functioned, in conformity with the expectations of Ran Hirschl's 'hegemonic preservation' thesis[4] as one of the chief spokesmen of the state elites. Thus, while particularly cautious and timid in matters related to the fundamental rights and liberties of citizens, it acted as the ultimate guardian of the official ideology, namely, a staunchly secularist, overly centralized, unitary nation-state (Arslan 2002; Özbudun 2006; Örücü 2008). This attitude became even more marked during periods when the military's political role was at its peak, namely the periods immediately following the military interventions of 1960, 1971, 1980, and 1997. Thus, in the words of

Ceren Belge, the Court has become an important actor in 'the republican alliance', together with the military and the CHP, the principal political representative of the state elites (Belge 2006).

The excessive judicial activism of the Court, interfering with the legitimate margin of appreciation of the legislature, often put it in a collision course with the elected parliamentary majorities, some of which resulted in constitutional amendments (Özbudun 2009: 261–70). The Court's ruling in 2008 in which it claimed the competence to review constitutional amendments in terms of their conformity with the unamendable clauses of the Constitution carried this clash to new heights, and severely limited the constituent power of parliament. The changes in the composition of the Court introduced by the 2010 constitutional amendment is a limited response by political elites designed to make the Court more pluralistic in composition and more representative of the society in general. The pro-state activism of the Constitutional Court is a part of the more general attitude of the Turkish judiciary as will be discussed below.

The triple headed judiciary

As in most Continental European countries, in Turkey administrative disputes are resolved not by the general courts, but by a system of administrative courts. The beginning of the administrative justice system goes back to 1868, when the Council of State was established to try disputes between government and individuals, inspired by the French *Conseil d'État*. This system was maintained by all three republican constitutions. Military courts, also existent since the late Ottoman times, were given constitutional status for the first time by the Constitution of 1961, and such status was maintained by the Constitution of 1982. Thus, the Turkish judicial system has a triple-headed structure. One may also argue that the Court of Accounts (*Sayıştay*) can be considered a fourth branch of the judiciary, since, in addition to its administrative functions, it is empowered to render final judgements concerning the responsibility of public accountants, and such judgements cannot be appealed against before the administrative courts (Art. 160).

At the apex of the general (civil and criminal courts) court system, is the Court of Cassation (*Yargıtay*). The Court of Cassation is the court of last resort deciding the legality of civil and criminal lower court judgements. At the moment, work is under way to introduce courts of appeal between the first instance courts and the Court of Cassation. The judges of the Court of Cassation are chosen by the HSYK from among civil and criminal judges and public prosecutors who are promoted to the first degree, by secret vote and the absolute majority of its full membership. The chief public prosecutor of the Court of Cassation and his deputy are appointed by the President of the Republic from among five candidates nominated by the plenary session of the Court of Cassation (Art. 154).

At the apex of the administrative justice system is the Council of State (*Danıştay*). Similar to the French *Council d'État*, its source of inspiration, the Council of State has both administrative and judicial functions. In its first capacity, it reviews and gives its advisory opinion on government bills submitted to it by the Prime Minister or the Council of Ministers, regulatory acts (by-laws) prepared by the Council of Ministers, and public service concession contracts. In its judicial capacity, in some cases it is the final court of appeal concerning the decisions of lower-level administrative courts (administrative courts, tax courts, and regional administrative courts), and in others it is the first and the last instance court.

Three-quarters of the judges of the Council of State are chosen by the HSYK from among administrative justice judges and public prosecutors assigned to the first degree; one-quarter are appointed by the President of the Republic from among qualified public servants as defined by law (Art. 155). The President's role in this regard is justified by the fact that the Council of State has administrative, in addition to its judicial, functions.

The division of labor between civil and administrative courts is defined on the basis of the legal nature of the dispute. If the resolution of the dispute involves the application of administrative or public law rules, namely prerogatives and obligations deriving from public law, then it is within the competence of administrative courts. Not all acts and actions of administrative authorities belong to this category. Such authorities may carry out certain activities within the rules of civil law, in which case disputes arising out of such actions are within the competence of civil courts.

Obviously, the dividing line between the two categories is not very clear. Therefore, in all countries with a dual judicial structure, there is need for another court to resolve conflicts of competence. In Turkey, this function is performed by the Court of Conflicts (*Uyuşmazlık Mahkemesi*). According to Article 158 of the Constitution, the Court of Conflicts has the power to resolve conflicts of competence and of judgements among civil, administrative, and military courts. The Court is composed of judges chosen by the HSYK from among candidates nominated by the Court of Cassation and the Council of the State, and those appointed by the President of the Republic from among candidates nominated by the Military Court of Cassation and the High Military Administrative Court. It is chaired by a judge chosen by the Constitutional Court from among its own members.

The administrative courts exercise their judicial review over the acts and actions of administrative bodies either through suits of annulment (*recours en annulation*), or suits of compensation (*recours de plein contentieux*). In either case, the competence of administrative courts is limited to the review of legality, and should not extend to the review of expediency. This is clearly stated in Article 125 which stipulates that

> judicial competence is limited to the review of administrative acts and actions in terms of their conformity to law. No judicial decision can be

taken that will restrict the performance of the executive function in accordance with the principles and procedures specified in laws, or in the nature of administrative acts and actions, or in a manner that will nullify the discretionary powers [of the administration].

(Art.125, 1982 Constitution)

Nevertheless, there is a tendency on the part of the administrative courts to exercise a review of expediency, that is, to evaluate a law or an administrative act in terms of their conformity to their own conception of 'public interest', thus interfering with the legitimate margin of appreciation of the administration. This tendency will be explored in greater detail in the last section pp. 287–88 of this Chapter.

As it was pointed out above, the military courts were given constitutional status for the first time by the 1961 Constitution. Under Article 145 of the 1982 Constitution,

military justice is administered by military courts and disciplinary courts. These courts are competent to try military offences committed by military personnel, their offences against other military persons, or committed in military locations, or connected with their military services and duties. Military courts are also competent to try military offences committed by non-military persons as defined by a special law, or against military persons during the exercise of their duties as defined by law, or in military locations as defined by law.

(Art. 145, 1982 Constitution)

Their area of competence has been somewhat limited, however, by the constitutional amendment of 2010. The amended Article 145 deleted the phrase 'committed in the military locations', thus considerably narrowing down the competence of military courts, and totally abolished their competence on civilians except in cases of war. It also stipulated that 'cases involving crimes against the security of the state, the constitutional order and its functioning shall in all cases be tried by civilian courts'. This amendment is particularly important in that it brought crimes against the constitutional order, such as preparations or attempts at coups, clearly under the jurisdiction of civilian courts. Another improvement introduced by the amendment is that while in the old text of Article 145 it was stipulated that the structure and functioning of military courts shall be regulated by law in accordance with the principles of the independence of the courts, security of tenure for judges, and the 'requirements of military service', the last phrase was deleted, thus removing the incompatibility between it and the other two criteria. The same was done with regard to the Article 156 on the Military Court of Cassation, and Article 157 on the High Military Administrative Court. This amendment will require an almost total revision of the current laws on military justice.[5]

The final court of appeal against decisions of the military courts is the Military Court of Cassation (*Askerî Yargıtay*). There is no appeal against its decisions before the civilian Court of Cassation. The judges of the Military Court of Cassation are appointed by the President of the Republic from among three candidates for each vacant seat nominated by the plenary of the Military Court of Cassation by secret vote and an absolute majority of its full membership (Art. 156).

Until the constitutional amendment of 1971, administrative disputes concerning the personnel matters of the military were resolved by the civilian Council of State. The amendment, however, created a High Military Administrative Court competent to resolve such disputes, and it was maintained by the 1982 Constitution. Under Article 157, the High Military Administrative Court resolves disputes on administrative acts and actions involving military persons and concerning military services, as the first and the last instance court, even if those acts are committed by a non-military authority. Disputes involving the military service obligation are also within the competence of this Court, even if the person concerned is not a military person. The members of the High Military Administrative Court belonging to the class of military judges are appointed by the President of the Republic from among three candidates nominated by the Court, and those members who do not belong to this class from among three candidates nominated by the Chief of the General Staff. The establishment of the High Military Administrative Court was a major encroachment into the area of the competence of the civilian judiciary, and is an important dimension of the growing autonomy of the military from civilian control.

Another such encroachment brought about by the constitutional amendment of 1973, also adopted during the semi-military rule of 1971–73, was the establishment of the State Security Courts to deal with crimes against the security of the state (the amended Article 136 of the 1961 Constitution). These were mixed courts composed of civilian and military judges and public prosecutors. The civilian judges were appointed by the HSYK upon the nomination of the Council of Ministers, and the military judges by the Chief of the General Staff. The Constitution of 1982 maintained these courts (Art. 143). However, many judgements of these courts were found in violation of Article 6 of the ECHR by the ECtHR, on the grounds that the military judges did not have the same independence and tenure guarantees as the civilian judges. Consequently, the State Security Courts were civilianized by the constitutional amendment of 1999 which eliminated the military judges and public prosecutors, and were totally abolished by the constitutional amendment of 2004.

Finally, martial law military courts constitute another encroachment into the area of competence of the civilian judiciary. Under the Law No. 1402 (dated May 13, 1971), martial law courts are established in regions under martial law to try offences defined by that Law. Offences related to events that caused the declaration of martial law are also tried by these courts even if they are committed at most three months before the declaration of martial law. This is a clear violation of the principle of 'natural judge', since a crime committed before the declaration of martial law and therefore subject to the jurisdiction of civilian courts may automatically become subject to the jurisdiction of military martial law courts with the declaration of martial law.

Thus, it may be concluded that the division of labor between civilian and military courts is far from the standards in established democracies. While military courts exist in many European democracies, their competence is normally limited to purely military or disciplinary offenses of military personnel, and often their decisions are subject to the review of civilian appeal courts. In contrast, the Turkish Constitution (Art. 145) defines their area of competence very broadly, even after the constitutional amendment of 2010, and provides for no possibility of appeal against their decisions before a civilian court.

The independence of the courts and the security of tenure for judges

The Constitution of 1961 had taken special care to protect and safeguard the independence of the judiciary vis-à-vis the legislature and the executive. The 1982 Constitution broadly maintained the same principle with some modifications. The basic principle on the independence of the judiciary has been stated in Article 138, which is identical with Article 132 of the 1961 Constitution. Thus, judges are independent in the discharge of their duties; they render judgement in accordance with the Constitution, law, and their conscientious opinions in conformity with law. No authority or individual may give orders or instructions to courts or judges concerning the exercise of judicial power. No questions can be asked, debates held, or statements made in the legislative Assembly in relation to the exercise of judicial power in a case under trial. Legislative and executive authorities must comply with court decisions. They cannot alter them or delay their execution. Security of tenure for judges and public prosecutors has also been recognized by the Constitution (Art. 139) in identical terms with the Constitution of 1961 (Art. 133), according to which

> judges and public prosecutors shall not be dismissed, or retired before the age prescribed by the Constitution; nor shall they be deprived of their salaries, allowances, or other personnel rights, even as a result of the abolition of a court or a post.
> (Art. 139, 1982 Constitution; Art.133, 1961 Constitution)

Personnel matters for judges and public prosecutors, such as appointments, promotions, transfers, disciplinary actions, and dismissals are within the exclusive jurisdiction of the HSYK (*Hâkimler ve Savcılar Yüksek Kurulu*, High Council of Judges and Public Prosecutors), itself composed mainly of judges. Indeed, the composition and the functions of the HSYK has become one of the most hotly debated constitutional issues, in the last decade and one of the most controversial items in the constitutional amendment package adopted in 2010. Amid these controversies, the 2010 constitutional amendment adopted by the votes of the AKP (*Adalet ve Kalkınma Partisi*, Justice and Development Party) majority changed radically the structure and functions of the HSYK, as described in Chapter 15 p. 298.

Clearly, the present arrangement has the advantage of representing the entire judiciary, not only the two high courts. Indeed, close to half of its regular members (10 out of 22) are elected by all general and administrative judges and public prosecutors, in addition to five regular members elected by the two high courts, without any interference by the executive branch. Thus the judge members constitute an almost two-thirds majority of the Council. With regard to the four members elected by the President of the Republic from among qualified persons, it can be argued that this is a quite common practice in European democracies with a high council of judiciary. The reports of the two important Council of Europe bodies, the Venice Commission and the Consultative Council of European Judges, express a preference for a mixed judicial council, composed of judges and non-judges and the appointment of some of its members by political bodies. Thus, the Venice Commission argues that

> A balance needs to be struck between judicial independence and self-administration on the one side and the necessary accountability of the judiciary on the other side in order to avoid the negative effects of corporatism within the judiciary ... One way to achieve this goal is to establish a judicial council with a balanced composition of its members ... In general, judicial councils include also members who are not part of the judiciary and represent other branches of power or the academic or professional sectors. Such a composition is justified by the fact that the control of quality and impartiality of justice is a role that reaches beyond the interests of a particular judge. The Council's performance of this control will cause citizens' confidence in the administration of justice to be raised. Moreover, an overwhelming supremacy of the judicial component may raise concerns related to the risks of 'corporatist management'.
>
> The participation of the legislative branch in the composition of such an authority is characteristic. In a system guided by democratic principles, it seems reasonable that the Council of Justice should be linked to the representation of the will of the people, as expressed by Parliament. In general, the legislative bodies are entitled to elect part of the members of the high judicial councils among legal professionals.
>
> (Venice Commission 2007)[6]

Thus, the constitutional amendment of 2010 concerning the HSYK seems to be in conformity with the guidelines of the two expert Council of Europe bodies, making the HSYK a council more broadly representative of the entire judiciary. Another improvement introduced by the amendment opens the dismissal rulings of the Council to judicial review. Furthermore, the amendment meets some of the criticisms directed against the previous arrangement, such as stipulating that the Council shall have its own secretariat, justice inspectors shall be attached to the Council; and the Minister of Justice, while remaining as the President of the Council, shall not take part in the work of the sections. Thus, his role has been reduced to a more symbolic and representative one.

Other improvement brought about by the constitutional amendment of 2010 in the field of the judiciary included the abolition of certain immunities from judicial review. Thus, dismissal rulings of the Supreme Military Council and the HSYK shall from now on be subject to the review of the administrative courts. They were previously excluded from such review by Articles 125 and 159 of the Constitution. The Supreme Military Council is a body composed of all four-star generals, and admirals in the Turkish Armed Forces under the chairmanship of the Prime Minister, and is authorized to make high-level appointments, promotions, retirements and transfers in the Armed Forces, and to dismiss military personnel from the service. Indeed, so far the Council has dismissed hundreds of officers and non-commissioned officers for allegedly having Islamist connections, without any judicial recourse. Similarly, some dismissals of the members of the judiciary by the HSYK have been highly controversial, and considered by many as being politically motivated, such as the dismissals of the two public prosecutors, Sacit Kayasu and Ferhat Sarıkaya. Therefore, subjecting such decisions to judicial review is a welcome development. Finally, an amendment to Article 129 stipulated that all disciplinary actions against civil servants and other public personnel shall be subject to judicial review, including warnings and reprimands that were so far left out of such reviews.

The constitutional amendment of 2010 also abolished the provisional article 15 that granted immunity from criminal and civil proceedings for the members of the MGK of 1980–83, the members of the Consultative Assembly, the ministers, and all those who acted on the orders of these bodies, an important exit guarantee for the responsibilities of the military regime. This may have no practical consequences, however, since the crimes committed during this period seem to have been covered by the statute of limitations. Nevertheless, the abolition of this article is likely to discourage future attempts at a coup and is a symbolically important step to liquidate the legacy of the MGK regime.

Debates on the political role of the judiciary

The political role played by the Turkish judiciary has recently become a hotly debated political issue. In the words of a leading Turkish constitutional law professor, the judiciary has impeded the development of political liberalism. The main reason for this impediment may be found in the self-declared mission of the courts in Turkey, which is to protect the state and its official discourse rather than the individual and his/her rights and liberties. The adoption of such a mission inevitably brings about the politicisation of the judiciary according to which the political convictions of judges play an increasingly important role in deciding the cases. The negative effect of the politicisation of the judiciary has been accelerated by the expansion of judicial power to cover more social and political issues, and by the judicial involvement in politics which is generally known as the judicialisation of politics.

(Arslan 2007: 220 and passim.)

Given the fact that in most Western democracies the judiciary has been the foremost defender of individual rights and liberties, 'the least dangerous branch' in other words, such a statement may sound surprising and paradoxical. Yet it is an observation shared by an increasing number of legal scholars, and in line with the rather peculiar course of Turkish political development, which followed the pattern of 'revolution from above' engineered by the military and civilian state elites. This sense of mission to protect the 'supreme interests of the state', if necessary at the expense of individual rights and liberties, was constantly inculcated into the minds of the members of the state elites, both during the Ottoman and the republican periods. A recent sociological study on the self-role perceptions of the members of the judiciary supports this observation. Many interviewees have stated that they give priority to the protection of the 'interests of the state' whenever these were at stake, and expressed doubts about the applicability of the ECtHR decisions in Turkey. Some others who have criticized this mentality have, nevertheless, observed that it is quite widespread within the judiciary (Sancar and Atılgan 2009). This mind-set explains the reluctance of many Turkish judges and public prosecutors to give due weight to the ECHR and to the case-law of the ECtHR, even though they are supposed to have precedence over Turkish domestic legislation under the 2004 amendment concerning Article 90 of the Constitution. It is particularly pronounced in cases involving the safeguarding of the two pillars of the 'founding philosophy of the Republic', namely the unitary nation-state and the principle of secularism. This is evident in generally harsh judgements concerning the crimes that allegedly undermine or weaken these principles.

In conclusion, the judiciary has become one of the most hotly debated issues in recent Turkish politics. This can only be understood in the light of the tutelary mentality of the state elites described in Chapter 15 p. 297. Thus, the judiciary has been conceived, and has perceived itself, as the ultimate citadel of the founding official ideology of the Republic, namely its staunchly secularist and strongly nationalist characteristics. This perception grew rapidly when the AKP with Islamist roots came to power in November 2002, and an armed Kurdish movement, PKK (*Partiya Karkerên Kurdistan*, Kurdistan Worker's Party), seemed to threaten the national and unitary character of the state, even its territorial integrity. The fact that a politician of Islamist roots, Abdullah Gül, was elected the President of the Republic in August 2007, following a severe constitutional crisis, carried these fears and anxieties to even greater heights, since the Presidency was customarily conceived as one of the main tutelary institutions, another 'citadel of the secular Republic'. The third pillar of tutelarism, the armed forces, also had to retreat to some extent because of the criminal proceedings against many retired and active duty high-level officers (the *Ergenekon* case) for having been involved in coup attempts.

It remains to be seen whether the reforms brought about by the constitutional amendment of 2010 will lead to a significant change in the attitudes of the judiciary in a more liberal direction. While there is a marked retreat by the Constitutional Court and HSYK from their tutelary/activist tendencies, the judiciary still occupies a center place in the political debates. Thus, the opposition argues that, as a result of changes introduced in 2010, the judiciary has become a handmaiden of the governing AKP, surely a highly exaggerated claim. On the other hand, there arguably remains a strong statist-illiberal streak within parts of the judiciary. Especially, the conduct of the 'criminal courts with special powers' continues to raise concern within a large part of the public. These courts replaced the 'state security courts', with practically the same broad powers to try cases involving the security of the state. At present, many cases involving conspiratorial schemes within the military, terrorist activities (mainly by the violent Kurdish organization, PKK), terrorist propaganda, and aiding and abetting such activities are being tried by these courts, often with exceedingly long detention periods and an apparently careless attitude towards defendants' rights. This has become a matter of embarrassment even to the Government, and various Government spokesmen uttered critical remarks about such excesses. Thus, a recent law (Law No. 6352, dated 2 July 2012) attempted to bring about some improvements by facilitating trial without detention. Ironically, however, this law did not seem to have created an observable change in the attitudes of the courts (Özbudun 2012). Apparently, old habits do not die quickly.

Notes

1 This chapter draws partly from my book (2011) *The Constitutional System of Turkey: 1876 to the Present*, New York: Palgrave Macmillan, Chs. 6 and 7.
2 For example, Constitutional Court decision, E. 1990/36, K. 1991/8, April 9, 1991, AMKD, no. 27, vol. 1, pp. 285–323.
3 Constitutional Court decision, E. 1993/33, K. 1993/40–42, October 21, 1993, *AMKD*, no. 29, vol. 1, pp. 574–81.
4 Ran Hirschl, R. (2004) *Towards Juristocracy: The Origins and Consequences of New Constitutionalism*, Cambridge, MA and London: Harvard University Press, pp. 50–59 and passim. Thus, he argues that 'unless proven otherwise, the most

plausible explanation for voluntary, self-imposed judicial empowerment is ... that political, economic, and legal power-holders who either initiate or refrain from blocking such reforms estimate that it will serve their interests to abide by the limits imposed by increased judicial intervention in the political sphere' (p. 39).

5 See especially Kardaş, Ü.(2006) 'Military Judiciary', in Cizre, Ü (ed.) *Almanac Turkey 2005: Security Sector and Democratic Oversight*, İstanbul: DCAF-TESEV, pp. 50–55.

6 Venice Commission 2007 'Judicial Appointments', Report adopted at its 70th Plenary Session, Venice, March 16–17, CDL-AD (20017)028, paras. 27–31. The Commission reiterated its opinion in a more recent report, stating that 'in all cases the council should have a pluralistic composition with a substantial part, if not the majority, of members being judges. With the exception of ex-officio members these judges should be elected or appointed by their peers', Venice Commission (2009) 'Report on the Independence of the Judicial System: Part I: The Independence of Judges', December 11–12, CDL (2010) 006, para. 32. Also in favor of a mixed composition for the judicial council, Consultative Council of European Judges (2007) *Opinion No. 10*, Strasbourg, November 21–23.

References

Arslan, Z. (2002) 'Conflicting Paradigms: Political Rights in the Turkish Constitutional Court', *Critique: Critical Middle Eastern Studies* 11, no.1.

—— (2007) 'Reluctantly Sailing Towards Political Liberalism: The Political Role of the Judiciary in Turkey', in Halliday, T. C., Karpik, L. and Feely, M. M. (eds) *Fighting for Political Freedom: Comparative Studies of the Legal Complex and Political Liberalism*, Oxford and Portland OR: Hart Publishing.

Belge, C. (2006) "Friends of the Court: The Republican alliance and selective activism of the constitutional court of Turkey," *Law and Society Review* 40, no.3.

Consultative Council of European Judges (2007) *Opinion No. 10*, Strasbourg, November 21–23.

Kardaş, Ü.(2006) 'Military Judiciary', in Cizre, Ü (ed.) *Almanac Turkey 2005: Security Sector and Democratic Oversight*, İstanbul: DCAF-TESEV.

Örücü, E. (2008) 'The Constitutional Court of Turkey: Anayasa Mahkemesi as the Protector of the System', *Journal of Comparative Law* 3, no. 2.

Özbudun, E. (2006) Political Origins of the Turkish Constitutional Court and the Problem of Democratic Legitimacy', *European Public Law* 12, no. 2.

Özbudun, E. (2009) 'Judicial Activism v. Judicial Restraint and Collisions with the Political Elites in Turkey' in Van Dijk, P. and Granata-Menghini, S. (eds) *Liber Amicorum: Antonia La Pergola*, Lund: Juristförlaget i Lund.

—— (2011) *The Constitutional System of Turkey: 1876 to the Present*, New York: Palgrave Macmillan.

—— (2012) 'Yargı Reformunda Beklenen Adımlar', *Star, Açık Görüş* (daily), 22 July.

Ran Hirschl, R. (2004) *Towards Juristocracy: The Origins and Consequences of New Constitutionalism*, Cambridge, MA and London: Harvard University Press.

Sancar, M. and Atılgan, E. Ü. (2009) *Adalet Biraz Es Geçiliyor: Demokratikleşme Sürecinde Hâkimler ve Savcılar*, İstanbul: TESEV Yayınları.

Venice Commission (2009) 'Report on the Independence of the Judicial System: Part I: The Independence of Judges', December 11–12, CDL (2010) 006.

—— 2007 'Judicial Appointments', Report adopted at its 70th Plenary Session, Venice, March 16–17, CDL-AD (20017)028.

Part VI
Rule of law

15 Democracy, tutelarism, and the search for a new constitution

Ergun Özbudun

Three dimensions of democratic consolidation

Juan Linz and Alfred Stepan define a consolidated democracy, referring to its behavioral, attitudinal, and constitutional dimensions. Thus,

> behaviorally, a democratic regime in a territory is consolidated when no significant national, social, economic, political or institutional actors spend significant resources attempting to achieve their objectives by creating a nondemocratic regime or turning to violence or foreign intervention to secede from the state.
>
> Attitudinally, a democratic regime is consolidated when a strong majority of public opinion holds the belief that democratic procedures and institutions are the most appropriate way to govern collective life in a society such as theirs and when the support for antisystem alternatives is quite small or more or less isolated from the pro-democratic forces.
>
> Constitutionally, a democratic regime is consolidated when governmental and nongovernmental forces alike, throughout the territory of the state, become subjected to, and habituated to, the resolution of conflict within the specific laws, procedures, and institutions sanctioned by the new democratic process.'
>
> (Linz and Stepan 1996: 6)

Turkish democracy seems to be a borderline case on all three accounts. Indeed, this is a rather surprising situation, since Turkey is a 'second-wave' democracy that made its democratic transition in the aftermath of the Second World War. Furthermore, Turkey maintained its competitive political system throughout this period despite two full (1960 and 1980), and two partial (1971 and 1997) breakdowns, all of which were of relatively short duration. Interestingly, despite this reasonably long experience with democratic government, Turkey is still far from democratic consolidation, and lays behind many newer, 'third wave' democracies of Southern, Central, and Eastern Europe.[1] Thus, according to the Freedom House ratings, Turkey is still a 'semi-democracy', or a 'partially free' country with a score of 3 for both fundamental and political rights in its 2009 report (Puddington 2009: 27).

Consolidation of Turkish democracy presents problems in all three dimensions alluded to by Linz and Stepan. Behaviorally, since 1984, Turkey has had to face with a violent, secessionist Kurdish movement, the PKK (*Partiya Karkerên Kurdistan*, Kurdistan Worker's Party). Even though in recent years the PKK seems to have dropped its secessionist claims, it still is difficult to meet its maximalist demands within the present structure of the Turkish Republic. Furthermore, this cannot be dismissed as a marginal movement, since a series of legal Kurdish political parties with hardly hidden sympathies for the PKK, receive about 5 percent of the total vote in parliamentary and local elections.

Even more ominously, the loyalty of the armed forces to democracy is not at all unquestionable. The so-called 'February 28' 1997 process that ousted the coalition Government of Islamist Necmettin Erbakan is usually considered a 'soft' or a 'post-modern' coup. Even though the process was supported by many civilian political forces and the leading NGO's and the change of government took place within established constitutional rules, it is widely believed that this could not have happened without a credible threat of coup.[2] Following the coming to power in 2002 of the AKP (*Adalet ve Kalkınma Partisi*, Justice and Development Party), in the eyes of the military the successor to Erbakan's banned RP (*Refah Partisi*, Welfare Party) and an equally Islamist party with a 'hidden agenda' of establishing an Islamic regime in Turkey, conspiratorial activities within the military seem to have gained ground again. Recently, many such coup plans were disclosed and a major criminal case (the so-called *Ergenekon* case) is currently going on against the suspects. A positive element in this rather black picture is the repeated statements by the former-chief-of the general staff Hilmi Özkök and his successor İlker Başbuğ, declaring their commitments to democracy.

Attitudinally, public opinion research in recent years has consistently shown that a strong majority of Turkish voters are committed to democracy. Thus, according to a 2006 survey, 76.9 percent of the respondents think that democracy is the best form of government, 79.9 percent support the freedom of expression, 76.6 percent are against restrictions on the freedom to live according to one's religious beliefs, 76.1 percent are against restrictions on the use of one's mother tongue, 73.2 percent are categorically against torture, 61.8 percent support the freedom of assembly and demonstration for radical and extremist groups provided that they do not disturb public order. However, 26.8 percent rather disquietingly believe that Turkey's problems can be solved not by elected governments but by a military regime (Çarkoğlu and Toprak 2006: 51). A 1999 survey by the same authors also demonstrated the incompatibility between liberal democratic values and those religiously inspired conservative ones. Thus, they found that 58.9 percent of all respondents think that all Muslim women should cover their heads, 57.1 percent are against short skirts, 66.5 percent are in favor of banning books which deny God or the Prophet, and 70.5 percent favor the banning of alcohol sales in the month of Ramadan (Çarkoğlu and Toprak 2000: 59). As Guillermo O' Donnell rightly observes in regard to the new South American democracies, 'the current prestige of democratic discourses, and conversely, the weakness of openly authoritarian political discourses' are major factors working to the advantage of democratic actors. These factors, however, are 'subject to withering by the passage of time ... The influence of democratic discourse depends ... in part on their capacity to be translated into concrete meanings for the majority of the population' (O'Donnell 1992: 21).

The history of constitution-making in Turkey

Of all three dimensions of democratic consolidation, however, the constitutional dimension is the most urgent and most problematic. Historically speaking, none of the five Ottoman-Turkish constitutions, those of 1876, 1921, 1924, 1961, and 1982, were made by broadly representative constituent assemblies through a process of genuine negotiations and compromises. The Ottoman Constitution of 1876 was prepared by a committee appointed by the Sultan and proclaimed by him with an imperial rescript. The short and short-lived 1921 Constitution was a partial exception to the generalization above, and can be explained by the extraordinary circumstances of the War of Independence period. The following Constitution of 1924 was adopted by an ordinary legislative assembly strongly dominated by Kemalists. The 1961 and 1980 Constitutions followed military interventions. They both were adopted by constituent assemblies that were not popularly elected. In both cases, the military committee that carried out the coup constituted one of the chambers of the bicameral constituent assembly. In the case of the 1960–61 constituent assembly, the civilian chamber was not based on popular elections; rather, it was essentially a co-opted body, including the representatives of the two opposition parties, the CHP (*Cumhuriyet Halk Partisi*, Republican People's Party) and the CKMP (*Cumhuriyetçi Köylü Millet Partisi*, Republican Peasants' Nation Party) as well as those of certain civil society institutions, but excluding the representatives of the ousted DP (*Demokrat Parti*, Democratic Party) which at that time represented about half of the Turkish voters. The military rulers of the 1980–83 period, MGK (*Millî Güvenlik Kurulu*, National Security Council), went much further than their predecessors in this direction by not even resorting to co-optative methods. Indeed, the civilian wing (Consultative Assembly) was composed of 160 members, all of whom were appointed by the ruling military council. Furthermore, no political party members were eligible for the Consultative Assembly. Consequently, it had a much more bureaucratic composition than its predecessor and much more limited powers vis-à-vis the MGK. At best, it performed only a consultative-advisory function as its name indicated.[3]

As expected, all three republican constitutions of Turkey, as a result of the method of constitution-making, strongly reflected the interests and values of the dominant state elites. In none of the three cases, was there a genuine process of negotiations and compromises among different social and political forces. Constitutional choices were one-sidedly imposed upon the civil society that had little or no role in constitution-making. Therefore, all three constitutions enjoyed little democratic legitimacy, and relatively short lives. Thus, while the Constitution of 1924 remained in force for 36 years, only the last 14 years of this period was combined with multi-party, competitive politics and it witnessed intense and polarized constitutional debates. The Constitution of 1961, in many ways the most democratic and liberal constitution that Turkey has ever had, survived only for 19 years, and underwent two radical amendments in 1971 and 1973 under the strong influence of the military.

The current constitution of 1982 was made by even much less representative and democratic methods as alluded to above. For all practical purposes, the ruling military council (MGK) had the ultimate say in its making. Consequently, the Constitution reflected the authoritarian, statist, and tutelary values of the state elites even more strongly than its predecessors.

The tutelary character of the 1982 constitution

The military founders of the 1982 Constitution had very little trust in civilian politicians and civilian politics which they often expressed in quite blunt terms. Thus, they designed a constitution that would limit the area of civilian politics as much as possible. Under the original version of the Constitution, all civil society organizations other than political parties were banned from engaging in political activities. Trade unions, voluntary associations, foundations, public professional organizations, and cooperative societies were not allowed to support, or receive support from, political parties, or to engage in joint action among themselves. These restrictions were repealed by the constitutional amendment of 1995.

The military founders of the 1982 Constitution also restricted the activities of political parties by a long list of vague party bans in the Constitution and even more draconian restrictions in the Law on Political Parties. Thus, so far 25 political parties (6 under the 1961 Constitution and 19 under the 1982 Constitution) were banned by the Constitutional Court, and many leaders and members of such parties were banned from political activities for a period of five years from the prohibition ruling of the Court. Despite some limited improvements brought about by the constitutional amendments of 1995 and 2001,[4] the legal regime of political parties still constitutes one of the most objectionable 'democracy deficits' in the Turkish political system. Thus, a recent (March 2009) report by the Venice Commission (European Commission for Democracy through Law) of the Council of Europe strongly criticized the Turkish constitutional and legal rules concerning the prohibition of political parties. The report concludes that 'the basic problem with the Turkish rules on party closure is that the general threshold is too low, both for initiating procedures and for prohibiting or dissolving parties. This is in itself *in abstracto* deviating from common European democratic standards, and it leads too easily to action that will be in breach of the ECHR, as demonstrated in the many Turkish cases before the European Court of Human Rights.'[5]

With this aim in mind, the Constitution established a number of tutelary institutions designed to check the powers of the elected agencies and to narrow down the space for civilian politics. Foremost among such institutions was the Presidency of the Republic. The combination of the constitutional referendum with the election of the next President of the Republic gave General Kenan Evren (the sole candidate) the possibility of exercising tutelary powers over elected Governments for a period of seven years (1982–89). In fact, he often described himself as the 'guarantor' of the Constitution. This tutelary role was strengthened by the broad powers given to the President by the Constitution, as will be alluded to below. The military founders of the Constitution might have possibly thought that after Evren's term came to an end, his successor would again be a military person or at least someone acceptable to the military. Another one was the strengthened MGK. The original text of the Constitution gave the military members a majority in the Council and stipulated that the decisions of the Council should be given priority consideration by the Council of Ministers, thereby rendering such decisions binding if not in theory, at least in practice. A third tutelary institution was the YÖK (*Yükseköğretim Kurulu*, Higher Education Council) that was designed to put universities in order and under strict discipline. The President of the Republic was given the power to appoint the chairman and some members of the YÖK and the university rectors. Finally, the President of the Republic was given broad discretionary powers with regard to the judiciary, such as appointing the judges of the Constitutional Court (three of them directly, and eight of them from among three candidates nominated by the other high courts and the YÖK), one-fourth of the members of the Council of State (the highest administrative court), the members of the Supreme Council of Judges and Public Prosecutors (from among three candidates nominated by the two high courts) and the Chief Public Prosecutor of the Court of Cassation (the Supreme Court) and his deputy from among five candidates nominated by the Court of Cassation. Thus, the judiciary was conceived as another tutelary institution designed to protect the values of the state elites against the actions of elected governments.

The composition of the Constitutional Court and the Supreme Council of Judges and Public Prosecutors is radically changed by the constitutional amendment package adopted in the referendum of 12 September 2010 without, however, reducing the role of the President. Under the new arrangement, the number of the Constitutional Court judges is raised from 11 to 17, three of whom shall be elected by parliament from among three candidates for each seat nominated by the Court of Accounts (two) and the presidents of the bar associations (one). Four members shall be directly selected by the President from among judges and public prosecutors, reporting judges of the Constitutional Court, practising lawyers, and high level public administrators. The president shall choose three members among three candidates for each seat nominated by the YÖK. YÖK's nominees have to be professors in the fields of law (two of the three must be in this field), economics, and political science. Finally, the President shall choose three members nominated by the Court of Cassation, two by the Council of State, one by the Military Court of Cassation, and one by the High Military Administrative Court, again from among three nominees for each vacant seat. Thus, the President maintains his strong role in the selection of the Constitutional Court judges, directly or indirectly selecting 14 out of 17 members. These changes were intended to limit the tutelary role of the Constitutional Court in line with widely accepted European standards.

The 2010 constitutional amendment also changed the structure of the High Council of Judges and Public Prosecutors. Under the new arrangement, the number of members is raised from seven to twenty-two. Seven regular and four substitute members shall be elected by the judges and public prosecutors of all ordinary courts, three regular and two substitute members by the judges and public prosecutors of administrative courts, three regular and three substitute members by the Court of Cassation, two regular and two substitute members by the Council of State and one regular and one substitute member by the Academy of Justice. The President's role in the selection of these members coming from the judiciary is eliminated. On the other hand, the President is entitled to appoint four regular members from among law professors and practising lawyers. The Minister of Justice and the Undersecretary of the Ministry of Justice remain as *ex-officio* members The Minister is still the president of the Council; however, his role is reduced to a mainly symbolic and ceremonial one. The change was intended to break the monopolistic domination of the two high courts over the Council, and to make it more representative of the judiciary as a whole by allowing the judges and public prosecutors of the lower-level courts to be strongly represented in the Council.

Finally, the military obtained important powers, privileges, and immunities as a price for relinquishing power to elected civilian institutions (exit guaranties as they are commonly called). In addition to the MGK mentioned above, the military was exempted from the review of the Court of Accounts, the High Board of Supervision; and the decisions of the YAŞ (*Yüksek Askerî Şûra*, High Military Council) regarding high-level military appointments, promotions, and expulsions from the military were closed to judicial review. The laws and law-amending ordinances (decree-laws) passed by the MGK regime (1980–83) were exempted from the review of constitutionality by the Constitutional Court. Furthermore, the Law on the General Secretariat of the MGK provided that the Secretary General shall be a high-level military person and endowed the Secretariat with broad executive powers.

The politics of constitutional amendments

It is no wonder that the 1982 Constitution met with severe criticism almost from its inception. In the following years, most political parties and the leading civil society institutions such as the TBB (*Türkiye Barolar Birliği*, Turkish Bar Association), the TOBB (*Türkiye Odalar ve Borsalar Birliği*, Union of Chambers and Commodity Exchanges of Turkey), and the TÜSİAD (*Türk Sanayicileri ve İşadamları Derneği*, Association of Turkish Businessmen and Industrialists) proposed entirely new constitutional drafts or at least radical changes in the Constitution. Consequently, starting from 1987, the Constitution has undergone 18 amendments. The general direction of these amendments was to improve liberal-democratic standards, although some of them dealt with rather trivial matters. Despite these positive changes, it is generally agreed that it was not possible to completely liquidate the illiberal and tutelary spirit of the 1982 Constitution. In the summer of 2007 constitutional debates took a new turn when the governing AKP initiated a process for the making of an entirely new constitution, as will be analyzed below.

The constitutional amendments of the 1990s, as well as those of 2001 and 2004 were accomplished through a process of intense inter-party negotiations and compromises and adopted by strong majorities in parliament.[6] Thus, it was hoped that after so many decades of internecine inter-party conflict, time had come for a period of 'elite convergence,' that would result in the making of a liberal and democratic constitution based on a broad consensus.[7] However, the constitutional crisis of 2007 seems to have reversed this trend towards elite convergence, as will be spelled out below. Indeed, the major amendment package involving 23 articles adopted in the 12 September 2010 referendum displays the extent of polarization on constitutional issues. The amendment package was adopted by 58 percent of the vote, after perhaps the most virulent and divisive campaign in Turkish political history. At the moment of this writing Turkey seems to be in a deep constitutional crisis and deadlock with little hope of achieving a broadly based constitutional consolidation in the near future.

The constitutional crisis of 2007–8[8]

A constitutional crisis erupted in the spring of 2007 over the question of presidency. At the end of President Ahmet Necdet Sezer's term of office, the governing AKP seemed to have enough votes in Parliament to elect its own candidate. Indeed, the Constitution of 1982 (Art. 102) clearly described the procedures for the election of the President, according to which a maximum number of four parliamentary rounds were foreseen for the election. The decisional quorum was two-thirds of the full membership of the TBMM (*Türkiye Büyük Millet Meclisi*, Turkish Grand National Assembly) on the first two rounds, and the absolute majority of the full membership on the third and fourth rounds, a minimum of 367 and 276 votes, respectively. The Constitution contained no special quorum rule for the meeting of the TBMM, in which case the general rule in Article 96 should apply, i.e., the quorum should be one-third of the full membership (184 votes). The parliamentary arithmetic then gave the AKP the power to elect the President alone on the third or fourth rounds, but not on the first two rounds. Thus, there seemed to be no constitutional obstacle to the election of an AKP candidate.

At this point, maneuverings of dubious legal validity started in order to 'save the last citadel of the secular republic' from the occupation of an alleged 'Islamist'. A retired chief Prosecutor of the Republic (Sabih Kanadoğlu) put forward an argument that the two-thirds majority is not only the decisional quorum, but also the necessary quorum for the opening of the session. The main opposition party, the CHP, embraced the argument after hesitating for a few days. After the first round on which the two-thirds quorum was not obtained because of the boycotting of the opposition deputies, the CHP carried the case to the Constitutional Court, and the Court in an extremely controversial ruling rendered on May 1st, endorsed the claim of unconstitutionality.[9] The ruling of the Constitutional Court put an end to the election process since the required quorum (367 votes) was not obtained on the first round and the AKP's candidate Abdullah Gül failed to get elected. This deadlock obliged the Parliament to call new elections as required by the Constitution. A full analysis of the Constitutional Court's decision is beyond the scope of this study. If suffices to say here, however, that it is found inconsistent with the literal, teleological, and historical interpretations of the Constitution by a majority of constitutional law scholars, and described as based on political rather than legal considerations.

As a result of the deadlock over the presidency, the TBMM decided unanimously to call new elections, and fixed the date at 22 July 2007. At about the same time, the AKP leadership reacted to the new situation by proposing a constitutional amendment package that involved changes in five articles and the addition of two provisional articles. The proposal involved the shortening of the legislative period from five to four years, the popular election of the President of the Republic for a maximum two five-year terms, and an amendment to Article 96 according to which the meeting quorum for the TBMM shall be one-third of its full membership for all business including elections. The proposal was strongly opposed by the CHP, but supported by the minor opposition party ANAP (*Anavatan Partisi*, Motherland Party). Therefore, all were adopted in the second reading by more than a two-thirds majority. The amendment package was designed with a view to preventing the reoccurrence of the parliamentary deadlock in the election of the President. During the debates, the CHP deputies argued that the real intention of the proposed change was to create a semi-presidential system, since popular election would increase the political weight of the President already endowed with broad constitutional powers. Indeed, the establishment of a presidential or semi-presidential system had long been advocated by such center-right leaders as Turgut Özal and Süleyman Demirel.

The amendment bill was returned to Parliament for reconsideration by President Sezer on 25 May 2007. Sezer argued in his reasoning that changing the method of election of the President is not a simple procedural change, but one directly related to the political system preferred by the Constitution. The present Constitution conceives the presidency as an impartial office, an element of 'balance and stability' vis-à-vis the power of the majority party. The proposed change means a departure from the parliamentary government system without, however, adopting the main features of a presidential or semi-presidential system; thus, it will be a system 'with no example or practice'. Sezer warned that a popularly elected President will 'easily become the dominant element of the political system', and the system will lead to conflicts and frictions within the executive. He also objected to the nomination of presidential candidates by political parties and the possibility of getting elected for a second five-year term as measures likely to weaken the impartiality of the President and to politicize his office. Finally, Sezer argued that such a fundamental change in the political system should not be introduced in haste without sufficient consideration and deliberation.[10]

Upon reconsideration, the TBMM readopted the amendment bill verbatim. All articles, expect Article 1 concerning the shortening of the legislative period from five to four years, were adopted by more than the requisite two-thirds majority (i.e. 367 votes). That Article 1 received only 366 votes led to a procedural debate on the question of the constitutionality of the voting, as will be spelled out below.

This conflict over the constitutionality of the proceedings was carried to the Constitutional Court by President Sezer and the CHP deputies. The claimants argued that, under Article 175 of the Constitution, the required quorum for the bill upon its being returned to Parliament by the President for reconsideration is the two-thirds of its full membership, and that this requirement is valid for every article of the bill, as well as for its whole. Therefore, according to the CHP deputies, the fact that Article 1 of the bill received only 366 votes made the adoption of that Article unconstitutional; it also made the final vote on the whole of the bill (which received 370 votes) unconstitutional since the rejected Article 1 was not dropped out of the bill. President Sezer went further arguing that the adopted bill should be considered 'null and void' (in Turkish law it is different to being subject to annulment) since the quorum rules for constitutional amendments were not complied with. Both claims were ultimately based on Article 148 of the Constitution which allows the Constitutional Court to review constitutional amendments from a strictly procedural point of view, i.e. whether the amendment bill is debated twice and whether the quorum rules for the proposal and adoption of the amendment bill are complied with.

The Constitutional Court rejected the claim of unconstitutionality, however, in its ruling on 5 July 2007.[11] Meanwhile, President Sezer had already submitted the readopted amendment law (Law No. 5678) to referendum as he was entitled to under Article 175 of the Constitution. The parliamentary elections of 22 July gave the AKP a strong mandate with 46.7 percent of the vote and 340 out of 550 seats. One of the first items on the agenda of the newly elected TBMM was to elect a President. However, given the Constitutional Court's decision discussed above, the same problem persisted. The AKP had enough votes to elect its candidate on the third or the fourth rounds, but not on the first two rounds. Since the required quorum for the starting of the first round was the two-thirds majority according to the Constitutional Court's interpretation, the AKP needed to secure the attendance of at least some of the opposition deputies. At this point, the second largest opposition party, the ultra-nationalist MHP (*Milliyetçi Hareket Partisi*, Nationalist Action Party), decided to attend the parliamentary sessions in order not to create a second constitutional crisis. The MHP's lead was also followed by the Kurdish nationalist DTP (*Demokrasi ve Toplum Partisi*, Democratic Society Party) and the DSP (*Demokratik Sol Partisi*, Democratic Left Party) whose deputies were nominated on the CHP lists but resigned from the CHP immediately after the elections. The MHP and the DSP deputies attended the parliamentary sessions but voted for their own candidates. On the third round held on 28 August, Abdullah Gül was duly elected the eleventh President of the Republic with 339 votes out of a total of 448 votes. On 21 October, the constitutional amendment Law No. 5678 was adopted by referendum with a 68.95 percent majority which a turnout rate of 67.51 percent.

The year 2007 can indeed be characterized as period of 'constitutional battles'. The bitterness and intensity of these battles can only be understood in terms of the peculiarities of Turkish politics. The secularist state elites who have always enjoyed a controlling influence on Turkish politics see the presidency as their undisputable domain and as a guarantee against anti-secular tendencies. The broad powers granted to it by the 1982 Constitution makes it a particularly important prize in political competition. The secularist camp often expresses the fear that an Islamist president can gradually Islamize the Constitutional Court, the judiciary, and the universities through his broad appointive powers. This fear is more dramatically expressed in the often-heard slogan that the presidency is the last citadel of the secular Republic which should not be surrendered to an Islamist at all costs. The secularists' and the 1982 Constitution's conception of the presidency is an office of tutelage or a mechanism of check and balance over elected politicians on behalf of the state elites, hence the bitterness of the opposition to Abdullah Gül's election as the President of the Republic. The same opposition is also evident in the reaction shown to the AKP's initiative for a new constitution.

The AKP's 2007 election manifesto contains a strong promise for a new constitution which is described as 'civilian' and as a 'social contract'. It should protect fundamental rights and liberties in the most effective way in accordance with the standards of the Universal Declaration of Human Rights and the ECHR, while preserving the unamendable characteristics of the Republic such as the democratic, secular, and social state based on human rights and the rule of law. The manifesto promises to regulate the relations among different branches of government in line with the parliamentary model and to redefine the powers of the President accordingly. The new constitution should be based on the broadest possible consensus (AKP 2007: 12).

The AKP started to work on the new constitution even before the 22 July 2007 elections. On June 8, Prime Minister Erdoğan asked a group of constitutional law professors to prepare a draft constitution within the parameters in the party's election manifesto. The drafting committee presented its draft to the AKP leadership on 29 August 2007. Some of its main novelties are as follows:

(a) Standards for fundamental rights and liberties are improved in the light of the European Convention of Human Rights. The Constitutional Court is empowered to annul a law that conflicts with an international human rights treaty of which Turkey is a party. Political rights are broadened by making the prohibition of political parties more difficult and abolishing the five-year political ban for individual party members resulting from the closure of their party. New rights are added such as the right to receive information, children's rights, the right to a fair trial, and the right to the protection of personal data. The provision on equality is amended to allow positive discrimination (affirmative action) for women and the other disadvantaged groups. Religious education that was made compulsory by the 1982 Constitution is made optional. The protection of human dignity is emphasized as one of the fundamental duties of the state both in the Preamble and in the text.

(b) The principle of the rule of law is bolstered by removing certain restrictions on judical review, such as on the decisions of the HSYK (*Hâkimler ve Savcılar Yüksek Kurulu*, High Council of Judges and Public Prosecutors), of the YAŞ (*Yüksek Askerî Şûra*, High Military Council), and the decree-laws passed during martial law and the state of emergency.

(c) The democratic legitimacy of the Constitutional Court and the HSYK is strenghtened by allowing the parliament to elect some of their members (eight out of 17 in the case of the Constitutional Court, and five out of 17 in the case of the HSYK).

(d) The excessive powers of the President of the Republic are eliminated making the system of government much closer to a classical parliamentary model, although the popular election of the President is maintained.

The original declared intention of the AKP leadership was to present the draft (after they finalized it) to a fairly long period of societal debate and then to present it to the Parliament as a formal amendment proposal. It was hoped that debates both in the pre-legislative and the legislative stages would make it possible to reach a broader consensus. The final stage would be a referendum regardless of the extent of the majority obtained in parliament. However, the developments that will be spelled out below, and possibly some differences of opinion within the AKP itself, caused the project to be silently shelved at least for the time being.

The constitutional debates took on a new intensity over the so-called 'headscarf issue'. The roots of the problem go back to the mid-1980s, when the Constitutional Court annulled a law (No. 3511) permitting female university students 'to cover their hair and neck because of their religious convictions.' The AKP government made no attempt to lift the headscarf ban during its first term of office. Prime Minister Erdoğan and other party spokesmen often stated that there was a social consensus for the lifting of the ban, but not an 'institutional consensus', obviously referring to the opposition of the CHP, military and the judiciary, and promised that they would seek to obtain institutional consensus as well. Indeed, survey research has shown that over 70 percent of the respondents (76.1 percent in 1999 and 71.1 percent in 2006) were in favor of allowing female university students to wear headscarves (Çarkoğlu and Toprak 2006: 71). An institutional consensus, however, has ever materialized.

The headscarf issue, dormant during the first term of the AKP government, suddenly became the number one issue of the political agenda in early 2008. Erdogan in a press conference in Madrid stated that the ban should be lifted even if the headscarf is used as a 'political symbol'. He added that there was no need to wait for the adoption of a new constitution and that the problem could be solved by a simple, 'one sentence', constitutional amendment. The Prime Minister's statement was strongly criticised by the CHP, but surprisingly supported by the second largest opposition party, the ultra-nationalist MHP. The MHP leader Devlet Bahceli argued that the ban could be lifted by a change in the constitutional Article on equality. Following intensive talks between the two parties, they agreed on an amendment proposal concerning Articles 10 and 42 of the Constitution, and the proposal was submitted to the TBMM with the signatures of 278 AKP and 70 MHP deputies. The change in Article 10 concerning equality involved the addition of the phrase 'in the use of all kinds of public services'. Article 42 on the right to education was also changed by adding a new paragraph: 'No one shall be deprived of his/her right to higher education for any reason not explicitly specified by law. The limits on the exercise of this right shall be determined by law'. At the end of the first round of debates, Article 1 was adopted by 401 (with 110 opposing deputies) and Article 2 by 404 (with 99 opposing deputies) votes. On the second round, both articles received 403 votes, and the entire bill 411 votes. It was not clear whether the amendments automatically lifted the ban, or that would require a new implementing legislation. In any case, the CHP and the DSP deputies challenged the constitutional amendment before the Constitutional Court arguing that it was against the unamendable articles of the Constitution (i.e. secularism) and therefore null and void.

On June 5, 2008, the Constitutional Court annulled the amendments.[12] The decision was based on the alleged incompatibility of the amendments with the principle of secularism referred to in the unamendable Article 2 of the Constitution. In fact, Article 4 states that the first three articles of the Constitution are unamendable and that no proposal can be made to amend them. On the other hand, Article 148 of the Constitution limits the Court's competence regarding constitutional amendments to a merely procedural (i.e. not substantive) review. Moreover, unlike its predecessor, the Constitution of 1982 explicitly specifies the procedural defects that can be reviewed by the Court. These are the quorums for the proposal (it must be signed by at least one-third of the full membership of the TBMM) and for its adoption (it must be adopted by at least a three-fifths majority), and the requirement that the proposal be debated twice. Article 148 explicitly 'limits' the procedural review of the Court to these three dimensions. Since Article 148 is the 'special provision' relevant to the case, according to the well-known rule *lex specialis derogat legi generali*, Article 4 cannot be invoked as a basis for broadening the competence of the Court over constitutional amendments.

The Constitutional Court's ruling created a serious constitutional impasse. The Constitution has no explicit or implicit rule allowing the Court to review to compatibility of a constitutional amendment with the first three unamendable articles of the Constitution. Indeed, under the 1982 Constitution, the Court rejected three requests (one in 1987 and two in 2007) for such review quoting the provisions of Article 148. Therefore, the recent decision of the Court is not only inconsistent with its earlier rulings, but it also amounts to a 'usurpation of power' since it is in violation of the explicit text of Article 148. The resulting situation gives the Court almost total power of control over constitutional amendments. Since the characteristics enumerated in Article 2 and 3 ('a democratic, secular and social state governed by the rule of law, respectful of human rights, committed to Atatürk nationalism, and based on the principles specified in the Preamble within an understanding of social peace, national solidarity, and justice.') are so vague and broad that almost no constitutional amendment can be conceived as not in one way or another related to one of these characteristics. Thus, this interpretation amounts to an almost complete usurpation of the constituent power by the Constitutional Court which can only be described as an extreme example of 'juristocracy'.

The constitutional crisis was further aggravated by the closure case against the AKP. On March 2008, the Chief Public Prosecutor of the Court of Cassation started prohibition proceedings against the AKP. He claimed that the AKP had become a focal point of anti-constitutional activities intended to undermine the secular character of the state. Although evidently he had been collecting evidence against the AKP for a long time, the start of the proceedings seems to have been triggered by the constitutional amendment concerning the headscarf issue.

On 30 July 2008, the Constitutional Court announced its ruling.[13] Even though a majority of the judges (six out of eleven) voted in favor of banning the party, the qualified majority (three-fifths or seven members out of eleven) required by the Constitution was not obtained. Therefore, the party was not banned, but ten members concluded that the AKP had become a focus of anti-secular activities, and decided to deprive it partially of state funding (a sanction also provided by the Constitution for less severe cases of violation).

The Constitutional Court's ruling conforms neither to the European standards for party prohibitions developed by the European Court of Human Rights (ECtHR) and the Venice Commission of the Council of Europe, nor even to the much more restrictive provisions of the Turkish Constitution (Art. 68). It is based on a certain assertive and authoritarian understanding of secularism without any parallel in any Western democracy. One of the main justification for its ruling, according to the Constitutional Court, was the constitutional amendment concerning the headscarf issue, although the amendment was adopted by a nearly three-fourths majority of the TBMM that included not only the AKP deputies but also those of the MHP and the DTP. At any rate, condemning a party for an act of Parliament that clearly is within the limits of its constituent power is unheard of in the practice of European democracies. Furthermore, many of the accusations in the indictment of the Chief Public Prosecutor are statements by party leaders and members within the universally acceptable limits of the freedom of expression.

Constitutional issues and political cleavages

The overtly antagonistic nature of the recent constitutional debates cannot be properly understood without an analysis of political cleavages in Turkey. Most Turkish observers agree that the basic social cleavage that produced the present-day Turkish party system is a center-periphery cleavage.[14] It should be pointed out that here the terms center and periphery are not used in a geographical sense, but refer to an essentially cultural cleavage whose roots go back to the Ottoman times. Under the sharp dichotomy between the rulers and the ruled in the Ottoman Empire, the center was composed of the military-bureaucratic state elites headed by the sultan, while the periphery referred to the rest of the society who had no role in conducting the government affairs. The absence of powerful intermediary institutions in the Ottoman Empire made this cleavage much sharper than in Western Europe.[15] Starting with the late nineteenth century Ottoman reforms and continuing with the Republic, the center became increasingly nationalistic and secularist, against 'a culturally heterogeneous, complex, and even hostile periphery' with religious and anti-statist overtones (Kalaycıoğlu 1994: 403).

Whether the center-periphery cleavage is still dominant in Turkish politics is open to debate. While this cleavage is not identical with the one between Islamists and secularists, one should not overlook a large degree of overlap. Indeed, when the center became increasingly secularist during the late Ottoman times and even more radically so in the early republican period, the periphery increasingly identified itself with Islamic values and practices. With the rise of an Islamic bourgeoisie and an Islamic intellectual class in the post-1983 period, the center is no longer as united and cohesive as it used to be. Thus, argues Kalaycıoğlu, 'to complicate the picture further, the center is no longer what it used to be: Turkey lacks a coherent and compact elite group occupying the center and defending the collective interests of the center' (Kalaycıoğlu 1994: 407).

Still, it may be argued that the present Turkish party configuration reflects many of the characteristics of a center-periphery cleavage. While the CHP seems to be the strongest defender of the centrist values, the AKP appears to be the leading representative of peripheral forces. Although the AKP was able to forge a broadly-based cross-class coalition, the common element among them is the sense of having been excluded and discriminated against by the secularist center. The AKP is, in a real sense, the party of the excluded or marginalized sectors of the society, imbued with religious and conservative social values. For example, according to a 2006 survey, while the average value on the secular-Islamist scale is 7.1 (10 is the maximum) for the AKP supporters, this value is only 2.8 for the CHP supporters. 60 percent of the AKP supporters identify themselves as primarily Muslim, as opposed to 20.9 percent of the CHP supporters. Whereas close to half of the CHP supporters believe that secularism is under threat, only 12 percent of the AKP supporters think so. Similarly, according to the same public opinion survey, 50.2 percent of all respondents think that the AKP intends to impose an Islamic way of life (not to be confused with a *sharia*-based government), 43.8 percent think that it seeks to infiltrate the public bureaucracy with Islamic elements, and 36.7 percent are of the opinion that it intends to reverse the advances concerning women's rights (Çarkoğlu and Toprak 2006: 40, 42, 76, 87–91). These findings reveal a wide ideological gap between the AKP and its main rival CHP along the center-periphery or secularist-religious dimension. On all these issues, the supporters of the minor center-right parties (MHP, DYP, ANAP) occupy an intermediate position.

The superimposition of the class, center-periphery and the secularist-religious cleavages has led to a particularly deep and a potentially explosive division, a real dichotomy, in Turkish politics. As is well-known, mutually reinforcing cleavages, as opposed to cross-cutting ones, pose a particularly serious challenge to democratic stability. This has become strikingly clear in the constitutional crisis of 2007–8 as described above. The present political configuration of Turkey pits the AKP against an alliance of the strongly secularist CHP, the armed forces, the Constitutional Court and a large part of the judiciary, sometimes called 'the Republican alliance'. The conflict has righty been described as a 'zero-sum' game. Thus, it has been argued that 'the source of the secular establishment's threat perception is not the policies but the alleged Islamist identity of the AKP. Hence, the establishment persistently warns the public about the worrying magnitude of reactionism ... The second defensive strategy of the establishment involves the imposition of institutional limits on the political sphere ... The emphasis on the AKP members' Islamist pedigree and conservative lifestyles rather than on its policy proposals has reinforced the definition of the secular state as a community of devout believers of Kemalism. In fact, this 'communitization' of the state during the AKP Government has reached unprecedented levels' (Çınar 2008: 112–20). The threat perception by the secularist state elites has strengthened their tutelary attitudes and led them to manipulations of dubious democratic legitimacy, as it has been spelled out above.

In addition to increasing polarization along secularist-Islamic conservative lines, another challenge to constitutional consolidation is posed by the rise of Kurdish nationalism. Kurds represent the only large linguistic minority group in Turkey (an estimated 10–15 percent of the population). Although Kurdish speakers constitute a majority in many eastern and southeastern provinces, a large part of them live in other regions of the country and are fairly well integrated into Turkish society. Since the late 1970s a separatist violent organization, the PKK (*Partiya Karkerên Kurdistan*, Kurdistan Worker's Party) has emerged in the southeastern region, and the armed conflict is still going on.

Kurdish demands vary between relatively modest ones such as the recognition of their separate cultural identity and the cultural rights associated with it, to such maximalist ones as regional autonomy, federation, and even secession from Turkey. Since the late 1980s, Kurdish nationalism has been represented by a number of successive ethnic parties, each of which was closed down by the Constitutional Court on account of activities against the territorial and national integrity of the country. At the moment, this trend is represented in the parliament by the BDP (*Barış ve Demokrasi Partisi*, Peace and Democracy Party). To meet the maximalist demands of the PKK and of the Kurdish nationalist parties with hardly hidden sympathy for that organization is impossible within the present constitutional structure of Turkey, and it is most unlikely that they will be met in the foreseeable future. The question is whether more modest constitutional reforms such as more extensive cultural rights and greater administrative decentralization will satisfy a majority of Kurdish speakers and thus politically isolate the more extremist elements. The AKP started in the summer of 2009 a 'Kurdish' or 'democratic opening' with the aim of finding a peaceful solution to the problem, but this initiative was faced with the staunch opposition of the CHP and the MHP. Both parties argue that even modest concession to Kurdish demands will destroy the national and territorial integrity of the state.

The third obstacle to democratic consolidation is the continuing influence of the military over civilian politics. The constitutional amendments of 2001 and the following reforms have eliminated some of their constitutional privileges. These reforms do not reflect, however, a parallel decrease in the *de facto* political weight of the military. The significant role of the military in Turkish politics is due partly to historico-political factors, and partly to the two challenges discussed above. As regards the former, the military played a very significant role in the founding of the Republic and have since then been the staunchest defenders of the Kemalist legacy, most importantly his principles of a unitary, secular, nation-state. This historical role gave the military a strong sense of mission of protecting the Kemalist principles and the national interest against, if necessary, 'unprincipled, corrupt, power-hungry, and particularistic politicians'. This sense of mission led the military to three interventions (1960, 1971, and 1980; four, if we count the 28 February 1997 process as a military intervention) in the last 50 years, and on each of those occasions they obtained new constitutional privileges and immunities and increased their political influence. With regard to the latter factor, it can be argued that the military's continuing political influence is closely related to the two challenges mentioned above. Clearly, the demands both of political Islamists and of Kurdish nationalists run counter to their cherished values such as a unitary, secular, nation-state, hence, their desire to preserve their tutelary role with as little civilian control as possible. To make things even more complicated, certain civilian actors (the CHP, the higher judiciary, and part of the mainstream media) seem to be favourable to the continuation of this tutelary role.

Under these circumstances, it seems difficult to arrive at a broad-based constitutional consensus in the short and medium term. There is a wide gap between the constitutional positions of the AKP and its liberal allies on the one hand, and those of the CHP and its allies among the state elites, namely the armed forces and the higher judiciary, on the other. While the former intends to remove these tutelary vestiges, the latter favors to preserve them for fear that the AKP will establish a majoritarian version of democracy that will pave the way for an authoritarian Islamic regime. Thus, Turkey seems to be as far away as ever from constitutional consensus and consolidation. The only way out of the present impasse seems to be a clear and strong mandate from the people for a new and truly democratic constitution.

Notes

1 On the waves of democracy, Huntington, S. P. (1991) *The Third Wave: Democratization in the Late Twentieth Century*, Norman and London: University of Oklahoma Press, esp. Chapters 1 and 2.

2 On the '28 February process', Özbudun, E. (2000) *Contemporary Turkish Politics: Challenges to Democratic Consolidation*, Boulder and London: Lynne Rienner Publishers, pp. 120–21.

310   *Ergun Özbudun*

3 For details, see Özbudun, E. and Gençkaya, Ö. F. (2009) *Democratization and the Politics of Constitution-Making in Turkey,* Budapest and New York: Central European University Press, pp. 19–20.
4 For details, see Özbudun, E. and Yazıcı, S. (2004) *Democratization Reforms in Turkey, 1993–2004,* Istanbul: TESEV
5 Venice Commission (2009) *Opinion on the Constitutional and Legal Provisions Relevant to the Prohibition of Political Parties in Turkey,* Venice, 13–14 March, CDL-AD (2009)006, paras 30, 107.
6 For details, Özbudun and Gençkaya (2009): chapters., 2 and 3.
7 For 'elite settlements' and 'elite convergences', see Burton, M., Gunther, R. and Higley, J. (1992) 'Elites and Democratic Consolidation in Latin America and Southern Europe: An Overview', in Highley, J. and Gunther, R. (eds) *Elites and Democratic Consolidation in Latin America and Southern Europe,* Cambridge, Cambridge University Press, pp. 323–24, 339.
8 Here, I draw partly from Özbudun and Gençkaya (2009): ch. 6; also, Özbudun, E. (2009) *Türkiye'nin Anayasa Krizi,* Ankara: Liberte Yayınları
9 Constitutional Court's decision (2007a) E. 2007/45. K. 2007/54, 1 May, *Resmi Gazete* (Official Gazette), 27 June, No. 26565.
10 Sezer's statement, 25 May 2007, 3/1281, *TBMM Tutanak Dergisi* (Minutes of the TBMM), Period 22, Legislative Year 5, Vol. 159, Session 113, 26 May 2007.
11 Constitutional Court decision (2007b), E. 2007/72, K. 2007/68, 5 July, *Resmî Gazete,* 7 August, no. 26606.
12 Constitutional Court decision (2008a) E. 2008/16, K. 2008/116, 5 June 2008, *Resmî Gazete,* 22 October, no. 27032.
13 Constitutional Court decision (2008b), E. 2008/1, K. 2008/2, 30 July 2008, *Resmî Gazete,* 24 October, no. 27034.
14 Mardin, Ş. (1972) 'Center-Periphery Relations: A Key to Turkish Politics?', *Deadalus* Winter, pp. 169–90. Mardin was the first scholar who applied this dichotomy to Turkish politics. See also, Özbudun, E. (1976) *Social Change and Political Participation in Turkey,* Princeton: Princeton University Press, 1976, ch. 2; Heper, M. (1980) 'Center and Periphery in the Ottoman Empire with Special Reference to the Nineteenth Century', *International Political Science Review* Vol.1 No. 1, pp. 81–105.
15 For a fuller discussion, see Özbudun, E. (1996) 'The Ottoman Legacy and the Middle East State Tradition', in L. Carl Brown, ed., *Imperial Legacy: The Ottoman Imprint on the Balkans and the Middle East,* New York: Columbia University Press, pp. 133–57.

References

AKP (2007) *Nice Ak Yıllara: Güven ve İstikrar İçinde Durmak Yok, Yola Devam* [To Many Bright Years: Non-stop Ahead in Confidence and Stability], Ankara: AK Parti.
Burton, M., Gunther, R. and Higley, J. (1992) 'Elites and Democratic Consolidation in Latin America and Southern Europe: An Overview', in Highley, J. and Gunther, R. (eds) *Elites and Democratic Consolidation in Latin America and Southern Europe,* Cambridge, Cambridge University Press.
Çarkoğlu, A. and Toprak, B. (2000) *Türkiye'de Din, Toplum ve Siyaset,* Istanbul: TESEV.
—— (2006) *Değişen Türkiye'de Din, Toplum ve Siyaset,* Istanbul: TESEV.
Çınar, M. (2008) 'The Justice and Development Party and the Kemalist Establishment', in Ümit Cizre, ed., *Secular and Islamic Politics in Turkey,* London and New York: Routledge.

Constitutional Court decision (2007b), E. 2007/72, K. 2007/68, 5 July, *Resmî Gazete*, 7 August.
—— (2008a) E. 2008/16, K. 2008/116, 5 June 2008, *Resmî Gazete*, 22 October, no. 27032.
—— (2008b), E. 2008/1, K. 2008/2, 30 July 2008, *Resmî Gazete*, 24 October, no. 27034.
Constitutional Court's decision (2007a) E. 2007/45. K. 2007/54, 1 May, *Resmi Gazete* (Official Gazette), 27 June.
Heper, M. (1980) 'Center and Periphery in the Ottoman Empire with Special Reference to the Nineteenth Century', *International Political Science Review* Vol.1 No. 1.
Huntington, S. P. (1991) *The Third Wave: Democratization in the Late Twentieth Century*, Norman and London: University of Oklahoma Press.
Kalaycıoğlu, E. (1994) 'Elections and Party Preferences in Turkey: Changes and Continuities in the 1990s', *Comparative Political Studies* Vol. 27, October.
Linz, J. J. and Alfred Stepan, A. (1996) *Problems of Democratic Transition and Consolidation: Southern Europe, South America, and Post-Communist Europe*, Baltimore and London: The Johns Hopkins University Press.
Mardin, Ş. (1972) 'Center-Periphery Relations: A Key to Turkish Politics?', *Deadalus* Winter.
O'Donnell, G. (1992) 'Transitions, Continuities, and Paradoxes', in Mainwaring, S., O'Donnell, G. and Valenzuela, J. S. (eds), *Issues in Democratic Consolidation: The New South American Democracies in Comparative Perspective*, Notre Dame IN: University of Notre Dame Press.
Özbudun, E. (1976) *Social Change and Political Participation in Turkey*, Princeton: Princeton University Press.
—— (1996) 'The Ottoman Legacy and the Middle East State Tradition', in L. Carl Brown, ed., *Imperial Legacy: The Ottoman Imprint on the Balkans and the Middle East*, New York: Columbia University Press.
—— (2000) *Contemporary Turkish Politics: Challenges to Democratic Consolidation*, Boulder and London: Lynne Rienner Publishers.
—— (2009) *Türkiye'nin Anayasa Krizi*, Ankara: Liberte Yayınları.
Özbudun, E. and Gençkaya, Ö. F. (2009) *Democratization and the Politics of Constitution-Making in Turkey*, Budapest and New York: Central European University Press.
Özbudun, E. and Yazıcı, S. (2004) *Democratization Reforms in Turkey, 1993–2004*, Istanbul: TESEV.
Puddington, A.(2009) *Freedom in the World 2009: Setbacks and Resilience*, Freedom House, July.
Venice Commission (2009) *Opinion on the Constitutional and Legal Provisions Relevant to the Prohibition of Political Parties in Turkey*, Venice, 13–14 March, CDL-AD (2009)006.

16 Human rights in Turkey

Senem Aydın-Düzgit

Introduction

Although Turkey has been exposed to human rights language and claims for decades through its founding membership of the UN and its signing of the Universal Declaration of Human Rights as well as the European Convention of Human Rights, its human rights record has often been severely criticized on the grounds that these rights have not been fully enjoyed by its citizenry. Turkey's human rights record was particularly poor in the 1990s, mostly owing to measures taken to combat the PKK (*Partiya Karkerên Kurdistan*, Kurdistan Worker's Party)–the terrorist-guerrilla organization that launched a violent secessionist campaign in the South-East. Among such measures, the state of emergency which extended to cover 10 cities where the military and governors enjoyed immense powers, the establishment of the 'village guards system' and the Anti-Terror Law which contained severe restrictions on human rights and liberties were the most significant, paving the way for very serious human rights violations.

In the period following 1999 when the PKK was militarily defeated and the European Union (EU) accession perspective came into being, important steps have been taken to strengthen human rights and fundamental freedoms in Turkey. This article focuses on the state of human rights in Turkey in the period following the introduction of EU conditionality at the Helsinki Summit of December 1999, when Turkey was declared as an official candidate destined to join the EU. This chapter will first provide a brief account of the EU-induced reform process that accelerated in the 1999–2005 period. It will then shed light on the impact of the Union on various dimensions of human rights reform in Turkey, including the fight against torture, freedom of expression and of association, and the rights of minorities. The current state of affairs in these areas will be identified, followed by a discussion on the prospects of human rights reform in Turkey against the framework of the given structural constraints in the country, the current stalemate with the EU and the challenges posed by the low degree of socialization in the field of human rights, mainly through the medium of education policy.

EU conditionality and human rights reforms in Turkey

Since late 2001 in particular, fundamental reforms in the area of basic human, civil and political rights have been undertaken in Turkey. After the Helsinki Summit of 1999, the European Commission published the first Accession Partnership document in March 2000, which was followed by the preparation of the Turkish 'National Program for the Adoption of the *Acquis*' by the Turkish authorities in March 2001. These first signs of EU membership conditionality provided the initial trigger for change. Immediately following the approval of the National Program, political reform was initiated with 34 constitutional amendments in October 2001, a new Civil Code in January 2002 and three 'harmonization packages' adopted in the follow-up to the Copenhagen Summit of 2002. The legislative changes introduced significant reforms, most particularly in the fields of human rights and the protection of minorities, freedom of expression and freedom of association.

These reforms were the first crucial responses to EU conditionality and culminated in the Copenhagen Summit of 2002, at which the EU decided to open negotiations with Turkey as and when it fulfilled the Copenhagen political criteria. The summit decision reinforced the EU's commitments by providing Turkey with the prospect that full EU membership is indeed a real possibility (Keyman & Öniş 2004). Meanwhile, the EU also decided to increase significantly the amount of financial assistance to Turkey (European Commission 2003). Hence, the EU impact was not confined to pure conditionality, but extended to cover financial and technical aid. Pre-accession financial assistance would reach €250 million in 2004, €300 million in 2005 and €500 million in 2006 to help Turkey prepare to join the EU as quickly as possible (European Commission 2003). Given the size of the Turkish economy, which was about 300 billion Euros at the end of 2005, such assistance might mean little. Despite its relative modesty in financial terms, however, the new pre-accession aid was important in signalling the shift in Turkey's status and EU commitment, raising the credibility of EU conditionality. Similarly, administrative and judicial capacity-building mechanisms, primarily through the Twinning instrument, were now made available to Turkey. The strengthening of the credibility of conditionality was reflected in the adoption of four subsequent harmonization packages and two sets of constitutional amendments, leading up to the decision to open accession negotiations at the Brussels Summit of 2004.

Important legislative reforms followed in 2005, such as the new Penal Code and the Code of Criminal Procedure among others (European Commission 2005). With respect to training in basic rights and freedoms, the Turkish authorities have pursued a number of programs targeting relevant personnel in the Ministry of Interior Affairs, Ministry of Justice, the gendarmerie and the police. These reforms have led to significant improvements, specifically in the areas of the fight against torture, freedom of expression, freedom of association, minority rights and gender equality.

It needs to be underlined that the EU was not the only actor, but a crucial facilitator, in this process of human rights reform. It is evident that the prospect of membership becoming more 'real' clearly contributed to the emergence of effective conditionality in the case of Turkey. Nevertheless, human rights reform had already been on the agenda of Turkish politics and society, especially since the late 1980s. The Turkish Constitution that was drafted in 1982 in the aftermath of the military coup under the military regime had for some time been subject to intense domestic and international criticism for its shortcomings on human rights and liberties, which led to a number of important constitutional changes in the course of the 1990s (Özbudun 2007). In a related fashion, the European Court of Human Rights (ECtHR) also played an important role in reforming parts of Turkey's legal system, primarily in the fields of pre-trial detention, trial procedures, freedom of expression, and freedom of assembly and association (Smith 2007). The impact of ECtHR rulings even became stronger when compliance with them became a material condition for Turkey's EU membership. In the second harmonization package which passed in May 2004, Article 90 of the Turkish Constitution stated that 'should the international treaties on fundamental rights and freedoms that are duly put into effect and national laws contain contradictory stipulations on the same subject, the provisions of international law would prevail'.

Furthermore, the profound political and economic transformation initiated in the 1980s, where de-ruralization was coupled with the failed policies of the strong state and the increasingly corrupt parties of the centre, had already paved the way for an emergence of a stronger civil society and identity politics in Turkey, most notably regarding political Islam and the Kurdish identity. The EU, by helping to create a 'strong language of rights' in the country, started to play an important role in furthering the change in state–society relations and provided legitimacy for a vast amount of civil society organizations calling for a more democratic Turkey and demanding recognition of cultural and civil rights and freedoms (Keyman and İçduygu 2003).

In a similar sense, the EU has also provided increasing legitimacy for the heavy emphasis placed by the governing party, the AKP (*Adalet ve Kalkınma Partisi*, Justice and Development Party), on democracy and the protection of individual rights and freedoms, reflected in the speed of political reforms after the party came to power in November 2002. Democracy as advocated by the EU became the 'catchword and the strategy through which the former Islamists seek to change the system at the same time as they change themselves' (Bazoğlu Sezer 2002). It can be argued that the AKP, particularly in their first term in government (2002–7), relied heavily on the discourse of human rights and liberties alongside the heavy emphasis on EU membership as a strategy of systemic survival vis-à-vis the secularist state and military establishment.

Another factor that facilitated the reforms was the perceived decrease in adoption costs with respect to the concerns of the military/security establishment. Since in the Turkish context, the issue of human rights is very much linked with the treatment of minorities, particularly the Kurds, the end of the armed conflict proved to be crucial in the creation of a window of opportunity for the reform process. The political costs of compliance were reduced by the decline in PKK violence in the late 1990s, weakening the previous opposition of the military/security establishment and strengthening the view that national unity can be preserved through further democratization, rather than via military means.

Despite the progress that has been made, it has been widely argued that reform zeal has waned in the post-2005 period (Aydın-Düzgit and Keyman 2012), leading to the persistence of problems in the legislative framework regarding the human rights regime in Turkey as well as the implementation of the new legal mechanisms and measures in this field. This may be observed in the number of applications (allocated to a decision-making body) to the ECtHR which have increased progressively since 2005, reaching a record high 8,702 applications in 2011, more than double the average annual number of applications filed in 2005–10 (European Court of Human Rights 2005–11).

Current state of the reform process

Fight against torture and ill-treatment

The Government has committed itself to a policy of 'zero tolerance' for torture and ill-treatment. Accordingly, legislation in this area has been considerably strengthened particularly through the fourth, sixth and seventh harmonization packages. All detained persons now have a formal right of access to a lawyer from the outset of their custody; prosecutors no longer need to seek authorization from an administrative authority to instigate proceedings under Articles 243 (torture) and 245 (ill-treatment) of the Criminal Code; procedural amendments have been adopted to ensure the speedy investigation and prosecution of offences under Articles 243 and 245, and sentences imposed under those Articles can no longer be converted into fines or be suspended. One of the most crucial developments has been the reduction in custody periods to 24 hours (extendable to a maximum of four days, upon the written order of the public prosecutor, in the case of collective offences). Considering the close relationship between the length of pre-trial detention periods and incidences of torture and mistreatment, this amendment deserves special attention for its contribution to the fight against torture and ill-treatment.

Reports of torture incidents have consequently decreased in Turkey since 2002 and the downward trend in both the incidence and severity of torture and ill-treatment cases appears to be continuing (Council of Europe 2011a). This is partly due to the advanced set of provisions in this area introduced via strict EU conditionality. The EU has been dynamic in strengthening institutional capacity on this front by being actively engaged in the training of medicine forensic experts and judges/public prosecutors through TAIEX (Technical Assistance and Information Exchange) seminars and large-scale Twinning projects, in combination with the extensive training programmes of the Ministry of Health in this area. Hence growth of knowledge resources and a certain degree of value diffusion have been facilitated by the EU in this regard. Similarly, this issue is one where adoption costs were not high for the governing party in question and thus did not necessitate a shift of cost–benefit balance to begin with.

Despite considerable progress, the fight against torture and ill-treatment is not over. First of all, some of the current legal measures introduced by the 2006 amendments to the Anti-Terror Law have the propensity to create an environment more conducive for torture and ill-treatment. The article that raises the risk the most is Section 10 (e) of the Anti-Terror Law, which stipulates that upon the order of a public prosecutor, a detainee may be denied access to a lawyer during the initial 24 hours of custody if suspected of committing a terrorism-related offence. There are also remaining legislative obstacles untouched by the 1999–2005 reforms. For instance, forensic medical doctors, with the exception of those that operate under the Forensic Medicine Council, and thus the Ministry of Justice, are still not recognized by the courts, leading to a lack of independent forensic services and allegations of partiality in the deliverance of medical reports.

Importantly, more than these new and remaining legislative provisions, it is the 'culture of impunity' which allows the police and the gendarmerie to escape accountability for torture, that continues to represent the main hindrance to further progress in this area. For instance, a report by the Human Rights Investigation Commission Report found that, between 2003 and 2008, only 2 per cent of the 2,140 personnel who were investigated on accusations of torture and ill-treatment were given disciplinary sentences (US Department of State 2009). In some cases, it is the lack of a normative shift among the public officials and the political elite towards the unacceptability of torture, even in cases where the interests of the 'state' are perceived to be at stake, which provides the main hindrance to the eradication of torture, such as in the case of the law enforcement officers being present during medical examinations despite the legal reforms that forbid this, or the hasty and superficial examinations and reports of medical doctors who are not willing to deliver detailed evaluations (Council of Europe 2011a). In most cases, however, this problem of normative internalization is combined with legal loopholes to provide full effect to impunity for perpetrators of torture and ill-treatment despite the undertaken reforms. For instance, in some cases the public prosecutors choose to bring charges of torture and ill-treatment under those articles of the Turkish Penal Code (such as Article 256, 'excessive use of force' or Article 86, 'intentional injury' rather than Article 94, 'torture' or Article 95, 'aggravated torture due to circumstances') where relatively lighter sentences can be delivered and/or where there is an obligation to obtain prior administrative authorization for investigation. This is despite the fact that the sentences for torture cases have been increased and the requirement for prior administrative authorization for torture and ill-treatment cases has been lifted through legislative reforms (Council of Europe 2012: para. 46).

Freedom of expression

A number of existing restrictions were lifted in the 1999–2005 reforms. Amendments in particular to Article 312 of the Penal Code (inciting people to enmity and hatred by pointing to class, racial, religious, confessional or regional differences), Article 159 of the Penal Code (insulting the state and state institutions and threats to the indivisible unity of the Turkish Republic), Article 169 of the Penal Code (aiding and abetting an illegal organization), Article 7 of the Anti-Terror Law (propaganda encouraging the use of terrorist methods) and the abolition of Article 8 of the Anti-Terror Law (propaganda against the indivisible unity of the state) constituted important progress in meeting the ECtHR standards on freedom of expression. The EU-led reform process not only resulted in legislative changes, but was also translated into practice, resulting in a substantial decline in the number of individuals arrested for expressing their opinions (Alpay 2010). According to Human Rights Watch (2006), as of November 2005 there were no individuals serving prison sentences for the non-violent expression of their opinions.

However by June 2012, 95 journalists alone were reported to be imprisoned, 62 of whom were detained in relation to their reporting on the Kurdish issue. This increase has been progressive, from 15 imprisoned journalists in June 2009 to 57, 68 and 95 respectively in the three years that followed.[1] Freedom of expression is thus an area in which the progress that was made with the 1999–2005 reforms has been substantially reversed, to the extent that the curtailment of this freedom has now become one of the major sources of domestic and international criticism of the current state of Turkish democracy.

The current stalemate in this area stems from the combination of a multitude of legal provisions and the mind-set of the judiciary, that serve to restrict the freedom of expression against the background of key political developments in the country. As for the legislative provisions, the Constitution itself (in particular Articles 26 and 28) serves to provide the main hindrance with the limits that it imposes on the freedom of expression on the bases of national security, public order and national unity that in effect place the interests of the state above those of the individual and the society. Although a new Penal Code was passed as a part of the EU reform process in 2005, it retained key provisions of the old Penal Code that served to restrict the freedom of expression in the past such as Article 215 (praising a crime or criminal), Article 216 (inciting the population to enmity or hatred and denigration), Article 301 (insulting the Turkish nation, the Turkish Republic, the TBMM (*Türkiye Büyük Millet Meclisi*, Turkish Grand National Assembly), the government or the judicial organs of the state) and Article 318 (discouraging persons from doing their military service). While the retention of these articles and their widespread usage in limiting the freedom of expression testifies to the effects of incomplete legal reform, the case of the Anti-Terror Law demonstrates a reversal in the sense that the amendments made to this law in 2006 introduced new limits to fundamental rights and freedoms including the freedom of speech (Aytar 2006). For instance, with the 2006 amendments, the punishment for crimes under Article 6 (printing or publishing of declarations or leaflets emanating from terrorist organizations) was changed from a fine to imprisonment from one to three years.

These legal provisions became prominent instruments in curbing the freedom of expression, particularly against the background of KCK (*Koma Ciwaken Kurdistan*, Kurdistan Communities Union) operations initiated in April 2009 and the *Ergenekon* case launched in 2008. While the former case saw the prosecution of prominent political leaders and activists of the Kurdish movement on the grounds that they constitute the urban wing of the PKK, the latter led to a mounting pressure on the journalists covering the case, which involved alleged plans to stage a violent uprising against the government. Violations of free speech through these cases implied that the existing legislative provisions and the new legal measures are being utilized in curbing freedom of expression primarily in cases where the government's authority is severely under attack and/or its increasingly securitized Kurdish rights policy is being challenged.

In addition to legal provisions, the mind-set of the Turkish judiciary has also played a key role in stagnating and reversing reform on this front. For instance, in contrast to ECtHR case law, the Turkish judiciary is commonly found to apply a very wide interpretation of 'incitement to violence' and to disregard the 'defence of truth' ('assessing whether the content of journalistic reporting is true') and 'defence of public interest' ('assessing whether the public has a legitimate interest in and a right to obtain the information in question') in delivering its judgements on cases relating to the freedom of expression (Council of Europe 2011b: 10). Most violations, by Turkey, of Article 10 of the European Convention of Human Rights (ECHR) are in fact found to emanate from a lack of proportionality in the interpretation and implementation of these legal provisions by the judges and the public prosecutors.

Freedom of association and the protection of minorities

With respect to freedom of association, the New Law on Associations that entered into force in November 2004 constituted a major step in expanding the freedoms accorded to civil society organizations by reducing the possibility for state interference, and thus helped resolve many of the state restrictions that hampered civil society activity until recently. The more problematic aspect of the right of association however is very much linked to the debate on the protection of minorities (in particular the non-Muslim communities) in Turkey.

The legal status of minorities in Turkey was established by the 1923 Treaty of Lausanne, which defined minorities on the basis of religion. The Treaty of Lausanne grants non-Muslim minorities (applied in practice to Jews – approx. 23,000; Greeks – approx. 1,700; and Armenians – approx. 65,000) substantial negative rights as well as positive ones, with obligations on the Turkish Government to undertake measures for the enjoyment of those rights. Most significantly, the Treaty gives non-Muslim minorities the right to equal protection and non-discrimination, the right to establish private schools and provide education in their own language, the conditional entitlement to government funding to receive instruction in their own language at the primary level in public schools, the right to settle family law or private issues in accordance with their own customs, and the right to exercise their religion freely. There have been two sets of problems with the practical implementation of these rights. First was the selective application of these rights to the three non-Muslim communities, hence excluding other non-Muslim minorities such as the Assyrians (approx. 15,000). The second problem related to shortcomings in the implementation of these rights, especially regarding property issues and religious/educational institutions.

Little has been done to address the problems of non-Muslim minorities regarding their educational and religious institutions that are both regulated by the Directorate General of Foundations, a government agency that must approve their operations, despite the fact that this direct state interference violates the Treaty of Lausanne. In a similar vein, restrictions on the training of clergy remain. Resistance to reforms on these fronts is very much related to the perception of non-Muslim minorities as 'foreign' threats to national security that need to be controlled. The reform process initiated with the prospect of EU accession has aimed to resolve some of the issues related to property rights, thus largely excluding these issues.

Regarding property-related matters, the main problems suffered by religious minorities in Turkey have been lack of legal personality and the impossibility of acquiring and selling property. Under Turkish Law, religious institutions do not have legal personality and they can only be incorporated as 'foundations', falling under the jurisdiction of the Law of Foundations. Thus, their property rights were significantly limited since under Turkish Law, only properties declared under Law No.2762 of 1936 were legally recognized (160 minority foundations), and all properties not listed in 1936 could be confiscated by the Turkish state.

Despite the fact that the reform packages (specifically the third, fourth and sixth) have addressed the problem by allowing non-Muslim minorities to register the property they actually use as long as they can prove ownership, the regulation that was issued following the amendment required foundations to follow incredibly lengthy and cumbersome bureaucratic procedures as well as creating the mechanisms for further bureaucratic intervention in the process. Moreover, it failed to bring a just solution regarding the return of their already confiscated properties by the state. Thus, implementation on this front had been very slow, until the entry into force of the new Law on Foundations in February 2008, which not only improved the legal framework in freedom of association, attaining a broad alignment with the ECHR, but also addressed a number of property issues regarding non-Muslim foundations, mainly over management and acquisition of property. The Law was further revised with the amendments introduced in August 2011, which widened the scope of the new Law by providing for the return of the properties that were registered in 1936 but not specifically described in the original documentation, and permitted the foundations to receive financial compensation in cases where their property was sold to a third party and could not be returned. Nonetheless, the return of the property of merged foundations still remains outside the confines of the law and the Turkish government retains the right to seize land from religious communities (US Commission on International Religious Freedom 2012: 203).

The progress in reform was also mixed for the most numerous Muslim minority in Turkey, namely the Kurdish minority. The eventual capture of the PKK leader, the emergence of EU conditionality and the growing attraction of Northern Iraq for Turkey's Kurds contributed, in Turkey, to the increasing perception of the Kurdish problem as a minority issue with socio-economic and identity-related dimensions to it, rather than just a military matter. This led to gradual shifts in the official views on this front, leading to certain reforms that directly intended to improve the lives of the Kurdish minority. The most notable of these reforms concerned the right to broadcast in Kurdish, the right to learn the Kurdish dialects in private institutions and the right to name children in Kurdish.

Human rights reforms in general have also had a significant impact on the lives of the Kurds in the country, as the major restrictive measures that have been repealed in the reform process had mostly been used in the past for those who spoke for a distinct Kurdish identity. Similarly, the lifting of the death penalty also had a positive impact as almost all the prisoners on Turkey's death row were convicted for crimes related to terrorism and separatism. The lifting of Article 8 of the Anti-Terror Law thus expanding freedom of speech and the gradual lifting of the state of emergency from all ten provinces by November 2002 were also noteworthy developments. The lifting of the state of emergency deserves special attention here as it not only paved the way for the extension of rule of law in the conflict-ridden regions but also had a positive psychological impact in the region despite the increased tension caused by the events related to the Iraq war and the concerns over the possible resurgence of terrorist activity.

This virtuous cycle of reform was soon to be replaced by a vicious cycle of violence and the rise of Turkish and Kurdish nationalism, which stalled any substantial progress on this front. Against the background of weakening of EU conditionality (see below), the renewal of PKK attacks on civilian and military targets in 2005 and the ensuing operations contributed to the rise of Turkish nationalism that was already underway as a response to the EU-led reform process in the country. No further reforms were undertaken until January 2009, when the state-owned Turkish Radio and Television (TRT) established a new channel to broadcast exclusively in Kurdish. The government's Kurdish opening in July 2009 did not produce any concrete results and the situation started to closely resemble the state of affairs in the 1990s, when the Kurdish issue marked by intense violence was dealt with solely as a security matter and used to restrict fundamental freedoms. The limited reform that had been achieved was overcome by the reversals in human rights reforms outlined in the previous sections, such as in the case of the 2006 amendments to the Anti-Terror Law which imposed further restrictions on the fundamental freedoms of those who speak for expanded Kurdish rights. The State Security Courts entrusted to deal with crimes against the state, which were abolished in 2004, were now replaced by '"heavy penal courts with special powers" ... bearing continuity in mandate, rules of procedure, judges, personnel, archives and case files' (Kurban and Gülalp forthcoming).[2] Although the state of emergency was lifted in 2002, the Government has repeatedly authorized the military to declare 'temporary security zones' in which the military can freely conduct its operations (Kurban and Gülalp forthcoming).

This brief analysis of the current state of human rights reform in Turkey suggests that despite considerable progress, Turkey still has a long way to go to reach a human rights regime that is broadly aligned with the ECtHR. The reasons behind the stagnation in human-rights-related reform and its future prospects should be sought in a variety of interrelated factors that can be grouped under three main headings: normative appeal and socialization, structural constraints and weakening of the EU as an external anchor.

Human rights in context

Normative appeal and socialization

It can be argued that the normative appeal of human rights in Turkey is in fact weak at the level of political parties, civil society institutions and the society at large. In the case of the AKP, it was often argued that the reform process with crucial implications on the basic rights of the population would be continued regardless of the prospect of EU accession. Prime Minister Erdoğan's repeated statement that in the case of a rebuff from the Union, they would continue the reform process by naming the Copenhagen criteria as the 'Ankara criteria' was probably the most commonly cited evidence in that respect (Emerson et al. 2005: 189). Despite these claims, with the exception of progress in some issues such as the Law on Foundations and the launching of a state channel that broadcasts solely in Kurdish, little was done in human rights reform in the second half of the AKP's first term in office as well as during the party's second and third terms in government. Thus the waning of reform zeal has clouded the assumption that human rights reform in Turkey rests on the normative commitments of the government elite, as they themselves have claimed in the past. It is now widely argued that especially after its second electoral victory in 2007, the AKP became much stronger both in society and against the secularist establishment, and thus became less dependent on the EU and its democratization agenda (Öniş 2010: 369).

Furthermore, it can also be observed that the previous institutional measures which the party elite has heavily criticized in the past for being undemocratic and in violation of fundamental liberties, are now utilized by the AKP itself to strengthen its authority over the political system and the masses. For example, one of the public institutions much criticized in the past by the AKP was the office of the Presidency, which was attacked for utilizing its undemocratic powers granted by the 1982 constitution in exercising its control over universities by appointing rectors who were not democratically elected, but who were closer to the ideology of the state establishment. The main legitimating discourse of the party in such criticisms relied heavily on democracy and human rights. In its second term in Government, however, instead of making any attempt to reform the undemocratic powers of the presidency, the party condoned the new president from the AKP cadres, Gül, continuing to make full use of his powers of favouring rectors known to be closer to the party ranks or its ideology, regardless of the elections in universities (Ergin 2012). Thus, instead of reforming the key undemocratic measures of the 1982 constitution that are in violation of fundamental rights, the party in some cases makes full use of them to strengthen its own hold on power.

There is a mixed picture when one observes where the civil society stands with respect to commitment to human rights. It is largely accepted that civil society activity in Turkey has increased considerably from the late 1980s onwards. However, analyses reveal that such increase has not necessarily led to an increased internalization of democratic norms by the civil society actors. In fact, studies demonstrate that these actors overwhelmingly 'instrumentalize' democracy and human rights for their own rational ends with low degrees of normative commitment (Keyman 2008). A similar case exists with respect to the state of human rights NGOs in Turkey. It can be argued that particularly since the mid-1980s human rights NGOs in Turkey have played an important role in strengthening a 'domestically grown human rights perspective' in Turkish politics, by 'framing issues as human rights issues' in the domestic political context (Çalı 2007: 217). Nevertheless, human rights activism in Turkey has long upheld a sectarian understanding where the rights that were defended focused on specific groups (on the basis of ethnicity, religion, ideology) in different NGOs (Hale 2010). While human rights activism in Turkey is slowly moving from 'the advocacy of particular group's rights towards a more encompassing deliberation of human rights theory and praxis' (Çalı 2007: 232), this development seems to be limited and is evolving only very slowly.

This is no surprise, given the normative appeal of democracy and human rights among the masses in general. A prominent study suggests that a majority of the Turkish population does not uphold democracy as a 'normative value', but instead has a 'sectarian' approach to democracy, meaning that the rights of those who are perceived as one of 'us' are upheld while the rights of those denoted as 'others' are disregarded. For example, while 43 per cent of the respondents in the study are in favour of the abolition of the headscarf ban in universities, only 11.4 per cent of the public seem to support the right to education in Kurdish (Çarkoğlu and Toprak 2006: 27–28). In the words of the authors of the study, while 'issues of importance to citizens of Sunni Muslim faith and ethnic Turkish background, such as Imam Hatip High Schools or the turban ban in universities, are evaluated as part of basic human rights ... when asked about issues of relevance to Alevis, non-Muslim Turkish citizens or citizens of Kurdish origin, the same sensitivity to their basic rights is not expressed' (Çarkoğlu and Toprak 2006: 12). In a similar vein, in another study, it was found that around 62 per cent of the respondents argued that 'minority views should not be tolerated', and a similar majority supported the view that freedom of speech should be restricted for certain groups (Çarkoğlu and Kalaycıoğlu 2009: 51). Both political and social intolerance thus seem to be high among the masses.

Part of the explanation behind this intolerance at the mass level as well as the reluctance to reform at the elite level, particularly regarding minority rights which infiltrate into almost every sub-area of the human rights reform process in the Turkish context, lies in what is now commonly called the 'Sèvres Syndrome', named after the Sèvres Treaty that partitioned the Ottoman Empire among the European powers after its defeat in the First World War. The 'Sèvres Syndrome' in general refers to the fear of separatism and partition of the country among different ethnic groups, and underlines arguments within an isolationist and nationalist framework, hindering the reform process. It is particularly significant in fortifying a monolithic understanding of the nation, with little scope for diversity, which hinders in particular the implementation of reforms as well as the continuation of the reform process.

It can be argued that socialization into democratic norms via education would be the key to the comprehensive reform of the human rights situation in the country. Nevertheless, studies suggest that this is far from being the case. Çayır, for example, in his study on the state of human rights education in high schools in Turkey, finds that human rights education in Turkey rests on an 'elitist/nationalist political culture', 'prioritiz(ing) duties over rights', where the 'pedagogical approaches employed in formal education and training seminars remain at cognitive level rather than being transformative'

(Çayır 2007: 234). Thus, collective security and national duties are privileged over individual liberties and rights in the school texts, placing further question marks on the normative bases of the future state of human rights in Turkey.

Structural constraints

There are currently certain structural constraints that limit progress in human-rights-related reform. One of the main drivers of human rights reform in the Turkish case was the military defeat of the PKK in the late 1990s. The ceasing of terrorist activity significantly aided in lowering the adoption costs of the reforms undertaken in the field of human rights and the protection of minorities. Largely thanks to political instability in Iraq, the PKK renewed its terrorist activities in 2005, intensifying in 2007 and pushing the Government into taking military action against the PKK bases in Northern Iraq in February 2008. Violence continued up until the 2011 general elections and has been compounded since then with developments in Turkey's southern neighbourhood, where the PKK has recently found refuge in the political vacuum opened by the Syrian civil war. The renewal and rise of PKK terrorism enhances the nationalist fervour among the public and political parties, hindering substantial reform particularly in the field of minority rights. The 'peace process' initiated in 2013 may provide an important window of opportunity on that front, the ramifications of which remain to be seen.

The state of Turkish foreign policy also needs to be mentioned in assessing current and future prospects of human rights reform in the country. As the Turkish policy makers often emphasize, Turkey's growing links with the Middle East can be considered an asset for the EU in terms of having a future member 'acting as a European country' that resorts to soft power, diplomacy and multilateralism in the 'non-European Middle East' (Oğuzlu 2008). There are, however, two problems that can follow from this. One is that this perceived quality may in time make European powers less attentive to the state of the reform process in Turkey. A second possibility is that with a further severing of relations with the EU, the close relations developing with the Middle East may in time be considered as alternative, rather than complementary, foreign policy options to relations with the EU, which could further diminish the prospects of human rights reform in the country.

Probably the most important of all, the increasing degree of political and societal polarization along the axis of the Islamist–secularist divide as well as that of Turkish–Kurdish nationalism, is inhibiting the process of reform in Turkey (Çarkoğlu and Kalaycıoğlu 2009). This polarization is acutely visible at both the public and the elite level. For instance both the 2007 and 2011 elections as well as the Constitutional Referendum in 2010 were fought in highly polarized (and personalized) political contexts (Aydın-Düzgit 2012, Çarkoğlu 2007, Kalaycıoğlu 2011). At the societal level, public views on key issues of democratic consolidation are now largely divided along and determined by partisan lines. For instance, on a 1-to-10 scale that measures satisfaction with the functioning of democracy in Turkey, those who had voted for the AKP were found to score on average 6.6 whereas the degree of satisfaction with democracy among those who had voted for the main opposition party, the Republican People's Party (CHP), was found to be on average 2.9 (Kemahlıoğlu and Keyman 2011: 14). The same study found that among those who stated that freedom of expression exists for writers and journalists, 55.6 per cent had voted for the AKP while only 19.6 per cent were reported to be CHP voters (Kemahlıoğlu and Keyman 2011: 15).

Europe as an external anchor?

There is no doubt that the EU played a crucial role in the triggering of the democratic reform process between 1999 and 2005. It can be argued that one of the main ways it did this was the application of a relatively credible policy of conditionality: by making EU accession a more realistic prospect mainly through granting candidacy status to the country and taking the decision to open accession negotiations. Turkish accession has always been a subject of controversial debate in the EU. The intensity of the debate, however, grew as the accession perspective of Turkey became more 'real' (especially with the opening of accession negotiations) and as the internal discussions regarding the future of the European order were put in the spotlight with the referenda over the Constitutional Treaty. The debate particularly focused on Turkey's unchangeable features: its size, population, culture and unpopularity with the EU citizens, conveying the message that, unlike the Eastern enlargement, complying with the formal criteria alone might not be sufficient for Turkey's full accession to the Union. The mixed signals on the future of Turkish accession turned more for the negative when prominent EU leaders like Nicolas Sarkozy and Angela Merkel expressed their reluctance to have Turkey as a full member. In fact, upon Sarkozy's coming to power in 2007, the French Government blocked negotiations on five chapters of the *acquis* on the grounds that the chapters were directly linked to full membership.

Another crucial factor that has hampered conditionality in the case of Turkey is the Cyprus conflict. In December 2006, the European Council decided not to open negotiations on eight chapters of the *acquis* relevant to the issue and not to close any of the chapters provisionally until Turkey opens its seaports and airspace to Cyprus as required by Turkey's customs union agreement with the EU. This has, to a large extent, served to block progress in accession negotiations and substantially fed into the perceptions in Turkey that the country is being treated unfairly, with the EU using Cyprus as a tool to block Turkey's accession (Öniş 2010: 365).

This was clearly reflected in the surveys designed to gauge the attitudes of the Turkish public towards the EU and the accession process. These suggest that public support for Turkey's EU accession remained quite high until the second half of 2005. The data suggest that from the second half of 2004 onwards (with slight exceptions in 2006, 2009 and 2010), the Turkish public increasingly found EU membership to be not necessarily a good thing. By the first half of 2011, support levels fell to 41 per cent (European Commission 2004–11). This in turn implies that EU conditionality has been, for some time now, facing a lack of societal legitimacy in Turkey, whereby Turkish citizens are becoming increasingly estranged from the European project. The danger that this holds for human rights reform is that it reduces the incentive for the adoption of costly reforms to attain EU accession, ties the hands of domestic reformers and thus also undermines the power of the Union as an effective external anchor for democratic reform in Turkey.

On top of this general problem of the credibility of EU conditionality, there is also a more specific problem that weakens the power of the EU in human rights reform. It can be argued that the *Leyla Şahin v. Turkey* case where the ECtHR in November 2005 rejected the appeal to allow wearing of the headscarf in universities can be considered a 'turning point' for the AKP's perception of Europe in the promotion of human rights and civil liberties in Turkey. A study suggests that this case led to a serious reassessment among certain segments of the party as to how far Europe could contribute to changes in Turkish secularism through an agenda of democratization and human rights (Aydın and Çakır 2007).

Overall, it needs to be emphasized that the weakening influence of the 'Europeanization' process on democratic practice matters significantly for the fate of human rights in the Turkish context. This is not a judgement that derives solely from the transformative impact of the EU on human rights reform in Turkey in the first few years of the twenty-first century, but also rests on the observation that the EU is in fact the only external actor that has ever managed to exert any substantial influence on the democratic process in Turkey. The impact of other international actors, most notably the IMF and the World Bank, has been confined to combating corruption and increasing state accountability together with improving institutional/administrative capacity. Even then, the impact was limited, where the reforms (albeit incomplete) were in fact greatly facilitated by a fluid political and economic environment in the aftermath of the 2001 economic crisis in Turkey (Aydın-Düzgit & Çarkoğlu 2009).

Conclusions

The state of human rights in Turkey presents a mixed picture. Despite the various reforms discussed above, there are still remaining problems with the legal framework as well as the implementation of already-reformed laws in the areas of the fight against torture, freedom of expression, freedom of association and minority rights. Especially since 2005, Turkey has been experiencing a stalemate in human-rights-related reform. Part of the explanation lies in the low degree of normative commitment to human rights as a value to be upheld among the masses as well as the political elite. The problem is compounded further by structural constraints in the political realm, such as the revival of PKK terrorism, new orientations in Turkish foreign policy, and societal polarization along the axis of secularism and religiosity as well as ethnicity. Furthermore, the credibility of EU conditionality, which played the role of a key facilitator between 1999 and 2005, is severely hampered, mainly due to mixed signals from the Union regarding Turkey's ultimate goal of full accession.

Whilst these factors suggest a pessimistic outlook on the future of human-rights-related reform in Turkey, one could argue that there are also grounds for optimistic scenarios to be fostered. There is growing human rights activism in the country, which interacted with the EU in the first years of the century with enhanced legitimacy in pushing for human rights reform in Turkey. There is also a more open discursive sphere on human rights issues whereby democratic and public deliberations and discussion of 'sensitive' matters such as the Kurdish question have nevertheless become the accepted norm in Turkey. Furthermore, the legal system problematic with respect to human rights has been replaced with a partially reformed legal framework, largely thanks to the application of successful EU conditionality between 1999 and 2005. The 'peace process' which has currently halted violence may also provide an opening for reforms. The ultimate goal should be to complement a further reformed legal framework with the necessary changes of mind-set in society for a sustainable human rights regime and culture to take root in the country.

Notes

1 Figures were retrieved from the annual BIA Media Monitoring Reports, available online at www.bianet.org.tr
2 These courts were abolished with the third reform package adopted in July 2012 and replaced by Anti-Terror Courts.

References

Alpay, Ş. (2010) 'Two faces of the press in Turkey: the role of the media in Turkey's modernisation and democracy', in Kerslake, C. Öktem, K. and Robins, P. (eds) *Turkey's Engagement with Modernity. Conflict and Change in the Twentieth Century*, Basingstoke: Palgrave Macmillan.
Aydın, S. and Çakır, R. (2007) 'Political Islam in Turkey', *Insight Turkey*, 9 (1): 38–55.
Aydın-Düzgit, S. (2012) 'No crisis, no change: the third AKP victory in the June 2011 parliamentary elections in Turkey', *South European Society and Politics*, 17 (2): 329–46.
Aydın-Düzgit, S. and Çarkoğlu, A. (2009) 'Turkey: reforms for a consolidated democracy', in Leonardo Morlino and Amichai Magen (eds) *International Actors, Democratization and the Rule of Law: Anchoring Democracy?*, London: Routledge.
Aydın-Düzgit, S. and Keyman, E. F. (2012) *EU-Turkey Relations and the Stagnation of Turkish Democracy*, IPC-IAI Working Paper No.2. Online. Available HTTP: <http://www.iai.it/pdf/GTE/GTE_WP_02.pdf> (accessed 2 January 2013).

Aytar, V. (2006) *Daha Karanlık bir Geleceğe Doğru mu? Terörle Mücadele Kanununda*.

Bazoglu Sezer, D. (2002) 'The electoral victory of reformist Islamists in secular Turkey', *International Spectator*, 37 (4): 7–19.

Çalı, B. (2007) 'Human rights discourse and domestic human rights NGOs', in Arat, Z. K. (ed.) *Human Rights in Turkey*, Philadelphia: University of Pennsylvania Press.

Çarkoğlu, A. (2007) 'A new electoral victory for the "pro-Islamists" or the "new centre-right"? The Justice and Development Party phenomenon in the July 2007 parliamentary elections in Turkey', *South European Society and Politics*, 12 (4): 501–19.

Çarkoğlu, A. and Kalaycıoğlu, E. (2009) *The Rising Tide of Conservatism in Turkey*, New York: Palgrave Macmillan.

Çarkoğlu, A. and Toprak, B. (2006) *Değişen Türkiye'de Din, Toplum ve Siyaset* (Religion, Society, and Politics in a Changing Turkey), Istanbul: TESEV.

Çayır, K. (2007) 'Tensions and dilemmas in human rights education', in Z. Kabasakal Arat (ed.) *Human Rights in Turkey*, Philadelphia: University of Pennsylvania Press.

Council of Europe (2011a) *Report to the Turkish Government on the Visit to Turkey Carried out by the European Committee for the Prevention of Torture and Inhuman or Degrading Treatment or Punishment (CPT) from 4 to 17 June 2009*, Strasbourg, 31 March. Online. Available HTTP: <http://www.cpt.coe.int/documents/tur/2011-13-inf-eng.pdf> (accessed 27 September 2012).

—— (2011b) *Report by Thomas Hammarberg, Commissioner for Human Rights of the Council of Europe, Following his Visit to Turkey from 27 to 29 April 2011: Freedom of Expression and Media Freedom in Turkey*, Strasbourg, 31 March. Online. Available HTTP: <http://www.cpt.coe.int/documents/tur/2011-13-inf-eng.pdf> (accessed 27 September 2012).

—— (2012) *Report by Thomas Hammarberg, Commissioner for Human Rights of the Council of Europe, Following his Visit to Turkey from 10 to 14 October 2011* (CommDH(2012)2), Strasbourg, 10 January. Online. Available HTTP: <https://wcd.coe.int/ViewDoc.jsp?id=1892381> (accessed 27 September 2012).

Emerson, M., Aydın, S., Noutcheva, G., Tocci, N., Vahl, M. and Youngs, R. (2005) 'The reluctant debutante: the EU as promoter of democracy in its neighbourhood', in Emerson, M. (ed.) *Democratisation in the European Neighbourhood*, Brussels: Centre for European Policy Studies.

Ergin, S. (2012) 'Gül'ün rektör tercihleri çok tartışılacak' (Gül's choice of rectors will be heavily discussed'), *Milliyet* daily, 17 July.

European Commission (2003) *EU-Funded Programmes in Turkey: 2003–2004*, Ankara: European Union Delegation of the European Commission.

—— (2005) *Turkey: 2005 Progress Report*, Brussels: European Commission, SEC (2005)1426, COM (2005) 561 final.

——, *Candidate Countries Eurobarometer*, various years. Online. Available: http://ec.europa.eu/public_opinion/archives/cceb2_en.htm, (accessed 27 September 2012).

European Court of Human Rights EctHR, *Annual Statistics*, various years. Online. Available HTTP: <http://www.echr.coe.int/ECHR/EN/Header/Reports+and+Statistics/Statistics/Statistical+data> (accessed 27 September 2012).

Hale, W. (2010) 'Human rights and Turkey's accession process 2005–10', paper presented at the Workshop on Whither Turkey? Taking Stock of the Dynamics that Shape EU Reforms, Sabancı University, Istanbul, January 2010.

Human Rights Watch (2006) *Turkey: Human Rights Overview*. Online. Available HTTP: <http://hrw.org/english/docs/2006/01/18/turkey1220.htm> (accessed 27 September 2002).

Kalaycıoğlu, E. (2011) 'Kulturkampf in Turkey: the constitutional referendum of 12 September 2010', *South European Society and Politics*, 17 (1): 1–22.

Kemahlıoğlu, Ö. and Keyman, E.F. (2011) *Türkiye'de Demokrasi Algısı* (Democracy Perception in Turkey), İstanbul: İstanbul Politikalar Merkezi. Online. Available HTTP: <http://ipc.sabanciuniv.edu/publication/turkiyede-demokrasi-algisi> (accessed 27 September 2002).

Keyman, E.F. (2008) 'Civil society and democratisation in Turkey', paper presented at Seminar on Democracy and Democratization in Turkey, Universidad Autónoma de Madrid, November 2008.

Keyman, E.F. and İçduygu, A. (2003) 'Globalization, civil society and citizenship in Turkey: actors, boundaries and discourses', *Citizenship Studies*, 7 (2): 219–33.

Keyman, E.F. and Öniş, Z. (2004) 'Helsinki, Copenhagen and beyond: Challenges to the new Europe and the Turkish state', in M. Uğur, M. and N. Canefe, N. (eds) *Turkey and European Integration: Accession Prospects and Issues*, London: Routledge.

Kurban, D. and Gülalp, H. (forthcoming) 'A complicated affair – the Court and the Kurds: the role of the European Court of Human Rights in the broadening of Kurdish rights in Turkey' in Anagnostou, D. (ed.) *The European Court of Human Rights: Implementing Strasbourg's Judgments on Domestic Policy*, Edinburgh: Edinburgh University Press.

Oğuzlu, T. (2008) 'Middle Easternization of Turkish foreign policy: does Turkey dissociate from the West?', *Turkish Studies*, 9 (1): 3–20.

Öniş, Z. (2010) 'Contesting for Turkey's Political 'Centre': Domestic Politics, Identity Conflicts and the Controversy over EU Membership', *Journal of Contemporary European Studies*, 18 (3): 361–76.

Özbudun, E. (2007) 'Democratization reforms in Turkey, 1993–2004', *Turkish Studies*, 8 (2): 179–96.

Smith, W.T. (2007) 'Leveraging norms: the ECHR and Turkey's human rights reforms' in Arat, Z. K. (ed.) *Human Rights in Turkey*, Philadelphia: University of Pennsylvania Press.

US Commission on International Religious Freedom (2012), 'Turkey', in *2012 Annual Report*, March. Online. Available HTTP: <http://www.uscirf.gov/reports-and-briefs/annualreport.html> (accessed 27 September 2012).

US Department of State (2009) *2008 Human Rights Report: Turkey*, Washington: Bureau of Democracy, Human Rights, and Labor.

17 The paradox of equality

Subjective attitudes towards basic rights in Turkey

Ayşen Candaş and Hakan Yılmaz

Our aim in this chapter is to focus on *two paradoxes* that emerge from a survey that was conducted by Hakan Yılmaz (2006)[1] concerning the attitudes of Turkey's constituency with regards to basic rights. The first paradox is as follows. On the one hand, Turkey's inhabitants, by a rate of 51 percent, think that 'equality before the law' is by far the most important right they want to keep, compared to freedom of faith and religion (20 percent), electoral rights (10 percent), freedom of association (6 percent), and property rights (5 percent). On the other hand though, most do not seem ready to recognize the inviolability of others' rights. Hence, a cluster analysis over a series of questions regarding the inviolability of rights, which are perceived to be 'others' rights', show that a great majority of the respondents, close to 65 percent, reported that those rights can be totally suppressed by the state, if the state deems that it is required to do so. Only 35 percent of the respondents declared that the state should in no way violate 'others' rights'.

How come in Turkey the regularly stated 'strong preference' for – some notion of – equality's significance does not shape the political agenda and prepare the ground for a societal consensus on equal rights? Can we interpret the existence of this strong preference for equality as the existence of a fertile ground for instituting an indivisible set of basic rights (with their civil, political, social, cultural and economic components) in Turkey?

The second paradox that emerged from the survey and we want to focus on involves regional aspects of equal basic right internalization of Turkey's inhabitants. Marmara region (which excludes Istanbul in this study) and Southeastern Anatolia's attitudes toward basic rights are calling for revisiting generally accepted beliefs with regards to the Western and the Eastern regions' liberal/illiberal attitudes towards basic rights. The Southeastern Anatolia scores much better and is more liberal compared with the Marmara region on the recognition of others' rights such as with regards to the right to difference and the right to political dissent, while the Marmara region which is predominantly illiberal on other accounts shows more liberal attitudes in recognition of differences in sexual identity and orientation.

The study that was conducted in 2006 by Yılmaz was covering a nationwide sample of 2,000 people. Unlike similar studies of its kind that focus on political attitudes and values in general, the study under consideration specifically sought to assess the attitudes of the public towards a variety of sets of 'basic rights' and aimed to evaluate the causes of variation in those attitudes. In order to analyze the meaning of the data, there is need for further research, as it is the case with most opinion surveys, but the data nevertheless provides some interesting and politically significant tendencies, some of which are paradoxical enough to call for – if not readily deliver – explanation. In this paper, we would like to highlight a few of the findings that emerged within the context of this study and assess their plausible explanations. While examining the data on basic rights and the discrepancies of attitudes towards rights of difference and dissent, we will specifically focus on what emerges as 'the paradox of strong preference for equality' that reappears in this study as a strong preference for equality before the law (see figures below). Furthermore, we will focus on the paradoxical outcome that emerges when we analyze the data on a regional basis. Southeastern Anatolia appears to be the most ardent advocate of certain sets of basic rights and their inviolability compared with the Western Anatolia, which reveals much less liberal and even illiberal attitudes towards the rights to difference and dissent. The region-based finding only reverses itself on the attitudes towards the rights of difference and dissent on the basis of sexual orientation, and on that count only, the Western Anatolia scores better than the Southeastern Anatolia.

In the first part we will give an outline of the study and lay out its relevant findings. In the second part we will explain what emerges as the two paradoxical outcomes that emerge out of the data. Finally, in the third section, we propose some plausible explanations and evaluate these to uncover the direction of further research that this study must lead on the internalization of basic rights among of the inhabitants of Turkey.

Attitudes towards basic rights as *my* rights and *others'* rights

The design of the survey was as follows: The respondents were asked to evaluate 13 individual rights and freedoms one by one. In each case they were given the alternative to choose between 'indifference' when the state abolishes that particular right or 'object or protest' if the state were to interfere with or ban that particular right. The 13 individual rights that the respondents were asked to evaluate were electoral rights, equality before the law, freedom of communication, property rights, freedom of speech, freedom of religion and conscience in general, freedom of religion and conscience for non-believers and tolerance toward members of other religions, freedom of association, cultural rights for minority groups, freedom of the press and the media, the right not to be subjected to torture and degrading behavior, freedom of protest and demonstration and finally freedom of sexual orientation or LGBT individuals' rights. These rights are then grouped under two clusters by way of a two-step cluster analysis.

In the first cluster were included the rights that are of a more general character. These would roughly correspond to what T. H. Marshall (1959)

Table 17.1 My Rights vs. Others' Rights

	People reporting that this right CAN BE TOTALLY SUPPRESSED by the state, if the state deems it necessary	People reporting that this right SHOULD NEVER BE SUPPRESSED by the state under any circumstances
"My Rights": Basic Civil-Political Rights in general		
The right for the individuals to vote in the elections and to stand for elected offices	12%	87%
Freedom of religion in general	10%	89%
The right not to have a religious belief	10%	88%
Freedom of Speech	9%	89%
Freedom of communication through letters, telephone, internet and other means	7%	91%
Property and entrepreneurship rights	7%	89%
Equality before the law, irrespective of one's family, place of origin, religion, gender and ethnicity	7%	91%
Equality before the law irrespective of one's level of income and education	7%	91%
The right for the individuals to express their political choices in free and fair elections	7%	92%
"Others' Rights": Basic Civil-Political Rights to difference and dissent		
The right to live by one's own sexual choices, even if they differ from those of the majority (i.e. homosexuality)	58%	37%
Freedom of protest and demonstration	28%	66%
The right not to be subjected to torture and degrading behavior	23%	74%
Freedom of the press and the media	21%	76%
The right for non-Turkish speaking minority groups to use their own mother tongues and to express their cultures freely	20%	76%
Freedom to form and join civic associations and labor unions	17%	75%
Freedom of faith and prayer for non-muslims	15%	81%
The right for the political parties to have a fair and free competition in the political arena	12%	85%

called civil and political rights. In the second cluster were included the rights that are also civil and political rights but of the sort that are needed mostly by dissenters, and all sorts of minorities, i.e. rights and freedoms that are exercised to express difference and political dissent. Assuming that expression of difference, either in identity, aspirations, preferences or political opinions are crucial for the well-being of, first and foremost, 'minorities' within the larger population, we grouped the rights that are more likely to be needed by the minorities together. Thus, the first cluster included the following *basic* civil and political rights: electoral rights, equality before the law, freedom of communication, property rights, freedom of speech, freedom of religion and conscience in general. The second cluster, on the other hand, included again basic rights but those that we can expect to be most crucial especially for the dissenters and the minorities, such as freedom of religion and conscience for non-believers and members of minority religions, freedom of association, cultural rights for minority groups, freedom of the press and the media, the right not to be subjected to torture and degrading behavior, freedom of protest and demonstration and finally freedom of sexual orientation or LGBT individuals' rights. We call the first cluster 'Basic Individual Rights' and the second cluster 'Rights of Difference and Dissent'.

Recall that both clusters are comprised of basic civil and political rights. The clusters are only different with regards to the individuals and groups that are most likely to need them. In this sense, the first cluster of the basic set has a more generalizable character whereas the second cluster comprises the rights of the opposition and the right of being different from the majority in cultural, sexual, religious, political and ethnic terms.

The public's attitudes for these two composite rights can be traced in the Table 17.2:

Sixty-five percent of the respondents seem to support the very basic set of individual rights, while 35 percent seem to agree that basic individual rights *can be totally banned* by the state. These figures are *exactly reversed* when the respondents are asked to evaluate the rights of difference and dissent. In this case, only 35 percent of the respondents happen to be supportive of this second set of rights that have so much to do with the right to difference and dissent, while 65 percent seem to agree that the state can suppress difference and dissent whenever and wherever it deems necessary. Which social and political groups are more sensitive towards which sets of rights?

Table 17.2 The "My Rights" Cluster vs. the "Others' Rights" Cluster

	People reporting that this group of rights CAN BE TOTALLY SUPPRESSED by the state, if the state deems it necessary	*People reporting that this group of rights SHOULD NEVER BE SUPPRESSED by the state under any circumstances*
The "My Rights" Cluster (Involving 9 Rights)	35%	65%
The "Others' Rights" Cluster (Involving 8 Rights)	65%	35%

Table 17.3 TOP Groups Who Think That "MY RIGHTS" SHOULD NOT be suppressed by the State

People living in ONE OF THE THREE BIG CITIES (Istanbul, Ankara, Izmir)	84%
People living in the AEGEAN region	84%
Supporters of the Pro-Kurdish parties	80%
People ranking LOW in the "Religious Conservatism" and "Religiosity" indexes	78%
People whose mother tongue is KURDISH	78%
People living in the SOUTHEAST ANATOLIAN region	76%
People ranking LOW in the "Nationalism" index	76%
People with UPPER MIDDLE CLASS monthly household incomes (1200–2400 YTL)	75%
People who place themselves on the LEFT of the LEFT-RIGHT axis	75%
AVERAGE	**65%**

As it can be observed from Table 17.4, the top groups which think that basic individual rights (MY RIGHTS) should not be limited or infringed upon by the state are mainly people living in one of the three metropolitan cities (Istanbul, Ankara, Izmir), people living in the Aegean region, supporters of the pro-Kurdish parties, people ranking low in the religious conservatism and religiosity indexes, people whose mother tongue is Kurdish, people living in the Southeast Anatolian region, people ranking low in the nationalism index, people with upper-middle-class monthly household incomes (1200–2400 YTL) and finally, people who place themselves on the left of the political spectrum. On the other hand, if a respondent happens to live in Marmara (in this study Marmara region excludes Istanbul, which is analyzed separately), Central Anatolian or Eastern Anatolian regions, or if they are supporters of the Turkish Nationalist Action party (MHP) they are more likely than the average person to support the state's limitation of the basic individual rights and advocate the ban on rights to difference and dissent.

When we separately assess the rights to difference and dissent (OTHERS' RIGHTS), those who are willing to support the total restriction of those rights are exactly the same people who would favor state's ban of basic individual rights. The top groups who are 'in favor of rights of difference

Table 17.4 TOP Groups Who Think That "MY RIGHTS" CAN BE suppressed by the State

People living in the MARMARA region	71%
People living in the CENTRAL ANATOLIAN region	61%
People living in the EASTERN ANATOLIAN region	56%
Supporters of the Turkish nationalist MHP (Nationalist Action Party)	46%
AVERAGE	**36%**

Table 17.5 TOP Groups Who Think That OTHER PEOPLE'S RIGHTS SHOULD NOT be suppressed by the State

Supporters of Pro-Kurdish Parties	67%
People living in the SOUTHEAST ANATOLIAN region	64%
People whose mother tongue is KURDISH	59%
People living in the AEGEAN region	51%
People ranking LOW in the "Religious Conservatism" and "Religiosity" indexes	51%
People who place themselves on the LEFT of the LEFT-RIGHT axis	50%
People ranking LOW in the "Nationalism" index	50%
People living ONE OF THE THREE BIG CITIES (Istanbul, Ankara, Izmir)	48%
People ranking LOW in the "Political Conservatism" index	46%
Supporters of the Kemalist CHP (Republican People's Party)	45%
AVERAGE	**35%**

Table 17.6 TOP Groups Who Think That OTHER PEOPLE'S RIGHTS CAN be suppressed by the State

People living in the MARMARA region	88%
People living in the CENTRAL ANATOLIAN region	86%
People living in the EASTERN ANATOLIAN region	86%
Supporters of the Turkish nationalist MHP (Nationalist Action Party)	78%
AVERAGE	**65%**

and dissent' included supporters of pro-Kurdish parties, people living in the Southeast Anatolian region, people whose mother tongue is Kurdish, people living in the Aegean Region, people ranking low in the religious conservatism and religiosity indexes, people who place themselves on the left of the political spectrum, people ranking low in the nationalism index, people living in one of the three metropolitan cities (Istanbul, Ankara, Izmir), people ranking low in the political conservatism index and the supporters of the Kemalist CHP (*Cumhuriyet Halk Partisi*, Republican People's Party).

Two axes of differentiation: Turkish nationalism and individuation

To summarize the observable tendencies inherent in those findings, we can say that there are mainly 'two axes of differentiation' that would indicate whether a given person in Turkey would be more or less supportive of basic rights and freedoms for all. One of these axes is the 'level of Turkish nationalism' and the other axis is the 'level of individuation'.

The level of Turkish nationalism can be determined on the basis of the following criteria: Where a person places himself/herself on the nationalism index, where he/she places himself/herself on the left-right spectrum, whether the person is a supporter of (Turkish) MHP (*Milliyetçi Hareket Partisi*,

Nationalist Action Party) and whether a person defines himself/herself as pro-Kurdish or not. Hence, those who rank low in the nationalism index and place themselves on the left of the political spectrum as well as those who consider themselves pro-Kurdish are more likely to support basic rights and freedoms 'for all with no exceptions'. Those who tend to vote for MHP on the other hand, are more likely to approve of the state's ban on rights and freedoms.

The second axis of determination of the support for rights and freedoms involves 'the level of individuation'.[2] We define 'individuation' as an unceasing process during which culturally and socially, and consciously and unconsciously inherited and acquired traits, perspectives, beliefs and behavioral patterns get questioned, reflected upon, sorted out and as a result more authentic approaches and modes of behavior are embraced that distinguish the person as someone with particular attitudes towards his/her life world and the social, political and cultural context that surrounds it.

In that regard, residents of the regions with higher opportunities for individuation, that offer a variety of experiences, lifestyles and stimulating cultural alternatives, i.e. the three metropolitan areas and the Aegean Region in Turkey's case, turn out to be more supportive of basic rights and freedoms for all whereas people living in the regions which offer less opportunities for individuation are more in favor of state's limitation of rights and freedoms. The anomaly in this regard appears in the Marmara region (which excludes Istanbul in this study). Marmara region's inhabitants seem to be residing in one of the most individuation-generating regions in Turkey yet they also seem to be highly (Turkish) nationalist and thus favor the ban on cultural minorities' rights and freedoms while at the same time being more liberal in terms of their attitudes towards other types of minorities, such as those with non-heterosexual sexual orientation. In other words, the inhabitants of Marmara region are exposed to both axes of differentiation (Turkish nationalism and individuation) as a result of which one axis cuts across the other one and results in the selective adoption of basic rights to difference and dissent displaying much more liberal attitudes towards gender equality and right to sexual orientation while also resulting in illiberal attitudes towards the Kurdish ethnic minority.

East is West!

A similar anomaly appears again on the regional level and attests that, contrary to the common belief that geographic divisions between the East and the West correspond to the divisions between modernity and tradition, Turkey's Southeast, at least in the sphere of basic rights and freedoms (with the exception of women's and non-heterosexuals' freedoms) shows more 'Western' characteristics, whereas geographically Western regions, particularly Marmara has politically become 'Eastern' or pro-status quo in their denial of the rights and freedoms of the minorities (again with the exception of women's and non-heterosexuals' freedoms). In other words, with regards to internalizing the freedom from torture, freedom of the critical press and the media, freedom of protest and association and right to cultural freedom, Eastern and particularly Southeastern Anatolia displays much more liberal attitudes, while the same regions' inhabitants seem to be more illiberal in terms of their internalization of gender equality, and right to freedom for non-heterosexual sexual orientation. Marmara and the Western regions in general display the opposite tendency: The inhabitants that dwell in these regions support gender equality and the right to sexual difference and are more tolerant towards alternative life styles, while they seem to be illiberal towards the rights of cultural minorities, Kurds in particular. This finding can be explained by the high concentration of Kurds in South Eastern Anatolia and complements the finding that those who state that they are Kurdish, who vote for HADEP (Halkın Demokrasi Partisi, People's Democracy Party)/DTP (*Demokrasi ve Toplum Partisi*, Democratic Society Party) and who speak Kurdish are heavily represented in the 35 percent of respondents who support rights of difference and dissent. The relative homogeneity of the Western regions with respect to their ethnic dimension is also once again verified by their attitudes towards the rights of difference and dissent that are most frequently needed to be exercised by Kurds in the Turkish context. We can argue that Kurdish as opposed to Turkish nationalism results in adoption of basic rights with particular emphasis on right to cultural difference and dissent, while the relatively low level of individuation that characterizes this region (perhaps excluding Diyarbakir) results also in illiberal attitudes this time toward women and those with non-heterosexual sexual orientation.

MY RIGHTS vs. OTHERS' RIGHTS?

The cluster we called Basic Individual Rights or 'MY RIGHTS' (Table 17.2) seems to have been internalized by a larger portion of Turkey's population (65 percent). We grouped electoral rights, equality before the law, freedom of communication, property rights, freedom of speech and freedom of religion and conscience in general under this cluster. These rights correspond to the most basic sets of civil and political rights. Although we included almost all civil rights, political rights are represented here in their thinnest form, namely as the right to vote in elections. This set is basic and can be coined as 'my' rights for two reasons, one conceptual and the other one historical. Conceptually, civil and political rights, especially in this thin version, are rights that an ordinary citizen expects to exercise regularly and without any interruption during the course of his/her life time within a complex society in today's socio-economic and political context in any country which is, or strives to be, a constitutional democracy. Historically, civil and political rights have been the outcomes of the struggles of the past. Once they appeared on the world stage especially through the French

Revolution and the American Independence War that immediately followed it, the idea of citizen as an equal member of society with equal civil and political rights turned into a normative as well as a historically valid principle. The universality of equal rights principle accordingly has been documented by the Universal Declaration (1948) which was then followed by separate conventions on civil and political rights and economic, social and cultural rights (1966).

Recognition of fellow citizens as equal members endowed with the same and equally exercisable civil and political rights constitute at least half of what we call a basic rights system today. Unlike social, economic and cultural rights, the question of whose validity have proven to be socially divisive in a variety of contexts, this thin version of civil and political rights are perhaps the most widely shared, proven to be widely shareable, and typically least socially or politically divisive sets of rights. These prove to be socially divisive only in contexts in which either legally engendered forms of discrimination as in apartheid regimes are in place, or in which, despite legal and formal equality, certain classes and status groups are systematically but informally discriminated against within the society. If 35 percent of Turkey's population is in favor of state's banning, limiting or arbitrarily interfering with the basic set of civil and political rights, there would be two ways of understanding this phenomenon. It could be that there are groups of people who have not at all made the transition from a consciousness of subject (*kul*) to a consciousness of citizenship and remained as passive recipients of state-bestowed rewards and punishments that they accept as if these were gifts of grace. Or, the groups who do not support basic civil and political rights might be composed of people who are content to experience themselves as privileged, and are thus unwilling to grant equality to those and do everything in their power to prevent equalization of those who are currently underprivileged and thus refuse to give up 'privilege' for the sake of 'equal citizenship'.

The paradox of equality without rights

The first possibility, the idea that these groups experience themselves as subjects of the state rather than as citizens, is a plausible explanation. Yet our data also revealed that the respondents are strongly (51 percent) in favor of equality before the law, when compared to other rights and freedoms. Hence, equality before the law is by far the most important right they want to keep, compared to freedom of faith and religion (20 percent), electoral rights (10 percent), freedom of association (6 percent), and property rights (5 percent). If there are stages of internalizing the notion of equal rights for all, equality before the law must be the first and possibly the most significant threshold that must be left behind. Since a strong preference for equality before the law gives the immediate impression that it would correlate with the idea of equal citizenship, the strong preference that seems to be typical of Turkey's inhabitants would translate itself into a defense of equal rights for all. Yet our data *also* reveals that this is not at all the case. In fact, among the respondents who think that equality before the law is the most important right for them, a proportion (69 percent) higher than the national average (65 percent) think that what we have called 'my rights', i.e. basic individual rights and freedoms, can be violated by the state if the latter deems it necessary to do so. Moreover, among those who reported equality before the law as their most important right, a significant proportion (58 percent) oppose what we have called 'others' rights', or rights of difference and dissent, accepting that others' rights can be overstepped by the state at will. How to explain this paradox of favoring equality but not equal rights for all?

There might be various reasons why equality affirming attitudes do not get translated into rights-affirming attitudes in Turkey's constituency and perpetuate the self-perception of Turkey's inhabitants as being 'subjects' (*kul*) rather than citizens. Historical factors might be one explanation. The paternal state figure or 'father' state weighing over the shoulders of Turkey's inhabitants since the Ottoman times which has consistently proved its arbitrariness and 'easy to anger impulsive authority' image may be a factor that cannot be readily reversed. Even the relatively long history of constitutionalism in this land since the Tanzimat (1839) period may not have been consequential in this respect given the incessant interruptions of the relatively rights-recognizing constitutions that were accompanied by a series of coups d'etat during the republican period. These may have led the inhabitants to internalize the permanence of an impulsive, omnipotent and arbitrary regime in this land.

Another historical factor that might be reinforcing the consciousness of subject rather than equal citizen might be the role of Islam. Culturally, folk Islam with its obedience and meekness-praising, modesty and total-conformity-preaching teachings may have prepared the inhabitants to perceive the State as a wrathful but deeply compassionate, arbitrary, but ultimately just semi-divine figure. Again historically, the tested wrath and vengeance of the state and its ability to crush disobedient groups, or the militarily strong state tradition may have led people not to demand rights but be content with whatever is bestowed from above.

All of these factors which are counterfactuals and thus can neither be falsified nor proven, even if they were true in fact do *not* shed light on the strong preference for equality. After all, the internalization of the permanence of an arbitrary and potent State as if it were a demi-god might also mean the internalization of *in*equality, and result in meek acceptance of the pre-eminence of superiors over the rest. Is the regularly revealed and apparently widely distributed preference for (some notion of) equality then indicating the slow but persistent emergence of an authentic criticism of the asymmetry of power between the rulers and the ruled? Or is the preference for equality based upon a different notion of equality that correlates with a subject attitude rather than with a citizen attitude precluding a defense of equal rights for all from the beginning?

Equality of being leveled down?

Assuming that preference for equality is more or less equally distributed among all classes, ethnic groups and all sorts of minorities, a high preference for equality may in fact refer to two different notions of equality. The first notion of equality is a Hobbesian one: Insofar as people experience themselves as subjects (rather than agents or citizens) who need to be protected by the almighty Leviathan in exchange for absolute obedience, they would favor 'equality in their equal subjection'. They might accept that they only have the right to live within the political context that is made available by the arbitrary Leviathan, while they might see their equal subjection and subjection in general as the guarantee of *salus populi* or public safety. The demand for extended freedoms for some, or extensive and equal freedoms for all groups might be experienced as the fear of losing public safety and the subjects may become proactive in leveling the activists down at level with them.

This Hobbesian notion of equality is in contrast with the 'liberal' notion of equality. According to the liberal notion, which gradually and not without bloodshed evolved first in England, while having been established after the revolution and war in France and North America, citizenship entails equal liberties for all. These 'liberties', after having been translated into the constitution and/or laws become sanctionable rights, and are primarily conceived as rights 'against' the state. Political union of people is primarily motivated to 'limit' the reach of the political authority while the political authority is deemed to be legitimate 'only insofar as' it safeguards the equal freedoms that the citizens are entitled to have.

Hobbesian and liberal notions of equality: A sequential equality model?

Contra absolutist and monarchist Hobbesian notion of equality that legitimizes subjection and the necessity of instituting equal subjection 'for public safety', the liberal 'response to discrimination and intolerance' has been to set civil and political rights as the limits and side-constraints that the legitimate political authority cannot trespass without undermining its authority and legitimacy. Times of emergency such as attacks, wars and revolutions prove over and over again that Hobbesian and Lockean or liberal notions are not completely separated types of equality. Whenever and apparently wherever there is a perception that public safety is under duress, even countries which are historically proven to display strong preference for liberal rights have succumbed to a Hobbesian notion of equality, as the period immediately following the September 11, 2001 attacks proved in the US and elsewhere. We could say that the two notions of equality are sequential yet reversible as well depending on the context, whenever the popular perceptions with regards to the stability of *'public safety'* are intact, and only then, the 'concern about discrimination and intolerance' finds the opportunity to gain a priority in the majority's attitudes.

Turkey: The long journey from exclusive concern for public safety to a more refined concern about discrimination and intolerance

It could be that in Turkey, given the large yet declining weight of traditional social relations, attitudes of complete abandonment to political authority alongside with the attributes of an increasingly salient complex society, a Hobbesian notion of equality currently coexists with a more recently flourishing sense of a liberal notion of equality. Coexistence of Hobbesian as well as liberal understandings of equality, when combined as a sum within the population may explain why an overwhelming majority of survey respondents in Turkey seem to favor equality while how they perceive equality seem to be radically at odds, and why, in terms of values and attitudes, the inhabitants might be severely divided among themselves. A preference for a Hobbesian notion of equality would justify equality at the bottom, equality of subjection, and may even demand the people to proactively level down the freedom-demanding groups, while precluding the liberal suspicion from the state to emerge or preventing inhabitants to critically re-assess the state's arbitrary and paternal power or may pre-empt the possibility of guarding one's rights against the political authority. A preference for a liberal notion of equality on the other hand, requires jealously guarding one's rights against the state and expanding the scope of these liberties especially because it is the state itself that can most readily, arbitrarily, and with ease infringe upon equality, freedoms, pursuit of happiness and systematically and formally discriminate at will and it is the state which has the means to institute privileges while undermining equal rights.

Under the light of the analysis above we can look at our findings once again: it seems that the 65 percent who are in favor of defending basic individual rights must have more or less internalized a liberal notion of equal liberties. Does that mean they are against all forms of discrimination? The findings also show that only 35 percent are in favor of supporting the second cluster of rights that we called Rights to Difference and Political Dissent. In this first level of analysis it is clear that more people have generated a consciousness as to the value of their own basic rights and want to protect these 'against' the state, but a second level of analysis shows that this consciousness as to the value of MY rights has not reached to a level of consciousness that would culminate in defending others' rights as if they were 'my own'. Hence, of those who would defend 'my rights' against the arbitrary interventions of the state, only half (51 percent) would also defend others' rights, while the other half (49 percent) would accept it if the state decided to suppress others' rights. On the other hand, of those who said they would be defensive of others' rights, 93 percent also said that they would not accept any state intervention in their own rights too.

It would not be accurate then to claim that those who have internalized what basic rights refer to within the liberal context of the equal citizenship principle, since a genuine internalization of the universality of basic rights necessarily entails recognizing perhaps *especially* the rights of others as if they were 'my own'. Internalization of 'my rights' as entitlements while rejecting 'others' rights' and admitting to their dispensability shows that 'especially the equality principle that attaches to rights, and especially their universality', has 'not' been internalized. Only 35 percent for one reason or another seems to have internalized the liberal and normative principle of equal rights of citizenship. If rights are not universalized, their equality is not acknowledged and once their equality is not acknowledged, even an endorsement of 'my rights' is an endorsement of 'my privileges' rather than 'rights'. Conceptually, to be considered as a right at all, a principle has to be universally applicable across the population.

What are the social indicators that correlate with defending others' rights? Why does a group affirm its own rights as 'rights against the state' while failing to acknowledge the same as others' entitlements? The data affirms that the minority 35 percent who seem to be ready to defend others' rights or Rights to Difference and Political Dissent are primarily those who are 'already different or in the minority' either because of their politicized ascriptive identities or their politically critical standpoints. At least 3 of the 10 categories of respondents who are fervently (above the standard deviation) in favor of defending others' rights indicate that being Kurdish in Turkey is an important variable in having generated a sensitivity and consciousness regarding equal citizenship principle as equal rights for all. Again expectedly, those who rank low in religious conservatism and nationalism indexes and those who consider themselves to be on the left of the political spectrum are similarly in favor of equal rights for all.

Conclusion

Since we began to write this chapter, another survey by Hakan Yılmaz,[3] which was conducted in 2010, showed that even the support for what we have called MY RIGHTS has deteriorated and declined. Given that basic rights in a democracy are foundational and constitute the counter-majoritarian side-limits that have to be sanctioned regardless of their present level of popularity, it seems apt to emphasize the deficiencies in the roles of the ruling AKP (*Adalet ve Kalkınma Partisi*, Justice and Development Party) and the opposition CHP in bringing about this deterioration in terms of the internalization of basic rights in Turkey.

AKP is a party whose constituency is less liberal compared with its leadership and CHP is a party whose constituency is more liberal compared with its leadership. AKP, as the governing party has played a pivotal role in the EU accession process which was opposed by the CHP leadership. Yet instead of regarding the foundational role of basic rights in a democracy as intrinsically valuable political goals, AKP seems to have embraced the EU led reforms on the issue of basic rights as an instrumental and contingent factor that is but one obstacle on the way of accession. In other words, instead of prioritizing the constitutional and institutional changes that would expand the scope and definition of basic rights in Turkey, AKP seems to have approached this issue from an instrumentalist perspective. Politicization of basic rights' reforms in Turkey has happened in such a way that the whole process was as if these were merely the bitter pills that one must swallow in order to get accession. Thus when the accession process came to a halt for various reasons, the initial politicization of the basic rights issue and the instrumentalist tilt involved in it produced an unintended ill outcome for the prospect of basic right reform in Turkey. Had the basic rights and their indivisible nature been politicized in such a way that would emphasize the foundational significance of these for the prospect of genuine democratization in Turkey, this attitude that would underline the basic rights' intrinsic value for a democracy would have been a positive externality of the EU accession process, though long halted. Right now, on the contrary, basic rights and the recognition of equal rights for all seem to be less and less internalized by a public who feels discriminated against and cold-shouldered by the EU and whose way of in turn cold-shouldering the EU and what it represents involves de-internalizing the significance of equal basic rights.

Opposition parties play a tremendously significant role in democracies by providing constructive criticism to the ruling party, by enabling the ruling party to check their reasons in public and become self-reflective and by pulling the ruling party to the center of societal issues instead of letting the ruling party to set the political agenda. CHP's monopolization of the social democratic left and its being ruled by a nationalist and rightist leadership who provided not constructive criticism but conservative attacks has played a tremendous role in the politicization of basic rights reforms in Turkey. Even an instrumentalist AKP could have been pushed to embrace a more intrinsic attitude toward basic rights reforms had they found any credible social democratic opposition set against them. Considering CHP leadership's proven and highly consistent Hobbesian attitude towards equality and its strong preference for prioritizing status quo perceived as public safety, we can suggest that had the party leadership been more representative of its base, the CHP supporters would not have appeared in the list of 35 percent who favor defending others' rights. As CHP supporters are more likely to rank low in religious conservatism indexes, they may be strongly favoring freedom of conscience as freedom for nonbelievers and non-Muslims as well as recognizing the freedom for non-heterosexual sexual orientation which are important components of liberal rights. Yet given that cluster analysis only picks out the groups who favor *all* rights within the cluster without exceptions, the group that vote for CHP while defending the rights of others must have categorically supported all the rights within the cluster called Rights to Difference an Political Dissent. This group represents 45 percent of the population who vote for CHP. In other words, '55 percent those who vote for CHP are not supporting the rights of others or tend to support these selectively'. Given that the party is called Republican People's Party, it is ironical to observe that a majority of so called republicans are *against* defending others' rights as their own which undermines the liberal as well as the Kantian republican idea of equal rights of citizenship.

Notes

1 Hakan Yılmaz. 2006. 'Major Variants of Conservatism in Turkey'. Research project jointly supported by a grant from the Open Society Institute Assistance Fund (Grant No:20014746) and Bogazici University Research Fund (Project No: 05M103). Access to data: Online. Available HTTP: <www.hakanyilmaz.info> (accessed 30 June 2013). For a brief commentary on the survey findings see Yilmaz, H. (2008) 'Conservatism in Turkey', *Turkish Policy Quarterly*, Spring 2008: 57–65.
2 Although there are philosophical, for example Hegelian, or psychological, for example, Jungian definitions of individuation in the literature, here we are using the definition we author specifically for the purposes of this article.
3 Hakan Yılmaz. 2010. 'Between Hospitality and Hostility: Determining the Processes of Othering in Turkey and Developing Policy Proposals for the Prevention of Discrimination'. Research project supported by a grant from Açık Toplum Vakfı (Open Society Foundation) (Grant No: 2009001) and Boğaziçi University & State Planning Organization (Grant No: 07K120620). Date of completion: February 2010.

References

Yılmaz, H. (2006). 'Major Variants of Conservatism in Turkey'. Research project jointly supported by a grant from the Open Society Institute Assistance Fund (Grant No:20014746) and Bogazici University Research Fund (Project No: 05M103). Date of completion: July 2006. Access to data: Online. Available HTTP: <www.hakanyilmaz.info> (accessed 30 June 2013).
—— (2008). 'Conservatism in Turkey', *Turkish Policy Quarterly*, Spring 2008: 57–65.
—— (2010). 'Between Hospitality and Hostility: Determining the Processes of Othering in Turkey and Developing Policy Proposals for the Prevention of Discrimination'. Research project supported by a grant from Açık Toplum Vakfı (Open Society Foundation) (Grant No: 2009001) and Boğaziçi University & State Planning Organization (Grant No: 07K120620). Date of completion: February 2010.

18 The Kurdish question

Law, politics and the limits of recognition

Dilek Kurban

Introduction

One principal factor that renders the Kurdish question unique in Turkey has been the distinct spatial/territorial nature of state oppression. The majority of the Kurds have lived in their homeland in Eastern and Southeastern Turkey until the late 1980s and the early 1990s, though an increasing number immigrated for economic reasons to the western parts of the country from the mid-1950s onwards.[1] The latter group of Kurds by and large 'agreed' to the tacit deal they were forced to make, suppressing their distinct identity in exchange for integration and upward mobility. Those who refused or were unable to do so faced persecution. Scores of Kurdish activists, politicians and journalists were charged under anti-terrorism laws, Kurdish newspapers were banned, and a number of political parties established by the Kurds and/or advocating their rights were abolished. As far as the Kurdish homeland was concerned, however, there was an additional collective and spatial dimension to state oppression. In the name of combating the 'PKK (*Partiya Karkerên Kurdistan*, Kurdistan Worker's Party) terrorism,' the state treated the civilian population in the Kurdish region as an internal threat, subjugating it to collective punishment through forced evictions in rural areas and grave human rights abuses in urban centers in the form of political assassinations, enforced disappearances, summary executions and torture.

Related to this spatial/territorial dimension, the distinct nature of the Kurdish question also stems from the duality the state has created in the law. Certainly, Turkey's long-standing policy of making an exception to the rule of law has not been exclusive to the Kurdish region. What distinguishes this region from the rest of the country is that it has been subject to longer periods as well as unique regimes of 'state of exception'. Turkey's legal order has subjected the Kurds to a permanent state of exception, where exceptionality has been the rule. While the persecution of the Kurds has increased and intensified at times when a *de jure* emergency regime was in force, it has not withered away with the return to 'normalcy'. During periods when a special legal regime was not formally operative, routine human rights violations continued.

When the EU membership process started, many assumed that Turkey would have to undertake a radical overhaul of its constitutional and legislative order. After decades of forcefully assimilating its Kurdish subjects, the state would now be obliged to ensure the equal treatment of all its citizens, in law and in fact. In reality, Turkey's policies on the Kurdish question have remained by and large intact. Certainly, some restrictions on the Kurdish language were lifted, Kurds were granted limited rights to teach, learn and broadcast in their mother tongue and a number of safeguards against human rights violations were introduced. However, the change has not been radical. The 'Kurdish opening' that the AKP (*Adalet ve Kalkınma Partisi*, Justice and Development Party) government initiated in 2009 failed to meet the Kurds' basic demands for the provision of mother tongue education, the removal of all restrictions on Kurdish, the abolishment of the excessive limitations on political freedoms and the redefinition of citizenship. The exceptional treatment of the Kurds continues, in law and in fact, as evident in the detention on remand of thousands of Kurdish politicians, journalists, students, lawyers and activists on the basis of police investigations based on unlawfully gathered evidence shielded from public scrutiny by secrecy orders.

The Kurdish question in the legal framework: An overview

It is commonly assumed that the exceptional treatment of the Kurds under the law is a provisional phenomenon that occurs during interim regimes and ends with the return to normalcy. In reality, the Kurdish region has always been governed by some form of state of exception. The Turkish state has always deviated from its fundamental duties vis-à-vis its Kurdish citizens. What has changed at times when a special legal regime was *de jure* in force was the intensity and scale of human rights violations against civilians committed through emergency regimes, forced displacement and cultural assimilation, processes which were often in place simultaneously. Law has served an indispensable role in the design and implementation of each of these mechanisms.

Emergency regimes

Since the establishment of the Republic in 1923, some form of state of exception was operative in Turkey most of the time.[2] At many times, anti-democratic regimes were operative across the country. Sometimes, however, they were effective exclusively in the Kurdish region. Noteworthy in the latter group is the 1935 Tunceli Law which was adopted to establish the state's control over the Dersim region populated by the Alevi Kurds.[3] The law established and designated as the highest provincial authority the office of the Governor of Tunceli and stipulated the appointment to this office of a military commander with extraordinary powers. Individuals prosecuted under the law were not granted the most basic due process rights, including the right to be notified of the charges against them or to appeal against the verdict when convicted.

The most recent universal martial law declared across Turkey after the 1980 military coup was gradually abolished from 1984 onwards and formally brought to an end in 1987. And yet, in the Kurdish region, it was replaced by a state of emergency regime, justified in the name of combating the PKK. Declared on 10 July 1987,[4] the state of emergency was extended by the parliament 46 times until it was formally abolished on 30 November 2002 (Balzacq and Ensaroğlu 2008: 11). The law established the office of the Governor of the State of Emergency which was hierarchically superior to the provincial governorships in the region. This governor was equipped with extraordinary powers, including evacuating villages, temporarily or permanently suspending the print media, expelling from the state of emergency region individuals deemed to threaten public order, banning labor union activities and restricting the exercise of the rights to assembly and demonstrate. The decisions and acts of the State of Emergency Governor as well as the provincial governors were exempt from judicial review.

Unlike in the 1930s, the Governor of the State of Emergency region did not formally resort to his powers under the law. Instead, the eviction of civilians from their homes in villages and urban centers in the Kurdish region took place outside of the realm of the law. Human rights abuses committed by security forces were not limited to forced displacement. Villages were burnt down; properties were destroyed; individuals were disappeared, summarily executed and tortured; Turkish press was censored;[5] Kurdish press was often banned and its members killed, intimidated and tortured;[6] freedoms of assembly, association and expression were restricted and many times suspended.[7] While the PKK also committed crimes against civilians, in most cases the perpetrators were the security forces, as documented by national (Türkiye İnsan Hakları Vakfı 1995) and international (United States Committee for Refugees 1999; Kurdish Human Rights Project 2002) human rights organizations, the Turkish Parliament and the European Court of Human Rights (ECtHR)[8] (Kurban *et al.* 2007: 119–44). A clandestine criminal unit within the Turkish military, the *JİTEM* (*Jandarma İstihbarat ve Terörle Mücadele* Gendarmerie, Intelligence in Combatting Terrorism), was the principal perpetrator of the crimes in the urban centers.[9]

Despite having lost dozens of cases before the ECtHR and having paid large sums of compensation to victims, the Turkish Government has never assumed its responsibility and persistently denied that it had pursued policies of displacement, torture, summary execution, forced disappearance and arbitrary deprivation of liberty. Although Turkey has over time admitted that its security forces committed human rights abuses in 'isolated and regretful incidents,'[10] it has never accepted that the army had a policy of evicting civilians from rural areas nor its responsibility in these abuses.

One notable aspect of the state of emergency regime of the 1990s was that, in theory, the Kurdish civilians had the right to seek the judicial review of state acts. However, in practice, the *de iure* existence of this right did not translate into legal protection for the Kurds. In virtually all cases where civilians attempted to file complaints with the authorities in the state of emergency region, either the prosecutors refused to bring charges against security officers accused of having committed human rights violations or the State Security Courts issued lack of jurisdiction in rare cases where prosecutors opened up investigations. Thus, the right to effective legal remedy did not *de facto* exist. National courts' reluctance to review the state's acts was so blatant that the ECtHR, in its precedent setting *Akdıvar* judgment, made an exception to the rule of exhaustion of domestic remedies by deciding to directly review, on a case by case basis, petitions concerning the incidents in the state of emergency region. The Court took particular note of the fact that despite the gravity and high number of allegations of village destructions, there was not a single domestic court decision compensating the victims for their losses and prosecuting the perpetrators. The ECtHR's findings concerning the reluctance of national courts to review the security forces' conduct in the state of emergency region remain a striking testament to the exceptional treatment of the Kurds by the judicial authorities in Turkey.

Forced displacement

The first instance of Turkey's pursuit of forced displacement for suppressing Kurdish resistance is the 1926 Settlement Law.[11] Yet, the initiation of forced displacement as a systematic policy targeting the masses started in 1934 when a law was adopted for the forced resettlement to designated areas of those 'who do not share the Turkish culture and are not of Turkish origin'.[12] In identifying the objects of the resettlement program as those 'whose mother tongue is not Turkish', 'is not tied to the Turkish culture', or 'who are not of the Turkish race', the law made an implicit reference to the Kurds.

Following the adoption of the 1934 Settlement Law and until 1947, a total of 25,831 individuals were forcefully displaced from the region and resettled in the western parts of Turkey (Tekeli 1990: 64). The state provided the displaced with housing and financial assistance to enable them to rebuild their lives in their new places of residence. Following the containment of the Kurdish rebellions in eastern Turkey, the 1934 law was abrogated in 1947 and the displaced were given the right to return. As a result, a total of 22,526 Kurds returned to their homelands (Yeğen 2006: 66).

The most recent instance of forced Kurdish displacement took place between the late 1980s and the late 1990s in the context of the armed conflict between the PKK and the Turkish armed forces.[13] Civilians in thousands of villages and hamlets (Türkiye Büyük Millet Meclisi 1998) were forcefully evicted by security forces in accordance with the 'field domination doctrine' (Jongerden 2007: 91). The 15 years of armed conflict which came to a halt in 1999 with the arrest of the PKK leader, Abdullah Öcalan, left around 1 million civilians displaced.[14] The largest group of these was those evicted by security forces, often in retaliation for their refusal to join the state-sponsored village guard force for fighting against the PKK.[15] According to a survey commissioned by the government to the Hacettepe University, nearly half of the displaced received 'verbal instructions' prior to their displacement (Hacettepe Nüfus Etütleri Enstitüsü 2006: 98). Neither the Hacettepe University nor the Government has released the findings of the qualitative component of this research. A summary of the qualitative findings the Hacettepe University has released, however, shows that 'unwillingness to become village guards and eviction orders has been identified in majority of the interviews as among the most important reasons for leaving the villages' (Hacettepe Nüfus Etütleri Enstitüsü 2006: 129).

Various Government programs have been adopted since the mid-1990s with the stated goal of enabling the return of the displaced. Most recently, the KDRP (*Köye Dönüş ve Rehabilitasyon Projesi,* Return to Village and Rehabilitation Project) was adopted in 1999. Implemented in 14 provinces in the state of emergency region, KDRP provides limited in-kind aid to those who wish to return to their villages. However, rather than a law granting the right to return to the displaced, KDRP is a project, whose purpose, budget and scope remain ambiguous and non-transparent. Research findings show that KDRP is a failed project.[16] According to the Hacettepe survey, half of the displaced were not aware of the aid distributed by the state under KDRP, while 88.5 percent of those who have returned to their villages have not received any assistance from the state (Hacettepe Nüfus Etütleri Enstitüsü 2006: 90, 93).

Subjugation of the Kurdish identity and language

The third main mechanism through which the state has violated the Kurds' citizenship rights has been the subjugation of their identity and culture. Until recently, the denial and suppression took place through simultaneous processes; the state has on the one hand denied the existence of Kurdish as a distinct identity and language, and on the other adopted legal measures to eliminate its visible traces. The names of places in the Kurdish region were 'Turkified,' Kurds were prohibited to give Kurdish names to their children, speaking Kurdish at schools and public offices were banned and official documents were cleared of references to 'Kurd' and 'Kurdish' (McDowall 1996; Yeğen 1999).

The constitutional order established after the 1980 military coup furthered the state's policies towards the Kurdish identity (Taşpınar 2005: 97). Once again, no explicit reference was made to the Kurds or the Kurdish language in the legal texts. The 1982 Constitution prohibited the expression of opinions[17] and broadcasting[18] 'in any language prohibited by the law'. A legislation adopted in 1983 expanded the scope of this ban to include the use of 'any language other than Turkish' as mother tongue, or in the expression and dissemination of opinions.[19] These bans were lifted in 1991 and the use of Kurdish in communication, media and arts was legalized, resulting in the flourishing of books, newspapers and music albums in Kurdish. In liberalizing the use of Kurdish in social and cultural life, however, the state did not assume any obligations for the protection of the Kurdish language and culture. Furthermore, restrictions on the use of Kurdish in political life were not abolished. Despite the EU-induced democratization process, there remain significant bans on the use of Kurdish in the exercise of political rights. The only reform made in the area of political freedoms was the 2010 amendment of the Law on the Fundamental Provisions Governing Elections and Voter Registration, lifting the ban on the use of Turkish in election campaigns. According to new Article 58, candidates and political parties 'shall primarily use Turkish'.[20] However, a similar ban continues to exist in the Law on Political Parties, prohibiting the political parties' use of 'any language other than Turkish' in their statutes, programs, congresses, meetings, propagandas or any written, audio and visual material.[21]

The EU process: 'Reforming' the Kurdish question

It was against this background that Turkey has found itself obliged to develop a solution to the Kurdish question. Two principal external factors account for the measures adopted by successive Turkish Governments during the past decade for the recognition of the Kurdish identity, the easing of legal restrictions on the Kurdish language and the provision of a remedy for compensating the displaced Kurds: the cases pending before the ECtHR and the EU accession process.

The ECtHR's fact findings in the 1990s revealed a pattern of routine violations by security forces, the impunity of perpetrators, and the unavailability of domestic legal remedies for victims. The Court's case law also demonstrated the lack of an impartial judiciary upholding the principles of the rule of law.[22] Regardless of the awareness the ECtHR's judgments created in the international community, the real improvement in law and practice only came with the emergence of the EU as an external actor. The EU pressured Turkey not only to execute the ECtHR case law regarding the Kurdish question, but also to go beyond it and grant the Kurds their cultural rights.[23]

Turkey's EU process formally started in 1999, when it was declared by the Union an official candidate for membership. The decision triggered a legislative process, which gained further speed with the AKP's victory in the national elections of November 2002. Before the AKP came to power, the preceding government had removed the constitutional restrictions on the use of 'languages prohibited by law' (i.e. Kurdish) in the expression of thought and broadcasting, and introduced higher constitutional standards for the dissolution of political parties.[24] In August 2002, death penalty in peacetime was abolished and in November 2002, the state of emergency was formally brought to a complete end.

Regardless, it has been the AKP Governments which introduced the most tangible changes in state policies. In its first two terms in office, the AKP followed a two-tiered approach to the Kurdish question. During its first term, particularly between 2002 and 2004, the AKP's approach was legalistic. A series of amendments were introduced in critical laws through 'reform packages' adopted by the parliament. During its second term, particularly after the launch of the 'Kurdish opening' in 2009, the AKP's approach was political, where rhetoric replaced concrete action and a deliberative process substituted legal reform.

The legal process: 'Reform' packages (2002–4)

After coming to power in 2002, the AKP Government initiated a legislative process with an unprecedented breadth and speed. With the goal of opening the accession negotiations with the EU, it introduced successive 'reform packages' within a very short time. In the area of human rights, safeguards against ill treatment and torture were introduced, a number of restrictions on political freedoms were removed, state security courts were replaced with heavy penal courts with special jurisdiction and the Press Law was liberalized. Relatively significant laws were adopted to appease the Kurds. They – and a number of select minorities-were granted the right to broadcast in and to teach/learn their mother tongue in private courses. A new law entitled the Kurdish displaced to monetary compensation for the pecuniary losses they had suffered since 1987.[25]

None of these laws, however, even those granting the Kurds limited language rights, contained an explicit reference to the Kurds or the Kurdish language. Characteristic of Turkey's policy of regulating the Kurds without explicit acknowledgment, the objects of the rights granted under the new laws were rendered obscure. The August 2002 'reform package'[26] allowed 'broadcasting in different languages and dialects 'Turkish citizens traditionally use in their daily live' (Kurban 2006: 341–72). The wording leaves uncertain which language(s) are entitled to benefit from the law and depicts Kurdish as a traditional language used exclusively in the private sphere as opposed to one with practical use in the public realm. Similarly, both the title and the text of the 2004 'Law on the compensation of losses arising from terrorism and the fight against terrorism' does not refer to the Kurds or even the displaced, its principal right-bearer.

In a characteristic fashion of lawmaking in Turkey, the package laws introduced new rights and subjected them to significant restrictions at the same time. For example, broadcasts that 'contradict the fundamental principles of the Turkish Republic and the indivisible integrity of the State' were prohibited under a law adopted in August 2002. In the past, prosecutors and judges have consistently applied the principle of 'national unity and territorial integrity' for banning political parties which advocated peaceful solutions to the Kurdish problem, prosecuting individuals who expressed non-violent dissenting opinions on the Kurdish question, and shutting down pro-Kurdish press organs.

The limited rights introduced by these laws were further restricted by executive regulations. A 2002 regulation established state control over broadcasting in Kurdish, introduced time and content restrictions (such as a ban on children's programs), and imposed stringent preconditions on televisions and radios, such as simultaneous and consecutive Turkish translation, respectively (Kurban 2007: 17). A 2004 regulation allowed national private broadcasting in Kurdish for the first time, but, again, subject to time and content limitations. Local and regional broadcasters were required to submit the state an audience profile in order to receive permits. The red tape made it very difficult for small private broadcasters with limited human and financial resources to comply with these requirements. In response to Kurdish broadcasters' complaints regarding the incompatibility of the legal framework with media freedom, a new regulation was adopted in 2009. The time and content restrictions and the translation requirements were lifted, allowing 24-hour broadcasting in Kurdish and the broadcasting of children's programmes.

The legislative changes of 2002–4 were hastily adopted by the parliament in late night sessions, without going through the democratic deliberation processes. The laws were not adopted with a rights-based approach, as evident in the extensive limitations they contained and the wide margin of appreciation granted to bureaucrats tasked with their implementation. Still, in recognition of the progress Turkey made, the EU decided to open the accession talks in 2005. Relieved by having secured a date from the EU, the AKP Government turned its focus on the upcoming general elections of July 2007.[27] Motivated with the interest of attracting nationalist votes, the Government rolled back many of the rights it had granted in earlier years. The principal legal instruments of this roll back were a new Penal Code in 2005, the amendments to the Anti-Terrorism Law in 2006 and the changes to the Law on the Duties and Authority of the Police in 2007 (Kurban and Gülalp 2012, forthcoming). The amended Anti-Terrorism Law treated minors over the age of 15 as adults, requiring their prosecution in heavy penal courts with special powers instead of juvenile courts. This has had dire consequences for Kurdish minors, thousands of whom were arrested and put on trial after 2006 for participating in anti-government protests, pro-PKK demonstrations or celebrations.[28] In response to strong protests at the national and international level, a new law passed in 2010 limited the applicability of the Anti-Terrorism Law, which requires the prosecution of all minors at juvenile courts and allows the postponement or reduction of their sentences. A further result of the regression in mid-2000s has been a sharp increase in police brutality. Equipped with new powers, the police started to resort to disproportionate force in putting down riots and taking civilians into custody simply for having participated–or even for being presumed to have participated–in public demonstrations. The high number of civilians, including minors, apprehended during peaceful protests in the Kurdish region was an outcome of the expanded powers of law enforcement.

As the July 2007 general elections approached, the security situation deteriorated in the Kurdish region. Following the expiration of the PKK declared ceasefire in May 2007, the fighting between the Kurdish militants and the armed forces resurfaced. The AKP faced anti-government protests across the country and a growing criticism by the army and the political opposition for the failure of its anti-terrorism strategy. In June 2007, the army declared a designated area in the region as a 'temporary security zone', restricting access of civilians and the media. Security forces started to routinely stop and search civilians, restrict freedoms of association and assembly and raid houses without a court-issued search warrant, practices that the Kurdish lawyers interpreted at the time as signs of a *de facto* state of emergency in the region.

The political process: 'Kurdish opening' (2009-)

In early 2009, the Government launched a 'Kurdish opening' with the stated goal of bringing a political solution to the conflict.[29] The strategy was based on a deliberative process where the Minister of Interior tasked with leading the initiative consulted, in a number of closed meetings, academics, civil society members, experts and, in rare cases, Kurdish politicians and opinion leaders on the solution of the Kurdish question. Mindful that any reform laws it would introduce to the parliament might not pass the opposition parties, the Government prioritized the adoption of executive measures in the short term and postponed the most critical reforms that required legislative and constitutional reforms to the future. By 2011, the initiative was by and large withered. The consultation process lasted too long without having produced a road map for the future and the government has never disclosed any conclusions it may have reached as a result of the deliberations.

The sole outputs of this process were executive measures, which fell far below the Kurds' demands for structural constitutional and legal reforms. On 1 January 2009, the state-owned Turkish Radio and Television (TRT) launched a new channel, TRT 6 (*Şeş*), which broadcasts exclusively in Kurdish. The initiative was criticized by the Kurdish political movement in that the channel lacked a legal basis, which they argued made its longitude subject to the political will of governments. Second, the government approved the establishment of Kurdish institutes and departments at public universities. The Mardin Artuklu University, located in the Kurdish region, had earlier applied for the establishment of a Kurdology Institute and an undergraduate program in Kurdish Language and Literature. This petition was declined by the YÖK (*Yükseköğretim Kurulu*, Higher Education Council) in 2009. The university, supported by the Kurdish movement, persisted and YÖK eventually approved the establishment of the 'Institute of Living Languages' and the opening of a master's program. Again, no explicit reference to the

Kurdish language was made and the scope of the decision was expanded to include other minority languages so as not to grant the Kurds an exclusive right. In 2011, YÖK approved the establishment at the same university of the Department of Kurdish Language and Literature, which started to provide the first undergraduate program on Kurdish in Turkey.

Two developments have greatly undermined the Government's initiative in the eyes of the Kurds and wider democratic society in Turkey. The first was the launch in of a criminal case in Diyarbakır in April 2009, a few months after the Government had launched the 'Kurdish opening'. Fifty-three Kurds, including elected mayors and local politicians from the BDP (*Barış ve Demokrasi Partisi*, Peace and Democracy Party), lawyers, activists, trade union members and women's rights activists, were detained in the first wave of arrests. Between June 2009 and February 2010, another 50 Kurds with the same profile were taken into custody. Suspects were accused of being leaders or members of the KCK (*Koma Ciwakên Kurdistan*, Kurdistan Communities Union), the alleged urban branch of the PKK. In 2011, the number of defendants in the 'KCK case' reached thousands, hundreds of whom were held in pretrial detention for periods ranging from fifteen months to two years.[30] The timing of the first arrests, two weeks after the BDP won a number of municipalities in the Kurdish region in local elections, was interpreted by the Kurds as the proof of the AKP's intention to penalize the Kurds for having voted for BDP.

The second development was the AKP's exclusion of the Kurds' principal demands from the constitutional reform package it introduced to the parliament in March 2010. While the package touched upon a wide range of issues, including the establishment of an ombudsman's office, affirmative action for disadvantaged groups, the redesign of the Constitutional Court and the High Council of Judges and Prosecutors, it did not involve the recognition of the right to mother tongue education, the redefinition of citizenship and the decentralization of Turkey's administrative system. Nonetheless, while the other opposition parties declared their negative vote to the package they deemed to be a government plot to control the judiciary, the BDP set preconditions to lend support to the package which it did not oppose 'in principle'. In exchange for its support, the BDP asked the revision of the Anti-Terror Law and the Penal Code to ensure the release of its members detained under the KCK case, the lowering of the 10 percent electoral threshold which precludes the Kurdish parties from entering into the national parliament and a fairer distribution of the Treasury's assistance to political parties. Upon the AKP's refusal to negotiate over these demands, the BDP bloc voted against the package, which failed to receive the two-thirds majority required to be adopted directly by the parliament and had therefore to be submitted to popular vote, and called on its constituencies to boycott the referendum held on 12 September 2010. Although the package was approved in the referendum, a significant portion of the electorate in the predominantly Kurdish provinces did not go to the ballots.[31]

Conclusion

In the ever globalized world of the 1990s, it had become increasingly difficult for the Turkish state to further its assimilationist and repressive policies against the Kurds. The ability of the Kurdish *diaspora* in Europe and the Kurdish activists in Turkey to bring to the world's attention the grave human rights abuses in the state of emergency region placed Turkey under international spotlight. The petitions that human rights lawyers filed with the ECtHR in the early 1990s displayed the state of terror reigning on civilians in the Kurdish region, galvanizing the international community, particularly in Europe, to put pressure on the Turkish state. With its declaration as an official candidate for EU membership, Turkey could no longer escape facing the Kurdish question and liberalizing its discriminatory policies. The twin goals of diminishing the number of unfavorable ECtHR judgments and sufficiently fulfilling the Copenhagen political criteria of the EU have made the liberalization of government policies on the Kurdish question inevitable. The challenge facing the AKP Government was and is to achieve these goals without compromising the official policies towards the Kurds.

The limited constitutional and legislative reforms adopted during the AKP's first term in government were followed and replaced in its second term by a political approach which emphasized discourse over concrete legal measures. While the legal framework in Turkey is still 'ethnic-blind' vis-à-vis the Kurds, politics no longer is, as evident in the AKP Government's new discourse based on brotherhood, and shared history and religion between the Turks and the Kurds. In a series of historical speeches, the Prime Minister made references to the Kurdish identity, history and culture; admitted the crimes the state had committed against the Kurds in the 1990s, explicitly referring to disappearances and extrajudicial killings; promised the Kurds equality and prosperity and addressed them in their mother tongue on the occasion of the launch of TRT 6. However, the progress did not bring a drastic overhaul of the official line on the Kurdish question or end the institutionalized state of exception against the Kurds. The state of emergency regime is *de facto* operative in the body of heavy penal courts with special powers which have jurisdiction over terrorism offences, there remain legal restrictions on the use of the Kurdish language in political life and thousands of Kurds are being prosecuted for their lawful political activities.

Even if the Government had been bold and daring in its 'Kurdish opening', however, mere legal reforms would have failed to restore the Kurds' faith in the state. The century-old experience with the republic has created a deep distrust among the Kurds vis-à-vis the state. Unlike in the 1990s, today, the Kurds' political demands go beyond and above the protection of their first generation rights. To feel themselves as true and equal citizens, Kurds demand constitutional reforms to ensure, as a matter of priority, mother tongue education in Kurdish and decentralization. The 'democratic autonomy' models proposed by various entities within the Kurdish political movement are based on the principle of self-rule. Proposing a radical restructuring of the political system based on the transfer of key competences from the center to the regions, the Kurds want the (BDP-run) municipalities to have exclusive mandate over, among others, health, education and social affairs.

A greater challenge to the state is the Kurds' demands for truth, justice and peace. The EU process has opened up a political space for the Kurds to express their demands more vocally and persistently. While the public discussion on the Kurdish question has not necessarily been free, as evident in the continuing restrictions on political speech, it has certainly been unstoppable. Perhaps the greatest cost of the EU process for the Turkish state has been the loss of its ability to dictate the 'truth' and subjugate the society to intimidation. In the past decade, the Kurds have started to speak up, to narrate their stories of state oppression and to claim justice and truth. Today, the Kurdish society is united in its demands for the prosecution of state officials who committed crimes against the Kurds, the excavation of mass burials to identify the whereabouts of their forcefully disappeared fellows and the establishment of truth commissions to look into state atrocities since 1980s. The Kurds' demand for peace is not only on the cessation of the armed conflict, but also on an amnesty to allow the return of the PKK militants dispersed in the mountains of the Kurdistan Regional Government, the Turkish prisons and in *diaspora*. In the eyes of the Kurds, an 'honorable' peaceful solution must provide all PKK militants, including their leader Abdullah Öcalan who has been in solitary confinement since 1999, the opportunity to reintegrate into society and to make politics through non-violent means.

After a century of oppression and denial, the Kurds, as never before, challenge the moral and political authority of the state in Turkey. Decades of legal and political resistance and armed fighting gave the Kurdish people the upper hand vis-à-vis the state. It is no longer the state that sets the agenda, but the Kurds who increase the stakes by the day. Conscious of their political power in the region and the moral supremacy of their position, the Kurds are determined to set the agenda of a possible solution to the conflict. With increasing persistence and clarity, the Kurdish political movement has made it clear that they would not accept as a solution any 'deal' which does not involve structural constitutional and legislative reforms. The government, on its part, is torn between its efforts to stay in tune with the status quo in order to preserve its power, its awareness of the need or developing a democratic solution to the Kurdish question and its determination not to lose political capital to the BDP by 'giving in' to the latter's demands. The interplay of political maneuvers by multiple political actors on the one hand and the Kurds' demands for equality, autonomy and justice on the other will set the direction of the events in the time to come.

Notes

1 The same region has also been the historical homeland of various other people, first and foremost the Armenians, Ezidis, Assyrians and Arabs, though most of these groups have nearly been diminished from these lands.

2 The first instance was the adoption of martial law through Law no. 785 of 3 March 1925 (*Takrir-i Sükûn Kanunu*) in the aftermath of the suppression of the Sheikh Said Rebellion. The most recent incident was the declaration in 1987 of a state of emergency in select provinces in the Kurdish region in the name of fighting against the PKK.

3 *Tunceli Vilayetinin İdaresi Hakkında Kanun* (Law on the Administration of the Province of Tunceli), no. 2884, 25 December 1935, Official Gazette, no. 3195, 2 January 1936.

4 The legal basis of the state of emergency regime was a 1983 law. *Olağanüstü Hal Kanunu* [State of Emergency Law], no. 2935, 25 October 1983, Official Gazette, no. 18204, 27 October 1983.

5 For a first hand account of the censorship in the mainstream Turkish media by journalists who covered the atrocities of the military in the Kurdish region, see Solmaz 2012.

6 During its short life between May 1992 and April 1994, a total of 27 reporters, editors and distributors of daily *Özgür Gündem* were killed in the Kurdish region. By the time the paper was suspended by court order in 1994, there was a case opened against 486 out of its 580 issues and its journalists and editors were sentenced to a total of 147 years of imprisonment (Aydemir 2011). For the striking story of the Diyarbakır office of the Kurdish daily *Özgür Gündem* in the 1990s, see Yılmaz 2010.

7 There are no reliable official statistics regarding the gross human rights violations committed during the state of emergency. The Ministry of Justice has reported that between 1987 and 2003, 1,248 killings by unidentified perpetrators were committed in the state of emergency region. Ministry of Justice, formal reply to the query of Mesut Değer, Diyarbakır deputy of the Republican People's Party, 23 May 2005. A special commission established by the Turkish Parliament found the number of such killings between 1975 and 1994 to be 908, most of which were committed in 1992 (316 killings) and 1993(314 killings). An independent project run by the Istanbul Bar Association during 1998–2002 continued the research of the parliamentary commission and identified the total number of killings by unidentified perpetrators between 1975 and 2000 to be 2,435. In general, murders whose perpetrators remain unidentified and disappearance under custody are being grouped under the same category. For figures regarding forced displacement, see below.

8 See for example, AİHM (1998), *Selçuk ve Asker Türkiye'ye Karşı*; AİHM (1997), *Menteş ve Diğerleri Türkiye'ye Karşı*; AİHM (1996), *Akdıvar ve Diğerleri Türkiye'ye Karşı*.

9 JİTEM had in its payroll military officers, PKK militant-turned-state informants and village guards.

10 See friendly settlement declarations issued by the Turkish government in ECtHR cases concerning village destructions. See e.g. ECtHR (2002), *Kınay ve Kınay Türkiye'ye Karşı*.

11 *İskân Kanunu* (Settlement Law), no. 885, 31 May 1926, Official Gazette, no. 409, 1 July 1926.

12 *İskân Kanunu* (Settlement Law), no. 2510, 14 June 1934, Official Gazette, no. 2733, 21 June 1934. According to Mesut Yeğen, both the letter and the implementation of the law shows its principal purpose to be the Turkification of Kurds

through resettling them in regions populated by the Turks or resettling Turks in regions populated by the Kurds (Yeğen 1999).

13 For more on the nature of the forced displacement of 1990s and government responses to it, see Kurban *et al.* 2007.

14 A government commissioned academic survey by Hacettepe University's Institute of Population Studies estimated the number of individuals displaced during the armed conflict between 1986 and 2005 to be between 950,000 and 1,200,000 (Hacettepe Nüfus Etütleri Enstitüsü 2006). However, the government has not adopted the official figures to the findings of the Hacettepe survey and continues to claim that the real number of the displaced ranges between 350,000 and 380,000.

15 In addition to this large group of displaced forcefully evicted by the state security forces and village guards, others were obliged to leave their homes due to lack of security arising from the armed conflict and/or inability to maintain a livelihood due to food embargos and bans on access to pastures imposed by the government. Finally, a third category of displaced persons are those who were forced by the PKK to migrate for refusing to cooperate with the PKK or for fighting on the side of the state against the PKK.

16 For findings of field research conducted in Diyarbakır, Batman and Hakkari regarding IDPs' access to assistance provided under KDRP, see Kurban *et al.* 2007.

17 Former Article 26.

18 Former Article 28.

19 *Türkçeden Başka Dillerde Yapılacak Yayınlar Hakkında Kanun* (Law on Broadcasting in Languages Other than Turkish), no. 2932, 19 October 1983, Official Gazette, no. 18199, 22 October 1983. This law was abolished in 1991 through the Anti-Terrorism Law no. 3713, removing the legal bans on the speaking of and broadcasting in Kurdish.

20 *Seçimlerin Temel Hükümleri ve Seçmen Kütükleri Hakkında Kanun ile Milletvekili Seçimi Kanununda Değişiklik Yapılmasına Dair Kanun* [Law on the Amendment of the Law on the Fundamental Provisions Governing Elections and Voter Registration and the Law on Members of the Parliament], no. 5980, 8 April 2010, Official Gazette, no. 27548, 10 April 2010, art. 7.

21 *Siyasi Partiler Kanunu* [Law on Political Parties], no. 2820, 22 April 1983, Official Gazette, no. 18027, 24 April 1983, art. 81(c).

22 In finding Turkey to have violated some of the most fundamental rights protected under the European Convention, the Court did not, however, address the petitioners' claims under Article 14 of the Convention that Turkey had a discriminatory policy of forced displacement targeting the Kurdish population.

23 However, in requiring Turkey to fulfill the minority protection conditionality for accession, the EU has never explicitly elaborated what exactly 'respect for and protection of minorities' entailed, and left a considerable room for discretion to the government in determining that. The ambiguity of the EU's Copenhagen criteria is of course not restricted to Turkey, but a general problem concerning its accession process.

24 Making it no longer possible to close parties solely on the basis of their programs and requiring the consideration of sanctions short of dissolution, such as withdrawal of public funding. This was followed by an amendment to the Law on Political Parties in 2003 which required qualified (rather than simple) majority vote by the Constitutional Court for the dissolution of a political party.

25 *Terör ve Terörle Mücadeleden Doğan Zararların Karşılanması Hakkında Kanun* [Law on Compensation for Losses Resulting from Terrorism and the Fight against Terrorism], no. 5233, 17 July 2004, Official Gazette, no. 25535, 27 July 2004.

26 *Çeşitli Kanunlarda Değişiklik Yapılmasına İlişkin Kanun* [Law on the Amendment of Various Laws], no. 4771, 3 August 2002, Official Gazette no. 24841, 9 August 2002.
27 The EU's ambivalent approach and the increasing opposition of various EU member states to Turkey's accession also played a role in diminishing the political will and ability of the AKP Government to further the reform process.
28 The first public protests where Kurdish minors participated in mass numbers took place on 28–29 March 2006 in Diyarbakır in the aftermath of the funeral of 14 PKK fighters who were killed by security forces. The police used disproportionate power against civilians who demonstrated on the streets after the funeral, killing 10 civilians, including minors. The incidents sparked mass riots in the region and expedited the adoption on 29 June 2006 of amendments to the Anti-Terrorism Law which had been pending before the parliament. In 2006 alone, 295 minors were taken into custody in 27 provinces across Turkey on the ground of having committed 'crimes of terrorism' and 719 minors were prosecuted by heavy penal courts with special powers. In 2007, the latter number increased to 869 (UNICEF 2010: 6).
29 The government subsequently changed the name of the initiative first to 'The Democratic Opening' and finally to 'The National Unity and Brotherhood Project'.
30 In reality, there are a number of interrelated but separate cases. The prosecutorial investigation against the suspects started in May 2007. Yet, the first police operation was carried out on 14 April 2009, followed by others in 2009 and early 2010, resulting in the apprehension of thousands of suspects and the detention of hundreds. It was only on 9 June 2010, when the indictment was issued, that defendants were formally informed of the charges against them. As of October 2010, there were ten separate but related KCK cases in the following provinces: Diyarbakır (hosting the principal KCK case), Batman (hosting two separate cases), Şırnak, Mardin, Van, Adana (hosting two separate cases), Mersin and Gaziantep. In Kars and Siirt, the KCK investigations did not yet result in the launching of a legal case. Information based on the legal brief presented by defendants' counsel to the Diyarbakır Sixth Heavy Penal Court with Special Powers, 18 October 2010.
31 The turnout rate in some of the Kurdish cities was as follows: Hakkari, 9,1 percent; Diyarbakır, 35,2 percent; Batman, 40,3 percent; Şırnak, 22,5 percent; Van, 43,6 percent. The nationwide turnout average was 77,4 percent.

References

——(2006) *Müstakbel Türk'ten Sözde Vatandaşa: Cumhuriyet ve Kürtler* (From Prospective Turk to So-Called Citizen), İstanbul: İletişim Yayınları.
—— (2007) *A Quest for Equality: Minority Rights in Turkey*, London: Minority Rights Group International. Online. Available: <http://www.bianet.org/files/doc_files/000/000/105/original/kitap_tamamı.pdf> (accessed 14 February 2013). Online. Available HTTP: <http://www.hips.hacettepe.edu.tr/tgyona/TGYONA_rapor.pdf> (accessed 14 February 2013).
Aydemir, Ş. (2011) 'İki yılda 27 çalışanı öldürüldü', *Radikal*, 18 March. Online. Available: <http://www.radikal.com.tr/Radikal.aspx?aType=RadikalDetayV3&ArticleID=1043304& CategoryID = 82> (accessed 14 February 2013)
Balzacq, T. and Ensaroğlu, Y. (2008) *Human Rights and Security: Turkey, England and France*, Istanbul: TESEV Publications.
Hacettepe Nüfus Etütleri Enstitüsü (2006) *Türkiye'de Göç ve Yerinden Olmuş Nüfus Araştırması* (Turkey Migration and Internally Displaced Population Survey), Ankara: Hacettepe Üniversitesi.

360   *Dilek Kurban*

Jongerden, J. (2007) *The Settlement Issue in Turkey and the Kurds: An Analysis of Spatial Policies, Modernity and War*, Leiden: Brill.

Kurban, D. (2006) 'Unraveling a Trade-off: Reconciling Minority Rights and Full Citizenship in Turkey', *European Yearbook of Minority Issues*, vol.4, 2004/5: 341–72.

Kurban, D. and Gülalp, H. (2012) 'A Complicated Affair-the Court and the Kurds: The Role of the European Court of Human Rights in the Broadening of Kurdish Rights in Turkey,' in Anagnostou, D. (ed.) *Domesticating the European Court of Human Rights: Implementation, Legal Mobilization and Policy Reform*, Edinburgh: Edinburgh University Press.

Kurban, D., Yükseker, D., Çelik, A.B., Ünalan, T. and Aker, A.T. (2007) *Coming to Terms with Forced Migration: Post-Displacement Restitution of Citizenship Rights in Turkey*, Istanbul: TESEV Publications, 119–44. Online. Available HTTP: <http://www.tesev.org.tr/Upload/Publication/9327b591-52c8-4392-8dc2-821a2c1a764a/zgo-c_yuzlesmek_ENG_kitap_24_10_08_pdf.pdf> (accessed 14 February 2013).

Kurdish Human Rights Project (2002) *Ülke İçinde Göç Ettirilen İnsanlar: Türkiye'deki Kürtler*, London: Kurdish Human Rights Publications.

McDowall, D. (1996) *A Modern History of the Kurds*, New York: I.B. Tauris.

Solmaz, S. (2012) *Savaşın Tanıkları Gazeteciler Anlatıyor* (Witnesses of War: Journalists Narrate). Documentary.

Taşpınar, Ö. (2005) *Kurdish Nationalism and Political Islam in Turkey: Kemalist Identity in Transition*, New York: Routledge.

Tekeli, İ. (1990) 'Osmanlı İmparatorluğu'ndan Günümüze Nüfusun Zorunlu Yer Değiştirmesi' [The Forced Relocation of Populations from the Ottoman Empire to Present Day], *Toplum ve Bilim*, 50: 49–71.

Türkiye Büyük Millet Meclisi (1998) *Doğu ve Güneydoğu Anadolu'da Boşaltılan Yerleşim Birimleri Nedeniyle Göç Eden Yurttaşlarımızın Sorunlarının Araştırılarak Alınması Gereken Tedbirlerin Tespit Edilmesi Amacıyla Kurulan Meclis Araştırma Komisyonu Raporu* [Report by the Parliament Research Commission Formed with the Objective of Researching the Problems of Citizens in Eastern and Southeastern Anatolia who Migrated because their Places of Settlement were Evacuated, and of Establishing the Necessary Measures], *Tutanak Dergisi* 53, vol: 20.

Türkiye İnsan Hakları Vakfı (1995) *İnsan Hakları Raporu-1995*, İstanbul: Türkiye İnsan Hakları Vakfı Yayınları.

UNICEF (2010) *Gösterilere Katılmaları Sebebi ile Terör Suçlusu Sayılan Çocuklar Hakkında Saha Ziyareti Raporu* [Field Visit Report on Children Deemed to be Terrorist Offenders for Participating in Demonstrations].

United States Committee for Refugees (1999) *The Wall of Denial: Internal Displacement in Turkey*, Washington, D.C.: United States Committee for Refugees.

Yeğen, M. (1999) *Devlet Söyleminde Kürt Sorunu* (The Kurdish Question in State Discourse), İstanbul: İletişim Yayınları.

Yılmaz, S. (2010) *Press*. Documentary.

19 Non-muslim minorities in the Turkish democratization process

Samim Akgönül

Introduction

According to the commonly accepted nationalist paradigm, minorities do not form part of the unity that nations aspire to. In a way, their existence runs counter to the supposed will of the nation and their very existence is tolerated but not accepted by the majority. While the nineteenth-century nationalist dream of a so-called pure nation seems to have resurfaced in the twenty-first century, this dream has become nearly impossible to achieve in Europe, for at least three reasons. First, the progressive denationalization of governance has imposed the transfer of sovereignty to supranational political, cultural and economic structures. Second, access to transportation, although it exposes the huge and persistent gap in wealth between North and South, has empowered transnational communities. Third, there has been a shift towards micro or autonomous entities (e.g. regions, federate entities, Euroregions), which has promoted the ongoing creation and reshaping of entities within the nation. Thus, the democratization process of a country, especially in the case of Turkey, can be seen in its attitude towards minorities. The treatment of minorities becomes a measure of the degree of democratization.

The vague concept of democratization is difficult to define. The process of political modernization as suggested by Lucian Pye proposes (Pye 1966:45):

1 A general inclination towards equality, which allows participation in politics and competition for government office;
2 The capacity of a political system to formulate policies and to have them carried out;
3 Differentiation and specialization of political functions, though not at the expense of their overall integration; and
4 The secularization of the political process, separation of politics from religious aims and influence.

Under these considerations, the long road to democratization in Turkey seems like a liberalization process of the Turkish political system from

Ottoman societal rules. Briefly, it must be seen as an attempt to guarantee the supremacy of politics over society's will. While the Ottoman societal system was based on religious and ethno-religious divisions (the *millet* system),[1] the formulation of a new type of politics in the recently established Republic of Turkey principally built a new imagined community called a nation where affiliation was individual and not collective. Thus, the one and a half century-long Turkish democratization process has not been a political process per se (i.e. the authoritarian character of the regime has been protected), but a societal one where the first aim is to erase differences throughout the society, especially religious ones. Paradoxically, this forced homogenization has failed, creating resistance and improving, by reaction, democratization by means of civil society. This chapter aims to analyze the Turkish nation-state building process and the place of minorities, the development of a pluralist democracy with minority policies and the role of minorities in Turkish democracy during globalization.

The nation-state building process and minorities

All political systems are built in opposition to the previous one. To be able to understand the place and role of religious minorities in the democratization process in Turkey, one must remember that the first aim of the Kemalists at the beginning of the twentieth century was not to build a democratic system but to create as homogeneous a nation as possible from the ashes of the Ottoman society. Thus, the Turkish state was not built by the Turkish nation but rather built in order to construct a new nation. In addition, the political system of modern Turkey was not configured in an opposition of 'authoritarian monarchy versus democracy', but in an opposition of 'monarchy plus imperialism versus authoritarian republic'. Consequently, the political system in Turkey, with all its components including democracy, has always been a tool to keep and protect the national question. This question leads to the nation-building process in Turkey and, consequently, to the issue of what is called 'Turkishness'.

The period of building the nation-state took less time than the nation-building itself and witnessed the dismantling of a 500-year-old empire and the founding of a new state in the form of a secular republic in which the ultimate power would remain in the hands of an undetermined Turkish elite. This tour de force was made possible by forging an authoritarian bureaucratic elite not based on any powerful social group. The political dominance of the bureaucrats was kept intact and the pre-revolutionary distribution of power remained more or less the same. The only difference compared to the nineteenth century was the Turkish and civil secular character of the new leading class.

The defeat of the Ottoman Empire, the fierce War of Independence and the collaboration of the sultan/caliph with the occupying forces led, astonishingly quickly, to the total dissolution of all institutions belonging to the past. The ongoing ideological controversy between Islamism, Ottomanism and Turkism during the decline of the empire gave rise to a synthesis of the three, where the nation had to be Turkish, but with an invisible tie to Islam. The indivisibility of the nation was reasserted on every occasion.

Clearly, the indivisible identification of Turkishness cannot be analyzed without placing it in a more general context: the birth of nations and consequently of nation-states. The thesis of the modernity of the concept of nation is well known, Deutch (Deutch 1953), Gellner (Gellner 1989), Hobsbawm (Hobsbawm 1992) and Schnapper, (Schnapper 1994) propose the concomitance of national construction and the creation of political organizations. In both cases, one can easily talk about the nineteenth century as a century of nations. Indeed, it was during this century, especially during the second half, that the Turkish nation began to be built and adapted to the political system.

The question of the definition of a nation brings forth the definition of a minority. Who are the individuals living surrounded by a nation and forming a distinct group? If, according to Emile Giraud, we consider that in order to form a nation it is necessary for the individuals to 'have the same origin, to speak the same language, to have received the same moral and intellectual heritage, to have lived under the same laws and to have known the same joys and the same pains' (Giraud 1924: 8), what do we do about the individuals who do not share one or more of these criteria? We have to consider them as belonging to the group known as minorities. Thus, all the attempts to define this concept start from a negative definition, i.e. finding a definition of the nation, taking those who do not tally there, and putting them in the category of minority. The minority is then inseparable from the majority. In this context of coercive nation-states, where there is no nation, there are no minorities. Given the fact that in empires, and, *a fortiori*, in the Ottoman Empire, one cannot speak of a nation, it would make no sense to speak of minorities.

The problem of minorities appeared in the nineteenth century with the emergence of the concept of the nation-state (Thornberry 1991:25 *et passim*). In international law, the first case of attributing the title of nation to a distinct group within a nation-state took place at the Congress of Vienna in 1815, when the Polish right of national representation and right to establish their own national institutions was recognized (Öktem 1996–97: 62). But it was not until a century later that the term minority appeared, when the United Kingdom addressed a note to Greece in 1914 about the protection of Muslim minorities on its territory. Indeed, in a very few happy cases, the state and the nation emerged in a spontaneous and synchronic way in a country (Öktem 1996–97: 60). However, if the state was preceded by the emergence of the nation, wars of independence took place, which were often seen as rebellions by the dominating power. To conclude these wars of independence, the leaders needed to unify their lands, and the cement of this unification was nationalism.

Within the territories of the created state, distinct groups always remained, who the founders of the nation-state always considered as different. In addition to the majority in that given nation-state, there were minority members. In the nationalist paradigm the difference is interiorized both by the majority and the minority. Therefore, the matter of perception and of self-perception is encountered at the same time.

If the state was established before the nation, then this nation had to be built. In other words, it was necessary for the already founded state to correspond to a so-called pure nation that was as homogeneous as possible. Again, the main ideology of this construction is nationalism. Thus, for those who did not correspond to the definition of this pure nation, four alternatives could be applied:

- Eliminate them physically by means of extermination, expulsion, exile or population exchange;
- Try to divide the group in order to create sub-groups, if possible antagonistic ones for better control;
- Try to meld the group into the nation by imposing a dominant language, a dominant religion and/or a dominant culture, i.e. forced assimilation;
- Accept the minority as is and encourage it with a series of rights, in order to attach it definitively to the state (multiculturalism).

The last choice of the four led to a series of agreements, treaties, legislative acts, and other various manoeuvres, all of which comprised the bases of what is known as a 'regime of minorities' in international law. Minorities in the Turkish Republic

These theories establish the bases for a more specific discussion of the Turkish case at the turn of the twentieth century. The political and legal framework was that of an empire, but not a colonial one in the sense of Western European empires, where colonial possessions were remote and more or less preserved their cultural and ethnic characteristics. In the eighteenth and even the nineteenth centuries, the Ottoman Empire's centre of gravity was the Aegean Sea. On the three shores and in the middle of this sea (islands, especially Crete), the population was religiously mixed while the way of life or the culture was shared. Cretan Muslims for example, spoke the same language, listened to the same music, ate the same local foods, etc.

Thus the modernization of Turkish politics first required a homogenization based on religious belonging (neither belief nor practice) and not on a cultural level. After the Armenian massacres and exile in 1915, the compulsory exchange of populations between Greece and Turkey determined in January 1923 was exceptional in its compulsory nature. The exchange convention had legitimated a *de facto* situation since 1920: the mass escape of the Greek Orthodox populations from Western Asia Minor. But by including groups such as the Turkish-speaking Christians of Cappadocia or the

Greek-speaking Muslims of Crete in this exchange, the two countries clearly showed their understanding of the 'unmixing of populations' (the expression comes from Dr. Nansen, Aktar A. 2005: 61): The Turkish nation would be modern with a westernized visibility, but it would be Muslim.

The Turkish nation-building process in the first two decades of the twentieth century was not complete (there is, of course, no such thing as a complete homogenization process). Thus, the very much desired homogenization could not be carried out. In 1923, apart from the Turkish Sunni Muslims, four groups remained as obstacles to building this modern homogeneous nation:

- Some ethnically non-Turkish Muslim populations such as Bosnians, Laz, Circassians and Greek Muslims came into Anatolia during the nineteenth century or after the compulsory exchange. These groups were the main object of linguistic and national assimilation policies during the first decades of the republic. These policies succeeded in making these populations, in the words of some, 'more Turkish than the Turks';
- The Alevis supported the nation-building process in addition to the Sunni character of the new nation, mainly because the Kemalists were trying to establish a 'secular' system where the Sunnis would be under state control;
- The Kurds, who are ethnically different, for the most part belong to Sunni Islam although some are aligned with the Alevis. They are the main group that resisted assimilation. This ethnic and violent resistance may reveal that the first criterion of Turkishness, i.e., belonging to Islam, has its limits.
- Finally, despite the ethno-religious cleansing of the first two decades of the twentieth century, marginal non-Muslim groups have remained, especially in Istanbul but also in Thrace (rural Jews) and Southeastern Anatolia.

The presence of non-Muslim Turkish citizens on the margins of the Turkish nation was institutionalized by the Lausanne Treaty of 1923.[2] The main group, formed by the Istanbul Greeks, remained as *établis* (established) and had Turkish citizenship. At the beginning of the Lausanne negotiations in 1923, the Turkish delegation opposed the maintenance of a Greek population in Turkey, which was seen as a main obstacle to the homogenization of the population (Meray 1973: 121). In his memoirs, Ismet Pasha recalls how he had to yield to the insistence of Eleftherios Venizelos and George Curzon on the question of this maintenance, which went along with the maintenance of the patriarchate (İnönü 1987: 133–132). Indeed this was the real question. What could have been important for Greece and for part of the Western powers about maintaining a Greek community in Turkey, and, more so, the patriarchate? (Arı 1995: 17). For the Turks, the starting point of the negotiations was to exempt the Muslims living in western Thrace from the exchange, but to integrate the Istanbul Greeks and especially the patriarchate. Finally, as a compromise solution, both communities remained in a reciprocal way (Akgönül 2006: 3–17), the word reciprocal being key here.

Thus the Istanbul Greeks, at least those who had lived there since 1918, had the right to be *établi*,[3] forming a material justification for the maintenance of the patriarchate. Upon the insistence of Western powers, the Turkish delegation agreed to maintain it as long as it remained a purely religious institution. For the patriarchate, dealing with the internal religious affairs in Turkey required a consistent Orthodox community. Besides the Istanbul Greeks, two other communities were exempt from exchange. The small Orthodox community on the two islands situated at the entry of the Dardanelles Strait, Imvros and Tenedos, also obtained this right under more complicated circumstances. The problem lay in the fact that other non-Muslim groups such as Armenians and Jews were also subject to coercive policies in the framework of this reciprocity despite their lack of links with Greece.

Under these circumstances, the democratization of Turkey in the 1930s was seen as dangerous by the founders of the republic for three main reasons. A democratic opening could reinforce:

- Muslim believers who supported the Sultan because he was the Caliph;
- Kurds who supported the national struggle expecting autonomy, although this claim would be crushed violently after 1925;
- non-Muslim minorities considered potential traitors.

All three groups were under pressure from the Turkish bureaucratic and military elite to be removed from power. Therefore, non-Muslim groups were placed sociologically in what could be called a double minority position. A minority does not emerge *sui generis*. Two simultaneous processes have to take place in order for a group to be qualified as a minority. The first is a quantitative process. A group is either diminished through massacres, exiles, population exchanges, etc. or the group flees from a country due to economic and political conditions as well as ethnic persecution, finding itself a minority in the host country. The second is a qualitative process.[4] The majority, i.e. the group that considers itself the legitimate ruler of a territory, marginalizes non-dominant groups. The majority constantly expects proof of the loyalty of the minority so the minority is put in the position of constantly having to prove it belongs to the nation without ever having that belonging affirmed (Rabinowitz 2001: 64–65). A minority comes into existence with the combination of these two processes, as was the case in Turkey. In nation-states, multiculturalism is regarded as potentially destabilizing. Thus, the exclusion of the minority becomes a vital component of the majority's own existence. In this respect, the 'other' that emerged within the context of the nineteenth-century continues to have implications for the twenty-first century. Groups such as Turkey's non-Muslims, who feel threatened as groups, stick all the more to their characteristics, thus creating what could be termed an inflation of identity. This identity inflation is necessary to keep and reinforce the feeling of otherness. Because the Turkish nation needed this otherness to define itself and to maintain (as much as the groups in a minority position) a kind of jealousy of membership, it used otherness to avoid disintegration, agitating the spectrum of supposed acculturation. The result was an identity spiral in which the nationalist paradigm, like monotheist religions, refuses dual membership. In this vision of the world, one cannot be at the same time non-Muslim and Turkish in spite of an undeniable common way of life and common so-called culture.

This otherness has a double effect in the nation-making process and therefore in the reinforcement of the feeling of membership or non-membership. When the Turks think about the 'Greek' or the 'Armenian', they see the 'other', the different one, threatening the very existence of the Turkish nation itself. However, even if this otherness is necessary for sincere (or instrumentalist) nationalists of both groups, it becomes problematic when it is applied to minorities. When speaking of an enemy, one speaks of a distant person; therefore it is impossible to verify the supposed difference. In the case of minorities assimilated to the otherness of the enemy, the entire set of characteristics imputed to the group is verifiable in everyday life. This situation leads to a reaction of marginalization on behalf of the dominating group. The majority is under constant demand to allow members of the minorities to join them, but when those people abandon their group to approach the majority in a highly visible way (by abandoning their religious practices, by using the language of the majority, participating in mixed marriages, adopting ideological attitudes that conform with those of the majority, etc.), this same majority takes refuge behind the most rigid aspects of its identity. Fearing the dilution of the group, they create an otherness of proximity that is even stronger than the distant otherness. The individuals or groups in these situations are thus doubly marginalized, by the majority group because public opinion doubts their sincerity and prefers them to belong to the different group, but also by the minority because, by betraying their original identity, they threaten the existence of the group.

Minority policies in the democratization process: exclusion from the national life

Throughout the history of the Turkish Republic, minority policies have formed a double movement, seemingly contradictory but quite common in majority and minority relations in other contexts as well. This double movement can be summarized in a few words: the dominant majority constantly requires signs of loyalty from the minority, but the very same majority never accepts or considers these pledges sufficient.

This double movement is embodied on the one hand in sociological and political marginalization and the permanent exclusion from the idea of

Turkishness. On the other hand, it manifests itself in a policy of assimilation, especially towards other ethnically non-Turkish Muslims. The aim of these minority policies is to 'Turkify' all Muslims and to make all non-Muslims invisible.

In this dialectic between exclusion and assimilation, tensions have arisen whenever there is a societal crisis in Turkey, during bilateral disputes with the country where the minority is close (Greece, Armenia, Israel) or in a generally difficult international situation (the Cold War, European integration process, etc.). Sometimes these tensions become repressive policies. This applies to the Second-World-War period, when Turkey was not a part of the war but suffered from the economic and political influences of the belligerents. During these five years, harassment policies such as taxes on capital and unarmed military service were applied to visible minorities.

Similarly, during the 1950s and 1960s, with the deterioration of Greek-Turkish relations in the context of the Cyprus dispute, a whole series of events marked the history of Turkish non-Muslims, especially Greeks, such as the events of 6–7 September 1955 and the expulsion of Greek nationals in 1964.[5]

On the other hand, the situation of minorities improves in times of bilateral or international détente, which shows that they are considered and treated as if they were external to the Turkish nation, while at the same time Turkish nationals. The frequent use of the concept of *içerdeki Yabancılar*, i.e. internal foreigners, is due to that very view.

New political claims

In the ongoing construction of the Turkish nation and its effect on minorities, the 1990s brought an upheaval. This radical turnover was due to:

- The complete restructuring of the regional situation;
- (Re)awakenings of particular identities in Turkey as well as in the Balkans and the Middle East;
- The democratization of Turkey, which allowed more open and stronger expressions of identity claims.

Throughout the Cold War period, political and ideological confrontations between the two blocs were somehow able to conceal other types of otherness. The temporary loss of ideological rivalries contributed to the creation of new types of otherness or the reactivation of old ones, reinforcing ethnic and especially religious enmities. The Yugoslavian war crisis and the Caucasian conflicts are some of the examples.

These new cleavages had multiple consequences for the Turkish nation-building process and for the idea of Turkishness at two levels: ethnic and religious. At the ethnicity level, participating in Turkishness took on a new meaning beginning in the 1990s, when the Turkic groups that were inaccessible for decades became suddenly tangible. Thus, not only were the Turkish/Muslim minorities of the Balkans and the Caucasus fully integrated into the imagined Turkish world, but the Turkic republics of Central Asia also attracted the attention of policymakers and entrepreneurs in Turkey. Quickly, the horizon of Turkishness expanded spectacularly with the concept of *Dış Türkler*, i.e. external Turks. This ethnicization of the national membership inevitably had important consequences within Turkey: the exclusion of non-Turkish ethnic groups, especially the Kurds, who had started to rediscover their ethnic identity in the second half of the 1980s. The tension between Kurds and Turks turned into an armed struggle that has intensified with this ethnicization of Turkishness. Nevertheless, the significance of minority status was and is so pejorative in the Turkish context that the Kurds never claimed it. The most radical Kurds fought for autonomy, while others claimed the title of what they called 'co-founding people'.

Another cleavage appeared during the same period between the Sunnis and the Alevis. Alevism is the second largest religion in the country, estimated to have 12 to 15 million followers. The external perception is not completely identical to the internal perception insofar as a great number of Alevis in Turkey consider themselves Muslim. Thus, like other current religious persuasions in Turkey, it would be wrong to see the Alevis as monolithic in both practical and doctrinal terms. Indeed, Alevism refers to mutated heterogeneous belief systems as well as to disparate practices that vary across groups and over time (Zarcone 2004: 297).

Since the 1990s, the Alevis in Turkey have been in a process of legitimation vis-à-vis the overall Turkish society and the government. Indeed, after having been despised under Sunni Ottoman rule, the Alevis have been able to enjoy secularist Kemalist Turkey since the authority attempted to relegate religion to the private sphere. Thus, the Alevi vote is often Kemalist and secular. Since the revival of religious identities in Turkey, starting with the Sunni identity in the 1980s, Alevi identity has also begun to take on a more confessional meaning. These two religious identities have created tensions between the Alevis and Sunnis but also between the Alevis and the state. Sometimes, these tensions have resulted in physical violence, as was the case in 1993 in Sivas where Sunnis attacked and killed Alevis gathered in a hotel for a cultural festival.

The Alevis are now divided about the strategy to follow in a process of public and official recognition of Alevism in a more democratic Turkey, especially in the process of European integration, with relatively greater religious freedom. A number of Alevi NGOs claim this recognition on at least three levels:

• The possibility of no longer being treated as Sunnis during compulsory religious instruction at schools. A breakthrough has occurred in this area since, at least in some cases, these courses are no longer confined to Sunni-Hanafism but include some history of Ali as well. By contrast Alevi students are still not exempt from these courses.

- The ability to write Alevi in the religious affiliation section of identity cards. There has been a recent development here; since a decree published in the Official Gazette of 23 October 2006, it is now possible to leave this blank or change the word to Islam.
- And finally and most importantly, a number of Alevis are demanding state subsidies from the Directorate of Religious Affairs, which reports directly to the prime minister and which funds all Sunnis. Other Alevi leaders, on the contrary, are refusing public funding, which they consider equivalent to state control.

Non-Muslims: Fewer but audible

For non-Muslims in the same process of democratization and the development of liberal views in public opinion, a number of cyclical changes have been observed during the last two decades. Discussions on non-Muslims, who could betray Turkey, still exist, of course. But this debate is sometimes modulated by another, more concrete, more realistic and sometimes even more humanistic one.

Three main non-Muslim communities (Greeks, Armenians and Jews) are, again, at the centre of the more or less controversial public debates. However, compared to the 1950s or 1960s, one can see a plurality of views rarely observed before, especially in the direct participation of stakeholders, i.e. the minorities themselves.

Above all, the common problem with these three minorities concerns the properties belonging to religious foundations. These foundations form the pillars of minority institutions from not only a religious perspective, but a symbolic and financial one as well. These institutions were harassed throughout the 1970s and 1980s and even in the 1990s. They were banned from acquiring new properties, including through donation, and other properties that had been acquired since 1936 were expropriated. The legal changes of the last decade have resulted in a more flexible situation. But the problem remains that non-Muslim non-laic foundations are still classified in a category separate from other Muslim foundations and are therefore subject to special treatment. However, on this point, conflicting dynamics are complicating this development.

On the one hand, pressure from the European Union focused on this issue irritates nationalist circles which see evidence that the West is trying to disintegrate the unity of the Turkish Republic. Nationalists draw attention to similarities with the period of disintegration of the Ottoman Empire when Western powers are considered to have destroyed the empire using non-Muslim groups. The minorities themselves are no longer silent either, but defend their rights in public spaces and are being heard, particularly by democrats and the liberal left. This dynamic inevitably creates tension.

The specific situation for each of the three groups can be summarized as follows.

The small Greek Orthodox minority (over 100,000 in 1923, nearly 5,000 in 2010) has problems in two distinct categories. First, there are concrete problems related to everyday life such as the issue of minority schools, textbooks and the personal property of Greek citizens expelled in 1964. Almost all of these problems are due to the negative and restrictive interpretation of the principle of reciprocity established by Article 45 of the Treaty of Lausanne. This article, interpreted as the reciprocity of two minorities, actually refers to the 'mutual obligations' of two states towards their own nationals, i.e. the reciprocity is not between two minorities, but between the two states in giving the usual citizenship rights to their nationals, including minority members. Second, there is a complex situation regarding the status of the Greek Orthodox patriarchate, which remained in Istanbul in 1923, is considered a local church by the Turkish authorities and which plays an undeniable role on the international and ecumenical level. Turkish public opinion in this case agrees with the state, believing that this internationalization is harmful to national interests.

In the same context, since 1971, the Orthodox Church in Turkey no longer has a theological school in which to educate the ministers necessary for religious practice. The reopening of the Halki Theological School (on an island near Istanbul) was the subject of intense debate in both Turkish public opinion and in terms of Turkey's relations with the EU and the United States. As of 2011, despite many promises, the Halki theological school was still closed.

The Armenian minority in Turkey suffers in a complex international environment. This minority of approximately 50,000 members, mostly living in Istanbul, carries the memory of the 1915 massacres, qualified as genocide by some Western states. Due to this qualification, Armenians feels trapped during every Turkish-European crisis because they are targeted, especially by the mainstream media but also by Turkish political leaders. For Turkish public opinion, there is no difference between Armenians of Turkey (Turkish citizens), of Armenia, and of the *diaspora*.

Furthermore, - relations between Turkey and Armenia complicate links between the Armenians of Turkey and the Armenians of Armenia. The Nagorno-Karabakh conflict between Azerbaijan and Armenia also continues to poison relations. But, via a newspaper that belongs to the Turkish minority, *Agos*, and its figurehead, Hrant Dink, Turkish mainstream public opinion has been informed of the existential and practical problems of this minority. Many Turkish intellectuals have rallied to the cause of the Armenian minority through the dynamism created by *Agos*. In the first decade of this century, Hrant Dink became one of the most followed and prominent intellectual figures in contemporary Turkey until his assassination in January 2007. This murder, followed by a spectacular funeral, can be seen as an electroshock for Turkish public opinion. As of that murder, thanks to Dink's courageous position, Armenians in Turkey can express themselves more openly. Specific demands are concentrated on the election of a new

Armenian patriarch and on the status of Armenian foundations but more generally against the negative image of Armenians in the country and the associated hate speech in the media.

Turkish Jews, mostly descendants of the Sephardic Jewish community expelled from Spain in the fifteenth century, form a small minority of approximately 30,000 members. However, this minority, and especially its elites, presented a very close position to the official Turkish view, as seen in its newspaper *Salom*, at least until the recent clash between Turkey and Israel in 2009. Since this clash, which is related to the Palestinian issue, a two-directional change has occurred. On the one hand, Turkish public opinion supports the Palestinian cause more and more openly (this is also expressed by the political powers that be). This new situation has given rise to an anti-Semitic discourse that is freely expressed. On the other hand, several voices from the minority have challenged the usual view of a minority that is happy and grateful to Turkey. Some Turkish-Jewish circles have claimed that history has been rewritten, in part to confront the historical realities of the treatment of the Jewish community, especially in the 1930s and 1940s. However, Jews have also suffered from the anti-Semitic discourse of the mainstream media.

Therefore, during the democratization process, it is possible to perceive three kinds of transformations for the three minorities at the discursive level:

- Minorities now appear as actors in the deep societal changes that Turkey is undergoing;
- Turkish public opinion has varied attitudes towards non-Muslim minorities ranging from racist hostility to indifference or solidarity, which was not the case until the 1990s;
- Public policies have taken tentative steps towards these minorities, partly under European pressure.

Conclusion

The transformation of Turkish society and changes in perceptions and self-perceptions show that Turkish democratization is taking new steps. This period is characterized by a tension between blurred identifications. These identification currents can be described as either exclusivist, supporting a rigid definition of Turkishness often based on language, religion, Turkish culture and attachment to Central Asian and Ottoman origins, or inclusivist, which relinquishes the ethnic meaning of Turkishness and supports a national identity based on territory that can encompass all ethno-religious components, such as the Kurds and Alevis but also non-Muslim minorities (Oran 2005: 131 *et passim*).

Since 1999, the third phase of the Europeanization of Turkey (the first one was in 1920s, the second in the 1950s) has brought new perspectives to Turkish identity as well as to the Turkish political system. In the Ottoman

Table 19.1 Four phases of democratization in Turkey and identity issues

	Ottoman Empire	*1920s Foundation of a nation-state*	*1950s Participation in Western structures (NATO, Council of Europe)*	*2000s Process of integration into the European Union*
Political system	Semi-feudal empire	Monist nation-state / single party	Monist nation-state / political plurality	Pluralist democratic state
Status of the individual	Subject / Protected	Compulsory Turkishness (ethno-religious cleansing and assimilation)	Compulsory citizenship in the Turkish state	Voluntary citizenship in a European candidate / member state
Status of the community	Muslim millet (dominant nation) / non-Muslim millets (dominated / protected nations)	Turkish nation (homogeneous, secular and coercive)	Turkish nation (homogeneous, secular and coercive)	Voluntary membership in many groups (political, ethnic, religious, professional, gender, ideological, etc.)
Identity	Religious (collective)	Ethno-religious (collective)	Ethnic, religious and political (collective)	Individual

system, an individual belonged first to his/her *millet* and then to the Empire, at least until the Tanzimat period. In the Turkish Republic, being Turkish became a requirement for direct links with the state. The European view focuses more on the individual than on the state. Thus, it is possible for Europeanization to create a new definition of Turkishness, related more to the individual will to participate in a democratic and public life than to ethno-religious belonging.

In contrast, a new situation is undermining this phase of democratization, which was intended to ease tensions and create a new national unity that respects the particularities of each component. During the 1970s, the main cleavages that created violent tensions were political and ideological. It is this climate of violence that led Turkey to be trapped in the destabilizing military regime of the 1980s established after the coup of 12 September 1980. The second half of 1980s and first half of the 1990s depoliticized the masses, and tensions have turned into ethnic conflicts, especially with the Kurdish question. This racialization of social relations continues, but is gradually being replaced by a new divide which is religious this time. From the mid-1990s on, the interpretation of all economic or social problems became increasingly religiously oriented. This new view has created a growing opposition between groups, not between Muslims and non-Muslims, or between believers and nonbelievers, but between the defenders of an increased role of religion in political orientations and socialization on the one hand and those who want to confine religion to the private sphere as in Western secularized societies, by coercive policies if necessary, on the other. It is through this new phase of identity between individualization and social communitarization that Turkish democratization must pass.

Notes

1 In the dynamic Ottoman *millet system*, society was divided according to religious affiliation. Muslims, despite the fact that different religious orders were categorized under the label of *Islam milleti*, was the dominant one in the society. Non-Muslims (*Zimmi* or 'protected') had autonomy but also an inferior position under Islamic law.
2 A former Turkish diplomat, who reflects the official view of the presence of non-Muslim minorities in Turkey perfectly, qualifies the presence of these minorities and rights granted as 'debts', (Akşin 1991:134).
3 On the debates concerning the qualification of *établis*, see, Ari. (1995), p. 18, Gönlübol (1982): 56–57, Erim (1944): 62–73.
4 The distinction between quantitative and qualitative processes has been elaborated by Serge Moscovici who, following Max Weber, introduced a concept of domination as the essential element to qualify a group as a minority (Moscovici 1976). The terms "minoriation" and "minorization" are frequently used in French sociology. For a theorization of this dual process, refer to Blanchet (2005): 17–47.
5 For a detailed analysis of these two events see Akgönül (2001): 37–51.

References

Akgönül, S. (2001) 'Chypre et les minorités gréco-turques: chronique d'une prise d'otage', *Gremmo-Monde arabe contemporain. Cahiers de recherches,* 29 'Recherches en cours sur le problème chypriote': 37–51.
Akgönül, S. (ed.) (2006) *Recpirocity: Greek and Turkish minorities. Law, religion and politics*, Istanbul: Press of Bilgi Universty.
Akşin, A. (1991) *Atatürk'ün Dış Politika ilkeleri ve diplomasisi*, Ankara: Türk Tarih Kurumu.
Aktar, A. (2005) 'Türk Yunan nüfus Mübadelesinin ilk yılı' in Pekin M. (ed.), *Yeniden Kurulan Yaşamlar: 1923 Türk-Yunan Zorunlu Nüfus Mübadelesi*, Istanbul: Bilgi Üniversitesi Yayınları.
Arı, K. (1995) *Büyük Mübadele. Türkiye'ye Zorunlu Göç*, Istanbul: Tarih Vakfı Yurt Yayınları.
Deutch, K. W. (1953) *Nationalism and Social Communication*, New York: Wiley.
Erim, N. (1944) 'Milletlerarası Daimi Adalet Divanı ve Türkiye, Etabli Meselesi', *Ankara Üniversitesi Hukuk Fakültesi Dergisi*, 2 (1): 62–73.
Gellner, E. (1989) *Nations et nationalisme*, Paris: Payot.
Giraud, E. (1924) 'Le Droit des nationalités. Sa valeur, son application', *Revue Générale de Droit International Public*, 31:17–71.
Gönlübol, M., Sar, C. (1982) *Olaylarla Türk Dış Politikası*, Ankara: Ankara Üniversitesi Siyasal Bilimler Fakültesi Yayınları

Hobsbawm, E. (1992) *Nations et nationalismes depuis 1789*, Paris: Gallimard.

Huck, D., Blanchet, P. (ed.) (2005) *Minorations, minorisations, minorités: études exploratoires*, Rennes: Presses Universitaires de Rennes.

İnönü, İ. (1987) *Hatıralar*, Ankara: Bilgi.

Meray, S. (1973) *Lozan Barış Konferansı*, Ankara: Siyasal Bilgiler Fakültesi Yayını.

Moscovici, S. (1976) *Psychologie des minorités actives*, Paris: PUF.

Öktem, E. (1996/97) 'L'évolution historique de la question des minorités et le régime institué par le Traité de Lausanne au sujet des minorités en Turquie', *Turkish Review of Balkan Studies*, 3:59–87.

Oran, B. (2005) *Türkiye'de azınlıklar, Kavramlar, Teori, Lozan, İç mevzuat, İçtihat, Uygulama*, İstanbul: İletişim.

Pekin, M. (ed.) (2005) *Yeniden Kurulan Yaşamlar: 1923 Türk-Yunan Zorunlu Nüfus Mübadelesi*, Istanbul: Bilgi Üniversitesi Yayınları.

Pye, L. (1966) *Aspects of Political Development*, Boston: Little Brown & Company.

Rabinowitz, D. (2001) 'The Palestinian Citizens of Israel, the Concept of Trapped Minority and the Discourse of Transnationalism in Anthropology', *Ethnic and Racial Studies*, 24(1): 64–85.

Schnapper, D. (1994) *La communauté des citoyens*, Paris: Gallimard.

Thornberry, P. (1991) *International law and the Rights of Minorities*, Oxford: Clarendon Press.

Zarcone, T. (2004) *La Turquie moderne et l'Islam*, Paris: Flammarion.

20 Democratization in Turkey?

Insights from the Alevi issue

Elise Massicard

The last few decades are often perceived as a time of liberalization and democratization in Turkey, even more so since they coincided with the end of the military regime in 1983. This development is largely considered to be an outcome of two different processes. First, many movements for recognition have developed since the 1980s, in Turkey as elsewhere in the world, contributing to the weakening of the constraints on public discourse, and to the empowerment of silenced or oppressed groups. Second, Turkey reiterated its candidacy to European integration in 1987, obtained the status of an official candidate at the Helsinki Summit in 1999, and finally began accession negotiations in 2005.

This chapter aims to analyze the question of democratization from the perspective of the Alevi issue. As a consequence, it pays special attention to the evolution not only of the legal framework affecting their rights, but also to the integration of Alevis, in particular to the Alevist movement that appeared in the late 1980s, in the political process. Therefore, this chapter analyzes the way in which Alevi organizations channel their claims, the main constraints they face, and the political and official answers to those claims. Which constraints–legal, but also discursive and informal–do they face, and how do they deal with them? Second, this chapter sheds light on the ways in which the perspective of European integration affects the situation of Alevis and their scope for action. Since Turkey's status as a candidate was recognized in 1999, Alevist organizations have presented their claims to European Union officials and therefore brought their claims into Turkey's EU agenda. This chapter, accordingly, gives an account of the EU-induced reform process from the perspective of the Alevi issue.

Looking at recent evolutions of the Alevi issue leads one to nuance somewhat the statement of an overall democratization (Massicard 2005a). Aleviness is no longer denied and indeed has become an acknowledged fact and even a public issue that is publicly debated and is being addressed by all political actors. However, Alevist claims have hardly any response from state authorities. Besides, Aleviness has still not been given any kind of recognition or official status, the legitimacy of identity-based claims remains problematic, and the unitary nature of the Turkish state and people remains an official dogma. Some changes in both legal framework and practice can be observed, especially concerning freedom of organization and the growing legitimacy and visibility of Alevi culture. However, most of these limited changes result not from the mobilization of activists, but from the European perspective and pressure. Finally, the very support of European institutions for the Alevi issue tends to undermine the legitimacy of Alevist claims.

Mapping the Alevi issue: Marginalization and mobilization

Mapping Alevis: invisibility and marginalization

Alevis are a heterodox group consisting of Turkish and Kurdish-speaking, as well as some Arabic-speaking members. There is no statistical data available that would help to evaluate the actual population of Alevis in Turkey but estimates range from 5 to 25 million, while the European Commission estimates them at between 12 and 20 million.[1] However, these estimates have always been controversial, and most commentators tend to over or under-estimate these figures according to their positioning. Alevis are geographically spread throughout Turkey, their traditional presence being stronger in Central and Eastern Anatolia as well as on the Mediterranean Coast. Since urban migration however, the majority of Alevis live in cities.

The Alevi cult is both heterodox and syncretistic. It is characterized by diverse influences, especially from Shi'a Islam (the cult of Ali and the twelve imams, *muharrem* fasting) and Islamic mysticism (strong esoteric features). However, the requirements of Sunni Islam bear little on Alevi life: Alevis do not fast during *Ramazan* – the holy month for Sunni Muslims-, and they do not perform *namaz* as a prayer. Instead, Aleviness is characterized by specific rituals (the *ayin-i cem,* or *cem,* being its main ceremony), institutions (the *dede* from holy lineages being its religious authorities) and cultural practices (especially oral poetry and music) which are hardly linked to Islam. Finally, Aleviness is quite diverse in terms of beliefs and practices, and has hardly established itself as a formal religion. This internal diversity and the existence of subgroups is the reason why I prefer not to speak about an 'Alevi community'.

Alevis were stigmatized as heretics under the Ottoman Empire since the early sixteenth century, i.e. since the Empire became a defender of Sunni Islam. Although most Alevis welcomed the creation of the Republic, they enjoyed no official status or recognition, contrary to some non-Muslim groups who gained the status of minority.[2] One reason for this denial lies in the fact that Muslimhood was accepted as a kind of national marker of Turkishness. This nation-building perspective involved a stress on unitarism (of state, language, people and religion), and the fact that difference was considered a potential threat. While this is commonly acknowledged regarding the ethnic dimension, especially as far as Kurds are concerned, this is also the case in the religious field. The place of religion in the nation-building process signifies that speaking about a separation of state and religion in the Republic of Turkey would be misleading, despite the principle of secularism (*laiklik*) present in the Constitution since 1937. Rather, one should speak about a domestication of religion by the state. This control manifests itself through the Directory of Religious Affairs (Diyanet İşleri Başkanlığı, DİB, from now on the *Diyanet*). This state institution in charge of religion manages both cult places (mosques) and clergymen, whom it nominates and pays. Far from being religiously neutral, the Turkish state has therefore endorsed and institutionalized a particular religious identity, the Sunni interpretation of Islam, as a kind of official denomination by default (Bozarslan 1994) – thus perpetuating, in a way, the privileged place Sunni Islam enjoyed under the Ottoman Empire. According to this difference-blindness, the DİB considers Alevis to be Muslims who have somehow been pushed aside from the 'true path', and that it is its task to bring them back to 'true Islam'. No different treatment is reserved nor allowed to them: the mosques built by the Diyanet are supposed to be a public service rendered to them like to all other Muslims, too. Therefore Aleviness enjoys no official visibility or representation: while mosques, churches and synagogues alike enjoy the status of worship places, Alevi *cemevi* do not.

Furthermore, the marginal place Alevis have long occupied in Turkish society is also due to their social origins. Most of them hail from relatively poor villages and migrated to the cities mostly in the 1960s and 1970s, then becoming workers or civil servants. While access to political and economic resources is not officially blocked by law, it is usually limited by the weakness of networks connected to power centres and by prevailing prejudices (Göner 2005: 115). As a matter of fact, the social prejudices against Alevis, often considered to be disreputable people of doubtful sexual morality, have in part endured. Finally, the public invisibility of Aleviness is also due to the fact that Alevis themselves have concealed their religious identity, in accordance with the tradition of *takiyye* (dissimulation), which allows one to conceal one's true faith when revealing it could involve danger.

Mobilization for recognition: The Alevist movement

It is only recently that Alevis have expressed identity-related claims, simultaneously with the apparition of identity issues on the public agenda. In the late 1960s a first Alevist public movement appeared.[3] It was first centered around reviews and cultural events (Massicard 2005b). The movement also gained political dimensions with the first 'Alevi party', The Unity Party (BP/TBP).[4] However, this movement was limited to elite and religious circles, and many Alevis were more active in left-wing political activism until the early 1980s.

A stronger Alevist recognition movement developed in the late 1980s, parallel to the growing visibility of the ethno-linguistic diversity of Turkey, and Kurdish and Islamist claims against the homogenizing dimension of Turkish identity. This revival has resulted in increased public visibility of Alevis (especially through the creation of Alevi organizations and growing media presence), heightened group consciousness, greater ease to express their identity in public, and claims over Alevi identity in social and political arenas. The main objective of Alevist identity politics is to create the conditions for the maintenance of the Alevi identity in the modern context and to get recognized and accepted as equal actors by the Turkish state as well as by the other social and political actors. Therefore, the Alevist movement can be considered an affirmative 'politics of recognition', voicing demands in order to be recognized as a specific group and to obtain equal participation in all spheres of life without facing discrimination.

Alevis are unanimous in blaming institutions—both of the Ottoman Empire and of the Republic of Turkey—for favouring Sunni Islam and denying Aleviness as a constitutive element of the country. According to popular Alevi narratives, for centuries Alevi identity, culture, and institutions were either denied recognition or assimilated into the majority Sunni identity. Likewise, most Alevis share feelings of marginalization, discrimination, persecution and victimhood, as well as collective traumas.[5] Consequently, Alevis agree on claims like the end of discriminatory practices and the acknowledgement of the crimes and grievances against the Alevis caused by the Turkish state, the extreme right and Islamist groups. Likewise, Alevists unanimously seek public recognition of Aleviness as an equal and legitimate element of Turkish society, and an equal representation of Alevi culture in public. They blame the Diyanet for representing the Sunni interpretation of Islam only. In the same way, almost all Alevi organizations and a considerable number of Alevis alike criticize the 'Religious Culture and Morals' course that is compulsory in the curricula of primary and secondary public schools, for not teaching different religions and cultures, but instead Sunni beliefs and practices alone – thus for being biased and assimilatory. Most Alevists also demand that *cemevi*s be given the status of places of worship (*ibadethane*), and benefit from the privileges that provides, including free electricity, free water, and the allocation of free building sites. Before rural-urban migration, in most Alevi villages, there was not a separate religious space since *cem* ceremonies were held secretly, only a few times a year, mostly in the largest hall or house of the village. After having settled in cities, since the early 1990s, Alevis have established community premises. These places, which have the status of associations or foundations, are multi-functional: religious ceremonies are held; they also offer a wide range of services such as lute (*saz*) classes, ritual dance (*semah*) classes, computer courses, and kitchens where free food is distributed to people in need or for religious ceremonies. The recognition of *cemevi*s as cult places is one of the main claims of the Alevist movement.

Poor achievements

After more than 20 years of mobilization however, one has to conclude that the Alevist movement has achieved little. The main change is that the taboo around Aleviness has weakened a lot: it is now much easier to speak about it than it was before. Aleviness has now become a public and debated issue, and Alevists have done much to destroy the prejudices Alevis have been suffering. However, practices like hiding one's Aleviness in order not to lose one's job, or turning the light on early in the morning during Ramadan even if one does not fast, so that the neighbours may not realize one's Aleviness, still exist in some settings.

The most important achievements are in the cultural realm. Alevi culture is now celebrated including by state institutions. In fact, in the early republican period, some cultural elements which can be attributed to Alevis, like songs or poems, were integrated into the official national culture and broadcasted officially. However, they had often been cleaned of any Alevi component beforehand and thus 'neutralized' in terms of particularism (Coşkun 1995: 208, 214). More recently, following the Alevist movement, institutions like the Ministry of Culture have attempted to 'rehabilitate' Alevi culture within the framework of Turkish national culture, whilst denying it any specific character outside this framework. As a matter of fact, the Ministry of Culture has promoted the main Alevi festival, the Hacı-bektaş annual festival. This is most probably linked to the fact that cultural claims such as the representation of Aleviness on public channels are more legitimate, in comparison, say, to religious claims. In a way, the Diyanet also fosters this process by asserting that the specificity of Alevis is cultural and not religious. However, these cultural achievements also accompany a process of (self-) folklorization.

Some minor public subsidies have been distributed to mostly state-friendly Alevist organizations for cultural or social activities – especially at a local level, or in times of general mobilization against Islamists. State institutions no longer deny the existence of Aleviness; they mostly defend an Aleviness moulded in Islam and Turkish nationalism, but remain distant from Alevist claims.

On the whole however, the main Alevist claims (recognition, specific treatment by the Turkish state) have not been fulfilled. The parliamentary debate on the exact content of the term 'worship place' in 2006 ended in the exclusion of *cemevis* from this category. Alevis have also failed to obtain the abolition of either the Diyanet or the compulsory religion classes. The only change is that in 2005, and again in 2012, some modules on Aleviness were introduced into the compulsory religious education syllabus. However, their content is very controversial among Alevis, since they consider the way Aleviness is presented–mainly stressing its similarities with mainstream Islam and framing its specificities as cultural–as a further attempt for assimilation.

Internal obstacles: A divided movement

One further explanation for the poor achievements of the movement lies in some features of Alevism itself. Beyond the unanimously recognized need for recognition, diverse groups – to some extent identifiable with organizations – have emerged in the course of the movement's development. A wide range of disagreements have appeared among them that, interestingly enough, include the very definition of Aleviness and the claims to be made. Some claim Aleviness is a purely religious matter. However, they disagree over the question of whether it is inside or outside Islam. A majority of Alevis argue that Aleviness is a specific interpretation of Islam—or even 'true Islam'. Some claim that it is a separate religion–the 'real religion' of Turks or of Kurds. For others, Aleviness is not chiefly a religious phenomenon but is a political philosophy of liberation, resistance and democracy. For yet another group, Aleviness is mainly a culture, a way of life characterized by critical-mindedness. It is not our aim to describe here this diversity of positions, which has been discussed solidly in various works (Vorhoff 1995). Suffice to say that the lack of consensus on the definition of Aleviness is a striking feature of contemporary Alevism. These different groups try to establish a monopoly over the definition and over the right to represent Aleviness. It is not just about politics of recognition; it is also–and maybe above all–about politics of recognition *as* a particular kind of Aleviness. Even after 20 years of mobilization, this debate over the definition of Alevi identity and its boundaries is not settled.

These debates are not just theoretical. Depending on their interpretation of Aleviness, Alevists differ in terms of the issues they address and the corresponding direction of attribution and solutions they propose. This is especially the case regarding the 'Religious Culture and Morals' course that is compulsory in the curricula of primary and secondary public schools, including for Alevi children, opposed by almost all Alevi organizations and a considerable number of Alevis alike. However, different organizations disagree on the solution to be adopted: while most are firmly against the existence of religion classes in a secular state and think this course should be simply abolished or at least made optional, others argue its content should be changed to more religious neutrality, by, for instance, including some teachings on Aleviness and possibly other religions as well.

These conflicts are even more obvious regarding the Diyanet. For leftist and secular-minded Alevists, Alevis' problems stem from Islamists having taken power, destroyed Turkey's secular heritage and introduced discrimination against Alevis; thus, secularism and the impartiality of the state should be restored. This position is best represented by the Alevi Bektaşi Federation (ABF), which claims the Turkish State should refrain from all activities related to religion, as a requirement of secularism. Consequently, the ABF does not want Aleviness to be integrated into Diyanet in any form, but opposes its very existence, suggesting its property should be confiscated by the Treasury. It also opposes the existence of compulsory religious courses. More religious-minded Alevists, however, claim Aleviness is a religion and should be recognized as such. They consider the secular state oppressive regarding religion, and suggest this is what should be changed in a liberal manner, so that Alevis, as well as other Muslims, can practice their religion freely. For example, the CEM Foundation (Cumhuriyetçi Eğitim ve Kültür

Merkezi Vakfı/ Republican Education and Culture Center) and the Ehl-i Beyt Foundation demand that Aleviness be included in the state institutions dealing with religion, either in the form of the representation of Alevis within the Diyanet, or of a separate directorate for Alevis, similar to the Diyanet. They also claim that Alevi *dede*s, like imams, should be paid salaries by state institutions. Hostility towards the Diyanet is shared among the diverse views, but there is disagreement as to what needs to be done. On the whole, these groups are not static communities with clearly defined boundaries, but rather dynamic political locations where certain views and sometimes organizations ally (Erman and Göker 2000: 105).

Charles Tilly distinguished between 'reactive' or 'defensive' claims (aiming at the redress of grievances), 'competitive' claims (i.e. demands for resources claimed by other groups), and 'offensive' claims (i.e. rights that have not been exercised before) (Tilly 1978). In the Alevist case, demands for the redress of perceived discriminations and the restoration of the neutrality of state institutions, for example to punish slanders against Alevis, can be considered reactive; demands for the same rights as Sunnis, such as the teaching of Aleviness at school or the free practice of religious rituals, can be considered competitive; finally, the official recognition of Aleviness and permission for it to organize separately can be considered an offensive demand. On the whole, defensive claims are quite consensual, while competitive and to an even greater extent, offensive demands, are contested in the Alevist movement itself and even more so in Turkish society.

Therefore, unity and competition are a significant challenge for the Alevist movement, making it less powerful. Whereas this debate is often understood as concerning Alevis alone, it has a broader scope. Not only activists and Alevi citizens, but also the media, different political groups, and state institutions take an active part in these contests. The numerous articles published in daily newspapers and national TV programs on this topic attest to the public character of this debate. In the end, institutions define legitimate categories to be claimed, and criteria to be fulfilled.

The political process

Besides the mere outcome – if claims have been met or not – another dimension is crucial to understanding democratization: the political process, i.e. the way in which claims and answers are politically expressed and channelled. I shall here address the enduring lack of legitimacy of identity claims, the enduring lack of channelling of Alevist claims by political parties, and tendencies like the judicialization of the Alevi issue, and its extraversion.

The lacking legitimacy of identity-based claims

First, the enduring illegitimacy of particularist claims constitutes an important obstacle to improvements in the situation of Alevis. On the whole, despite the growth of identity claims and debates since the 1980s, Turkish state institutions have continued to stress nationalism and national unity. Turkish unity still denies any group-specific features, provides very narrow opportunity for the recognition of specificities, and criminalizes particularism as 'separatism'. These constraints impact the ways in which Alevists act, as well as their discourses and framings. Only defensive claims have some legitimacy, if ever, since they can be framed as facing discrimination against part of the people, thus threats against national unity. But competitive and offensive claims can easily be understood as challenging national unity. They are not argued and legitimized publicly in the frame of diversity, as would be the case in a multicultural context or a system accepting diversity, but in reference to the unity as a supreme value of the nation. For example, the claim for recognition of *cemevi* as places of worship is mostly framed as follows: Alevis, who are loyal Turkish citizens, cannot practice their religion freely and are therefore discriminated against, which constitutes a threat to national unity. Therefore, the defence of the nation's supreme values, especially Turkish nationalism, remains the legitimizing frame for claim-making, even (or especially) for identity claims. This shows that difference, and particularist claims even more so, remain illegitimate and stigmatized despite the fact that they have become widespread, as have debates on identity and diversity, since the 1980s. These constraints strongly influence and limit the expression of difference and demands for recognition for Alevis, as for similar groups.

As a consequence, it is difficult for most Alevi organizations to ally or collaborate with non-particularist or 'universalist' political forces (parties, labour unions, NGOs, etc.), which fear a loss of legitimacy if they cooperate with particularist groups (Schüler 2000). For example, Alevists often support or participate in activities like demonstrations or manifestos organized by other 'universalist' political actors (for example demonstrations for Human Rights or May Day), whereas these universalist political actors more rarely support publicly Alevist claims, which contributes to their marginalization

The lack of channeling by political parties

This has consequences on the way Alevist claims are channelled, or not, by political parties. A further explanation of the poor achievements is that there are major legal obstacles that prevent the fulfilment of Alevist claims, since they address the very bases of the relationship between state and religion and, judicially, the Constitution itself. The compulsory status of the course in religion and ethics in public schools is regulated by the 24th article of the 1982 Constitution. Likewise, changing the legal status of the Diyanet is legally very difficult, since it is regulated by an article of the Constitution that cannot be changed. Meanwhile however, many Constitutional revisions have been passed regarding crucial issues, but not those addressed by the Alevist movement. This leads to the question of the relationship between Alevist claims and political parties.

In this respect, it is crucial to make clear that Alevist demands have hardly been supported or relayed by political parties, even by those that Alevis most supported.[6] Likewise, almost all parties promise to improve the situation of Alevis in electoral campaigns – especially in the provinces where Alevi constituencies are important. For instance, before the 1995 elections, Tansu Çiller, the leader of the centre-right True Path Party, promised to give Alevis an enormous amount of money. Almost all parties have nominated Alevis on their tickets – including the AKP (*Adalet ve Kalkınma Partisi*, Justice and Development Party) with Reha Çamuroğlu and İbrahim Yığıt in 2007. Until now however, no party in power has officially endorsed or enacted Alevist demands, which would bring the risk of being identified as an 'Alevi party', or of losing their Sunni constituents.

Some gestures are being initiated, most of them remaining symbolic. In 2007, the AKP Government launched an 'Alevi opening' (*Alevi açılımı*) as part of the broader policy of 'democratic opening', aiming to reconcile marginalized segments of society (including Kurds, religious minorities and Roms) with the Turkish state. For the first time, ministers, including Prime Minister Erdoğan, apologized on behalf of their government and the Turkish State for the oppressions and violence that the ancestors of the Alevis had suffered, and acknowledged Alevi victimhood. Prime Minister Erdoğan voiced a commitment to accommodate Alevi requests. The hotel that was set into fire in Sivas was bought by the state in order to become a museum in the future. A series of workshops were also set up and high-ranking politicians and statesmen made symbolic and discursive gestures.

Beyond that however, no concrete step has been taken to address Alevist claims. The Government considered the recognition of *cemevi*s as worship places[7] and the creation of an Alevi unit in the Diyanet, but has not allowed legal amendments and seems to have abandoned these claims. Furthermore, the government revised the content of the compulsory religion classes on Aleviness, in consultation with some Alevis. Although some Alevi leaders responded positively, most Alevi organizations rejected these initiatives: first, because they interpreted them as assimilatory tricks since they stressed similarities between Aleviness and Sunni Islam and aimed to bring Aleviness under state control; second, because most Alevi organizations were not even consulted. In the same way, opinions of Alevi citizens about these gestures reflect widespread scepticism and a deep mistrust towards the governing party. According to an opinion poll, 49.2 per cent of Alevi citizens expressed their discontent with the Alevi opening, while only 14.9 per cent said that they were happy about the situation. According to this report, 59.8 per cent of the Alevi respondents said AKP 's Alevi opening was a policy of 'Sunnification' whereas only 21.9 per cent of the Alevi respondents disagreed with this statement (Stratejik Düşünce Enstitüsü 2009: 50).

However, one of the outcomes of this move is that the Alevi issue is on the political agenda again. Even the nationalist MHP (*Milliyetçi Hareket Partisi*, Nationalist Action Party) launched a new Alevi policy somewhat parallel with the AKP's, promising the allocation of a budget to *cemevis*, the representation of Aleviness within the *Diyanet*, the teaching of Alevi culture and beliefs in religion classes, the opening of government-funded Alevi research centers and institutes, and the broadcast of documentaries about Alevi culture on the official state channel. Since the 1990s, therefore, the Alevi issue is much debated by political actors, but very few steps have been taken.

Weakening obstacles to possibilities of organizing

However, some changes can be traced concerning the institutional and legal regulations of the possibilities of organizing for Alevis. Legal constraints tend to diminish as a result of both Alevist activism and the European harmonization process. Firstly, the Law on political parties prohibits religious groups from organizing themselves as parties. The three political parties close to Aleviness that existed in the past[8] could neither really present themselves as Alevi parties while being too Alevi-oriented to defend convincingly a general political orientation, resulting in their rapid failure (Massicard 2006: 72–73). Another legal constraint influencing the ways Alevists claim recognition, are limitations on the possibilities of organizing. According to the 1983 Law on Associations, it is forbidden to form associations aiming to create differences of race, religion, *mezhep* (religious orientation) and region, or minorities based on these, and to demolish the unitary state structure of the Republic.[9] Moreover, the Civil Code restricts the creation of foundations (*vakıf*) contrary to the characteristics of the Republic, constitutional rules, national integrity and national interest, or with the aim of supporting a distinctive race or community.[10] Therefore, religious groups cannot organize formally as associations or foundations.

This does not mean that there are no such organizations, but these organizations cannot openly express objectives linked with religion. As a consequence, most Alevi organizations have been avoiding mentioning the word 'Alevi' in their name or statutes. Still, most of them express this dimension through circumlocutions or allusions, for example by mentioning the names of figures symbolizing Aleviness, such as Hacı Bektaş or Pir Sultan Abdal. Many but not all organizations which have tried to inscribe the term 'Alevi' in their name, or objectives linked with Aleviness in their statutes, have had legal problems or have simply not been registered.[11]

Alevi organizations have resorted to legal means in the first place as a means of defence and have conducted long legal struggles, leading to some changes, if not in law, at least in legal practice. Indeed, the decisions not to register organizations were often annulled. As a matter of fact, the action brought against the Pir Sultan Abdal 2 Temmuz Eğitim ve Kültür Vakfı in 1997 ended in the court finding against the Foundation in 2000. But the Court of Appeal finally decided in its favour, judging that its aim of "serving Alevi philosophy" did not infringe the law. In the summer of 1999, after a long legal struggle, the Alevi-Bektashi Educational Foundation (Alevi-Bektaşi

Eğitim vakfı) finally obtained the right to keep its name from the Supreme Court.

Reforms passed in the framework of harmonization with European Union legislation have also lead to legal developments. In 2002, a state court decision closed down a grouping of Alevi organizations, the Cultural Association of Alevi-Bektashi Formations (Alevi-Bektaşi Kuruluşları Birliği Kültür Derneği), considering that its objectives (including 'the construction of *cemevi*' and 'the fostering of cooperation between Alevi-Bektashi organizations') were contrary to the Law on Associations.[12] This case was mentioned in the European Commission's 2002 regular report (European Commission 2002: 37), and followed up by the German government, mainly because the biggest Alevi organization in Germany was involved in this association; the issue thus gained a European dimension. The Association appealed against the decision at a time when Turkey's projected accession was a burning issue; in the end, it was registered in 2003. In the same way, the second harmonization package passed in March 2002 removed the prohibition for founding an association aiming to protect, develop or expand languages or cultures other than the Turkish language or culture, or claiming the existence of minorities based on racial, religious, sectarian, cultural or linguistic differences.[13] The recent legal developments toward more organizational facilities result from the perspective of accession to the EU and the external constraints associated with it, more than from Alevist activism itself.

However, the decrease of legal constraints on the formal organization of Alevism is partial and ambiguous, and can be in no way be considered a settled matter. For instance, contradictions remain between different legal texts or between texts and their application, which contributes to the existence of a grey area where many things are not clearly authorized without being really forbidden. For example, the preparatory laws for the enactment of the constitutional changes decided in 1995 that broadened the scope of action for associations and foundations were passed only years later. As late as in December 2010, Ankara provincial authorities moved to close down an Alevi association because the latter aimed to build a *cemevi* as a worship place, while *cemevis* are not recognized as such. In this zone of legal insecurity, activists know that if they act in a given way, they may or may not be sanctioned. This state of affairs still has a strongly inhibiting effect on leading officials, who know that their organizations could be quite easily closed down by the authorities and that they personally could be held responsible and incur punishment. As a matter of fact, this situation points to two tendencies that are revealing of the place of Alevism in the political process: judicialization, and the importance of extraversion.

Judicialization and extraversion as a lever for change?

Alevis and Alevi organizations resorting to European institutions in order to use Turkey's EU accession process as a lever for change in Turkey dates back to the early 2000s. It has an important juridical dimension, namely the resort to the European Court of Human Rights. In two major cases, Alevi citizens resorted to ECHR: on the exemption of Alevi children from compulsory religious education (Eylem Zengin vs Turkey, 2007), and on the suppression of the inscription of religion on Turkish ID cards (Sinan Işık vs Turkey).[14] In both cases, the ECHR stated in favour of the applicant. Hasan Zengin, an Alevi citizen, submitted requests in 2001 to the Directorate of National Education and before administrative courts for his daughter to be exempted from lessons in religious culture and ethics. He claimed that, under international treaties such as the Universal Declaration of Human Rights, parents had the right to choose the type of education their children were to receive. He also alleged that the course was incompatible with the principle of secularism and was not neutral as it was essentially based on the teaching of Sunni Islam. On appeal to the Supreme Administrative Court in 2003, all his requests were ultimately dismissed on the grounds that the course in religious culture and ethics was in accordance with the Constitution and Turkish legislation. The applicant then resorted to the EHRC, notably alleging that the course's syllabus lacked objectivity because it included no detailed information about other religions and it was taught from a religious perspective which praised the Sunni interpretation of Islam. The EHCR found that the syllabus and the textbooks indeed gave greater priority to Islam than to other religions and philosophies. Besides, pupils received no teaching on the confessional or ritual specificities of the Alevi faith. The Court therefore found that religious culture and ethics lessons could not be considered to meet the criteria of objectivity and pluralism necessary for education in a democratic society and for pupils to develop a critical outlook towards religion. In March 2008, the Turkish Council of State also issued a ruling declaring that religion courses could not be obligatory in their current form.[15] With arguments similar to those of the ECHR, it stated that the current curricula focused solely on Sunni Islam; therefore, students should not be required to attend religion courses.[16] The President of *Diyanet* criticized the Council of State's decision, arguing that the purpose of compulsory religion courses is not to raise devout Muslims. Interestingly, however, Turkish authorities hardly changed the curriculum.

The same can be said about the outcomes of the entrance of the Alevi issue on Turkey's EU agenda. Since 2000, the Alevi issue has been mentioned in all regular reports of the European Commission on Turkey's progress towards accession. In November 2000, the first Regular Report referred to it in the following terms:

> The official approach towards the Alevis seems to remain unchanged. Alevi complaints notably concern compulsory religious instruction in schools and school books, which would not reflect the Alevi identity, as well as the fact that financial support is only available for the building of

Sunni mosques and religious foundations. These issues are highly sensitive; however, it should be possible to have an open debate on them.

(Commission of the European Communities 2000: 18)

This statement is reiterated in almost the same words in later reports, which are critical of the absence of improvement and the lack of formal recognition of Alevis, the fact that they are not represented by the *Diyanet*, the fact that compulsory religious instruction in schools still fails to acknowledge the Alevi identity, and their difficulties in opening places of worship. The European Commission has thus legitimized Alevists' demands.[17] However, except in the case mentioned earlier of the legalization of the Cultural Association of Alevi-Bektashi Formations, this has hardly had any concrete consequences.

Finally, one could expect the support of European institutions for Alevi rights to expand the legitimacy of Alevist claims. On the contrary, the very fact that many of these changes have been initiated by the perspective of EU accession or external constraints fosters resistance. This was obvious with the very controversial public debates following the 2004 EU Commission Report on Turkey's progress towards accession, calling Alevis a 'non-Sunni Muslim minority' (Commission of the European Communities 2004: 44). Interestingly, this qualification raised much opposition from Alevists themselves. Due to this perception and the negative connotations of the term 'minority' in Turkish, even groups like Alevis who experience non-representation and exclusion refrain from calling themselves minorities and from claiming a minority status. Instead they claim 'full citizenship'.

Conclusion

Analyzing the Alevi issue and its development over the last decades prompts some caution concerning statements of an overall democratization in Turkey. Debates on identity and diversity have indisputably become more widespread, and Aleviness has become acknowledged and even a public issue addressed by all political actors. However, difference and particularism even more so, are still to some extent illegitimate, and the unitary nature of the Turkish state and people remains an official dogma. As a consequence, Alevist claims have hardly been addressed by state authorities, and Aleviness has still not been provided any kind of official recognition. Some changes in legal framework and practice have evolved, in particular as far as organizational freedom and the growing legitimacy and visibility of Alevi culture are concerned. However, most of these minor changes have resulted not from the mobilization of activists themselves, but from the European perspective and pressure. Finally, the very support of European institutions for some Alevi claims tends to undermine their legitimacy. By way of a conclusion, some positive outcomes and developments may reinforce an analysis in terms of democratization. However, integrating not only outcomes, but also the political process to the analysis, prompts further nuance.

Notes

1 Interestingly enough, the French version of the 2004 report estimates them at between 12 and 15 million (Commission des Communautés Européennes 2004: 45, n14), whereas the English version estimates them at between 12 and 20 million (Commission of the European Communities 2004: 44, n14).
2 The list of recognized religious minorities, all of them non-Muslim, was fixed by the 1923 Lausanne Treaty. Interestingly, the first official recognition Alevis ever obtained occurred in Berlin, Germany in 2000, where an Alevi association was given the status of a 'religious community'. On this point see Massicard (2003).
3 I distinguish Aleviness, which covers the social fact, from Alevism, which designs the movement in the name of Aleviness.
4 *Birlik Partisi* (BP) created in 1966, later changed to TBP (*Türkiye Birlik Partisi*, Unity Party of Turkey). On this party see Ata (2007).
5 Particularly important in this respect are some bloody episodes of recent Turkish history: during the politically polarized and violent late 1970s, pogroms by Sunni nationalists targeting leftist and especially Alevis ended in the death of more than hundred Alevis. Alevis often draw a continuity with the 'Sivas events' and with the 'Gazi events'. On July 2, 1993, 37 intellectuals and artists, most of them Alevis, who had gathered for a cultural festival in Sivas, were killed when a mob of radical Islamists set fire to the hotel where the group had assembled. In March 1995, unknown gunmen in a stolen taxi drove through the Gazi neighborhood of Istanbul and riddled five tea-houses with bullets, killing one and wounding numerous people. The police were slow in taking action, resulting in clashes between the police and Alevi demonstrators ending in the death of 17 demonstrators.
6 For social-democratic parties see Schüler (1998: 242–45); for other parties see Massicard (2012: 111–29).
7 'Erdoğan: Cemevi talebine uzak kalmayız', *Radikal*, 14 January 2008.
8 The TBP was active between 1966 and 1980, and the Barış Partisi (Peace Party), between 1996 and 1999. The EDP (Eşitlik ve Demokrasi Partisi, Equality and Democracy), again a leftist party with a concern for the Alevi issue, was again very short-lived (2010–12).
9 Art. 5, Law on Associations n°29008, 6 October 1983.
10 Art. 101. A similar ban has existed in the Civil Code since 1967.
11 For an overview of the 10 years legal struggle of a foundation, see Kaleli (2000: 220–82).
12 'Alevi-Bektaşi Kültür Derneği kapatıldı', *Radikal*, 13 February 2002.
13 See the new law on associations n°5253 passed in November 2004.
14 The Court found that the mere fact of having an identity card with the 'religion' box left blank, obliged the individual to disclose, against his or her will, information concerning an aspect of his or her religion or most personal convictions; and that this was at odds with the principle of freedom not to manifest one's religion or belief.
15 'Danıştay: Din dersi hukuka aykırı', *Hürriyet*, 4 March 2008.
16 'Danıştay: Zorunlu din dersi hukuksuz', 4 March 2008. Available HTTP: <http://arsiv.ntvmsnbc.com/news/437852.asp> (accessed 2 January 2013).
17 The Commission implicitly recognizes Aleviness as a religious phenomenon within Islam. These statements are found in the section concerning freedom of religion, itself included in the chapter on 'civic and political rights', not in the chapter on 'rights and protection of minorities', which deals mainly with Gypsies and Kurds. The 2003 report refers to Alevis as a 'non-Sunni Moslem community' (Commission of the European Communities 2003: 36).

References

Ata, K. (2007) *Alevilerin ilk siyasal denemeleri: (Türkiye) Birlik Partisi (1966–1980)*, Ankara: Kelime.

Bozarslan, H. (1994) 'Au-delà de l'abolition du Khalifat. Laïcité, Etat-Nation et contestation kurde', *Les annales de l'autre islam*, 2: 225–35.

Commission des Communautés Européennes (2004) *Rapport Régulier 2004 sur les progrès réalisés par la Turquie sur la voie de l'adhésion*, Brussels.

Commission of the European Communities (2000) *2000 Regular Report from the Commission on Turkey's progress toward accession*, Brussels. Online. Available HTTP: <http://ec.europa.eu/enlargement/archives/pdf/key_documents/2000/tu_en.pdf> (Accessed 12 October 2011).

—— (2003) *2003 Regular Report on Turkey's progress toward accession*, Brussels. Online. Available HTTP: <http://ec.europa.eu/enlargement/archives/pdf/key_-documents/2003/rr_tk_final_en.pdf> (Accessed 12 October 2011).

—— (2004) *2004 Regular Report on Turkey's progress toward accession*, Brussels. Online. Available HTTP: <http://ec.europa.eu/enlargement/archives/pdf/key_-documents/2004/rr_tr_2004_en.pdf> (Accessed 12 October 2011).

Coşkun, Z. (1995) *Aleviler, Sünniler ve … öteki Sivas*, Istanbul: İletişim.

Erman, T. and Göker, E. (2000) 'Alevi politics in Contemporary Turkey', *Middle Eastern Studies*, 36(4): 99–118.

Göner, Ö. (2005) 'The transformation of the Alevi Collective identity', *Cultural Dynamics*, 17(2): 107–34.

Kaleli, L. (2000) *Alevi kimliği ve Alevi örgütlenmesi*, Istanbul: Can.

Massicard, É. (2003) 'Alevist movements at home and abroad: mobilization spaces and disjunction', *New Perspectives on Turkey*, 28–29: 163–87.

—— (2005a), 'Les mobilisations "identitaires" en Turquie après 1980: une libéralisation ambiguë' in G. Dorronsoro (ed.) *La Turquie conteste. Action collective et régime sécuritaire*, Paris: CNRS Editions.

—— (2005b) 'Alevism in the 1960s: Social Change and Mobilisation', in H. I. Markussen (ed.), *Alevis and Alevism, Transformed Identities*, Istanbul: Isis.

—— (2006) 'Claiming Difference in an unitarist frame: the case of Alevism' in H.-L. Kieser (ed.) *Turkey Beyond Nationalism: Towards Post-Nationalist Identities?*, London: IB Tauris.

—— (2012) *The Alevis in Turkey and Europe: Identity and Managing Territorial Diversity*, London: Routledge.

Schüler, H. (1998) *Die türkischen Parteien und ihre Mitglieder*, Hamburg: Deutsches Orient-Institut.

—— (2000) 'Secularism and ethnicity: Alevis and social-democrats in search of an alliance', in S. Yerasimos, G. Seufert, K. Vorhoff (eds) *Civil Society in the Grip of Nationalism*, Istanbul: Orient-Institut.

Stratejik Düşünce Enstitüsü (2009) *Alevi Raporu*, Ankara.

Tilly, C. (1978) *From Mobilization to Revolution*, Reading: Addison-Wesley.

Vorhoff, K. (1995) *Zwischen Glaube, Nation und neuer Gemeinschaft: alevitische Identität in der Türkei der Gegenwart*, Berlin: Klaus Schwarz.

21 The political economy of the media and its impact on freedom of expression in Turkey

Ceren Sözeri

Introduction

Freedom of expression and freedom of the media have always been caught between political and legal pressures and structural problems. Even it is described as a 'no-man's land' located somewhere between south-eastern Europe and the Middle East' (Christensen 2007: 180) or treated as idiosyncratic by the experiences inside and outside the Turkey (as cited in Christensen 2011: 182), the media structure of Turkey is similar more to that of the Mediterranean or Polarized Pluralist Model of Hallin and Mancini even though it is not a part of their research. As in many other Mediterranean countries, the media in Turkey developed as a political institution more than a market, and it has been used by various actors as tools to intervene in the political area (Hallin and Mancini 2004: 90–113).

From the outset, the suppression of the state has been well documented (Christensen, 2007: 195); however, the clientelist relationship which creates a climate of self-censorship, unqualified content and inconvenient working conditions in the journalistic profession still need to be discussed.

This chapter analyzes the freedom of expression and freedom of media within the political, structural and legal issues in Turkey. To understand the main concerns about the media, first a brief historical perspective will be given. It is possible to read the history of media at the same time through the relationship between the state and the media owners. Hence, the political pressures on the media, censorship, and self-censorship are evaluated from within a political economic perspective in the following chapter. The jailed journalists and coverage of sensitive topics like the Kurdish issue are not only the current concerns in Turkey and outside of Turkey, as seen in the European Commission (2012) Turkey 2012 Progress Report, they also have attracted the international public opinion's attention. Therefore, the situations of the jailed journalists, the reasons for the detentions, and the risks of covering sensitive issues are discussed in part five. Turkey is still dealing with the ECtHR cases on the violation of the freedom of expression and freedom of media, despite the reforms packages adopted during the EU integration process. The improvements that emerged thanks to the integration process and the reasons for the ECtHR cases against Turkey are examined in the last part.

Historical overview

From the publication of the first official newspaper in the late Ottoman period to the industrialization process of the press in the1960s, journalists were part of the elite in society and played significant roles in the modernization of the state. They were assigned to educate people and to support the Kemalist reforms throughout the foundation of the Republic. However, their approaches to the political regime resulted in a distinction made between 'opponent' (Istanbul) and 'proponent' (Ankara) press. Membership in parliament was often used as award or punishment by the Government. Accordingly, between 1920 and 1957, 75 journalists sat in parliament. Furthermore, journalists occasionally were appointed to positions as civil servants, especially when they had been suspended during the single-party regime by the government (Gürkan 1998: 79–83). As a result, the journalists were excluded from the scope of the first Labour Law (no.3008) for many years.

Although in 1952 the first specific law regulating the profession of journalism allowed the establishment of a trade union, and a labour agreement among others came into effect, the rates of censorship and crackdowns increased and continued during the multiparty era. Following the 1960 coup d'état, the Committee of National Unity established the Directorate General of Press Advertisement to prevent arbitrary advertisement distribution practices by the governments. The Committee then made a remarkable amendment known as 'the 212' and favoured journalists within Law no. 5953, which served to protect journalists from political pressure and the negative effects of the industrialization process of the press. This amendment entitled journalists first and foremost to terminate their contracts by default without giving up their severance pay. These were known as 'conscience clauses' to protect them from the media owners and preserve their independence. The first and most serious reaction to this amendment came from the bosses. The owners of *Akşam, Cumhuriyet, Dünya, Hürriyet, Milliyet, Tercüman, Vatan, Yeni İstanbul* and *Yeni Sabah* newspapers protested the amendment by suspending publishing for three days. The journalists of these dailies issued a newspaper called *Basın* during those three days with the support of the Journalists' Union.

The coups staged in 1960, 1971 and 1980 were followed by a period of military rule, which had significant repercussions for media freedom in Turkey. After the third coup d'état, the family-owned media companies were replaced by new investors who already operated in other sectors as a result of neo-liberal policies. In addition, this commercialization also ended with an increase in the sensationalism and tabloidization of the press (Bek 2004).

In the 1990s, after the termination of the state monopoly over broadcasting, a few conglomerates that had increased their economic power through vertical and horizontal mergers came to dominate whole sectors of the media and pursued competition strategies by setting up cartels and engaging in promotion wars. Some media groups that had investments in the financial and banking sectors were affected by the 2001 financial crisis. Some of them were completely wiped out while others were seized by the Savings Deposit Insurance Fund (*Tasarruf Mevduatı Sigorta Fonu*) established by the government. These transfers were used as a tool for the reconfiguration of the mainstream media in accordance with the ideology of the ruling party from 2002.

The relationship between the state and the media owners

In the 1960s, despite the economic and political instability, the newspapers gave a relatively good account of themselves under the family-owned media. While their print qualities increased as a result of new press techniques, the quality of the content also was enhanced due to better-educated journalists and columnists. However, the second and third coup d'état ended up with suspended newspapers and jailed journalists once again. Accordingly, the neoliberal policies adopted by the ruling ANAP (*Anavatan Partisi*, Motherland Party) following the end of the military rule resulted in the shifting ownership structure in the media in 1980. The new owners who already had investments in other sectors of the economy carried the 'corporate mentality' into their media operations. With the end of the state monopoly over broadcasting, the media market started to be dominated by a few conglomerates that increased their economic power through vertical and horizontal mergers. The deregulation gave rise to the development of 'clientelist' relationships between the media patrons and the state, whereby the former exerted pressure on politicians to maximize their profits in other sectors of the economy (Christensen, 2007: 185). In 2002, the regulation that had come into force in 1994 regarding ownership restriction after the beginning of private broadcasting was amended to benefit the media bosses owing to effective lobbying on their behalf.[1]

In the 1990s, the media owners pursued balancing acts between the army, the government, and the opposition (Cemal 2012). In addition to promotion wars between themselves, the two big media groups, Doğan and Bilgin, took positions between the two big centre-right parties and did not resist the manipulative policies of the army against the coalition government composed of the Islamist RP (*Refah Partisi*, Welfare Party) and the centre-right DYP (*Doğru Yol Partisi*, True Path Party) during the February 28th process.[2] The most notorious incident of this period was the publication of news fabricated by a senior military official accusing Cengiz Çandar and Mehmet Ali Birand, two notable journalists working for a mainstream media, of being PKK (*Partiya Karkerên Kurdistan*, Kurdistan Worker's Party) agents based on the alleged testimony of a PKK militant in custody turned informant (Elmas and Kurban 2011).

These patronage relationships, or the 'vicious triangle' (Alpay, 2010) of the media conglomerates, the politicians and the businessmen,[3] also laid the ground for the 2001 financial crisis through widespread corruption in the banking sector. Some media barons like Dinç Bilgin, who had built up the second big media conglomerate, lost their banks and media outlets, which were later seized by the TMSF.

When the AKP (*Adalet ve Kalkınma Partisi*, Justice and Development Party) came to power in 2002, there was a positive atmosphere in terms of the relationship between state and the media owners. However, after the local elections victory of the AKP in 2004, the withdrawal of the support of the biggest media group (Doğan Group) ended up in irreversible conflicts between the government and the media. In response, the AKP government adopted a dual strategy to eliminate media opposition. It forced the Doğan Group to downsize its media investments by means of heavy tax fines and it reconfigured the main-stream media. In 2007, the second largest media group was bought by Çalık Holding, which has close ties to the government, thanks to credits provided by two major public banks. The chairman of the board of this group is the son-in-law of the prime minister. Thus, the power shifted from the opponent mainstream media companies to 'reconfigured' or 'proponent' media companies (Kurban and Sözeri, 2012: 50).

The domination of big conglomerates has continued in terms of advertising revenue distribution. Despite selling its second TV channel and two newspapers after the tax fines,[4] Doğan Group still has the biggest part of the advertising revenues. It may be more accurate to say that the advertising pie is almost entirely divided between the big media groups in all of the sub-sectors (except for cinema and outdoors) of the media. The regulations are mostly ineffective against preventing concentration in the market. For instance, such a highly concentrated market structure is observed in the newspaper sector such that most newspapers cannot generate optimal advertising revenues and therefore operate in the red (Kurban and Sözeri 2012: 28). Hence, these irrational market conditions have oriented the newspapers owners to own at least one TV channel to support the news-papers and to make a profit. Recently, the new proponent media owners and directors have revived the debate on unbalanced ads revenues among the outlets (Karaalioğlu, 2012). However, it should be observed that the arguments actually aim to obtain more ads in support of proponent media instead of requesting a more pluralistic distribution.

Censorship and self-censorship of the media

Journalists constantly struggle with state censorship and subsequently self-censorship in addition to the legal pressures that are the most significant press freedom concerns in Turkey. While the conflict between state and media are reflected on censored blank pages and suspended newspapers to begin with, the state mostly preferred to put direct pressure on the media owners who have been dependant on public procurement for their non-media operations from the 1980s onward. Therefore, self-censorship significantly expanded in mainstream media content.

In the 1990s, the media owners sought to engage with the army and the ruling party or the opposition depending on their interests, without neglecting the balance between them. During the reconfiguration of the media after the 2007 general election, the big media groups became too weak vis-à-vis the political power of the AKP (Cemal 2012). As one of big media owners pointed out, the huge size of the state in the economic area obliged businessmen to get along with it even though they did not participate in public procurement.[5] As a result, this dependence inevitably influenced the editorial policies. The most salient example of this submission was observed in a meeting of the Prime Minister Recep Tayyip Erdoğan with media owners and executives on 20 October 2011 on the media coverage of terrorism and violence incidents. Çongar contended that some media executives and owners were more willing to censor themselves than the prime minister (Çongar 2011). The following day, the five biggest news agencies[6] announced in a joint statement that they were going to 'comply with the publication bans of the competent authorities' (Söylemez 2011).

In recent years, some popular journalists and columnists have lost their jobs due to their critical comments on Government policies especially on Kurdish issues. Moreover, the prime minister has targeted some columnists and pleaded to media owners to keep their columnists under control or dismiss them for their negative coverage of the Government's policies (Söylemez 2012a). On 29 December 2011, the mainstream media including the television news channels were unable to cover the deaths of 34 Kurdish civilian by Turkish military fighter jets in a village of Hakkari province during the first 18 hours, i.e. until the Government's press release.

A recent survey (Arsan 2011) showed that a very high percentage of journalists complain about censorship and self-censorship in the media. They fear being taken to court and feel intimidated by the Government and patronage pressure. On the other hand, self-censorship results not only from Government pressure, but also from the unwillingness of the media executives, columnists and editors to risk their careers and high incomes. Moreover, as Hallin and Mancini pointed out, media owners and journalists also have political ties or alliances in Mediterranean countries (Hallin and Mancini 2004: 98). Likewise the ideological polarizations and political divisions among journalists prevent a collaborative struggle against censorship and self-censorship.

The practice of accreditation is also considered another form of censorship in the media. In accordance with the political polarization some media organs have been restricted in their access to official press meetings by some public authorities on a routine basis. While accreditation indeed is been known as a common practice of the army, recently this controversial practice has been adopted by the AKP, which denied accreditation to six national newspapers to its fourth annual party congress in September 2012. It should be added that the selective distribution of press cards by the Directorate General of Press and Information of the Office of the Prime Ministry also constitutes a form of accreditation. In many countries, this process is undertaken by industry associations, trades unions, and professional associations (Kurban and Sözeri 2012).

However, the working conditions of journalists must be examined to understand their submission to censorship and self-censorship. As Topuz (2012) contends an editor who prefers to maintain editorial independence at the same time has to face up to becoming unemployed. According to official statistics, the informal employment rate is very high in the media sector. The average wages are very low compared to those of other sectors (Sözeri and Güney 2011). The owners have adopted a highly discriminative wage policy that has been very effective in breaking down solidarity among the higher and lower levels of media employees (Alpay 2010). The weakening of horizontal solidarity among journalists due to the low rates of unionization also has worked to the benefit of the media owners.

Censorship is observed more significantly on Internet through blocking web pages. Internet Law no. 5651 authorizes the banning of access to websites where there are sufficient reasons for a 'suspicion' of crimes as enumerated[7] in Article 8. Moreover, web site access can be banned by a judge (in the investigation phase), a court (in the prosecution phase), or by TİB (Telekomünikasyon İletişim Başkanlığı, Telecommunication Communication Presidency) in cases in which the content provider is outside of Turkey or where the content concerns the sexual abuse of children or obscenity. In practice, the blocking of Internet sites often results in the blocking of content that has nothing to do with child pornography or hate speech inciting people to violence (Hammarberg 2011a). Therefore, the issue was eventually taken to the ECtHR and recently the Court found Turkey guilty of blocking Google Sites in its judgements in the case of *Ahmet Yıldırım vs. Turkey*, as can be seen in detail at the last section.

Jailed journalists and coverage of sensitive issues

In addition to censorship and self-censorship, the Turkish journalists also face prosecution and long-term detention on the grounds of journalistic activities in violation of the penal code and anti-terror law. According to Media Monitoring Reports of BİA (Independent Communication Network) at least 167 journalists have been detained on grounds of terrorist propaganda, coverage of unpermitted demonstrations, and relationships with illegal organizations in the last 10 years (Gülcan 2013). The Committee to Protect Journalists (CPJ) identified 76 journalists jailed as of August 1, 2012. At least 61 of them were being held in direct relation to their published work or newsgathering activities (CPJ 2012: 6). The BİA also declared that 104 journalists and 30 newspaper distributers had been imprisoned only in 2012 (Gülcan 2013) however, as stated in the Platform of Solidarity with Detained Journalists comprised of 14 professional press organizations under the direction of the TGC

(*Türkiye Gazeteciler Cemiyeti*, Turkish Journalists Association) there are 91 journalists in jail as of 5 May 2012. While the contradiction between the numbers arises from the definition of a journalist and the definition of journalistic activity, Justice Minister Sadullah Ergin responded to the list of 91 people, which was published on 5 May 2012 by 'the Platform of Solidarity with Detained Journalists' functioning in Turkey as follows:

> Four people in the list have no prison entry record. Twenty-four of the remaining are convicted; sixty-three are detainees and only six out of the total number (91) possess a press card"[8]

However, as mentioned above distribution of the press card is also quite problematic since, not all journalists have a press card and not every individual who has a press card is a journalist (Kurban and Sözeri, 2012). On the other hand Ergin defended the government's approach to the CPJ report asserting that

> all the people imprisoned in our country, the great majority of those who are tried to be linked with journalist identity are the ones who are deprived of their liberty on the grounds of serious offences such as membership of an armed terrorist organization, kidnapping, possession of unregistered firearm and hazardous substance, bombing and murder.
> (Government response to CPJ report by Justice Minister Sadullah Ergin, quoted in CPJ, 2012: 52)

Moreover, within an interview with Hard Talk broadcasted on BBC, Egemen Bağış, the Minister in Charge of EU Affairs, claimed without hesitation that the journalists in prison were charged with crimes such as 'rape, murder and robbery' (Söylemez, 2012b).

According to the CPJ report (CPJ 2012: 9), more than 70 per cent, and 64 per cent as reported by BİA (Gülcan 2013), of the jailed journalists are Kurdish or work for the Kurdish media. Most of them have been charged with aiding terrorist organizations by covering the viewpoints and activities of the banned PKK, and the KCK *Koma Ciwakên Kurdistan* (Kurdistan Communities Union). As stated in the CPJ report (2012:7), basic news-gathering activities, receiving tips, assigning stories, conducting interviews, and relaying information to colleagues were the basis of the prosecutions. Moreover, as the chief editor of the Kurdish daily *Azadiye Welat,* Vedat Kurşun, contended the courts impose the upper limit of penalties on the staff of Kurdish media compared to their Turkish counterparts.[9]

The coverage of Kurdish issues has also suffered from mainstream media disinformation in addition to state repression. Especially in the 1990s, reporters, editors and distributors of Kurdish publications faced the risks of death, torture, and detention and also they were unable to get their real stories published in the mainstream media (Solmaz 2012); in addition, when

Abdüllah Öcalan, the imprisoned leader of the PKK appeared in the news, adjectives such as 'baby killer' or 'the head of terrorists' would appear before his name (Aktan 2012; Solmaz 2012). In the same way, the phrase 'so-called' always qualified any reference to the Armenian genocide and it was inserted by the editors due to political repression and self-censorship.

The mainstream media owners and the chief editors mostly share a common mind-set, one that rests on protecting the 'state interest' concerning the coverage of sensitive issues (Kurban and Sözeri 2012: 49). The most vicious outcome of this alliance was observed before the assassination of an Armenian journalist Hrant Dink. After he published an article stating that the adopted daughter of Turkey's founder could have been an Armenian survivor of the 1915 genocide, the media targeted him as an object of hatred, even after his death (İnceoğlu and Sözeri 2012). The defamatory media campaign and the legal case against him based on Article 301 on the grounds of insulting Turkishness cannot be undervalued in the events leading to his assassination. The young nationalist murderer defended himself by blaming the newspapers which had shown Dink as hating Turks (Çandar 2011).

EU integration process and ECtHR cases

The problems concerning freedom of expression and freedom of press have often occupied the agenda both in Turkey and abroad since the country became a candidate to the EU in 1999 (Christensen 2010: 178). The integration process also gained an important dimension in Turkey's legislative system. The Government adopted a reform package to fulfil the Copenhagen Political Criteria in terms of freedom of expression and freedom of press. Accordingly, despite its shortcomings and the restrictions, i.e. many documents are unavailable on the grounds that they are considered to be a 'state secret', the Right to Information Act was implemented in 2003 to provide the accessibility of information from the public authorities to ordinary people and journalists. In addition, in 2004, broadcasts in 'languages traditionally used by Turkish citizens in their daily lives' were allowed as a part of the reforms (Alpay 2010: 382).

The impact of the EU integration on media policy making was perhaps most visible in the recent enactment of Law No. 6112 in 2011. In preparing the draft, Turkish policy makers strived to develop a text in harmony with the EU Directive (Kurban and Sözeri 2012: 32). However, different from the Directive, the excessively-detailed broadcasting principles cast in ambiguous wording provide potential loopholes to limit freedom of expression (Sümer and Adaklı, 2011). Finally, these principles contain references to notions subject to subjective interpretation, such as 'public morality,' 'family values,' and the 'trivialization of violence,' etc. (Hammarberg, 2011: para.32)

The reforms were left off after the second general election victory of the AKP in 2007. As Hammarberg (2011) pointed out, Turkey has not yet taken all of the necessary measures to effectively prevent violations of freedom of expression and freedom of the media. Especially the Penal Code and Anti-Terror Law still cause serious problems for freedom of expression despite the amendments adopted in 2004 and in 2006 (Hammarberg, 2011: para.15). Specifically, Article 215 (praising a crime or criminal), Article 216 (inciting the population to enmity or hatred and denigration), Article 301 (insulting the Turkish nation, the state of the Turkish Republic, the Turkish Grand National Assembly, the government of the Republic of Turkey or the judicial organs of the state), Article 318 (discouraging persons from doing their military service) of Penal Code increase the cases against journalists. Recently, it has been observed that Article 220 (forming organized groups with the intention of committing crime) of the Penal Code and its application are causing significant concerns about freedom of the media (Hammarberg, 2011, para.18). Article 301, with which Hrant Dink was tried, continues to be a thorn and threat to the freedom of expression (Christansen 2010: 182).

Similarly, the relevant paragraphs of Article 6 (such as para. 2: punishment for printing or publishing declarations or leaflets emanating from terrorist organizations; para. 4: imprisonment of owners and editors; para. 5: suspension by a judge of the publication of periodicals containing propaganda of a terrorist organization, incitement to commit a crime, or praising of a crime that has been committed) and Article 7 (para. 2: punishment for propaganda in favour of a terrorist organization increases by half if committed through the press, including punishment for the owner and editor of the periodical) of the Anti-Terror Law concerned particularly freedom of expression in Kurdish media. Although recently some new legal reforms including the relevant articles in of the Anti-Terror Law have been applied, these remain short-sighted and are not likely to provide more freedom of expression (HRW 2012).

These two laws have also been the reasons for the large number of freedom of expression cases in front of the ECtHR on the grounds of violations of Article 10 of the European Convention on Human Rights ('ECHR'). As Judge Karakaş[10] notes, Turkey has the worst record on freedom of expression and freedom of press cases at the ECtHR. There were 207 decisions against Turkey between 1959 – 2011. It is thought that this number will gradually increase in the near future because the Court is now giving priority to appeals concerning violations of the right to live and torture allegations.

The Court pointed out the chilling effects on press freedom of the rulings based on the Penal Code and the Anti-Terror Law such as *Ürper and Others* and *Turgay and Others*, which means dissuading journalists from publishing similar news in the future, which therefore constituted an indirect way of censorship (Kurban and Sözeri 2012: 43). In 2010, the Court found a violation of Article 10 ECHR in regards to Hrant Dink's conviction based on Article 301 despite the amendment adopted in 2008, which subjects prosecution to a prior authorization by the Ministry of Justice in each individual case. Then in 2011, in its judgment in the case of *Akçam vs. Turkey*, the ECtHR emphasized once more that the amendment to Article 301 is not a solution to the abusive application of Article 301; moreover, it is open to the interpretative attitudes of the Ministry of Justice. The ECtHR's judgments in the cases of *Dink vs. Turkey* (concerning Article 301 of the Turkish Criminal Code as amended) and *Gözel and Özer vs. Turkey* (concerning Article 6, para. 2 of the Anti-Terrorism Act as amended) indicate that 'the provisions in the amended texts have kept the contents of the former texts largely intact' (Hammarberg 2011: para.15).

At the end of 2012 the ECtHR delivered a very important judgement in the case of *Ahmet Yıldırım vs. Turkey* on the blocking of Google sites in Turkey to the effect that it violated the right to freedom of expression, i.e. Article 10 of the Convention. The decision is accepted as 'a strong message that wholesale blocking of Internet services is arbitrary, overbroad, and violates the freedom of expression online' (HRW, 2012). In addition to the violation of the applicant's right to access his own Internet site, the ECtHR's decision pointed out that Article 8 of Internet Law no. 5651, the Turkish Government 'had failed to meet the foreseeability requirement under the Convention and had not afforded the applicant the degree of protection to which he was entitled by the rule of law in a democratic society.' Thus, in addition to local NGOs like The Alternative Informatics Association (Alternatif Bilişim Derneği 2012), the OSCE Representative on Freedom of the Media, the Commissioner for Human Rights of the Council of Europe, and the European Commission have all called on the Turkish Government to revise Internet Law 5651 substantially or to repeal it altogether (HRW 2012).

Conclusion

From the outset journalists have belonged to an elitist group in charge of the modernization of society and of supporting state reforms. The media owners have always been dependant on the state in political and economic matters. Therefore, Turkey's media policies and some aspects of the regulation of freedom of expression have been considered a reflection of state-centric modernity (Kaymas 2011:62). While political engagement was significant for media-state relationships at the beginning, after the third coup d'état in 1980, the end of the military rule resulted in a shift in the ownership structure in the media. With the termination of the state monopoly over broadcasting in the 1990s, a few conglomerates that increased their economic power through vertical and horizontal mergers began to dominate whole sectors of the media. Later on, some media groups which had investments in both the financial and media sector were seriously affected by the 2001 crisis; some to such a degree that they were completely wiped out while others were seized by the Savings Deposit Insurance Fund.

The financial crisis played a significant role in the reconfiguration of the media in the 2000s. The AKP, which came to power in 2002, forced the biggest media group to downsize while supporting the reconfiguration of a proponent mainstream media. Although the power shifted from the opponent mainstream media to 'proponent' media companies, the media market remained dominated by the same big media groups who had already invested in other sectors. However, these groups became too weak vis-à-vis the political power of the ruling party because they no longer pursued the balance policy between the army and the ruling party or the opposition.

This dependence was reflected in the editorial policies. The opposition and the negative coverage of the government's policies by the mainstream media decreased substantially. Self-censorship became a significant problem as a result of political pressure and the unwillingness of the media executives, columnists, and editors to risk their careers and high incomes. On the other hand, it should be kept in mind that the average wages are very low and the informal employment rate is very high in media compared to other sectors. The vulnerable position of journalists vis-à-vis the media owners' self-censorship practices and the political pressure is also the result of the competition, the unionization practices and lack of horizontal solidarity in the profession.

Journalists also struggle with serious legal issues which have resulted in a large number of journalists being incarcerated for substantial periods of time. Although the reforms on freedom of expression and freedom of press created a positive climate in last decade, the violations of these freedoms and the increasing number of jailed journalists raise serious concerns inside and outside Turkey. Considering the problems arising from the Penal Code and Anti-Terror Law, it is clear that Turkey has not yet taken all of the necessary measures to prevent violations of freedom of expression and freedom of the media effectively.

As a result, as Miyase Christensen (2010: 181) pointed out, state-centric modernization has produced state-controlled media discourse and banal nationalism. In addition, after the shifting ownership-structure, the media came under the sway of corporate interests, nepotism, and clientelist relations, which are always in accordance with 'state interest.' The lack of unionization and horizontal solidarity among the journalists prevent an effective struggle concerning political pressure that appears as censorship and self-censorship and even enhances their working conditions against the media owners and the state. As in other Southern European countries, the state plays a large role in the media and the political polarization and lack of political consensus block off to overcome in a comprehensive manner all the obstacles for freedom of expression and freedom of media in Turkey.

Notes

1 The new amendment also removed the restrictions on cross ownership and participation in public tenders and the stock market. However, the Constitutional Court cancelled relative clauses of Article 29 of the new broadcasting law no. 4756 on the grounds that they caused monopolization in the Turkish broadcasting market and violated Article 167 of the constitution, which tasks the state with the prevention of 'the formation, in practice or by agreement, of monopolies and cartels in the markets.

2 It was called the February 28th process because of the 'post-modern military coup' of 28 February 1997.

3 The information recently revealed by the criminal investigations into the February 28th process indicates that the military was also a part of the coalition to

which Alpay (2010:378) refers and was engaged in 'rampant corruptions' in the period running up to the 2001 financial crisis.

4 After the elimination of some dissident journalists and columnists and shifting the editorial policies towards a positive outlook to the Government, a large portion of these fines were included in the scope of a tax amnesty law of October 2012 (Dorduncukuvvet Medya, 2012).

5 Turgay Ciner; Written reports of the Parliamentary Coup and Memorandum Investigation Commission, Istanbul, 05 October 2012.

6 These were Anadolu, Turkish News, Ankara News, Cihan News, and İhlas News.

7 These are incitement to suicide, sexual exploitation and abuse of children, facilitating the use of drugs, obscenity, prostitution, arranging a place or facility for gambling, and crimes defined in the Law on Crimes Committed against Atatürk (no. 5816).

8 'Turkey's press freedom crisis,' *CPJ Special Reports*. Online. Available HTTP: <http://www.cpj.org/reports/2012/10/turkeys-press-freedom-crisis-appendex-ii-government-responses.php> (accessed 8 July 2013).

9 Minutes of the Conference and Panel: Media in the Claws of Market, Power and Ownership: Freedom of the Press in Turkey, Istanbul, 23 November 2012.

10 Minutes of the panel discussion of the Friedrich-Ebert-Stiftung, Umut Foundation, Bianet and European Federation of Journalists on 'Media Freedom and Freedom of Expression in Turkey Current Developments,' Istanbul, 24 November 2012.

References

Alpay, Ş. (2010) 'Two faces of the press in Turkey: the role of media in Turkey's modernisation and democracy', in C.J. Kerslake, K. Öktem & P. Robins (eds.), *Turkey's engagement with modernity,* Oxford: Palgrave Macmillan.

Aktan, H. (2012) *Kürt Vatandaş* [The Kurdish citizen], Istanbul: Iletisim Publishing.

Arsan, E. (2011) 'Gazeteci Gözüyle Sansür ve Otosansür' [Censorship and self-censorship in the Turkish news media], *Cogito*, 67:56.

Bek, M.G. (2004) 'Research note: Tabloidization of news media: an analysis of television news in Turkey', *European Journal of Communication*, 19(3): 371–86.

Cemal, H. (2012) 'Büyük Medyanın Eski Gücü Neden mi yok?' [And why does the big media no longer have the power of its hey days?], *Milliyet*, 4 May 2012. Online. Available HTTP: <http://siyaset.milliyet.com.tr/buyuk-medyanin-eski-gucu-neden-mi-yok-/siya-set/siyasetyazardetay/04.05.2012/1535945/default.htm> (accessed 7 May 2012).

Christensen, C. (2007) 'Concentration of ownership, the fall of unions and government legislation in Turkey', *Global Media and Communication*, 3(2): 179–99.

Christensen, M. (2010) 'Notes on the public sphere on a national and post-national axis: Journalism and freedom of expression in Turkey', *Global Media and Communication*, 6(2): 177–197.

Committee to Protect Journalists (2012). 'Special reports: Turkey's press freedom crisis'. Online. Available HTTP: <http://www.cpj.org/reports/2012/10/turkeys-press-freedom-crisis.php> (accessed 14 December 2012).

Çandar, T. (2011) *Hrant*, Istanbul: Everest Publications.

Çongar, Y. (2011) 'Millî' gazetecilik ve 'gayrımillî' hislerim' [National journalism and my non-national feelings] *Taraf,* 21 October 2011. Online. Available HTTP: <http://www.taraf.com.tr/yasemin-congar/makale-milli-gazetecilik-ve-gayrimilli-hislerim.htm> (accessed 10 January 2013).

Dorduncukuvvet Medya (2012) 'Doğan Yapılandırmadan Faydalandı, Borçlarını Ödedi' [Doğan benefitted from debt restructuring and paid its debts], *Dorduncukuvvet Medya,* 1 October 2012. Online. Available HTTP: <http://www.dorduncukuvvetmedya.com/

index.php?option=com_content&view=article& id = 4736:aydin-dogan-devlete-olan-borclarini-odedi& catid = 34:medyajans& Itemid = 53> (accessed 14 December 2012).

Elmas, E., and D. Kurban (2011) *Communicating democracy-Democratizing communication. Media in Turkey: Legislation, policies, actors*, Istanbul: TESEV Publications.

European Commission (2012) *Turkey 2012 Progress Report*. Online. Available HTTP: <http://ec.europa.eu/enlargement/pdf/key_documents/2012/package/tr_rapport_2012_en.pdf> (accessed 14 December 2012).

Gülcan, E. (2013) 'İfade Özgürlüğünün On Yılını Okumak' [Reading the 10 years of freedom of expression] *Biamag*, 5 January 2013. Online. Available HTTP: <http://www.bianet.org/biamag/kitap%25E2%2580%25932/143165-ifade-ozgur lugunun-on-yilini-okumak#.UOhidCu6ycA.twitter> (accessed 10 January 2013).

Gürkan, N. (1998) *Türkiye'de Demokrasiye Geçişte Basın (1945–1950)* [The Press in Turkey during transition to democracy (1945–50)], Istanbul: Iletisim Publishing.

Hallin, D.C., and P. Mancini (2004) *Comparing media systems: three models of media and politics*, Cambridge: Cambridge University Press.

Hammarberg, T. (2011) 'Freedom of expression and media freedom in Turkey'. Online. Available HTTP: <https://wcd.coe.int/ViewDoc.jsp?id=1814085> (accessed 20 November 2011).

Human Rights Watch (2012) 'Turkey: End Overly Broad Website Blocking: European Court Rules Against Government in Google Sites Case'. Online. Available HTTP: <http://www.hrw.org/news/2012/12/21/turkey-end-overly-broad-website-blocking> (accessed 10 January 2013).

İnceoğlu, Y., and C. Sözeri (2012) 'Nefret Suçlarında Medyanın Sorumluluğu: 'Ya sev ya terket ya da … ' [The role of the media in hate crimes: 'Love it or leave it or …], in Y. Inceoglu, (ed.), *Nefret Söylemi ve / veya Nefret Suçları [Hate Speech and / or Hate Crimes]*, Istanbul: Ayrıntı Publishing.

Karaalioğlu, M. (2012) 'Reklam bütçeleriyle korunan eski medya düzeni' [The old media order that protected by advertising budgets], *Star*, 10 December 2012. Online. Available HTTP: <http://haber.stargazete.com/yazar/reklam-butceleriyle-kor-unan-eski-medya-duzeni/yazi-710609> (accessed 10 January 2013).

Kaymas, S.A. (2011) 'Media Policy Paradigm Shift in Turkey: Rethinking Neo-Authoritarian Media Systems in the Age of Neo Liberalism', Acta Universitatis Danubius. Communicatio, 5(1): 40–69.

Kurban, D.and C. Sözeri (2012) *Caught in the Wheels of Power: The Political, Legal and Economic Constraints on Independent Media and Freedom of the Press in Turkey*, Istanbul: TESEV Publications.

Savaşın Tanıkları Gazeteciler Anlatıyor [Witnesses of War]. [Documentary] Directed by Sami Solmaz. Istanbul.

Söylemez, A. (2012a) 'Başbakan'dan "Medya Kılavuzu"' [Media guidance from Prime Minister], *Bianet*, 15 August 2012. Online. Available HTTP: <http://bianet. org/biamag/bianet/140332-basbakandan-medya-kilavuzu> (accessed 14 December 2012).

Söylemez, A. (2012b) 'Kim bu "Tecavüzcü" Gazeteciler?' [Who are these 'rapist' journalists?], *Bianet*, 7 March 2012, http://www.bianet.org/bianet/ifade-ozgurlugu/ 136753-kim-bu-tecavuzcu-gazeteciler, (accessed 26 May 2012).

Söylemez, A. (2011) 'We will comply with official publication bans … ', *Bianet*, 24 October 2011. Online. Available HTTP: <http://www.bianet.org/english/freedom-75of-expression/ 133600-we-will-comply-with-official-publication-bans> (accessed 14 December 2012).

Sözeri, C. and Z. Güney (2011) *The Political Economy of the Media in Turkey: A Sectoral Analysis*, Istanbul: TESEV Publications.

Sümer, B. and G. Adaklı (2011), 'Ankara Üniversitesi İletişim Fakültesi'nin Radyo ve Televizyonların Kuruluş ve Yayın Hizmetleri Hakkındaki Kanun Tasarısı Taslağı Değerlendirme Raporu' [Evalua-tion Report of the New Broadcasting Law Draft]. Online. Available HTTP: <http://ilef.ankara.edu.tr/gorsel/dosya/1275562046RTUK_ TASLAGI – ILEF_GORU-SU_2010.pdf> (accessed 24 December 2011).

The Parliamentary Coup and Memorandum Investigation Commission. (2012) *Written reports*, Istanbul, 05 October 2012. Online. Available HTTP: <http://t24. com.tr/haber/turgay-ciner-komisyona-neler-anlatti/217367> (accessed 10 January 2013).

Topuz, H. (2003) *II. Mahmut'tan Holdinglere Türk Basın Tarihi* [Turkish press history from Mahmut II to conglomerates], Istanbul: Remzi Kitabevi.

Part VII

Conclusions

22 Some observations on Turkey's democratization process

Carmen Rodríguez, Antonio Ávalos, Hakan Yılmaz and Ana I. Planet

Turkey is in the midst of a process of democratization. The political regime that emerged after the 1980 coup d'état produced a defective democracy of an illiberal and tutelary nature. Since the first elections held after the coup in 1983, Turkey has undergone important transformations during which – for both internal and external reasons – the regime's democratization process has advanced. The most important of the external causes, of course, is Turkey's candidacy for EU membership, which was solidly promoted by the 1999 Helsinki European Council, resulting in the opening of negotiations between Ankara and Brussels in October 2005. The EU's influence has been notable, especially because it came to serve as a catalyst at a specific point in time for a broad political and social spectrum, contributing to a consensus in favour of far-reaching political reforms. Turkey's candidacy to the EU and the need to fulfil the Copenhagen criteria fostered a deeper overall review of the Turkish political system. Until that time, advances in democratization had been characterised by piecemeal reforms.

Indeed, the regime that resulted from the 1980 coup d'état did undergo changes and experience a slow, progressive return to electoral normalcy. However, it did not manage to fulfil all of the criteria supposedly inherent in a liberal democracy, according to the terminology of embedded democracies put forth by Merkel (2004).

This book makes it clear that, as in the Chilean case, Turkey underwent an incomplete transition, since the military maintained prerogatives in the political sphere that allowed it to have the final say in the regime and held on to key spheres of power which were, furthermore, protected by the 1982 Turkish Constitution. All of this resulted in a defective democracy that was tutelary (controlled by the military establishment) and illiberal (in which there were severe limitations on the exercise of public freedoms and fundamental rights and the effective rule of law). However, especially in recent years, important transformations have taken place in this defective democracy. How should this process of transformation and change be analysed? We have chosen to use the theoretical framework of democratic consolidation, while qualifying that in Turkey, a process of democratic consolidation *per se* is not taking place.

Borrowing from Valenzuela (1992), we have come to understand that with this type of regime–where an incomplete transition gives rise to a hybrid regime – if a democratization process takes place, it does not consist of consolidating existing dynamics and institutions, but rather of dismantling the institutions that stand in the way of a fully operative liberal democracy that incorporates the following characteristics: inclusive and fair competition for power, that, once achieved, allows democratic governments to be fully capable of administering and making political decisions that guarantee fundamental rights and freedoms. Our approach, therefore, complements Schedler (1998), who argues that the type of democratization process that affects semi-democratic regimes cannot be understood as a consolidation of the regime, but as a process of "democratic completion."

Linz and Stepan (1996a) defined five arenas which can be used to examine the dynamics of democratic consolidation: political society, civil society, economic society, state apparatus, and the rule of law. These can be of great assistance when analysing the democratization processes that affect hybrid regimes, particularly when they are identified as defective democracies, as in this case. Using these five arenas, the changes and transformations involved and the factors that promote or hamper them can be observed.

Before beginning the analysis of the five arenas, however, the book's authors consider two macro variables that affect democratic transitions and democratic consolidation, the question of "stateness" (the state in which the process is taking place) and the nature of the prior regime, along with one contextual variable, international influence.

The chapter by Ibrahim Saylan considers exactly how the process of modernization promoted by the Turkish state since its early stages "claimed the congruence of nation and state", resulting in policies of homogenization designed to establish a monolithic nation that ignored or assimilated cultural, religious and ethnic differences. The citizenship policies put into practice, far from protecting this diversity, marginalised or assimilated non-Muslims and non-Turkish Muslims. In his article, the author argues that if the democratization process is to be fostered in Turkey, the civic dimension of the citizenry must be emphasised. This would permit the integration and inclusion of different gender, linguistic, ethnic and religious identities. Indeed, this is the issue that seems to be at the root of the problems inherent in reaching a consensus on a new Turkish constitution: the political elites responsible for the process are finding it difficult to accommodate the demands for recognition related to questions of identity, as Saylan explains. Despite these difficulties, however, it should be noted that this requirement for democracy is a growing topic of discussion in the public debate.

For Linz and Stepan, another key macro variable is the nature of the prior regime, a crucial variable to understanding the possible consequences of democratization processes. İlter Turan's chapter analyses not only Turkey's democratic experiences but also its authoritarian legacy, inviting readers to reflect on a visible shift in the political paradigm in recent years, "a long-term transition from a security maximization to a prosperity maximization paradigm." This is an important step if Turkish politics are to be more pragmatic and less ossified in terms of the ideological questions that have preserved the status quo until now. This and other chapters explain how a predominant political view developed in Turkey over decades in which the state took precedence over society, whose autonomy was reduced and whose political action was limited. A specific way of understanding the preservation of the state prevailed at the expense of fundamental rights and freedoms. The 1980 coup d'état continued and notably reinforced this view, suppressing some of the democratic achievements reached in earlier decades. After the coup, the political system was reformed and important changes were adopted aimed at depoliticising citizens. At the same time, however, economic liberalization and the elimination of protectionist barriers in the economy were promoted. Although the coup d'état sought to moderate political options and put an end to the ideological polarization of the 1960s and 1970s, in the 1990s political polarization began to develop around two main questions: ethnic identity and religious identity.

Turan's argument leads to the idea that what is required for a successful democratization process is not so much the absence of conflicts, but the knowledge of how to establish the necessary democratic mechanisms to resolve them. Dismantling the authoritarian legacy is difficult; inertia persists and important sectors oppose change, but the malleability of Turkish society and politics is particularly important in this respect. In recent years, the sectors that defended their conception of the state against the rights of citizens have lost clout (though not importance). Furthermore, the arena for political wrangling has grown larger, and actors from both political and civil society without any deep-rooted ties to the state (or that even suffered state repression) are facing off there. The question is whether these new actors are capable of acting within a new legal framework.

The chapter by William Hale deals with a contextual variable: external factors in the process of Turkish democratization. This variable has been extremely important since the time of the Ottoman Empire for different reasons and the new Turkish state has also undergone significant transformations due to external influence, either to adapt itself to the spirit of the times or for more tactical reasons. When the synergies of change coincide inside and outside the country, as occurred after the Second World War and during Turkey's candidacy for EU membership, the external impact is certainly much greater. Although the United States has been a powerful influence at key moments, the relationship with European countries and especially the process of joining the EU has had a much more significant overall impact. The democratization process cannot be imposed from outside, but outside influence can positively encourage internal changes. Beginning in 1999, the EU was a key catalyst for the Turkish reform process; however, as Hale notes, it has lost weight in Turkey. On the one hand, this has given the country greater autonomy in the democratization process, allowing Turks to assimilate and see it as *sui generis* instead of directed and demanded by external factors. On the other more negative hand, the external reinforcement to push the process forward in difficult times would seem to be lost.

After the analysis of these two macro variables and the contextual variable of international influence, the book analyses the five arenas delineated by Linz and Stepan in order to study the dynamics of democratic consolidation. The section on political society begins with the chapter by Sabri Sayarı, which focuses on the Turkish party system and its recent transformations.

As Sayarı discusses in the chapter, studying political parties requires analysing not only their ideology and organization, but also how the party system itself functions. In the Turkish case, the political society is undergoing a remarkable renewal among its elites. In addition to the traditional elites which arose under the aegis of Kemalism, other recently consolidated groups have emerged from what is known in the Turkish political and social sphere as the periphery (Mardin 1972). These include most notably the political elites of the AKP (*Adalet ve Kalkınma Partisi,* Justice and Development Party) who belonged to the Islamist parties led by Necmettin Erbakan that were successively banned and the difficult grouping of politicians from pro-Kurdish parties.

In the first case, the AKP has managed to position itself as the top centre-right party in Turkey, roundly supplanting the parties that had filled this space on the political spectrum before and after the 1980 coup d'état, after winning three consecutive general elections with an overwhelming majority far above the nearest opposition party, the CHP (*Cumhuriyet Halk Partisi,* Republican People's Party). The constitutional court's decision to hear a closure case against the AKP in 2008 was a challenge backed by some sectors of the judicial system that appeared to have the power to debilitate the party in government, which had been accused of anti-secular activities. In the end, the AKP was not banned and its position was strengthened after the shock passed. There has been some speculation about the impact that this case against the AKP might have had on its later reactions to the judiciary and the military establishment (Jenkins, 2009: 46).

The pro-Kurdish BDP (*Barış ve Demokrasi Parti,* Peace and Democracy Party) – the other sector that had traditionally belonged to the political periphery – won significant parliamentary representation after the 2011 legislative elections. This party faces difficulties carrying out its political activity. In Turkey, the BDP is a survivor party, the heir to successive banned pro-Kurdish parties accused of collaborating with the PKK (*Partiya Karkerên Kurdistan,* Kurdistan Workers Party). It is severely limited by the 10 per cent electoral threshold, which its candidates work around by putting forward individual candidates in specific constituencies. During the 2011 campaign, members of the BDP reported that the authorities put a number of impediments in their way when they tried to hold campaign rallies and that their headquarters were searched. Additionally, the BDP, which occupies an essential place on the political spectrum – it is needed to channel the demands of an important part of the population and to play a constructive role in the Kurdish conflict – is also limited by the impact and presence of the PKK as a key actor in the resolution of the Kurdish question. Members of the BDP have had no qualms about naming Abdullah Öcalan as the leader for Kurdish demands on a number of occasions.[1]

The BDP and PKK share a common social base and the former has not hesitated to recognise the relevance of the latter and let it take the leading role, all of which has complicated how it is received in the Turkish political party system. This leads to problems of inclusivity in the system, as Sayarı discusses in his article. These are not only motivated by the institutional limitations that make it difficult to normalise the activities of one or more pro-Kurdish parties in Turkey, but also by the very position of the BDP, overshadowed by the enormous influence of the PKK and its leader Abdullah Öcalan.

The main opposition party, the CHP, under the leadership of Deniz Baykal until 2010, developed a growing nationalist and secular rhetoric, which brought it ideologically close to the ultranationalist MHP (*Milliyetçi Hareket Partisi*, Nationalist Action Party) party and distanced it from the characteristics supposedly inherent in a centre-left social democratic party. When Kemal Kılıçdaroğlu became leader of the CHP in May 2010, the party changed its rhetoric and positioned itself much more clearly in favour of democratic reforms and Turkey's candidacy to the EU, as can be seen in the fact that one of Kılıcdaroğlu's first trips after succeeding Baykal was to Brussels. He also wasted no time in calling for a decrease in the electoral threshold from 10 per cent to 7 per cent or 5 per cent.

While Baykal strongly criticised the government for its attempts at conciliation in 2009 regarding the Kurdish question, Kılıçdaroğlu in contrast announced the following at the beginning of January 2013 with respect to the new peace initiative recently launched between the Turkish Government and the PKK leader Abdullah Öcalan: "Despite all the mistakes it has made in the past, we are issuing the AKP new credit. So solve the problem". It remains to be seen how far an agreement between the AKP and CHP on the peace plan will go, but there has been a clear change in attitude on the part of the CHP leader, who is developing a more sensitive discourse towards democratic demands on this topic, than the one held by his predecessor.

The ultranationalist MHP party formed part of the Government coalition from 1999–2002 and in that role, it also contributed to advancing Turkey's candidacy to the EU and supported some of the political reforms necessary to achieve that. In the legislative reforms of summer 2002, however, it expressed its direct opposition to abolishing the death penalty for cases of terrorism and to supporting cultural rights that would primarily affect the Kurdish population, alluding to the possible Balkanization of the country.

The MHP defends a rhetoric that constantly draws on the fear of the possible territorial disintegration of the country and the erosion of national sovereignty. It is consequently very reluctant to support some democratization reforms, especially those related to cultural rights and greater regional autonomy.

Within the sphere of political society – and bearing in mind the objective of establishing an embedded democracy as defined by Merkel (2004) – the Turkish party system must first lower the electoral threshold from 10 per cent to provide greater inclusivity. The political system must also remove the formal and informal obstacles that make it difficult for a pro-Kurdish party to function and become normalised in the system. In this respect, it is also the responsibility of the pro-Kurdish parties, in this case the BDP, to develop constructive policies that are decoupled from the PKK's shadow of violence. The BDP also forms part of the new peace talk process with the PKK and its support will be essential.

The current party system is less fragmented than in earlier times, as Sayarı explains, and enjoys greater stability. However, it is often noted that Turkish democracy would be better off if the AKP had a clear political adversary in the CHP that could serve to balance power. At this time, there is a considerable gap between the AKP and the opposition, which is especially problematic given that, as the author discusses, the AKP has developed an understanding of democracy over the last few years that is based on the power of the majority. This attitude is not amenable to conflict resolution via negotiated pacts and agreements in a country that requires inclusive politics to promote democratic participation and respond to the demands of very different sectors. Sayarı also notes one more key fact: the loss of military power vis-à-vis the political arena in recent times has given greater autonomy to the parties, which must fill the entire political space effectively.

While the dynamics of the party system per se are important, any observation of how the democratization process is evolving must also analyse the consenting or dissenting positions that the parties have taken in promoting or supporting democratization reforms. To what extent do they advance or impede the democratization process? As previous authors have noted, parties must channel society's demands, govern independently after winning at the polls, promote regime reforms, grant them legitimacy and contribute to their successful implementation. It is the responsibility of the parties in government to lead this process while the opposition parties either support the party in government in its democratization reforms, hamper them or apply pressure to encourage new changes if the effort made by the party in government is insufficient in this respect.

In recent years, democratization reforms have been highly influenced by Turkey's candidacy for EU membership. Under the 1999–2002 coalition led by Prime Minister Bülent Ecevit, who was leading a tripartite government, the Turkish democratization process was inextricably linked to the political conditions established by Brussels to begin membership negotiations. During this period, the idea was put forward among the political elite and society that changes needed to be made to the system. The tripartite government managed to stay in power until 2002, although it ended its term fatally damaged by the 2001 economic crisis. Looking at the period between 1999 and 2002, it is interesting to observe how very dissimilar parties came together over the need to reform the political system. The 1990s, in comparison, was a "lost decade" in this respect: the parties would not or did not want to reach any substantial agreements on these questions.

In its position as a party in government during 1999–2002, even the ultranationalist MHP favoured Turkey's candidacy to the EU and contributed – although not without problems – to having some important legislative changes approved. However, the MHP made its limits very clear in the laws approved in the summer of 2002, just a few months before the following general elections held in November. The party opposed the abolition of the death penalty for cases of terrorism, the official teaching of languages spoken in Turkey other than Turkish, and radio and television broadcasts in these other languages. Consistent with its ultranationalist ideology, the MHP also opposed the extension of cultural rights, believing that this process might promote separatism under the aegis of the rise of national identities, as occurred in the Balkans. It was also a way of guaranteeing its niche in the elections and setting it apart from the other parties in parliament. In the end, despite their ideological differences, the rest of the parties approved the reform package, either because they believed that the reforms were good or because they considered it the price to pay to gain membership in the EU.

After the 2002 elections, only the AKP and CHP surpassed the electoral threshold that allowed them to share a portion of the seats. In the 2002–7 legislative term, the AKP, backed by a solid absolute majority, managed to open negotiations with the EU in October 2005. From this date on, a slowdown in the government's reform process could be detected. The polarization between the AKP and the main opposition party, in turn, increased considerably.

The research done by Isik Gürleyen shows that although a quarter of the AKP's election manifesto in 2002 was devoted to the issue of democratization, only one eighth of the 2007 election manifesto dealt with it. The data also indicates accordingly that more space was dedicated to fundamental rights and freedoms in the AKP's 2002 electoral manifesto than in 2007. The CHP's manifesto followed this trend, including more proposals on democratization in 2002 than in 2007. As Gürleyen observes, in its 2007 election manifesto the party put special emphasis on threats to territorial integrity, which it believed emanated from the AKP's reformist proposals in certain areas, and more emphasis was placed on questions of security and terrorism in the 2007 elections. The party in government and the main opposition party both decreased the number of political proposals aimed at promoting substantial legislative changes for the democratization of the political system in the AKP's second legislative term. Polarization between the ruling party and the main opposition party also prevented consensus on key issues. This research opens an area that cries out for further investigation at a later date, as do the actions of the MHP and BDP.

The second arena discussed is civil society. The mere fact of having a civil society that can openly question the functioning of the regime and demand substantial transformations in the sphere of democratization is clearly a positive indicator that reveals advances in the democratization process. To begin, it is important to study civil society's possibilities for action. Limitations on the rights of association and freedom of expression can severely constrain the reach of the organizations of civil society. It is therefore important to analyse the context in which they operate. Clearly, their work and impact benefit from an environment that encourages their formation and expansion.

In the Turkish case, the reforms carried out in recent years with respect to freedom of association have clearly encouraged the operability of civil society organizations, although much remains to be done. LGTB organizations, for example, have been subject to important limitations and human rights organizations have encountered restrictions in their activities.

The chapter by Fuat Keyman and Tuba Kancı discusses the fact that no sufficiently clear legal framework exists to protect association activities. The authorities continue to exercise important controls over the movements of different associations, most notably human rights associations. The 2011 report prepared by the U.S. Department of State on human rights in Turkey[2] stated that 'a number of domestic and international human rights groups operated in many regions but faced government obstruction and restrictive laws regarding their operations, particularly in the southeast.' It added that, 'government officials were generally uncooperative and unresponsive to their views, although cooperation increased during the year'.

Civil society is clearly influenced, therefore, by the institutional framework in which it operates and by the action of other actors. The absence of a legislative framework with clear constitutional guarantees does not encourage free action in a country like Turkey with a legacy of restricting rights and significant political repression. On the other hand, civil society can become a force of change and promote significant transformations in defective democracies when it comes to demanding reforms.

The most thoroughly analysed case in the book is that of feminist demands in Turkey presented in the chapter by Pınar İlkkaracan. This study shows how women's organizations have promoted substantial changes in the institutional framework, both in the civil and penal codes. This article also highlights an issue repeated in other chapters: how a slowdown in democratization reforms began to take place in 2005. In any case, civil society, with the advances and limitations discussed by Keyman and Kancı, has become a more vocal actor in recent years.

More peripherally, but very graphically, this trend can also be seen in the art world described by Marcus Graf. The depoliticization of the 1980s found its expression in more conceptual and less political art movements. Later on however, starting in the 1990s, more critical art began to appear. In recent years, the Istanbul Biennials can be analyzed as a reflection of this trend, as they have welcomed questions related to politics, society and urbanism – a sign of greater political openness.

The third arena analysed deals with economic society. For Linz and Stepan, although a consolidated democracy is impossible with a command economy, democratic regimes must deploy an entire set of regulations and institutions that allow for and mould market action. For the authors, moreover:

> Democracy entails free public contestation concerning governmental priorities and policies. If a democracy never produced policies that generated government-mandated public goods in the areas of education, health, and transportation, and never provided some economic safety net for its citizens and some alleviation of gross economic inequality, democracy would not be sustainable.
>
> [1996b: 5]

When referring to the economic arena, Turkey is considered by the European Commission to be a "functioning market economy". In the book, among the different aspects that link the economy to democratization, Mine Eder's analysis focuses on the provision of social services by the Turkish state. In recent years in the country, neoliberal policies promoting the privatization of social services have been combined with an increase in the role of non-governmental organizations in social assistance. Some of the NGOs are religious in nature and tend to promote Islamic communitarianism. The author describes this transformation as "neoliberal populism" with an Islamist ethos.

If social services are provided in a discretionary and arbitrary manner by NGOs, this clearly erodes the concept of a citizenry with universal rights, as Eder notes. Then, access to certain goods and services does not emerge from the demands of a community of citizens, articulated through an active civil society, but rather results in "individual" salvation, subject to agreeing with the conditions that NGOs can impose unilaterally. This promotes a type of social homogenization by necessity, which makes some fundamental citizens' rights secondary to the interests of the most basic survival.

In the fourth section, the different authors look at the state administration, the military establishment, the judiciary and the perception of the state administration among citizens.

As Linz and Stepan have noted, a democratic regime requires a state apparatus that functions correctly and can deliver services to its citizens. This regime must also have extractive capacities that ensure state resources. The article by Süleyman Sözen looks at the important transformations experienced by the state administration that were promoted by the AKP government consistent with the reforms demanded by international actors like the International Monetary Fund and the World Bank due to the 2001 economic crisis and by the EU through the harmonization packages. With these reforms, the administration has sought to be more efficient and accessible to its citizens. Good governance indicators show positive changes in this respect in recent years.

On the other hand, important sectors of the bureaucracy often opposed the political elite in earlier eras. Bureaucracy in Turkey has been marked by a strong state tradition in which state security policies have predominated over welfare policies. In a democratization process, the bureaucracy must be malleable to change and become an agent at the service of the political elite that is responsible for governing. If good governance indicators have improved, it would seem that the bureaucracy has been open to the changes proposed by the AKP. However, Sözen delves into an important question here: bureaucracy in the sense of the Weberian model requires that meritocracy prevail over party patronage. Advances are required in this area in today's Turkey, however. If bureaucrats opposed to the government are replaced by pro-government bureaucrats, the result will once again be a partisan bureaucracy, when what is needed is the enhancement of the role of the bureaucracy as a neutral actor.

Along these same lines, armies–which in an authoritarian regime preserve a tutelary position in the decision-making process–in democratization processes must make a transition from "principal" to "agent," subject to civil authority. In the relationship between principal and agent, the principal needs to establish a relationship in which the agent acts in accordance with the principal's preferences and directions (Kassim and Menon, 2003: 122–24). The principal has the authority, while the agent has the know-how. In Turkey, the military establishment has been a principal. The 1982 constitution approved after the coup d'état conferred enormous power on the National Security Council. As Yaprak Gürsoy discusses in her chapter, Turkey's candidacy to the EU has contributed considerably to decreasing the political prerogatives held by the army in earlier decades. In addition to this external factor, a growing sector of Turkish society is unwilling to accept the participation of the military in politics. The AKP government has significantly subordinated the military establishment, although steps still remain to be taken in this respect, and the political elite, as Gürsoy notes, must be able to render any political action of the military non-viable and prevent the space left by the military establishment from being filled by civil agents who will reproduce the security vs. freedom models that the military applied in Turkey (Hakay, 2009: 27).

The judiciary, on the contrary, must not become an agent of the principal (the government), but as a state power must safeguard its independence and act in a manner that is consistent with democratization reforms. In Turkey, there is an open debate about the reach of the reforms undertaken by the AKP in this area. Traditionally in Turkey, the work of the judiciary, as Ergun Özbudun explains, has been one of guardianship of the system, with a rigid view of Turkish nationalism and the concept of secularism. This view has given precedence to the idea of preserving the state over individual rights and freedoms.

At this time, opinions on the judiciary differ and, as the author shows in this chapter, a debate has arisen between those who believe that the AKP is remodelling the judicial organization to create a judiciary that more closely shares its beliefs and those who believe that these reforms are making way for a more plural and independent judiciary. This topic, like others in the text, suggests further fields of research. Areas for further investigation may include the study of the sentences handed down by juries in the last few years related to relevant cases on fundamental rights and freedoms.

Finally, this section includes the study done by Ali Çarkoğlu and Fikret Adaman. The chapter focuses on the view that citizens have of the state administration, of the politicians that lead it and of their fellow citizens. Çarkoğlu and Adaman analyse how important sectors of the citizenry believe that there is a high level of tax evasion, which undermines their confidence in the efficiency of delivering public services and acts as a disincentive when complying with their own obligations, which can have a negative impact on tax collection. This chapter studies how political culture can influence the correct functioning of democratic institutions, where trust in one's fellow citizens and in the political class is important.

The fifth arena of analysis focuses on the legal framework, the situation of fundamental rights and freedoms in the country, and on the demands for rights that affect specific groups in Turkey.

In the first chapter in this section, Özbudun addresses the question of constitutional reform. Although the political groups that make up the Turkish parliament agree that a new constitution should be approved, the lack of agreement on key questions have slowed down the process up to the point of raising serious concerns about its future. One of the essential requirements to ensure that a defective democracy develops in the right direction is the dismantling of the institutional framework that is serving as an obstacle to full democratization. The constitution is the main framework that protects fundamental rights and freedoms and organises the functioning of the state and territorial organization.

The legislature resulting from the 2011 elections is made up of four parties that come from a very diverse political spectrum and an agreement between all of them would give the new constitution powerful legitimacy. However, to date, the political groups have not been able to come to an agreement on some important issues. The Kurdish question is particularly key in this respact. A new Constitution is an absolutely necessary step in order to establish a coherent legal system; if not, only piecemeal reforms will be made, which may result in ambiguous or even contradictory measures that can be applied or interpreted at the discretion of security forces and members of the judiciary.

In her chapter on the evolution of the protection of fundamental rights and responsibilities, Senem Aydın explains the advanced reforms in this area and the limits to their correct implementation. Ayşen Candaş and Hakan Yılmaz for their part, analyse attitudes towards human rights in Turkey. The three authors agree that there is no normative commitment to human rights either on the part of the political elite (reflected in the important gaps in this respect that can be seen in the AKP and CHP election manifestos) or of the citizens, although references to fundamental rights and freedoms have been inserted into the political discourse over the last few years. Aydın, Çandas and Yılmaz also discuss how a lack of credibility in the negotiation process between Turkey and the EU has negatively affected the effective protection of these rights.

Along with individual rights and freedoms in Turkey, the country must face specific demands from certain groups. Like the vast majority of states, Turkey does not have a homogenous population, and authors like Will Kymlicka (1996) argue from a position of liberal democracy for the need to promote and protect the cultural sphere that belongs to the individual, a key part of his or her identity. The Treaty of Lausanne recognises three minorities in Turkey: Armenians, Jews and Greeks. Samim Akgönül has analysed the problems faced by these three communities in Turkey, some shared and others unique. In recent years, their demands have become part of the political agenda, although the response to them is still limited. The different communities have become more vocal when raising their concerns. As Akgönül says, "minorities now appear as actors". However, much remains to be done. The perception still exists that the expansion of minority rights contributes to the disintegration of the state. The death of the Armenian journalist Hrank Dink in 2007 served as a tragic sign of how a hostile political and social attitude still exists towards these communities. Citizen demonstrations after his death also revealed that this type of event produces repulsion in broad swaths of society.

Changes in this arena cannot be limited to legislative action and the implementation of institutional policies. The political elite and the media share a large part of the responsibility when it comes to promoting a political culture that fosters a varied and heterogeneous reading of Turkish society.

The cultural demands of the Alevis in Turkey, analysed by Elisse Massicard, were also adversely affected for decades by a monolithic vision of the state, although it is possible to detect some improvement in the situation, given that they now have more freedom to participate in the public arena. Much work remains, however, in terms of officially recognising their distinctiveness within the Muslim world and responding to their claims.

Kurdish demands, however, constitute a qualitative leap in that they do not only include cultural rights but also political demands for decentralization and greater autonomy for the regions, as Dilek Kurban explains. On this key point in the Turkish democratization process, there is still a long way to go. Greater democratization throughout the political system would make it possible to decidedly advance the Kurdish question and vice-versa: this question must be solved if there are to be overall advances in Turkish democratization. Constant allusions to the danger of the separatist threat have severely limited fundamental rights and freedoms in Turkey, such as freedom of expression, association, and the rights of the detained. This fact has also led to the development of illegal structures that have become embedded in Turkey's so-called *deep state*.

The difficulties in this area are augmented by the need to resolve the armed conflict between the Turkish state and the PKK. The year 2013 started with renewed hope in this respect, since a new peace process between the Turkish government and the leader of the PKK, Abdüllah Öcalan, was made public. Although from the outset this process had substantial social and political support and a significant fund of goodwill, there are many dimensions involved in which domestic and foreign factors will influence the final outcome.

The last point analysed in this section regards the media and freedom of expression. The development of this right is fundamental if state powers are to be controlled and the demands of civil society and other political groups channelled. This right is influenced not only by the legal framework explicitly dealing with its exercise, but also by other factors such as economic models that affect the management of the media, an issue considered by Ceren Sözeri. Turkey, as noted in the introduction, has declined in international freedom of expression rankings, raising significant concerns about this question. The political elite has lacked the necessary will to promote advances in this sphere. The legal framework does not offer clear guarantees for the exercise of this right, reforms made to date have not been sufficient and even the advances that have been made in some areas are seriously limited by previous laws that have been retained or by new legislation that has been approved and that can be used against them.

Even in consolidated democracies, freedom of speech is clearly one of the most fragile but crucial rights, and constant vigilance is required to guarantee that it is properly administered. In general, the combination of the control of the media by large holding companies, self-censorship, attacks between parties masquerading as political communication – avoiding any serious, thought-out debate on public policy – and the frequent omission of important information from citizens, when accompanied by the insecurity of journalism as a profession, jeopardises access to critical, true information. Freedom of expression is key when measuring the quality of democracy in consolidated democracies and the real impact of democratization processes in defective democracies. Without this right, different groups cannot channel their demands and governments will not act with the required transparency.

The Turkish democratization process has experienced ups and downs, moments of acceleration and deadlocks. The Turkish political class at this time has unparalleled room to manoeuvre with respect to earlier periods after having limited the power of the military considerably. However, there is an important lack of unity between the parties in terms of objectives and the reach of legislative reforms related to the democratization process. The shortcomings in the process of adopting a new constitution after the 2011 elections are indicative of this.

The AKP has won three consecutive victories that have given it solid absolute majorities in parliament and made it the predominant party on the Turkish political spectrum. The risk inherent in this situation is that although the AKP is replacing the former political and state elite, it may continue and further develop the previous authoritarian attitudes instead of removing them altogether.

The political opposition, in turn, has an important responsibility to contribute positively to the democratization process, make proposals, check and balance the government and voice different demands from civil society. Although the MHP has always been characterized by its ultranationalist and conservative discourse, the CHP, as the leading opposition party and the only party that can occupy the centre-left position at this time, has a clear role to play in demanding fundamental rights and freedoms. The BDP could increase its impact notably, not only if it plays a constructive role in resolving the Kurdish conflict, but also if it mounts a comprehensive defense of fundamental rights and freedoms not only applied to the Kurdish population, which would broaden its base.

Although the political class has an extremely important role in the democratization process, civil society must be given the space to organize and articulate its demands independently. Democratization cannot be understood as only a top-down process in Turkey at this time.

The demonstrations and protests that emerged around Gezi Park and Taksim Square in Istanbul and extended to other parts of the country in May and June 2013, could signify a turning point in this sense. Numerous analysts and academics such as Nilüfer Göle, Ihsan Dagı or Edhem Eldem, have pointed out in different national and international news media like *Radikal Gazetesi, Today's Zaman, T24* or the *New York Times*, the enormous relevance and novelty of the phenomenon for Turkish politics.

The protests have constituted a break in Turkey's political trajectory, putting civil society at centre-stage in a country where major political and social transformations are usually managed by the ruling elite. The demands and discontent of protesters have touched on a variety of issues, among which criticism of an economic model that is leading to a breakneck gentrification of the city of Istanbul, by dint of exclusionary urban growth and privatization that is not readily compatible with sustainability criteria. Aside from the demands concerning Gezi Park and other specific demands such as the release of those detained in that period, the constant reference in the protests to shortcomings in the area of freedom of speech must be mentioned. It is important to emphasize that the people gathered in the country's squares demanded respect of their own individual freedom, but also that of "others" – a highly relevant phenomenon in a country that has witnessed sharp ethnic and religious polarization. The protests galvanized such disparate sectors of society as anti-capitalist Muslims, feminists, leftist groups, artists, LGTB movements, Armenians, Kurds, Turks, Alevis, Sunnis, veiled and unveiled women, pensioners, students, workers and even the supporters of the traditionally arch-rival clubs Besiktas, Galatasaray and Fenerbahçe. Their discontent did not level at other sectors of society, but instead against the policies of what is perceived to be an increasingly high-handed government.

While Taksim, Gezi and the rest of the protests across Turkey were something new, the response of the AKP and the executive however, was qualified in successive analyses as a repetition of the past – the Turkish elite's timeworn reflex of responding to mobilizations with violence by the state security forces and with further restrictions in the area of human rights and freedoms.

The prime minister meanwhile opted to polarize society through the speeches he gave to packed audiences at improvised rallies convened by his party to undermine the protests and stir up support. In these speeches, Tayyip Erdoğan accused the protesters of participating in an international plot to destabilize the country, and drew a line between his supporters and his opponents, who he criticized moreover, for their lack of religious belief, thereby making a distinction between good and bad citizens. His detractors were, according to the prime minister's vision, thereby excluded from the body politic (Polity).[3]

Looking ahead to future elections, the AKP would seem to have lost points in polls of voter intentions[4], but it is noteworthy that the CHP, the main opposition party, does not seem to be in a position to be able to channel the discontent voiced in citizen mobilizations, even if it has made symbolic advances toward the protesters' demands, roundly criticized the police repression and some of its members of parliament have played an active part in the protests[5].

The BDP for its part has also repeatedly condemned the police brutality against the protesters and several of its members of parliament such as Sırrı Süreyya Önder played a key role at Taksim. The Kurdish political movement opted to keep a low profile in case its active participation be used as an excuse to sabotage the ongoing peace process (Küçükkeleş, 2013). The leader of the MHP for his part outright rebuked the executive's approach and said of the AKP: "The party that does not accept democracy has nothing more to offer."[6] It will take some time however, until it becomes clear to what extent the events of May and June will make an impact on the opposition parties as regards their proposals for democratization and how they join forces with civil society.

At the international level, the EU has lost considerable leverage over the Turkish democratization process as compared with previous periods. Full adhesion is a distant and uncertain objective and Brussels' declarations on Turkish internal politics during the protests have not been welcomed. Turkey's prime minister reacted to the European Parliament's 12 June resolution condemning the repression of the demonstrations, retorting that he did not recognize that institution's resolutions and comparing the Turkish police's actions against demonstrators to that of police forces in other European countries[7].

By the same token, the impact of regime changes in neighboring countries remains to be seen. Turkey's role as a regional power, its positioning in balances of power in the region and the Turkish elite's own perception of the issue will affect its internal politics. The evolution of the conflicts taking place on its borders will in turn give rise to different scenarios with hugely relevant effects. Proof of this, is the existence of a Kurdish autonomous entity in Northern Iraq and the possibility that in a near future similar decentralized systems be set up in neighboring countries – something that would inevitably have an impact on the perspectives and demands of Turkey's Kurdish population.

Turkey is embedded in a process of change. If the country's democratization process concludes unsuccessfully, Turkey runs the risk of passing from being a defective democracy managed by the military, with severely limited rights and freedoms, to being another type of defective democracy, this time delegative. One in which once again, rights and freedoms are acutely limited, but where the executive is not obliged to subject itself to excessive constitutional provisions and its exercise of power is hardly limited by the legislative or judiciary. The outcome of the process still remains to be seen and it will depend on the positive interaction between the five arenas analyzed in this book.

To conclude we would like to underscore how reflecting on democracy in Turkey invites wider reflection on the evolution of democratic processes in other parts of the world. The wave of protests burgeoning on different continents (including in what are considered consolidated democracies) – each in a particular context and with specific demands – are evidence of discontent with the limitations and defects of the political system and, in some cases also, of an economic model that gives rise to greater social inequalities and is ecologically unsustainable. In the majority of these cases, demonstrators are calling for more democracy, more transparency, more citizen participation and more political accountability in their political regimes. As political systems go, representative democracy with universal suffrage is still quite a recent form of government in historical terms. As many academics and analysts point out, there is a need to keep reflecting on its deepening and improvement – limiting democratic practice to holding elections does not seem to suffice. If we take up the legacy of the social contract theorists and envisage democracy as a governing contract between the citizens and their governors, this contract has fine print and requires a detailed and comprehensive revision so as to avoid unfair terms.

Notes

1 For example, one party deputy, Pervin Buldan, said in a press conference in parliament: "We have never seen Öcalan as a murderer. We, the Kurdish people, have always seen Öcalan as a leader," adding that Ankara should hold talks on a possible settlement with Öcalan and not with the BDP. Buldan explained this position by saying that "If millions of people in Turkey have declared Öcalan as their leader, this reality must be acknowledged." Online. Available HTTP: <http://www.hurriyetdailynews.com/ocalan-is-leader-not-criminal-bdp-deputy.aspx?pageID=238&nID=21293& NewsCatID = 338> (accessed 4 July 2013).
2 "2011 Human Rights Report, Turkey", *U.S Department of State*. Online. Available HTTP: <http://www.state.gov/j/drl/rls/hrrpt/2011/eur/186414.htm> (accessed 4 July 2013).
3 "Başbakan Erdoğan Kazlıçeşme'de konuştu" [Prime Minister Erdoğan speaks in Kazlıçeşme], *CNN Türk*, 17 June 2013. Online. Available HTPP: <http://www.cnnturk.com/2013/turkiye/06/16/basbakan.erdogan.kazlicesmede.konustu/711858.0/index.html> (accesed 4 July 2013).
"Police lock down Taksim, PM shows off in Istanbul," *Hurriyet Daily News*, June 16 2013. Online. Available HTPP: <http://www.hurriyetdailynews.com/PrintNews.aspx?PageID=383&NID=48921> (accessed 4 July 2013).
4 "Survey reveals growing public apprehension over democratic process," *Today's Zaman*, 16 June 2013. Online. Available HTPP: <http://www.todayszaman.com/news-318446-survey-reveals-growing-public-apprehension-over-democratic-process.html> (accessed 4 July 2013).
5 "CHP moves for freedom of expression law reforms," *Hurriyet Daily News*, 27 June 2013. Online. Available HTTP: <http://www.hurriyetdailynews.com/chp-moves-for-freedom-of-expression-law-reforms.aspx?pageID=238&nID=49547&NewsCatID=338> (accessed 4 July 2013).
6 "Opposition leader says Turkish PM has become twitter police," *Hurriyet Daily News*, 25 June 2013. Online. Available HTTP: <http://www.hurriyetdailynews.com/opposition-leader-bahceli-says-turkish-pm-has-become-the-twitter-police.aspx?PageID=238&NID=49427&NewsCatID=338> (accessed 4 July 2013).
7 "I don't recognize European Parliament decision, Turkish PM Erdoğan says," *Hurriyet Daily News*, June 13 2013. Online. Available HTPP: <http://www.hurriyetdailynews.com/i-dont-recognize-european-parliament-decision-turkish-pm-erdogan-says.aspx?pageID=238&nID=48730&NewsCatID=338> (accesed 4 July 2013).

References

Akay, H. (2010) *Security Sector in Turkey: Questions, problems and solutions*, Istanbul, TESEV Publications. Online. Available HTTP: <http://www.tesev.org.tr/Upload/Publication/301a9c69-db25-41c5-bcc1-4c9d39a22438/ENGguvenRapor KunyaDuzelti10_03_10.pdf> (accessed 13 February 2013).
"Başbakan Erdoğan: Bir Besmele milyonlarca tweet'e bedeldirt" [Prime Minister Erdoğan: One formula (*Islam*) is worth a million tweets], *Radikal*, 22 June 2013. Online. Available HTPP: <http://www.radikal.com.tr/politika/basbakan_erdogan_bir_besmele_milyonlarca_tweete_bedeldir-1138705> (accessed 4 July 2013).

"Başbakan Erdoğan Kazlıçeşme'de konuştu" [Prime Minister Erdoğan speaks in Kazlıçeşme], *CNN Türk*, 17 June 2013. Online. Available HTPP:<http://www.cnnturk.com/2013/turkiye/06/16/basbakan.erdogan.kazlicesmede.konustu/711858.0/index.html> (accessed 4 July 2013).

"CHP moves for freedom of expression law reforms," *Hurriyet Daily News*, 27 June 2013. Online. Available HTTP: <http://www.hurriyetdailynews.com/chp-moves-for-freedom-of-expression-law-reforms.aspx?pageID=238&nID=49547&NewsCatID=338> (accessed 4 July 2013).

Kassim, H. and Menon, A. (2003) "The principal-agent approach and the study of the European Union: promise unfulfilled?," *Journal of European Public Policy*, 10(1): 121–139.

Küçükkeleş, M. (2013) "Istanbul protests: what consequences for Turkey's peace process?", *Open Democracy Essays*. Online. Available HTPP: <http://www.opendemocracy.net/m%C3%BCjge-k%C3%BC%C3%A7%C3%BCkkele%C5%9F/istanbul-protests-what-consequences-for-turkey%E2%80%99s-peace-process> (accessed 4 July 2013).

"I don't recognize European Parliament decision, Turkish PM Erdoğan says," *Hurriyet Daily News*, June 13 2013. Online. Available HTPP: <http://www.hurriyetdailynews.com/i-dont-recognize-european-parliament-decision-turkish-pm-erdogan-says.aspx?pageID=238&nID=48730&NewsCatID=338> (accessed 4 July 2013).

Linz, J. J. and Stepan, A. (1996a) *Problems of Democratic Transition and Consolidation: Southern Europe, South America, and Post-Communist Europe*, Baltimore, MD: The Johns Hopkins University Press.

——. (1996b) "Toward Consolidated Democracies," *Journal of Democracy*, 7 (2): 14–33.

Mardin, Ş. (1972) "Center-Periphery Relations: A Key to Turkish Politics?", *Deadalus*, (Winter): 169–90.

"Opposition leader says Turkish PM has become Twitter police," *Hurriyet Daily News*, 25 June 2013. Online. Available HTTP: <http://www.hurriyetdailynews.com/opposition-leader-bahceli-says-turkish-pm-has-become-the-twitter-police.aspx?PageID=238&NID=49427&NewsCatID=338> (accessed 4 July 2013).

"Police lock down Taksim, PM shows off in Istanbul," *Hurriyet Daily News*, June 16 2013. Online. Available HTPP: <http://www.hurriyetdailynews.com/PrintNews.aspx?PageID=383&NID=48921> (accessed 4 July 2013).

Schedler, A. (1998) 'What is democratic consolidation," *Journal of Democracy*, 9(2): 91–107.

"Survey reveals growing public apprehension over democratic process," *Today's Zaman*, 16 June 2013. Online. Available HTPP: <http://www.todayszaman.com/news-318446-survey-reveals-growing-public-apprehension-over-democratic-process.html> (accessed 4 July 2013).

U.S. Department of State (2011) "2011 Human Rights Report, Turkey." Online. Available HTTP: <http://www.state.gov/j/drl/rls/hrrpt/2011/eur/186414.htm> (accessed 4 July 2013).

Valenzuela, J. S. (1990) "Democratic consolidation in post-transitional settings: Notions, process and facilitating conditions," *Kellogg Institute Working Paper 150*. Online. Available HTTP: <http://kellogg.nd.edu/publications/workingpapers/WPS/150.pdf> (accessed 7 December 2012).

Index

For Product Safety Concerns and Information please contact our EU
representative GPSR@taylorandfrancis.com
Taylor & Francis Verlag GmbH, Kaufingerstraße 24, 80331 München, Germany

www.ingramcontent.com/pod-product-compliance
Lightning Source LLC
Chambersburg PA
CBHW071352290326
41932CB00045B/1453